CONTEMPORARY IRANIAN ART

HAMID KESHMIRSHEKAN

CONTEMPORARY IRANIAN ART

New Perspectives

New Edition

SAQI

SAQI BOOKS
Gable House, 18-24 Turnham Green Terrace
London W4 1QP
www.saqibooks.com

First published in hardback by Saqi Books 2013
This paperback edition published 2025

ISBN 978-0-86356-979-1
eISBN 978-0-86356-786-5

A full CIP record for this book is available from the British Library.

The EU GPSR authorised representative is Logos Europe, 9 rue Nicolas Poussin,
17000 La Rochelle, France. Email: contact@logoseurope.eu

Printed and bound by Printworks Global Ltd, London/Hong Kong

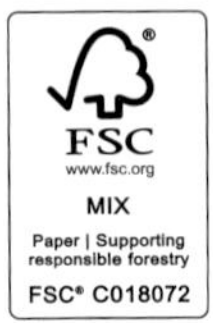

Contents

Note on Transliteration

The system of transliteration adopted in this thesis is based on *International Journal of Middle East Studies* with simplification in diacriticals. This system has been applied according to modern Persian. Persian words and phrases as well as titles of books and articles in Persian have been fully transliterated. In a number of cases, however, this system has been abandoned for the use of more familiar forms of certain Persian names, places and names of cities. For example: Heydarian, Seddighi, Zenderoudi, Niavaran and Isfahan. However, names in Arabic, especially those from before the twentieth century, have been transliterated strictly, for example: Mir ʿAli, Saniʿ al-Mulk and Dar al-Funun, *Nastaʿliq*.

Acknowledgments

The first edition of this book took shape in 2012, primarily during my research associateship at the Khalili Research Centre for the Art and Material Culture of the Middle East, Oxford University. This work was generously supported by the Barakat Trust, for which I am deeply grateful, especially to the Chairman of the Academic Committee at the time, Professor James W. Allan. This second edition presents a completely revised version of that book, with thorough updates to the texts and images throughout its chapters. Several sections have been revisited and expanded with new material, particularly reflecting recent developments since the last edition, especially from Chapter Four onward.

I am grateful to the libraries of Oxford University and the School of Oriental and African Studies, University of London, where I was able to access both older textual materials and the most up-to-date sources on Iranian history and socio-political culture. My association with a great number of Iranian artists and art professionals worldwide has significantly enriched my research. I am greatly thankful to these artists, curators and writers for their invaluable contributions and support.

I am deeply grateful to Ruin Pakbaz and Parviz Tanavoli for their invaluable insights and for generously sharing their memories of life in the art scene, along with those of their fellow artists and artistic enterprises, particularly from the pre-revolutionary period. Their willingness to provide documents and images has been instrumental to this work.

This publication would not have been possible without the generous support of institutions and collectors who granted permission for works in their care to be reproduced here for the first time. I would particularly like to thank the Tehran Museum of Contemporary Art, the Golestan Palace Museum, the Niavaran Museum, the Malek Museum, the Majlis Museum, the Museum of Fine Arts at Sa'ad Abad Palace, the Museum of National Arts, the Art Centre of the Islamic Propaganda Organisation, and the British Museum. My gratitude also extends to Mahnaz Sahaf from the Photography Department at the Tehran Museum of Contemporary Art for her patience in assisting with photographic orders and for providing excellent photographs from the Museum's collection.

Special thanks go to Vahid Kooros for his encouragement and generous support. I am also deeply indebted to those who helped secure rare photographs of works held in public or private collections, especially Majid Abd Amin and Mohammad Hossein Hamedi. Furthermore, I sincerely appreciate the artists who provided high-quality images for this publication, many of which are being published for the first time.

Finally, I would like to express my gratitude to Lynn Gaspard, the director of Saqi Books, for her warm support and professionalism throughout this project.

Introduction

During recent decades, interest in different facets of contemporary Iranian socio-politics, culture and art has significantly increased, along with the number of conferences, publications, major museum displays and exhibitions. Publications on modern and particularly contemporary Iranian art have proliferated, including bilingual journals, books and catalogues on various aspects of the genre. Those sources have largely focused on the works of expatriate Iranian artists now working in the West, also known as diaspora artists; however, in the midst of the most challenging social and political circumstances, Iran has experienced a remarkable artistic reinforcement.

One of the most pressing problems in the compilation of a well-balanced body of research on contemporary Iranian art is the scarcity of any precedent. This lack of literature underlines the neglect that has befallen the subject.[1] Although the aforementioned recent developments have played a key role in bringing current Iranian art into wider focus, a gap remains in scholarly discussion of certain aspects. No comprehensive study has ever been carried out on the subject, even though research on modern and contemporary art of the Middle East and North Africa, including Iran, is a fast-growing field in academia and the museum sector. Therefore, in many instances, this book treads on virgin territory. Indeed, one of its main objectives is to respond to the urgent need to fill this gap in scholarship. As well as using those few English and Persian sources and reliable documents currently in existence, this book relies heavily on personal documentation, observations and participation. Hence, material and data have largely been gathered through interviews with artists and visits to museums, institutions, galleries and private collections. My close association with the contemporary Iranian art community provided me with an exceptional opportunity to maintain a dialogue with several of the country's artists, art critics and historians, and administrative officers.

During the past decades Iranian artists inside the country have created works that reflect its social, cultural and political aspects. However, as in other art histories, it is not feasible to understand this development without delving into the historical backgrounds that have made it possible. This book therefore aims to explore modern and contemporary art over the past hundred years by examining the country's socio-cultural, political, and artistic transformations during this period. It also examines the neglected development of post-nineteenth-century Iranian art. In essence, this book intends to provide an introduction to and an understanding of the later developments and transformations of art during the modern and contemporary period.

The book is based on the premise that the twentieth century is a crucial period in the art and culture of Iran, when the legacies of tradition and modernism were being critically evaluated and reviewed. Moreover, as the text will explain, the artistic concerns during this period are indivisible from the ideological ones. Therefore, current problems and assumptions when studying the art of Iran will be introduced, followed by an examination of the relationship between art and various socio-cultural events in the twentieth and twenty-first centuries, represented as a series of case studies.

The book tries to explore fundamental questions such as: what could 'modern' and 'contemporary' really mean in the context of non-Western art, and what are the main issues that arise when dealing with this question? Are there non-Western varieties of modernism? Is there something in reference to the aesthetic quality, content or just a historical categorisation? Can modern art, in this context, be reconfigured? What does 'contemporary' mean? What is the meaning of contemporaneity in Iranian art? From where and how have Iranian artists drawn their new vision for art from contemporary life?

This book will also try to contextualise modern and contemporary Iranian art within the wider context of contemporary art worldwide. By analysing the ways in which socio-political contexts can be used to understand art and culture, as well as the conceptual structure of a given artwork, it will seek to explain how artworks are created as representations of critical junctures of Iranian society in different periods – for example, during the 1960s, 1970s, the post-revolutionary period, the so-called Reform period (1997–2005) and the subsequent period of cultural and political change from 2005 onwards. In other words, it seeks to contribute to the understanding of the evolving nature of contemporary Iranian art as a step towards understanding the situation of Iranian culture. It will examine how movements such as nativism, nationalism and anti-Westernism or anti-Westoxication were effective in the political arena, and affected art and artistic movements. The book, furthermore, explores how modernism, secularism, nationalism and Islamicism have affected art in Iran. Here, the treatment of Iranian art during this period will be selective rather than exhaustive, aiming to address certain problems rather than provide final answers. Also, according to the aim of the book, the treatment of the subject is thematic rather than essentially historical, although a certain chronological sequence has been observed.

Through formal analyses and close interrogation of key concepts, styles, movements and tendencies in Iranian art during the past century, the book will examine the social and historical relevance of varying ideas and their impact on artistic practices of the country: issues such as modernity and its relationship with Iranian society; nationalism in the socio-political context, religious/Islamic identity and its relation to Iranian culture; and the role of state patronage.

The main sections of this book explore and contextualise art produced inside the country. However, given that the 1979 Islamic Revolution and its aftermath profoundly transformed cultural and artistic practices within the country and gave rise to a plethora of diasporic art practices, the final chapter of the book is devoted to the work of Iranian artists in the West. As there is already a wealth of information on the diasporic artists and the associated discourses to which they are related, this chapter touches on the topics briefly and offers introductions to some artists as case studies.

Three major issues are discussed, all of which have functioned as dominant debates across Iranian socio-political and cultural domains. These are modern culture (modernity) and its place in Iranian politics and society; nationalism (in general but mainly secular nationalism); and Islamic/Shi'i identity (this includes Islamic nationalism). However, in recent decades there have been reproaches against a fixed definition of (collective) identity, especially when applied or imposed on individuals. Yet there are undeniable connections between the three aforementioned complex discourses that make it necessary to unravel them meticulously. For instance, modern Iranian nationalism is itself a product of modernism and Iranian acquaintance with modernity and, despite its criticism of the West, it is a kind of Western product that was adopted in Iran. Although Islamic nationalism genuinely differs from secular nationalism and in many cases is critical of it, it has its roots in nationalism. In other words, since nationalism cannot be considered as a total ideology, it can surface in a variety of ideological systems.

These ideological systems were active both before and after the Islamic Revolution and one can see their impact on the cultural and political agenda of twentieth-century Iran. Here are introductions to each fundamental theme; more comprehensive accounts will appear in the following chapters.

1.   Modern Culture and its Affinity with Iranian Context

Following the introduction of European thought into Iran in the nineteenth century, a debate arose as to whether and how to emulate or limit its intellectual capacity. Among different groups of intellectuals, some initially became overwhelmingly convinced that the only way to redemption was through a break with the past, a total emulation of the West and the avoidance of any indigenous innovations in this process of acculturation.[2]

In contemporary Iran, amid the ongoing process of development and social change, Iranians have been grappling with a myriad of complex forces, endeavouring to forge a new societal order aligned with their own values and preferences. The emergence of diverse and often unfamiliar elements of modernism – such as advancements in industries, technologies, arts and knowledge systems – has sparked a range of responses and reactions.

On one end of the spectrum were proponents of complete assimilation into modern Western society, known as the 'Westoxicated' or *gharb-zadigan*. Conversely, there were the *sunnat-parastan*, or traditionalists, who staunchly resisted anything perceived as exotic or foreign. Somewhere in between lied a moderate Iranian stance, acknowledging the inevitability of adopting new forms, techniques, and systems. The central tenet of this approach was to embrace external forms while preserving their 'own' values, heritage, and traditions, thereby infusing the new external structure with their distinctive character and identity.[3]

These moderate attitudes were commonly found among Iranians. Nevertheless, they prompted pertinent questions: to what extent has this 'outward form' been adopted and a new external structure established? Can traditional values, beliefs, and patterns of loyalty and behaviour be integrated into this new structure and contribute to its stability and reinforcement?[4]

It was inevitable that similar questions would occupy the minds of Iranian artists. Therefore, it is no surprise that many artists who embraced the framework of modernism for their artistic practice were also immersed in the intellectual debates surrounding cultural identity in their country.

It has been argued that, in the Pahlavi era, the preoccupation with the loss of socio-cultural identity and political sovereignty was rooted in the rapid and fundamental transformations taking place in Iran, mostly under the influence of the state.[5] The state developmentalist strategy could not succeed without concurrent political and socio-cultural 'modernisation'. The modernisation of the Pahlavi state (1925–79) undertook a form of modernism in imitation of certain Western developments and institutions. Most of the country's political, economic and even social apparatuses were overhauled based on these patterns. The sociologist Farhad Khosrokhavar argues that even the 1979 Islamic Revolution 'was the result of the modernisation

of Iranian society and as such it bore many features of this modernisation.'[6]

Recognising that modernity has integrated into Iranian society, one can view modernism as a cornerstone of Iranian socio-political culture. Like other cultural practices, art underwent a similar process of transformation alongside Iranian political and cultural shifts towards modernism. This gave rise to movements that shaped Iranian art throughout the twentieth century. Yet, a central question for Iranian intellectuals and vanguard artists until recently has been how to reconcile the dichotomy of 'modernism' with traditional cultural heritage.

2. Nationalism and its Place in Iran's Political Culture

The significance of nationalism as a central aspect of Iranian political behaviour emerged primarily in the twentieth century. According to political analyst Mehrdad Mashayekhi, the shift from an exaggerated fear of foreigners[7] to a modern nationalism – an independent nation-state in control of its resources and culture – was facilitated by two key episodes. The first occurred in the sixteenth century, marked by the reunification of Iranian territory under the Safavid dynasty (1501–1722), coinciding with the establishment of Twelver Shiism as the official state religion. The second episode unfolded in the latter half of the nineteenth century, characterised by increased interaction between Iranian society and European colonial powers, leading to the dissemination of modern values and ideologies such as liberalism, socialism, and nationalism among the intelligentsia. This contact fostered the rise of nationalistic sentiments and values.[8]

Although most nineteenth-century nationalist Iranian thinkers upheld the Islamic cultural identity of the Iranian nation, such intellectuals as Mirza Fath Ali Akhundzadeh (1812–78) and Mirza Agha Khan Kermani (1854–96) desired to re-establish the pre-Islamic cultural inheritance and attribute to it due credit for past splendour, while condemning Islam as the cause of national corruption.[9] They also found in the Western racist theories of the time the justification for disdain that they felt for the Arabs and a positive argument for their high respect of Iran: 'the noble Aryan nation' of the 'good Aryan people of good extraction.'[10] It seems however that neither this anti-Arab sentiment nor the cult of the Zoroastrian past had an effective response until the twentieth century. Nevertheless, at the time they laid down the foundation for a new nationalist and secular ideology that played a leading role in the shaping of Pahlavi cultural strategy.

In Iran, nationalism did not emerge as a resurfacing force from a long dormancy, but rather as a deliberate strategy embraced by ruling elites, the intelligentsia, the state, and ultimately the clerics, as anthropologist Mostafa Vaziri argues.[11] They recognised the advantage of unifying the population under the banner of nationhood. Vaziri maintains that:

> ...historical heterogeneity was immaterial to the process at hand, since modernization required that the unity of all communities – whether religious, regional, or tribal under the single territorial banner – be preserved. Under the influence of the European notion of nationalism the state territorial unit of Iran was used by the secularists to create a common feeling and identity among all the people.[12]

The hypothesis of an Aryan race[13] was, on the other hand, taken seriously in Iran by secular intelligentsia, who began to support their historical arguments by these conceptions. Owing to the lack of a strong countervailing theory or opposition, the Aryan racial theory was emphasised by the state in Reza Shah's reign[14] (1925–41) and subsequently in that of Mohammad Reza Shah (1941–79). Undoubtedly, the Aryan race and pre-Islamic history and civilisation, as highlighted by Orientalist excavations, became central themes in Pahlavi propaganda aimed at shaping an Iranian 'national' identity.

When Reza Shah, the founder of the Pahlavi dynasty, came to power, this trend was formally supported and even adopted as part of the state cultural and ideological policy. The powerful central government was basing the modernisation process upon the adoption of Western civilisation; it aimed at integrating it with the historical traditions and ancient ancestral honours of Iran. Reza Shah promoted a carefully crafted vision of nationalism, a so-called 'romantic nationalism' that celebrated Iran's pre-Islamic heritage.[15] On the other hand, it is argued that 'by stressing the institution of kingship and the panorama of Iranian history and culture, Reza Shah generated a deluge of nationalistic rhetoric and sentiment.'[16] In other words, the Pahlavi regime was quick to use this situation, by means of the hypothetical reconstruction of a distant dynastic connection, as the basis of its own legality and of claims about the continuity of monarchical rule in Iran.[17]

The Pahlavis' emphasis on the Persian language, recognised by the Orientalists as the national language and historical property of Iran,[18] was intended to be the key linking instrument for creating a national Iranian body and for instilling a cultural consciousness that Persian was the medium that brought cultural splendour. Furthermore, as Vaziri maintains, the Persian language was considered by the state to be historically enlarged as a sign of cultural resistance by Iranians in the face of the expansive Arab culture.[19] In the light of the importance of the Persian language (this is apart from the views held by some intellectuals during the 1950s and 1960s) against the background of Arab-Islamic culture, the Pahlavi government even decided to set up the Persian Language Academy (Farhangistan-i zaban-i farsi). This set out to purge borrowed Arabic and other foreign loanwords (mainly European and Turkish) from Persian and to replace them with 'pure' Persian words.

One of the other enterprises of the state was the glorification of the *Shahnameh* (book of king) as an immortal part of national culture. The *Shahnameh* was identified as a national symbol of the glorious heritage of the past. The establishment of Shahnameh Cultural and Scientific Foundation (Bunyad-i 'ilmi-farhangi-i Shahnameh) in 1971, three years after the inauguration of the Firdawsi monument in Tus (in 1968), resulted in the mass publication of the *Shahnameh*. The charter of the

Shahnameh Foundation mentions that the *Shahnameh* is cherished because it is the most important factor for the generation of national unity and equality.[20]

The fast rate of the Pahlavi modernisation process and mass integration also led to the arrival of urban middle-class individuals, among whom the meaning and aspects of modern nationalism were gaining power. On the other hand, their consciousness of their cultural heritage had an importance for nationalism closely paralleling that of their historical consciousness. Both were strongly unifying forces that helped to alleviate the many disruptions to national unity. The American political scientist Richard Cottam (1925–97) points out that the Iranians' cultural consciousness allowed them to perceive themselves as deserving respect and admiration from the international community. This sense of uniqueness played a significant role in embedding nationalism in the collective consciousness.[21] Territorial identity came to be included in their conversations, and the cultural achievements of past literary figures were lumped together as part of Iranian territorial heritage.[22] As a result of an intensive campaign in education and other state agencies, 'the stage had been set for cosmetically decorating the so-called age-old Iranian culture.'[23]

It is noteworthy that nationalists faced a dilemma as they found themselves caught between two civilisations, striving to reconcile modern rationalism with ancient traditions. However, they did not wholly align with either perspective. Their eclectic approach was evident in two ways: firstly, their promotion of pre-Islamic Persian grandeur coupled with a strong sense of Persian chauvinism; and secondly, their embrace of Enlightenment principles such as secularism, nationalism, democracy, socialism, and scientism.[24] This inherent inconsistency is also evident in the state's cultural and artistic policies, as we will explore in the following chapters. Consequently, there is not a singular unified ideology that can define official art. It is important to note, however, that while the state or its cultural custodians[25] never directly mandated the formation of dominant genres such as the neo-traditionalist *Saqqa-khaneh* in art, nationalist sentiments did influence all aspects of state propaganda. In literature, for example, as the social scientist Ali Gheissari observes, political writings during the Pahlavi period emphasised Iranian nationalism, particularly as awareness of Persian pre-Islamic history became more widespread.[26]

Although modern nationalism was mainly a Western creation, it then became a weapon that opposed the West and its domination. One prominent nationalist thinker was Seyyed Fakhroddin Shadman (1907–67), who was equipped with both traditional and modern training. He published his most important essay titled 'Taskhir-i tamaddun-i farangi' (The Conquest of Western Civilisation) in 1948. Reflecting on the nature of the challenges facing Iranian society, Shadman puts forward the following argument:

> In order for Iran not to be taken over by Western civilisation and made into a powerless captive, it should attempt to appropriate that civilisation willingly and thoughtfully.[27]

The only means to do that, however, is through the use of the Persian language, which he regarded as the common denominator of all Iranians and the embodiment of the ageless wisdom of the ancestors. In the same text, Shadman represents a characteristic treatment of the topics of social and literary modernism and the possibility of a synthesis between European advancement and Iranian identity which became a central intellectual dialogue of the late 1940s and 1950s. Shadman calls on Iranians to gain intellectual independence (*istiqlal-i fikri*) and self-confidence, so they can learn to distinguish between 'groundless adulation' of everything European and 'scientific criticism'.[28] Later, in the 1960s, such nativist intellectuals as Jalal Al-e Ahmad grappled with these same issues but with a different language.

In retrospect it becomes clear that Shadman was an intellectual successor to a movement that emerged around the turn of the twentieth century, embodying the essence of national identity. For Shadman and many others of his generation, language represented the timeless wisdom of their ancestors. Shadman advocated for the preservation of the Persian language as the most potent defense Iranians possessed against the encroaching Western civilisation.[29]

The popularisation of Iranian identity did not cease with the downfall of the Pahlavi regime; rather, it took a new trajectory with the emergence of fundamentalist values. Under the Islamic Republic, the strengthening of historical national identity was tethered to a shared cultural code centred around Islam, contrasting with the secularism of the Pahlavis.[30] Indeed, both preceding and following the Revolution, the study of Iranian nationalism has been significantly influenced by the nation's historical grandeur, as awareness of this history has greatly contributed to the current vigour and legitimacy of nationalism.[31]

During the early post-revolutionary period, the Islamic universalising trend[32] influenced Islamicists' views on patriotic values. However, the challenges of governing a modern state and dealing with various domestic and foreign issues, particularly the eight-year war with Iraq, reinforced the regime's nationalism alongside its Shi'i fervour. Over time, the Islamic Republic adapted its universalist Islamic ideology to fit the national context.[33] Mashayekhi notes that many political leaders and intellectuals associated with the Islamic Republic had strong nationalist sentiments even before the revolution. Consequently, many Islamic thinkers now speak of an 'Islamo-Iranian' culture and identity, seeing a symbiotic relationship between Islam and Iran.[34]

Modern Iranian nationalism had initially aimed at establishing a powerful modern Iranian state. This movement was based on an ancient Iranian awareness of ethnic identity that was cultural identity and, in its emphasis, relied upon pre-Islamic Iranian history. This history, most of which was unknown during the Islamic era or was lost in myths, was discovered in the nineteenth century through the efforts of European archaeologists and philologists. On one hand this nationalism was gradually searching for an Iranian origin with reference to the pre-Islamic period; on the other hand, it relied on the Iranian people and their culture during the Islamic period in which the Persian language and its literary heritage had a specific place. In fact, this kind of nationalism was continuously mixing the memory of the pre-Islamic Iranian political

empire with the flourishing period of the Persian language in the Islamic period.

Regarding the relationship between Iranian acceptance of Shi'ism and nationalism, Cottam argues that there is reason to believe that a strong sense of being a unique and culturally superior people was instrumental in the Iranians' acceptance of the Shi'i sect.[35] The very devotion to a sect that was not dominant in Islam probably reinforced the Iranians' feeling of independence. He concludes that 'it is in this close association of religion and nationalism that Iranian nationalism appears to be most anomalous.'[36] In relation to the post-revolutionary period, the cultural and political scientist Shireen Hunter maintains:

> The most important change for the Islamic regime has been to accept and legitimize the concept of Iran and Iranianism as a coequal focus with Islam of national loyalty and a component of Iranian cultural identity. The regime has now accepted the notion of an 'Iranian nation,' and it has also concluded that the nature of the Iranian culture is 'Iranian Islamic.' Of course, even now, the Islamic element is emphasized more.[37]

Generally, it seems that during the twentieth century nationalism led artists to pay more attention to national and cultural identity and artistic heritage. The use of ancient indigenous materials to construct indigenous works was undoubtedly the result of nationalist beliefs presented both before the Revolution, mainly during the 1960s, and echoed in the post-revolution and 1990s. A large store of such materials is accumulated in the past of any society, and an elaborate language of symbolic practice and communication is always available: from well-supplied stores of official ritual, symbolism and moral exhortation-religion and princely pomp, and national folklore materials. Those decades were also the years in which nationalist sentiment was in upheaval and spread through Iranian society and intellectual thought.

3. Religious Movements and their Relation to Iran's Socio-Political Culture

Among contemporary Iranian intellectual movements, a campaign was formed which has come to be known as 'Islamicism' or 'Islamic Modernism'. This group, influenced by nationalist ideas, embraced an Islamic view and political agenda, contrasting with earlier nationalists who primarily advocated for deism, secularism, and occasionally socialism.[38] Although this group had been influenced by European doctrines, it remained opposed to the cultural appropriation of the East through the dominance of Western culture. As Boroujerdi maintains: 'Viewing cultural abstinence as no longer a practical alternative, they advocated selective adoption of those Western scientific and cultural traits which were compatible with the Shariah.'[39]

During the late 1950s and particularly the 1960s, a prominent topic in Iranian intellectual discourse emerged: the notion of the 'other'. This discussion has had a profound impact on the social perception of the West. The emergence of an intellectual discourse known as *gharb-zadegi* ('Westoxification')[40] came to dominate the intellectual panorama of Iranian society (and remained present in the post-revolutionary period). Mohammad Ali Sepanlou (1940–2015), a leading Iranian poet and writer, believes that what distinguishes the 1960s from other periods is the decade's 'alertness regarding *gharb-zadegi* and transcending of inferiority complex towards the West's intellectual exports and gaining of an Eastern, Asian, Islamic, Iranian identity.'[41] The emergence of this new paradigm of thought can be attributed to two core and interconnected issues that modernist Iranian intellectuals had grappled with since the nineteenth century: questions surrounding self-identity and encounters with Western civilisation. A critical interpretation of the works of Iranian intellectuals during the 1960s, 1970s, and 1980s shed light on the ontological, epistemological, and political foundations of *gharb-zadegi*.

In the early 1960s, many intellectuals criticised superficial Westernism and advocated self-assertion when referring to an authentic identity.[42] In the autumn of 1962,[43] at a time of rapid transformation in the structure of Iranian society, a monograph entitled *Gharb-zadigi* was published by Jalal Al-e Ahmad (1923–69). Immediately after its publication the book created an intellectual shock, because it called into question the basic foundations of Iranian social and intellectual history. Boroujerdi believes that this quality caused *Gharb-zadigi* to be the intellectual bible of several generations of Iranian intellectuals.[44] This work gave birth to a discourse of the same name which in many scholars' views was the 'modern Iranian articulation of nativism'.[45]

In general, nativism[46] can be viewed as a reaction to Eurocentrism and colonialism, both on a textual and political level.[47] As British scholars Patrick Williams and Laura Chrisman noted in 1994, nativism broadly refers to the advocacy for the resurgence, restoration, or perpetuation of native or indigenous cultural customs, beliefs, and values.[48]

Al-e Ahmad and his contemporaries emerged as the vanguards of Iranian nativism during the 1960s. As a prominent intellectual figure, Al-e Ahmad embodied the complex mindset prevalent among Iranian intellectuals in the post-war era. He belonged to a generation that, while inspired by the West, harboured political opposition toward it. This generation exhibited a paradoxical relationship with the West – xenophobic yet drawing intellectual inspiration from its thinkers. Simultaneously, they grappled with conflicting attitudes toward religion and tradition, while aspiring to modernist ideals such as democracy, freedom, and social justice, despite doubts about their historical viability in Iran. Ultimately, this generation faced the challenge of defining concepts of 'self' and 'other',[49] a challenge mirrored in the artistic practices of the 1960s. Artists of this era sought to establish an artistic identity through the neo-traditional movement, a subject explored in Chapter Three.

Gharb-zadigi served a variety of important functions for the Iranian intellectual community. By offering a critical record of a century of Iranian enlightenment, it portrayed the quandary of a shifting society. Through a nativistic approach, it also put the question of national and ethnic identity once again on the agenda of Iranian intellectuals.

Moreover, it urged Iranian intellectuals to re-examine their inert devotion to Western ideas and culture and called them to an awakening and struggle against an alien culture that increasingly dominated the social, political, intellectual and economic scene of Iranian society.[50]

According to Al-e Ahmad, the source of many Iranian social and cultural problems was the abandonment of traditional heritage and submission to superficial imitation of the West without any genuine knowledge of the roots of Western achievements.[51] He used the term *gharb-zadegi* (the state which is being struck by the West) for an explanation of this condition.[52] He believed that this malady could result in the abolition of cultural authenticity, political independence and economic progress in Iran.[53]

Around the same time that Al-e Ahmad was exploring the relationship between Iran and the West, Ali Shariati (1933–77) was also engaged in this subject, but from a different perspective that embraced Islamic identity as the authentic foundation of Iranian culture.[54] He contended that to discover true Iranian identity, Iranians must first discern the reasons behind their historical disruptions and the suppression of the more favourable aspects of their national culture.[55]

It is important to note that the concept of *gharb-zadegi*, as proposed by intellectuals often described as 'religious intellectuals', did not stem from historical theories such as Marxism versus Western capitalism. Instead, it emerged as a quest to reclaim something lost and perceived as corrupted due to Western influence. From this perspective, *gharb-zadegi* was viewed negatively, signifying an unhealthy state of Iranian culture and life. It means that the authentic cultural heritage had been tainted by excessive Western influence. Therefore, the *gharb-zadegi* theory, largely influenced by Al-e Ahmad's ideas, aimed to elucidate the nature of the Iran-West relationship and its underlying causes, and propose a return to authenticity as a means of rectifying this situation.

This belief is evident in the prevailing artistic movements of the 1960s, where the issue of artistic authenticity and identity, rooted in traditional materials and artistic approaches, took centre stage.

Another commended book was very influential in Iranian intellectual coteries in both pre- and post-revolutionary periods: *Asiya dar barabar-i gharb* (Asia Facing the West) by Daryoush Shayegan (1935–2018), comprising a collection of essays on the socio-cultural transformation of the traditional societies of Asia. In this book, Shayegan maintains that the essence of philosophy and science in Asian civilisation is completely different from its equivalent in the West. Basing his analysis on a set of ideas that he has laid out in his previous works, Shayegan maintains that, while occidental philosophy is based on rationalist thinking, oriental philosophy is grounded in relation and faith. As a result, Asian philosophy has an essentially different character.[56]

To preserve their cultural identity, Shayegan believes, Asian intellectuals must first engage in a dialogue with their ethnic memories and then continue a dialogue with the West. He argues that ethnic memories can accelerate the flowering of Asia's ancient glorious heritage. The constitutive basis of Iranian collective ethnic memory, Shayegan claims, is Islam, and in particular Shi'ism. Just as with Al-e Ahamd, it is impossible now to distinguish between Islamic Iran and Iranian Islam, as they have been so intermingled over the centuries. Thus, his assertion of religion as the source of Iranian identity led him to the same position which had previously been taken by Al-e Ahmad in the 1960s. However, Shayegan does not abandon his quest to link modernity to tradition. For him, the past is still just around the corner. Even if it is buried, it can still be exhumed.[57]

In the period after the Revolution, especially in the 1980s, we face another leading Iranian religious intellectual and philosopher, Abdolkarim Sorush (b.1945), whose intellectual theories were quite influential on Iranian thinkers. He says that Iranians are successors to three cultures comprising pre-Islamic Iran, Islamic Iran and Western (modernism). He believes that Iranians should try to reunite and recreate all three, instead of favouring one over the others.[58]

Peter Chelkowski and Hamid Dabashi assert that 'the Iranian Revolution of 1979 revealed, in the most spectacular way, the deepest, most energetic, volcanic forces of the

Islamic culture of Iran.'[59] They further note that 'Although deeply rooted in material and ideological conditions of diverse nature and origin, the Islamic Revolution of Iran increasingly assumed the most radical rhetorics of Shiism as its defending character.'[60] Nikki Keddie, an authority on Eastern, Iranian, and women's history, also argues that:

> ...the Islamic state included many features of parliamentarism, nationalism, socialism, and a 'Third Worldist' reaction against the West [...], while at the same time retaining the Islamic identity that was still crucial to most Iranians. [61]

It is argued that the essence of the Iranian Revolution was not rooted in 'fundamentalism' but rather in a fundamental amalgamation of traditional and revolutionary ideals. Subsequently, the state tried to amalgamate Shi'i culture and politics into a unified political culture,[62] systematically seeking institutionalisation. This led to an Islamicisation process aimed at rehabilitating a society perceived as Islamically deficient. It is unsurprising that the influence of the Revolution and Islamic ideology permeated the artistic atmosphere of the period, evident even in the earliest official artistic events post-Revolution, such as national exhibitions in the 1980s.

Yet, in the process of permanent quest for cultural and cultural identity by reference to traditional heritage, the presence of Islamic/Shi'i iconographic characteristics could be understood even subsequently in the early 1990s when the post-Revolution modernism was reborn. The same can be seen in the works of neo-traditionalists in which modern western artistic characteristics and susceptibility were employed with traditional material from the repository of the past. It seems, however, as we will see, this theory is not valued in the recent history of Iranian culture and art, in particular among the new generation of artists. This new generation is willingly trying to be part of what is happening in the the new millennium in the world of contemporary art. However, what is also clear is that Iranian society is going through a self-criticising process, putting under discussion what it has experienced during the past century, including modernisation, revolutions, traditionalism, neo-traditionalism and their effect in different domains of culture and art.

Overall, the theoretical discourse and complex abstractions of themes such as authenticity, transnationalism, and contemporaneity, although understood, seem to be secondary to the issues of cultural and social concerns with which Iranian artists are engaged. Many artists are responding to more and more interwoven geographies with their global conversations. Their work shares a critical interest in the social dimensions, political realities and aesthetic history of Iran. While experiencing profound yet contradictory changes in the social and cultural spheres, the younger generation appear neither very eagerly revolutionary nor ideological. They seem to be inventing a new politics of identity for the twenty-first century; new cultural practices that have taken centre stage. This variation in contemporary Iranian art echoes the complexity and multiplicity of Iranian society, its diverse facets, its manifestations and its nuanced responses to instabilities and pervasive crises. All these processes have posed options and challenges for Iranian society at large and will continue to affect art and artistic production.

NOTES

1   Among others, the most reliable sources written on the subject are those of the art historian and critic Ruin Pakbaz. He has been active since the early 1960s with pioneering works in the field, which are published primarily in Persian. His acquaintance and close association with many distinguished modern and contemporary Iranian artists and artistic organisations, together with his involvement with various major artistic events and exhibitions, has enabled him to produce invaluable sources. Among others, the *Encyclopaedia of Art* (1999) is the most valuable in which Pakbaz presents documented sources, although encyclopaedically; there is a great lack of even well-balanced descriptive historical materials for research in this area. *Picturing Iran: Art, Society and Revolution* (2002), edited by Shiva Balaghi and Lynn Gumpert, is a scholarly book published on the occasion of the exhibition *Between Word and Image in the Grey Art Gallery* in New York University; it introduces the works of modern Iranian artists of the 1960s and 1970s in the Grey Art Gallery collection. As with similar sources published in the West, its approach to the art of the period after the 1979 Islamic Revolution limits itself to these initial years, specifically the late 1970s, in which the art of propaganda and revolutionary art mainly dominated artistic production. In addition to these early examples, there have been several other publications during the past decade, both in English and Persian. Among others are *Amidst Shadow and Light: Contemporary Iranian Art and Artists* (2011); *Iran Modern* (2013); *Amazingly Original: Contemporary Iranian Art at Crossroads* (2014); *Contemporary Iranian Art: From the Street to the Studio* (2014); *Persia Reframed: Iranian Versions of Modern and Contemporary Art* (2019); *Alternative Iran: Contemporary Art and Critical Spatial Practice* (2022); and *The Cultural Politics of Art in Iran, Modernism, Exhibitions, and Art Production* (2023). Moreover, a number of artist monographs have been published during this period, all contributing to the advancement of knowledge in this evolving field.

2   Mehrzad Boroujerdi, 'Gharbzadegi the Dominant Intellectual Discourse of Pre-and Post- Revolutionary Iran', in Smith K. Farsoun and Mehrdad Mashayekhi, ed., *Iran Political Culture in the Islamic Republic*, London and New York 1992, p.32.

3   See William G. Millward, 'Traditional Values and Social Changes in Iran', *Iranian Studies*, vol. no. 4, 1971, pp.2, 3, 11.

4   Ibid, p.3.

5   Mehrdad Mashayekhi, 'The Politics of Nationalism and Political Culture', 1992, p.94.

6   Farhad Khosrokhavar, 'Postrevolutionary Iran and the New Social Movements', in Eric Hooglund, ed., *Twenty Years of Islamic Revolution: Political and Social Transition in Iran since 1979*, Syracuse, New York 2002, p.18.

7   Here, it refers to the major invasions by Greeks, Arabs, Turks and Mongols that contributed to the formation of a foreign-suspicious collective memory of Iranians. (Mehrdad Mashayekhi, 'The Politics of Nationalism and Political Culture', 1992, p.85)

8   Ibid.

9   Mangol Bayat-Philipp, 'Tradition and Change in Iranian Socio-Religious Thought', in Michael E. Bonine and Nikki R. Keddie, ed., *Modern Iran: the Dialectics of Continuity and Change*, New York 1981, p.51.

10 Ibid.

11 Mostafa Vaziri, *Iran as Imagined Nation: The Construction of National Identity*, New York 1993, p.6.

12 Ibid. Consequently, the Turkish, Arab, Turkaman, Baluchi, Gilaki, Mazandarani, Kurdish, Luri, Armenian, Assyrian and other religious, linguistic, and tribal communities that lay within the administrative boundary demarcating the Iranian plateau during the transition to modernism were all termed 'Iranian'. (Ibid.)

13 Although the Aryan-race concept was hypothesised in early nineteenth-century Europe, it found its way into Iran slowly in the early twentieth century. One of the earliest references to the division between Aryan and Semitic races and civilisations (with Aryan standing for Iran) can be found in a history textbook in 1901 by Zaka al-Mulk Foroughi. (See Mostafa Vaziri, *Iran as Imagined Nation*, 1993, p.196.)

14 It was not, however, irrelevant when Reza Shah demanded that the international community use 'Iran' instead of 'Persia' for his country, both to emphasise the racial etymology and underscore the historical significance of the term Iran rather than the narrower Persia. (Mostafa Vaziri, *Iran as Imagined Nation*, 1993, p. 196.)

15 The enterprises were to be fulfilled by cultural planning and organisation, including the establishment of several cultural centres relating to the revival of ancient Iran's grandeurs. Some of these enterprises consisted of: approbation of a law respecting the preservation of historical antiquities in 1930; the establishment of the Iran-i Bastan (Ancient Iran, now changed to National) Museum in 1935 in Tehran; the Pars Museum in Shiraz in 1938; the Anthropology Museum in 1937; and National Library of Iran in 1939, both in Tehran.

16 Ali Gheissari, *Iranian Intellectuals in the Twentieth Century*, Austin USA 1998, p.46.

17 See Mostafa Vaziri, *Iran as Imagined Nation*, 1993, p.193.

18 According to Vaziri, 'Concomitantly, other languages in Iran were trivialized. The history of a single language (in this case, [Persian]) was linked to an entire geographical zone (Iran) in order to create the necessary nationalist basis between culture and territory.' (Ibid, p.5)

19 Ibid, p. 197.

20 See Yahya Aryanpour, *Az nima ta ruzigar-i ma: tarikh-i adab-i Farsi-i mu'asir* (from Nima to Our Time: History of Iranian Literature), Tehran 1374S/ 1995, p.205.

21 Richard W. Cottam, *Nationalism in Iran*, 1979, p.29.

22 Between the time of Reza Shah and the early period of his son's reign, the government used the millenial celebration of Firdawsi, Avicenna (*Ibn-i Sina*) and other figures as an occasion to rebuild their tombs, as well as those of Sa'di, Hafiz, and Omar Khayyam to glorify their national cultural achievements. (Mostafa Vaziri, *Iran as Imagined Nation*,1993, p.196)

23 Ibid.

24 Mehrzad Boroujerdi, 'Gharbzadegi: the Dominant Intellectual Discourse of Pre- and Post-Revolutionary Iran', 1992, p.34.

25 The term 'cultural custodians', which will be used through this book, refers to the government administrators who are mainly in charge of cultural and artistic planning and organisations.

26 Ali Gheissari, *Iranian Intellectuals in the Twentieth Century*, 1998, p.3.

27 Seyyed Fakhroddin Shadman, 'Taskhir-i tamaddun-i farangi (The Conquest of Western Civilisation)', in *Arayish va pirayish-i zaban*, Tehran 1326S/ 1947, p.23.

28 Ali Gheissari, *Iranian Intellectuals in the Twentieth Century*, p.84.

29 Mehrzad Boroujerdi, *Iranian Intellectuals and the West: The Tormented Triumph of Nativism*, New York 1996, p.61.

30 Mostafa Vaziri, *Iran as Imagined Nation*, 1993, p. 199.

31 For further description see Richard W. Cottam, *Nationalism in Iran*, 1979, p.26.

32 Pan-Islamism echoed in themes such as export of the Revolution and denunciation of secular nationalism.

33 Mehrdad Mashayekhi, 'The Politics of Nationalism and Political Culture', p. 111.

34 Ibid.

35 Richard W. Cottam 1979, p.134.

36 Ibid, p. 135.

37 Shireen T. Hunter, *Iran After Khomeini*, New York 1992, pp.94–95.

38 See Mehrzad Boroujerdi, 'Gharbzadegi: the Dominant Intellectual Discourse of Pre- and Post-Revolutionary Iran', 1992, p.34.

39 Ibid, p.35.

40 There is no general consensus about the exact translation of the title of this term. 'Gharbzadegi has been rendered into various English translations as "Weststuckness," "Occidentosis," "plagued by the West," "Western-mania," "Euromania," "Xenomenia," "Westamination," and finally, "Westoxication." In all instances, the term *ghabzadegi* was generally meant to convey Iranian society's and its intellectuals' indiscriminate borrowing from the West.' (Mehrzad Boroujerdi, *Iranian Intellectuals and the West: The Tormented Triumph of Nativism*, New York 1996, p.66)

41 Mohammad Ali Sepanloo, *Nivisandigan-i pishrow-i iran az mashrutiyat ta 1350: tarikhcheh-i ruman, qisseh-i kutah, nimayishnameh va naqd-i adabi dar iran-i mu'asir*, Tehran 1366S/ 1987, p.82.

42 For more explanation see Ali Gheissari, *Iranian Intellectuals in the Twentieth Century*, 1998, p.6.

43 Early chapters of *Gharb-zadigi* appeared in the spring of 1962 in the ill-fated *Kitab-i mah* (Book of the Month), a literary journal published by the daily *Kiyhan*.

44 Mehrzad Boroujerdi, 'Gharbzadegi: the Dominant Intellectual Discourse of Pre- and Post-Revolutionary Iran', 1992, p.36.

45 Ibid 1996, p. 53.

46 In his book *Iranian Intellectuals and the West*, Mehrzad Boroujerdi explains nativism thus: 'Nativism was born of the lamentable circumstance of colonialism and the agonizing milieu of the post-World War II period of decolonisation. It represents a cultural reflex on the part of many Third World intellectuals from Southeast Asia to the Caribbean eager to assert their newly found identities. The proponents of nativism were adamant about ending their condition of mental servitude and their perceived inferiority complex vis-à-vis [the] West.' (Boroujerdi 1996, p.14)

47 See Mehrzad Boroujerdi, *Iranian Intellectuals and the West*, 1996, p.17.

48 Patrick Williams and Laura Chrisman, *Colonial Discourse and Post-colonial Theory; a Reader*, Patrick Williams and Laura Chrisman, ed., New York 1994, p.14.

49 Mehrzad Boroujerdi, 'Gharbzadegi: the Dominant Intellectual Discourse of Pre- and Post-Revolutionary Iran', 1992, p.41.

50 Ibid 1996, p.67.

51 Jalal Al-e Ahamd, *Gharb-zadigi*, Tehran 1341S/ 1962, p.3.

52 Ali Gheissari, *Iranian Intellectuals in the Twentieth Century*, 1998, p.89.

53 Jalal Al-e Ahmad, *Occidentosis: A plague from the West*, translated into English by R. Campbell, Berkeley, California 1984, p.55.

54 For further critical explanation see Ali Gheissari, *Iranian Intellectuals in the Twentieth Century*, 1998, p.97.

55 Ali Shariati, *Baz-shinasi-i huviyyat-i irani-islami, majmu'eh*, vol. 27, Tehran 1361S/1983, pp.79–225.

56 Daryoush Shayegan, *Asiya dar barabar-i gharb* (Asia Facing the West), Tehran 2536=1356S/ 1977, p.109.

57 Ibid, *Cultural Schizophrenia: Islamic Society Confronting the West*, translated from the French by John How, London 1992, p.4.

58 Abdolkarim Sorush, 'Seh farhang', *Ayandeh-i Andisheh*, nos. 3–4, 1369S/ 1990, p.57.

59 Peter Chelkowski and Hamid Dabashi, *Staging a Revolution: The Art of Persuasion in the Islamic Republic of Iran*, London 2000, p.307.

60 Ibid, p.22.

61 Nikki R. Keddie, *The Iranian Revolution and the Islamic Republic*, Nikki R. Keddie and Eric Hooglund, ed., New York 1986, p.11.

62 According to Samih Farsoun and Mehrdad Mashayekhi, the Islamic political culture derived its legitimacy from thirteen centuries of Shi'i history and tradition with its affinity for political protest and oppositional values. (Samih K. Farsoun and Mehrdad Mashayekhi, 'Introduction' in Samih K. Farsoun and Mehrdad Mashayekhi, ed., *Iran: Political Culture in the Islamic Republic*, London 1992, p.9.)

CHAPTER ONE

Historical Background

I. A Transformation in Qajar Art

In tandem with other aspects of Iranian life, notably the political and economic spheres, the nineteenth century marked a time of cultural introspection and uncertainty in Iran. The Industrial Revolution that had originated mainly in France and Britain had gone on to transform all of Western Europe, and had begun to affect the rest of the world. As Stephen Vernoit argues, Iranians along with other Muslim societies were faced with a new phenomenon: an international political and commercial system that worked to the advantage of Europeans.[1]

Vernoit continues by saying that these societies also experienced a matchless accumulation of social changes; the rulers of colonised or independent lands in the Muslim world were affected by a new political and cultural order. Additionally, the import of manufactured goods and works of art from industrialised Europe started to influence traditional products and challenge the economic basis of Muslim life.

Vernoit further argues that prejudiced judgments were made by some European scholars of the nineteenth century when confronting the different approaches to art of non-Western societies. For example, when considering nineteenth-century Iranian paintings, Murdoch Smith (1876) suggests that:

The paintings on a large scale on canvas are very poor, especially as regards the drawing. The large pictures in the museum [South Kensington Museum, London] were bought,

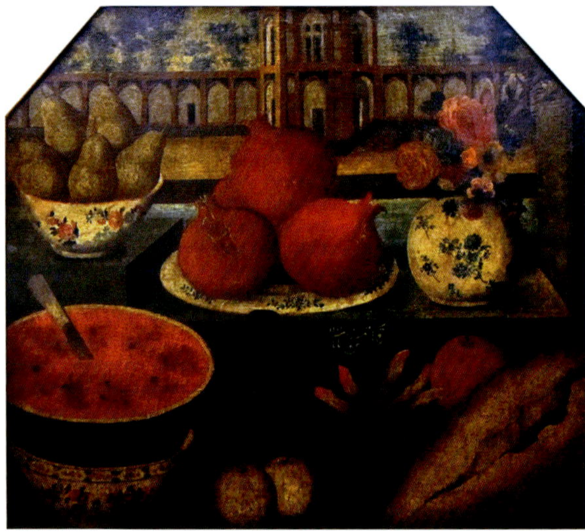

1.1
Mirza Baba, decorative still-life used on the wall, AH 1218/AD 1803, oil on canvas, no size, Museum of Fine Arts, Sa'ad Abad Palace, Tehran

not for any interest they might have from an artistic point of view, but rather as illustration of costumes, national types, &c.[2]

Another typical example is the assessment of Qajar painting made by Comte de Rochechouart in the 1860s: 'As for the paintings that the Persians themselves produce, they make one gnash one's teeth.'[3] De Rochechouart then focuses his critique thus:

> Having no idea of design, ignorant of the most simple laws of perspective, not understanding art in the way that we do and, consequently, lacking any critical faculty with which to focus their judgment and illuminate their taste, they copy the most flat and absurd compositions with minute care, and exert themselves to extinguish the brightness of their colors in order to approximate as closely as possible the gloomy and false color of polychromatic lithographs.[4]

As Finbarr Barry Flood convincingly argues, this sentiment finds its origin in the hybrid style of *Farangi-sazi*[5] (Europeanising) paintings, which were prevalent in Iran at the time. (Figure 1.1) 'For the count, as for other nineteenth-century commentators, a perceived absence of linear perspective, chiaroscuro, and verisimilitude in Qajar art obviated its classification as fine art, its interest lying primarily in a documentary value for the ethnographer.'[6]

All this suggests that Qajar artists would have to learn the appropriate Western conventions in order to produce work that could be accepted within the domain of fine art. Sheila Canby, however, believes that a capable *Farangi-saz* artist could consciously choose to follow only certain tenets of European art. She further contends that prior to the nineteenth century, Iranian taste never wholly embraced European art; instead, Iranian artists and their patrons selectively appropriated elements of European art that aligned with their own aesthetic principles.[7] If Iranian society was becoming increasingly fascinated and overawed by Western manufactured products, it was therefore not unexpected that indigenous forms of visual arts and architecture were slowly being influenced by new European styles. Often new patterns of taste and life were accompanied by a great attention to the artistic forms practised in the West, in literature, music and art.[8]

Indeed, the art of the Qajar period was characterised both by an engagement with the artistic legacies of the distant Iranian past and the artistic practices of contemporary Europe. So, diverging from their earlier painting traditions, the Qajar artists produced many large-scale paintings executed in oil on canvas. In addition, Qajar artists were quite capable of mining European royal portraiture for inspiration, adapting some details, poses and iconographic conventions.[9] (Figure 1.2)

In the initial years of the nineteenth century, the Qajar dynasty not only restored political and economic ties with Europe but also prolonged them as Iran was quickly drawn into European expansionism. These ties basically began with Western-style military and educational reforms in the early nineteenth century and opened the door to cultural changes. In art, as Maryam Ekhtiar points out, the royal *naqqash-khaneh* (house of painting), successor to the earlier *kitab-khaneh* (royal library workshop), stood as one of the initial beneficiaries of these innovations, serving as the primary conduit for the introduction of Western artistic styles, techniques, and materials into the country. By the latter half of the nineteenth century, pioneers introduced a novel system of art education inspired by European models, whose practices challenged traditional approaches and techniques.[10]

The increasing taste for European styles at court was more and more evident. One example is Lady Sheil's description of some palace rooms in Tehran in 1851 as an 'exact imitation of European drawing room; they were papered and hanging round the walls were some very inferior coloured engravings.'[11] One of the most significant innovations during this period was the introduction of canvas and its frame. This shift led to Persian painting being separated from its traditional album and manuscript context, with its scale expanded and its application broadened to include architectural decoration and interior design.[12]

It is stated that innovative reforms in the management, economy and education of the country were employed at the beginning of Nassir al-Din Shah's reign (1848–96) by his capable chief minister, Mirza Taqi Khan Amir Nizam (Amir Kabir) (1807–52). During that period, European-style painting, akin to European architecture and luxury goods, enjoyed appreciation across both the high and popular strata of Persian culture.[13] Nassir al-Din Shah, who himself was an amateur artist, patronised the new Perso-European style that was taught in the Dar al-Funun and popularised by lithographic reproductions in books and newspapers.

During this period the close contact and artistic exchange between Iran and Europe reached an unprecedented level, resulting in profound effects on the structure and content of art production and education in Iran.

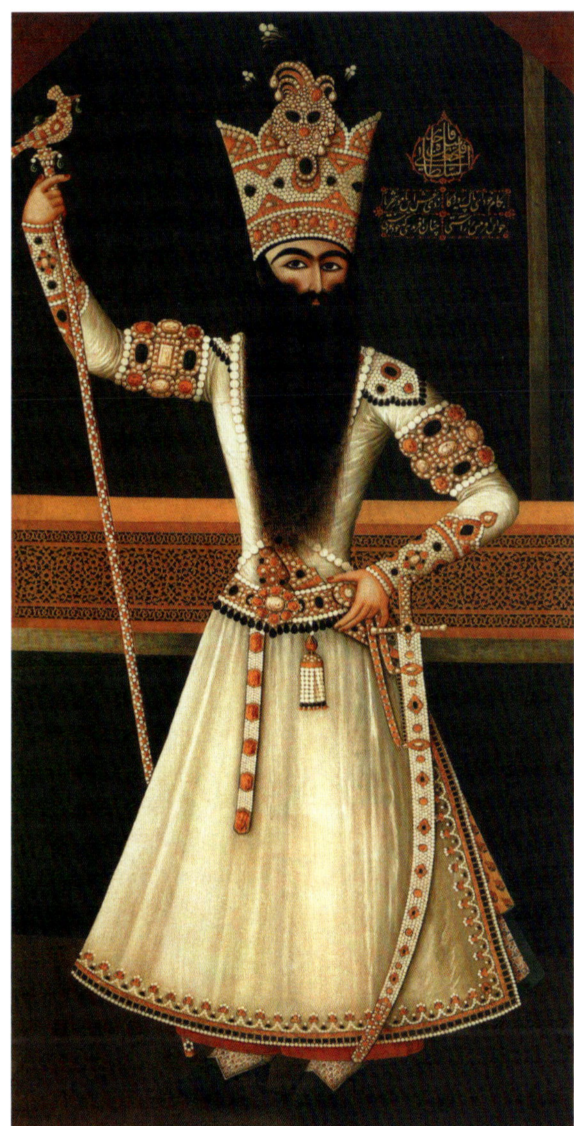

1.2
Mihr 'Ali, Portrait of Fath 'Ali Shah, AH 1224/AD 1809–10, oil on canvas, 253×124 cm, Hermitage Museum

1. The Dar Al-Funun

The Dar al-Funun, Iran's first institution of higher education, was founded in Tehran in 1851. Future military officers, engineers, doctors and also artists were taught there. European tutors were initially employed. As Layla S. Diba explains,

> [B]efore the establishment of the *Dar al-Funun*, art production and training took place in workshops located on the palace premises or in the bazaar. Artists were members of guilds and were trained in an apprenticeship system which emphasized a respect for tradition, versatility of styles, copying from models and replicating earlier styles of masters.[14]

The establishment of the Dar al-Funun was the motivating force in the subsequent distribution of art training and production in the European mode. It provided a new structure for the training of artists and introduced new technologies. It was at the Dar al-Funun that most of the leading figures of the next generation and leading court artists of Iran in the late-nineteenth century were trained, including Isma'il Jalayir[15] (d.1893), Abu-Turab Ghaffari[16] (1862–90) and the most famous and influential, Mirza Mohammad Ghaffari, alias Kamal al-Mulk (Perfection of the Kingdom) (1859–1940).[17]

It was not until 1861[18] that painting was taught at the Dar al-Funun the year in which Mirza Abu'l Hassan Khan Ghaffari (1814–66),[19] famous under the name Sani' al-Mulk, was appointed director of the state printing press and chief editor of the state newspaper. Thus, the introduction of the first art classes in the European mode in Iran was closely attached to the establishment of the printing press and formation of the first illustrated newspaper.[20] As Ekhtiar remarks, Abu'l Hassan's influential training in the *karkhaneh* (traditional workshop) system, combined with his grasp of European realistic portraiture, set him apart as an artist with a notably innovative approach.[21] (Figure 1.3) Records indicate that he played a pivotal role in establishing the inaugural painting classes as a part of the Dar al-Funun programme.[22] However, other sources suggest that during the 1860s, a French tutor named Monsieur Constant also instructed in painting and the French language at the College.[23] Within the Dar al-Funun, an outstanding school of portraiture flourished, blending elements of the classical Persian

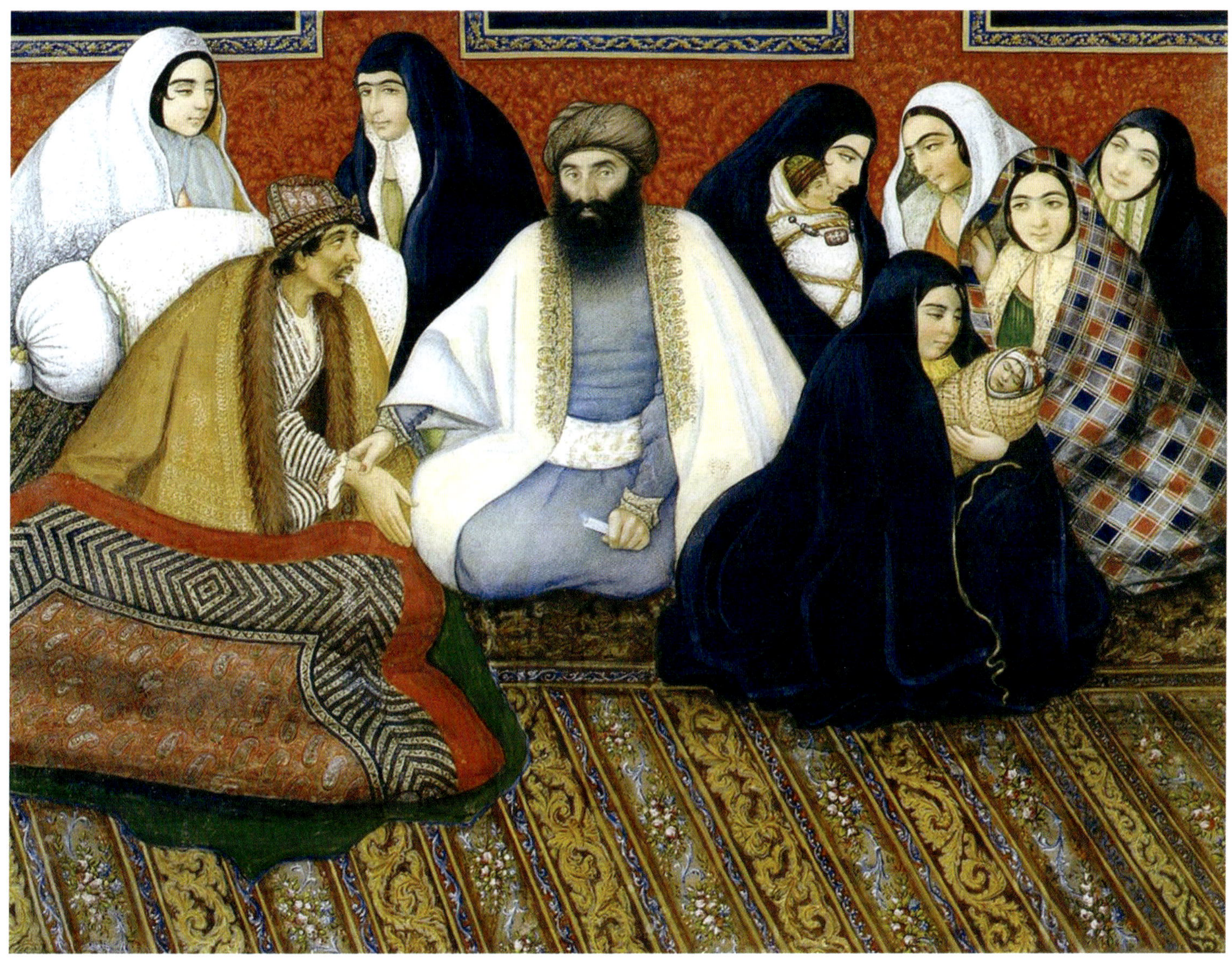

1.3
Mirza Abu'l Hassan Khan Ghaffari (Sani' al-Mulk), *Physician and Patient* (Mirza Abu'l Fazl-i Kashani), c. AH 1278/AD 1861, watercolour on paper, Malek Museum, Tehran

painting tradition with a new sensibility influenced by European art.

The documents suggest that the Dar al-Funun's classes were fashioned after the European academic system, akin to the education Sani' al-Mulk received during his journey to Italy. During his tenure as a teacher, he used various materials and tools imported from Europe, which encompassed printing equipment, paintings, drawings, sculptures, and engravings, along with replicas of works by Raphael, Michelangelo, and Titian. It appeared that several common theoretical courses, such as art history and anatomy, were omitted from the curriculum despite the primary focus mirroring that of European academies. Instead, a method of study was established to align with, rather than challenge, the existing system of art training

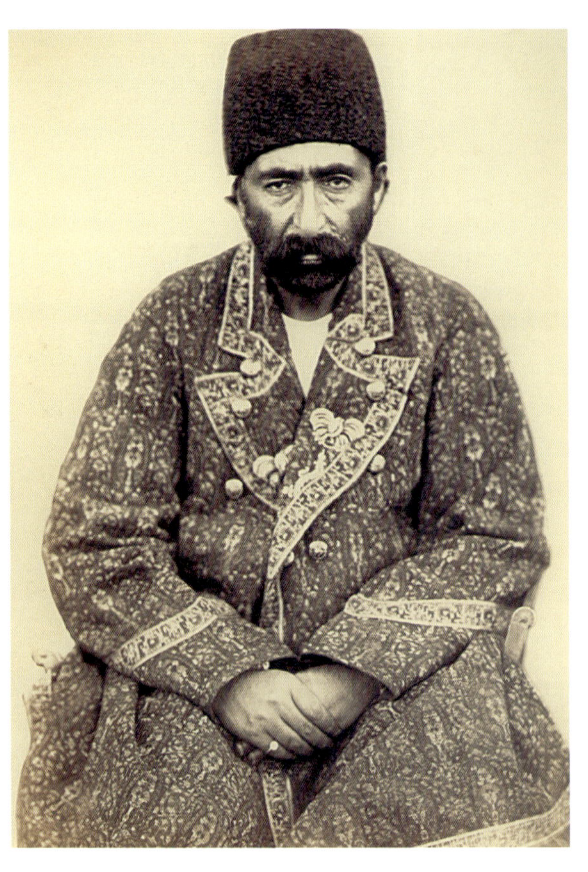

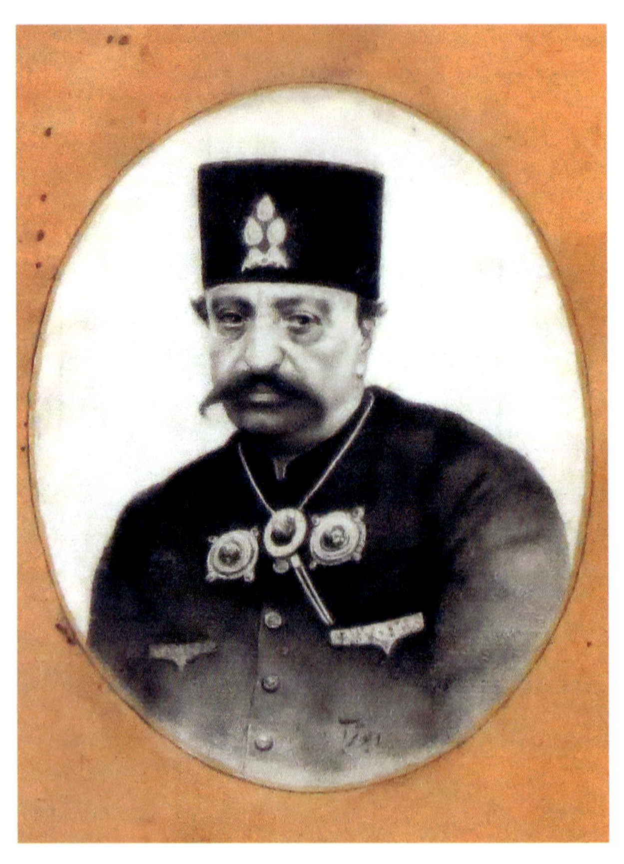

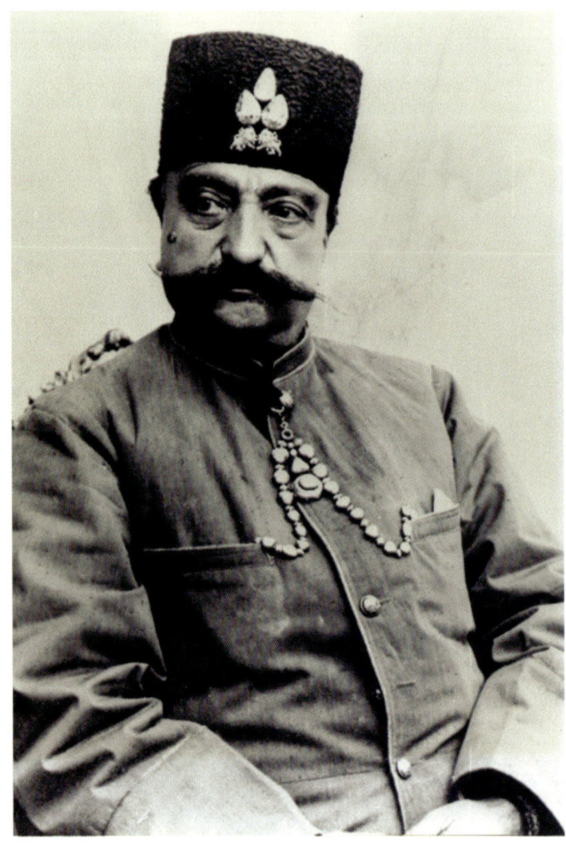

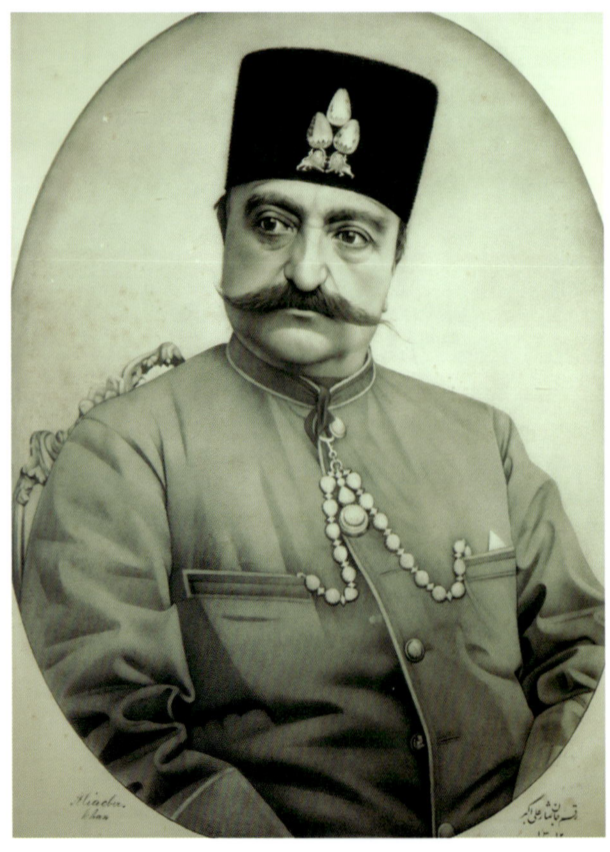

and production in Iran. It was during this period that the teaching of painting was integrated into the academic curriculum of a school for the first time, coming under the authority of the Vizarat-i 'Ulum (Ministry of Higher Education). Consequently, painting was clearly regarded as an academic discipline rather than merely a 'handicraft' as it had been perceived previously.[24]

In 1860 photography[25] was also taught as a part of Dar al-Funun's curriculum, both for its later use in printing material such as newly established newspapers and in order to assist artists during their training. As Diba explains:

> [P]hotography was considered by many as the essential tool for the advancement of Persian painting to the level of European painting, judged by Qajar art connoisseurs to be far superior. Although its impact is evident, we know little of the way it was actually used by painters. Photography may also have been used as a teaching tool for painting in the *Dar al-Funun*, to judge by surviving works. It could have been adapted to the academic teaching system and used along with models and replicas...[26]

I'timad al-Saltana wrote a basic Persian vocabulary for European terms and techniques related to painting and was also Nassir al-Din Shah's Minister of Publications. He mentions the close connection between the 'art of painting' and the 'science of photography' when stating that: 'Since photography was introduced into Iran, it has served the art of painting and portraiture vastly.'[27] A study by Shahryar Adle and Yahya Zuka confirms that many portrait paintings of late-nineteenth-century Iran were direct copies of daguerreotype photographs.[28] Therefore, the emergence of skilled painting in the naturalistic style locally was undeniably shaped by the advent of photography. Enabled to depict their subjects with precision and realism, Iranian artists embraced what was perceived as the 'perfect style'. Unlike Western avant-garde artists of the nineteenth century who rejected naturalism with the rise of photography, Iranian artists were captivated by the detailed imagery captured by the camera. This led them to transition from the idealistic portrayal characteristic of earlier Qajar portraiture to a more objective and realistic photographic style.[29] (Figures 1.4–7)

Copying European painting appears to have been a crucial part of the Dar al-Funun's curriculum. Sources suggest that anyone able to execute a perfect copy of a European painting was generously rewarded. For example, Nassir al-Din Shah requested that the painter Mirza Mahdi Khan Musavvar al-Mulk produce a replica of a painting that he had brought back from Europe 'so that one could not distinguish the replica from the original'. Musavvar al-Mulk replied: 'Of course, your Majesty...'[30] It seemed that by replicating those paintings an Iranian artist of that period was not only experiencing different styles and methods but also struggling to come to terms with his vague relationship with Europe and to redefine himself within a changing global context. When copying European paintings, he believed that he was placing himself on an equivalent position with the European artist. As Ekhtiar suggests, the artist no longer merely limited himself to producing a work that would embody a particular royal vision; he intended a painting that would measure up in his eyes to European 'standards' of representational naturalism, perspective and chiaroscuro.[31]

A new set of criteria for assessing instructors' qualifications was created at the Dar al-Funun. The fundamental requirements, according to the school's aims and preference, were knowledge of the conventions of European academic painting and skill in functioning with the new equipment. Therefore, the instructors were mainly elected from among European-educated Iranians. The *Naqqash-bashi* (chief court painter) was no longer elected by the members of his workshop, but was chosen by the Shah or the Ministry of Higher Education.

Shortly after Monsieur Constant assumed Sani' al-Mulk's role as the painting instructor, in 1871, the painting department at the Dar al-Funun came under the direction of Mirza 'Ali Akbar Khan-i Kashani Muzayyin al-Dawla (1847–1932). He was awarded the title *Naqqash-bashi* in the same year.[32] Muzayyin al-Dawla was a graduate of the Dar al-Funun and the École des Beaux Arts and was therefore considered automatically competent to teach painting and later French at the school.

While there is no substantial evidence confirming the curriculum of the painting department at the school during this period, it appears that there were no significant changes in the teaching method.[33] Muzayyin al-Dawla, however, had a markedly different style compared to Sani' al-Mulk. While Sani' al-Mulk's works show a nuanced assimilation of external influences, incorporating Europeanised forms while retaining certain features of Persian painting and subject matter (as evidenced by his disciples, like Isma'il Jalayir; Figure 1.8), Muzayyin al-Dawla's technique reflects a more conservative adherence to the prevailing academic style in Paris.

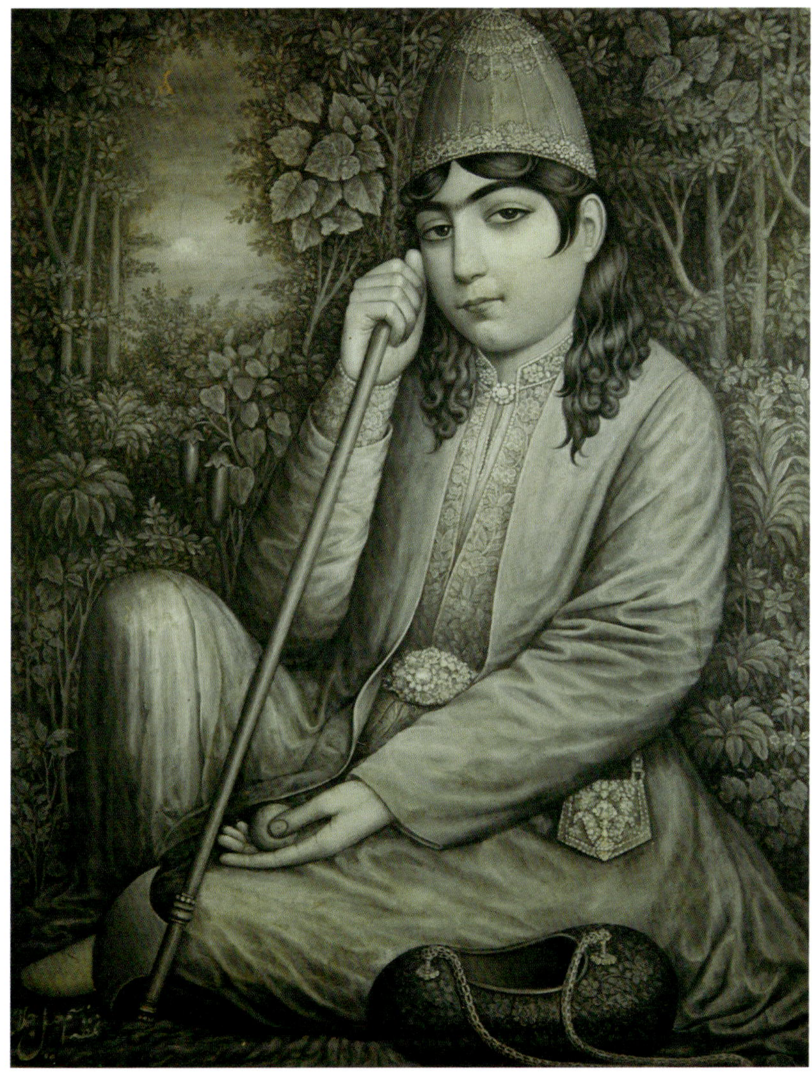

1.8
Isma'il Jalayir, *Portrait of a Dervish*, no date, oil on canvas, 69×49 cm, Golestan Palace, Tehran

(Figures 1.6, 9) Many of Muzayyin al-Dawla's students succeeded him as *Naqqash-bashi* or painting instructors at the Dar al-Funun. His most distinguished student, however, was Sani' al-Mulk's nephew, Mirza Mohammad Ghaffari, better known as Kamal al-Mulk.

Kamal al-Mulk worked across the late Qajar period and into the early twentieth century. In 1882 he graduated from the Dar al-Funun with skills in the fields of painting and history and was granted the title of *Naqqash-bashi* by Nassir al-Din Shah. He was later appointed as the leading artist of Nassir al-Din Shah's court.

As Kamal al-Mulk's reputation and abilities grew, he acquired new duties as a court painter. According to the Shah's tastes he was required to paint events, palace buildings, gardens and portraits of the Shah and royal residents, reproducing them with accuracy and detail as precise as in a photograph. (Figure 1.10) He was also asked

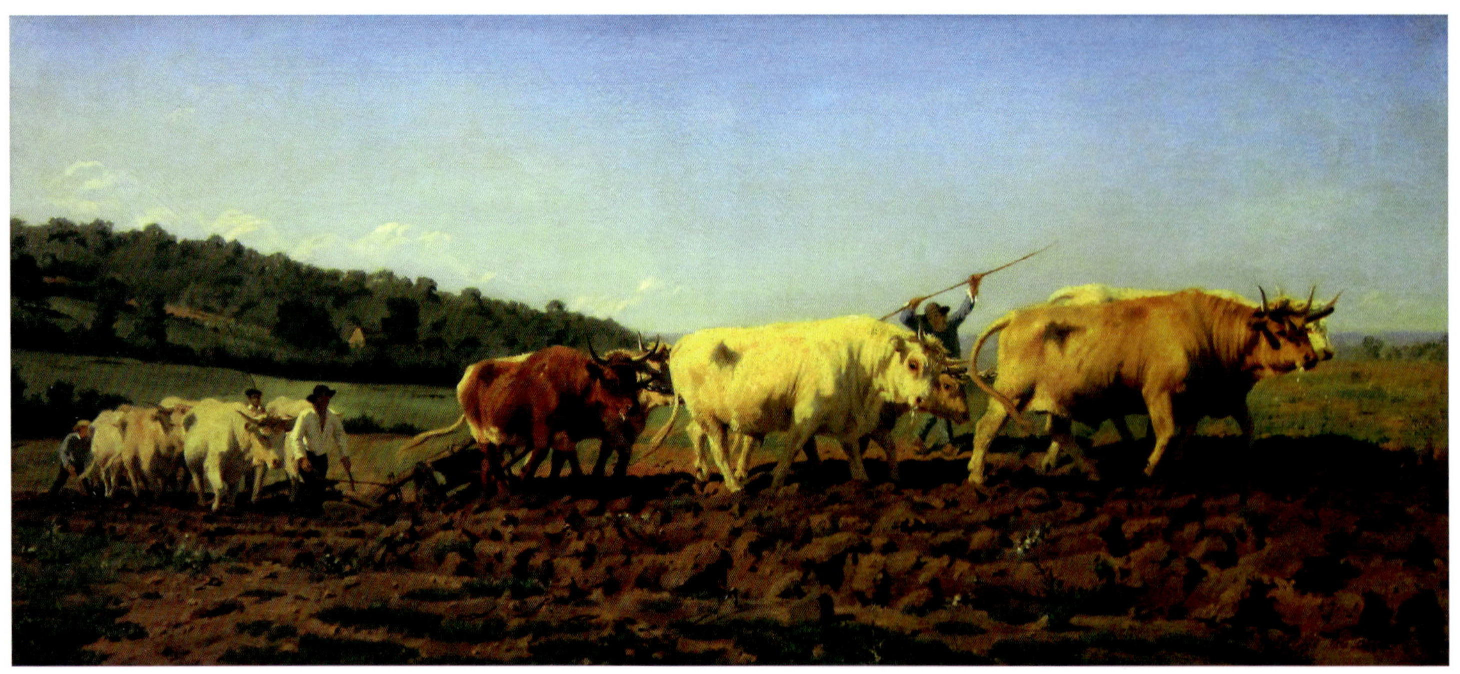

to make some historical documents of the customary life of the palace and its environment. (Figure 1.11)

As mentioned earlier, paintings by the generation before Kamal al-Mulk's, such as those of Sani' al-Mulk, show an interest in depicting the subject in a European naturalistic manner, sometimes with the aid of photography. At the same time, however, signs of the old Qajar eclectic style could still be found, resulting in a blended mixture of the two. (Figure 1.3) Examples of this eclecticism could be seen in Fath 'Ali Shah's court (1797–1835), in such works as Mihr 'Ali's (1795–c.1830) and later in particular in paintings of Sani' al-Mulk himself. (Figure 1.2) While Sani' al-Mulk's visit and potential study in Europe likely afforded him some knowledge of European techniques, evident in his portraiture, he did not wholly disregard Qajar pictorial traditions, such as the absence of accurate linear perspective. This suggests a reluctance to fully transition his work to a purely European mode. It is not until Kamal al-Mulk that we see Iranian norms of art appreciation turn rather significantly to European standards. His influential role ensured that traditional practices such as manuscript illustration and lacquer-work faded away and were replaced by European-style easel painting.[34] In fact it could be argued that Kamal al-Mulk effectively ended the eclectic style of *Farangi-sazi* which had started from the late Safavid period and continued through Qajar royal painting. *The Hall of Mirrors* (1885–90) (Figure 1.12) – the first painting signed by the artist as Kamal al-Mulk – exemplifies his

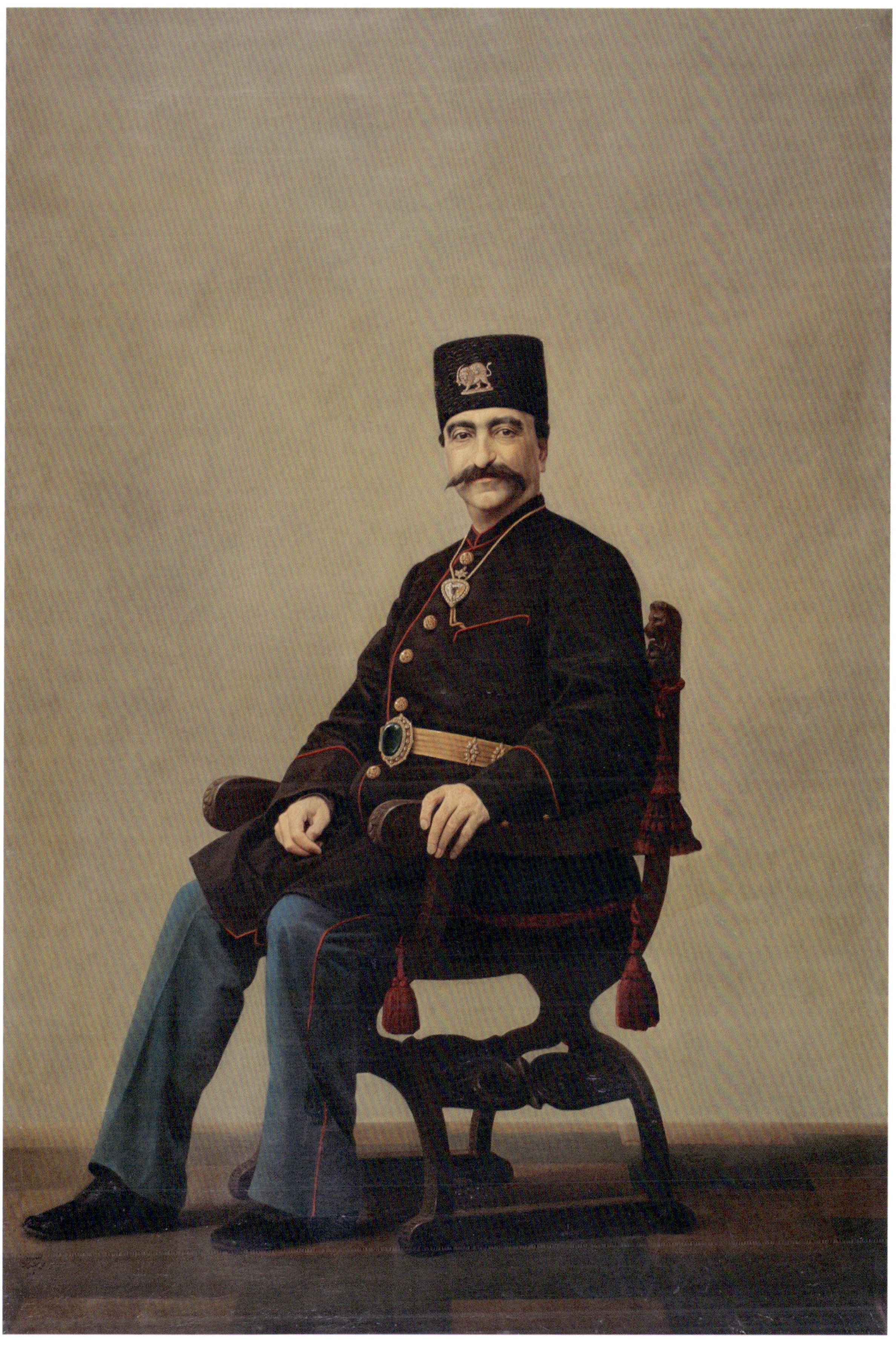

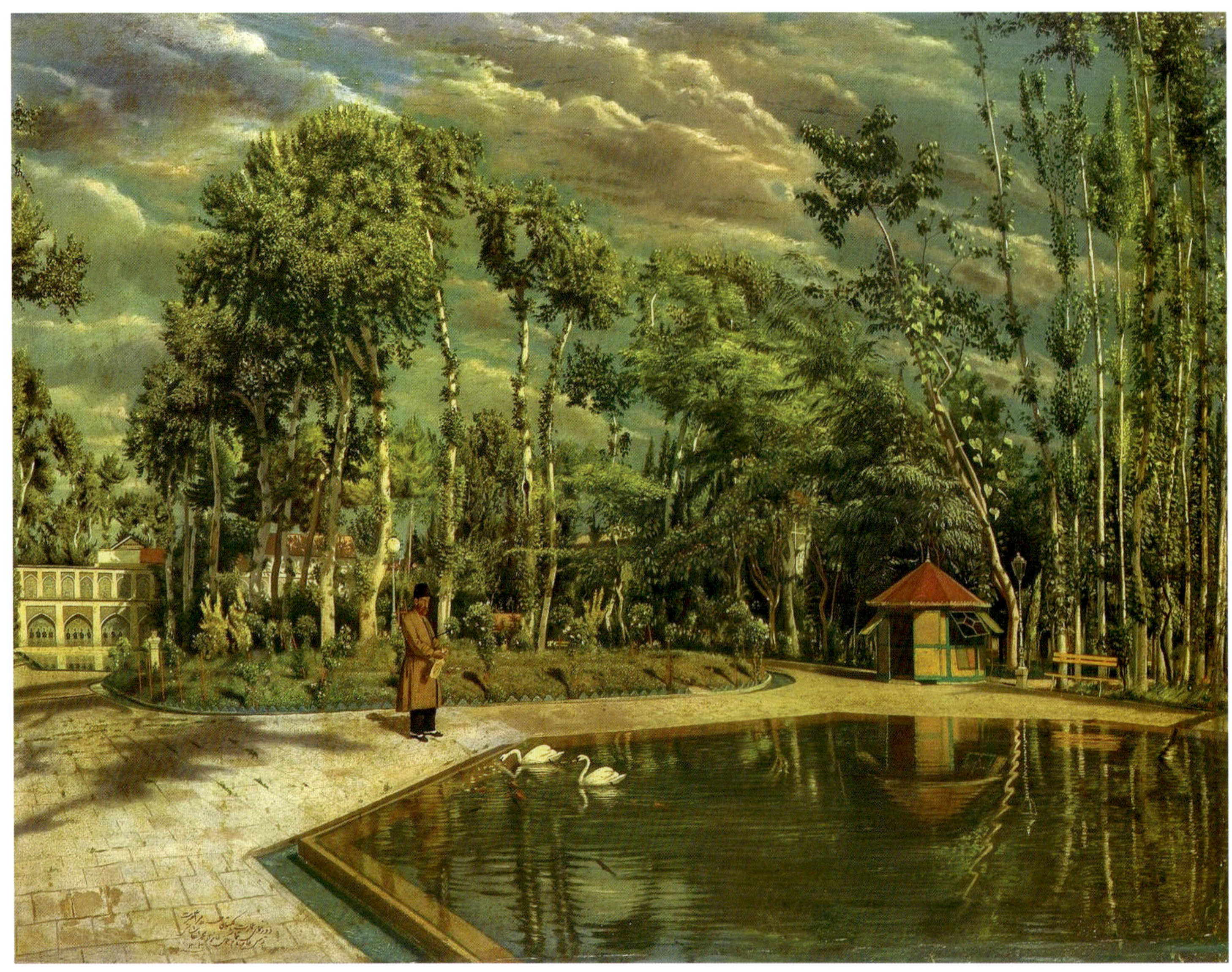

1.11
Kamal al-Mulk, *A view of the Golestan Garden*, 1885, oil on canvas, 92×108 cm, Niavaran Museum

naturalistic approach to painting and vividly demonstrates his effort to emulate nineteenth-century European academic painting. In this piece, he meticulously captures every detail of the Mirror Hall in the Golestan Palace, enhancing the grandeur of the scene by magnifying the room's proportions, the interplay of light and shadow, and the reflections in hundreds of mirrors.

Later, during the reign of Muzaffar al-Din Shah (1896–1907), Kamal al-Mulk had the opportunity to embark on a three-year government-sponsored educational mission (1898–1901), during which he travelled to Florence, Rome, Paris, and Vienna. Like his uncle Sani' al-Mulk (Abu'l Hassan), and perhaps influenced by Muzayyin al-Dawla's training, Kamal al-Mulk dedicated several hours to meticulously copying the works of European Old Masters.

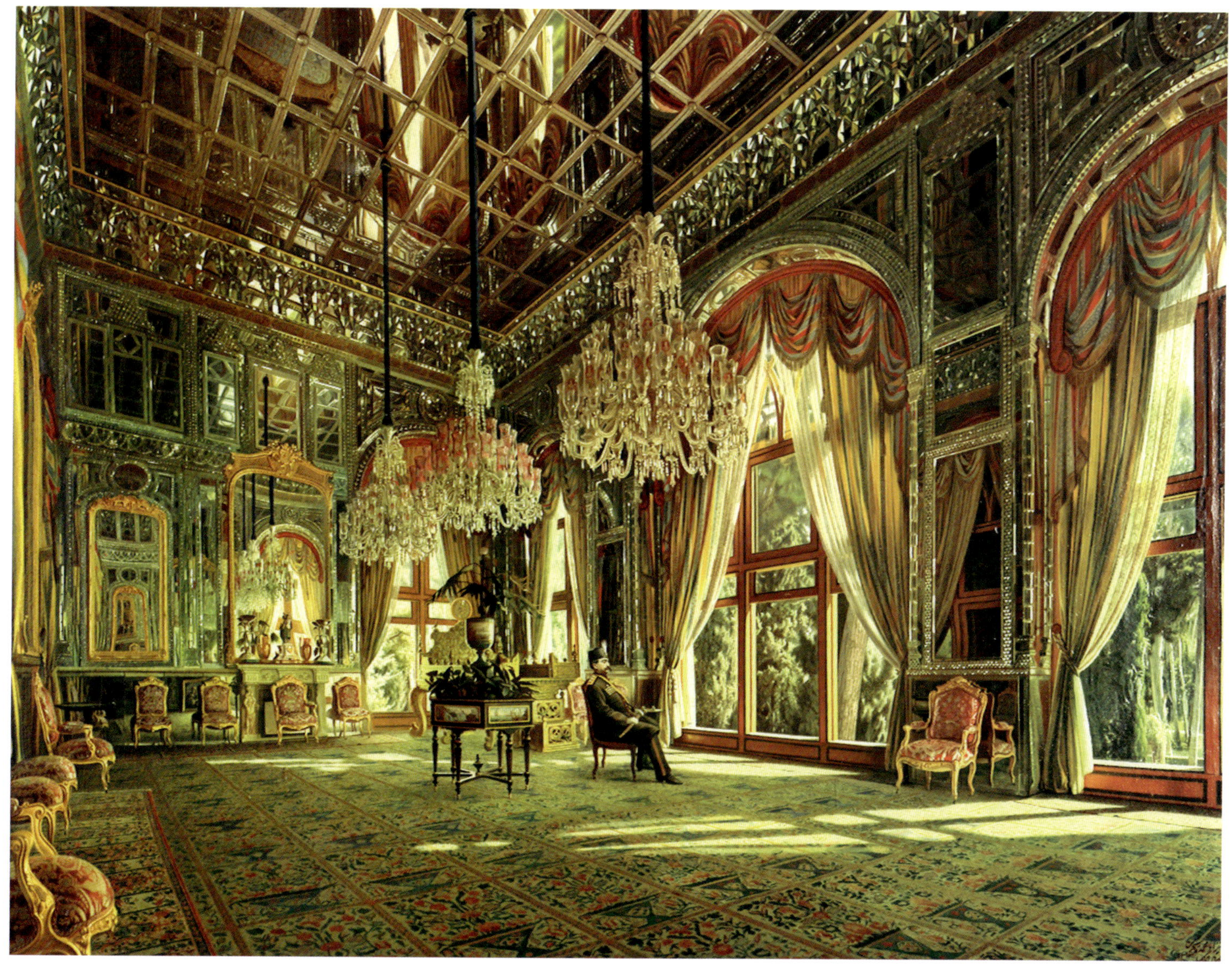

1.12
Kamal al-Mulk, *The Hall of Mirrors*, 1885–1890, oil on canvas, 91×120 cm, Golestan Palace

In his memoirs, he repeatedly emphasised his admiration for the paintings of Rembrandt, Raphael, and Titian, showing little interest in contemporary Impressionist works.[35] His journey to Europe was undertaken with the intention of expanding his technical proficiency as a royal artist rather than as an individual one. Therefore, his preference for the classical works of European Old Masters over contemporary artists should not come as a great surprise. He seemed drawn to the conservative art of the period, such as the nineteenth-century academic style or Salon paintings. While Kamal al-Mulk might have been aware of avant-garde movements emerging at that time, such as Impressionism and Post-Impressionism, possibly through his acquaintance with the French painter Henri Fantin-Latour (1836–1904),[36] he consciously chose not to align himself with these new movements.

Following his return to Iran in 1901, Kamal al-Mulk's adherence to nineteenth-century European academism in his painting style became even more pronounced than before. Even in his later works, after he left the royal court, where he effectively portrayed social scenes depicting indigenous themes, his aim was to present them in a pure, naturalistic style. Some of his most successful works in this genre, such as *Karbala Square* (1902), *Baghdadi Goldsmith* (1901), and *Baghdadi Jewish Fortune-Tellers* (1901), were created during his two-year stay in Iraq (1901–3, in Baghdad and Karbala). (Figure 1.13) Although Kamal al-Mulk had already depicted social scenes of the time earlier (such as *The Fortune-Teller*, 1891), it was mainly during this period that a noticeable shift in his choice of subject matter occurred, with a greater emphasis on urban scenes and images depicting the everyday life of ordinary people. This shift can be understood in the context of the collapse of the court patronage system that had existed since the Timurid period, following the death of Muzaffar al-Din Shah in 1907.

Indeed his later development in a purely Europeanised style represents a major evolution in the imagery of Persian painting[37] and would have a lasting effect on its subsequent development. It seems that this particularly occurred after his journey to Europe. Later in this period he chose a wider range of subject matter such as landscapes around Tehran, social scenes and also the dignitaries of the time. (Figure 1.14) Portraits such as Commander Asa'd Bakhtiyari and Azad al-Mulk (the two key figures in the 1905–6 Constitutional Revolution) signify this genre. (Figure 1.15) These were the dominant themes of his painting in this period.

1. The establishment of the Madrasa-i Sanayi'-i Mustazrafa (School of Fine Art) in 1911

Perhaps the most significant outcome of Kamal al-Mulk's journey to Europe was the establishment of Iran's first academy of fine art, the Madrasa-i Sanayi'-i Mustazrafa (School of Fine Art) in 1911. It was five years after the Iranian Constitutional Revolution[38] when, as Ruin Pakbaz argues, the first traces of a new development in Iranian arts and literature could be discerned. Pakbaz, nevertheless, remarks that the social and cultural changes resulting from this revolution provided an important background against which the arts could grow.[39] With the approval of the post-revolutionary government[40] and driven by

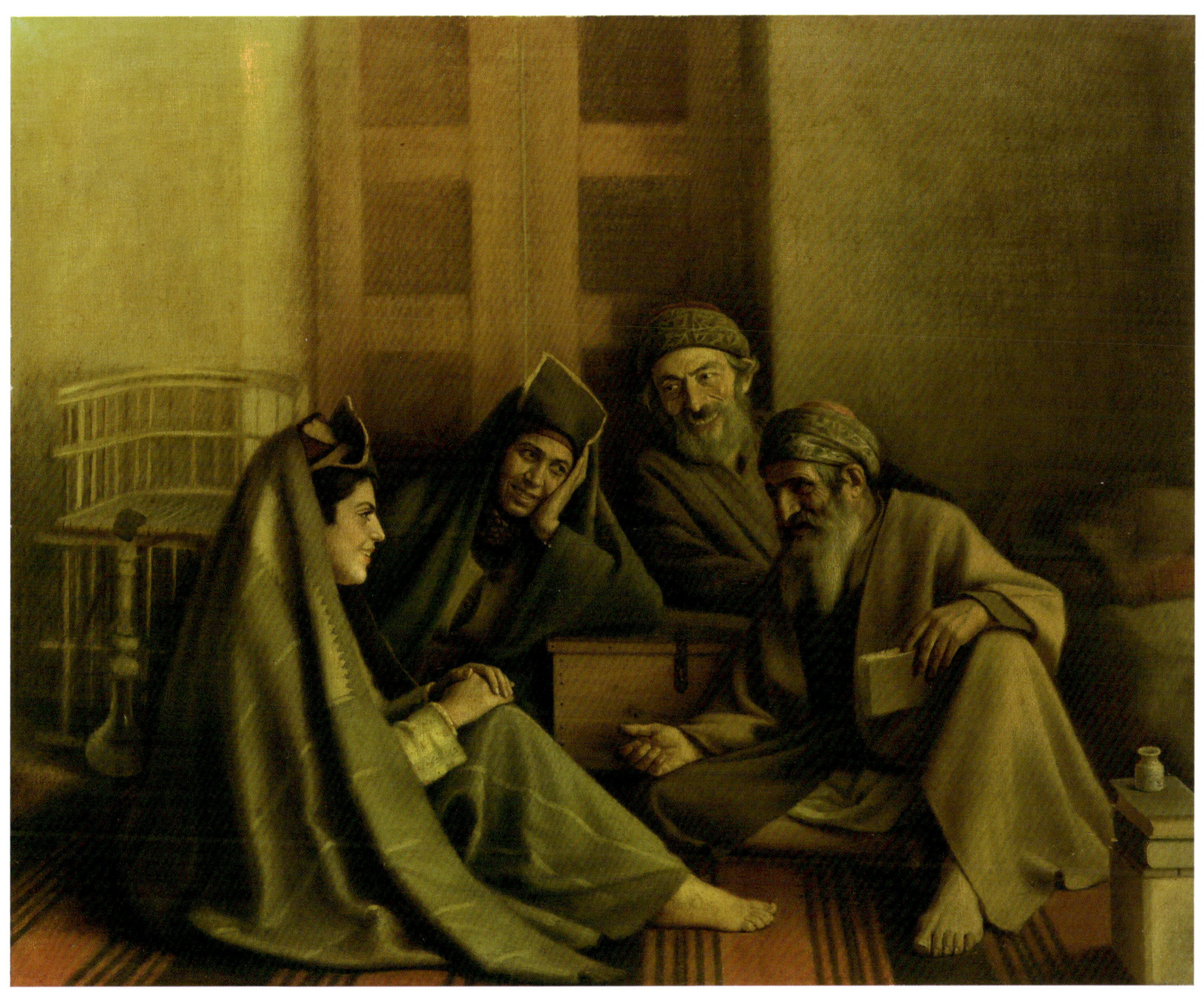

1.13

Kamal al-Mulk, *Baghdadi Jewish Fortune Tellers*, 1901, oil on canvas, 46×55.5 cm, Majlis Museum

his own artistic mission, Kamal al-Mulk attempted to introduce a European educational system of art in his Madrasa. The school, under the jurisdiction of the Vizarat-i Ma'arif (Ministry of Education), was intended to be devoted exclusively to the instruction and promotion of fine art, especially the 'science of painting'.[41] As painting classes at the Dar al-Funun were given increasingly less attention by the court in favour of new subjects such as music and theatre, the Madrasa-i Sanayi' i Mustazrafa became the sole new institution for the training of the visual arts in the country. The Madrasa's mission statement explicitly referred to painting as a science and delineated the school's primary function as the 'disseminator of this science'.[42] Among the

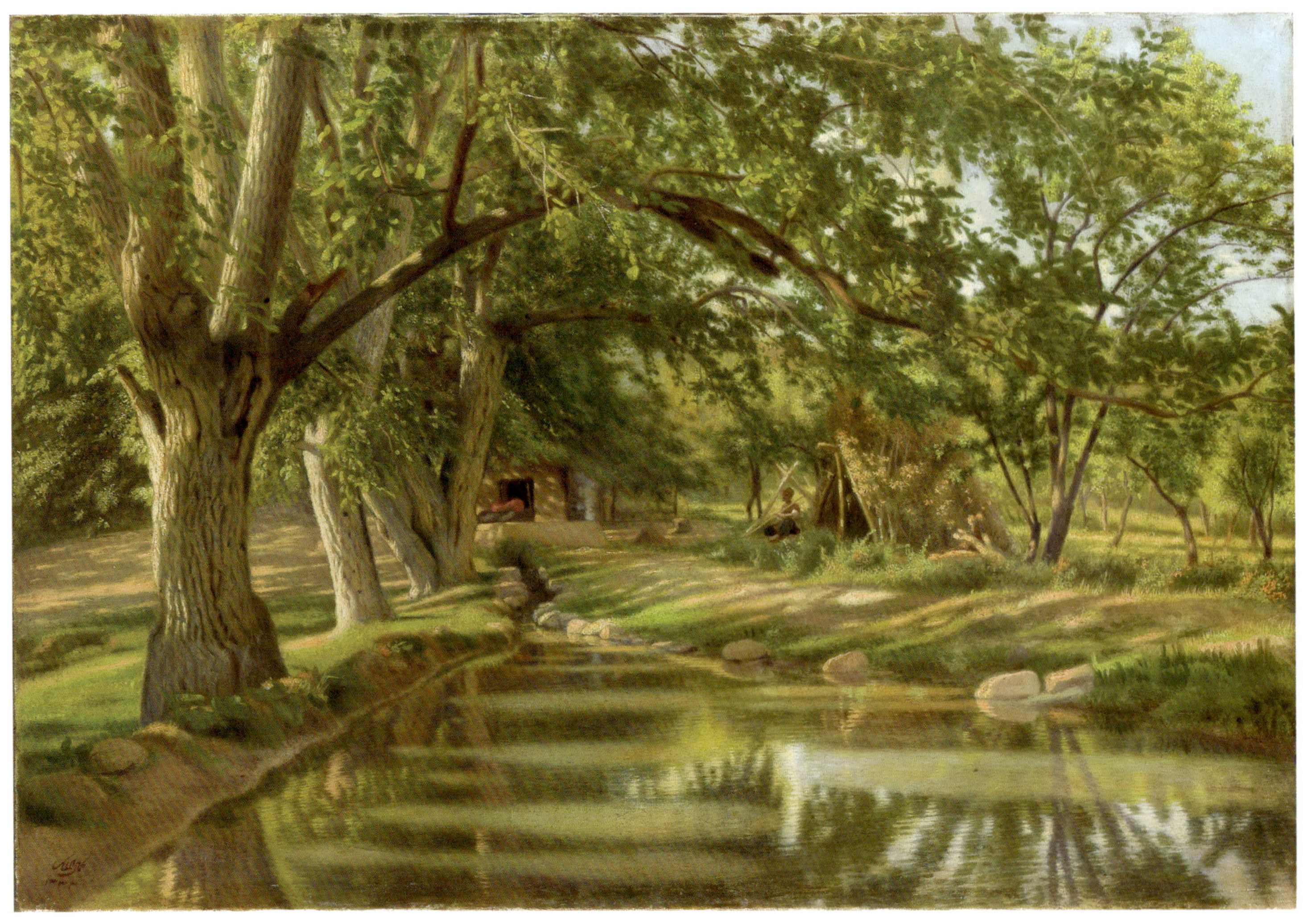

1.14
Kamal al-Mulk, *Mughanak Village*,
oil on canvas, 1915, 59.5×85 cm,
Majlis Museum

Facing page
1.15
Kamal al-Mulk, *Commander Asa'd
Bakhtiyari*, 1911, oil on canvas,
189×131 cm, Majlis Museum

courses were oil and watercolour painting, sculpture, carpet-weaving, drawing and, later, lithography.[43]

The published documents and announcements relating to the Madrasa reveal no particular indication or information about the school's curriculum. Rather, the documents mostly deal with administrative issues and budgetary questions. However, what seems obvious from the records is the presence of traces of both apprenticeship and the European academic systems. (Figures 1. 16–17)

Kamal al-Mulk's aim in establishing the Madrasa was to train students to follow European academic methods. He himself directed the school until his resignation in 1927.[44] It exerted a major influence in the promotion of European-style academic painting. Through the school he trained and launched a host of disciples who propagated and popularised the new style of painting at the expense of former ones. Although this school never developed into a fully fledged academy,

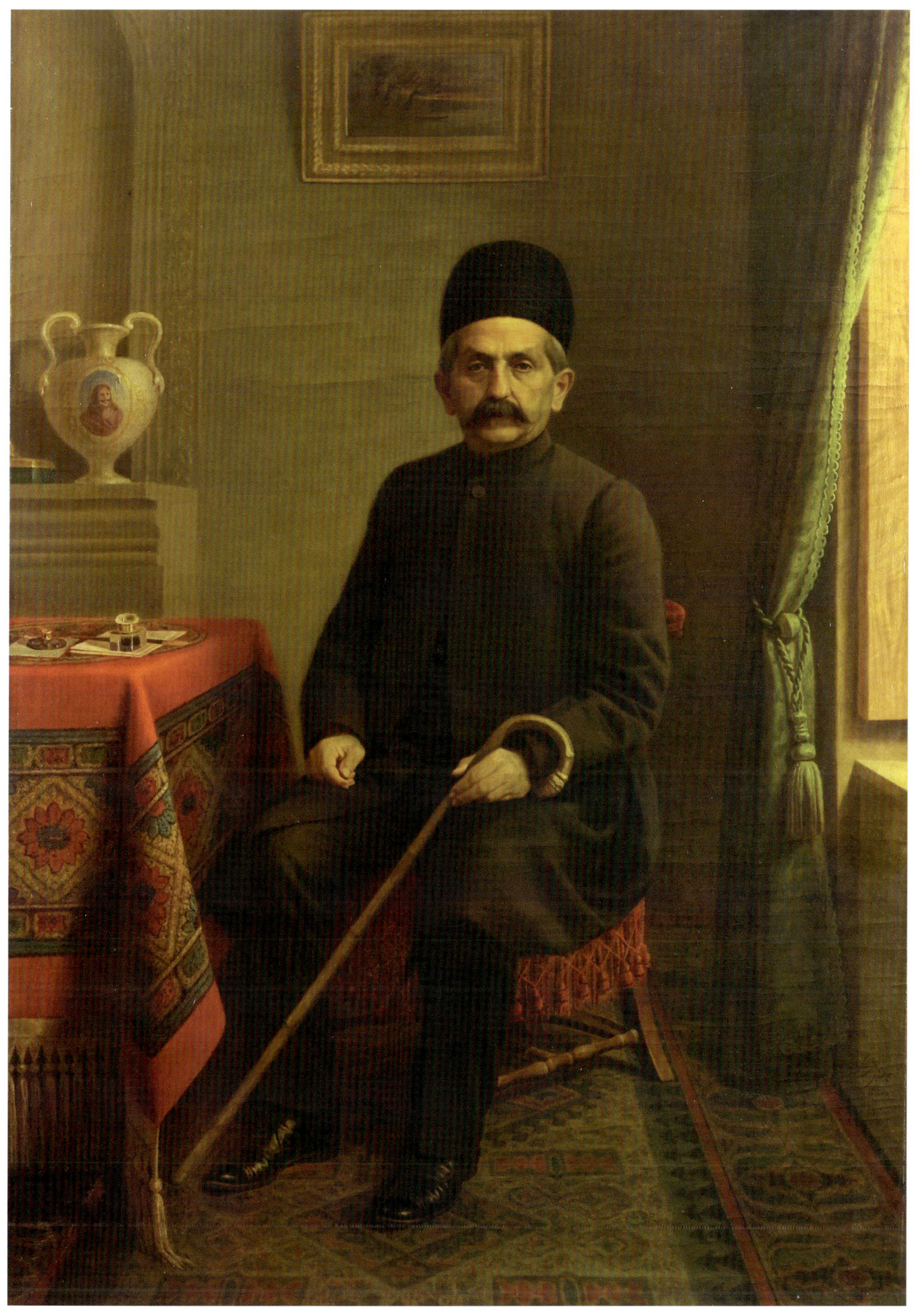

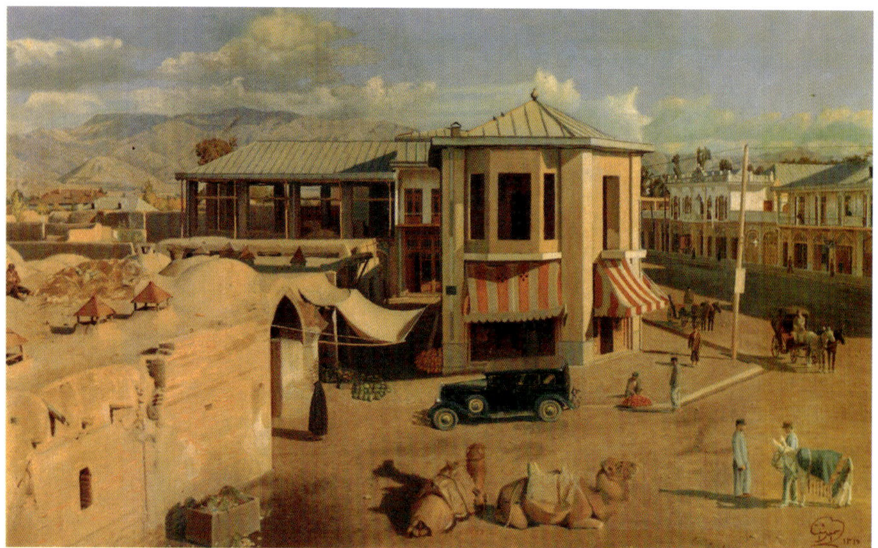

1.18
Ismail Ashtiani, *Chahar-rah-i Galubandak, Tehran*, 1938, oil on canvas, private collection, Tehran

Hassan Ali Vaziri served as the deputy of the Madrasa while Kamal al-Mulk was still the director. He also taught there and later at the Faculty of Fine Arts, Tehran University. Vaziri emerged as one of the pioneering artists of his generation, notable for his plein air landscape paintings that drew inspiration from the Impressionist style. His works are characterised by an abundance of light, vivid tones, and a meticulous emphasis on contrasting lights and shadows. (Figure 1.17) Ali Akbar Yasami who lived, worked and taught in Tabriz, was highly influential in training artists in Azarbaijan. His intimate subjects and style of painting, although much more humble than Kamal al-Mulk's, were not far in character from the master's either. (Figure 1.21) Abul Hassan Sedighi, a leading Iranian sculptor, launched the sculpture studio at the Madrasa and later the Sculpture Department at the Faculty of Fine Arts, Tehran University. Sedighi was appointed as the director of the Madrasa there in 1932. He made trips to Europe (Italy and France) and studied in the École des Beaux Arts (1928–31). Sedighi is recognised as the inaugural professional sculptor in twentieth-century Iran. His monumental marble statues honouring esteemed figures from Iran's past, including Ferdowsi, Sa'di, and 'Omar Khayyam, rendered with impeccable realism and installed in city squares across Iran, mark an unparalleled achievement in Iranian history. (Figure 1.22)

It seems that Kamal al-Mulk's efforts were influenced by broader transformations in Iran's socio-cultural domain. Both as an artist and an educator, he strove to cultivate a new artistic sensibility that resonated with the evolving context of a rapidly changing Iran. Indeed, the so-called 'School of Kamal al-Mulk' exerted significant

Facing page
1.19
Ali Mohammad Heydarian,
Philosopher, 1967, oil on canvas,
92×73 cm, TMoCA

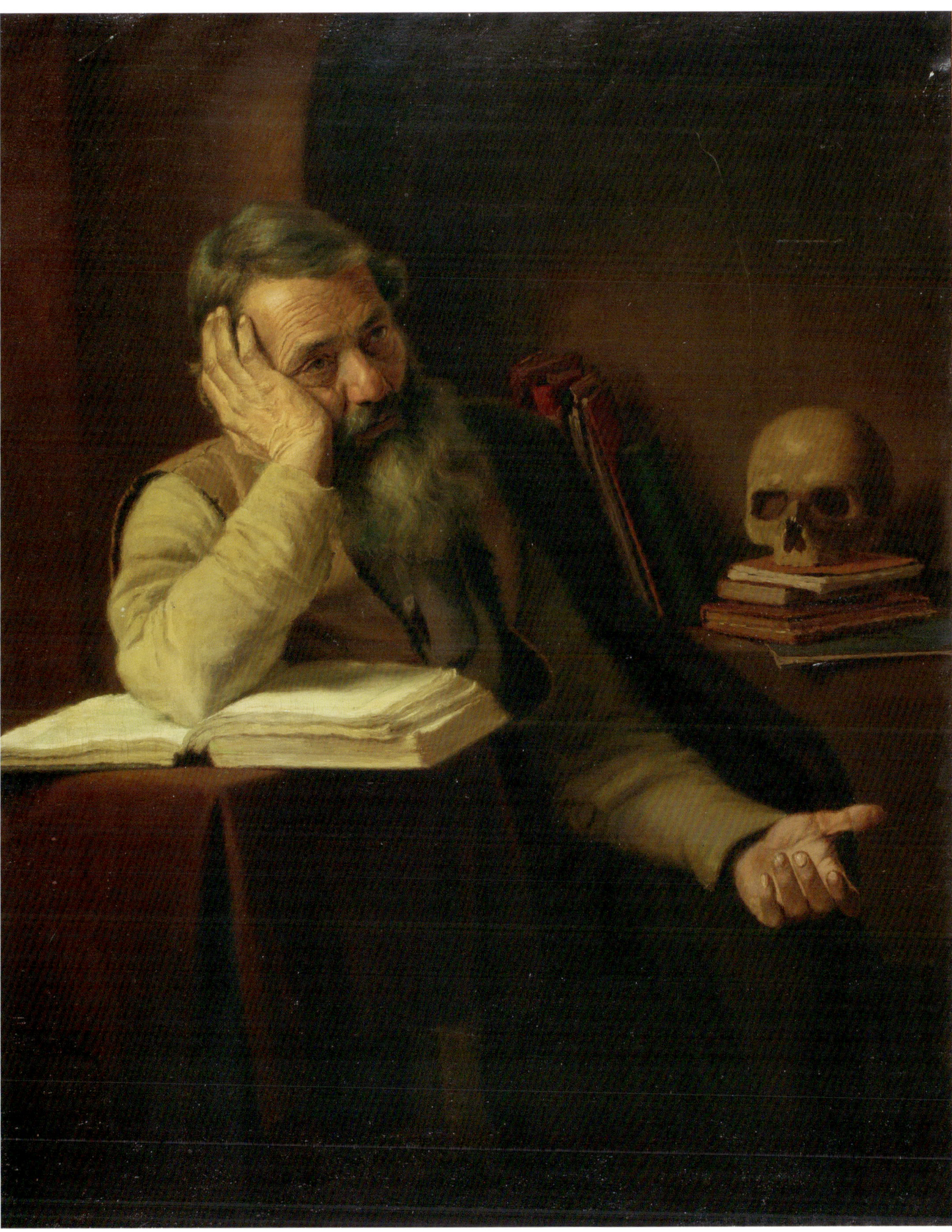

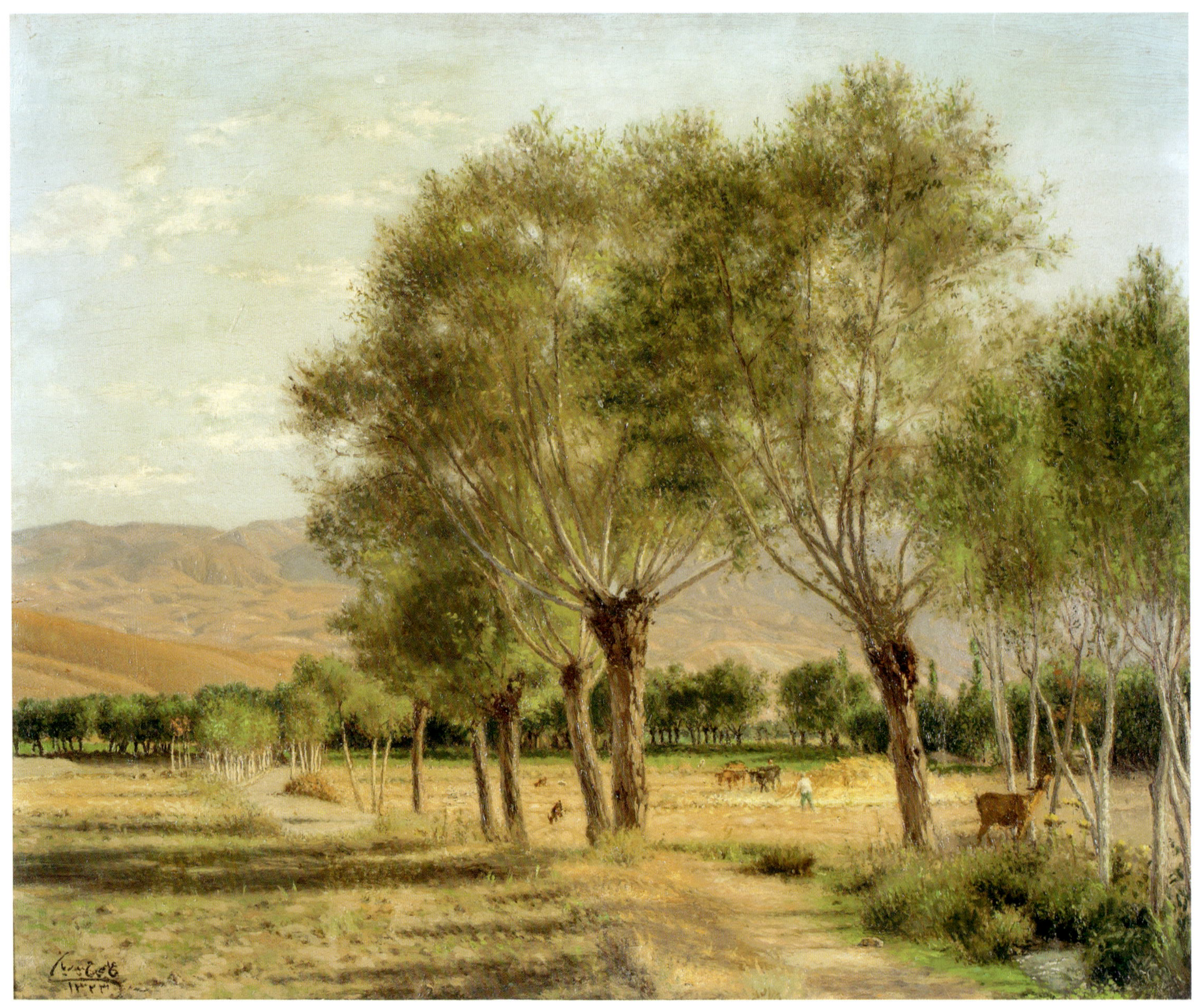

1.20
Ali Mohammad Heydarian,
Threshing, 1944, oil on board,
50×60 cm, TMOC

influence over the visual arts in Iran during the initial decades of the twentieth century (Figure 1.23). His profound impact extended far and wide, shaping the trajectory of subsequent artistic developments.

2. Madrasa Sanayi'-i Qadima (School of Traditional Arts) and the formation of the so-called School of Tehran

Considering the changes wrought in the previous century, it is somewhat paradoxical that during the early twentieth century the Iranian art scene witnessed the renewal of traditional miniature painting. However, it should be stated that this shift of focus was greatly influenced by the aesthetic system established by the Kamal al-Mulk School. A group of traditionalist artists, usually referred to as miniaturists, attempted to revive Timurid and late Safavid artistic traditions, in particular those of the so-called Tabriz and Isfahan Schools of the sixteenth and seventeenth centuries. Beginning in the late Qajar and early Pahlavi

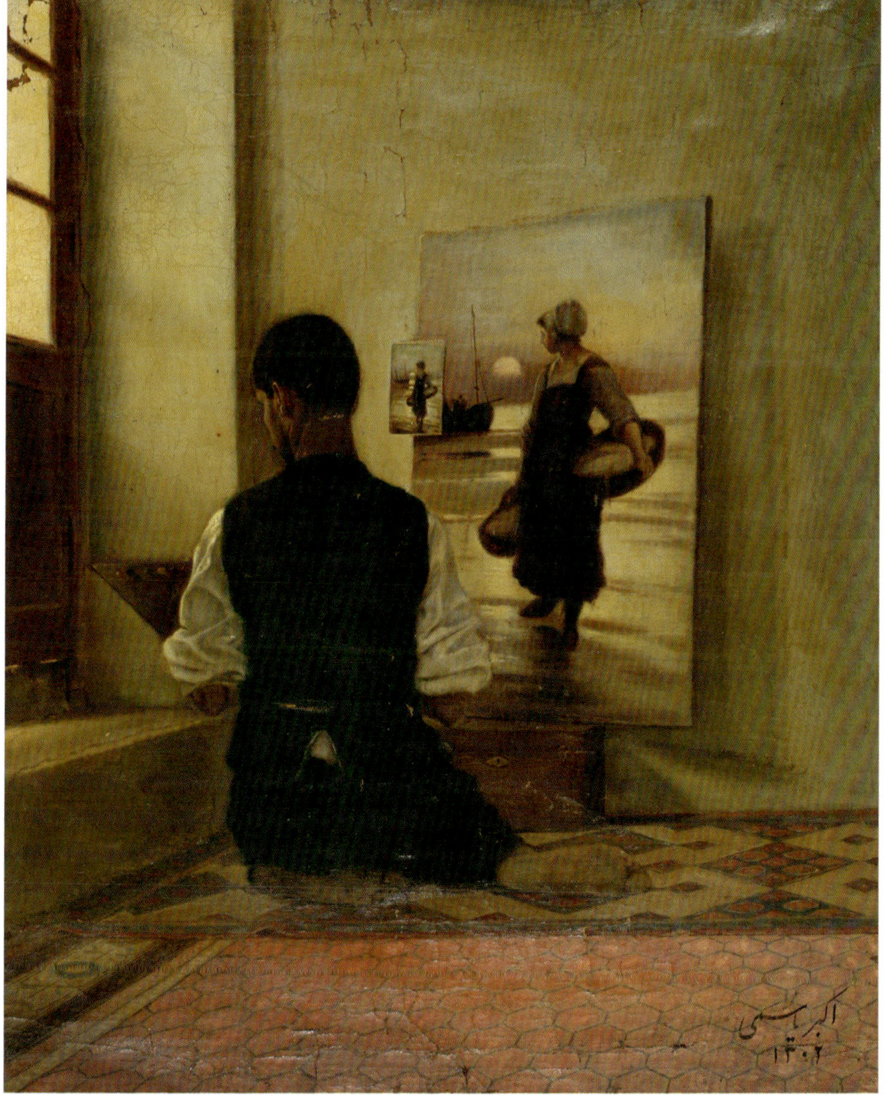

1.21
Ali Akbar Yasami, *Painter*, 1923, oil on canvas, 74×90 cm, TMoCA

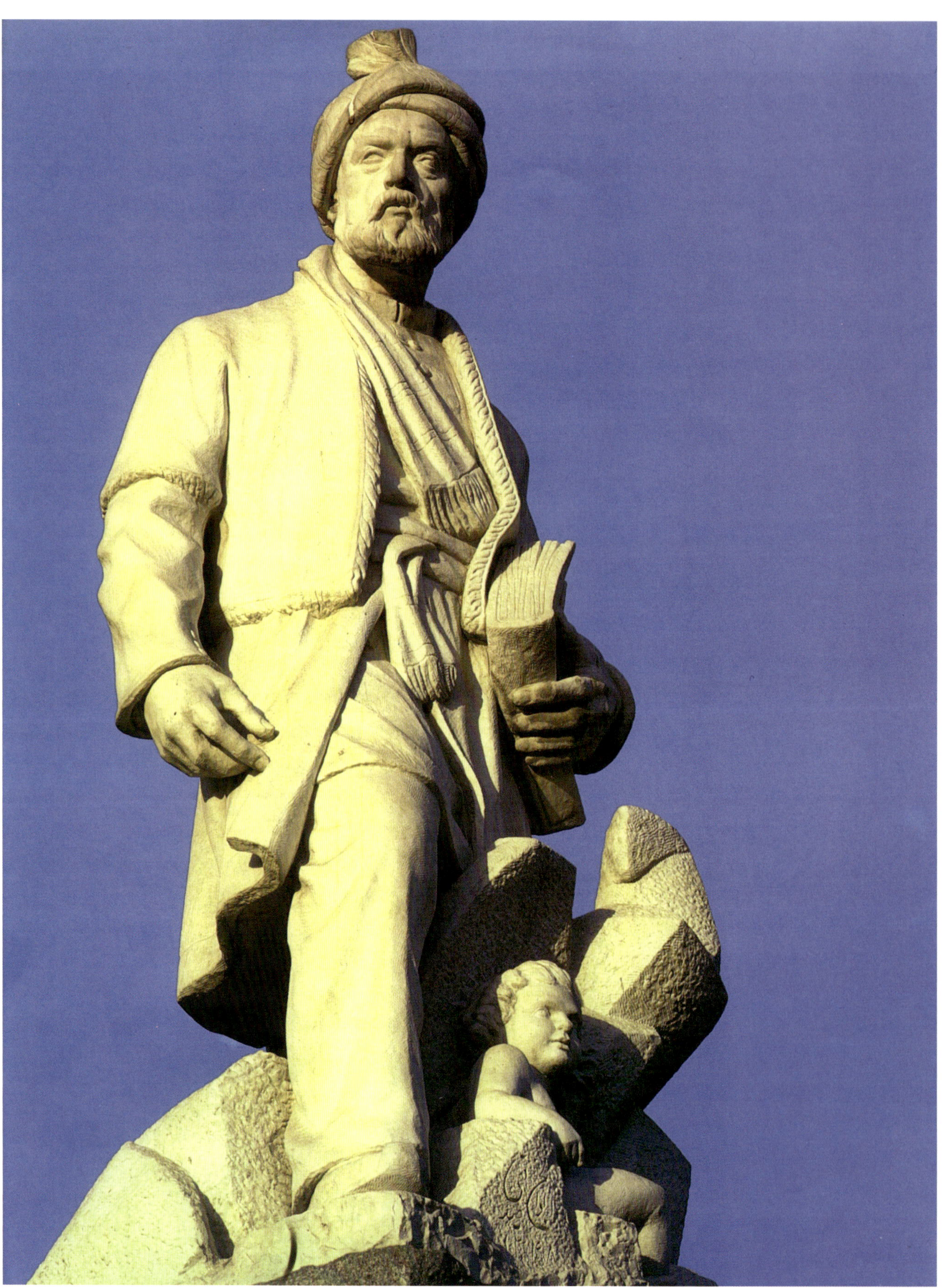

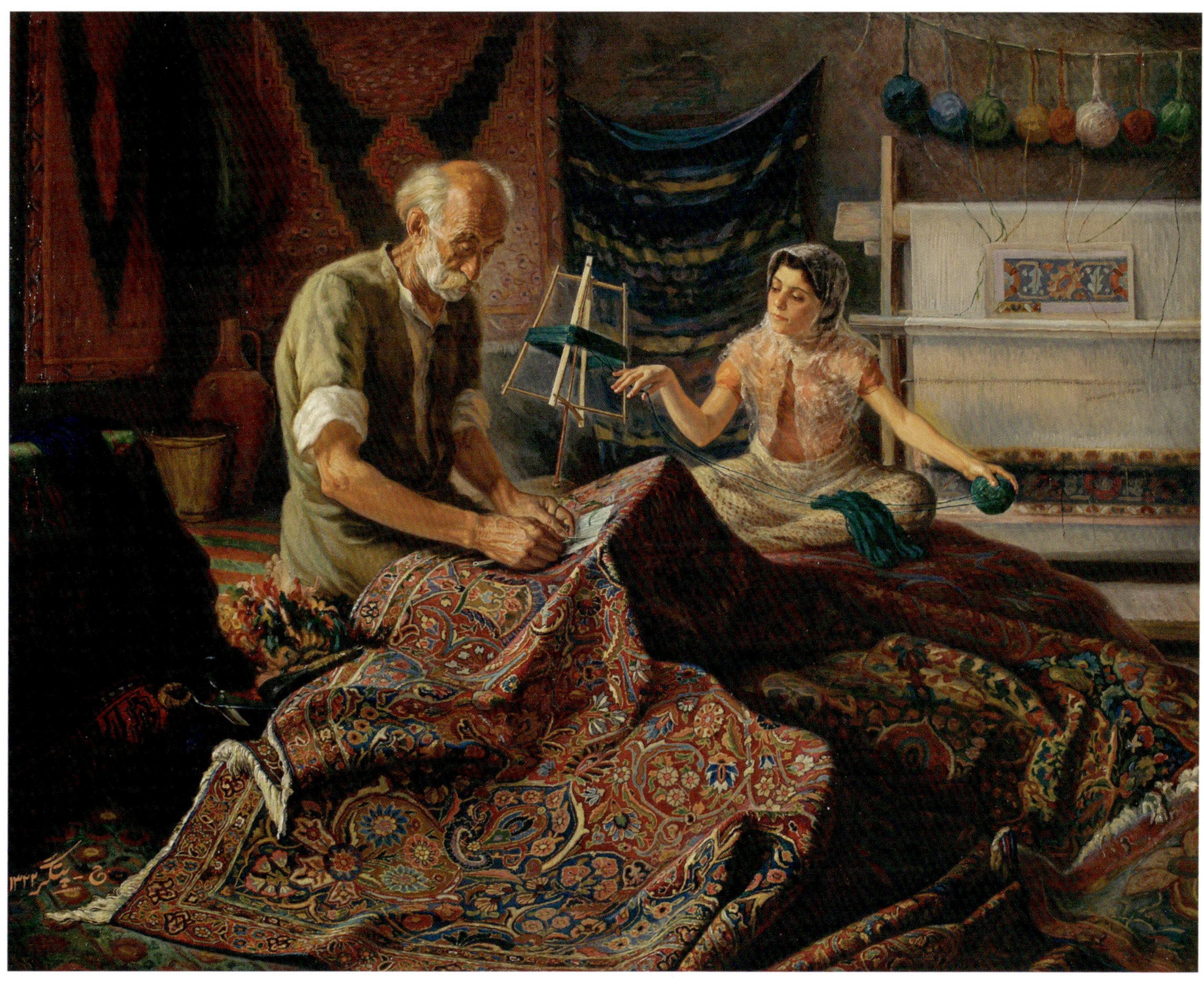

periods (1920s), these miniaturists taught several pupils who then went on to promote the style both in Tehran and in Isfahan. Thanks to the efforts of artists such as Hossein Taherzadeh Behzad (1887–1925) and Mirza Hadi-Khan Tadjvidi (1892–1940) (who had also attended Kamal al-Mulk's Madrasa-i Sanayi'-i Mustazrafa), the establishment of the Madrasa Sanayi'-i Qadima (School of Traditional Arts) in 1929 was followed by a period of renewed activity; this led to the formation of the so-called Tehran School of Miniature. The Madrasa Sanayi'-i Qadima, at least in the beginning, was a kind of artistic encounter with the other Madrasa-i Sanayi'-i Mustazrafa. Having said that, the Sanayi'-i Qadima and the style promoted by it never had the same hegemonic dominance and popularity of the Sanayi'-i Mustazrafa and Kamal al-

Facing page
1.22
Abul Hassan Sedighi, *Ferdowsi Statue*, 1971, Carrara Marble, height: 300 cm

Above
1.23
Jafar Petgar, *Darning*, 1943, oil on canvas, 107×133 cm, TMoCA

Mulk School.

This renewal of Persian painting was encouraged under the rule of Reza Shah Pahlavi, and by the creation of the Madrasa-i Sanayi'-i Qadima to train and support artists.[46] Several other centres and museums were formed, including various 'traditional art workshops' and the Iranian National Museum of Arts – the latter preserving many works by prominent artists of the School of Tehran.

Hossein Taherzadeh Behzad, a distinguished miniaturist and teacher, was the main founder of the Madrasa Sanayi'-i Qadima. His aim was to revive 'real' traditional and national Iranian art, which was believed to have been eclipsed for about three centuries. The other main figure was Mirza Hadi-Khan Tadjvidi, who had studied miniature painting in Isfahan under his older brother Mehdi (who signed his paintings as Mehdi Taeb), Agha Mohammad Ebrahim Nematollahi, Agha Mirza Ahmad and Hossein Haj Mossavar-ol-Molki (1889–1967); and later with Agh Mirza Yahya Khan Naqqash-bashi in Tehran, where he learnt techniques of Qajar painting and lacquerwork. He then attended the Madrasa Sanayi'-i Mustazrafa under Kamal al-Mulk, where he taught watercolour before being appointed as the first instructor at the Madrasa Sanayi'-i Qadima.[47] He especially admired the Herat (Kamal al-Din Behzad in particular), Tabriz and Isfahan schools. Later, his style of miniature painting and teaching methods were affected by his interest in and understanding of chiaroscuro, linear perspective and three-dimensional rendering. The absorption of these 'realistic' techniques was probably an effect of his studentship at Madrasa Sanayi'-i Mustazrafa. While the subject matter remains almost unchanged compared with classical Persian painting, the content and style of portraiture seem different in terms of characters and the depiction of social figures – in contrast to the traditional approach, which was to portray literary or mystical personalities. (Figure 1.24) Tadjvidi died at the age of forty-six but trained a number of distinguished miniaturists who continued in this style throughout the twentieth century. Mohammad Ali Zaviyeh (1912–90), Abutaleb Moghimi Tabrizi (1912–69), Ali Karimi (1913–97), Ali Moti' (1916–2008), Kelara Abkar (1915–96), Hossein Altafi (1906–79) and Ali Esfarjani (1920–2005) are examples worthy of mention.[48] (Figures 1. 25–26)

A parallel development of the renewal of miniature painting occurred in Isfahan. The key figures were Mirza Agha Emami (1882–1946), Hossein Haj Mossavar-ol-Molki (1889–1967) and Issa Bahadori (1906–86). Bahadori taught at the Madrasa Sanayi'-i Qadima and

1.24
Hadi-Khan Tadjvidi, *Shahnameh Majlis*, 1926, gouache and watercolour on paper, 34×44 cm, TMoCA

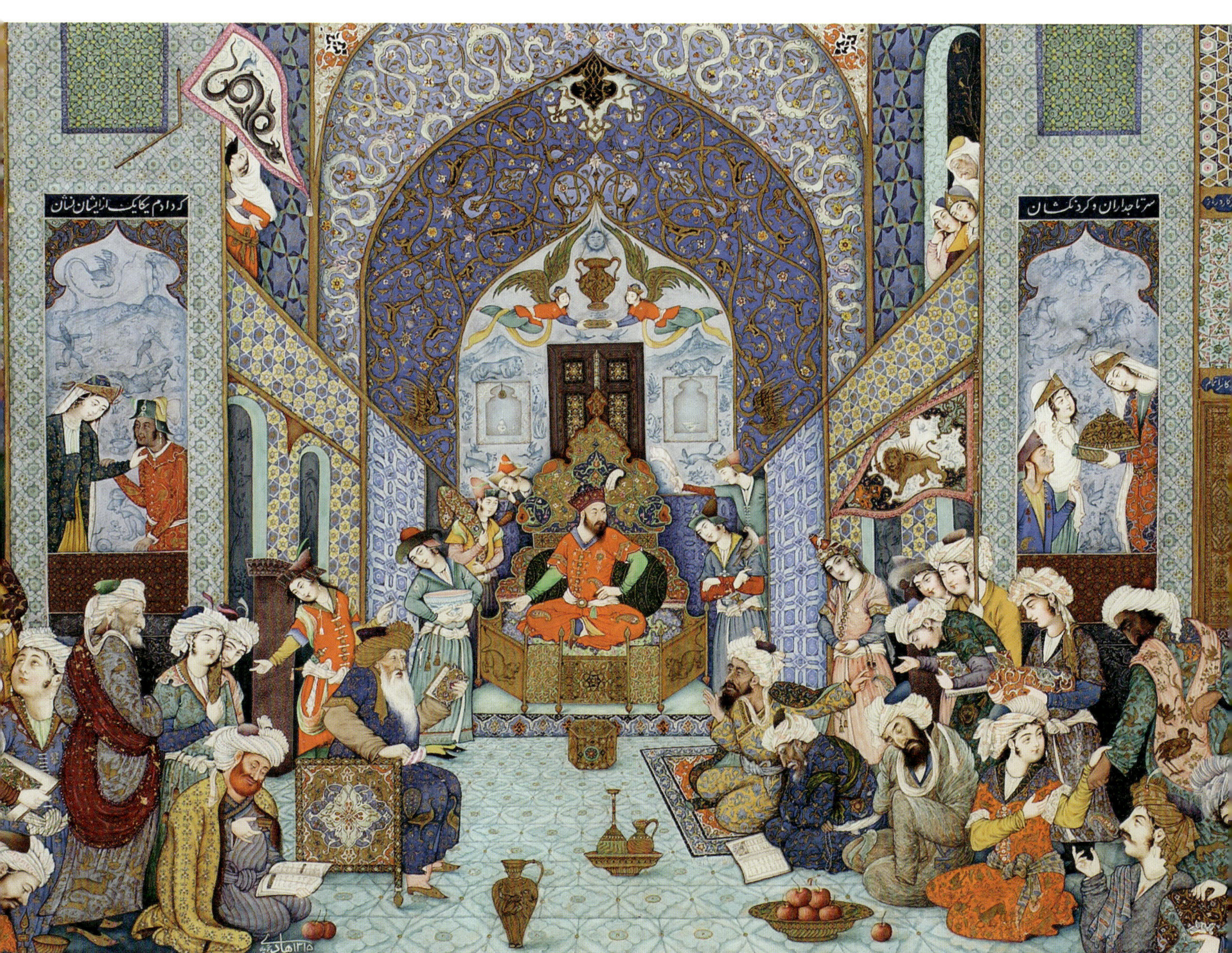

کدام یک یکایک از ایشان نشان
سرتاجداران و کردنکشان

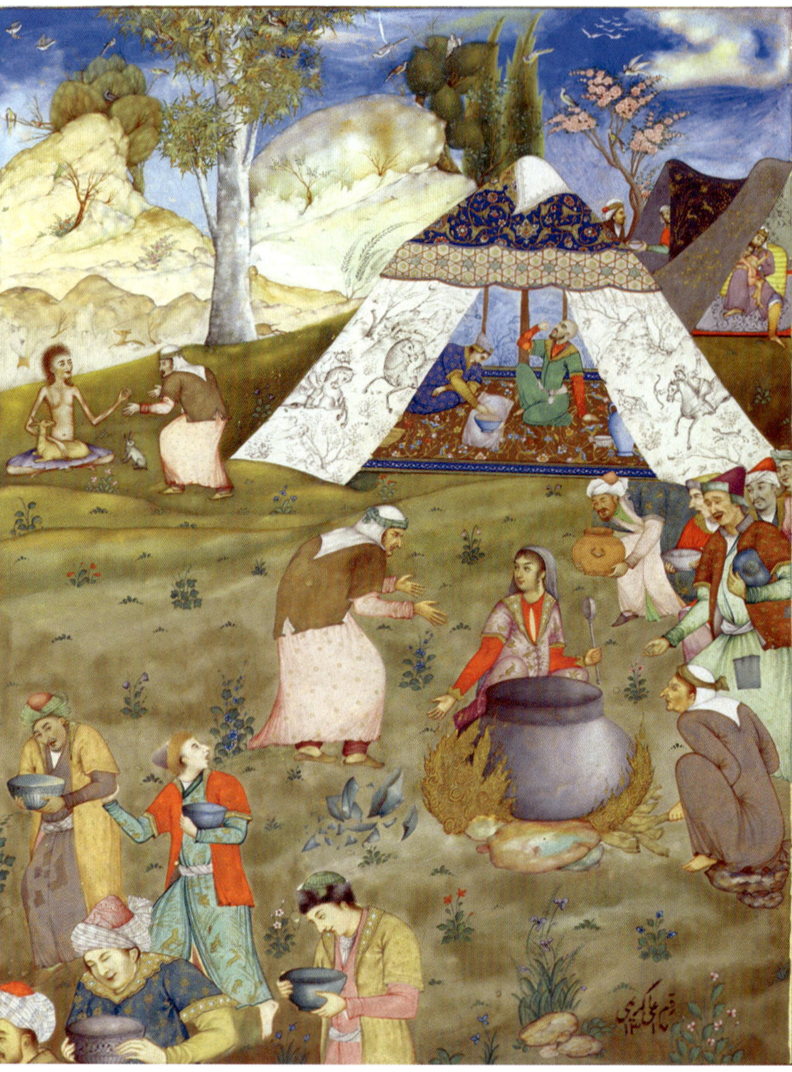

1.25
Ali Karimi, *Untitled*, 1938, gouache on paper, 40×29 cm, Museum of National Arts, Tehran

directed the Isfahan Fine Art High School for Boys where the next generation of miniaturists were trained. Emami studied in Isfahan and then in Tehran at the Majma' al-Sanayi' under Mirza Razi Sani' Homayoun, who was a maestro of traditional illumination. He then returned to his hometown and established a studio where several disciples were trained, including Hossein Eslamian (1911–81), Rostam Shirazi (1919–2005), Hossein Khataei (1908–75), Hossein Khoshneviszadeh (1909–94), Mahmoud Farshchian (b.1929) and Houshang Jazizadeh (b.1933).

Another distinguished figure working in the same manner was Hossein Behzad (1894–1968). Although he did not participate in either of these regional schools he played a key role in this period, and his highly personal style of miniature painting had considerable influence on the development of twentieth-century miniature painting. Behzad, who was famous for his detailed and mostly monochrome miniatures, did not have any formal education but taught at the Tehran Fine Art High School for Boys. (Figure 1. 27) André Sevruguin (1896–1996) is also named as an eminent artist of this genre, although his personal style of miniature is completely different from that of other more conventional artists of this trend.

These developments together shaped the first four decades of the twentieth-century Iranian art scene. The principles established would not, however, remain unchallenged in the 1940s, which saw the arrival of a new Western system of art education within the recently founded Tehran University and the coming generation of artists.

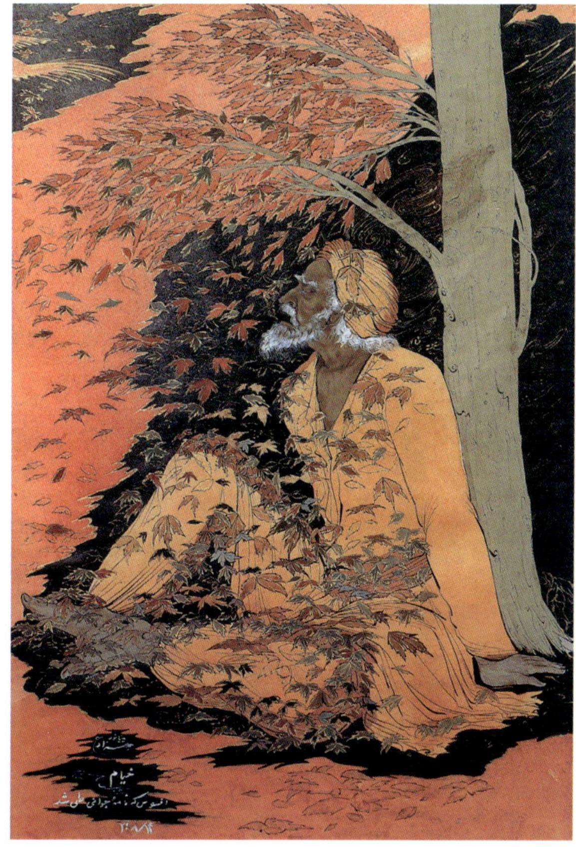

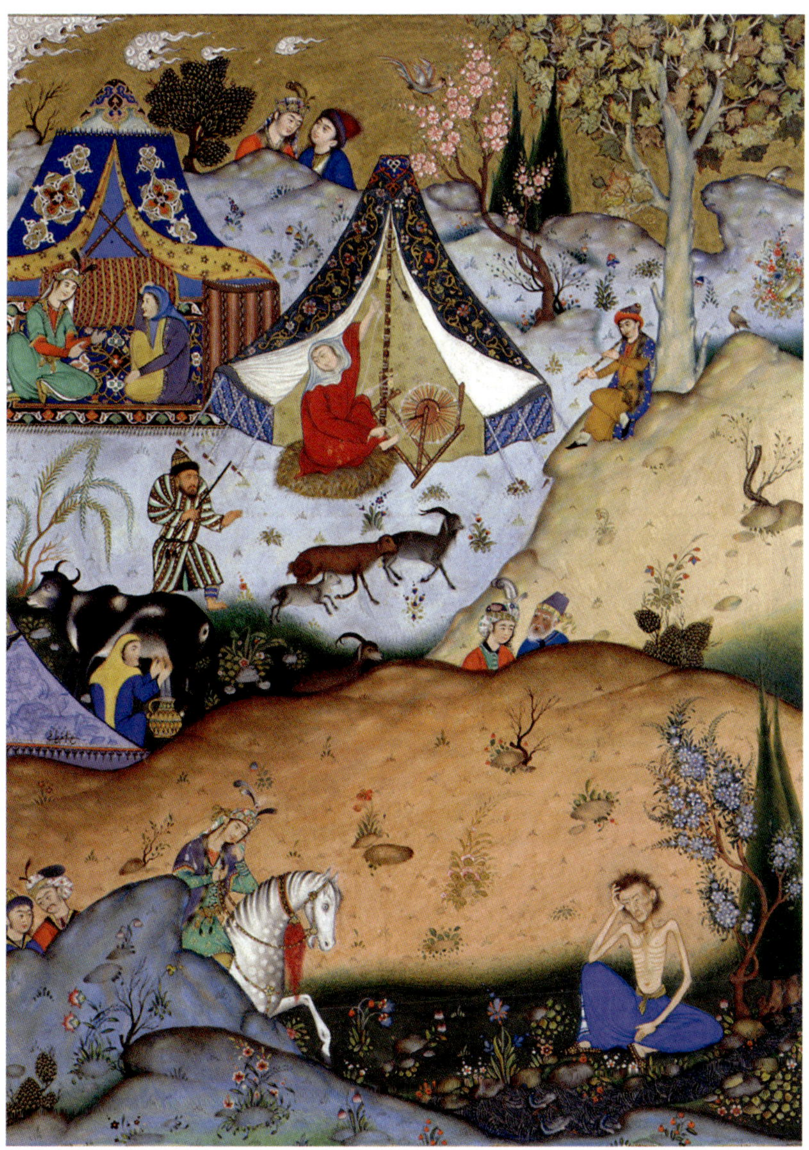

Left
1.26
Ali Esfarjani, *Majnun in the Desert*, *c.* 1951, gouache on paper, no size, Museum of National Arts, Tehran

Above
1.27
Hossein Taherzadeh Behzad, *Afsus keh nameh-i javani tiy shud …* (*Alas, the letter of youth passed …*; a verse from Khayyam), 1943, gouache and watercolour on paper, no size, Behzad Museum, Tehran

NOTES

1 Stephen Vernoit, *Occidentalism: Islamic Art in the 19th Century: The Nasser D. Khalili Collection of Islamic Art*, vol. 23, New York 1997, p. 10.

2 R. M. Smith, *Persian Art*, London 1876, p.78. Vernoit also writes that in the view of some European scholars 'such paintings had no artistic merit because they lacked a proper understanding of scientific perspective, chiaroscuro and verisimilitude'. (Stephen Vernoit, *Occidentalism*, p.12.)

3 Julien M. de Rochechouart, 'Quant aux paintures que les Persans produisent eux-mêmes, c'est à faire grincer les dents,' in *Souvenir d'un voyage en Perse*, Paris 1867, p.261.

4 Ibid, pp.264–265.

5 This term was used to explain a tendency throughout late seventeenth, eighteenth and nineteenth-century Persian painting that was described as a loose use of European styles by a number of Iranian and Indian painters. The main feature in these works was the use of typical techniques of post-Renaissance European painting such as the free use of chiaroscuro and perspective. This tendency to borrow also included the subject-matter of their works. (Sheila Canby, 'Farangi saz: the Impact of Europe on Safavid Painting', in Jill Tilden ed. *Silk & Stone: The Art of Asia*, London 1996, p.57 and Ruin Pakbaz, *Encyclopaedia of Art*, Tehran 1378S/1999, p.371)

6 Finbarr Barry Flood, 'From the Prophet to Postmodernism? New World Orders and the End of Islamic Art', in Elizabeth Mansfield, ed., *Making Art History: A Changing Discipline and its Institutions*, London 2007, p.37. Also see Stephen Vernoit, *Occidentalism*, p.12.

7 Sheila Canby, 'Farangi saz', London 1996, pp.58, 59.

8 See Stephen Vernoit, *Occidentalism*, p.10.

9 Finbarr Barry Flood, 'From the Prophet to Postmodernism? New World Orders and the End of Islamic Art', in *Making Art History: A Changing Discipline and its Institution*, London 2007, p.35

10 Maryam Ekhtiar, 'From Workshop to Bazaar to Academy: Art Training and Production in Qajar', in Layla S. Diba, ed., *Royal Persian Painting: The Qajar Epoch 1785-1825, Two Hundred Years of Painting from the Royal Persian Courts,* New York 1999, p.50.

11 Lady Sheil, *Glimpses of Life and Manners in Persia*, London 1856, pp.202–203.

12 Layla S. Diba, 'Muhammad Ghaffari: The Persian Painter of Modern Life', *Iranian Studies*, vol. 45, no. 5, September 2012, p. 650.

13 Abbas Amanat, 'Qajar Iran: A Historical Overview', in Layla S. Diba, ed., *Royal Persian Painting*, p.26.

14 Layla S. Diba, 'Muhammad Ghaffari', *Iranian Studies*, p.646.

15 Ism'il Jalayir, one of the early students of the Dar al-Funun, was a favourite artist in Nassir al-Din Shah's court.

16 Abu-Turab Ghaffari also studied at the Dar al-Funun and in 1887 was appointed *naqqash-bashi*. He was a fine portraitist and, like Abu'l Hassan, worked for an illustrated newspaper.

17 See Ahmad Ashraf, KAMĀL-AL-MOLK, MOḤAMMAD ĠAFFĀRI, https://www.iranicaonline.org/articles/kamal-al-molk-mohammad-gaffari

18 A document dated 1852 describes 'the initial production location as a *Hujra* in the newly established arts and crafts centre in Tehran, the Majma'-i al-Dar al-Sanayei.' (I'timad al-Saltaneh 1984–5, p.244.) The products manufactured in this centre included clocks, guns, carriages, European-style military uniforms, and paintings. (Maryam Ekhtiar, 'From Workshop to Bazaar to Academy: Art Training and Production in Qajar', p. 58). This college could be the initial form of artistic training in the academic mode before the formal foundation of painting classes at the Dar al-Funun.

19 Mirza Abu'l Hassan Khan Ghaffari, leading painter of Mohammad Shah (1834–48), was sent to Italy towards the end of the Shah's reign to study technical draughtsmanship and painting. During his sojourn in Italy (1846–50), Abu'l Hassan visited academies and museums in Rome, the Vatican, Florence, and Venice, meticulously replicating the works of Italian masters while also honing his technical skills in lithographic printing press operations. Upon his return, he was appointed as the illustrator for the state-sponsored gazette *Ruznama-i vaqayi'-i ittifaqiyya* and was commissioned by Nassir al-Din Shah to design and illustrate a seven-volume manuscript of the *Thousand and One Nights*, distinguished for its extensive pagination and ornate decoration.

20 Maryam Ekhtiar, 'From Workshop to Bazaar to Academy: Art Training and Production in Qajar', p.59.

21 Ibid.

22 Mohammad Ali Karimzadeh Tabrizi, *Ahval va asar-i naqqashan-i qadim-i iran va barkhi az mashahir-i nigaragari-i hind va 'usmani*, vol. 1, London 1985, pp.21–34.

23 Stephen Vernoit, *Occidentalism*, p.116.

24 For centuries, 'art' and 'handicraft' were interchangeable in Iran. (Seyyed Hossein Nasr, *Art and Spirituality*, New Delhi (Delhi) 1990, p.67.) An examination of the four Persian words for art or craft – *san'at, fann, pisheh*, and *hunar* – and a tracing of their usage back to the fifteenth century reveal that until the second half of the nineteenth century they were employed interchangeably. Similar to geometry and history for instance, at the time certain handicrafts, especially painting and related arts, were first observed as 'branches of knowledge'. As Ekhtiar remarks, an 1862 announcement in the state newspaper *Ruznama-i dawlat-i 'illiyeh-i iran*, inviting students to study painting, revealed the new tendency to associate 'art' with schooling. References to painting as 'a course of study' to be done 'in scientific and experiential manner' further supported this point. (Maryam Ekhtiar, 'From Workshop to Academy: Art Training and Production in Qajar', pp.50–51.) It seems that Europe, in particular Italy and France, served as a model to 'academize' art in the latter half of the nineteenth century Iran. (Ibid, p.51.)

25 According to Diba, shortly after photography was introduced to Iran by European photographers in 1840, Iranians quickly embraced the new technology. The daguerreotypes captured between 1844 and 1845 of members of Mohammad Shah's royal

household in Tehran by the Frenchman Jules Richard (1816–1889) coincided with the initial experiments in photographic techniques conducted by Malik Qasim Mirza (1807–1862), the son of Fath 'Ali Shah, in Azarbaijan. (Layla S. Diba, *Royal Persian Painting: The Qajar Epoch 1785–1825, Two Hundred Years of Painting from the Royal Persian Courts,* New York 1999, p.264). Soon afterward, the young Nassir al-Din Shah, son of Mohammad Shah, developed a keen interest in photography and became one of its earliest practitioners.

26 Layla S. Diba, 'Muhammad Ghaffari', *Iranian Studies*, p.651.

27 I'timad al-Saltana (Sani' al-Dowleh), M. H .K, *Matla' al-Shams*, vol. 3, Introduction by Teymour Borhan Limoudehi, Tehran 1363S/1984–5, p.268.

28 Shahriar Adle & Yahya Zuka, 'Notes et Documents sur la phtographie Iranienne et son historire: Les Premiers Daguerreotypistes', *Studia Iranica,* no. 12, 1983, pp.249–80.

29 The same happened with the introduction of lithography and the subsequent demand for realistic images to be published in newspapers.

30 Dust 'Ali Khan Mu'ayyir al-Mamalik, *Rijal-i 'asr-i nassiri: Kitab-i dahum (qajariyya)*, Tehran 1363S/ 1984, p.279.

31 Maryam Ekhtiar, 'From Workshop to Bazaar to Academy: Art Training and Production in Qajar', p.60.

32 Layla S. Diba, 'Muhammad Ghaffari', *Iranian Studies*, p.648.

33 Among those few descriptions about the painting classes at the Dar al-Funun, one was given in the 1890s by Curzon, who sarcastically commented on the models used in the painting classes as 'in the drawing classes models were European studies from the nude, classical hands and busts, drawings of Christ, pictures of subjects so various as His Majesty the Shah, Andromeda and Landseer's Challenge' (G. N. Curzon, *Persia and Persian Question*, London 1892, pp.494–9). This brief description, however, shows the atmosphere of the classes which was patterned on European academies.

34 His tendency towards naturalist painting could be realised even in his earliest works although one can still recognise the great influence of an earlier Qajar colour-scheme and detailed style. A look at his works before his journey to Europe in 1897 shows that he had gained some knowledge of post-Renaissance European techniques, indisputably at the Dar al-Funun.

35 Ahmad Soheyli Khansari, *Kamal-i hunar* (Perfection of Art: Life and Works of Mohammad Ghaffari Kamal-ol-Molk (1847–1940), Tehran 1989, p.179.

36 Henri Fantin-Latour, a French painter and lithographer who was best known for his luxurious flower pieces, though he also painted several group portraits that are important historical documents. During his artistic life, he showed his interest in avant-garde movements of his era through his friendship with leading Impressionist artists, although he never completely joined the movement.

37 For example, the self-portraits that Kamal al-Mulk executed represented another genre new to Persian painting and reflected his increasing self-awareness as an individual artist, 'They present him in elegant European garb, confidently gazing at the viewer. These self-portraits are a radical departure from tradition in Persian painting, where artists depicted themselves prostrating or humbly bowing before their ruler, and signed their works with demeaning phrases emphasizing their humility.' (Layla S. Diba, 'Muhammad Ghaffari', *Iranian Studies*, p.654)

38 The Revolution took place in 1905–6 in the last year of Muzaffar al-Din Shah's reign. It suggested a country with a constitution modelled on the Belgian and French examples. It also resulted in the establishment of Iran's first parliament, or *Majlis*, on 30 December 1906.

39 Ruin Pakbaz, 'Contemporary Art of Iran', *Tavoos*, no. 1, autumn 1999, p.168.

40 Diba maintains that 'It was […] at the *Dar al-Funun* that he was to be exposed to the liberalizing trends of the Qajar intelligentsia and where he made contacts with leading thinkers and political figures of the constitutional period such as Muhammad 'Ali Furughi, Zuka al-Mulk and Ibrahim Hakim, Hakim al-Mulk. These statesmen acted as patrons and supporters later in his career.' (Layla S. Diba, 'Muhammad Ghaffari', *Iranian Studies*, p.652.)

41 Ahmad Soheyli Khansari, *Kamal-i hunar*, p.194.

42 Ibid.

43 Ibid, p.50. Of the forty-seven students enrolled in the school, thirty-six were specialising in painting, (Ibid) and so the Madrasa-i Sanayi'-i Mustazrafa was basically a painting academy.

44 After founding the Madrasa he was also appointed for a while as the Deputy of the Sanaye' Mustazrafa (Fine Art Administration) which was in charge of all arts and craft activities in the country. Kamal al-Mulk, however, resigned from both the Madrasa and the Sanaye' Mustazrafa owing to some displeasure with the current Minister of Ma'arif, Suliyman Mirza, who was disrupting the school and its directorship. Kamal al-Mulk left for the Hossein Abad Nishabur, remaining there until his death in 1940.

45 Meanwhile, painters who had received training in Russian schools were also working in Tabriz, yet their artistic and teaching approaches did not diverge from those of Kamal al-Mulk and his students. The full integration of European naturalistic techniques and style was evident in the work of artists like Rassam Arjangi (1892–1975), who had studied in Moscow.

46 Although there is no precise document about this, it is stated that one of the main reasons for the establishment of the Madrasa was to train artists who could help decorate the newly built Green Palace in the traditional style.

47 Tadjvidi was chosen as the best artist in a national competition set up to select an instructor for the Madrasa.

48 Other instructors at the Madrasa included Ali Doroudi (teaching Tazhib, Tashir, carpet design Studios), Nosratollah Yousefi and Abdollah Bagheri, Ahmad Emami (teaching at Munabbat and Mushabbak studios), Sani Khatam and Ali Nemat (teaching Khatam-sazi). Other disciplines that were taught there were ceramics and tile making, *qalam-zani* (graver), enamelling, and traditional intinction. The Madrasa was later named as Hunaristan-i 'Ali Hunar-hay-i Irani under the General Fine Art Administration, and then Ministry of Culture and Art.

CHAPTER TWO

Decades of Hesitancy and Confrontation: Modernism Versus the Status Quo

1. The Beginning of the Modern Art Movement in Iran: the 1940s

As we have seen, the Kamal al-Mulk School and the artistic methods he taught at the Madrasa-i Sanayi'-i Mustazrafa eventually spread to Iran's formal art institutions and exhibitions and was popularised through the country.[1]

The most important and influential institute was the College of Fine Arts (Hunarkadeh-i hunar-hay-i ziba), which was established in 1940;[2] it was attached to Tehran University as a separate faculty in 1948/9 and renamed the Faculty of Fine Arts (Danishkadeh-i hunar-hay-i ziba). The institution taught fine art through an academic curriculum, and it was here that the influence of Kamal al-Mulk through his pupils – now key players in the Faculty – appears fundamental. Indeed, the Faculty was extremely influential in training artists who themselves played important roles in the next decades in the Iranian art scene.

The development of modernism in art in Iran can be seen as a consequence of the rapid modernisation processes occurring in other areas of Iranian life and culture. Attached to the first university in Iran, the Faculty encouraged the adoption of modern Western art through teaching and practising art. Consequently, it emerged as the nurturing ground for modern art in the country over the following decades.

Tehran University, founded in 1934, was designed as a centre for scientific and cultural modernism. It was a key part of the modernisation programme of Reza Shah. The state's education policies and university curricula were at the heart of this official strategy, in line with which, modern civic instructions were created one after another. As with other faculties of Tehran University, the Faculty of Fine Arts was initially created by integrating existing art institutions. This was achieved in 1940, on the proposal of Esmail Merat, the Minister of Education. Merat was also in charge of the administration of Tehran University and had already been keen on the École des Beaux-Arts during his years in Paris as the consultant of Iranian university students. The College of Fine Arts merged the School of Architecture (Madrasa-i ʿali-i miʿmari) with the School of Crafts and the Arts (Madresa-i sanayiʿ va pisha va hunar).[3] Now both schools were ordered closed, and their faculties and facilities were integrated into the newly established College. André Godard, the French archaeologist and architect who was acting as Iran's director of antiquities, was commissioned by Merat to structure the foundations of an art school modelled after the École des Beaux-Arts. The same method and curriculum were adopted, taking course outlines and projects translated into Persian[4] and used in teaching.[5] Thus, the state was effectively incorporating Western models and teaching methods in the most official manner possible.

The College established three branches of art education: painting, architecture and sculpture. Teaching and practical work were carried out in studios, each directed by a single professor.[6] André Godard, the first director of the Faculty, was in charge of arranging a curriculum for instruction and employing the teaching staff, which included former students of Kamal al-Mulk: Ali Mohammad Heydarian,[7] Hassan Ali Vaziri,[8] Abul Hassan Sedighi,[9] Mohsen Moghaddam (1900–87) and others such as Mohsen Foroughi (1907–83), Fath Allah Obad (1900–81), Yevginu Aftandilian and Marthe Célestine Éve (famous as Madame Ashub)[10], who were all graduates of the École des Beaux-Arts.

These appointments suggest that it was Godard's intention to incorporate current Euro-American art movements into the educational framework of the Faculty. Documents only indicate that European instructors did expose students to late-nineteenth-century French modern art. This period marks the beginning of artists oscillating between naturalist techniques and early modernist movements, experimenting within often unstable educational frameworks due to the differing approaches of tutors and teachers. According to Javad Hamidi, one of the first graduates of the Faculty, students were not granted much freedom to explore European modernist ideas or techniques at the time.[11] On the other hand, Mahmoud Javadipour, another graduate, remembers that French professors, including Madame Ashub and Dubreuil, actively directed students toward modernist techniques during their studio sessions.[12]

Although (at least at the beginning) the method of teaching employed at the Faculty was fundamentally patterned on the curriculum of the École des Beaux Arts, the important difference was that it lacked professional instructors and a well thought-out syllabus. The Faculty's functioning in practice oscillated between the poles of naturalist instruction and Impressionism under the influence of the school's visiting French professor, Madame Ashub Aminfar.[13] It seems, however, that the new generation gravitated towards the newer approach rather than the style associated with Kamal al-Mulk's legacy. The love for novelty and artistic creativity pushed the students forward even in this confusion of contradictory instructions, producing fresh artistic tendencies that appeared in the works of students such as Hossein Kazemi (1924–96), Ahmad Esfandiari (1922–2013), Abdollah Ameri (1922–2017), Mehdi Vishkai (1920–2006) and Mahmoud Javadipour (1920–2012).

The evidence suggests that this new generation began to reject Kamal al-Mulk's patterns and looked for new sources of inspiration, challenging the official, Salon-influenced or naturalistic art of that period.[14] This tendency could now even be seen in the works of some of Kamal al-Mulk's pupils, such as Mohsen Moghaddam, also a graduate of the Paris École des Beaux-Arts. (Before this, Hassan Ali Vaziri had also demonstrated clear tendencies towards impressionistic use of bright colour in a series of landscape paintings.) Their works show the influences of late-nineteenth-century French art, especially Impressionism and Russian Realism.[15] The most adventurous students were even influenced by Post-Impressionists such as Cézanne and Van Gogh.

In subsequent years, Faculty graduates such as Javad Hamidi (1918–2002), Jalil Ziapour (1920–99), Hossein Kazemi and Mahmoud Javadipour furthered their study in European institutes, mainly in France (especially the Paris École des Beaux-Arts) Italy and to a lesser extend Germany and UK. They were, in fact, the

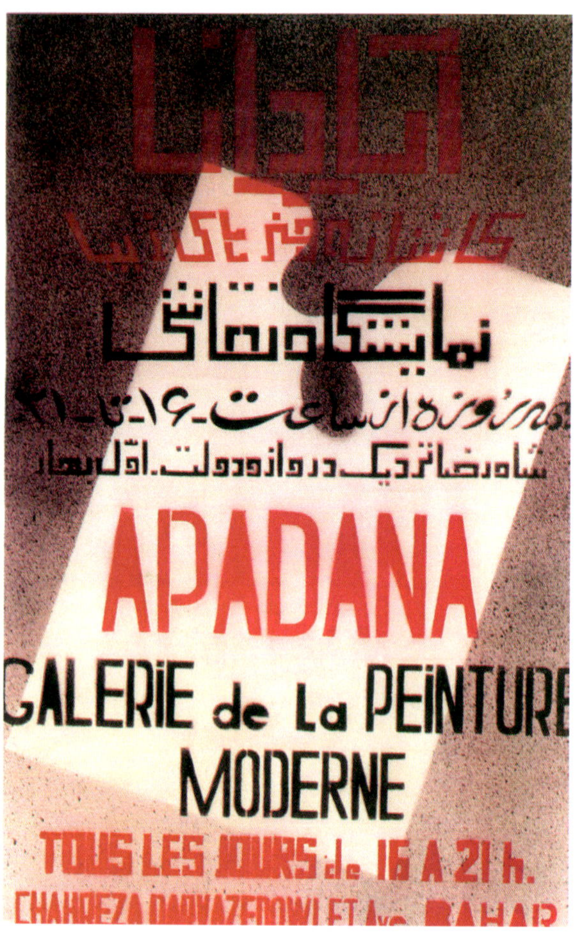

2.1

Mahmoud Javadipour, poster for the
Apadana Gallery exhibition, 1949

first Iranian artists who went to Europe in the post-war period to continue their studies at the chiefly French art institutes. These artists were joined by others, such as Houshang Pezeshknia (1915–72), who had graduated from the Istanbul Faculty of Fine Arts and who were equally keen to promote modernist styles.

During this period, Iran experienced a convergence of diverse ideas and ideologies. There was a keen pursuit of new directions and an enthusiastic embrace of novel concepts.[16] It is also important to note that Iran was occupied by the Allied Forces in 1941. Despite its brevity, this occupation facilitated closer contact with the West, leading to a growing familiarity with Western culture and art. The burgeoning intellectual atmosphere in Iran after Reza Shah's reign had strengthened the desire of young Iranian artists to experience new European artistic approaches. Moreover, in the post-war years, a huge number of famous European works – including novels, poems and philosophical writing – were being translated into Persian; analytical discussions on these materials increased. The tendency towards exploration of cultural, social and intellectual productions of the West appeared more clearly among the intelligentsia and also Iranian artists in this period. As will be discussed at greater length in the next section, during the 1940s and 1950s it was the Faculty's graduates – who had mainly studied in Europe – who shaped and promoted modernism, acknowledging various trends from Impressionism and Expressionism to Cubism and abstract art. These artists were thus the pioneers of the establishment and growth of modern art practices in Iran during the 1940s and 1950s.

2. The Development of Modern Art Practices During the 1940s and 1950s

The introduction of modernism was a groundbreaking concept in the Iranian art scene, and the modernists faced a considerable challenge in acquainting the audience with its stylistic intricacies. Evidently, there was a pressing need to familiarise the public with modern art, prompting the pioneers to advocate for its validity through their societies, magazines, and exhibitions.

During this period artists started to unite and share their interests through activities such as the *Khurus-jangi* (Fighting Cock) Association and the Apadana Gallery. Apadana Gallery, Home of the Fine Art, the first Tehran private gallery, was founded in 1949 by the Faculty graduates Mahmoud Javadipour and Hossein Kazemi, with the collaboration of Houshang Ajoudani. The gallery served as a centre for the promotion of modern art and provided a venue for exhibiting the modernists' works. It was there that the works of modernists such as Jalil Ziapour, Houshang Pezeshknia, Javad Hamidi, Ahmad Esfandiari, Mehdi Vishkai and Abdollah Ameri were exhibited. (Figure 2.1) Understandably, the 1940s created works mainly dependent on modern European models. The modernist camp swiftly endeavoured to bridge the gap between the naturalistic style advocated by Kamal al-Mulk's followers and modernist European artistic trends. The modernists were furthermore engaged on two fronts that were unexpectedly coexisting: Kamal al-Mulk's followers, whom they called 'conservative imitators', and the miniaturists or 'reactionary traditionalists'.

Another group was acting against these modernists' goals: the Tudeh Party of Iran (Party of the Masses of Iran) which was an Iranian communist party formed in 1941 but cracked down on after the 1953 Coup d'état. Its advocates upheld the idea that only art with a clear message could resonate with the general public, often viewing modern art as lacking this communicative power.

In the following decade, artists grappled with the dual challenge of traditionalism versus modernism, with modernist ideas ultimately prevailing. By the late 1950s, modernism in art had received official approval from the country's art custodians. It is noteworthy to explore the impact of exhibition spaces during the 1940s and their role in facilitating this transition.

A number of group exhibitions were organised in Tehran, in which most practising Iranian modernists participated. However, these first exhibitions were held in foreign institutes because of scepticism on the part of government officials concerning the new trends in artistic practice. Public officials often regarded these artists as anarchist figures capable of destroying the country's national and cultural heritage. The most noteworthy of these was the 1946 exhibition at the Iran-Soviet Cultural Society (VOKS)[17] and the series of exhibitions held at the Mehregan club (home of the National Teachers' Association) during the early 1950s. They were the most comprehensive exhibitions before the First Tehran Biennial in 1958. These exhibitions continued to be largely populated by the works of Kamal al-Mulk's disciples. Yet, they also featured pieces by modernist painters, including a considerable number of Impressionist works, juxtaposed with the classical pieces from Kamal al-Mulk's School.

These exhibitions frequently became arenas for conflicts between these two groups of artists.

Another early exhibition held by the young artists was in the Iran-France Institute in 1945. It became part of a wider project – lasting throughout the 1940s – to gain public acceptance for modern art. Later exhibitions were held in recently opened private galleries in Iran and group discussions and debates between artists took place there.

In 1953, just after the Coup d'état, the government began gradually to change its approach towards visual art, resulting in a series of official policies that effectively favoured and supported art and cultural activity. The Coup took place in August 1953 against the liberal Iranian Prime Minister Mohammad Mosaddegh and head of the National Front movement. This coup, allegedly with the support of the CIA and MI6, resulted in the overthrow of Mosaddegh's nationalist government and established an era now referred to as the second period of the Pahlavi monarchy. In 1953, two major exhibitions were held in which modern art was brought to the attention of official artistic circles and opened up from its limited existence in avant-garde spheres. The first was the art show in May at the Mehregan Club, in which the works of the graduates of the Faculty of Fine Arts were displayed side by side with the paintings of the best-known artists of the day such as Heydarian, Vaziri and Behzad. Another was an officially sponsored exhibition in the palace of Prince Gholam Reza Pahlavi (Mohammad Reza Shah's brother). The inclusion of the modernists' works suggested that the cultural authorities had signalled an end to the official policy of indifference towards modern art.[18] Moreover, during the mid-1950s, Iranian modernists started to receive official support from the General Administration of Fine Arts (Idareh-i kull-i hunar-hay-i zibay-i kishvar, later developed to become the Ministry of Culture and Art).[19] This trend culminated in the staging of the first Tehran Biennial in 1958 – a grand exhibition space that promoted a wide range of experimental approaches. (Figure 2.2)

The Biennial's founders were now the government's cultural officials.[20] Their main aims were to bring in opportunities for the critical evaluation of works of Iranian artists; to familiarise the public with the approval of new artistic styles; to create a closer understanding and rapport between them and the artists; and to select, through a judging panel that included well-informed national and internationally reputed foreign experts, several works of Iranian artists to represent the country at a number of foreign art festivals, notably the Venice Biennale.[21] The show brought together the works of forty-nine artists, both painters and sculptors. Judging by the exhibition catalogue, one could find several major modernist styles represented.

The show demonstrated the excited curiosity of artists using a wide variety of stylistic experiments, ranging from Impressionism to Cubism and Expressionism to Abstraction. Yarshater explains this variety of modernistic interests as:

> Originality was submerged in the effort to absorb new outlooks, and to learn and master new techniques. In the exhibitions of the 1940s, it was blatantly obvious which artists had been emulated. The post-Impressionist masters commanded the largest following; figurative painting was, by far, the most prevalent method and abstract painting made only modest appearance.[22]

This pivotal moment marked the triumph of the modernists over their adversaries, particularly those proponents of the academic style and miniaturists, relegating the latter groups to obscurity. As the art critic Karim Emami contends:

> It had become apparent that a major exhibition, organised nationally on a regular basis, was needed to give impetus to the modern art movement while paving the way for the participation of Iranian artists in such international venues as the Venice Biennale.[23]

However, in the 1950s, the modernist movement started to fracture into smaller factions. Divergent individual styles surfaced, each asserting its unique characteristics. This evolution gave rise to trends that would shape subsequent developments in the years to come.

Having considered the important influence of exhibition spaces, let us now turn to those key figures responsible for sharing and promoting Iranian modernism. One of the most active and contentious graduates of the Faculty was the artist and art critic Jalil Ziapour, who for about a decade was the acknowledged spokesman and unchallenged 'guru' of Iranian modernists.[24] A passionate advocate of modern art, Ziapour had studied at the Faculty of Fine Arts during the early 1940s. He pursued further studies in Paris at the École des Beaux-Arts from 1946 to 1948, supported by a government

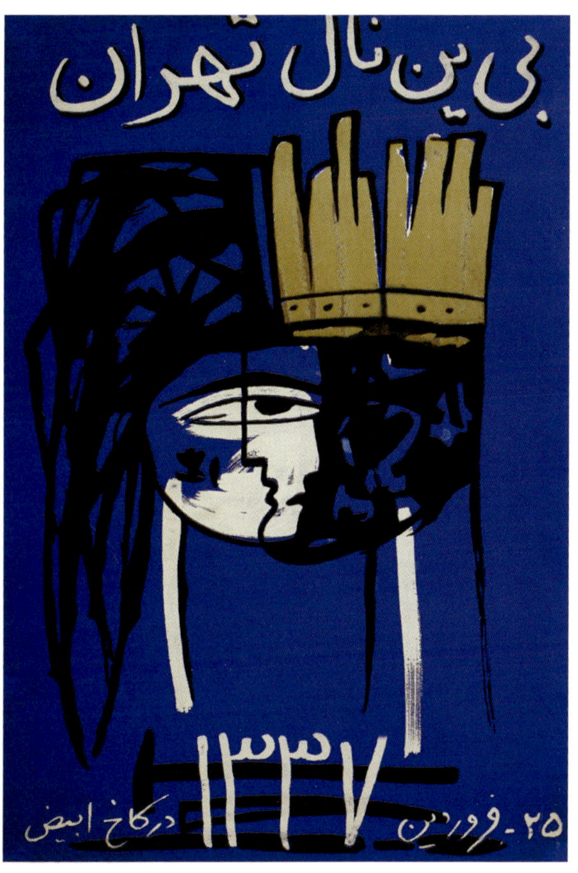

2.2
Marcos Grigorian, cover of the First Tehran Biennial catalogue, 1958

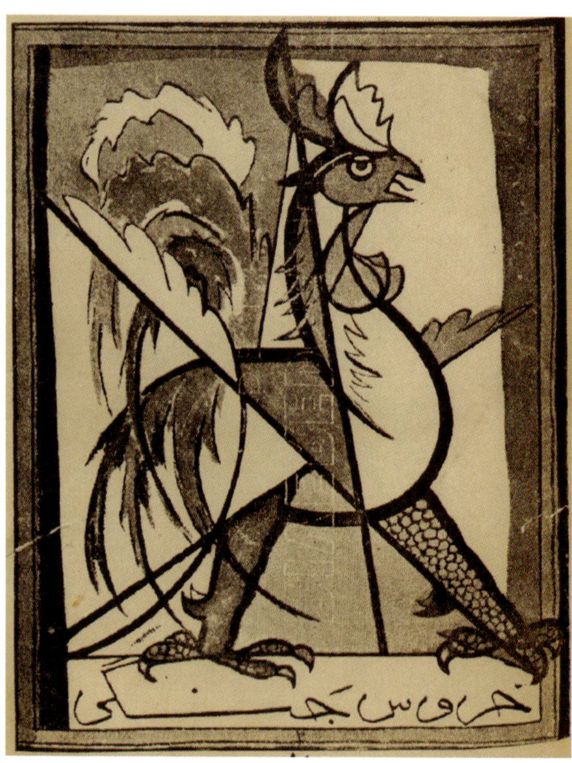

2.3
Jalil Ziapour, Logo for the cover
of *Khurus-jangi* (Fighting Cock)
magazine, 1949

scholarship. During this time, he studied under the tutelage of the influential French artist and educator André Lhote (1885–1962).[25] Upon returning, he taught history of art and styles at the Kamal al-Mulk Fine Art High School.

Upon his return from Paris in 1948, he joined forces with fellow modernists to spearhead a movement promoting modernist ideas. Their efforts included organising exhibitions of modern art, facilitating discussions and critical sessions, and delivering lectures on modern art. These initiatives undoubtedly sparked a newfound interest in visual art across Iran. Furthermore, Ziapour, in 1949, alongside other avant-garde poets, musicians and artists, established an association named the *Khurus-jangi* (Fighting Cock), a progressive body devoted to the promotion of modern arts, including painting, drama, music, poetry and literature. Other founding members of the Association were Gholamhossein Gharib Gorgani (literature), Hassan Shirvani (theatre), and Morteza Hannaneh (music). Ziapour's efforts aimed to garner support for modern art through his weekly lectures at the Association and other venues, as well as through his writings which featured both conceptual debates and technical critiques of works exhibited by fellow artists. Luckily, the social and political climate in Iran during that period was relatively tranquil, facilitating many discussion sessions.

The Association became more influential when further key literary and artistic figures joined, such as Nima Yooshij (1895–1960; the prominent avant-garde poet known as the father of Iranian New Poetry[26]), Manouchehr Sheybani (artist and poet), Sadegh Hedayat (novelist), Mohammad Ali Jamalzadeh (novelist), Houshang Irani (poet), Ebrahim Golestan and Farrokh Ghaffari (cinema), Mostafa Kamal Pourtorab (music), Bahman Mohasses (artist), and Sohrab Sepehri (artist). Importantly, the Association supported its activities by publishing a periodic magazine of the same name to disseminate its ideas. (Figure 2.3)

During the late 1940s, in both formal exhibitions and later private galleries such as Apadana, there were public debates concerning the necessity and virtues of modern art, and a parallel controversy in literature on the question of 'new poetry versus classical'.[27] When Ziapour returned home from his time in France, he arrived to find a growing verbal battle between supporters of modern Persian poetry and those of classical poetry. Ziapour, however, did not hesitate to side with the modernists, hence their contribution to the *Khurus-jangi* Association.

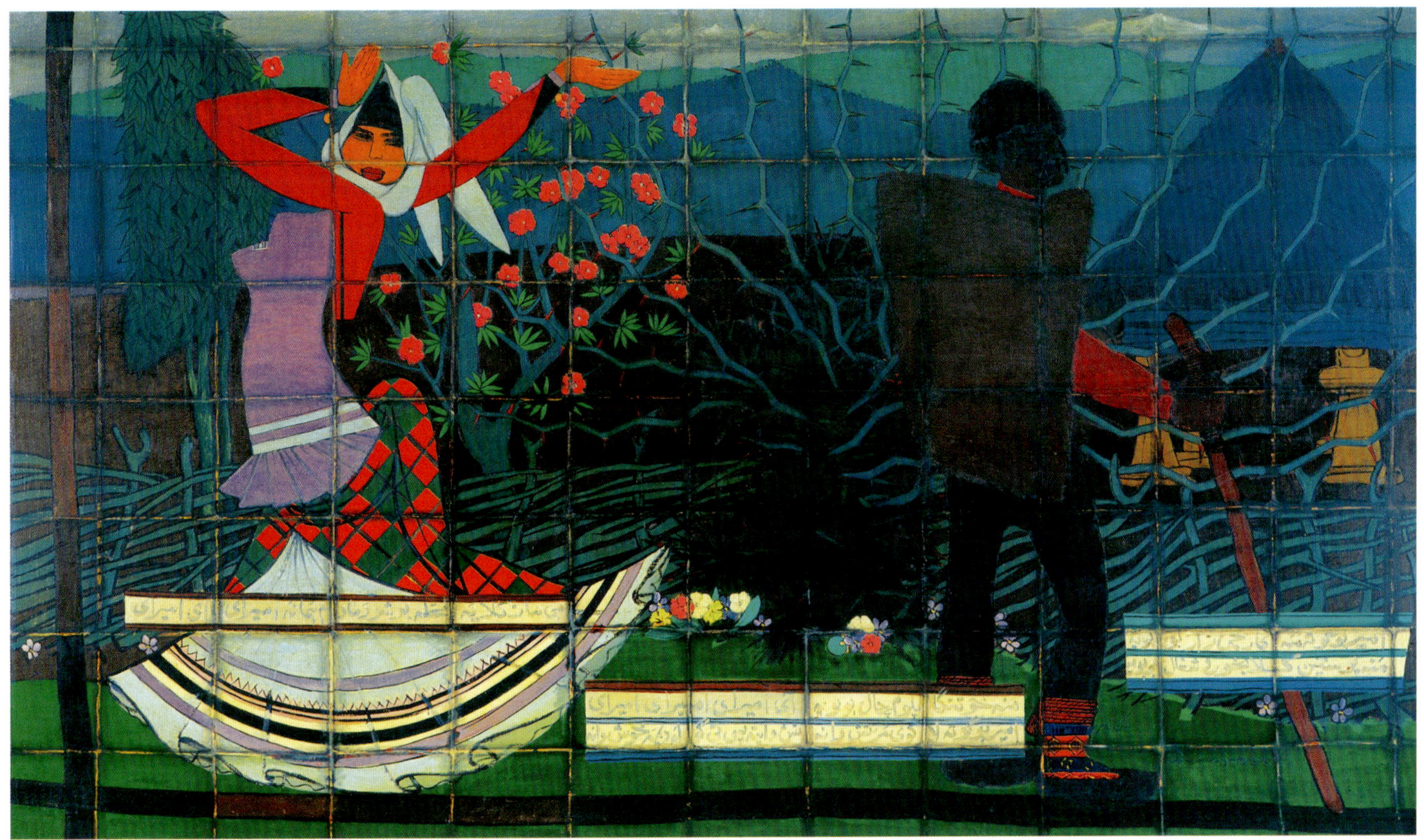

2.4
Jalil Ziapour, *Ey amir, amir*, 1958, oil on canvas, 122×207 cm, TMoCA

What stands out here is the distinction between the clash of modernist and traditional artists, including both followers of Kamal al-Mulk and master miniaturists who were still active to some extent, and the parallel conflict between 'new' and 'classical' poetry. While the conflict in poetry stemmed from the differences between modern Western literature and classical Persian poetry, in art, it primarily revolved around two Western artistic approaches: the academic art of nineteenth-century Europe and the cosmopolitan modern art movement. Yet, at this moment, modernist artists found themselves at odds mainly with the miniaturists, whose influence was relatively diminished. What bound together literary and artistic aspirations within the Association was a collective resolve against any traditionalist tendencies.

The ethos of modernism also grappled with a concurrent concern for cultural identity. Here artists harboured optimism, striving to grasp an understanding of their reality infused with the innate cultural and historical characteristics of their nation. It could be argued that during this period there was a significant burgeoning of self-awareness; and the artist began to take on the perspective of the 'other' as a way of articulating this new cultural self-knowledge. As we have seen, the earliest pioneers of this approach were those artists who had started meditating on what they had learnt in the West alongside the realities of what they were experiencing in their own country. A significant factor lay in the wider social changes taking place at the time – a time that witnessed widespread nationalist sentiments due to highly political and public events such as the Coup d'etat. Thus, nationalist sentiments motivated the young artists to refer to their roots and to seek an understanding of the national culture. These artists faced the challenge of merging national traditions with modern Western techniques, aiming not to become practitioners of creative subjectivity, a hallmark of Western art, but rather adherents to a form of objectivity that prioritises the visual elements of tradition.[28]

Many of the young modernists sought to distinguish their work from that of similar artists in other contexts, and to find a kind of picture that would identify them as 'Iranian'. A similar search for identity can be found in Iranian modernist literature. As Yarshater remarks, the pertinence of Iranicisation to the general artistic mood of the country had been confirmed by the parallels in Iranian literature. The work of Sadegh Hedayat (1903–51), for instance, largely concerns itself thematically with pre-Second World War Persian types and Persian environments (notably in *Dashakul, Buf-i Kur*, and *'Alaviyyeh Khanum*), and was followed by a number of Persian short story writers such as Sadegh Choubak, Jalal Al-e Ahmad and Beh-Azin, and also a number of younger fiction writers, particularly Houshang Golshiri (in *Shazdeh Ihtijab*).[29] The question was: what would define the 'Iranian' characteristics of their work? Or what was the relationship between the context in which they lived and the work of art that they were producing?

In an attempt to 'Iranicise' their works, these artists tended to embrace subjects or themes that would be immediately recognised as 'Iranian'. Some were captivated by the rural landscape of Iran, while others drew inspiration from traditional pictorial sources like the standard figures of Persian painting. Subjects such as tribal or village life, rural people and nomadic tribes, Iranian rituals, people in daily social contexts and women dressed in the *chador* can all be found, executed in different modernistic approaches (for example see Figures 2.4–5, 11). Now the challenge was to make their works visually recognisable as distinctly Iranian. According to Ziapour:

2.5
Jalil Ziapour, *Quchani Kurdish Girl*, 1965, oil on canvas, 171×121 cm, TMoCA

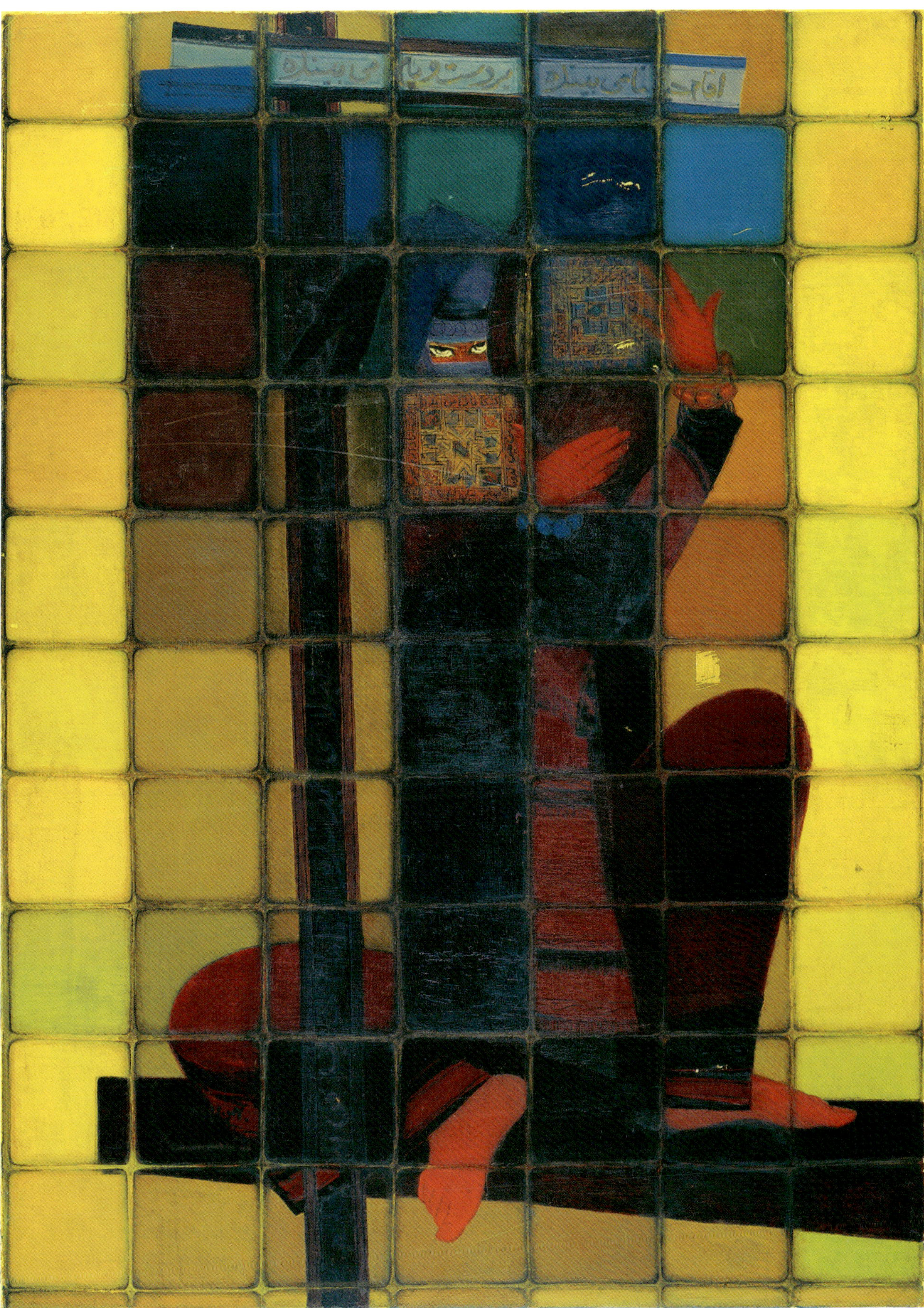
بردست و پا می بیند

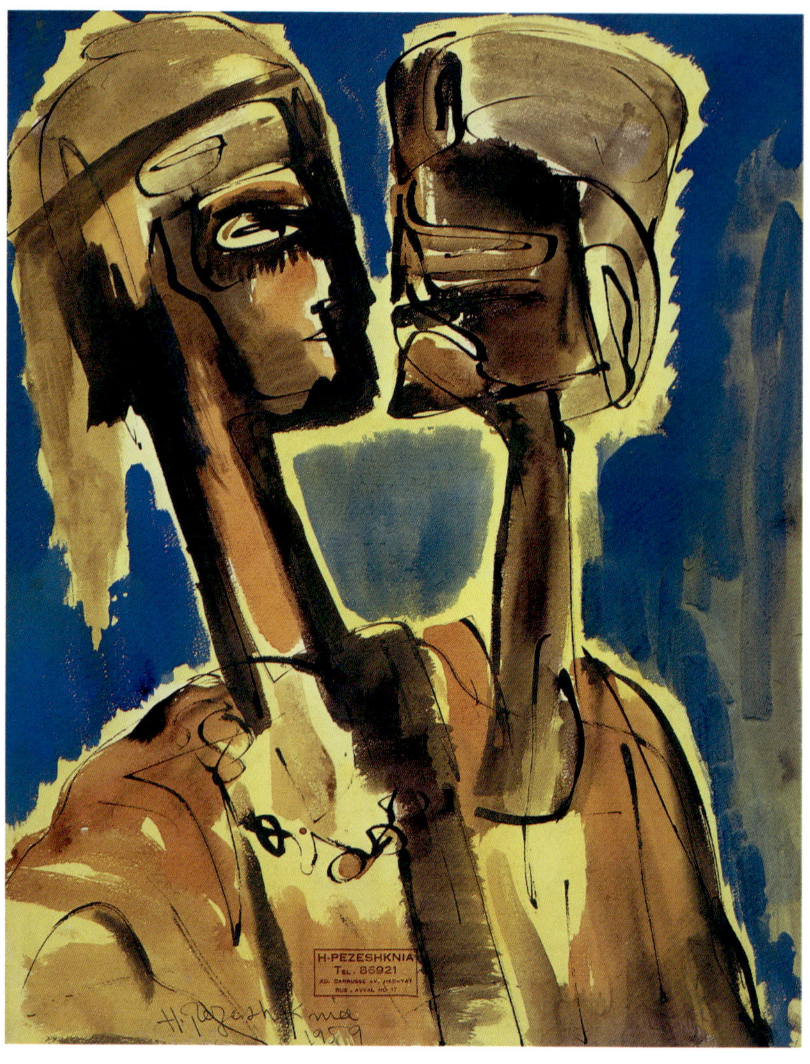

2.6
Houshang Pezeshknia, *Two profiles*,
1959, watercolour on paper,
61.5×47 cm, TMoCA

We should be moving to link up with the world culture
and we should try at the same time to preserve our identity.
When I came back to Iran [...] I was asking myself why we
are not drawing upon all these good things that we have
in our possession? I had seen how the Europeans reacted
to their own past, how they were reacting to the present
[...]. My task and my message was to try to find in our
own indigenous culture something that was still living
and had some compatibility with the universal language of
painting.[30]

Let us now consider some of the specific ways in which artists
articulated their preoccupation with Iranian subjects, starting with
Ziapour and Houshang Pezeshknia, both of whom were immensely
active during this time.

Ziapour initially concentrated on a kind of semi-Cubist style in which he tried to integrate some indigenous subjects. Although Ziapour's work did not align precisely with the typical definition of Cubism, as it lacked certain essential elements,[31] his intention was to achieve a synthesis between Cubism and traditional Iranian art, rather than simply imitate the Cubist style.

After years of grappling with this challenge, Ziapour engaged himself in a figurative style where reality was depicted as a blend of Qajar art and synthetic Cubism, a technique he learned from his teacher André Lhote. Stylisation and the use of colours such as ochre, red, and sienna characterise this period of Ziapour's work. In these paintings, he used the square module in the geometry of tiles and local crafts as the foundational unit of the composition, constructing his works around these dynamic units. These images were executed with broken, sharply angular lines, drawing from the formal structure of traditional tiles. (Figure 2.4, 5) His understanding of Iranian rural life and nomadic tribes, acquired through research in those areas, inspired him to choose these subjects for his canvases. These pictorial strategies were in line with the artist's efforts to develop a modern local visual language, a concept discussed in Iranian artistic circles as early as 1948.

Houshang Pezeshknia's artistic style was characterised by the use of expressionistic techniques and the portrayal of local subjects such as Khuzestani women, Muharram rituals, and women wearing *chador*s. A graduate of the Istanbul Academy of Fine Arts in 1946, Pezeshknia's canvases are considered early examples of Iranian Expressionism, also influenced by Social Realism. His paintings predominantly focused on the life of Khuzestani villagers, conveyed through a careful and economical use of colour. (Figure 2.6) As noted by Pakbaz, sunburnt, parched, and deeply creased faces set against the vast, open spaces of fields or under the shade of palms, oil derricks, and the maze of structures in petroleum refineries provided an effective medium of expression for his works.[32] (Figure 2.7)

It is worth touching on the work of other early modernists here, to demonstrate the ways in which artists were integrating their understanding of European styles while striving to find their own artistic voice. Javad Hamidi was a graduate and then lecturer of the Faculty of Fine Arts, who had also studied at the École des Beaux-Arts in Paris. He played an important role in teaching and training the next generation of Iranian modernists. Hamidi's painting can be characterised as a cross between Kamal al-Mulk's naturalist

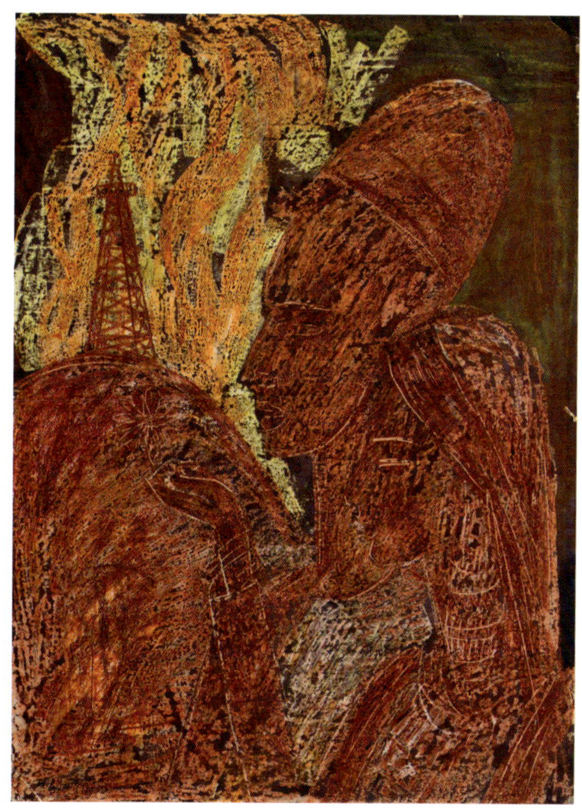

2.7
Houshang Pezeshknia, *Untitled*, 1963, oil pastel and watercolour on paper, 70x50 cm, private collection, Tehran

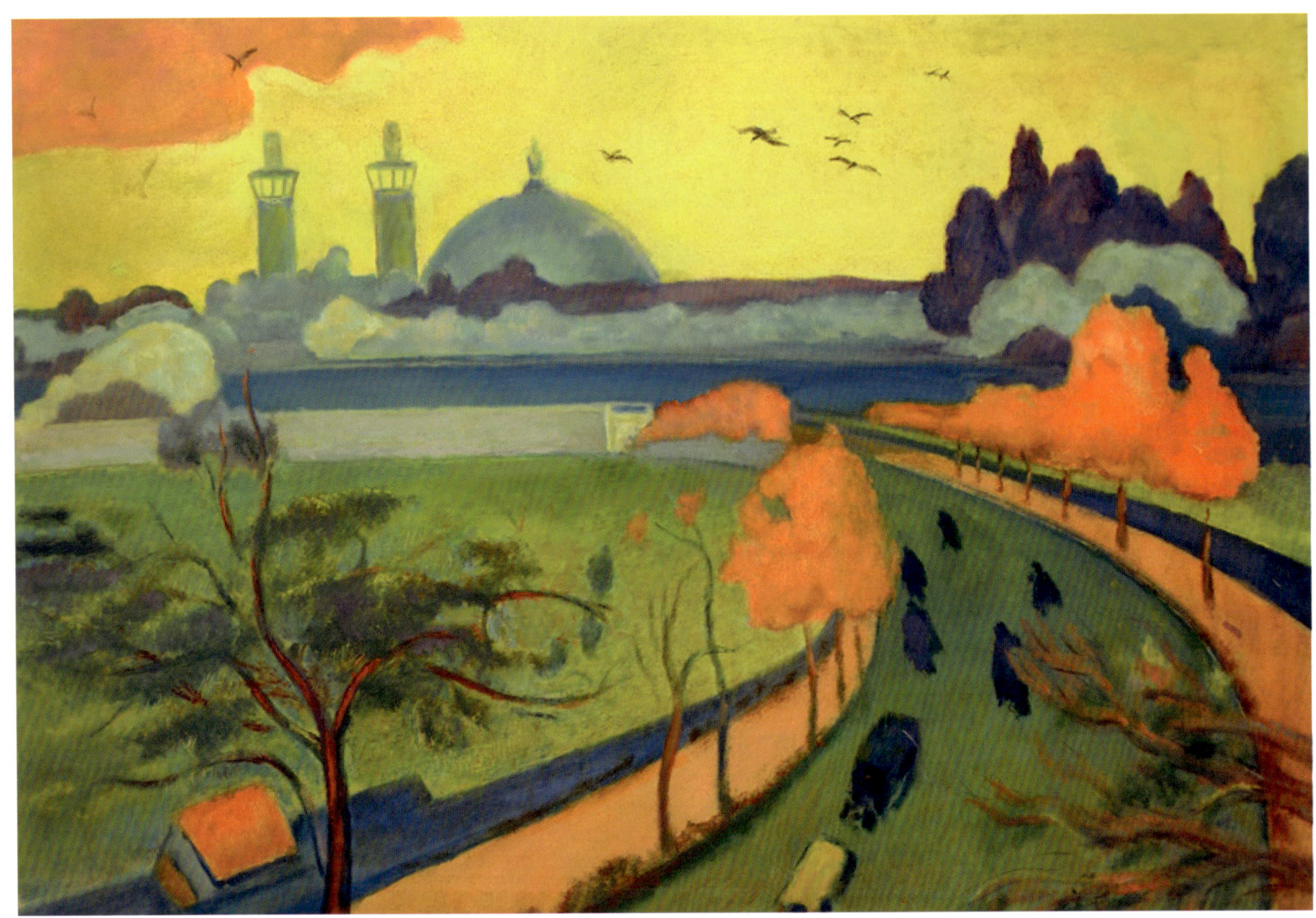

2.8
Javad Hamidi, *Landscape*, c.1950s,
oil on canvas, 81×100 cm, Iranian
Academy of Arts

painting and the modern tendencies developing at the time, such as Impressionism, Expressionism and also abstraction. Hamidi's work exhibits an experimental nature that transitions between symbolic realism, lyrical expressionism, and abstractionism across different periods, making it challenging to classify within a specific style. His later works display a masterful approach characterised by still life and lyrical concepts accentuated by vibrant colours. (Figure 2.8)

An influential art lecturer and artist, Hossein Kazemi initially explored delicate figurative painting before moving to bold, abstract works that reveal his interest in folk subjects, such as Iranian villagers and nature. Interestingly, while attempting to 'Iranicise' his works, Kazemi began incorporating formal characteristics and standard figures reminiscent of seventeenth-century Safavid painting, such as those seen in the works of Reza Abbasi including the use of lines in outlining figures, among other elements. His lyrical subject matter was rendered using exaggerated curved lines and a semi-Cubist style. During the 1950s his choice of subject matter changed, and was mainly inspired by contemporary Persian novels; he executed these works in a different style that came close to a kind of geometric Cubism. (Figure 2.9) His most distinguished works created during the 1970s onwards are his powerful abstract works inspired by the shapes of Iranian desert thistles. (Figures 2.10)

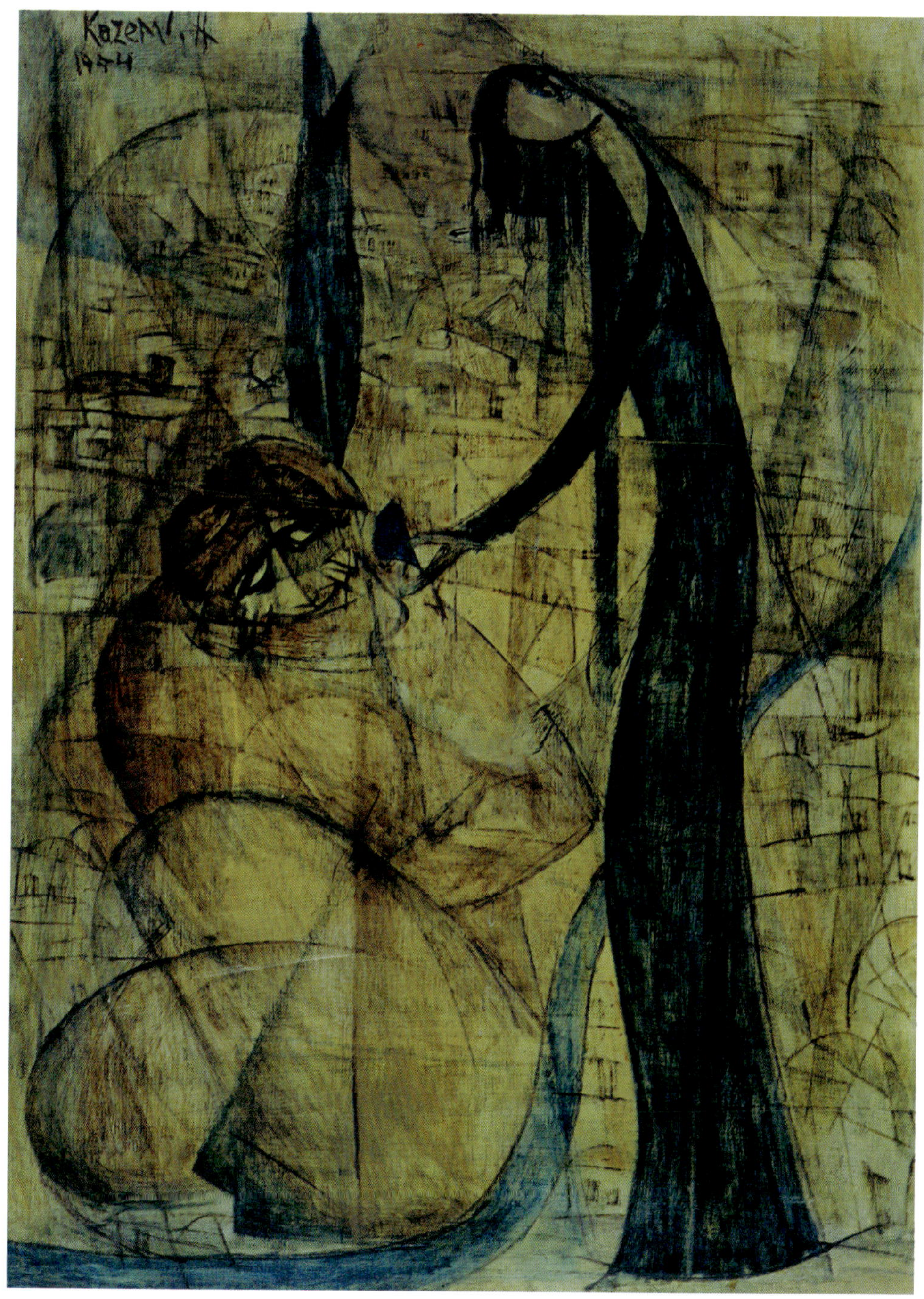

2.9
Hossein Kazemi, *Ethereal Girl and the Hunched-back Man*, 1954, oil on canvas, 65×46 cm, private collection, Tehran

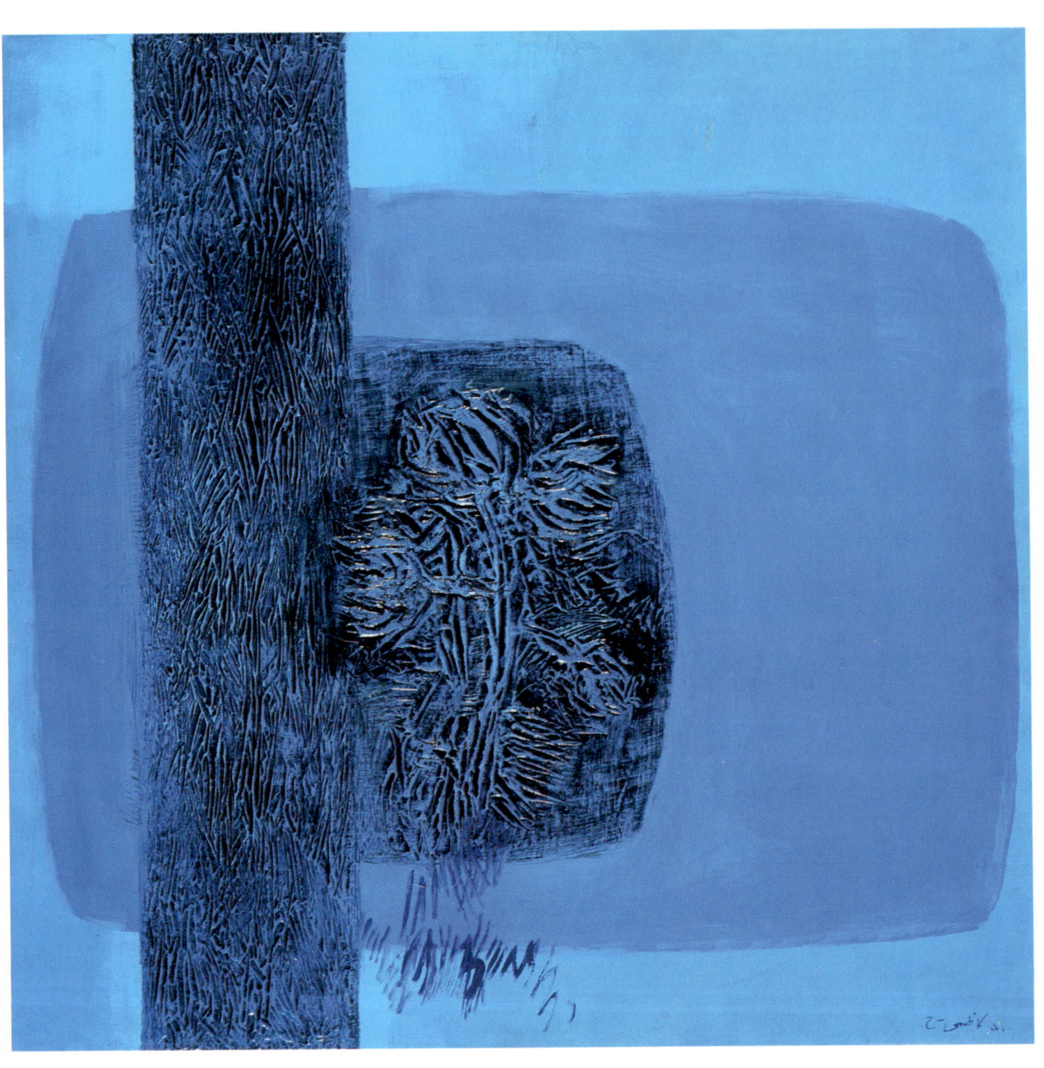

2.10
Hossein Kazemi, *Unttiled*, 1971, oil on board, 99×99.5 cm, TMoCA

Mahmoud Javadipour, another graduate of the Faculty of Fine Arts and later the Academy of Fine Arts, Munich, believed in the importance of native culture. He embarked on a journey to explore the lives of disadvantaged individuals in both urban and rural settings, capturing the scenes he encountered. Additionally, he depicted the natural landscapes of summer resorts surrounding Tehran. These subjects were portrayed in an impressionistic style, reflecting Javadipour's repertoire of paintings from this period. His works exhibited a fondness for ordinary people and traditional lifestyles. (Figure 2.11) Javadipour also experimented with formally appropriating Persian painting techniques for such subjects. (Figure 2.12) He believed that the people of untouched rural areas and specific indigenous cultures, such as the Kurds and Lurs, offered unique subjects worthy of being recorded using modern techniques.[33]

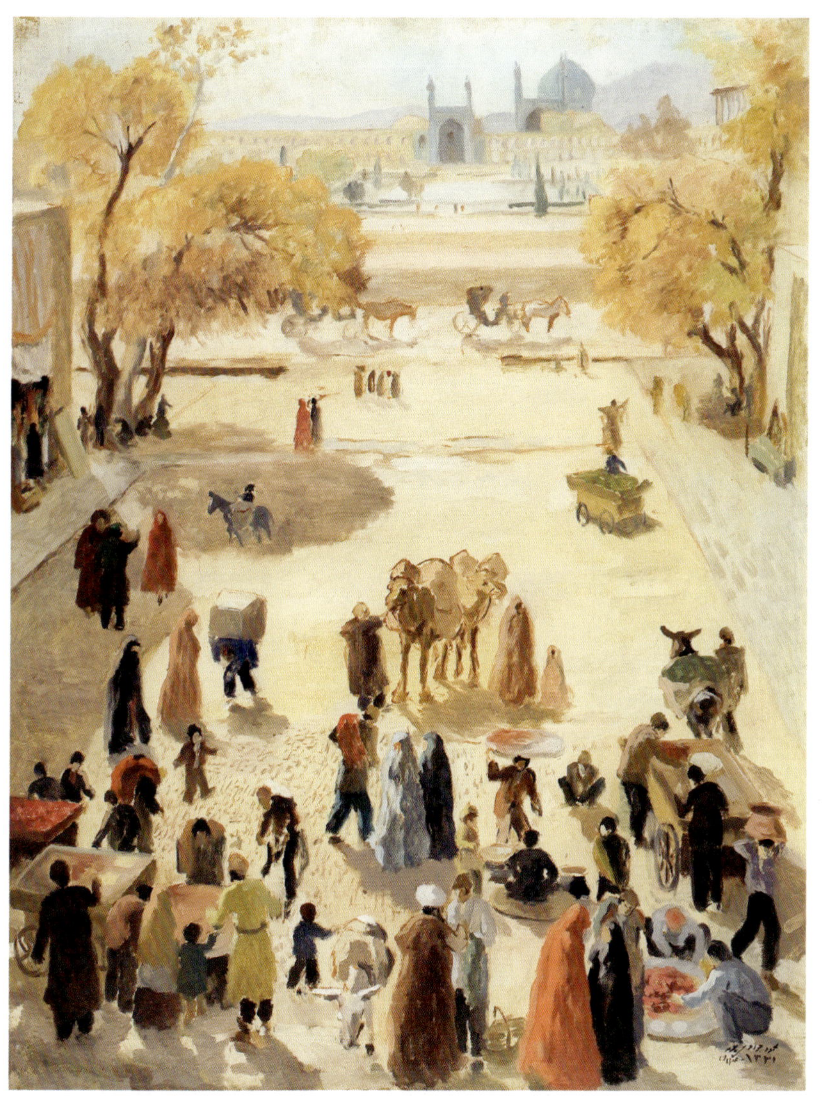

2.11
Mahmoud Javadipour, *Naqsh-e Jahan
Square, Isfahan*, 1952, oil on canvas,
81×61 cm, TMoCA

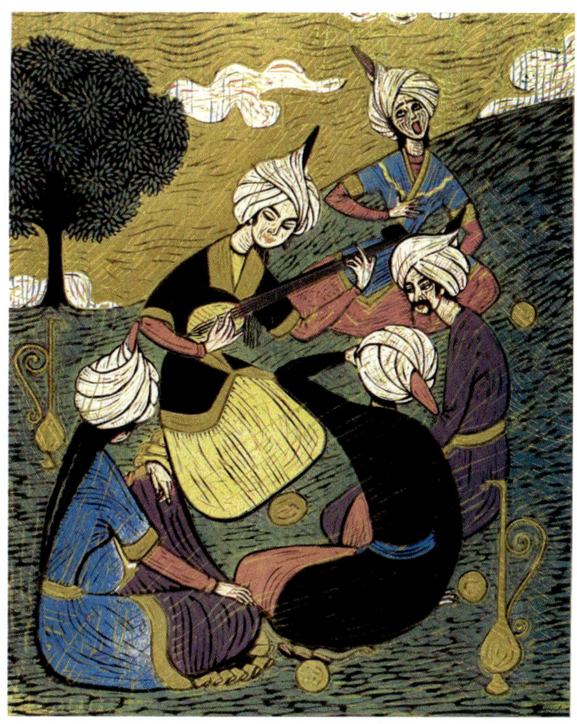

2.12
Mahmoud Javadipour, *Ramishgaran
(Musicians)*, 1958, linoleum print and
warecolour on paper, 75×63 cm

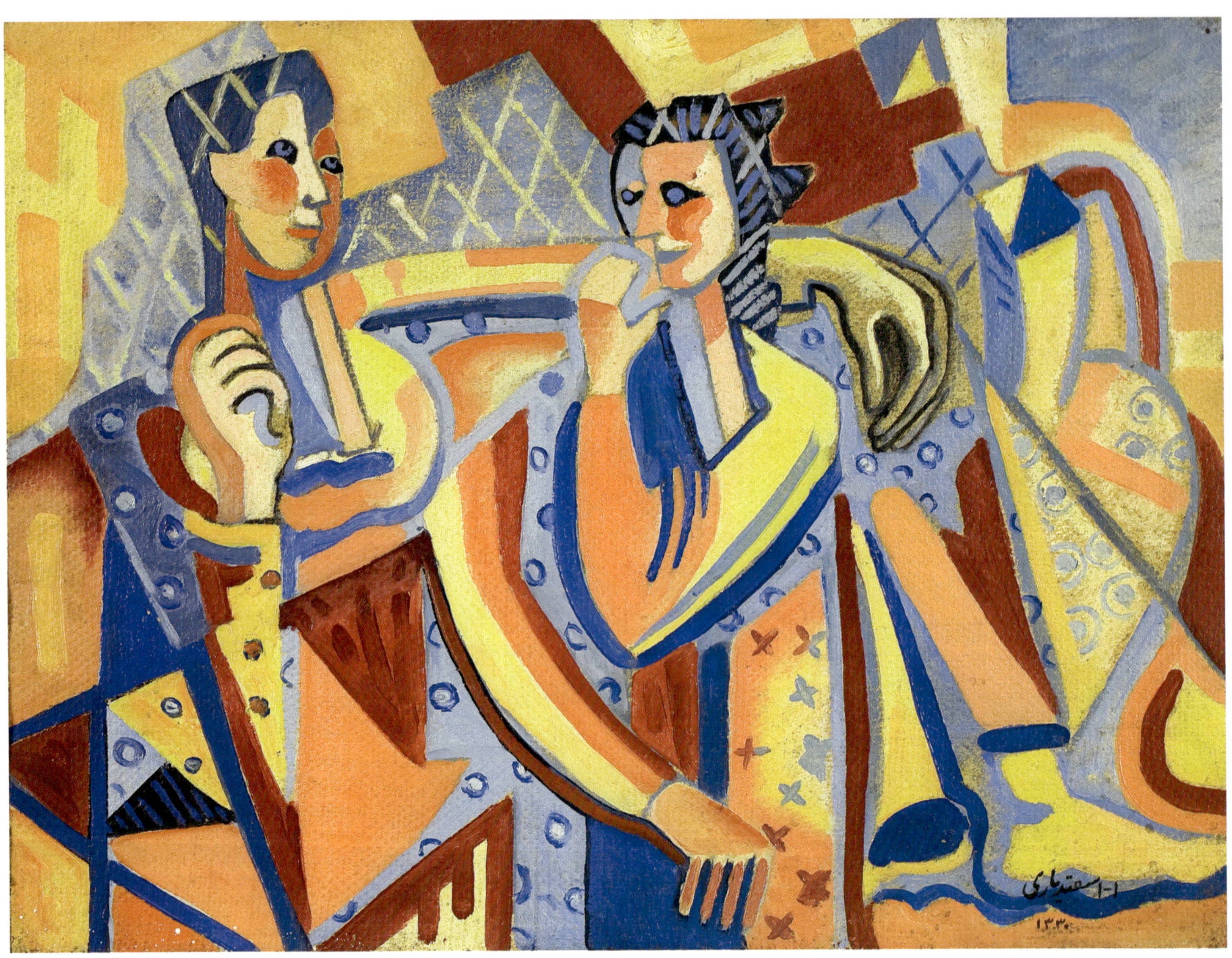

2.13
Ahmad Esfandiari, *Untitled*, 1951,
40×50 cm, TMoCA

Iranian nature, villages and agrarian scenes are the most common subjects in the paintings of Ahmad Esfandiari, another graduate of the Faculty. In the 1940s, following his graduation, his early works suggest an interest in various modernistic styles, showing affinities with Fauvism, Cubism, and Orphism. (Figure 2.13) Subsequently, after his attempt to 'Iranicise' his painting, as observed in other examples, Esfandiari shifted his focus to angular forms and arabesques, incorporating them into his works. Later, Esfandiari adopted Expressionism as his primary style while maintaining consistent subject matters. (Figure 2.14) Similar to Esfandiari, albeit in a more conservative manner, was his contemporary modernist Abdollah Ameri. Ameri was esteemed as one of the most dedicated Impressionist artists of the 1940s among his peers. His various

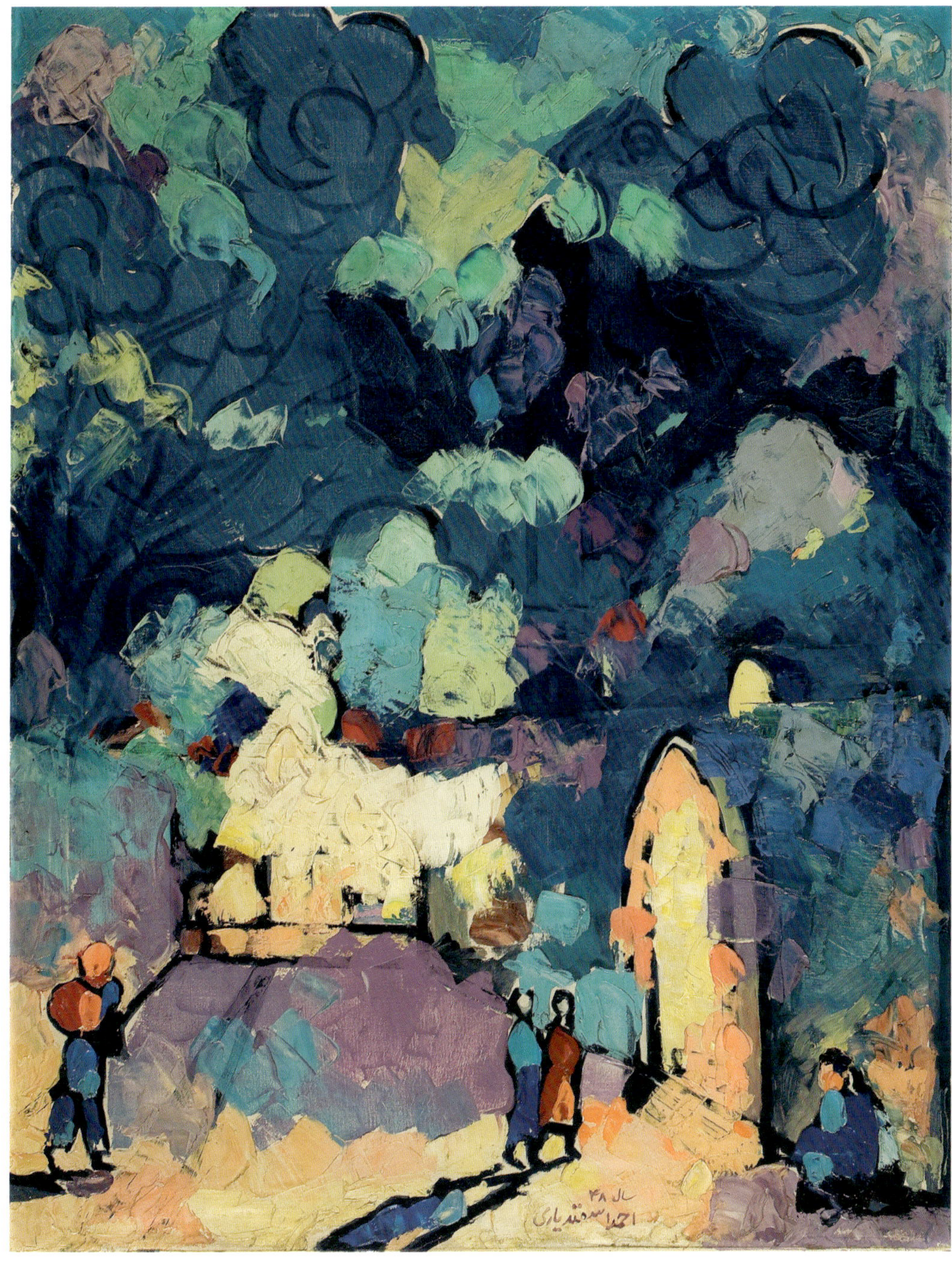

2.14
Ahmad Esfandiari, *Entrance to the Village*, 1969, oil on canvas, 90×70 cm, TMoCA

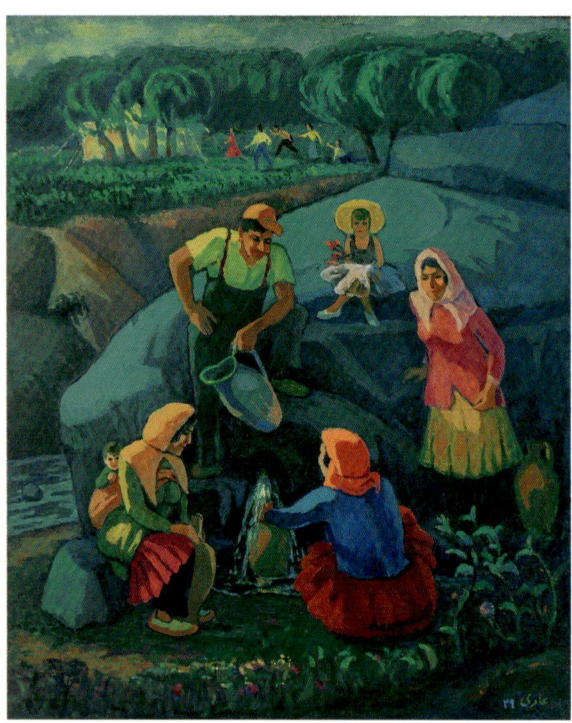

2.15
Abdollah Ameri, *Next to the Spring*,
1950, oil on sackcloth, 76×60 cm,
TMoCA

landscapes depicted gardens, cultivated fields, and countryside scenes bathed in bright sunlight, presenting a serene, idyllic, and colourful ambiance. (Figure 2.15)

Manouchehr Sheybani's (1924–91) artistic approach exhibited a discernible affinity with that of Ziapour, characterised by a diminished emphasis on clarity and objectivity in the portrayal of forms and figures. An avant-garde artist and poet, he studied at the Faculty of Fine Arts during the 1940s, then at the Accademia di Belle Arti in Rome and then France during the mid-1970s. Sheybani maintained a close association with the most vanguard movements and circles of the time, including the *Khurus-jangi* Association. The rural and tribal life of Iran was the typical subject of his works, rendered in geometrical, Expressionistic style. (Figure 2.16)

In contrast to prevailing tendencies that appropriated the forefront of modern Iranian art movement, another group of pioneers did not make significant efforts to assimilate Iranian or vernacular sensibilities into modernist frameworks and formats. It appears that for this group of artists, concerns and affiliations regarding nationality question in artworks do not hold as prominent a position in juxtaposition to the concerns of modernism and experimentation, and may even, according to their assertion, lead to artistic constraints. This approach can be observed in the works of pioneering figures such as Mehdi Vishkai and Manouchehr Yektai (1922–2019). Each presented notable examples of Expressionist art in familiar genres such as portraiture, landscape, and still life. While Vishkai's canvases were highly colourful, Yektai's, emphasising purity and self-expression, often displayed a more restrained use of the colour palette. (Figures 2.17–20) Yektai's bright canvases introduce exemplary instances of Iranian modernism without a concerted effort towards Iranicisation.

Having touched on those artists active during the 1940s, let us now consider the work of the next generation of artists similarly committed to promoting modernism. This group, who were active in the Iranian art scene during the 1950s, were mostly trained in Iran and Europe. Among them are Marcos Grigorian (1925–2007), Sohrab Sepehri (1928–80), Mohsen Vaziri Moghaddam (1924–2018), Abolghassem Saidi (b.1926), Sirak Melkonian (1931–2024), and Jazeh Tabatabai (1928–2008).

2.16
Manouchehr Sheybani, *Untitled*,
c. 1958, oil on canvas, 100×75 cm,
TMoCA

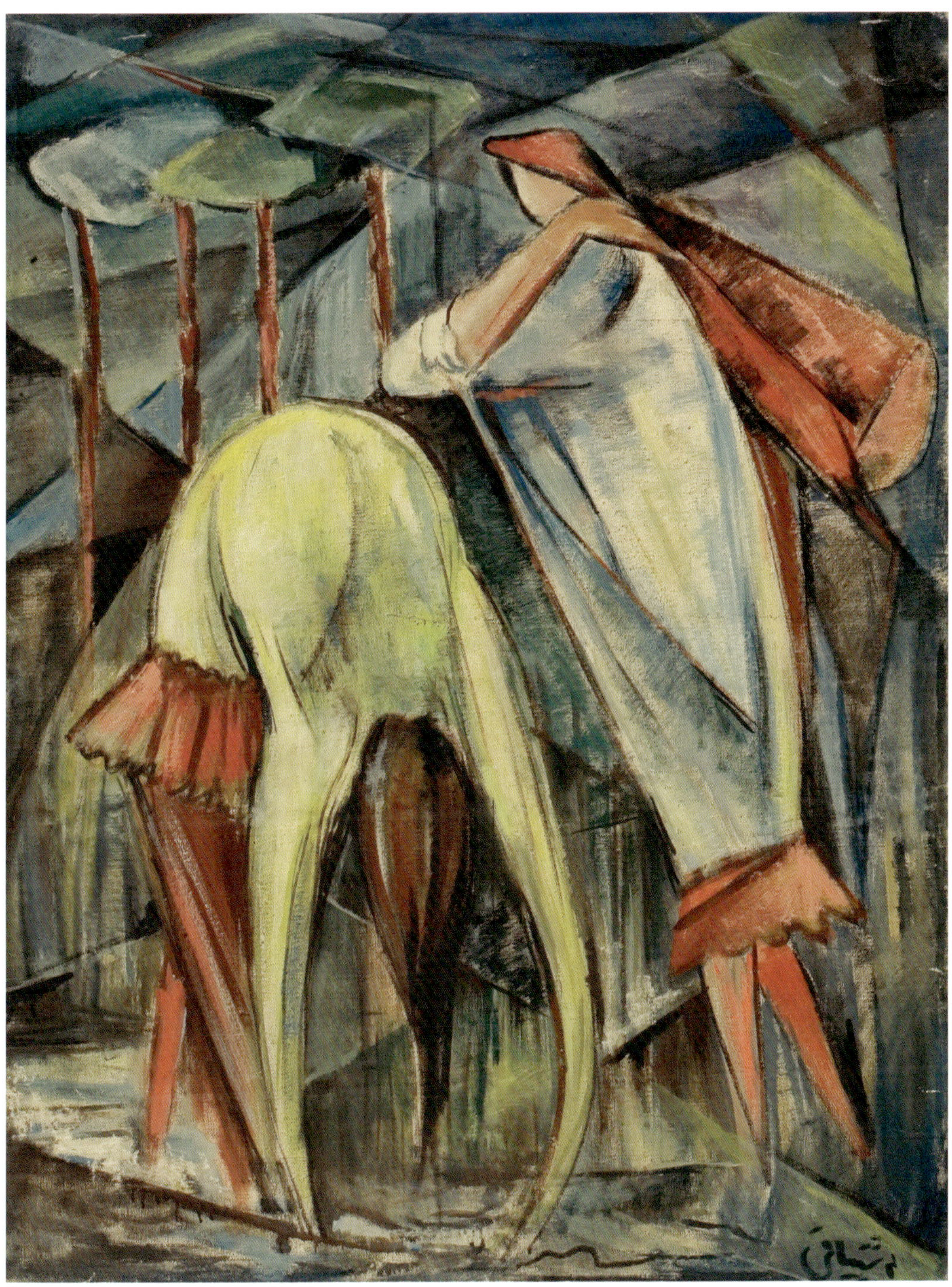

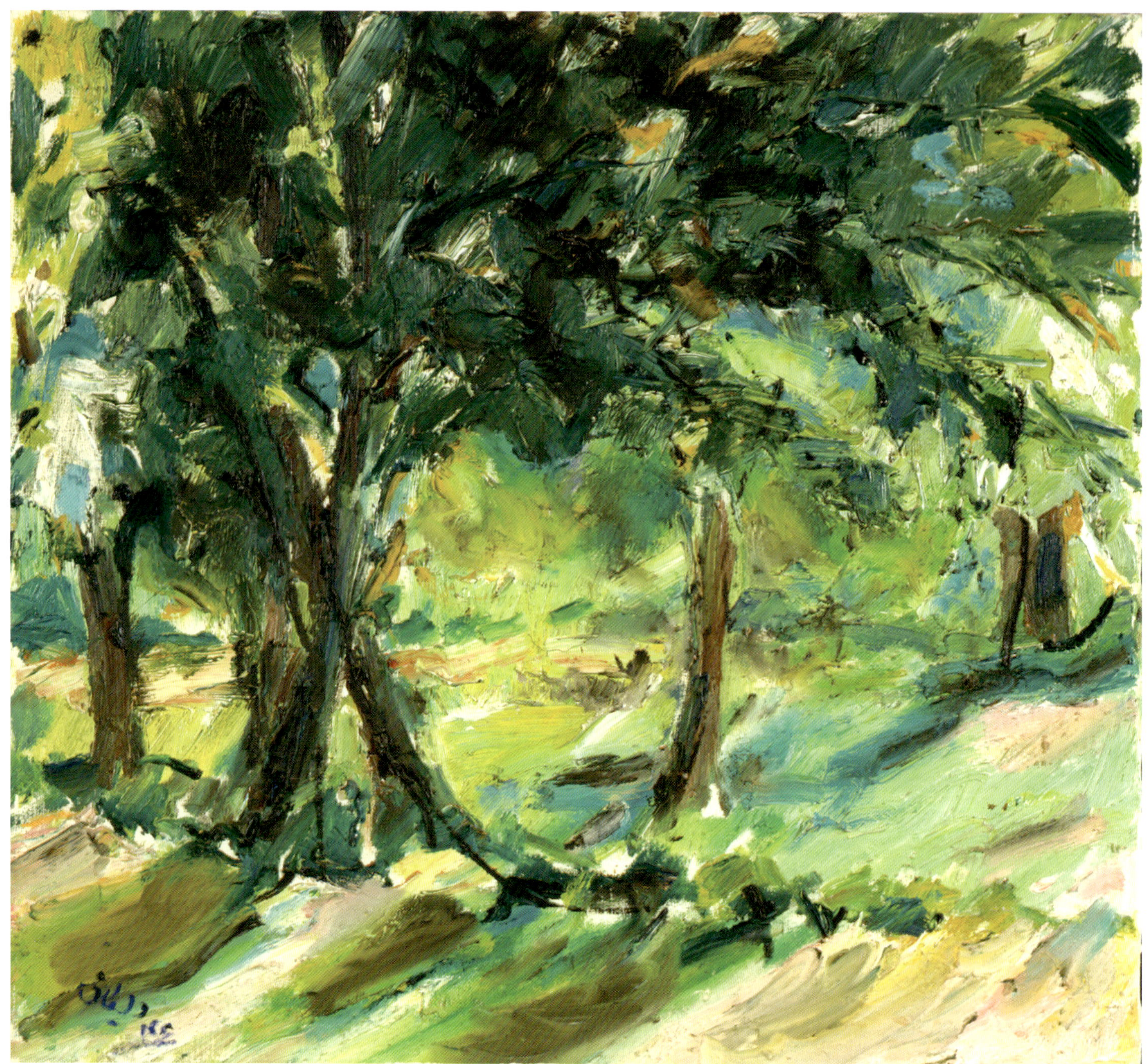

2.17
Mehdi Vishkai, *Untitled*, 1967, oil
on sackcloth, 75×71 cm, TMoCA

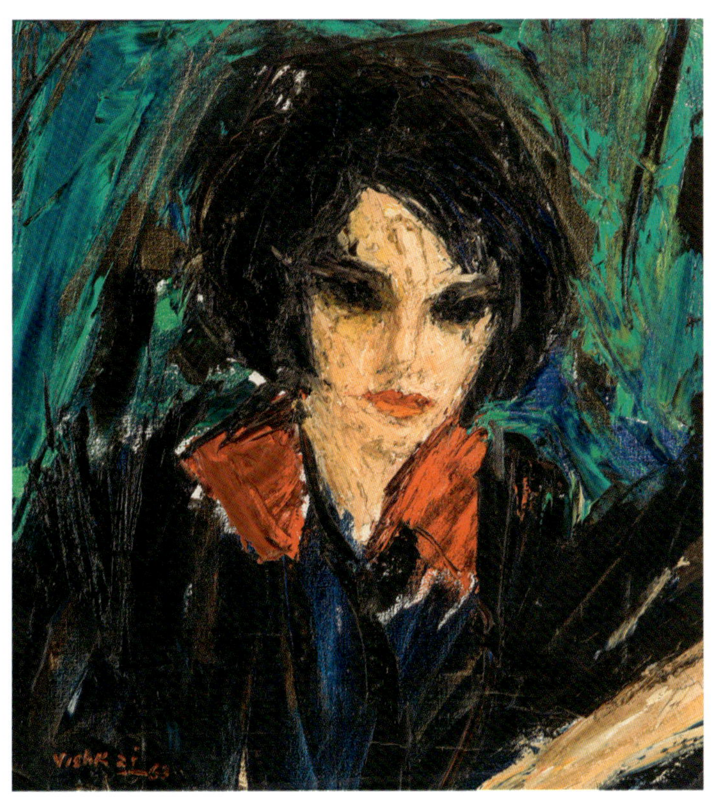

2.18
Mehdi Vishkai, *Portrait*, 1963, oil on
canvas, 65×58 cm, private collection,
Tehran

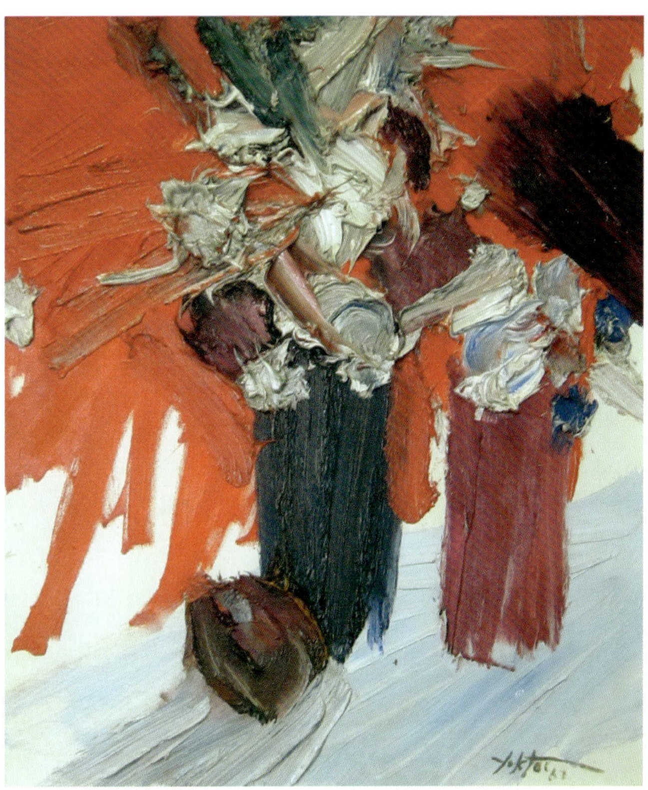

2.19
Manouchehr Yektai, *Still-life*, 1961,
oil on canvas, 88×65 cm, private
collection, Tehran

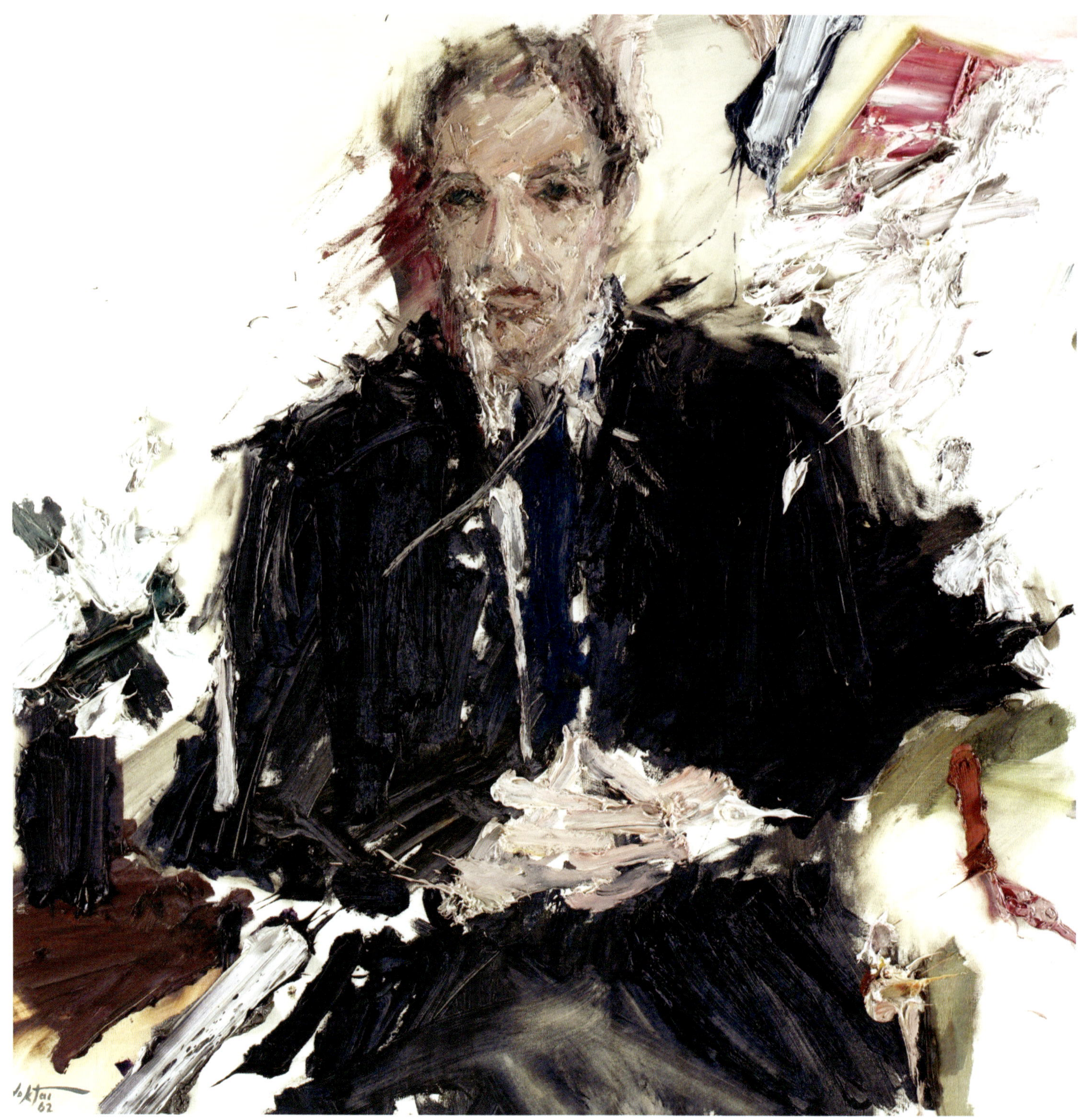

2.20
Manouchehr Yektai, *Portrait of Karl
Flinker*, 1962, oil on canvas,
100×100 cm, private collection,
Tehran

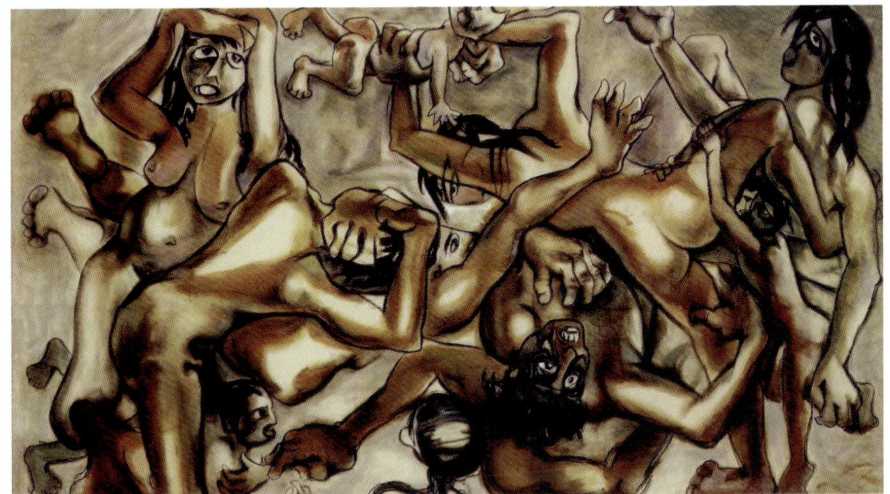

2.21
Marcos Grigorian, *The Gates of Auschwitz*, 1959, oil on linen, detail from a section of the twelve pieces, each visually narrates a scene of the event, 182.9×304.8 cm

Marcos Grigorian (1925–2007) should be regarded as one of the most influential artists of this period, and even in the decades that followed. A graduate of the Tehran Faculty of Fine Art and the Rome Accademia di Belle Arti, he played a pivotal role in solidifying artistic modernism in Iran, both as a pioneering artist and as an educator and active participant in the art scene. Initially, he gravitated towards a form of Expressionism with narrative themes, often imbued with bitterness, such as the event of Auschwitz. (Figure 2.21) In these examples, there is no evident inclination towards addressing Iranian subjects or scenes, but rather a clear narrative of his fervour for modernistic approach, particularly Expressionism. The impact of his potent style, notably observed in the monumental painting of *The Gate of Auschwitz*, can be discerned in the works of subsequent artists, many of whom were primarily his students in art school. However, Gregorian explored various approaches in the ensuing years, from abstract examples employing traditional materials like straw and mud to pop-art-inspired assemblages. This shift in trajectory, this time accompanied by the incorporation of indigenous elements and a concern for Iranicisation, was evident. Further elaboration on these pioneering experiences will be discussed in the subsequent chapter.

Undoubtedly, Gregorian was the foremost proponent of experimentation with new and unconventional materials in Iran, including blends of various soil compositions with pigments to create unconventional textural effects. (Figures 2.22–23) Gregorian also, upon returning from Italy, established one of Tehran's earliest galleries in 1954, the Galerie Esthétique, which served as a platform for promoting and exhibiting modern art. A few years later, he played a key role in organising the first national exhibition of modern art, known

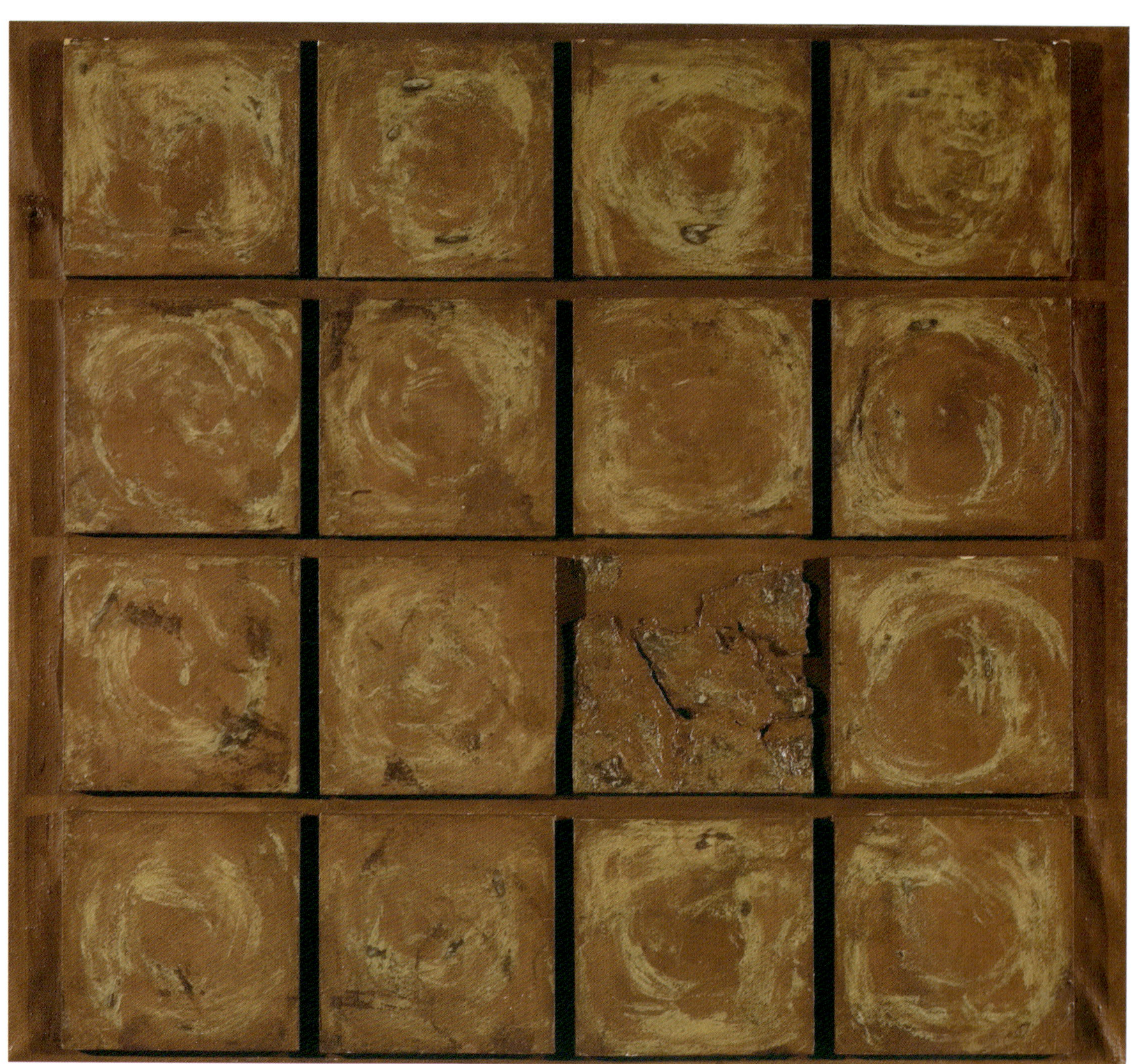

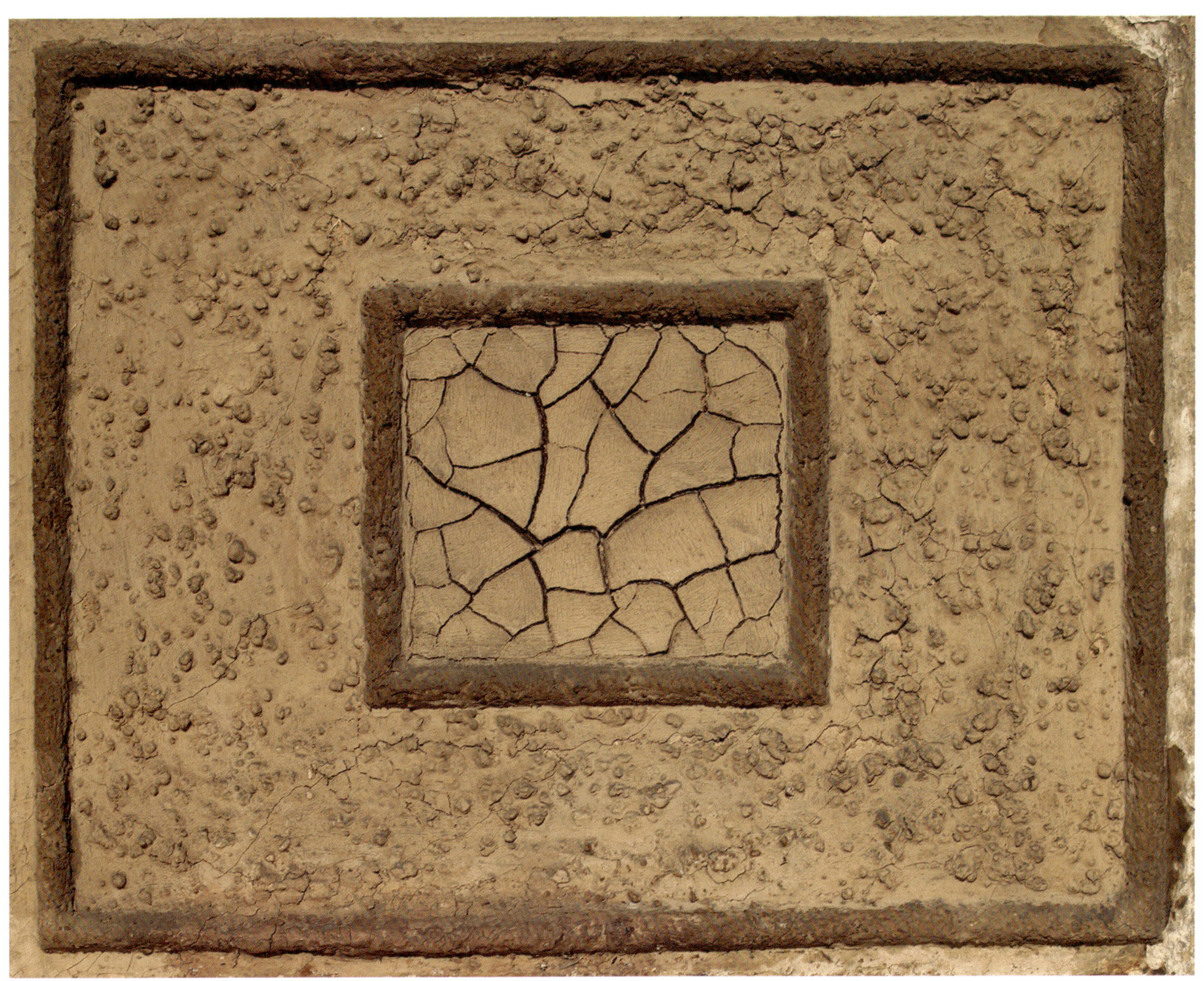

as the First Tehran Biennial in 1958. In the subsequent decades, his active involvement with younger, more avant-garde and experimental artists was evident through initiatives like the Independent Group of Painters and Sculptors, further solidifying his presence in the Iranian art scene. Additionally, another notable contribution of his was the introduction of Iranian Coffee-house painters to the international art scene through exhibitions in the 1960s.

Sohrab Sepehri, was another prominent and pioneering figure in modern Iranian art movement, presenting a personal and distinct style to the art scene: a style that emanated from his serious engagement with the question of how to incorporate modernism with a distinct Iranian sensibility. He graduated from the Faculty of Fine Arts in 1953

Facing page
2.22
Marcos Grigorian, *Fourfold Arenas*, 1964, mosaic on wooden panel, 147×137 cm, TMoCA

Above
2.23
Marcos Grigorian, *Untitled*, 1976, mixed media on board, 70×85 cm, private collection, Tehran

2.24
Sohrab Sepehri, *Untitled*, c. early
1960s, oil on canvas, 70×50 cm,
Kerman Museum

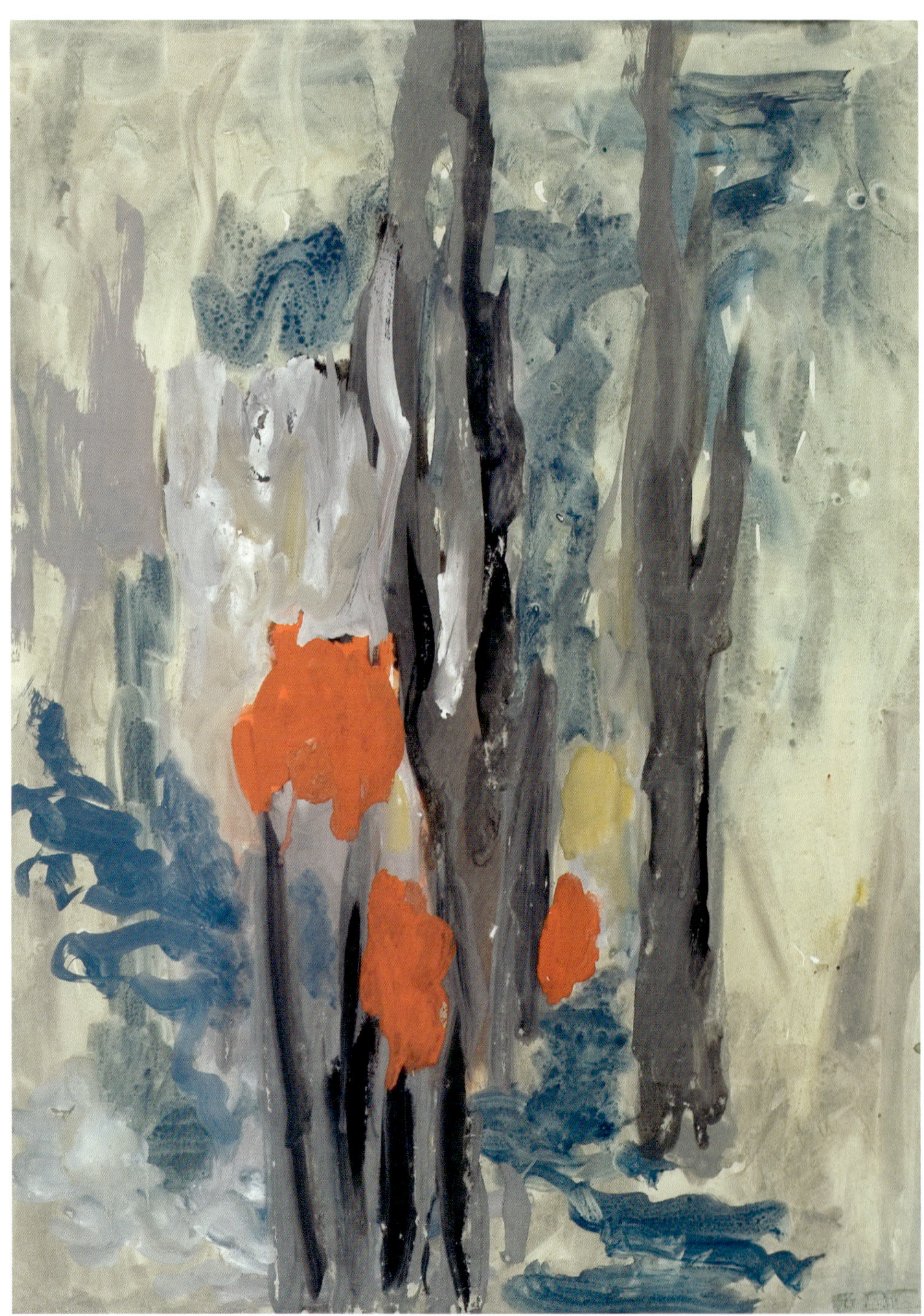

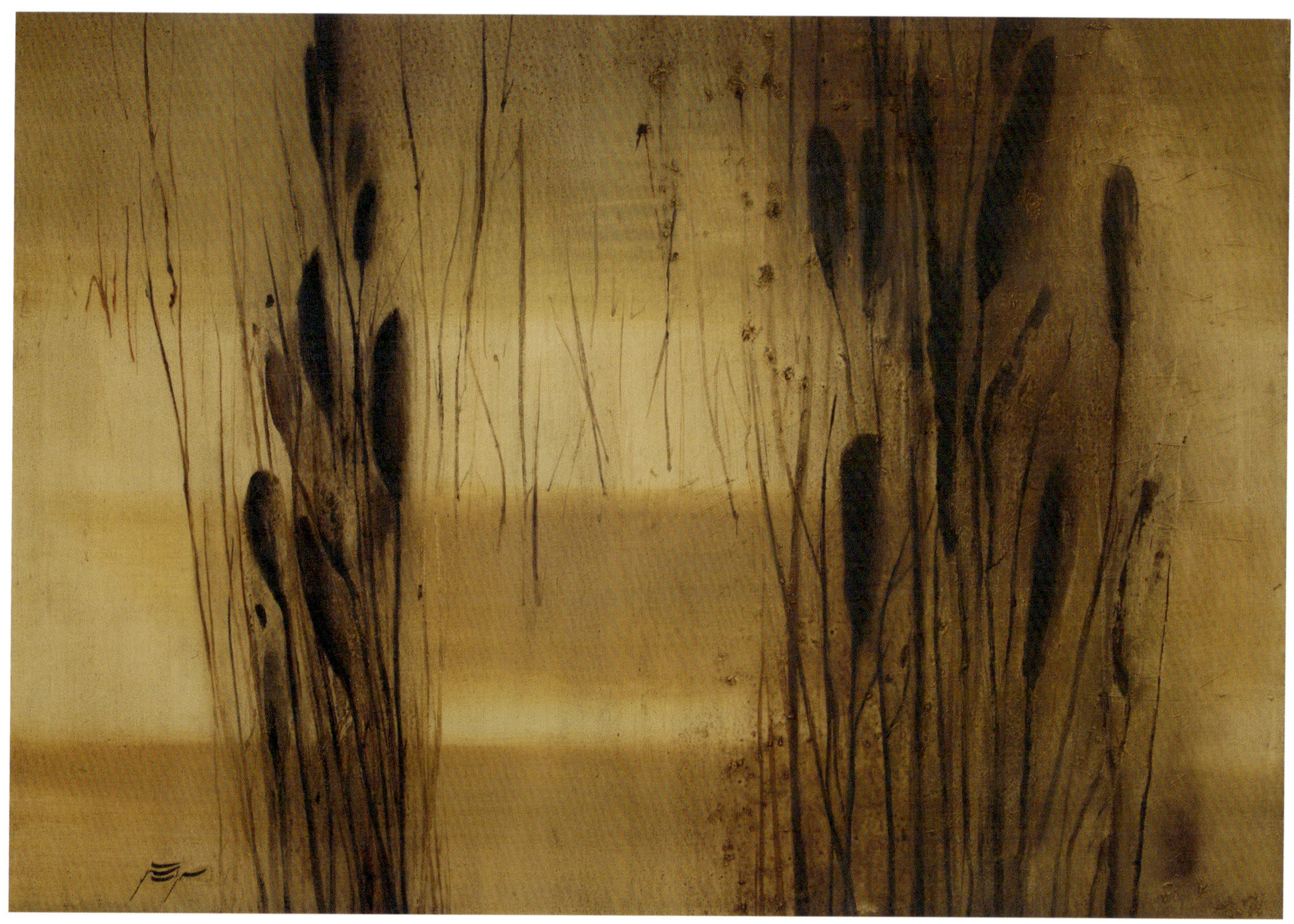

2.25
Sohrab Sepehri, *Untitled*, c. early 1960s, oil on canvas, 49.5×69.5 cm, private collection, Tehran

and pursued further studies for a brief period at the École des Beaux-Arts in Paris before learning hand-printing techniques in Japan. Sepehri explored various modernist stylistic approaches, from minimalist abstract forms to expressionist genres influenced by Japanese nature-oriented aesthetics. Ultimately, he adopted a personal approach that essentially depicted a simple and intimate representation of life with a mystical and introspective look, which was one of the main characteristics of his poems. Although the highpoint of his artistic career emerged in the 1960s and 1970s, he had collaborated with avant-garde artists of his time in the 1950s, notably within such circles as the *Khurus-jangi* Association. The works from this period reflect his initial fascination with Far Eastern art, particularly Japanese Zen painting, and his acquaintance with new techniques such as the 'Sumi ink' method and the *Sessho* attitude towards nature. While perhaps Sepehri, like other modernist artists of his generation and predecessors, did not find the solution to establishing a kind of local modernist art in direct appropriation of national-local forms or subjects, he tried in his art to present a harmonious combination of modernist aesthetic sensibilities with Far Eastern pictorial traditions. (Figures 2.24–25) As he gained more recognition, this tendency increased in his art in the following two decades. I will discuss his later works in the upcoming decades in the next chapter.

Mohsen Vaziri Moghaddam was another modernist artist who studied at the Tehran Faculty of Fine Arts and then the Rome Accademia di Belle Arti. Upon his return in 1958, he became an influential figure in the artistic and academic circles as an artist, writer, and educator during the subsequent decades. While his extensive body of work predominantly reflects preferences for European modernist stylistic inclinations, he consciously selected his artistic models and principles, avoiding strict adherence to any predefined pattern. As mentioned, the years of the 1950s and their continuation into the 1960s witnessed a particular emphasis on national and cultural identity, with a celebration of 'national art' and its representation in cultural and artistic forums, a characteristic that manifested diversely in the works of many artists. In his works during the 1950s, Vaziri Moghaddam too incorporated elements of traditional architecture and patterns, where familiar modernist traces such as Matisse's Fauvism and geometric, stylised and colourful shapes of Paul Klee were reflected. (Figures 2.26) However, he never reverted to this

2.26
Mohsen Vaziri Moghaddam,
Untitled, 1957, oil on canvas,
59×89 cm, private collection

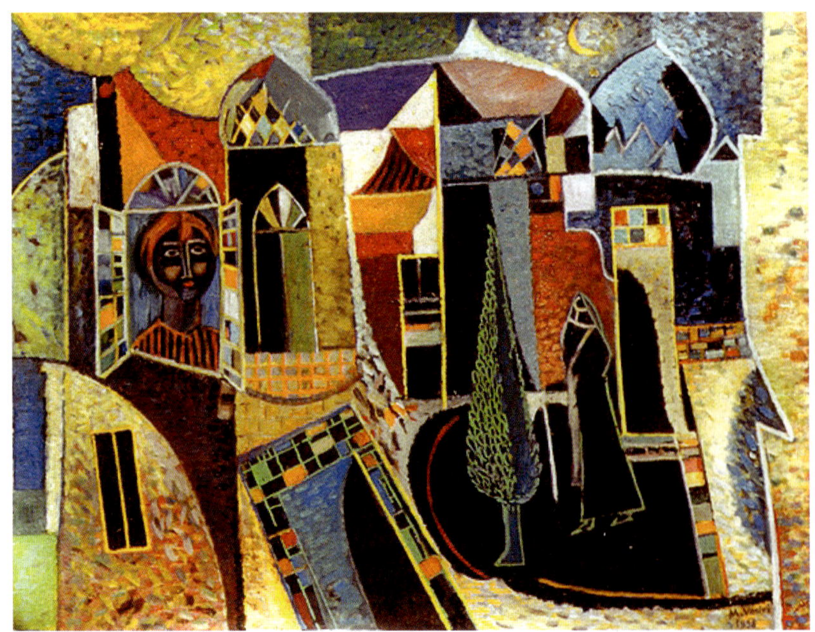

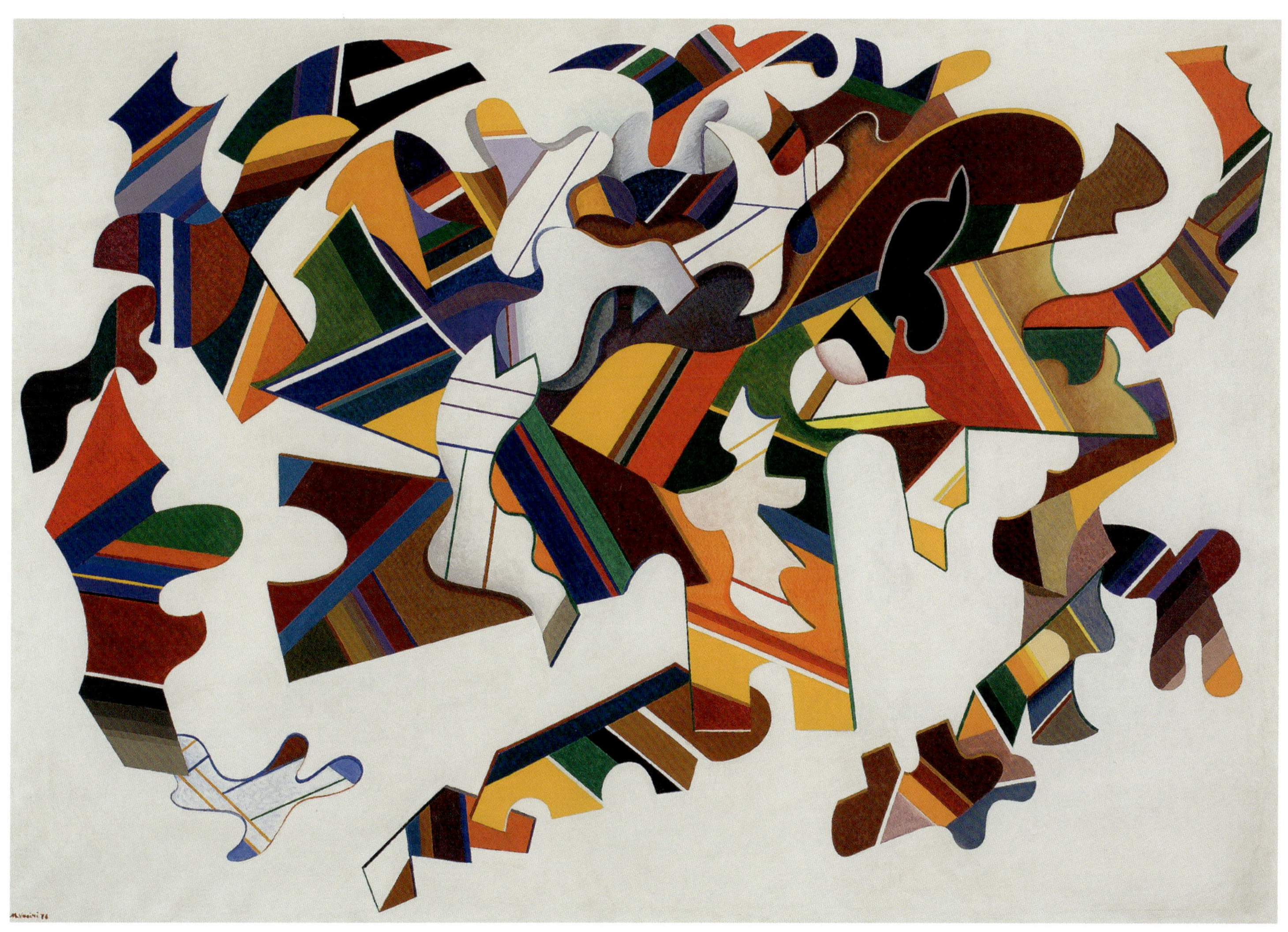

2.27
Mohsen Vaziri Moghaddam, *Untitled*, 1976, oil on canvas, 150×210 cm, TMoCA

approach in later periods. Consequently, the abstract shapes, colours, lines, rhythm, and the spatial movement within his works stand out as some of the most distinctive features throughout his long professional career. In his later works, he employed two-dimensional geometric shapes with bright and pure colours and concurrently created diverse experimental pieces using various materials and mediums. (Figures 2.27–28) In these works, unlike many of his contemporaries who were deeply engaged in the question of cultural identity, striving to adapt modernistic stylistic patterns and templates, he consciously distanced himself from the reflection of any local themes. He refrained from resorting to narrative and literary references to Iranian mythical or mystical connotations more than many Iranian avant-garde artists did. The main body of Vaziri Moghaddam's works denotes a sense of self-definition and singularity in artistic expression. Throughout the subsequent decades, his art offered an alternative form of modernism

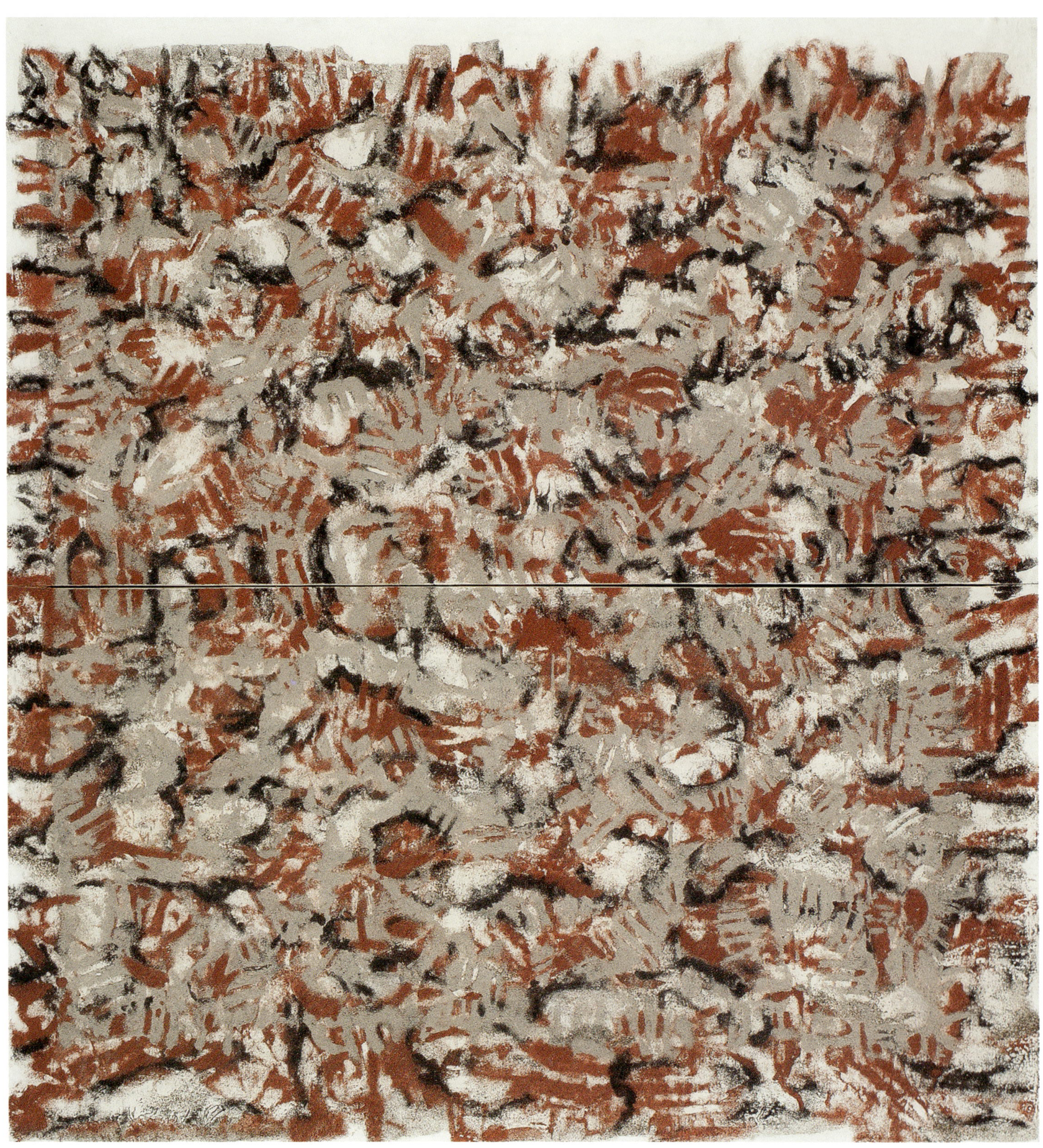

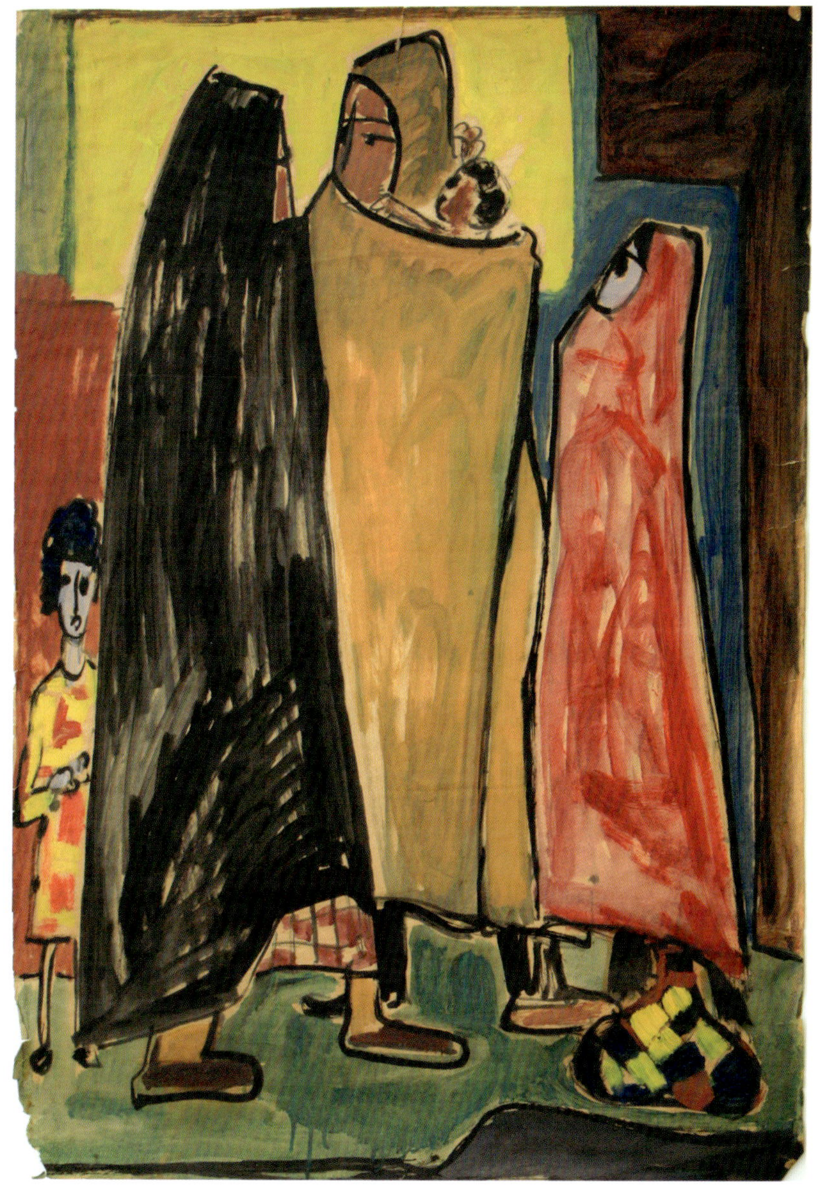

within the Iranian context, avoiding any nostalgic return to familiar clichés. During his years of teaching at the Tehran Faculty of Fine Arts and the Tehran College of Decorative Arts, he nurtured a group of emerging artists from the new generation, many of whom evolved to become the most influential artists of their time in the ensuing decades.

Sirak Melkonian, who also started his activity in the 1950s, drew inspiration from Grigorian initial expressionist paintings. Melkonian's early works showed a type of figurative Expressionism that bore this influence. The subjects of these works, reflecting his concerns about local subjects, often depicted ordinary people in his

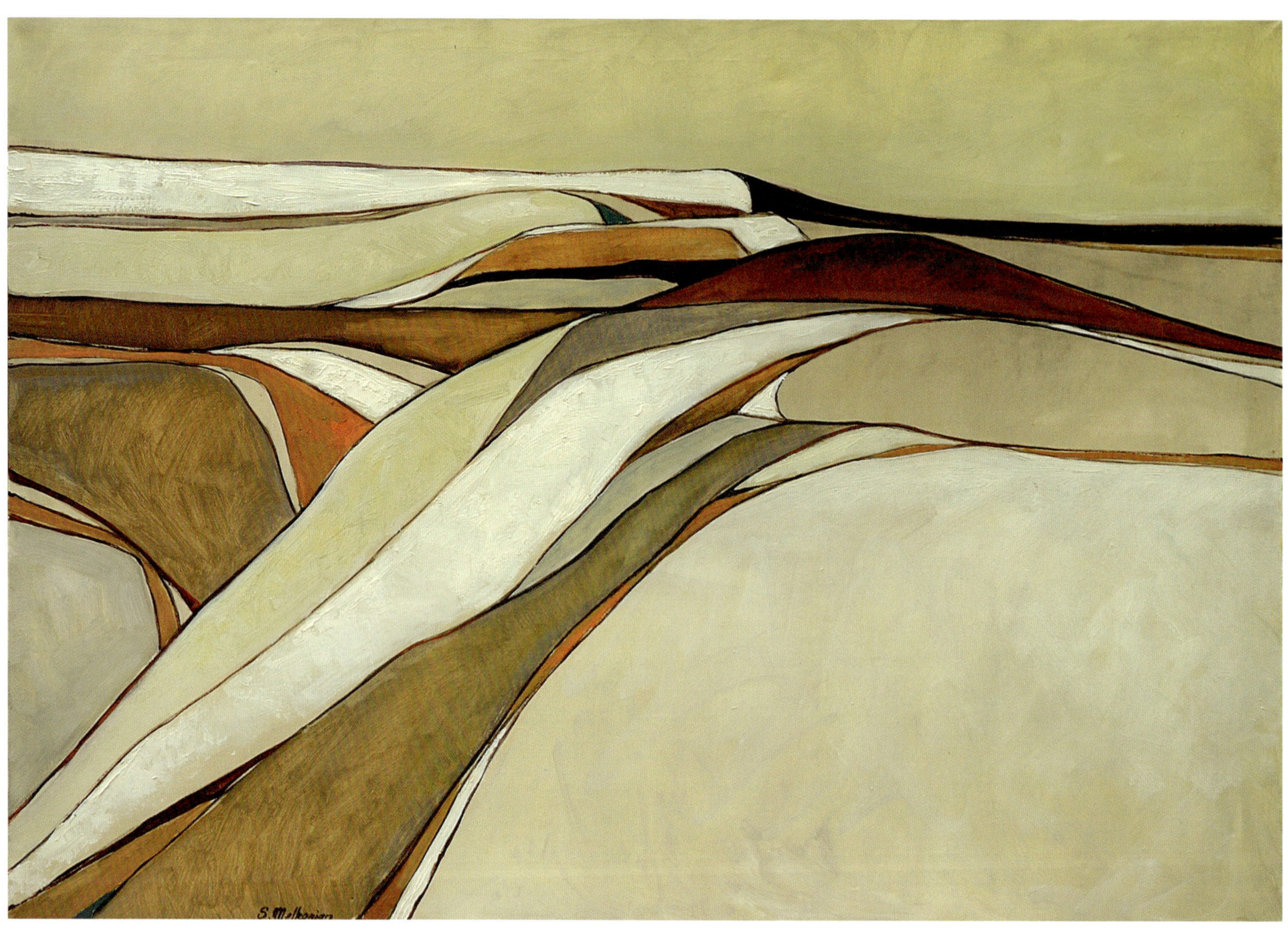

2.30
Sirak Melkonian, *Untitled*, 1973,
oil on canvas, 90×125 cm, private
collection, Tehran

surroundings in the alleys and markets, painted in expressionistic forms, often with dark colours. (Figure 2.29) In Melkonian's works, the artistic atmosphere of that period and the prevalent approach to modernism, with adaptation of national elements, can be seen prominently with the presence of veiled women and men in traditional attire. In subsequent years, this tendency transitioned into geometric and then abstract forms. Therefore, perhaps Melkonian can be considered one of the earliest figures of Iranian abstractionism. This abstract approach became apparent in the 1970s during his research trips to Sistan and Baluchestan and some other southern regions of the country, where he was influenced by the nature of these regions, achieving a personal style in his works. The predominant abstract forms, often monochrome and delineated by lines, resemble natural shapes such as mountains and desert hills. (Figure 2.30) These forms have been intricately incorporated into articulated networks, resulting in a harmonious interplay of elements within the composition. This minimalist abstract method gradually became the hallmark of Melkonian's paintings, evident in the diverse forms and combinations seen in his works over the subsequent decades. He also joined the Independent Group of Painters and Sculptors in the 1970s, which we will discuss further in the third chapter.

Jazeh Tabatabai, another graduate of the Tehran Faculty of Fine Arts, was a pioneer modernist artist who started his artistic activities in the mid-1950s, establishing one of Iran's first private galleries, the Modern Art Gallery (Galiri-i hunar-i jadid), in 1955. A versatile artist, embracing the disciplines of painting, sculpture, poetry, and writing, Tabatabaei initially focused on traditional Iranian imagery, drawing inspiration from various sources such as the formal characteristics of Persian painting, Qajar royal portraiture, and *Qahveh-khaneh* (Coffee-house) painting. (Figure 2.31) Subsequently, he integrated an expressionistic style into his artistic repertoire. Later, in the early 1960s, his interest in folk Shi'i religious art and folklore fables and maxims increased, which meant that he was able to play a key role as one of the main members of the forthcoming neo-traditionalist movement of *Saqqa-khaneh*.

Ziapour's belief that Iranian art needed to discover a *raison d'être* and a mode of expressing its distinctive identity to integrate into the global modern art scene was now endorsed by the art authorities, notably the Ministry of Culture and Art and later the Office of Empress Farah Pahlavi. These institutions actively promoted the pursuit of establishing a 'national school' of art, with evident connections to the illustrious eras of Persian art, particularly the Achaemenid, Sassanian, and Safavid periods.[34]

The artistic atmosphere of the 1940s and 1950s can be characterised as unstable, with artists often hesitant and unsure when it came to defining a specifically Iranian form of modernism. As we shall see, in the next decade this continuous search for artistic identity started to fuse with nationalist and also nativist sentiments.

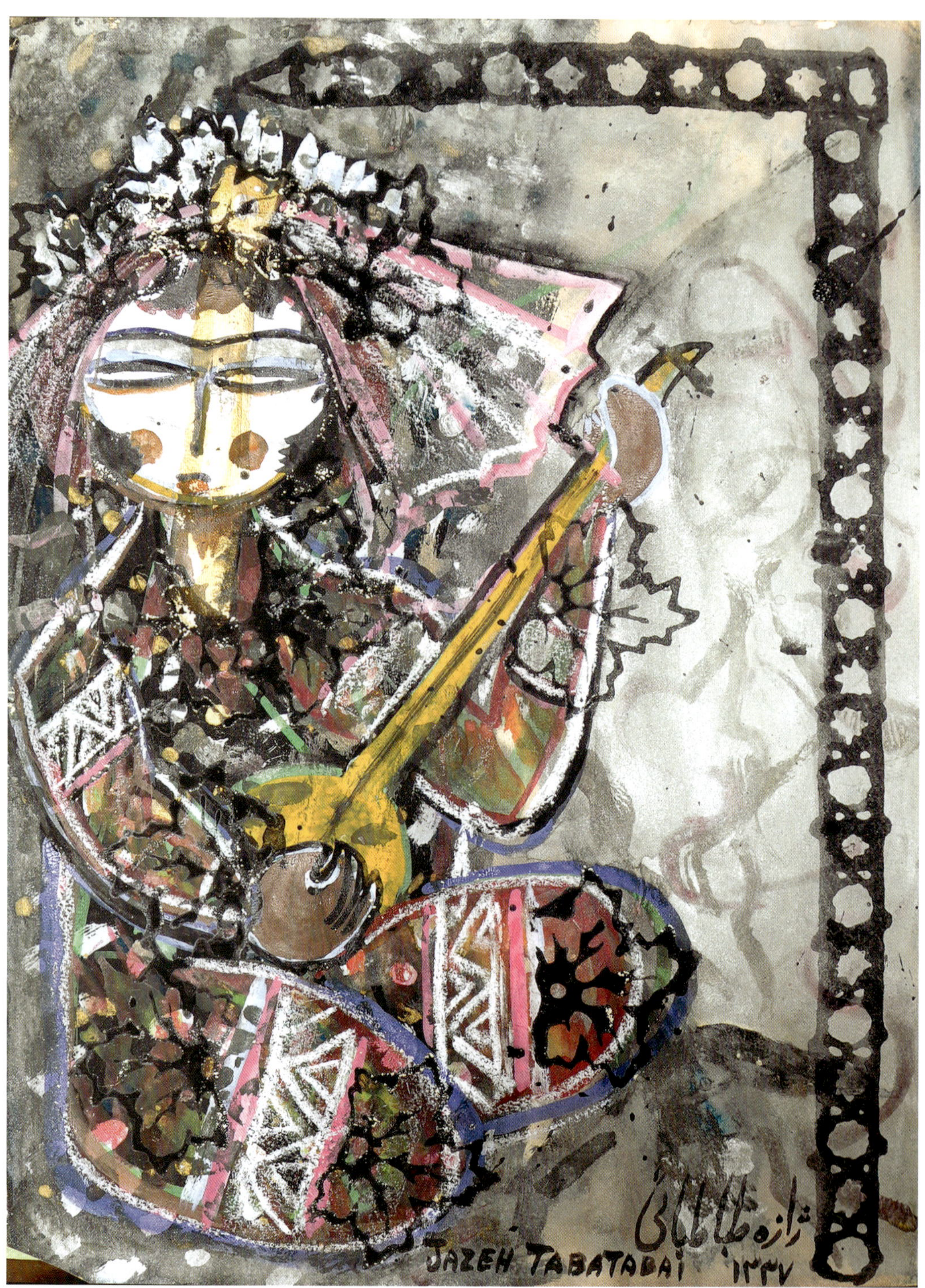

2.31
Jazeh Tabatabai, *A Girl Playing Sitar*, 1958, pastel and watercolour on paper, 40×33 cm, private collection, Tehran

NOTES

1   Although other sorts of traditional art were still being practised, including miniature painting and *Qahveh-khaneh* (depicting popular religious and folk themes in a style commonly known as Coffee-house painting), they did not enjoy the same level of popularity and widespread appeal as Kamal al-Mulk's naturalistic style.

2   The date accidentally coincided with Kamal al-Mulk's death!

3   After Kamal al-Mulk's resignation, the Madrasa-i Sanayi'-i Mustazrafa had been reorganised and renamed Madrasa-i sanayi' va pisha va hunar (School of Crafts and the Arts).

4   According to Mojabi, a set of Beaux-Arts textbooks were translated into Persian by contribution of university instructors and leading Iranian writers, including Sadegh Hedayat (one of the most eminent modernist Iranian novelists who worked in the education section of the Faculty). (Javad Mojabi, *Pioneers of Contemporary Persian Painting: First Generation*, Tehran, 1997 p.7.)

5   The new Faculty was temporarily housed in the old theological school, Madrasa-i Marvi, in the centre of Tehran; a year later it was transferred to the basement of the recently built Faculty of Engineering of Tehran University, which was being constructed on the main university campus. It finally moved to its present location in the south-eastern corner of the campus in 1948/9. (Morteza Momayyez, 'Faculty of Fine Arts', in Ehsan Yarshater, ed., *Encyclopaedia Iranica*, vol. X, New York 1999, p.142.) In the same year, the College's name changed from *Hunarkadeh* (college) to *Danishkadeh* (faculty) and was formally attached to the University of Tehran as the Faculty of Fine Arts. In the following year, Godard resigned his post as Dean of the Faculty of Fine Arts and returned to France. His successor was Mohsen Foroughi, who continued Godard's strategies.

6   At first the curriculum was planned in two parts, each taking two years and leading to a bachelor's degree. (Morteza Momayyez, 'Faculty of Fine Arts', p.142.)

7   He taught at the Faculty from 1941 to his retirement in 1966 and played a main role in its formation as Deputy Dean of the Faculty.

8   He was one of the founders of the Faculty and taught anatomy there for a period of time.

9   He was the founder of the department of sculpture and was active at the Faculty in training a new generation of sculptors.

10 She was French and this title referred to her Iranian husband, Dr Ashub Aminfar.

11 Javad Mojabi, *Pioneers of Contemporary Persian Painting*, p. 10.

12 Ibid.

13 Ruin Pakbaz, *Contemporary Iranian Painting and Sculpture*, translated into English by S. Melkonian, Tehran 1974, p.10. Ahmad Esfandiari, one of the students there, describes the contradictory instructions that they received at the Faculty: 'Each professor had a different style. Master Heydarian came from the Kamal al-Mulk School; he believed in it, and that was what he taught. Madame Ashub Aminfar, on the other hand, came from the *Beaux-Arts*, and she was trained in that system. [...] For us students, we could not fully grasp what the French professors said in class or in the atelier. The *Beaux Arts* programme which was presented to us was not clearly translated. The student was not able to grasp easily their views or viewpoints.' (Javad Mojabi, *Pioneers of Contemporary Persian Painting*, p.11.)

14 Throughout the 1920s, 1930s, and into the mid-1940s, Kamal al-Mulk's school, as official art, dominated Iranian art. Typical subjects such as landscape and portrait, academic renderings of subjects such as family gatherings, street scenes and still life compositions were the common subject matter that could be seen in many works of Kamal al-Mulk's disciples and those influenced by his school.

15 It is also worth noting that there were painters of this generation who had studied art at Soviet academies. Their works demonstrated Impressionist and post-Impressionist tendencies. Among them are such artists as Habib Mohammadi (1904–57) and Reza Forouzi (1911–67). See Ruin Pakbaz, *Contemporary Iranian Painting and Sculpture*, p. 11.

16 Ehsan Yarshater, 'Contemporary Persian Painting', in Richard Ettinghausen and Ehsan Yarshater, ed., *Highlights of Persian Art*, New York 1979, p. 363.

17 This exhibition continued to be held almost annually during the 1950s.

18 Now the number of exhibiting artists was growing. Among them one can find the following: Ahmad Esfandiari, Mahmoud Javadipour, Abdollah Ameri, Leili Taqipour, Shokouh Riazi, Fakhri Angha, Houshang Pezeshknia, Mehdi Vishkai, Hossein Kazemi and, from a younger generation, Manouchehr Sheybani and Sadegh Barirani.

19 In 1950 all the government offices and departments dealing with arts and crafts were unified as one agency called the Hunar-hay-i zibay-i kishvar, the General Administration of Fine Arts, in the Ministry of Culture. In 1961, the Fine Art section came under the supervision of the prime minister. In 1964, based on a parliamentary resolution, the Ministry of Culture and Art was established. The Ministry of Culture and Art, which was the responsibility of the Shah's brother-in-law, Mehrdad Pahlbod, was in charge of preparing and supporting the development of art and culture, and presenting and conserving the ancient heritage of the country.

20 The Biennial was inaugurated on 14 April 1958 in the Abyaz Palace within the Golestan Palace compound under the General Administration of Fine Arts, Public Relation and Publication Department. The second, third and fourth Tehran Biennials organised by the Public Relation and Publication of the General Administration of Fine Arts of the Country were all held in a regular basis at the Abyaz Palace. There was preparation for the Venice Biennale which would be held directly after the Tehran Biennial; after the Second Tehran Biennial it was hoped to have an Asian biennal. (Introduction to the *Nimayishgah-i naqqashi va piykat-tarashi; duvvumin biyenal-i Tehran*. (Catalogue of the second Tehran Biennial), 1339S/1960, p.14.)

21 Marcos Grigorian, Introduction to the First Tehran Biennial catalogue (exhibition catalogue), Tehran 1958, pp.4–8.

22 Ehsan Yarshater, 'Contemporary Persian Painting', p. 363.

23 Karim Emami, 'Art in Iran XI Post-Qajar', in Ehsan Yarshater, ed., *Encyclopaedia Iranica*, vol. II, London and New York 1987, p. 641.

24 See Ruin Pakbaz, *Contemporary Iranian Painting and Sculpture*, p.14.

25 Lhote was a French painter, sculptor, printmaker, art teacher and critic. He studied decorative sculpture at the *École des Beaux-Arts* in Bordeaux. Greatly influenced by Cézanne and by Cubism, he occupies an important place in the history of modern art as he was very active in developing the theoretical framework of Cubism. Lhote founded his own art school in 1918 and trained, taught and influenced a vast number of artists, reaching many more through his numerous books and frequent lecture tours.

26 The first modern poem was written by Nima Yooshij entitled *Afsaneh* (Legend) in 1921. However, it was during the period of the 1940s when the crucial battle between old and new took place.

27 See Karim Emami, 'Art in Iran XI Post-Qajar', p. 641.

28 See Javad Mojabi, *Pioneers of Contemporary Persian Painting*, p.15.

29 Ehsan Yarshater, 'Contemporary Persian Painting', p. 376.

30 Javad Mojabi, *Pioneers of Contemporary Persian Painting*, p.12.

31 Ruin Pakbaz, *Contemporary Iranian Painting and Sculpture*, p.14.

32 Ibid., pp.19–20.

33 See Javad Mojabi, *Pioneers of Contemporary Persian Painting*, p.15.

34 Karim Emami, 'Art in Iran XI Post-Qajar', p. 641.

CHAPTER THREE

Questions of Identity, Nativism and Nationalism Alongside Modernism in Art and Socio-Political Culture: Neo-Traditionalist Movements

1. The National School of Art and the Obsession with Identity and Cultural Concerns: *Saqqa-Khaneh* Movement

During the 1940s and 1950s, the terms 'national art' or a 'national school of art' were repeatedly used by both modernist artists and cultural administrators. Artists had made various attempts to produce what they considered to be this kind of art. As we saw in Chapter Two, the deliberate use of local material as a reference to the self and to cultural specificity dates back to the pioneers of modern Iranian art – to figures such as Jalil Ziapour. Yet the issue of identity in art (as in other fields of social activity) was in fact discussed in some artistic and intellectual gatherings before the onset of the state-assisted propagation of art in the 1960s. During the 1940s and 1950s, artists attempted to adapt to modernism; artists working in the 1960s, on the other hand, together with other intellectuals, found themselves caught between two polarities: traditionalism and modernism.[1]

The complex debate over these issues would eventually result in the growth of various new movements, and the formation of a modern approach towards traditional Iranian heritage, known as neo-traditionalism. This significant period in modern Iranian art

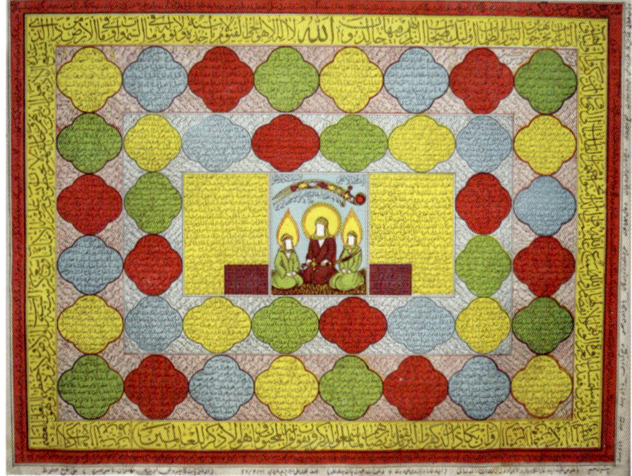

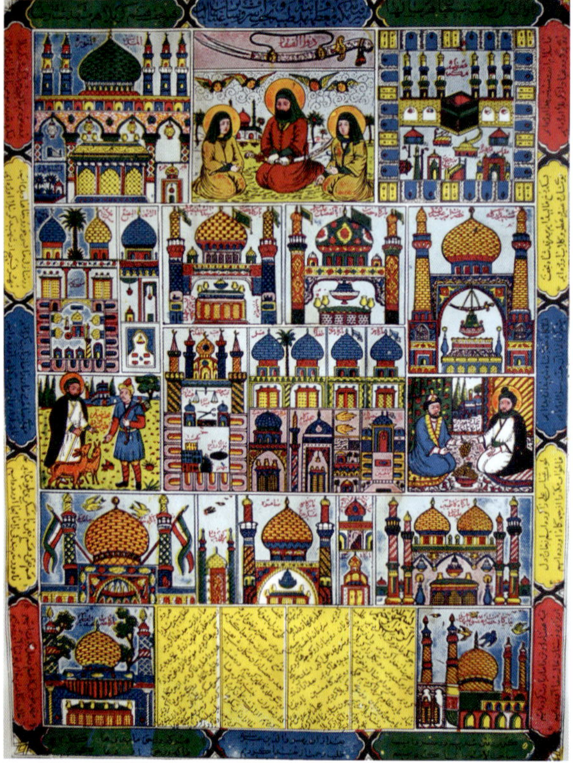

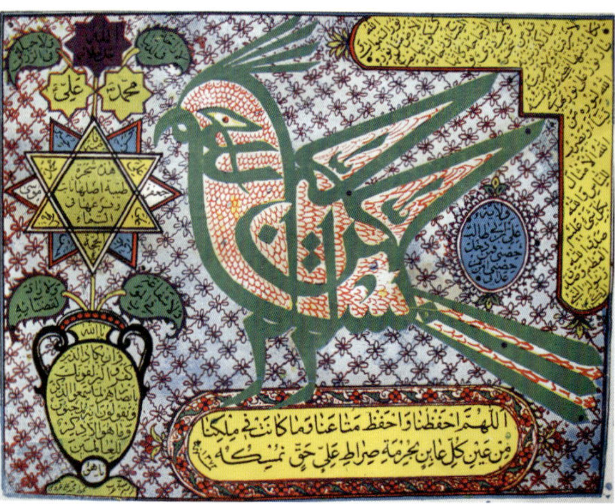

can be characterised by an increasing tendency to confront conflicts between past and present; it is when the quest for a national artistic identity coincided with the forces of modernity.

The first question that needs to be asked is: what is neo-traditional art? Accepted definitions involve a reinterpretation of the formal value systems that govern art, including technique and content, usually denoted by a set of style markers. However, it also involves a claim to authority over future forms by artists who interpret the values of the past. Reference to social aspirations focused on religion, politics, or on nationalist ideologies is reflected in this debate.[2]

Deeply affected by their contemporary intellectual, social, and political atmosphere, the neo-traditionalists attempted to create a synthesis between a pictorial heritage of the past and the new language of modern art. They realised that within modernist approaches, a distinct individual expression became a vital aspect of the artist's identity. Consequently, modernist artists frequently incorporated symbols or motifs from their personal or cultural background into their works to signify this expression.

Inevitably this section focuses on the most important movement during this period: the *Saqqa-khaneh* movement. The name *Saqqa-khaneh* was used for the first time by the art critic, journalist and lecturer in English, Karim Emami, at the Tehran College of Decorative Arts (Hunarkadeh-i hunar-hay-i taz'ini). The name was initially applied to the works of artists, both in painting and sculpture, that used existing elements of votive Shi'i art in their modern work. It gradually came to be applied to various forms of modern Iranian painting and sculpture that used traditional elements.

One of the main pioneers of the trend, the sculptor Parviz Tanavoli (b.1937), describes how he and Charles Hossein Zenderoudi (b.1937) became fascinated in the late 1950s by printed posters depicting religious scenes, talismanic seals and pictorial forms in the south of Tehran. They were searching for local Iranian raw material to be used and developed in their works.[3] The simplicity of forms, repeated motifs, and bright colours attracted them. Tanavoli believes that the first sketches Zenderoudi created on the basis of those materials could be considered as the very first examples of *Saqqa-khaneh* works.[4] (Figures 3.1–4)

Karim Emami, in describing one of the initial works of Zenderoudi a couple of years before the Third Tehran Biennial in 1962, maintains: 'It was a headless corpse of a Shi'i martyr from Karbala, covered in talismanic fashion with numbers, and words some written in earnest and some in jest.'[5] Another of Zenderoudi's works, a large linocut traced before 1962 which was familiar to Emami, presented some of the scenes from Karbala in different sequences, resembling a Coffee-house (*Qahveh-khaneh*) painting.[6] It refers to the work exhibited in 1960, together with a collection of Zenderoudi's latest oil paintings and linocuts displayed in the Talar-i Reza Abbasi (Reza Abbasi Hall).[7] It was a religious *pardeh*[8] that attracted considerable attention. This painting comprised ten illustrations of the Karbala tragedy and its aftermath and a verse in praise of Imam Hossein printed on canvas with linoleum blocks. This text reads: *In Hossein kist ke dilha hameh divaneh-i ust?* (Who is this Hossein with whom everyone is madly in love?). (Figures 3.5) This work displays Zenderoudi's special enthusiasm for folk art and religious topics and indicates the beginning of his interest in these topics, which emerged in subsequent canvases of this period.

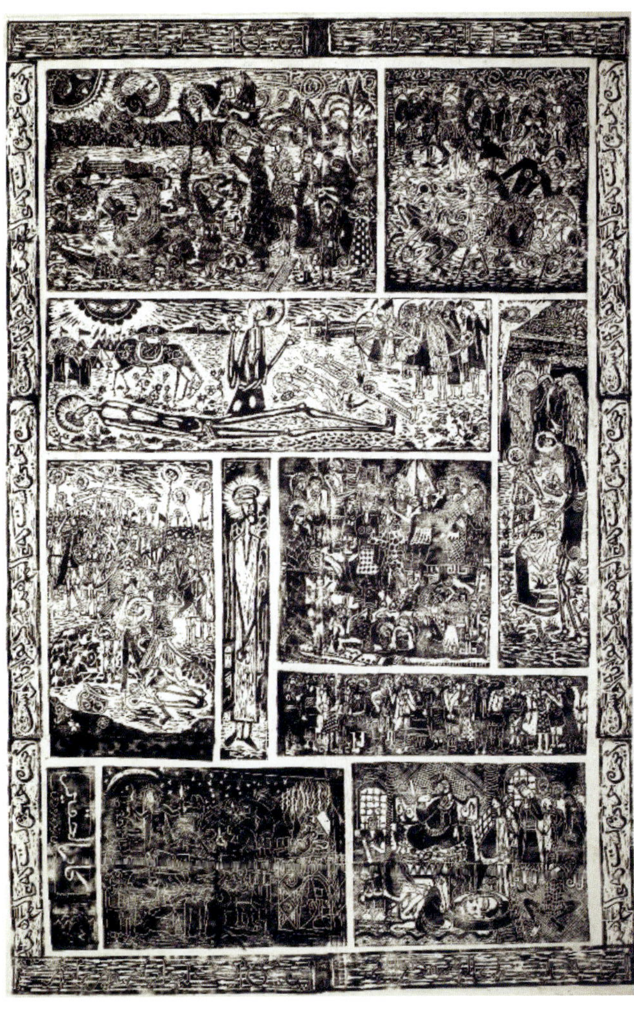

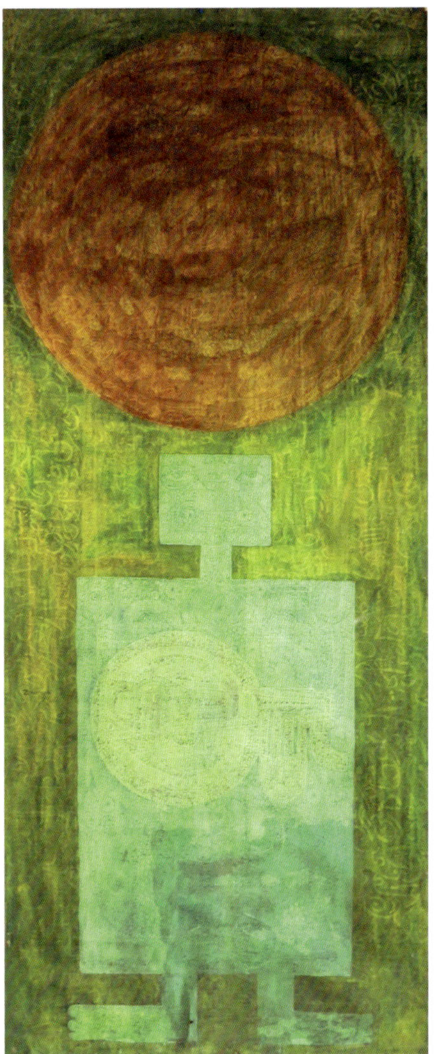

Facing page
3.1–3.3
Prints with religious and talismanic prayers, mid-twentieth century, Iran, private collection, Tehran

Above
3.4
Charles Hossein Zenderoudi, *Untitled*, 1960, natural pigments on paper.

Left
3.5
Charles Hossein Zenderoudi, *In Hossein kist keh dilha hameh divaneh-i ust?* (Who is this Hossein with whom everyone is madly in love?), 1958–9, linocut on linen, 228.52×148.50 cm, British Museum

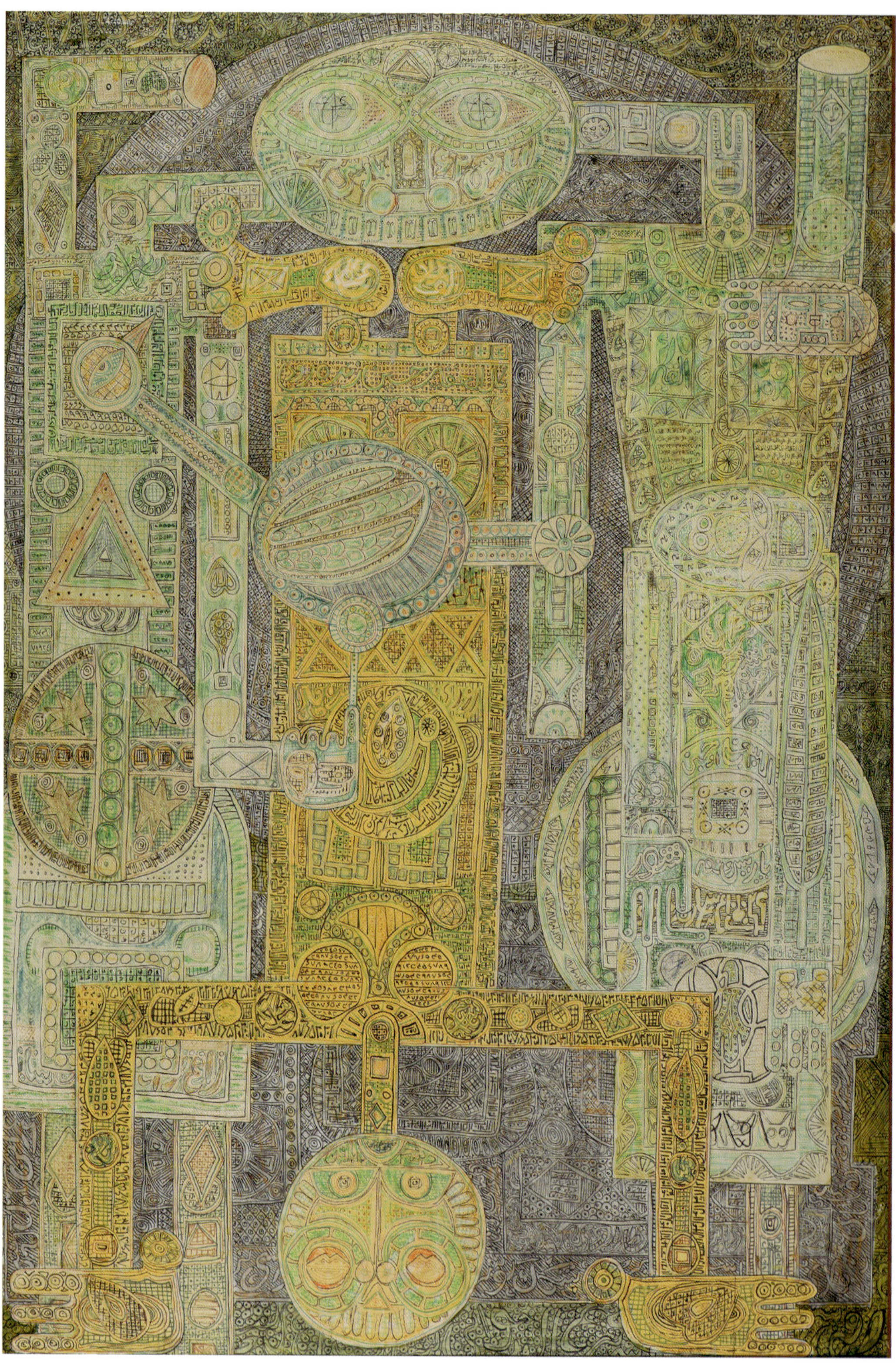

3.6
Charles Hossein Zenderoudi,
Untitled, 1962, natural pigments on
paper mounted on board, 225×150
cm, Iranian Academy of Arts

From Emami's point of view, however, the official birth of the *Saqqa-khaneh* movement occurred when Zenderoudi's canvases were exhibited at the Third Tehran Biennial.[9] These clearly showed the formal and stylistic developments that had emerged in his work. In these paintings, external lines of bodies were shaped in geometrical order, the alphabetical characters in the background were written carefully, and the squares, triangles, rectangles, and circles were coloured in hues of red, green, yellow ochre, and sometimes mild blue. (Figure 3.6) These colours accompanied with black had made up the Shi'i mourning colours.[10] Emami then explains the reason for choosing the name *Saqqa-khaneh* for art in this manner. He states that a viewer of Zenderoudi's canvases would be reminded of Shi'i shrines and assemblies. The atmosphere of the paintings was religious and reminder of Muharram mourning, of candles reflected in shiny brass bowls, of chants of '*Ya Hossein*' and 'Blessed be the Prophet'. The impression was not as lofty, grand, or spacious as some of the distinguished Iranian mosques, but as familiar and intimate as that of the (traditional) *Saqqa-khaneh*.[11] (Figure 3.7)

Saqqa-khanehs, literally, are votive fountains installed for public drinking, and can still be seen in Iranian towns and cities. Traditionally, in the older quarters of cities, each *Saqqa-khaneh* consisted of a small and inconspicuous niche within which a water tank, a copper or brass bowl, and some other equipment were supplied.[12] Small locks or pieces of rag were fastened to the metallic grid in the exterior part of some *Saqqa-khaneh*s for votive reasons. The interior of the *Saqqa-khaneh* often featured a portrait of an imam and metal trays with attached candleholders, creating a sacred ambiance. (Figure 3.8) Additional objects of religious significance, such as a hand crafted from brass or tin (associated with Abbas, the Shi'i martyr in Karbala), a string of beads, mirrors, and draperies embroidered with prayers or verses from the Qur'an, as well as small pictures or prints depicting events from Karbala or other popular religious episodes, further enhanced the devout atmosphere.

Within traditional Shi'i folk culture, *Saqqa-khaneh* (including a continuous link with Zamzam[13]) had an ultra-historical relationship with the martyrdom of Imam Hossein at Karbala in AD 680. Peter Lemborn Willson describes *Saqqa-khaneh* as:

> ... the "house" or "place of the water-bearer" and a symbolic tomb, a reminder of God's Mercy – which is epitomized for the dry lands of the Islamic world in the primordial

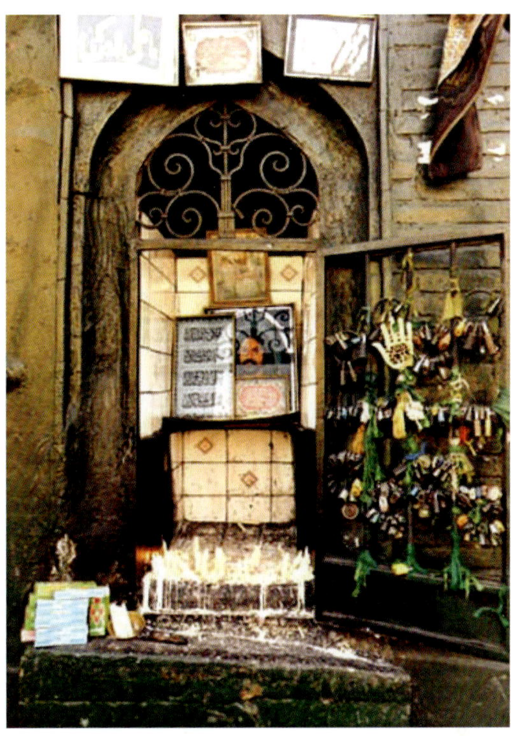

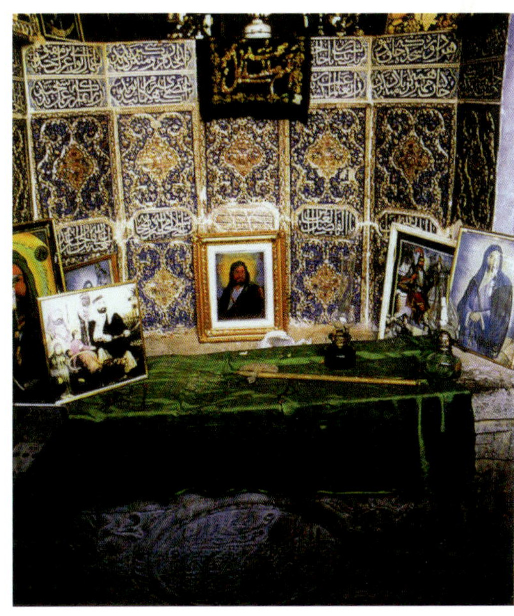

3.7
Saqqa-khaneh exterior, mid-twentieth century, Tehran

3.8
Saqqa-khaneh interior, c. 1980s, Tehran

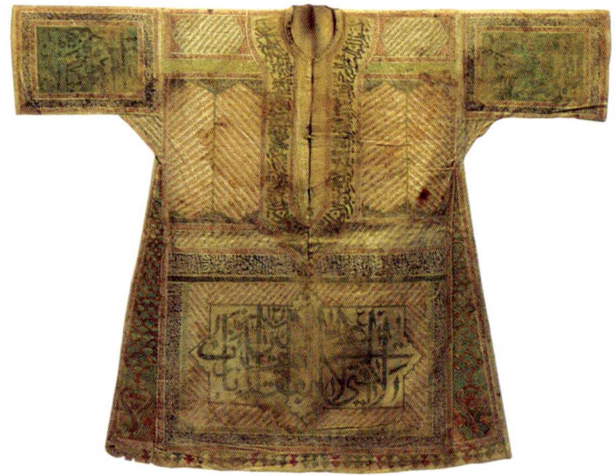

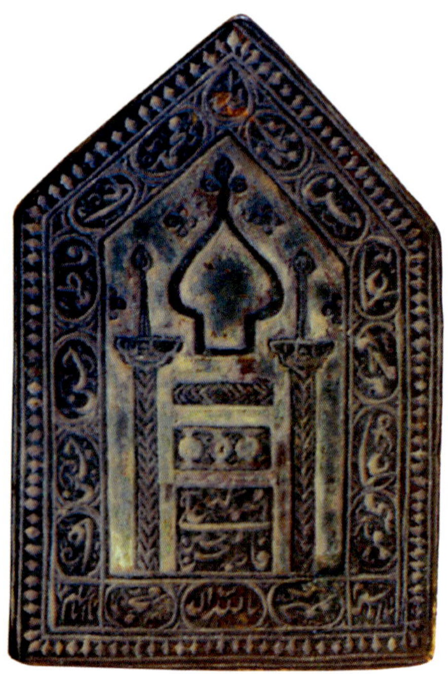

3.9
Talismanic shirt, 1787, ink on fabric, calligraphy Abdollah Akbar, 113×90 cm

3.10
Print seal with the shape of *Mihrab*, Iran nineteeth century, 8.3×6 cm

symbolism of the life-giving water of rain and rivers – and a reminder of the passion of Karbala.[14]

The artists affiliated to the *Saqqa-khaneh* movement looked to cults, rituals, and visual elements of folk and local vernacular culture for inspiration. Many of these items appeared crude in their execution, lacking the artistic polish of artefacts made by professional calligraphers and painters, and were often created collaboratively as a kind of street art; however, their true significance was not lost to these artists. From this perspective, *Saqqa-khaneh* artists could be considered successors to Iranian craftsmen of earlier centuries – miniaturist, illuminators, calligraphers and goldsmiths. For the above-mentioned modernists, however, these roots had to be linked to modern styles to create a distinctly national artistic expression. This, after all, was the age in which Iranian artists found themselves competing with and contributing to the international art scene.

In essence, then, the *Saqqa-khaneh* movement tried to find and establish a 'national' or 'Iranian' school of art. As John Clark maintains, '[a]n important feature of avant-garde practice found elsewhere in Asia is that artists who adopt avant-garde positions feel free to explore indigenous art forms alongside – rather than in opposition to – the discourse they operate on.'[15] In this, the movement was undoubtedly the most influential avant-garde movement of its time in the formation of neo-traditionalist art in Iran.

The *Saqqa-khaneh* artists believed could achieve a 'modern-traditional' synthesis that encompassed an Iranian identity and character. In exploring the movements and trends of Western art, they were striving for a balance between inherited specifics and pragmatic forms of modernism, which would constitute the Iranian art of their time.

Most members of the group had some affiliation with the Tehran College of Decorative Arts, either as students or teachers. The institution was established in Tehran in 1960 with the aim of training experts in the applied arts.[16] The College (*Hunarkadeh*), whose name was changed to the Faculty of Decorative Arts (Danishkadeh-i honar-hay-i taz'ini) a few years later, responded to the needs of the new generation by establishing alternative fields of study under the direction of foreign and Iranian instructors.[17] Several modernist painters, sculptors, and designers who played a crucial role in the development of contemporary Iranian visual art were trained there. Subjects such as decorative painting, graphic design, sculpture, industrial design and interior architecture were taught, with a major emphasis on applied arts. Students were encouraged to seek local sources of inspiration, symbols and idioms, and to familiarise themselves with Iran's decorative heritage. The Dean of the College, Houshang Kazemi (1923–2015), himself lectured on Decorative Arts and familiarised the students with the treasure house of Persian ornamental ware. As a result, *Saqqa-khaneh* artists, most of whom studied at this College, drew on the visual elements of Iranian folk culture and decorative forms.

According to Emami, the artists of the *Saqqa-khaneh* movement discovered a source in which they could experiment, analyse and combine those forms, colours and textures.[18] Materials were selected from folk art that was linked with traditional-national religious art. This art form was deeply ingrained within the public sphere. *Saqqa-khaneh* artists incorporated these elements, using them in innovative ways across a multitude of forms and structural compositions. Many types of traditional Persian arts and crafts were explored, including popular printed prayers; talismanic and magical seals; amulets; shirts; astrolabes; props used in mourning processions; motifs from local handicraft (rugs, carpets); ancient pottery motifs (such popular religious artefacts as the *jam-i chihil kilid*, the 'forty-key vessel', a brass talisman inscribed with forty Qur'anic verses); and the *panjeh-i panj tan*, the Hands of Fatima);[19] elements of Qajar art; enamelled bowls from Rey adorned with horse riders; Persian calligraphy and painting; Achaemenid and Sasanian inscription or epigraphy; and Assyrian bas-reliefs. (Figures 3.9–22) Persian poetry and mystical symbols also featured in the works of these artists.

The other facet of the *Saqqa-khaneh* tendency was the attention paid to modernism. The artists' work, however, 'suggests that modernity in the Iranian context was a complex field of negotiation and accommodation – and not a simple act of imitation and mimicry.'[20] Whereas all *Saqqa-khaneh* artists had created a modern idiom by adapting various traditional forms to their purposes, the pioneers attempted to find some harmonic familiarity with modern Western art (especially Abstract art), and to make a connection between the modern and the traditional. As Ehsan Yarshater remarks:

This occurred as a restatement of those sources or a re-working of them into new visual statements, or the conjuring-up of a vision of the past lost to modernized Persian life such as a Qajar dancer, a woman in veil, an old-

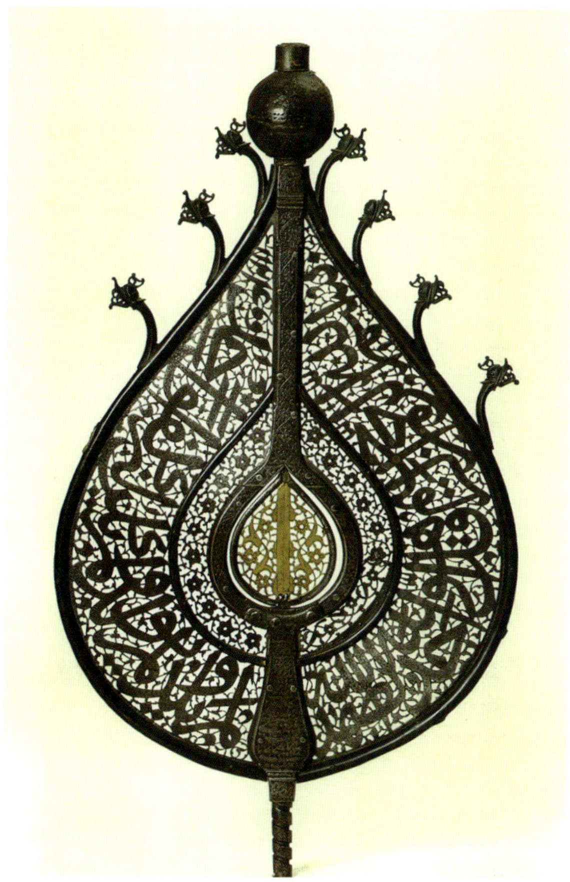

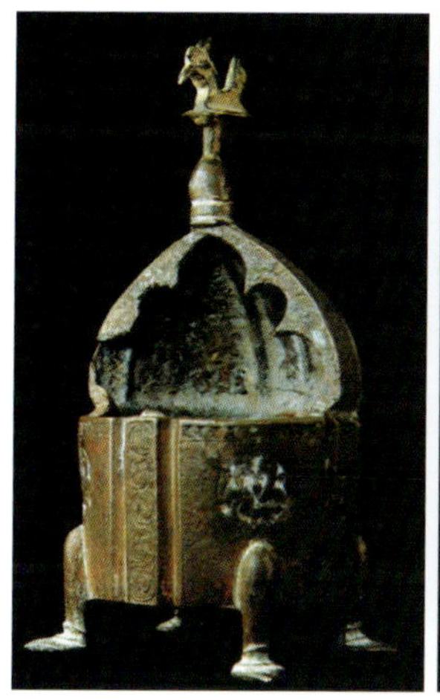

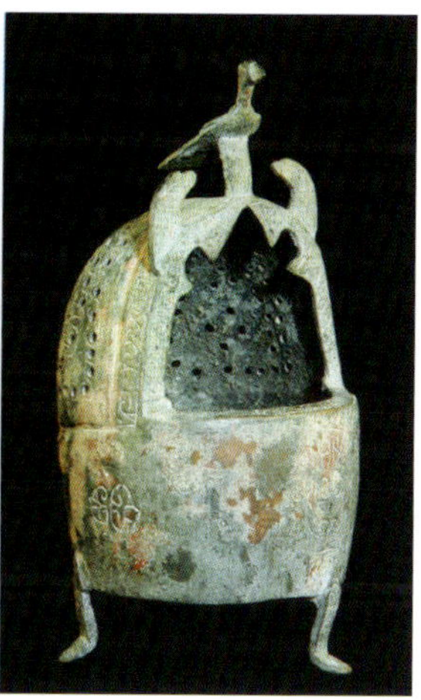

3.11
Steel Standard, Iran, 1712–13,
73.3×38.5 cm

3.12
Incense-burner, Iran, c. twelfth–
thirteenth century, cast bronze,
22×9 cm

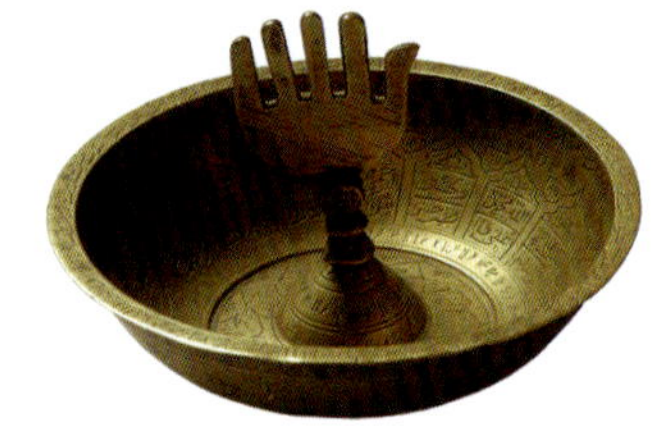

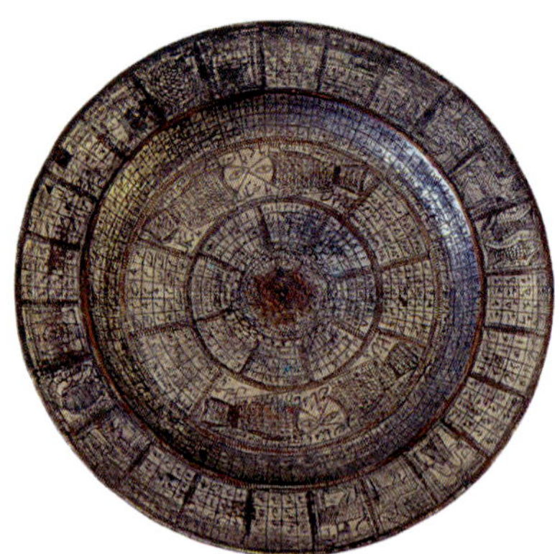

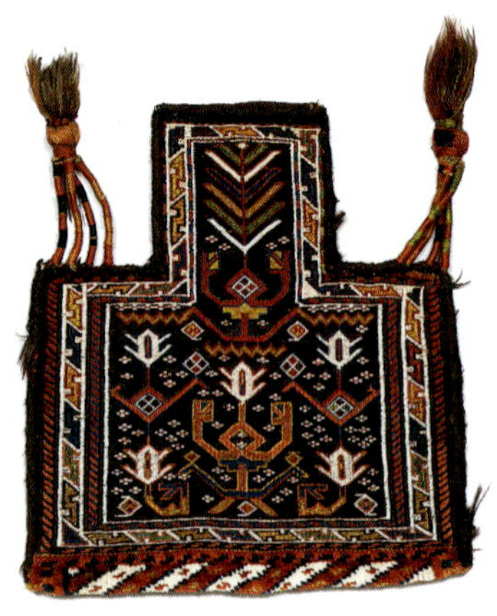

3.13
Saqqa-khaneh bowl with hand and talisman, brass, Iran, nineteenth century, diameter: 15 cm

3.14
Talismanic plate with astrolabe, copper, Iran, nineteenth century, diameter: 21.1 cm

3.15
Zarbaft salt container, c. 1920s, West of Iran, wool and linen, 53.3×48.3 cm, Metropolitan Museum

time musician, or an arrangement of votive objective and religious symbols in a non-religious context.[21]

The history of the movement can be classified into two periods: early (from 1962 to around 1964) and late (from 1964 onward). The first period was devoted mainly to the employment of votive Shi'i folk elements in the works of artists such as Zenderoudi, Tanavoli and Faramarz Pilaram. The later period involved all the artists, both painters and sculptors, who drew directly on the traditional art forms of Iran as raw material for their work. They were all adapting forms and themes gleaned from the past – even when unrelated to Shi'i iconography (from the Achamenids to the Qajar, for example). This was, however, not an official association with stated goals or a shared manifesto; and the imagery and vocabulary used by artists varied.[22] The pioneers consisted of Charles Hossein Zenderoudi, Parviz Tanavoli, Faramarz Pilaram (1938–83), Mansour Qandriz (1935–65), Nasser Oveissi (b.1934), Sadegh Tabrizi (1938–2017), Jazeh Tabatabai (1928–2008) and Massoud Arabshahi (1935–2019).

As Emami wrote in the *Saqqa-khaneh* exhibition's catalogue in 1977, and also as attested in statements by artists such as Oveissi, Tabatabai and Arabshahi, some of the artists were later unhappy about the inclusion of their names as members of the movement. However, they are listed here because of the affinities of their works to the *Saqqa-khaneh* trend, the presence of their works in the formal exhibitions of the group and, above all, because they appear to share the same artistic approach as the artists of the *Saqqa-khaneh* movement. Over time, the genre grew increasingly inclusive, encompassing various works by artists who referenced traditional materials in one way or another. Notably, artists like Siah Armajani (1939–2020) in the late 1950s and 1960s and Jafar Rouhbakhsh (1941–96) in the 1990s demonstrated a close affinity with this trend.

Sadegh Tabrizi believes that the *Saqqa-khaneh* artists, himself included, started their artistic careers independently.[23] Oveissi, for example, became involved earlier than the others in conservation work of Qajar paintings in the General Administration of Fine Arts and was thus influenced by their style from an earlier date. Zenderoudi had already shown his interest in religious images and rituals in his prints on the subject of Shi'i rituals, in particular in his 1960 work titled *In Hossein kist keh dilha hameh divaneh-i ust?* They were, however, probably aware of each other's activities through encounters at the College of Decorative Arts and also in

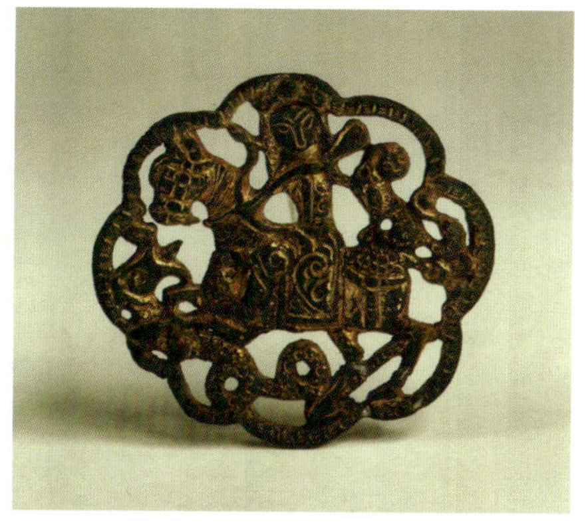

artistic clubs, particularly the Kaboud Atelier.[24] Tabrizi adds that, when the group assembled and exhibited together, a relationship between their works emerged, although the works had been created separately and none of the artists could be considered as following in the steps of the others.[25] It could be said that while Tabatabai and Oveissi or Zenderoudi and Pilaram were pooling their experiences, Tanavoli, Qandriz and Arabshahi appeared to be more independent in their approach.

The neo-traditionalist *Saqqa-khaneh* eventually became engaged with two main tendencies. Such artists as Zenderoudi, Tanavoli, Pilaram, Qandriz[26] and Arabshahi believed in the apparent similarity between abstract art and the stylised aspect of Iranian traditional decorative art. Various abstract forms were created in which the ornamental elements and geometrical shapes of Iranian Islamic art and Persian and Arabic calligraphy were selected and then spread throughout the whole space of the canvas, mostly in symmetrical constructions. On the other hand some artists, including Tabrizi, Oveissi and Tabatabai, found their inspiration in the existence of figurative forms such as human bodies and animals of different types in traditional Iranian art – from ancient stone relief and craft to the painting of the Qajar period. They attempted to use these to present the modern and transformed types through a multiplicity of elements

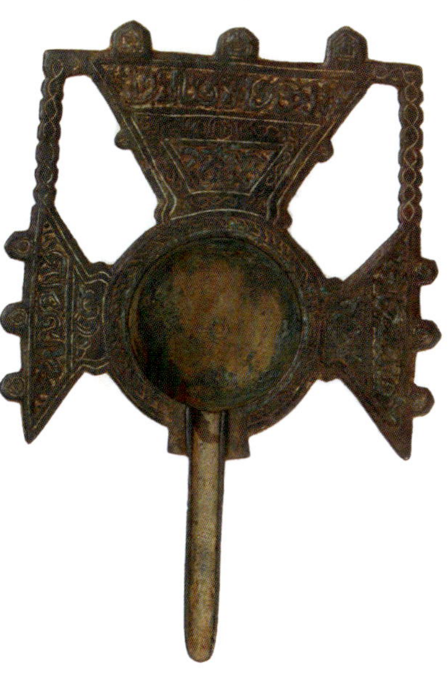

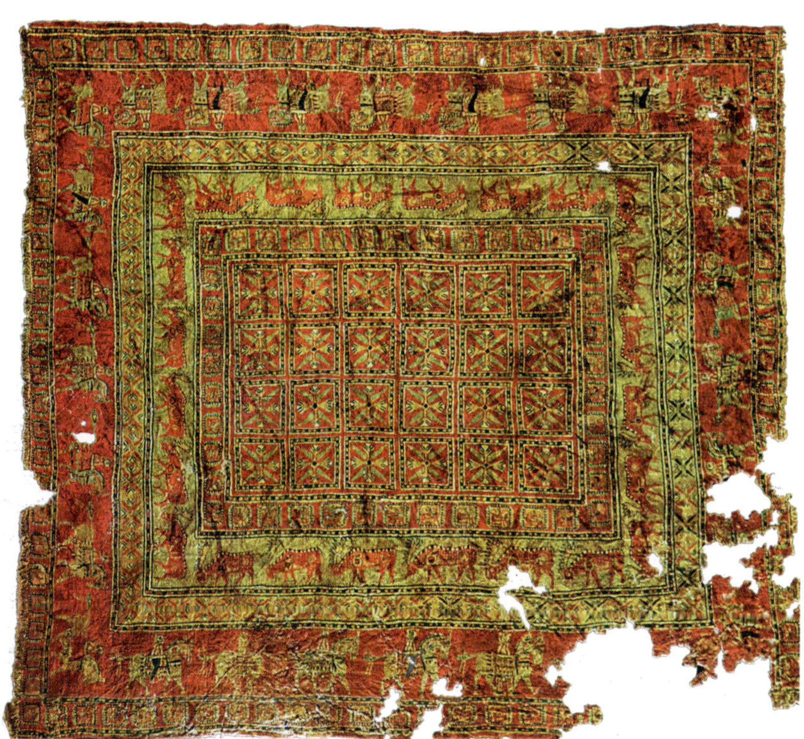

Left
3.16
Pazyryk carpet, Iran, c. fourth–fifth century B.C., Pile Carpet (Knotted Wool), Hermitage Museum, St. Petersburg

Above
3.17
Plaque, Iran, c. twelfth–thirteenth century, cast bronze, diameter: 6 cm

3.18
Medicinal mortar, Iran, twelfth century, cast bronze, 18.3×12.7×3.7 cm

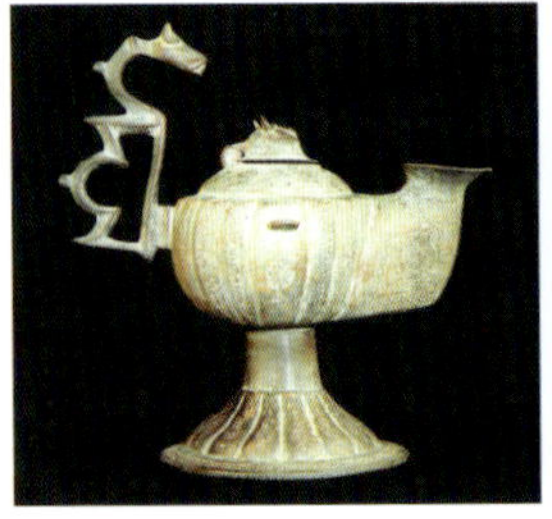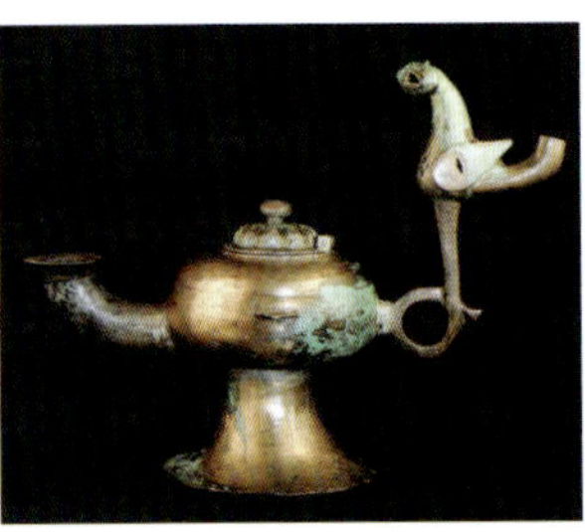

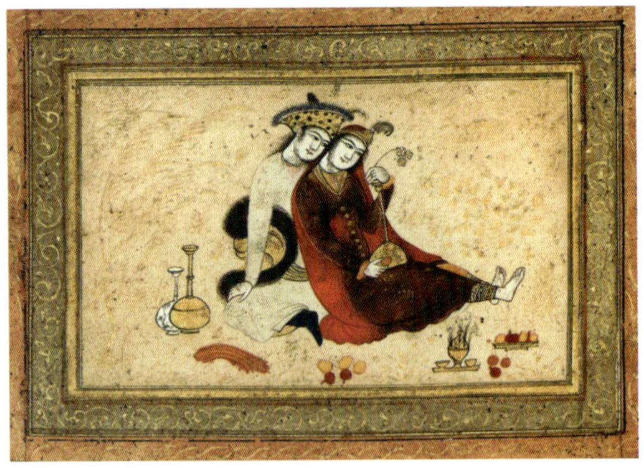

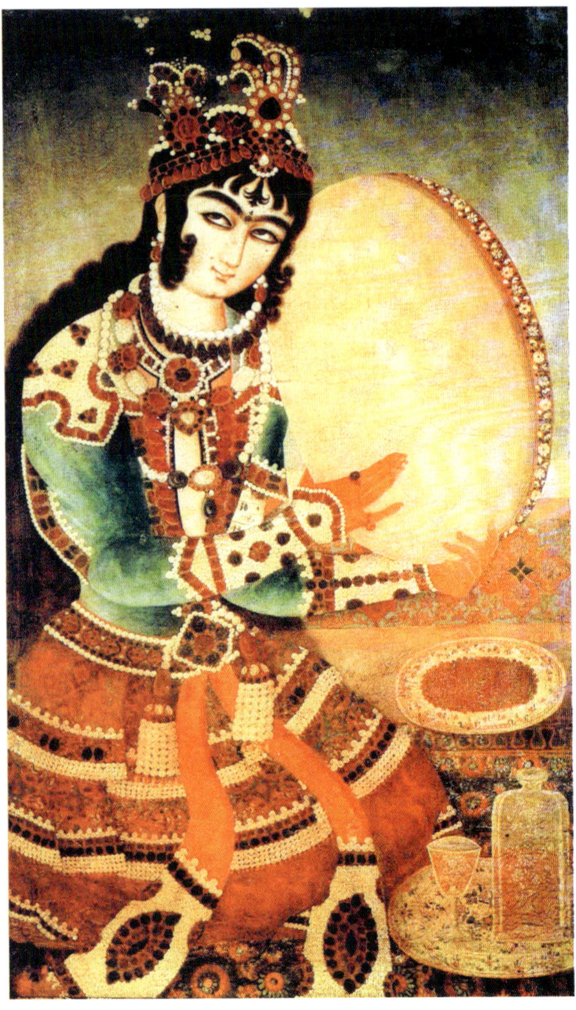

in a decorative mode with a generous use of calligraphic motifs in their canvases.

On the whole, these artists were making a formalistic reference to tradition rather than to subliminal associations or philosophical concepts. This quality is most apparent in the abstract branch of the movement.[27] In other words, they concentrated on forms, motifs and colours redolent of traditional and sometimes religious material rather than specific subject matter. Attention to traditional subject matter, apart from formal considerations, can also be found very occasionally in works by some of the artists. One could mention the mythical, traditional and literary subject matter exhibited in the *Ruba'iyyat* of 'Umar Khayyam, in the work of the legendary sculptor Farhad, and in the folk proverbs with modern outlooks found within Oveissi, Tanavoli and Tabatabai's works. Further examples are religious content in the initial works of Zenderoudi, before the formal introduction of the trend and during the early *Saqqa-khaneh* period; and also some of Pilaram's later works (in the late 1970s when he illustrated some Qur'anic stories).

Let us now consider the major artists of this movement. Parviz Tanavoli, a sculptor, painter, lithographer, collector, and scholar of Iranian folk art who has already appeared in this narrative, was a central figure of the movement. He was a graduate of the Tehran Fine Art High School in 1955 and in 1959 the Barrera Academy of Fine Art, Milan, where he studied with Marino Marini. He was active in the establishment of the Tehran Faculty of Decorative Arts as sculpture tutor. Tanavoli's effective presence in the Faculty during the early 1960s, and his sharing of avant-garde ideas with those fellow artists who were later considered the pioneers of the *Saqqa-khaneh* movement, was undoubtedly influential. His role as a forerunner of modern Iranian sculpture is significant too. He was a central figure of the movement and his work demonstrates the richness and validity of this genre. He emerged as a fervent believer in a kind of modernism attained through forms of popular visual culture, to which he added folkloric expressions.

Tanavoli has successfully evoked the multiple allusions and imagery of Persian language and literature. Such literary references appear for example in the hands of Farhad the Mountain Carver, Tanavoli's tribute to the legendary Iranian artist who, for love, accepted the impossible challenge of carving a channel through a rocky mountain. Tanavoli executed his series of sculptures in the early 1960s. Reworking tropes from classical Persian literature, Islamic folk

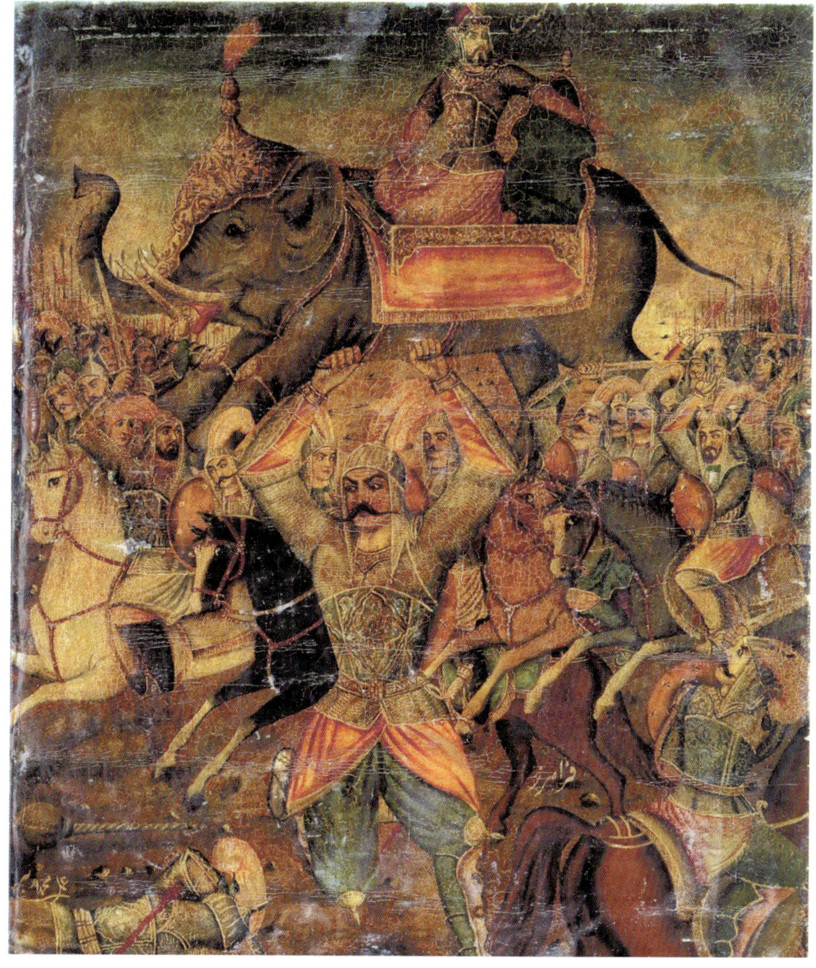

art and calligraphy, he produced works that provocatively unite style and meaning. (Figures 3.23–24) Throughout his long career, Tanavoli has rendered his subjects in drawings and paintings, monumental sculptures and delicate jewellery, as well as creating a mass-produced series in Plexiglas.

His *Heech* sculptures (*Heech* being the Persian word for nothing) – created since the 1960s[28] – transformed a nihilistic existentialist cry into a Persian allegory. The word had a spiritual dimension here, alluding to the theme of annihilation (*fana*), an important concept in Persian Sufi poetry. The *Heech* suggests a mystical condition beyond nothingness. Speaking of his work, Tanavoli states:

> My nothingness (...) was not tinged with the cynicism of Western artists. Mine was the nothingness of hope and friendship, a nothingness that did not seek to negate.[29]

As Abbas Daneshvari explains,

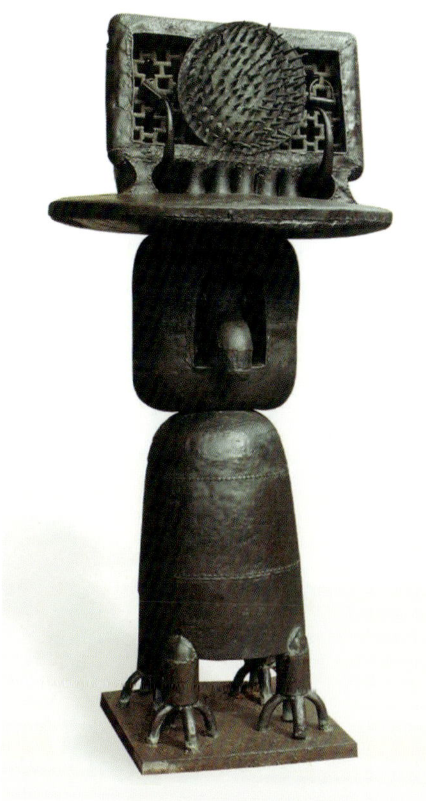

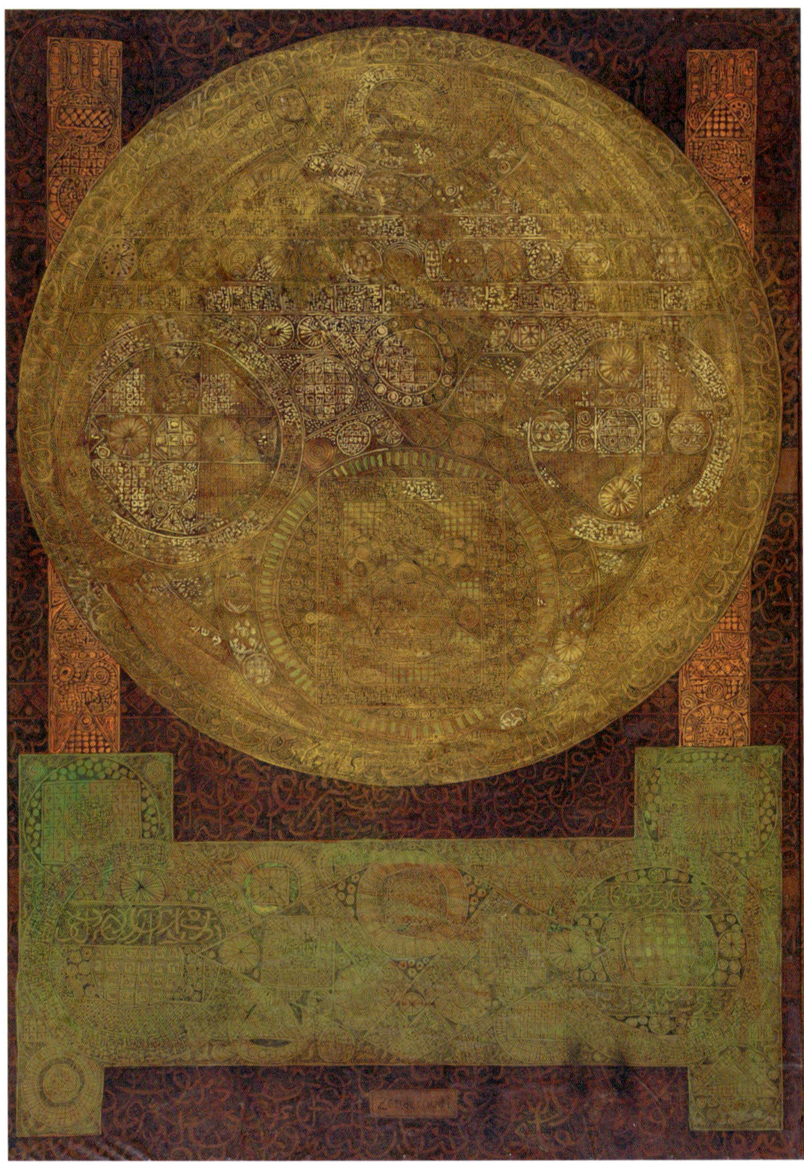

3.26
Charles Hossein Zenderoudi,
AB+35-0, 1962, natural pigments
on paper mounted on board,
145x98 cm, TMoCA

The influential artist and leading member of the group Charles
Hossein Zenderoudi studied at the Tehran Fine Art High School and
then briefly at the Tehran Faculty of Decorative Arts, but left Iran
in 1961 for France, where he has continued his artistic career, mainly
in Paris.[31] In fact, many critics, including Karim Emami, believe that
the term *Saqqa-khaneh* was initially coined for Zenderoudi.[32] Highly
influential, Zenderoudi was not only a versatile and exceptional artist
of the movement but also he advanced his artistic investigations
in different stages and guises and evolved an independent style in
his art. He started with some votive Sh'i iconography, geometrical
patterns, talismanic shapes, numbers, colours of religious folk art
and calligraphic ornaments. (Figures 3.6, 26) He then shifted to

using calligraphy as a major element of his canvases in various ways and stages.[33] In those works he presented the canvases using written forms of alphabetical characters in the background as texture-producing material for the squares, triangles, rectangles and circles juggling with them, then tinting them with the characteristic colours of religious folk art such as gold, green, yellow ochre, orange and red. The freshness, intuitiveness and originality found in his early works – inspired by these talismanic forms – are breathtaking and unique. One can also deduce from his creation the spontaneous graduation of these forms in their process of multiple evolutions. For example, he used motifs found on objects in folk art and similar motifs that appear on Persian painting, Islamic architectural ornaments, traditional carpets, rugs and astrolabes from the popular culture of Iran and then placed them within an abstract space.

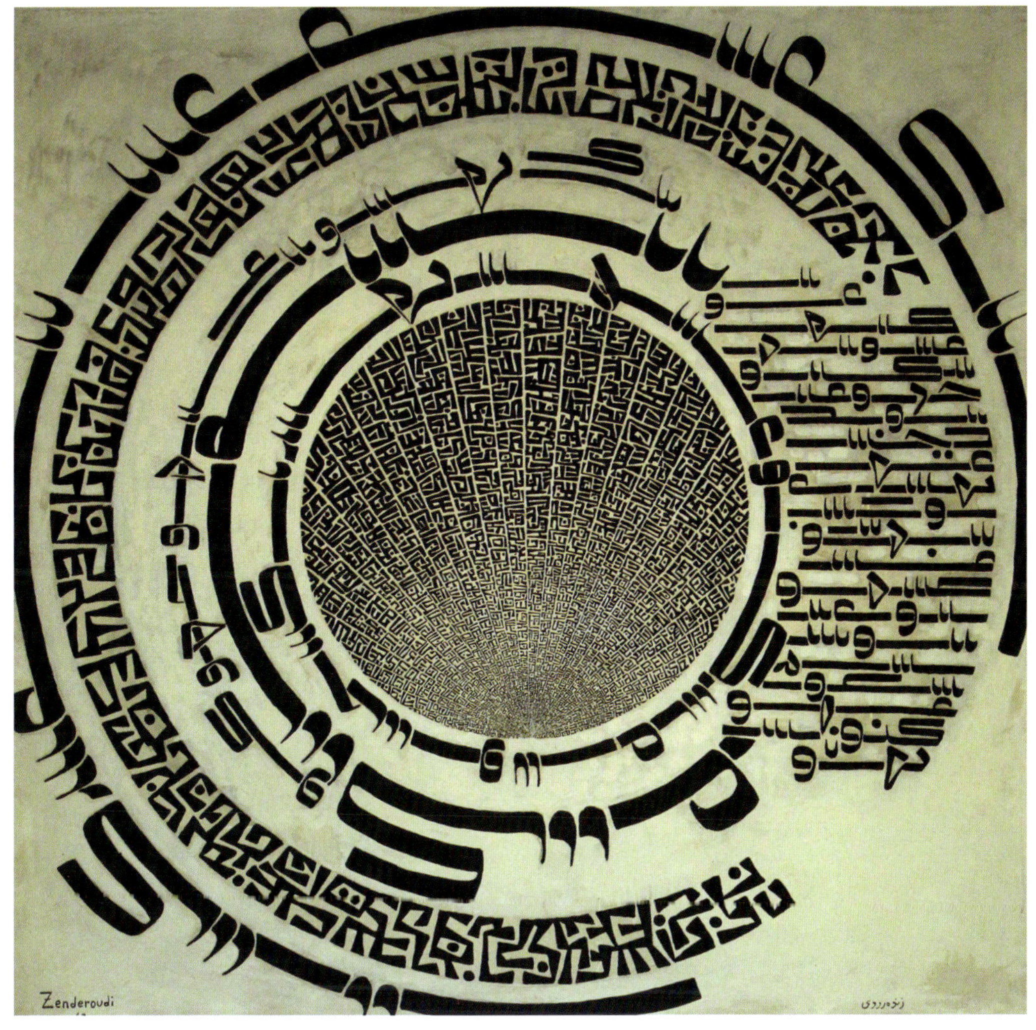

3.27
Charles Hossein Zenderoudi, *Untitled*, 1964, oil on canvas, 170×170 cm, Niavaran Museum

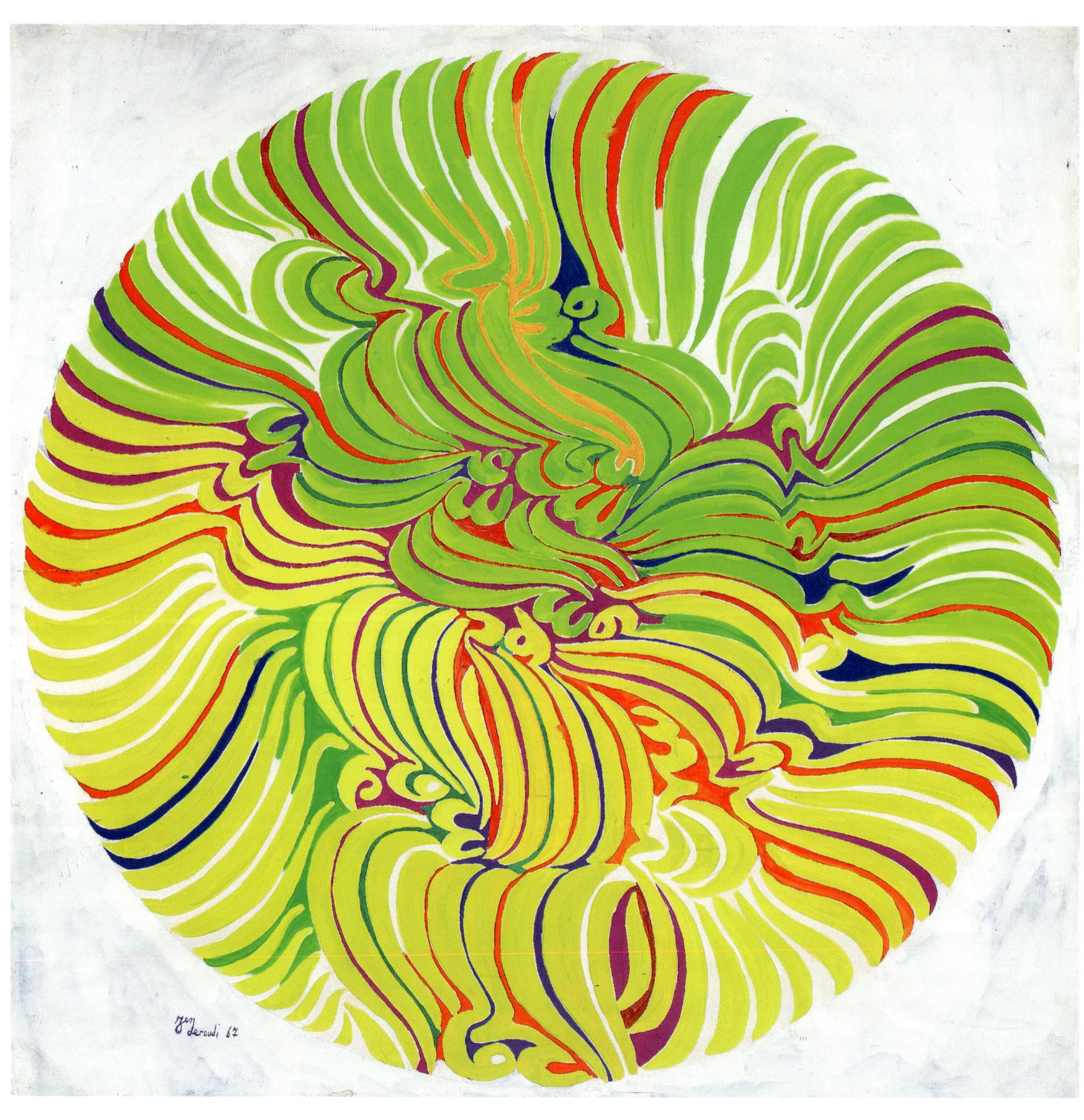
Zen
Deroudi 67

Later, in Zenderoudi's calligraphic paintings, with his pseudo-scripts, the characters in themselves carried no meaning but were meaningful as organic elements of visual art and alive with cultural connotations. At the juncture of calligraphy and geometry, we find these optic-art-like compositions of letters. (Figures 3.27–28) It is clear that among the founding members of the movement, Zenderoudi must be considered the pioneer of the calligraphic approach in terms of the use of calligraphy as the sole structural form. It is, however, worth noting that the artist's presence in Paris and the influences of such contemporary movements as *Lettrism* – the Paris-based avant-garde movement which was still at its apex when Zenderoudi moved there – would also have had a definite impact on him. With these influences combined, he seems to have developed the talismanic and calligraphic trends into a personalised pseudo-script of signs.

The artistic development of Faramarz Pilaram, a graduate of the Tehran Faculty of Decorative Arts, at one stage ran parallel to Zenderoudi's, and encompassed words, letters, and geometrical forms inspired by Shi'i iconography. (Figure 3.29) The prizewinner at the Third Tehran Biennial in 1962, Pilaram, whose use of old seals was a feature of the first part of his artistic career,[34] used these in his works as a connective texture in geometrical compositions. During his study in the Faculty, significant Western influences can be seen; he was introduced to the ontological and architectural aspects of Piet Mondrian's art and Alexander Calder's works and was fascinated by their geometrical structures. Later he became interested in three-dimensional wooden works intended for public spaces in cities, although his desire to create them never took shape.

An accomplished calligrapher, he later experimented with various styles in which calligraphy, especially the *nasta'liq* script, played a significant or central role. During the late 1960s and the early 1970s, he created several Expressionist calligraphic paintings and colourful *shikasteh*-like canvases with brushstrokes that can be associated with certain traditional inscriptions. In the subsequent stage of his painting, calligraphic elements played a textual role. They merged with the geometrical compositions as if they had been slid on to the transparent surfaces of the background. This technique ensures his art has a striking, three-dimensional appearance. The use of pure colour, in particular gold and silver, in his paintings from this period is another significant feature. (Figure 3.30) In his exhibition in the Iranian-American Society in 1975 he used single letters and monochrome paint, a gesture he himself interpreted as

3.28
Charles Hossein Zenderoudi, *Untitled*, 1967, oil on cardboard, 120×120 cm, TMoCA

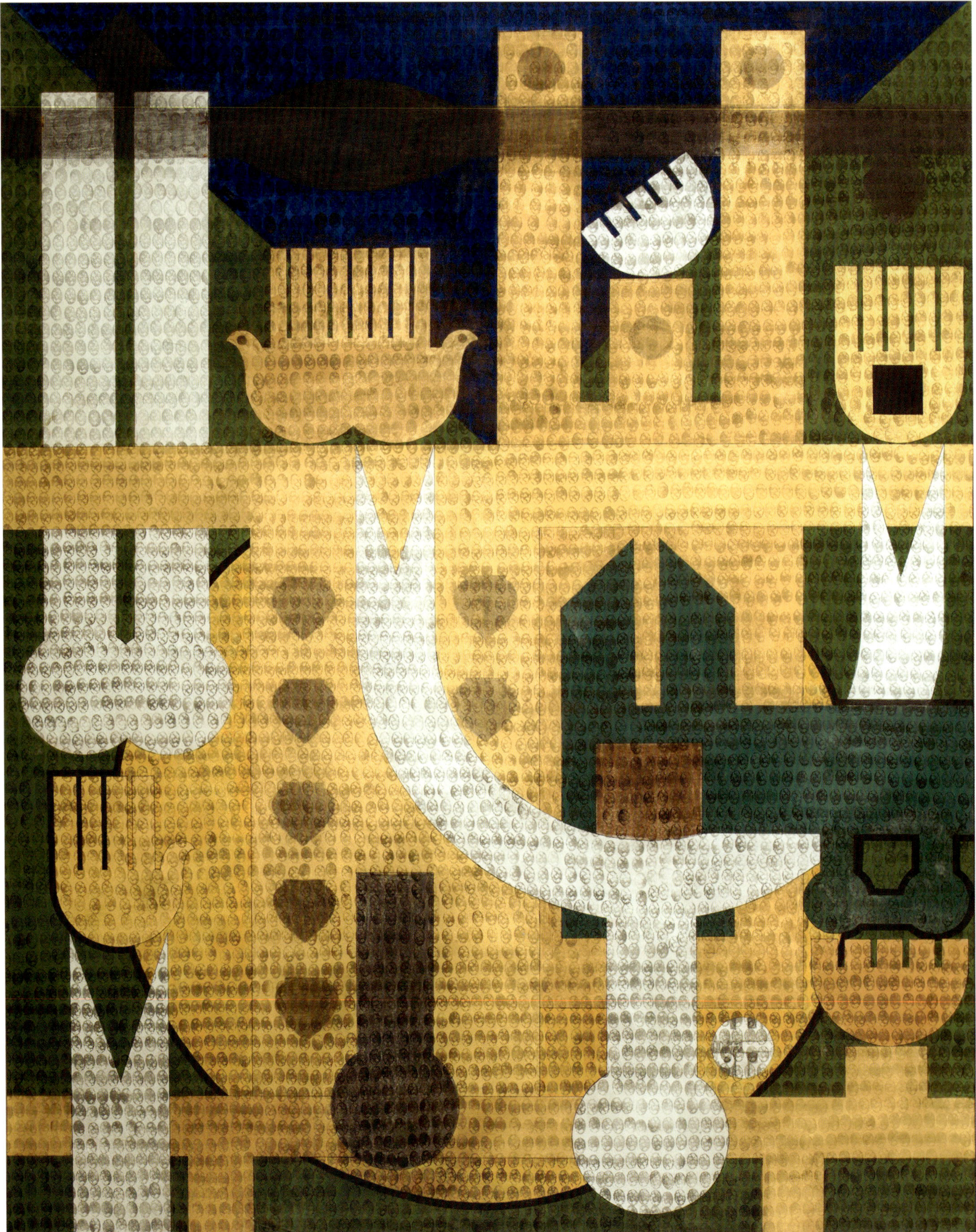

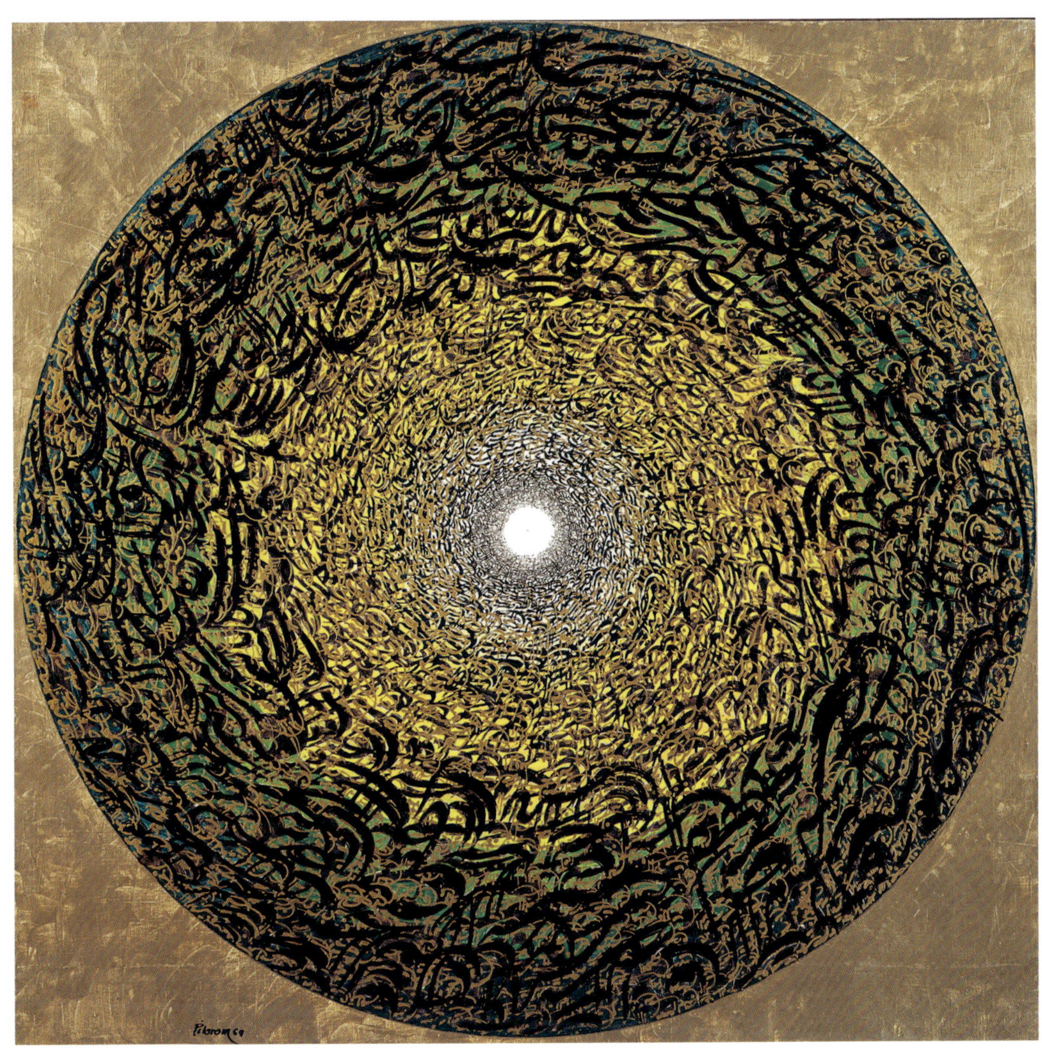

'unity'. Rhythm and visual movement were other common features in these works. He claimed that he was generating distance from calligraphic standards while creating his self-made letterism. In some paintings, which are part of the collection of the Tehran Museum of Contemporary Art, rhythmical words play visual movements in a symphonic space. (Figure 3.31) In fact, the homogeneous quality of indigenous arts, music, poetry and decorative painting consciously emerge with harmonic symmetries in his canvases. His drawings, infused with calligraphic elements, show his strong ability to compose masterly letters and figurative images. In his exhibition in 1977 Pilaram used familiar traffic signs with numbers, showing reference to his *Saqqa-khaneh* works.[35]

While the two artists mentioned above concentrated, to varying degrees, on exploring calligraphy, others used symbols to combine traditional and modern elements into abstract designs.

Facing page
3.29
Faramarz Pilaram, *Untitled*, 1962, tempera on paper, 152×119 cm, private collection, Tehran

Above
3.30
Faramarz Pilaram, *Untitled*, 1976, oil and colour ink on canvas, 105×105 cm, TMoCA

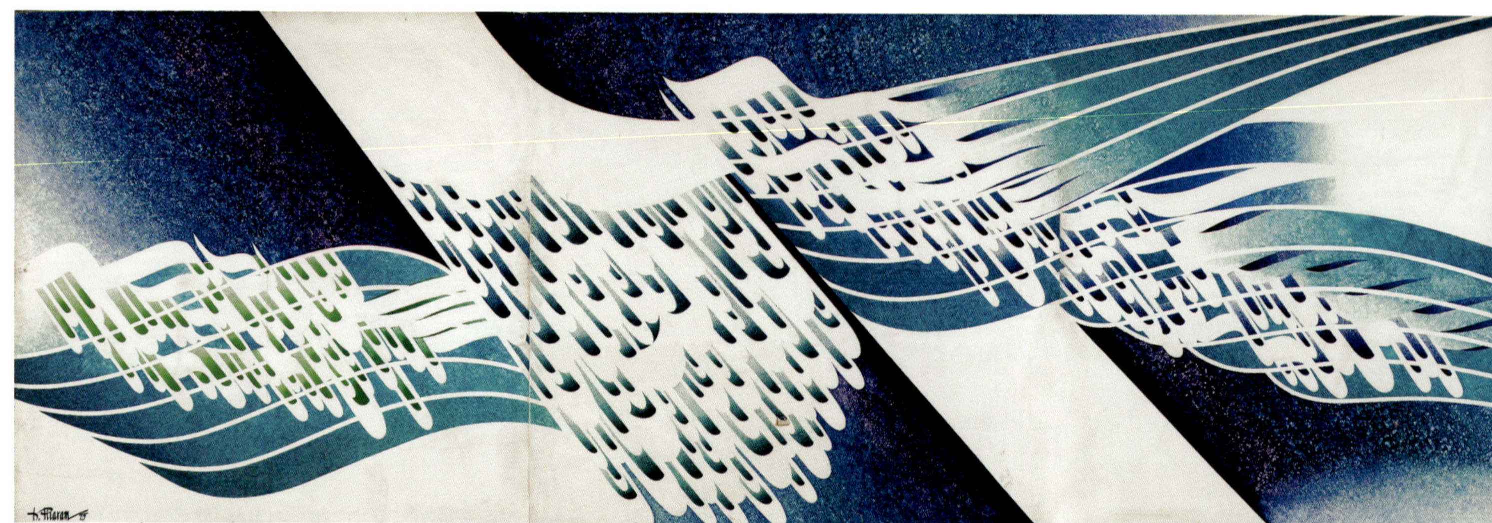

3.31
Faramarz Pilaram, *Fly*, 1975, oil on canvas, triptych, total size 150×450 cm, TMoCA

Another student of the Tehran Faculty of Decorative Arts, Mansour Qandriz, was a semi-abstract artist who used stylised Persian motifs, emphasising tribal forms, Iranian textiles and traditional metalwork through the employment of limited colours. His source of inspiration came from applied arts such as rugs, carpets and handicrafts.

Qandriz was also involved with existing (and somewhat contentious) issues surrounding Iranian art, such as cultural identity, the quest to create a national school of art and the revival of pictorial heritage. Like other neo-traditionalists, he primarily concerned himself with the complex problem of how tradition and modernity could coexist. Qandriz believed in a national art that could have an international language and that could advocate the individuality, nationality and universality of Iran.[36] In 1965 he wrote:

> We should start to search consciously rather than beating our head on fallacious and inconstant walls. One who is suspended in mid-air and claims to create an international language in art is unaware of his own mother language; in fact, he has not searched and known his own home. We should start with our own home if this kind of search is to be accompanied with healthy thoughts.[37]

He was an artist who 'had struggled in the various stages of his artistic development, with obsessive care and hesitancy, to elaborate and define a truly Iranian style'.[38] His early figurative images – painted in Tabriz (1957–59) before he joined the *Saqqa-khaneh* movement – reveal the influence of Matisse, Picasso and Persian painting. He was aware of the subjective concept of represented space in this kind of painting, i.e. the idealistic world coinciding with the artist's subjective imagination. In this period, one can see the constant presence of the sun, which is often red, coarse and shiny, and birds that emerge in the middle of the canvas.[39]

After the introduction of the *Saqqa-khaneh* movement in 1962, Qandriz stood out as one of its major figures.[40] In this period, using traditional textile and designs, he developed an individual semi-abstract style characterised by geometric patterns and stylised images such as humans, birds, fish, the sun and swords. In his early works of the *Saqqa-khaneh* period, images of a woman appear. The face is drawn by a circle; her shoulder, chest and midriff are drawn by

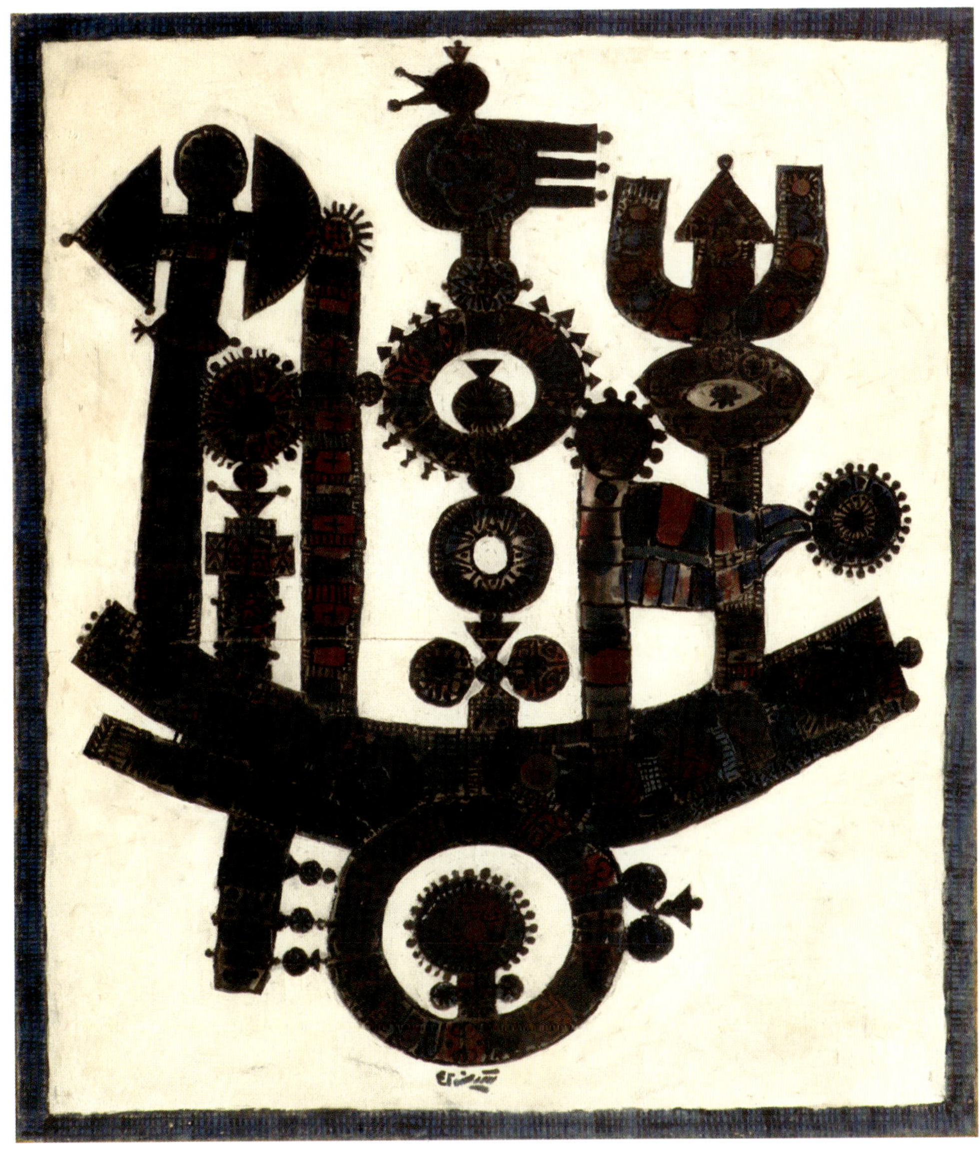

3.32
Mansour Qandriz, *Untitled*, 1963, oil on canvas, 200×170 cm, Niavaran Museum

a rectangle, and her pelvis and feet by an ellipse or circle. The effect seems to veer towards a stylised iconography. Accompanied by these images, religious folk motifs and symbols such as small minaret-like elements, candleholders, locks, reticulated glasses, small and big fish, and daggers can also be recognised. (Figure 3.32) Stylised forms such as birds' heads, martyrs' hands (*panj-tan*) and colourful glasses associated with religious meeting houses can also be seen. These elements altogether imply a religious and spiritual atmosphere – a common characteristic of the early works of the *Saqqa-khaneh* (1962–64).

Figures and objects now changed to decorative motifs and geometric forms. During this process the poetic spirit of Qandriz's previous paintings altered to an abstract structure of colour and form. Compositions tended to absolute symmetry and a mixture of colours rotating around a focal point. The image of birds in these paintings changed to fastenings that included only a sign of a bird. Similarly, the sun is sometimes a face, chest or abdomen and sometimes a mixture of the feet and pelvis of a human figure; whereas in other works it seems that it sits morbidly beside other ferrous motifs and elements. (Figures 3.33–34) Later, in 1964–5, these signs were gradually replaced by simple and more explicit forms. As Pakbaz remarks: 'In these canvases, the motifs are associated with mechanical objects, which perhaps show that civilisation has now dominated primitivism in his mind.'[41]

Massoud Arabshahi, who graduated from the same Faculty, delved even further back into history for his inspiration. He was inspired by the art of pre-Islamic Persia and Mesopotamia, as depicted in Achaemenid motifs, and by Assyrian and Babylonian rock carving and script. His drawings, inspired by Zoroastrian texts, resemble archaeological maps of ancient cities. Unlike other artists in the *Saqqa-khaneh* group he did not employ religious-folk-art, but his similar outlook and spirit set him close in *Saqqa-khaneh* exhibitions. Furthermore, his early works, and even the later ones, conform to some important *Saqqa-khaneh* aesthetic characteristics. In particular, one can cite the permanent presence of various motifs and ornaments and the multiplicity of elements in most parts of the canvas. Also to be noted is the use of the colour schemes of Iranian folk art: gold, green, red, black, lapis lazuli, turquoise and vermilion. A close relationship with Islamic architectural forms and crafts can be found in the forms and sometimes the colours that he employed in these works. (Figures 3.35–36) During the 1970s he decorated the walls and façades of public and private buildings with bas-reliefs of his own design.

Facing page
3.33
Mansour Qandriz, *Untitled*, 1963, oil on canvas, 200×170 cm, TMoCA

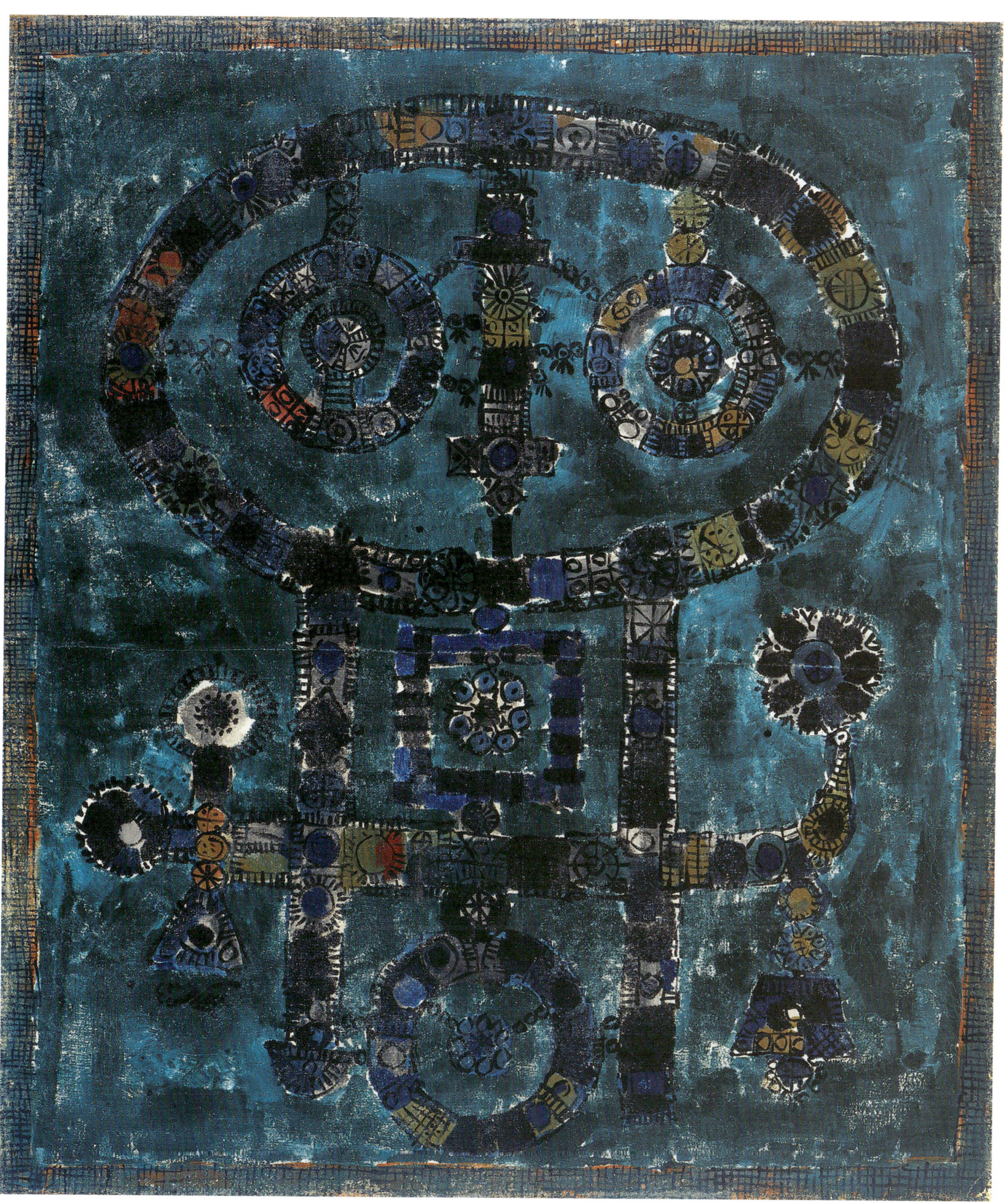

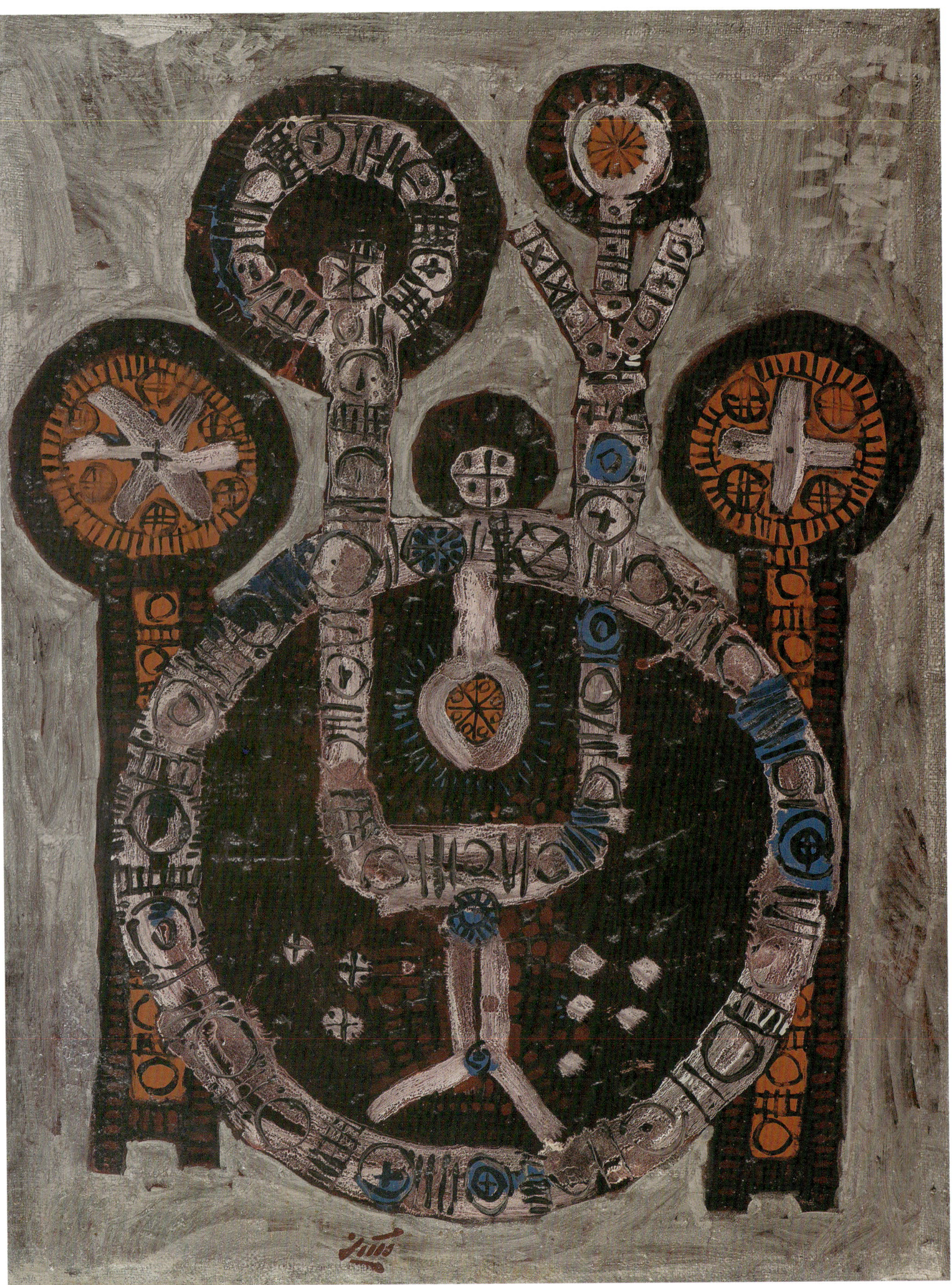

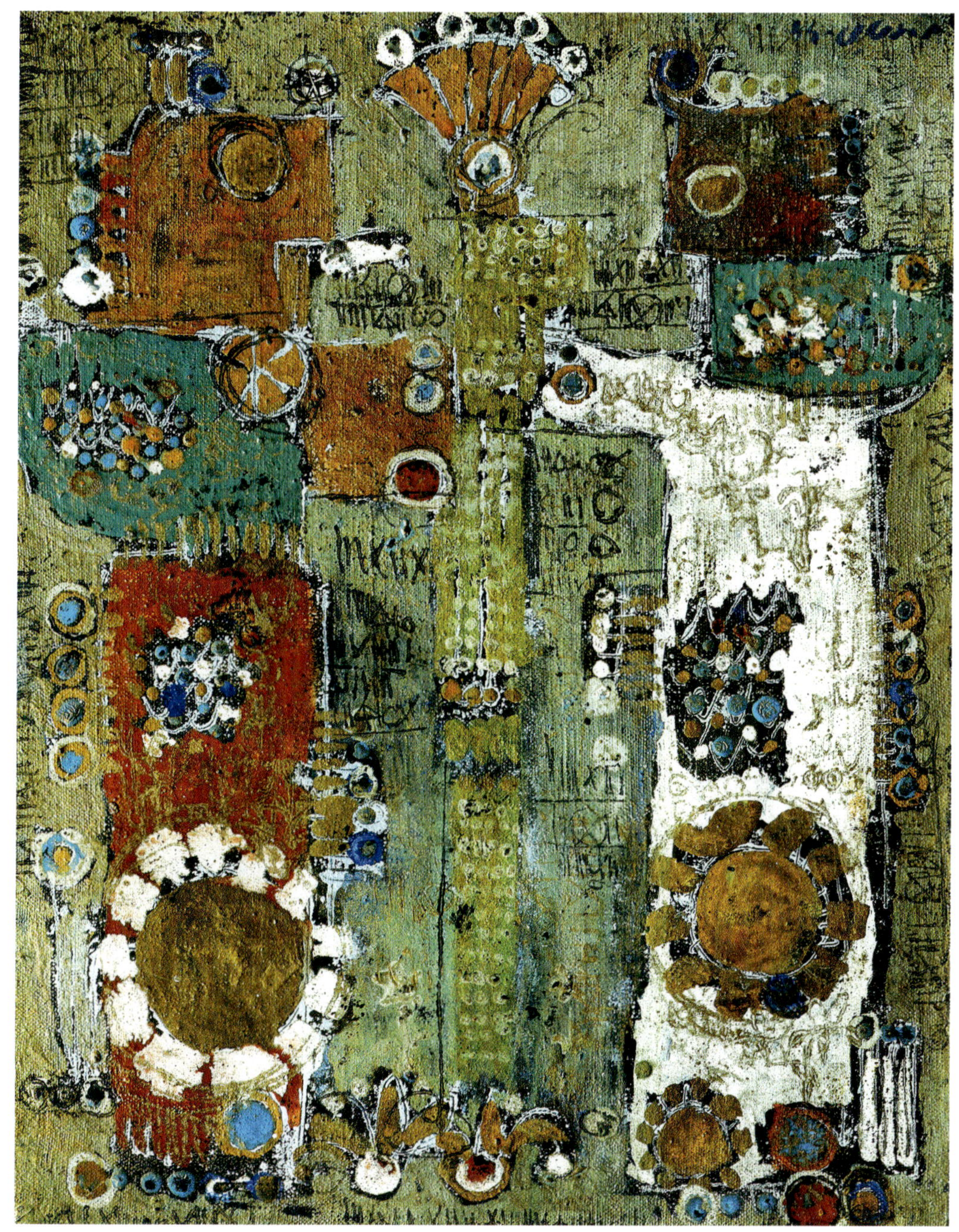

At the same time that these artists were dealing with abstraction, others like Nasser Oveissi chose figurative art. Motifs inspired chiefly by Persian paintings, ceramics, *qalamkar*s (hand-painted materials) and calligraphy all featured in his canvases. While he created complex designs, the formal elements of his paintings were few and simple. They included human figures, horses and painted pottery, inspired by Persian pottery. His women – single or in groups of two or three – with large oblong eyes and joined eyebrows were reminiscent of the

Facing page
3.34
Mansour Qandriz, *Untitled*, 1964,
oil on gunny, 120×90 cm, Iranian
Academy of Arts

Above
3.35
Massoud Arabshahi, *Untitled*, 1965,
oil on canvas, 40×28 cm

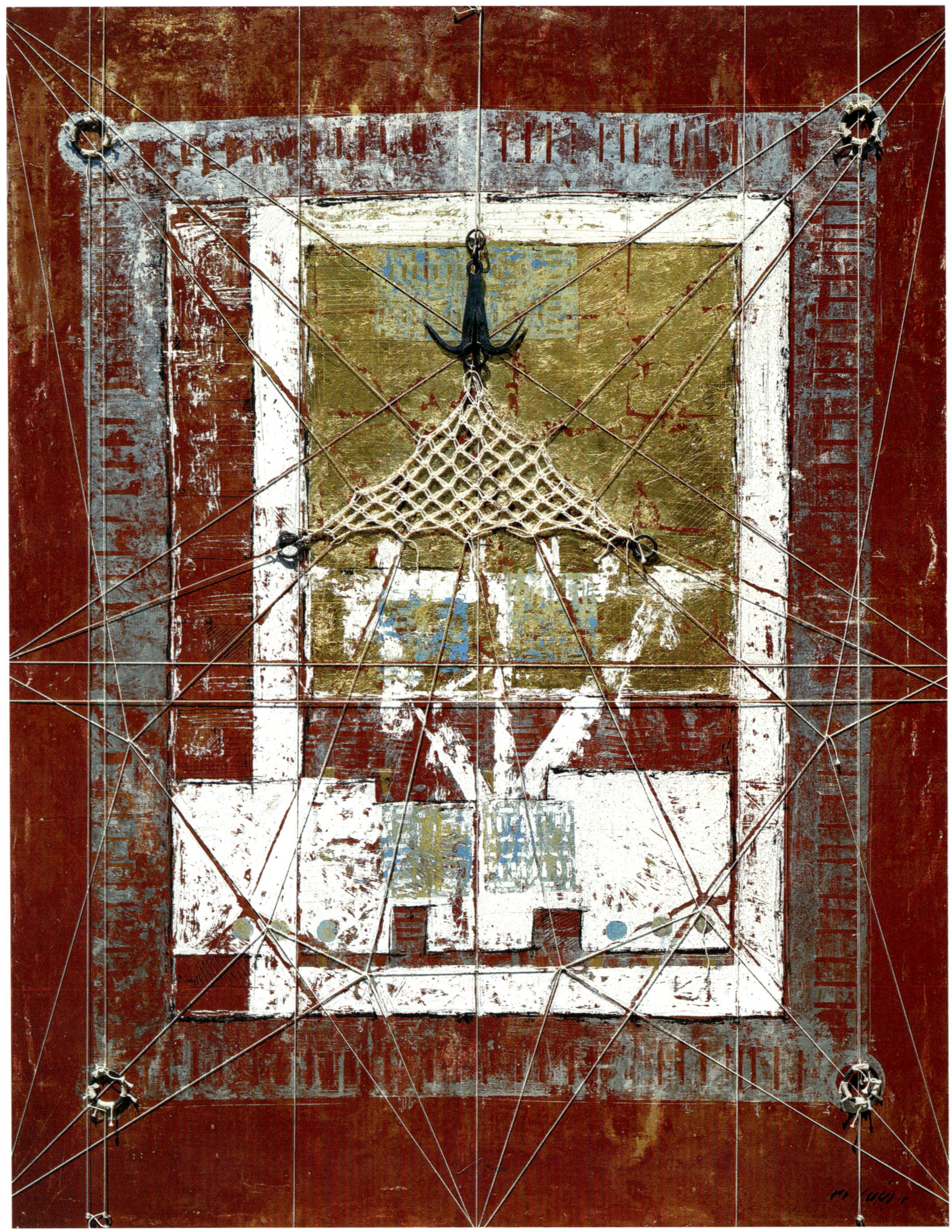

portraits in the Qajar royal paintings.[42] (Figure 3.37) His male figures, whether polo players, lovers or riders with falcons perched on their arms, brought to mind certain standard types of Iranian pictorial tradition and forms of Persian painting. In all cases, however, different sections of the figures were mostly adorned and illuminated by calligraphic or decorative patterns. (Figure 3.38)

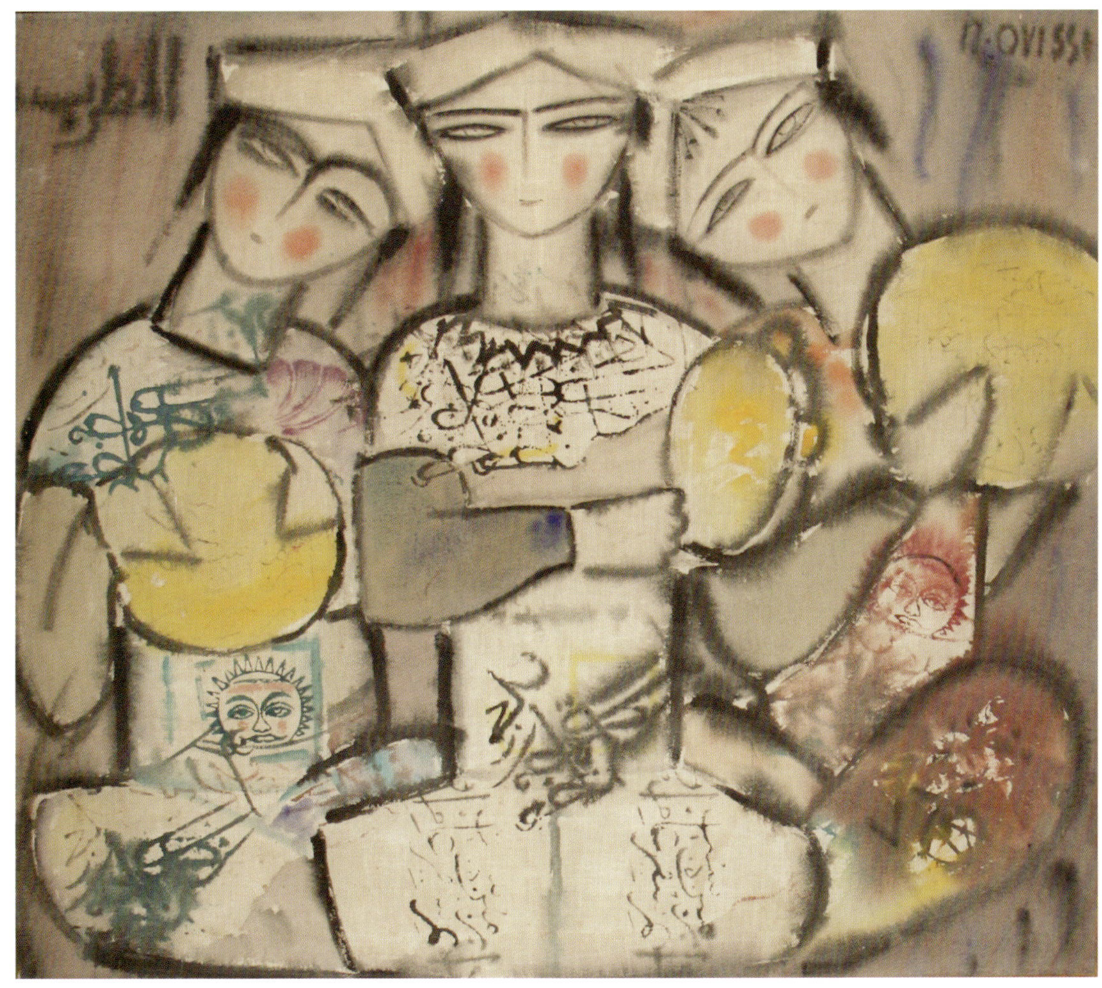

Facing page
3.36
Massoud Arabshahi, *Untitled*, 1977, oil, gold leaf, metal ring, threads and mesh on canvas, 177×135 cm

Left
3.37
Nasser Oveissi, *Untitled*, 1960, watercolour and oil on canvas, 80×90 cm, Iranian Academy of Arts

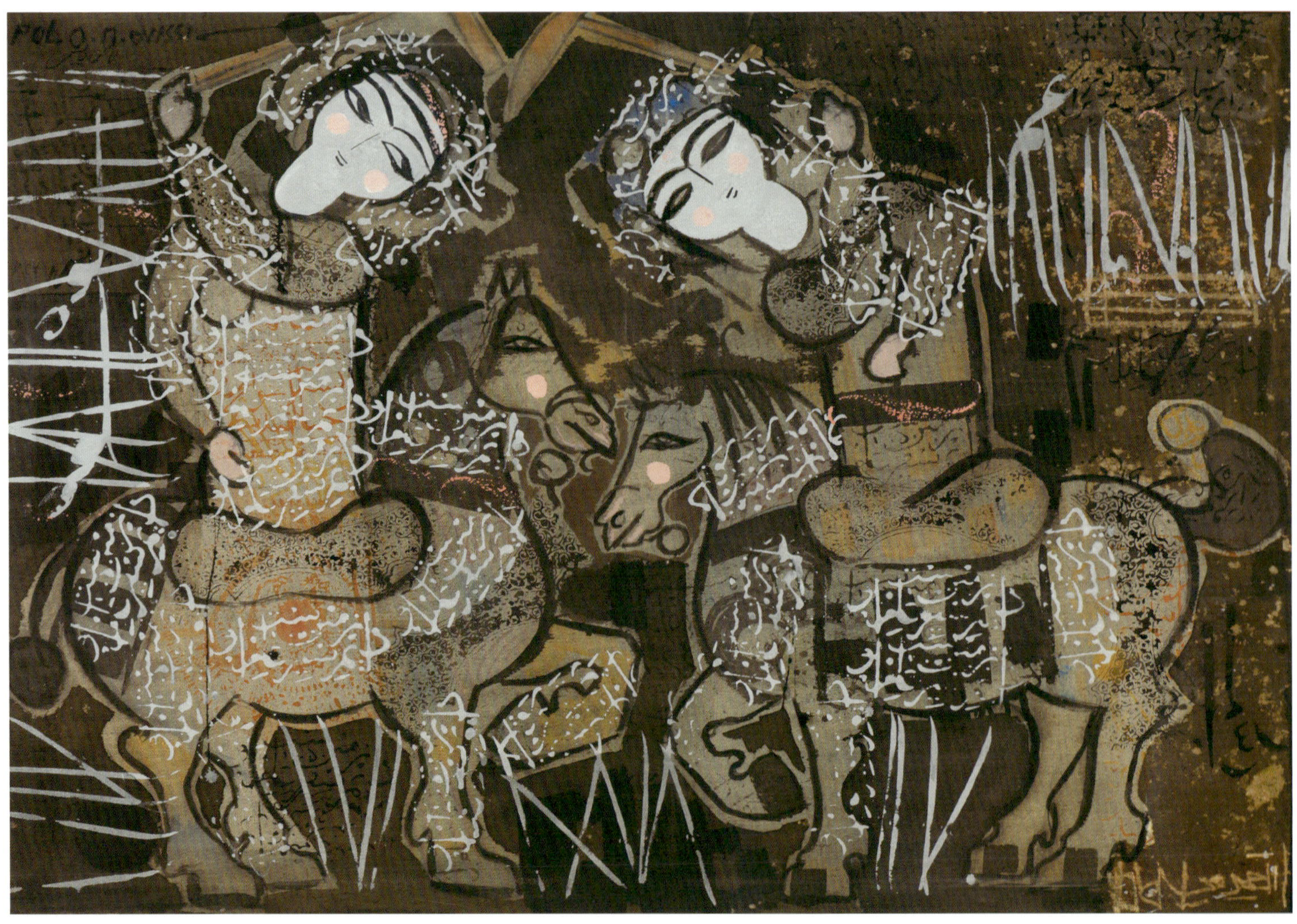

3.38
Nasser Oveissi, *Untitled, c.* 1964,
oil on canvas, 95×136 cm, Iranian
Academy of Arts

The horseback riders and lyrical couples populating Persian paintings and ceramics are also the themes of the paintings of Sadegh Tabrizi. The works of Tabrizi were first inspired by traditional symbolic articles found in such folk art as 'blue beads, old keys and locks, loose pages from manuscripts, penmanship practice sheets, old-fashioned signature seals, metal bowls with engraved rims, *qalyan* or *nargila* tops, coloured glass or bits of semiprecious stone'. [43] (Figure 3.39) They also draw upon Persian painting, Qajar portraits, and forms of religious and folk paintings of the Coffee-house (*Qahveh-khaneh*) genre. (Figure 3.40) In his works, one can observe the rhythmic repetition of motifs and calligraphic forms, often preserving the identifiable details of traditional objects. This allows the viewer's look to wander through his work, discovering familiar details imbued with tales of the past. And, as we have seen with the aforementioned artists, with his exhibitions of 1970–1, Tabrizi also started to utilise calligraphy as the sole element in his paintings.

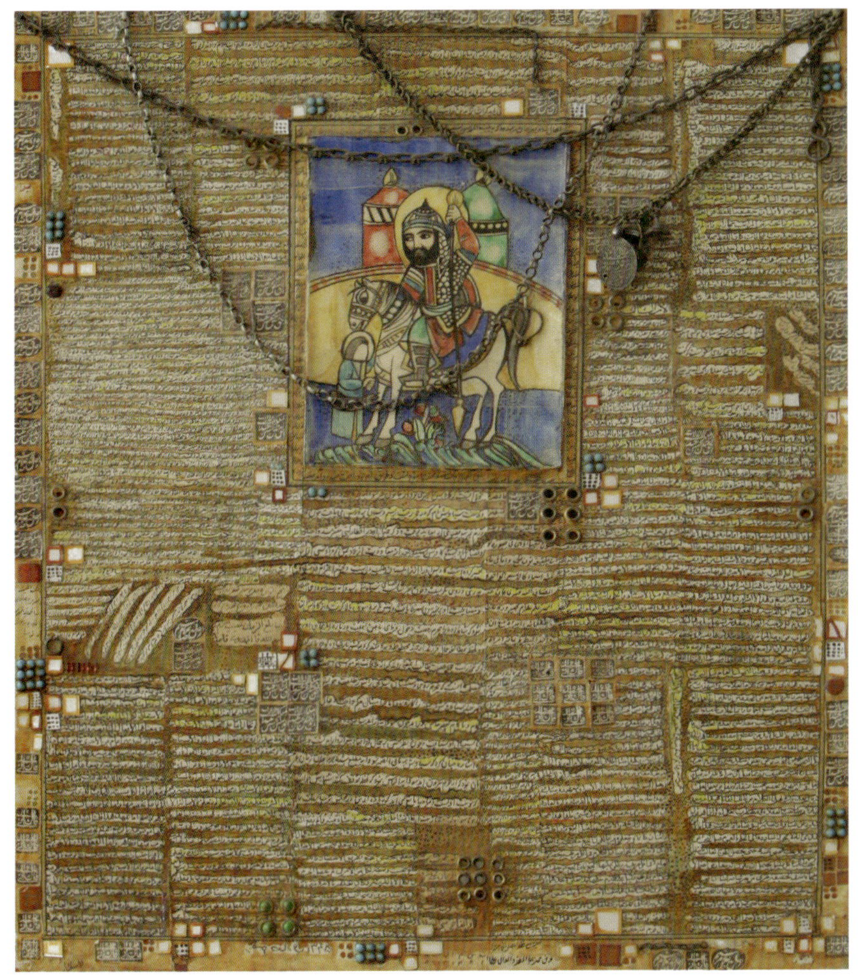

3.39
Sadegh Tabrizi, *Untitled*, 1966,
55×46 cm, collage and mixed media
on canvas, private collection, Tehran

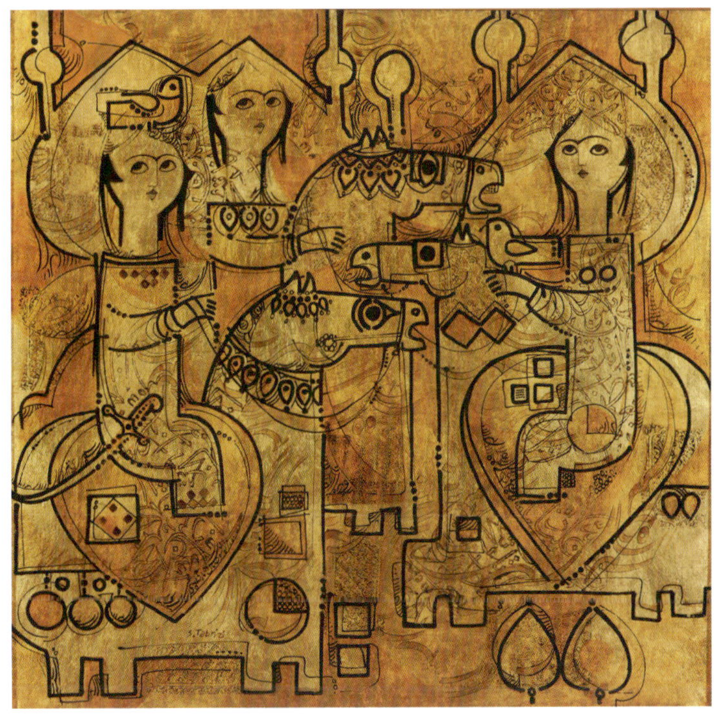

3.40
Sadegh Tabrizi, *Untitled*, mid-
1940s, mixed media on canvas,
100×100 cm, Iranian Academy
of Arts

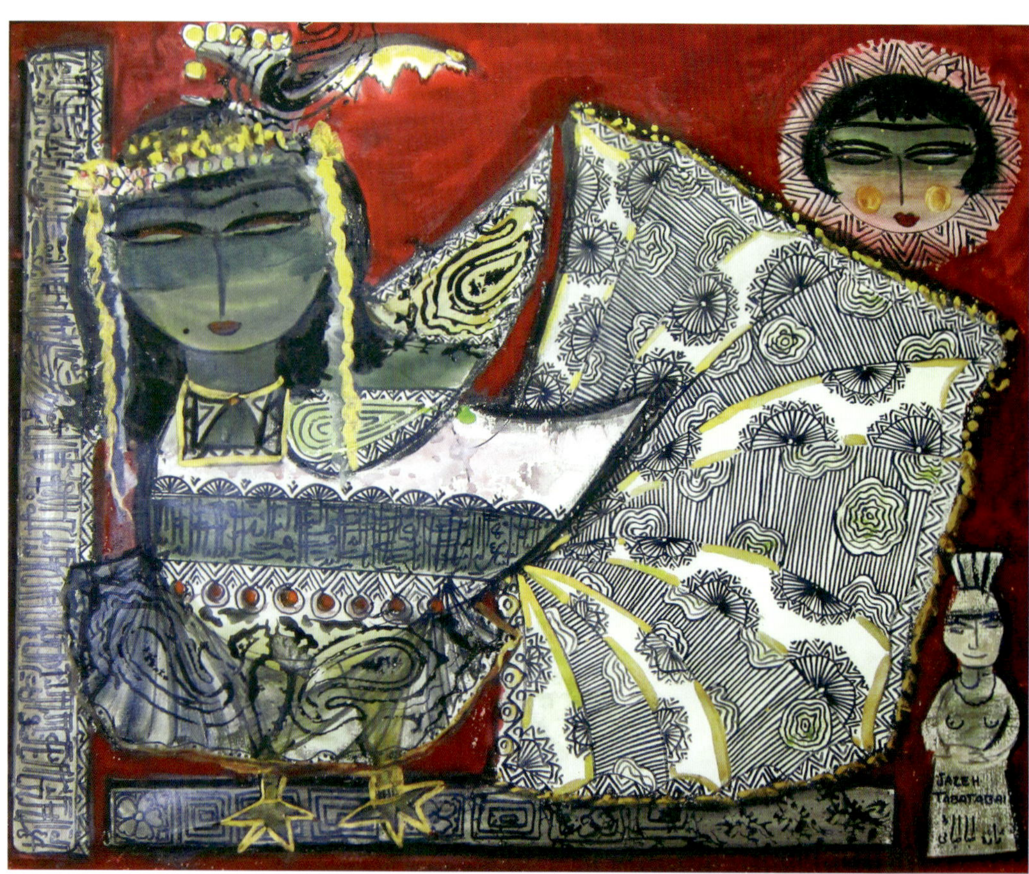

3.41
Jazeh Tabatabaei, *Untitled*, early
1960s, oil on canvas, 37×42.5 cm,
Museum of Fine Arts, Sa'ad Abad
Palace, Tehran

A graduate of the Tehran Faculty of Fine Arts, Jazeh Tabatabai began incorporating Qajar patterns into his work in the late 1950s, earlier than many of his contemporaries, but his style fell somewhere between caricature and more serious artistic expressions.[44] A serious sculptor and a prolific painter, Tabatabai had a wide scope and tried different styles; however, he was most recognisable in his bold restatements of Persian patterns such as Qajar females, decorative forms, calligraphic shapes and imaginative scenes. (Figure 3.41) He drew upon forms from Iranian folk art and culture a few years earlier than the trend was named, suggesting a forward-thinking approach. His sculptures were also combinations of various elements found in the scrap heap but imaginatively and humorously put together. (Figure 3.42)

A survey of the cultural atmosphere of Iranian artistic gatherings reveals two dominant topics. The same themes emerge when examining many written pieces in prominent art publications and from exhibitions during the 1950s and especially the 1960s (such as introductions to the Tehran Biennials and publications by independent non-governmental centres such as Talar-i Iran).[45]

(Figure 3.43) These dual subjects of debate are: the importance of current artistic achievements in the global art scene; and the formation of national and Iranian art. In the introduction to one of the publications produced by Talar-i Iran, it is stated that:

> There is no doubt that an artist anywhere in the world faces the challenge of defining their personal perspectives, artistic ideologies, and strategies. [...] To do so effectively, he must first possess a thorough understanding of his own expressive style and remain informed about new artistic inquiries and breakthroughs. This enables him to actively engage with these artistic achievements.[46]

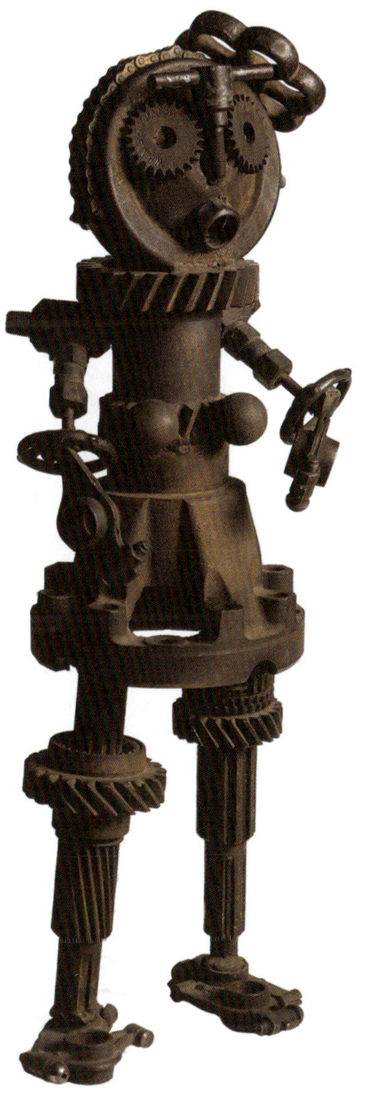

3.42
Jazeh Tabatabai, *Untitled*, 1977, iron pieces, height: 70 cm, TMoCA

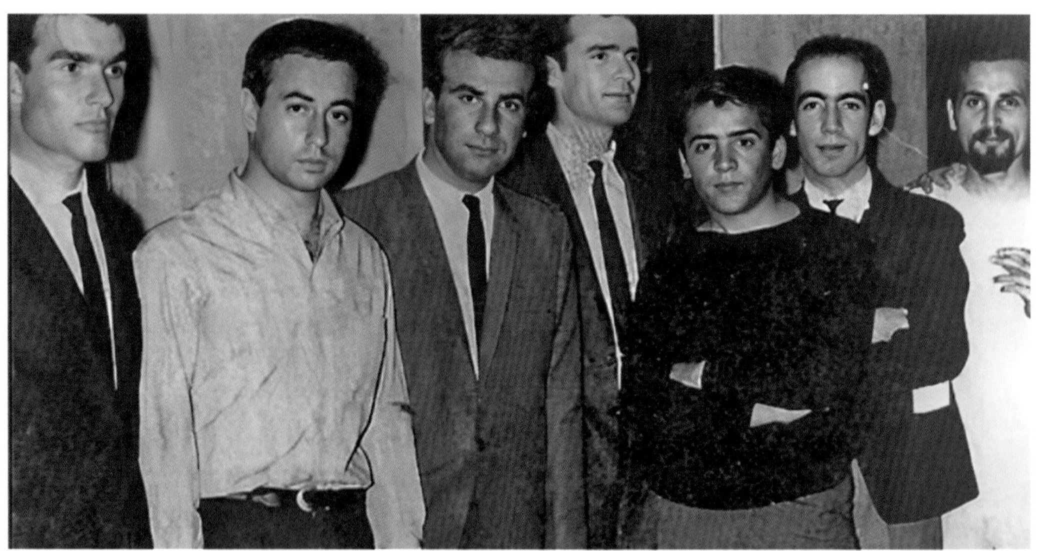

3.43
A group photo of a number of founders of the Talar-i Iran, from left to right: Hadi Hazavehi, Ahmad Aali, Fearamarz Pilaram, Sirous Malek, Ghobad Shiva, Mansour Qandriz and Ruin Pakbaz, 1964

On another occasion, it is argued that:

> ...We do not believe that national art should be confined to local contexts or divorced from global phenomena.
>
> Today, numerous remarkable discoveries and innovations emerge in the realms of knowledge and art, which should not and cannot be disregarded. Presently, the culture of nations transcends political and geographical boundaries. Artistic events rapidly disseminate worldwide; literary works are translated into diverse languages; international festivals showcase a myriad of sometimes contradictory ideas and evaluate them collectively; countries exchange cultural ambassadors; moreover, a group of artists, propelled by their international acclaim, perceive themselves as global participants...
>
> [...] Here, the artist's role in these societies would necessarily take on a distinct quality: he reflects his lived realities in the content of his art, and in framing this content appropriately, he would draw upon innovations from every corner of the globe. It is within this national and global context that he can truly find his place. In other words, when a nation's art enriches human culture that it embraces a sense of 'nationality'.[47]

What is emphasised here, and what was prevalent in those years, is the importance of the issue of new discoveries and an awareness of what was happening on the artistic scene, which mostly referred to Euro-American art. This somehow aligned with the cultural policies of the state during Mohammad Reza Shah's reign.

The state's sponsorship and support of other foreign and private institutes fostered the active development of art in the country during the 1960s. The role of the economic boom that occurred in the 1960s must also be taken into consideration. After the 'White Revolution' (*Inqilab-i sipid*) in 1962, and the subsequent economic splendour of the state, it was possible for the state to act as a patron of art in a much more effective manner. The economic development of the country had been made possible largely by increasing oil revenues. It was a strong factor in state's patronage of art, which the government cultural department now intended to support especially after the mid-1950s and particularly in the 1960s.[48]

In fact, one of the roles that the Cultural Reform (*Nowsazi-i farhangi*) played in the 1960s was to formalise modern art in the country. The General Administration of Fine Arts (subsequently the Ministry of Culture and Art, Vizarat-i farhang va hunar)[49] employed many of the modernist artists. Many initiatives combined to help modern Iranian art to become, a significant entity in the cultural life of the country. These included the state's sponsorship; support from other institutions such as the Iran-America and the Iran-Italy Societies, the Goethe-Institut, and the Cyrus Gallery in Paris (where modern Iranian painting, sculpture, and design were exhibited[50]), and private galleries in Tehran (including Saba, Mes, Litu, Borghese, Zarvan, Zand, Saman, Modern Art, and Talar-i Qandriz); the creation of several museums and artistic clubs in Tehran and other cities, including Isfahan and Kerman; and the establishment of the Faculty of Decorative Arts.

During the 1960s and 1970s, one of the state's most impactful cultural policies was the promotion of national culture. While the government primarily supported modern art, it also promoted traditional arts such as miniature painting, traditional calligraphy, and traditional music due to their connection to cultural heritage. From the 1950s to the 1970s several centres and organisations came into existence, including traditional art workshops, the Centre for Preservation and Promotion of Traditional Music (Markaz-i hifz va isha'ih-i musiqi) founded in 1968, the Behzad Art High School (Hunaristan-i Bihzad) in 1953 where miniature painting was at first the dominant subject of the school, and the Society of Iranian Calligraphers (Anjuman-i khushnivisan-i iran) in 1967.[51]

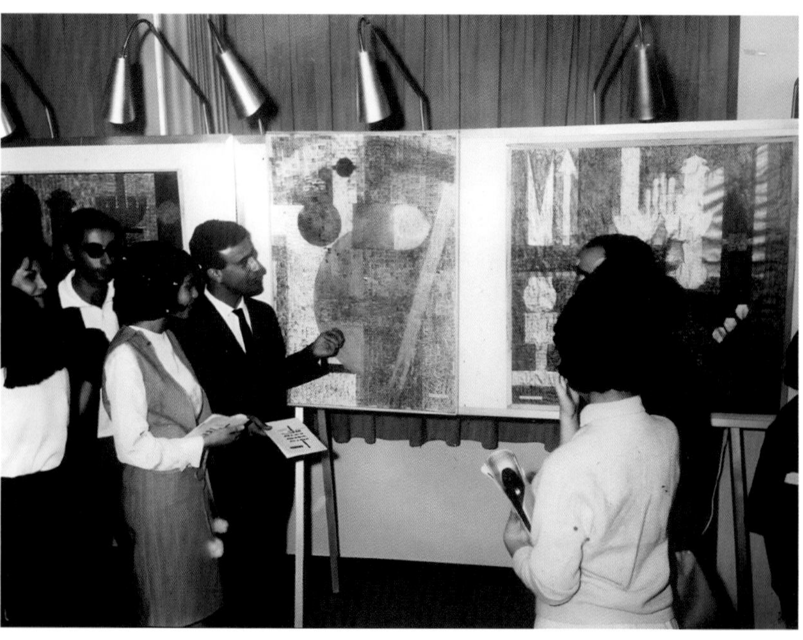

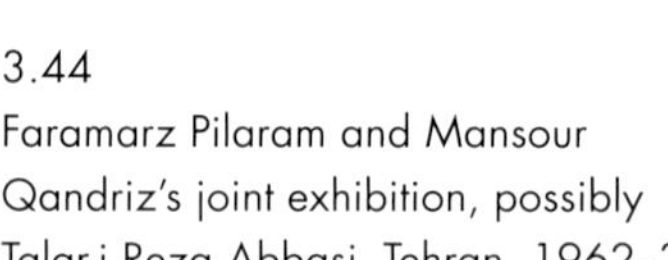

3.44
Faramarz Pilaram and Mansour
Qandriz's joint exhibition, possibly
Talar-i Reza Abbasi, Tehran, 1962–3

Here, the governmental cultural sections were the main leaders of artistic activities at that time. They tried to establish, through patronage of individual artists and movements, a 'formal art' that would form the basis of a sort of national school of art. Gradually, during the 1960s, this type of art was extensively disseminated and supported by governmental patronage. If we consider how the artists' works were selected, the awarding of prizes, and the manifestos written in formal exhibitions such as the Tehran Biennials, this trend can be readily apparent. (Figure 3.44) These external agents are inevitably of significance in the formation of the *Saqqa-khaneh* movement, which was regarded as a possible prototype for such a formal art. This issue was specifically addressed in the introduction to the Fourth Tehran Biennial. The passage mentions that the *Saqqa-khaneh* can embody all the characteristics that modern Iranian art requires.[52]

As a way of maturing the oil wealth in a way responsive to cultural needs during the economic boom of the 1960s, the state supported publications, festivals and commissions.[53] This movement was also helped by art clubs in Tehran and other cities. A growing number of art galleries and agencies defined and serviced new markets. This facilitated the (relatively) rapid establishment of reputations, and an interest that remained active and thriving in Iran in the 1960s and 1970s.

Among the formal artistic activities started and supported by the General Administration of Fine Arts of the Country (Idareh-i hunar-hay-i zibay-i kishvar) were the setting up of two public exhibition galleries, Aftab and Mehrshad, and the hosting of the Tehran Biennials. Through the five Tehran Biennials,[54] the aim was to foster the development of modern art while at the same time presenting the ancient heritage and civilisation of the country. What emerges is a strong and explicit relationship between nationally aware art and the cultural policies of the state. And, indeed, the *Saqqa-khaneh* could be an appropriate form of it. For example, the introduction to the brochure of the First Tehran Biennial in 1958 states that:

> We should have a deep understanding of our national art and prevent it from becoming trite. Our goal should be to establish an authentic school of visual arts, nurturing its growth and development, and ultimately guiding it towards perfection.[55]

In the introduction to the Second Tehran Biennial's catalogue, in a passage exploring the quality of artists' works, the same content can be perceived:

> [...] Most of the works share two common characteristics. Firstly, all artists strive to find fresh ways to express their unique 'perception', which embodies their 'artistic character'. Secondly, they attempt to convey a 'national' and 'Iranian' atmosphere in their works. Rather than merely focusing on superficial signs of 'nationality', they aim to incorporate the 'soul' of ancient national art into their innovative works.[56]

From the point of view of the biennial curators, the notion of national art appeared to represent an art form capable of catalysing artistic dynamism within society and safeguarding Iranian art from becoming solely derivative of global trends.[57] It seemed, however, that this kind of national art could not be acceptable without the employment of modern Euro-American art. After a period of time, the term 'national art' was replaced by 'art with inclusion of nationality'.[58]

It can be said that this analytical discussion of art ran parallel to the nationalist debates dominant in both the intellectual and political spheres during Mohammad Reza Shah's reign. We have seen how, following the adoption of modernism by Iranian artists in the 1940s, many pioneers attempted to examine modern Western art through an Iranian perspective, despite modernism and its reception by artists and Iranian society being the primary concern. In the 1950s, critics voiced significant criticism, arguing that the efforts of this group to establish a discernible national school of art were largely futile. They contended that artists were merely integrating local themes into pre-existing European art forms like Cubism, Impressionism, and Expressionism. While some artists used subjects unmistakably Iranian, others incorporated motifs drawn from old manuscripts. Such subjects as women with *chador*, villager men, local *bazar* and religious places were common themes in these paintings.[59] The main issue stemmed from their incongruous use of disparate and conflicting elements: pre-existing European styles alongside the pictorial material of Iranian traditional art.

Faced with the complexities of their artistic identity, the younger artists working during the 1960s were engaged in intensive experimentation, both intellectually and artistically. They now referred to Shi'i pictorial folk culture, which was still highly popular, especially among the middle and lower classes. These artists believed that such sources had a connection with their artistic roots.[60] At the same time, criticism of the West through anti-Western movements was growing among some Iranian intellectuals and artists. The nativist and nationalist debates prevalent in intellectual and political circles closely paralleled art-world discourses, and the effect of these debates on this group of artists should not be underestimated. These tendencies among the intelligentsia, which had originated in the 1940s and 1950s, manifested themselves in criticism of the insatiable desire among the majority to imitate and emulate the West and its products. This was known as *gharb-zadegi* ('Westoxification') in various scopes of life, literature, and art. According to Mehrzad Borujerdi:

> This period also represented the heyday of nativism and anti-orientalism in Iran. During this time, the question of self and other came to the forefront of intellectual deliberations and stayed there for good.[61]

The concept of nativism could be seen as a response to Eurocentrism and colonialism, both in textual and political terms. In essence, nativism serves not only as the manifesto of Third World intellectuals' resistance but also as the discourse through which their struggle is articulated.[62] In its broadest sense, nativism can be defined as the doctrine advocating for the resurgence, reinstatement, or continuation of native or indigenous cultural customs, beliefs, and values. Nativism is rooted in deeply held convictions such as resistance to acculturation, the privileging of one's 'authentic' ethnic identity, and a longing for a return to an untainted indigenous cultural tradition.[63]

While nativist beliefs were prominently present in the *Saqqa-khaneh* movement, none of these artists or their followers were anti-Western in their mindset or artistic approach. Instead, the question of cultural identity motivated them to draw from their own roots without completely rejecting the influence of the West. Fundamentally, these neo-traditionalist artists aimed to imbue their works with an Iranian essence and to cultivate an artistic style that originated in Iran.

Here, the question emerges as to whether the *Saqqa-khaneh* artists' treatment of traditional materials was a nostalgic approach towards their historical tradition. Furthermore, due to the modernistic nature of their art, another question can be posed: whether – as Kamran Diba believes – the ideals and motivations of the *Saqqa-khaneh* movement can be compared to the Pop Art movement in the West. He claims, 'if we simplify Pop Art as an art movement which looks at the symbols and tools of a mass consumer society as a relevant and influencing cultural force, *Saqqa-khaneh* artists looked at the inner beliefs and popular symbols that were part of the religion and culture of Iran, and perhaps, consumed in the same way as industrial products in the West (but for different reasons and under dissimilar circumstances).'[64] He names the *Saqqa-khaneh* movement 'in reference to Western art, "Spiritual Pop Art".'[65] While his assumption cannot be dismissed entirely, it also cannot be fully validated without considering the artistic circumstances of that period in Iran and the individual statements of the artists exploring their own motivations. The unique socio-political context, which differed significantly from that of the West, must also be taken into account. It is important to emphasise once again the influence of the intellectual and artistic atmosphere, as well as the significant role played by the government and custodians of culture.

After the success of the *Saqqa-khaneh* trend in winning over the cultural officials within the country a number of artists gained success in international art exhibitions such as the Venice and Paris Biennales. Critics in Iran argued that despite those artists' position against the Eurocentric art direction, they appeared to measure their success in accordance with Western standards. This type of position could be detected in most formal artistic exhibitions such as the

Tehran Biennials. It was according to these criteria that a number of artists selected by Tehran Biennial juries subsequently received awards. This approach was further criticised because it imposed a kind of tourist-orientated exotic trend[66] in Iranian art, rather than natural development within its own context. One example is a statement by members of Talar-i Qandriz's group exhibition in 1969:

> We advocate for the cultivation of a national artistic identity – one that, while not necessarily conforming to global trends, maintains its unique character. We believe that the challenges faced by Iranian painters should be addressed within the context of our own realities. Therefore, we view participation in international art festivals, biennials, and events as futile, and consider attempts to show these issues as a form of escapism [from our own realities].[67]
>
> … here [in Iran], vernacular art has yet to take shape – an art with a social function, characterised by its indigenous qualities, which would lend it validity and prevent it from becoming rootless, decadent, and devoid of value. However, it is important to clarify that by 'vernacular art', we do not mean the mere reproduction of existing cultural heritage, whether familiar or unfamiliar. Such an approach would represent a retreat into the past, allowing the artist to avoid engaging with present-day realities. We find this approach unacceptable. [68]

Although no one has yet claimed any exact date for the demise of the *Saqqa-khaneh* trend, it has been stated that the main movement did not survive because of the lack of concord between the members of the group. At present, its main doctrine[69] is continued through the individual artists of the trend and other artists who were influenced by it in different ways. From Emami's explanatory statement in the introduction to the *Saqqa-khaneh* exhibition's catalogue in the Tehran Museum of Contemporary Art in August 1977,[70] it appears that the trend had existed in a different manner, at least until that time. (Figure 3.45) He maintains that:

> What is the status of the Saqqakhaneh School today? Is it dead or alive? All but one of its members are luckily alive, [71] though some of them may not be currently in their best productive years. The mere fact that the present exhibition

is assembled on the occasion of the opening of Tehran Museum of Contemporary Art is itself an indication that the Saqqakhaneh School is a living presence in the arts of modern Iran...[72]

The exhibition consisted of works of the major *Saqqa-khaneh* affiliated members, including Zenderoudi, Tanavoli, Pilaram, Qandriz, Arabshahi, Tabrizi, Tabatabai and Oveissi. While there was no formal organisation for the *Saqqa-khaneh* group to exchange ideas, and their concrete activities did not persist beyond the mid-1960s, the core founders of the movement have continued to pursue their aspirations through their individual and diverse styles, even to this day. Essentially, though each artist associated with *Saqqa-khaneh* may have adopted a different approach and moved beyond the movement's initial boundaries, their subsequent development cannot be viewed as separate from the trend's primary objectives. For example, Zenderoudi, who has been working in Paris since

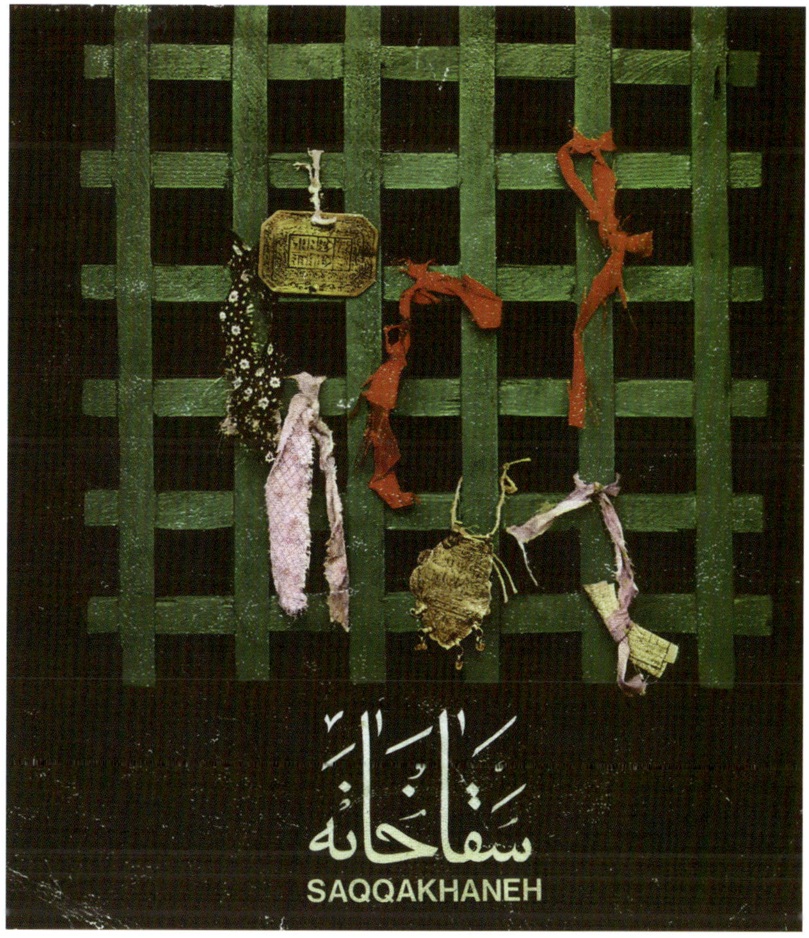

3.45
Cover of the catalogue for the *Saqqa-khaneh* exhibition at TMoCA, 1977

1961, soon gave up painting the talismanic compositions and folk motifs, and tended to concentrate on rhythmical bright colours and lines, and imagined constellation-like spaces. Tanavoli has been constantly finding new strategies and possibilities within his belief in folk culture, Persian literature and contemporary thought.[73] Pilaram, whose initial experiences paralleled with Zenderoudi's, tended to use calligraphy more than others. Arabshahi, who used to employ pre-Islamic motifs rather than Shi'i religious sources, created huge bas-reliefs with such materials as ceramic, copper and concrete during subsequent years.

From the mid-1960s onwards, increasing numbers of artists joined the *Saqqa-khaneh* movement. Many used calligraphic forms as the basis of their work. Distinguished figures such as Mohammad Ehsai (b.1939) and Reza Mafi (1943–82) belong to the genre then named *Naqqashi-khatt*. Hence the *Saqqa-khaneh* trend resulted in the emergence of other homogeneous tendencies in contemporary Iranian art in which the issue of identity was still a main concern.

Since the *Saqqa-khaneh* movement, no similar movement in Iran has had such a widespread national appeal and popularity. However, the dominant preoccupation of the modernist artists was to identify the specific characteristics of Iranian art, and in this continued quest the essence of the *Saqqa-khaneh* movement lived on, influencing subsequent artistic and cultural developments.

1.   Post-*Saqqa-khaneh* and other trends

2.1.   The Genre of 'Neo-Calligraphy'

As we have noted, the use of calligraphic forms in modern Iranian art first emerged in the works of pioneers of the *Saqqa-khaneh* trend as early as 1963–4. However, it is worth remembering that the *Saqqa-khaneh* artists chose a multitude of ways to communicate their ideas through the languages of modern art, in various forms and guises, including the adjustment of religious folk art to modern concerns. Calligraphic forms were among the later material that would feature in this exploratory framework. Although neo-calligraphy originated within the *Saqqa-khaneh* movement, it soon evolved into two main tendencies: one comprising the *Saqqa-khaneh* artists who exploited calligraphic forms as a primary pictorial material; and the other, *Naqqashi-khatt* (calligraphic painting), consisting of professional calligraphers who had an interest in employing calligraphy differently from those exclusive classical works.

These two types of neo-calligraphy developed distinct forms of expression. The *Saqqa-khaneh* artists and their followers veered in the direction of 'Letterism'[74]; meanwhile, the work of *Naqqashi-khatt*[75] artists was characterised by different forms. I use the Persian term *Naqqashi-khatt*[76] both to describe the works and to define the movement (for want of an adequate English term that could convey the appropriate meaning).[77] One can find artists outside these two tendencies whose works demonstrate an affinity with calligraphy. (The works of Mansoureh Hosseini (1926–2012) and Gholamhossein Nami (b.1936) are good examples.) Despite the vast diversity in content of artists' works, and the broader temporal reach of this tendency, this text deals mainly with the various forms of the movement and its characteristics from its beginnings in the 1960s through to the 1970s. The full breadth of this genre in the post-revolutionary period will be addressed in the next chapter.

In order to comprehend the concept of neo-calligraphy and its differences from various sorts of traditional calligraphy, a brief definition of the nature of classical calligraphy will prove helpful. In classical calligraphy any special script shows distinct characteristics in terms of style and even content,[78] which unifies the work of different calligraphers. As Anne-Marie Schimmel notes, 'the *Kataba* for a calligrapher could be restricted to certain kinds of writing (e.g. decorative pages, *hilyas*, or books), but it could also be valid for every kind of calligraphy in the special style that the newly graduated calligrapher would write.'[79]

Traditional calligraphy is ruled by strict regulations and principles and the mastery of a traditional calligrapher is indicated by his excellence of technique in accordance with these principles. In this way, a calligrapher is not expected to change the traditional procedures and order of calligraphy. To an established calligrapher, respect for the laws of his trade is just as important as respect for religious principles. Therefore, he is more interested in elaborating the art of calligraphy than fundamentally changing it; in softening its edges rather than carving new angles.

In the context of the history of Islamic art, calligraphy has long been used in various shapes, colours and compositions for decoration and the formation of compositional shapes. According to Anthony Welch:

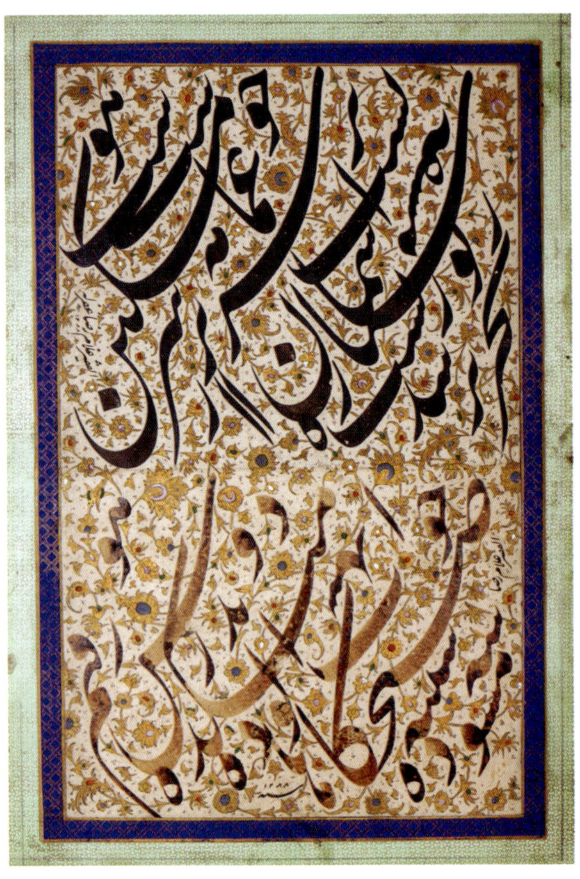

3.46

Mirza Ghulam-Reza Isfahani,
Nasta'liq Siyah-mashq, c. AH 1287
/AD 1870–71, private collection,
Tehran

Architectural inscriptions, like those on objects, were more often observed and admired than read. While their content was specific and often directed at a special and identifiable historical situation, to the mass of believers they served a symbolic function, asserting the power and rectitude of Islam simply by their presence. [...] To one who lived within the testimony of Islam, its religious and cultural belonging, and while the script had content and did serve to decorate and enliven the surfaces of buildings, this affirmation was its vital social function.[80]

A practice sheet of *Siyah-mashq,*[81] which is when the letters are written mostly without any special meaning, is a typical traditional calligraphic mode in which the meaning is secondary to the pictorial representation of calligraphy. It usually consists of a superimposition of lines and words without regard to continuity or meaning: the antithesis of the literary aspect of classical calligraphy. (Figures 3.46–47) Content is unimportant here because the forms themselves testify to the intrinsic value of the works.

Neo-calligraphy, however, is a modern approach to calligraphy that emerged in the early 1960s and then developed according to various approaches.[82] As Parviz Tanavoli, the pioneering artist of the *Saqqa-khaneh* movement, points out, it must be borne in mind that 'from the mid-1960s onwards, the *Saqqa-khaneh* movement was on the rise, with increasing numbers of painters joining its ranks or, if you like, jumping on its bandwagon. Most of them used calligraphy as the basis of their work and often simply covered their paintings with script.'[83] One of the most common and significant trends followed by *Saqqa-khaneh* was the *Naqqashi-khatt* tendency. Hence it was not surprising that the *Saqqa-khaneh*'s popularity throughout the country caused some to suggest that *Naqqashi-khatt* had been a part of the *Saqqa-khaneh* movement. Despite the undeniable and effective influence of *Saqqa-khaneh* on the formation of *Naqqashi-khatt,* careful consideration confirms that the artists of *Naqqashi-khatt* strove to apply a different strategy.

Pioneers such as Charles Hossein Zenderoudi, Parviz Tanavoli and Faramarz Pilaram began to use the calligraphic text as a primary reference of their works, and in their wake so did other artists, including Mohammad Ehsai, Reza Mafi and Nasrollah Afjei (b.1933), as major representatives of *Naqqashi-khatt.* However, there are distinct differences in their approach to calligraphy. The *Saqqa-*

khaneh artists and their followers drew inspiration from various aspects of Iran's pictorial tradition, including calligraphy. Likewise, in *Naqqashi-khatt*, calligraphy was primarily used and served as a pictorial source from tradition. However, in the latter tendency, the artist prioritised the sacred aspect of calligraphy over general or formal contents. The works of the letterists tended to be secular-oriented, while the artists of *Naqqashi-khatt* were fascinated by sacred or literary subject matter.[84]

Saqqa-khaneh letterists used elements of calligraphy as the primary constituent of an abstraction freed by their individual vision. The primary focus of this group was to produce artworks that exhibited a familiarity with modern art styles while retaining their own pictorial traces. Consequently, their approach to questions of cultural identity and the use of tradition was primarily secular.[85] As a result, their canvas constructions did not feature characteristics typical of traditional art, such as a commitment to incorporating religious or literary content, or specific subject matter, in a readable text. Instead, they predominantly emphasised basic shapes of simple letters or calligraphic forms, as well as various sorts of script, either individually or in combination, as structural elements of composition. However, their abstract works did not typically adhere to conventional rules of calligraphy.

Among the founding members of *Saqqa-khaneh*, Charles Hossein Zenderoudi was the pioneer of the calligraphic approach, insofar as he used calligraphy as the sole compositional element.[86] A prolific letterist, Zenderoudi branched out into calligraphy after his initial experiences in using local religious folk art. This period is a continuation of the previous one, in terms of his earlier attention to the use of letters and ornaments; it is known as the most characteristic period of Zenderoudi's artistic career. In Zenderoudi's canvases, unlike many others within this trend, calligraphy has lost its decorative function. The literary-religious content has become an element used for the creation of abstract and rhythmic spaces, yet sometimes showing similarities with those of the Dadaist approach. (Figure 3.48) Interestingly, it should not be forgotten that the *Lettriste* movement was still active when Zenderoudi moved to Paris in 1961.[87] Emphasising the visual effects of letters, words and signs, irrespective of their semantic content, *Lettristes* tried to bestow on them an expressive and communicative function. In the French critic Pierre Cabanne's view, 'this *Lettrisme* is the fundamental source of interest of Zenderoudi's art. This determination never relinquishes

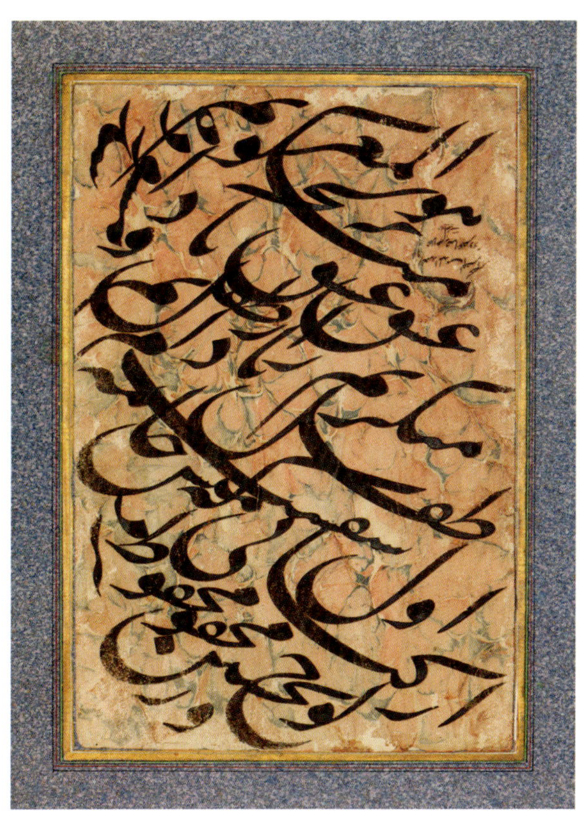

3.47
Mirza Ghulam-Reza Isfahani,
Nasta'liq Siyah-mashq, c. AH 1287
/AD 1870–71, private collection,
Tehran

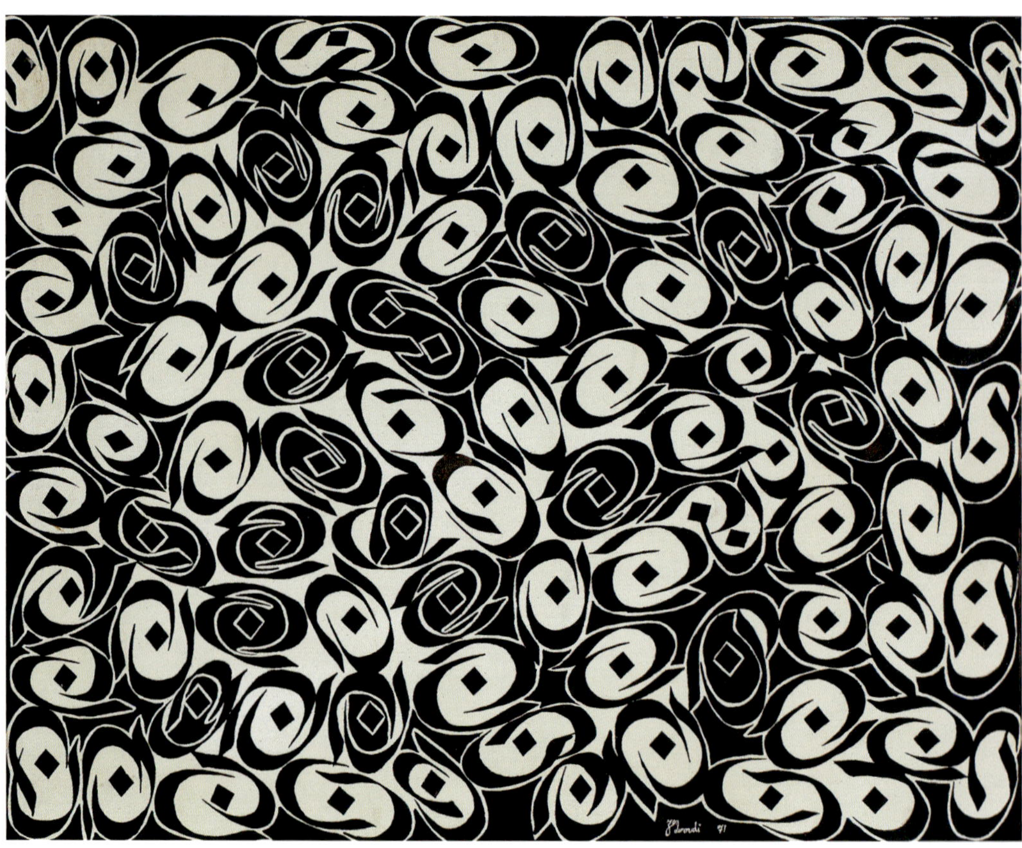

3.48
Charles Hossein Zenderoudi, *Noon*,
1970, oil and acrylic on canvas,
80×100 cm, TMoCA

its vigour nor its poetic intensity. The "message", a term much used and often misused, here takes in its true meaning – its ontological dimension.'[88] Influenced by the mid-twentieth-century modernists' motto, Zenderoudi believed in the absolute freedom of an artist, enabling him to make a complete commitment to his art without any external pressure imposed on him.[89] This attitude, which is a part of the radical manifesto propounded by abstract art (especially in the French *Art Informel* of the 1950s), can be clearly found during all his various artistic phases. He has disregarded all the conventions of calligraphy and has focused his efforts on exploring the visual characteristics of graphic elements and their potential for conveying meaning. (Figure 3.49)

Zenderoudi believes that depiction of the absolute beauty of epigraphy is not the main purpose of his use of calligraphy. Rather, it is the mental impression observed only in these calligraphic forms. Although in his paintings he uses some words and characters in styles, for example semi-*Thuluth*, semi-*Nasta'liq* or *Siyah-mashq*, which are typically associated with classical calligraphy, he prefers the word 'writing' instead of 'calligraphy' for these works. Yet he is heir to a great and magnificent graphic tradition in which the various arts of the book such as calligraphy, painting and illumination combine to convey beauty and meaning. When one examines any of Zenderoudi's paintings closely – for example his series of 1976–77 works filled with numbers and letters – one is struck by the illusion of reversibility; these pictures present simultaneously the appearance of a manuscript, astrological pictures and that of a talisman, a carpet or an arabesque.

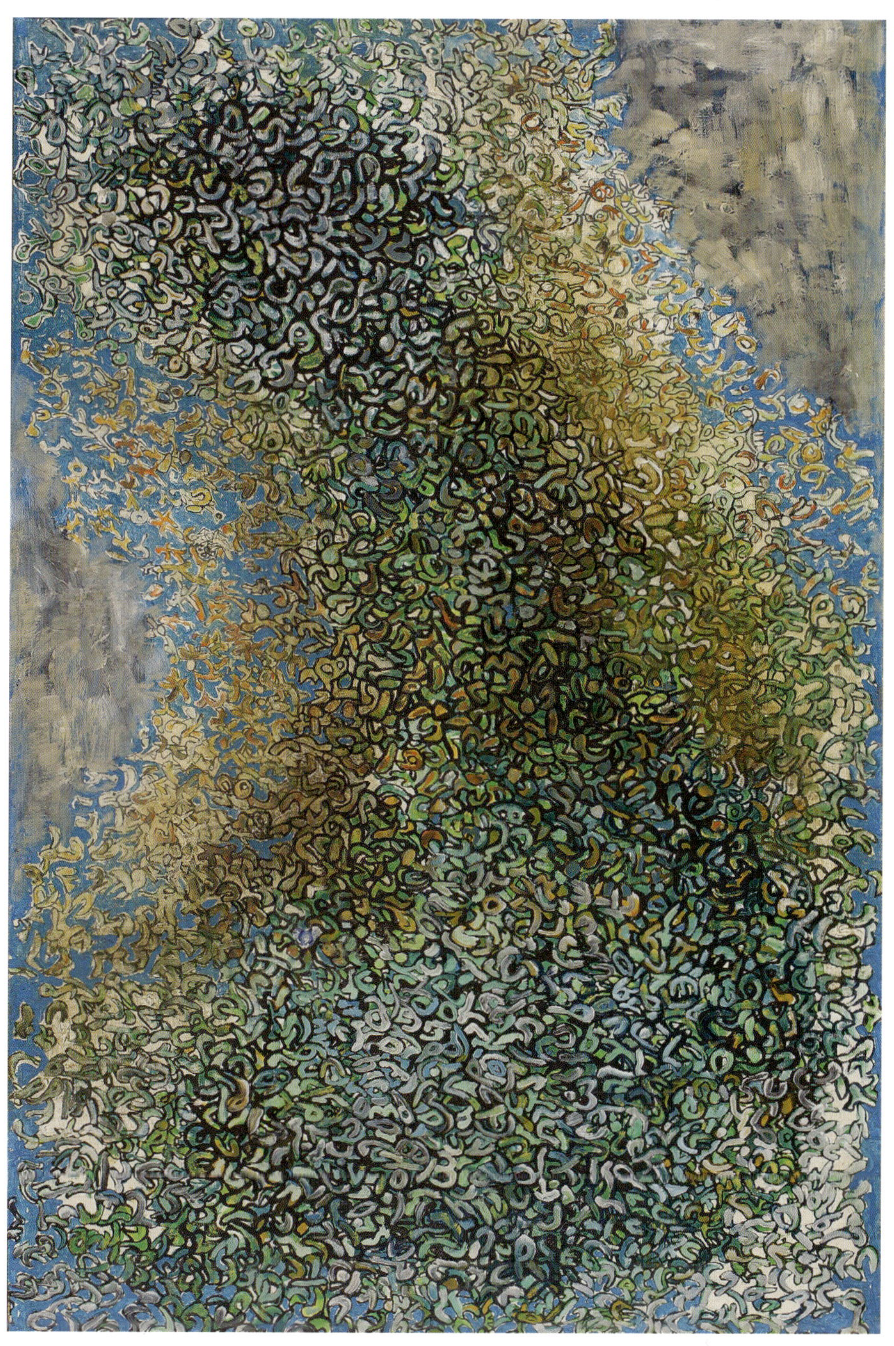

3.49
Charles Hossein Zenderoudi, *Untitled*, 1967, oil on canvas, 105×74 cm, TMoCA

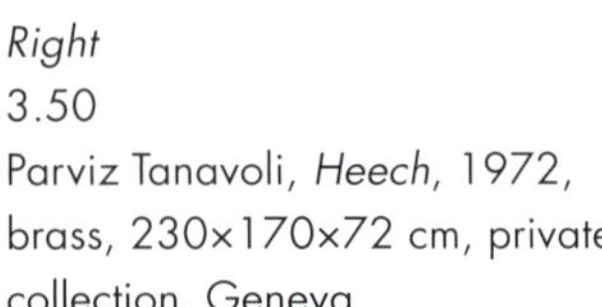

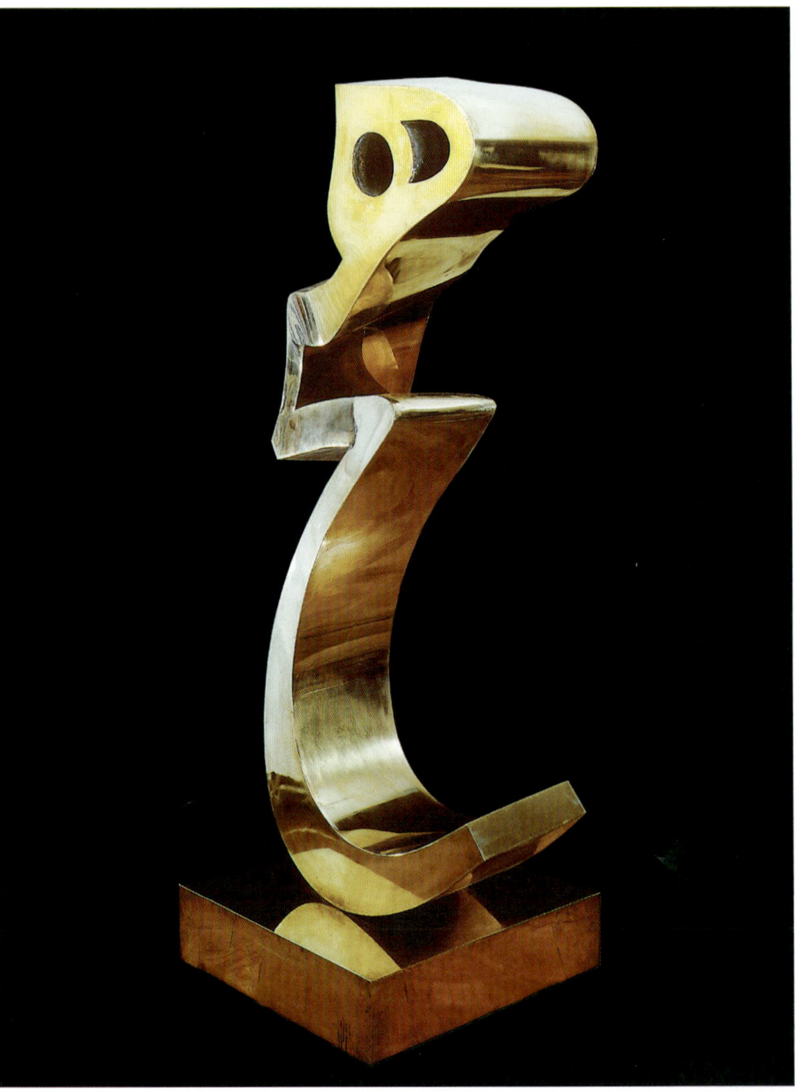

Parviz Tanavoli emerged as a passionate believer in a modernism attained through forms of popular visual culture; and he cited folk expression as his inspiration. After earlier use of unreadable letters or pseudo-script patterns in his abstract sculptures, Tanavoli began to make his sculptures *Heech* in the 1960s. (Figure 3.50) Another distinguished work in which Tanavoli focused on calligraphic patterns was the *Walls of Iran* series, produced in the mid-1970s and 1980s. Inspired by the artist's previous works and modelled after ancient Mesopotamian and Persian reliefs, this monumental series of bronze sculptures consists of the articulation of intricate inscriptions and pictograms. The richly structured walls ornamented with scripts echo the elaborate calligraphic patterns of Islamic buildings but, at the same time, other pictographic sources. (Figure 3.51)

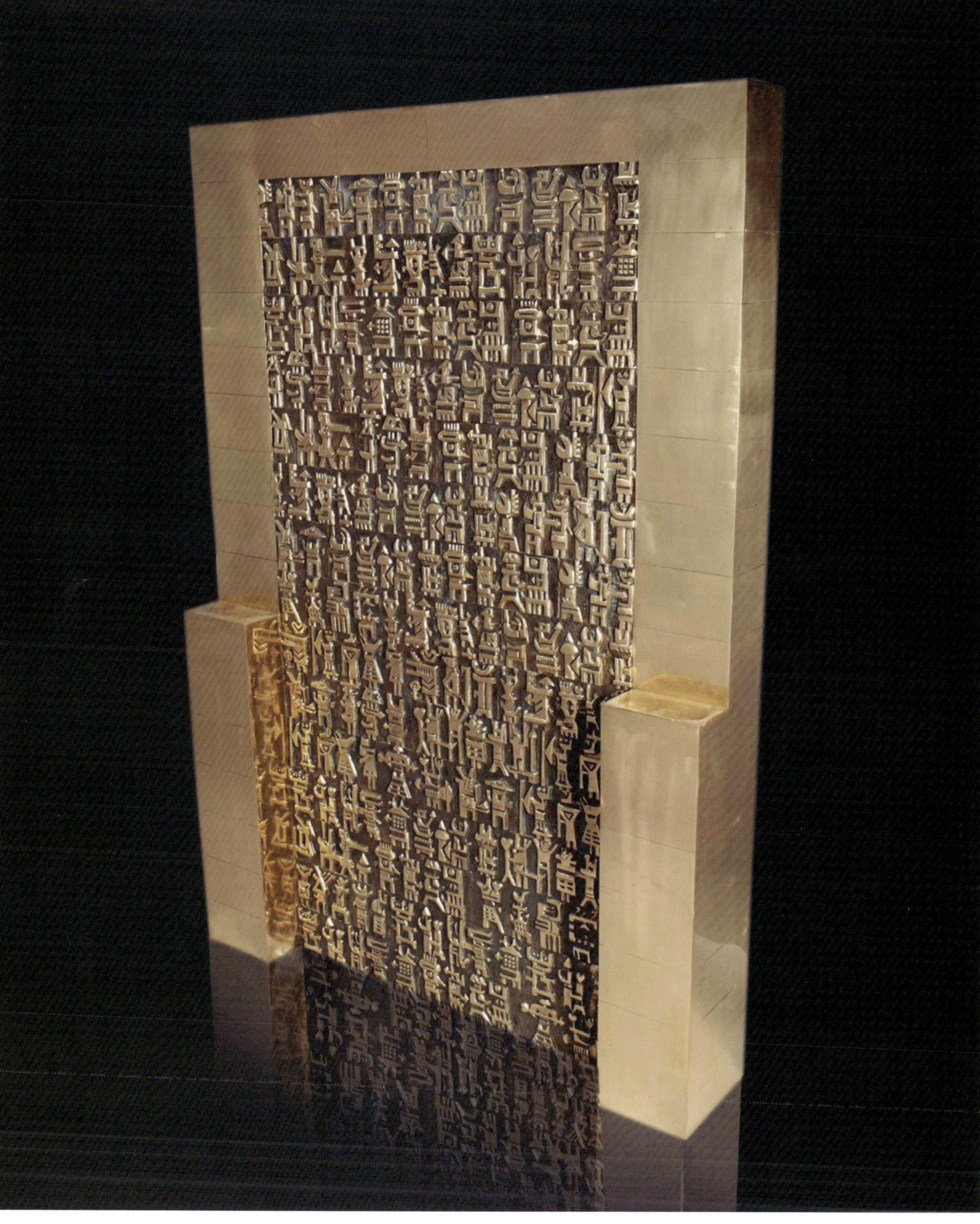

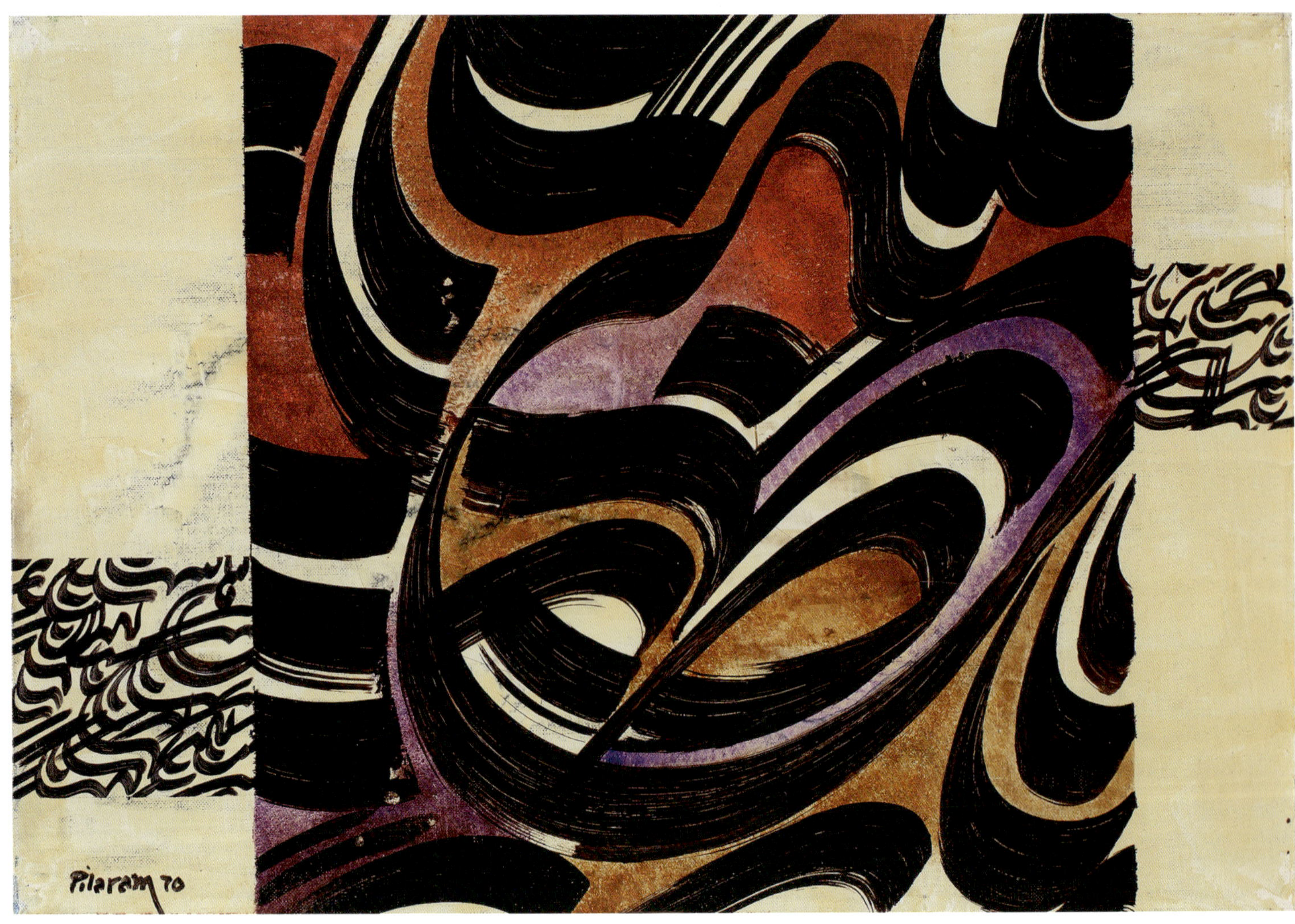

Above
3.52
Faramarz Pilaram, *Untitled*, 1970,
oil on canvas, 50×70 cm, TMoCA

Facing page
3.53
Faramarz Pilaram, *Untitled*, 1970,
oil on canvas, 105×105 cm,
TMoCA

Among other pioneers of neo-calligraphy, Faramarz Pilaram is best-known for his reference to classical calligraphic styles, although he avoided representing any specific style in his works.[90] In his canvases, calligraphy not only holds a traditional significance but also imbues the spontaneity of its interpretation into the lines. This includes their perpetual change, the juxtaposition of colours, the interplay of knots, circles, spirals, and straight lines, and the fusion of various volumes. (Figure 3.52)   What is most commonly found in Pilaram's neo-calligraphic paintings is the use of the *Nastaliq*-like and occasionally *Shikasteh*-like forms that associate the whole composition with *Siyah-mashq*, in which one can distinguish a few dominant meaningless forms of words or letters such as '*Sala*', and '*La*'. (Figure 3.53)   Expressing his displeasure for what a group of the Society of Iranian Calligraphers' graduates were producing as *Naqqashi-khatt* the artist says:

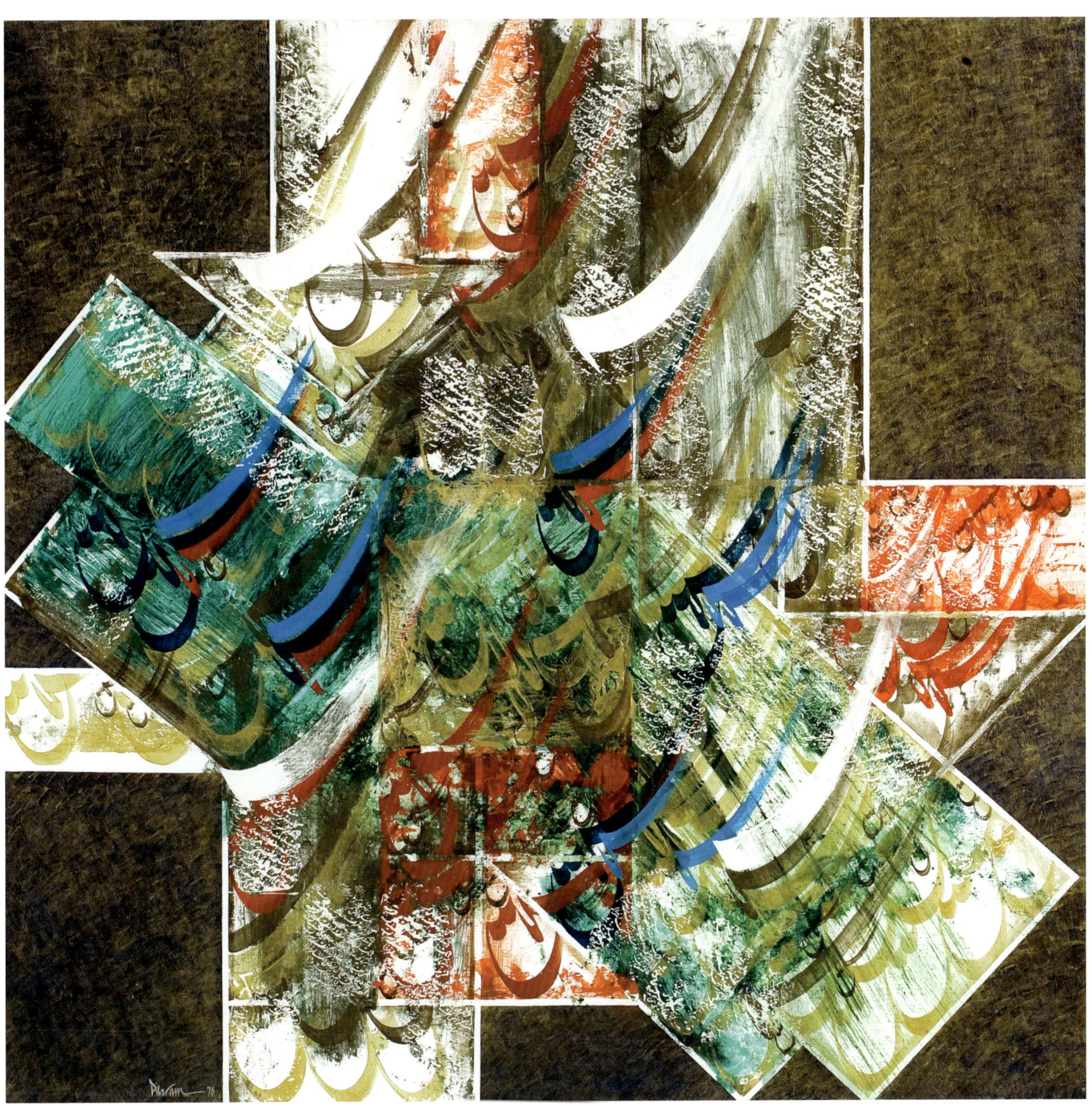

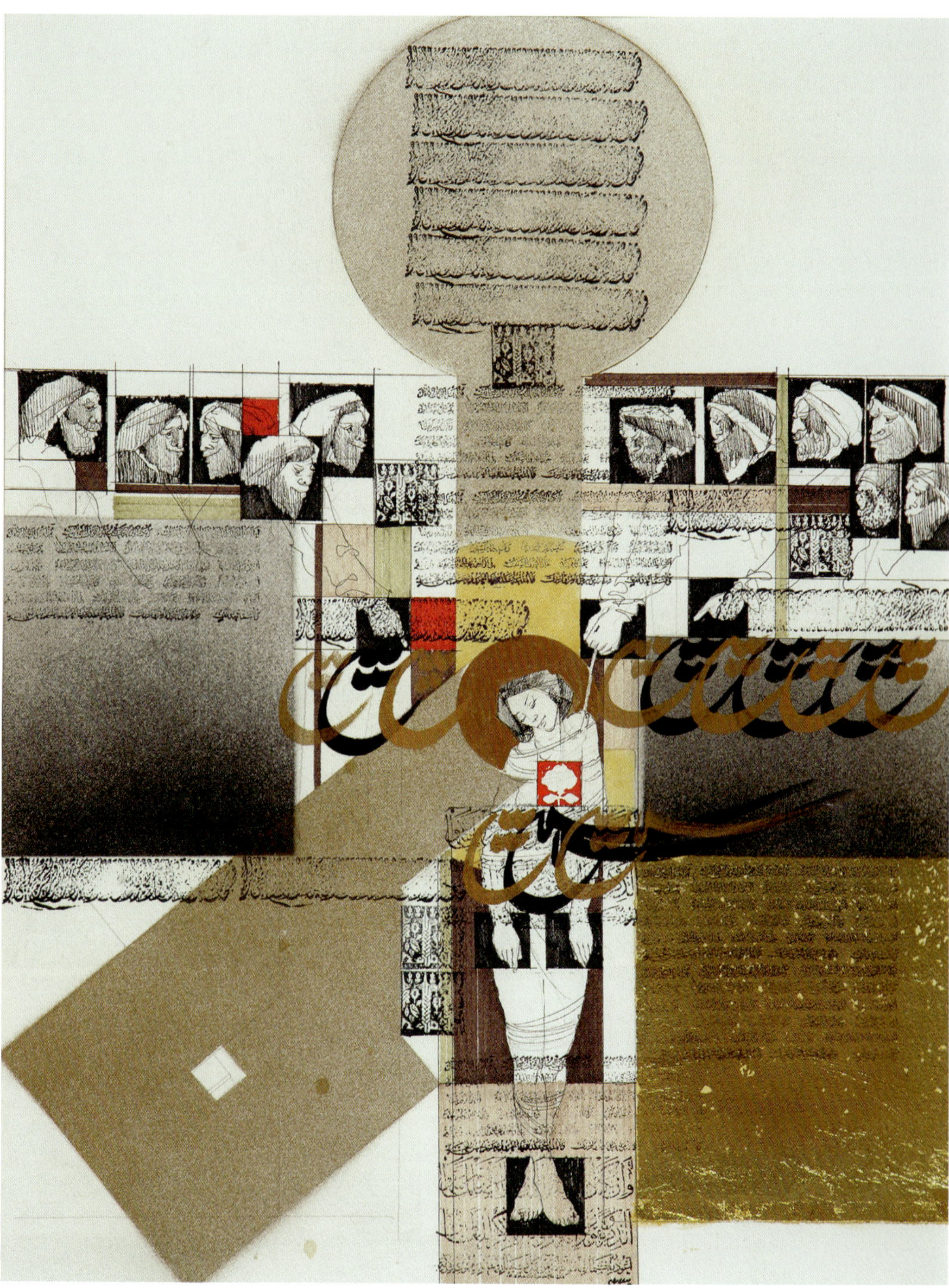

3.54
Faramarz Pilaram, *Yousef and Zuliykhah,* from the *Qur'anic Stories* series, 1977, ink, gold sheet and print on paper, 60×44 cm, TMoCA

I use calligraphy in a new abstract order whose purpose is quite different from the meaning of the words. [...] Here, there can be no judgment of my calligraphic words with regard to their correctness compared with the traditional standards of calligraphy, because this has not been of any interest to me. [91]

Pilaram continued his Letterist style later in 1975 when he participated in the foundation of the Independent Group of Painters and Sculptors (*Guruh-i azad-i naqqashan va piykareh-sazan*). Between 1976 and 1977, he created huge wooden sculptures while continuing to build on his previous experiences in letterism. It seems that his later works included an unfinished series of Qur'anic stories illustrations in 1978–79. In those paintings, Pilaram's utilisation of seals accompanied by geometrical space, which he had already used in 1974–75, re-emerged. Pilaram, who had used words as spontaneous elements based on traditional calligraphic forms, arrived at a reduction of calligraphic structure to the rhythm of the decorative shapes. (Figure 3.54)

Another *Saqqa-khaneh* artist who used elements of calligraphy as a main element in some of his canvases is Sadegh Tabrizi. A painter and ceramicist, Tabrizi graduated from the Tehran Faculty of Decorative Arts in 1967. He incorporates ornamental patterns, figures from the late Safavid period, texts, and stamps into his satirical paintings. Also, calligraphic elements with their essential forms were part of his paintings from his exhibitions of 1970–71.[92] In these neo-calligraphic works, Tabrizi avoids conveying any kind of readable message, emphasising instead the temporal quality of the calligraphic

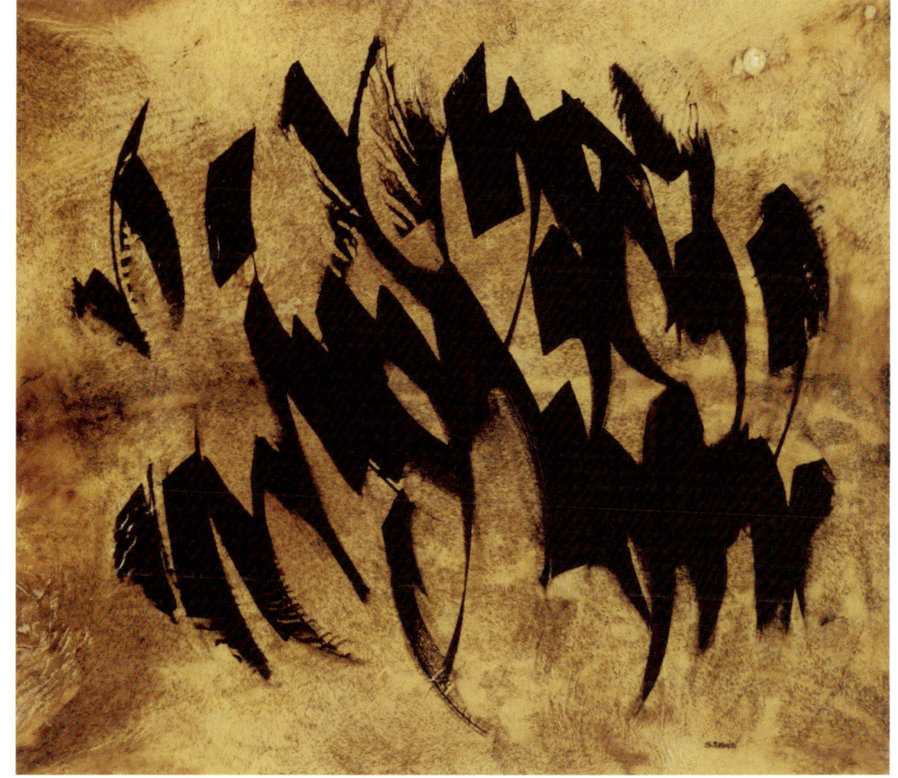

3.55
Sadegh Tabrizi, *Untitled*, ink on leather, 58×64 cm, TMoCA

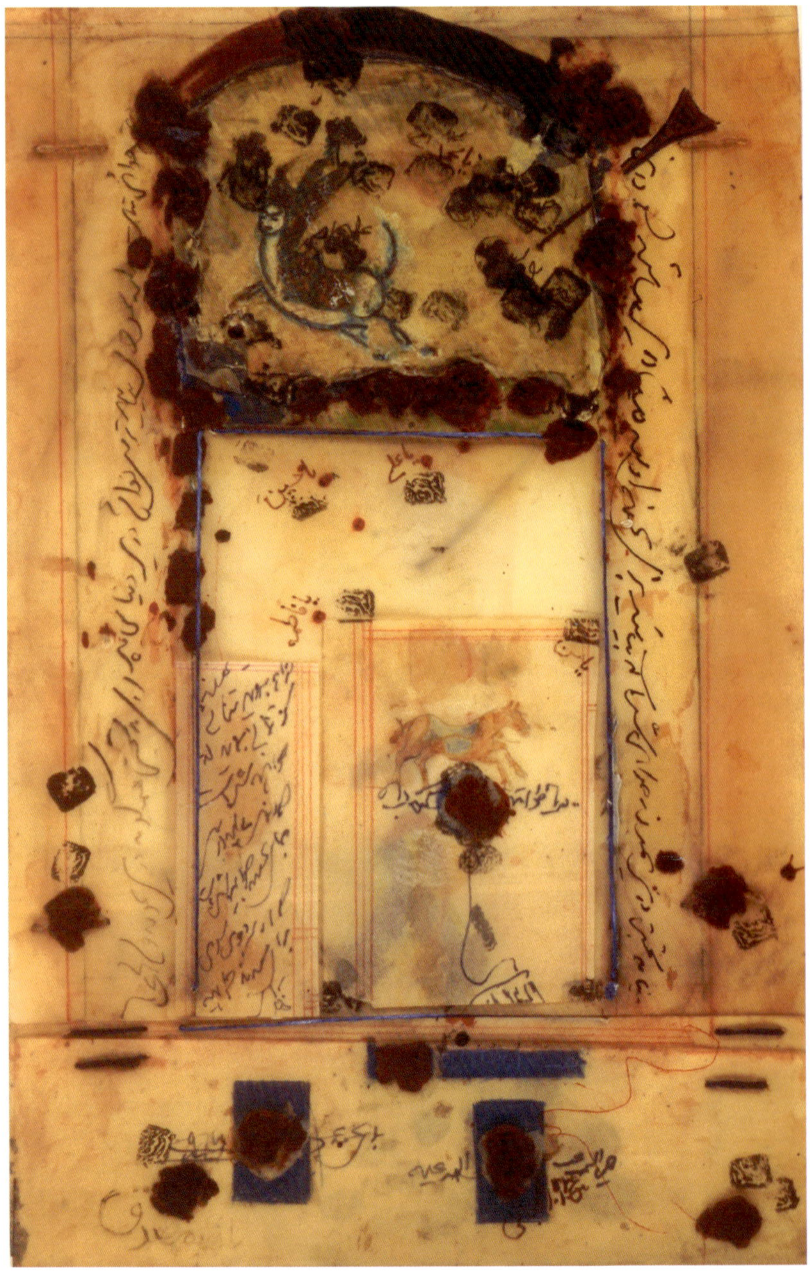

3.56
Siah Armajani, *The Way*, 1957,
45.72×29.2 cm, ink and mixed
media on paper, courtesy the artist

forms. (Figure 3.55) The contrast between black lines and forms on the ochre background, full and empty spaces which remind one of Chinese calligraphy, creates an expressionistic mood in his paintings. Having produced rhythmical and lyrical compositions using calligraphic elements, in particular during the 1970s and 1990s, he continued with this style in the latter part of his artistic career.

Although the works of Mansoureh Hosseini cannot simply be classified as Letterism or *Naqqashi-khatt*, her usage of calligraphic patterns is a dominant characteristic of her paintings. Hosseini, a graduate of the Faculty of Fine Arts, Tehran University and Rome's

Accademia di Belle Arti, had attempted to use forms of calligraphy in her paintings as early as 1959 (the *Saqqa-khaneh* was introduced in 1962). Indeed, according to Hosseini's words, she was not aware of the movement and its significant interest in and use of calligraphy. Her style developed while she was studying and working in Italy. She personally maintains that she was motivated by Professor Vantori, the Italian Cézanne expert and one of the eminent art critics in Italy at that time, who suggested that she employ the abstract motifs of calligraphy. This was when Vantori had recognised the similarity between her paintings and the calligraphic and arabesque-type elements.[93]

The abundance of paint soon prompted her transition from her earlier practices to an abstract expressionistic and subjective portrayal of emotional experiences. Subsequently, she drew inspiration from various forms of Arabic and Persian calligraphy, infusing her canvases with colourful forms and an expressionistic style. While her large, coloured, abstract paintings feature brushstrokes that defy readability and cannot be attributed to any specific calligraphic style, the dynamic, word-like forms they evoke align with a broader trend of calligraphic gestures. (Figure 3.57)

3.57
Mansoureh Hosseini, *Untitled*, 1960s, oil on canvas, 70×200 cm, TMoCA

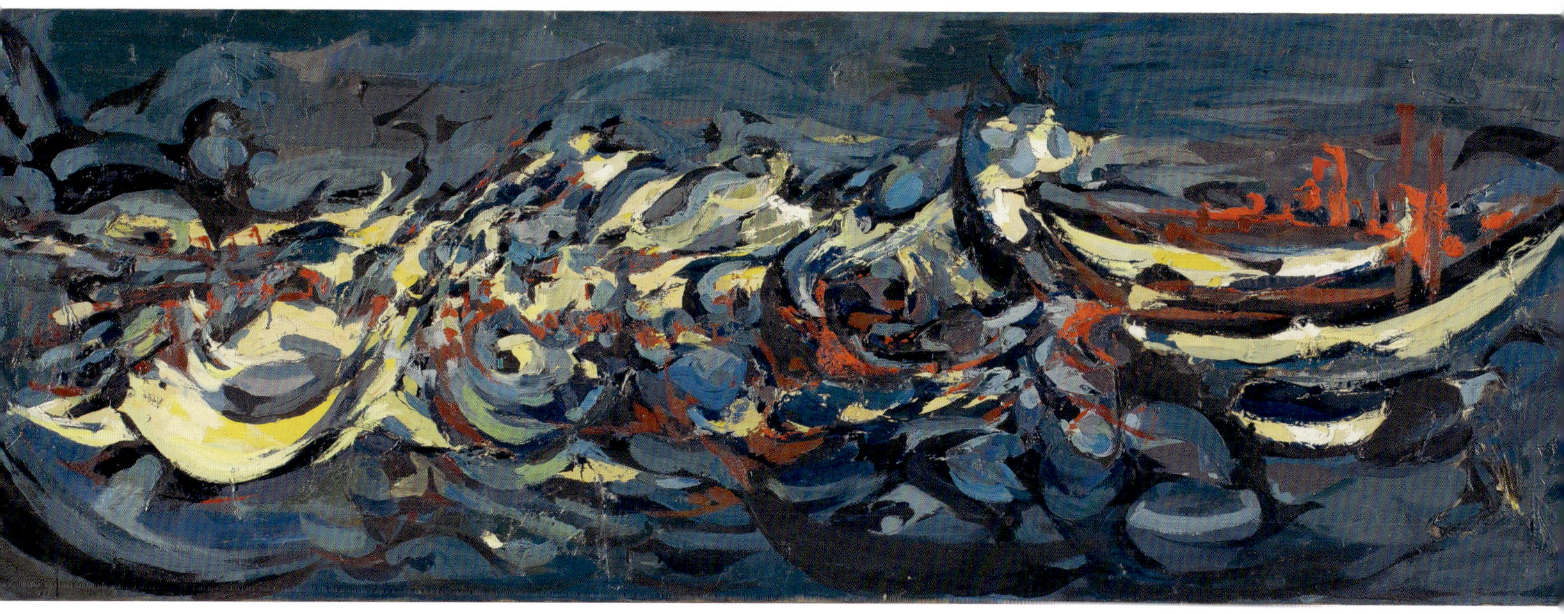

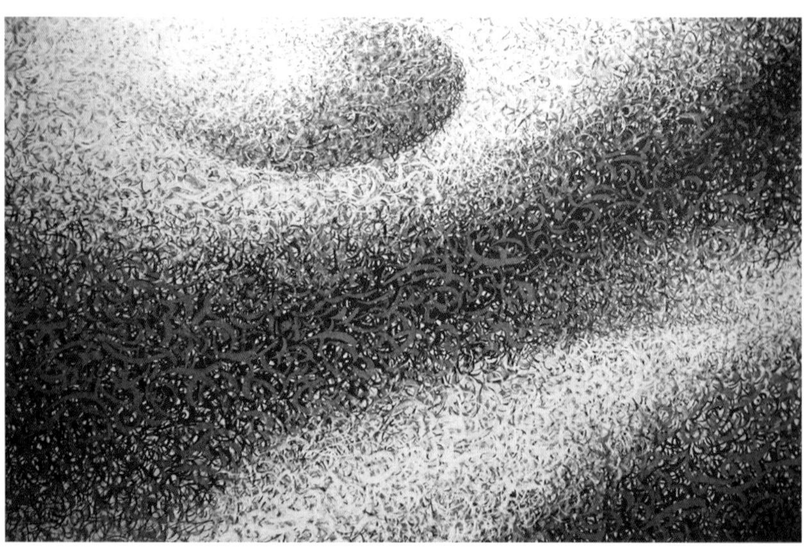

3.58
Gholamhossein Nami, *The Milky Way (1)*, 1977, oil on canvas, 100×150 cm, courtesy the artist

As mentioned earlier, while the *Saqqa-khaneh* movement's popularity was at its peak, more artists started to practise calligraphic idioms. A modernist artist who was mainly famous for his three-dimensional abstract works inspired by old Iranian gravestones, Gholamhossein Nami created works using patterns from calligraphy in his series of works in the 1970s. Highlighting the rhythm and motion in two-dimensional canvases, he was more concerned with the formal characteristics of letters and scripts than any specific literary meaning of those patterns. The spontaneous movements of these patterns on his canvases simply reincarnate familiar signs and calligraphic forms. (Figure 3.58)

Unlike the aforementioned artists, the artists of *Naqqashi-khatt*, who were mainly professional calligraphers, considered the traditional content to be a crucial component of their art. As a result, the dominant characteristic of their images has been their dependence on the standard rules of calligraphic form, its anatomical principles, as well as the communication with meaning. Having religious, literary or narrative concepts, their works mostly represent readable and meaningful words, including religious or poetic verses.

Mohammad Ehsai stands as a major member of the *Naqqashi-khatt* tendency and also as one of the pioneers of this trend in the late 1960s. A professional calligrapher, Ehsai attended Free Classes of Iranian Calligraphers in 1958 and then graduated from the Faculty of Fine Arts, Tehran University. He believes that in his neo-calligraphic style the pure usage of calligraphy, and its anatomy and atmosphere, is quite different from that of the *Saqqa-khaneh* in which calligraphy was used in painting simply as a form. Even though Ehsai denies any direct connection between his works and those of the *Saqqa-khaneh* artists, his use of calligraphy in new styles dominant at that time (1960s), and originally used by *Saqqa-khaneh*, cannot be disguised. His works, like those of his fellow *Naqqashi-khatt* artists, were appreciated in formal exhibitions; they were awarded a medal in the 1974 National Exhibition of Iranian art. He acknowledges that, in the years between 1959 and 1960, he met the sculptor Parviz Tanavoli, when they were working together at an institution in Tehran; and it was Tanavoli who encouraged him to utilise the capacity of calligraphy in new shapes. It was in 1967 that his first *Naqqashi-khatt* came into existence. Ehsai also admits that he was completely aware of the popularity of *Saqqa-khaneh* and its artists' achievements in terms of their neo-traditionalist approach. Hence, despite his status as a pioneer of the *Naqqashi-khatt* trend and his lack of involvement in the *Saqqa-khaneh* movement, the influence of the movement's artistic approach has undeniably shaped his emerging interest in neo-calligraphy.

Using the pure structure of traditional calligraphic forms in his canvases, an artist with firm religious beliefs, Ehsai has achieved an aesthetic synthesis between traditional calligraphy and the graphics of letters. In his works, the ability to modify the form of the script has been employed so that he can create his innovative visual settings. In his early works, he broke the traditional discipline of the 'written word'. He tore the words into pieces and reconstructed them into various combinations. In these canvases, he mainly used colour as a background and black for his letters, which echoes traditional uses of colouration. (Figure 3.59) His compositions of brown, green, black and white resembled the designs of classical architecture, where a single letter had the importance of a main foundation column and could not be displaced. In some of these paintings, executed over many years (1968–2000s), the artist has created three-dimensional forms with scripts and monochromatic scales. The stiletto-like forms of the *Thuluth* and *Muhaqqaq* scripts have been arranged in a systematic order that generates the overall structure of the paintings. (Figure 3.60)

In terms of subject matter, Ehsai is mostly inspired by classical Persian poetry and also contents based on Qur'anic verses and *Hadith*, especially in his works created in the post-revolutionary period. For him, just as for his calligrapher ancestors, the content of the writing is significant, but he does not try to make the meanings of his *Naqqashi-khatt* clear by using recognisably distinctive words or verses. According to him, in his works, he uses the forms of letters and the narratives, signifying the composition of letters in Iranian culture, as a means of expression.[94] For Ehsai, although there are similarities between abstract art and *tajrıdi* (stylised) art in Muslim artists' work in their non-representational characteristics of objective realities, there are important differences between them in terms of the artist's perception. He quotes a twelfth-century source, *Maqamat-i Hamidi* as: a real person is one who does not expect anything in his departure from this world, but his goal must be to approach the omnipotent.[95] He deems that if there is a definite and intrinsic relationship between calligraphy's etiquette and holy culture, the artist's education and mentality must develop within this context in order to be able to create an authentic work. From his viewpoint, when a work *Naqqashi-khatt* is authentic and meritorious, it has an affiliation with its origin which is unchangeable.[96]

In his poetic representations, black and white are two separate parts of a narration, leading the viewers to a conceptual, pure and magic world of the letter. He believes that, because these works are inspired by a kind of 'holy art' (i.e. calligraphy), they originally represent the supernal *Kalam*.[97] This unique characteristic, common to all of Ehsai's *Naqqashi-khatt*s during different periods, suggests his deep respect for traditional calligraphy and at the same time his continuous attempt to innovate within the genre of neo-calligraphy.

3.59
Mohammad Ehsai, *Untitled*, 1977,
oil on canvas, 50×110 cm, private
collection, Tehran

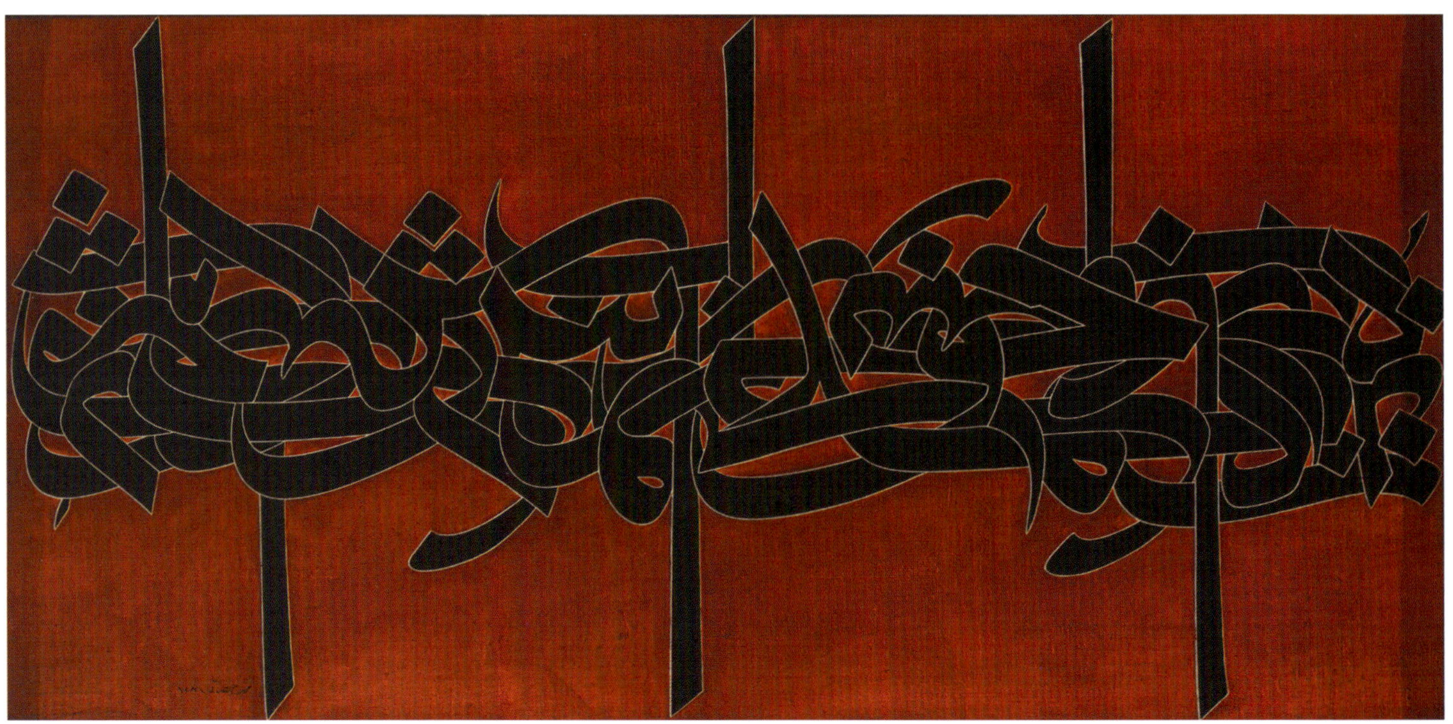

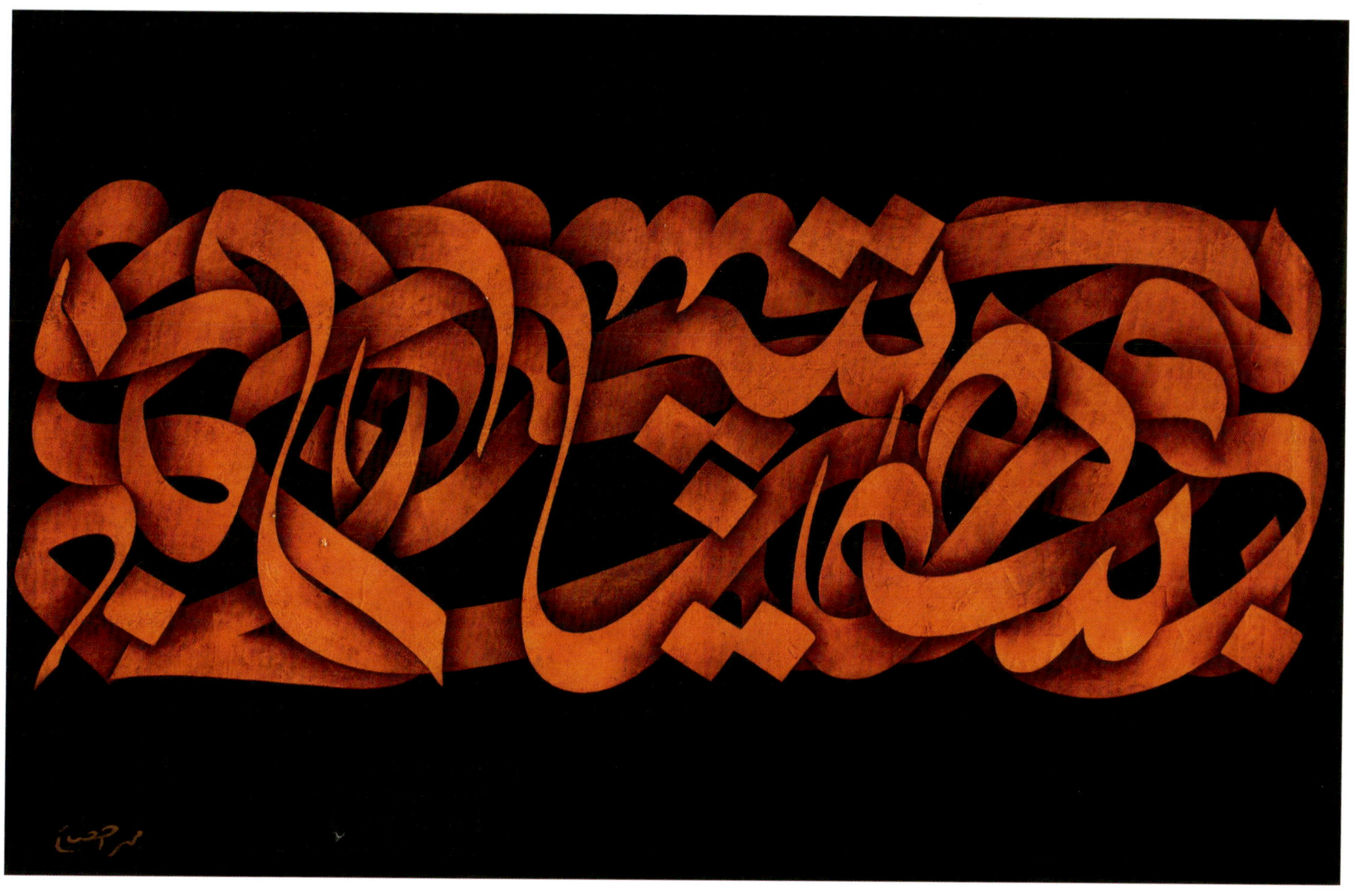

3.60
Mohammad Ehsai, *Untitled*, 1977, oil on canvas, 50×100 cm, private collection, Tehran

Ehsai was close friends with Reza Mafi, another leading member of the *Naqqashi-khatt* trend. They had a shared ideology when it came to their works. Mafi had finished a course at the Society of Iranian Calligraphers in 1968–69 when he began his major *Naqqashi-khatt* experiences. But his initial *Naqqashi-khatt* works date from slightly earlier, in 1966, while he was still studying at the Society. He continued his career with monochromic *Siyah-mashq* paintings in the early 1970s, but soon changed his style. While his initial attempts were comparable to some of the famous *Siyah-mashq*s of the traditional masters of the *Nastaliq* script, these works differed from those original calligraphies in the different size of letters and in his rhythmic composition. (Figure 3.61) The pictorial standards of the elements (calligraphic letters) and their compositional function were more important than calligraphic skill. This tendency further increases in his later works. Towards the end of his life, he used elegant brown and beige curves with great freedom of expression. (Figures 3.62–63)

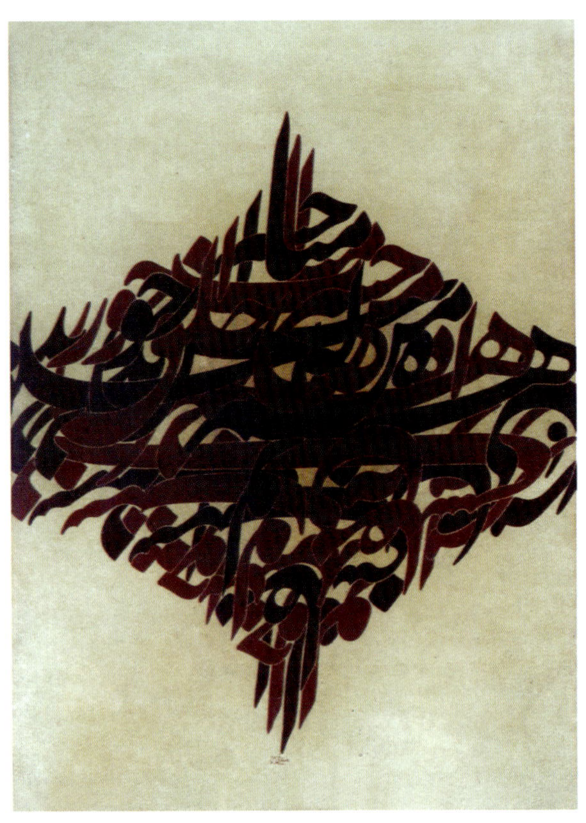

Above
3.61
Reza Mafi, *Untitled*, 1973, gouache
on paper, 61×44 cm, private
collection, Tehran

Right
3.62
Reza Mafi, *Untitled*, 1975, oil on
canvas, 50×70 cm, TMoCA

As a neo-calligraphist, Mafi brought a fresh attitude to the aesthetics of traditional handwriting during his professional career. In the latter years of his life, Mafi also created a series of monochrome *Naqqashi-khatt*s inspired by the poems of the famous Iranian modernist poet and painter, Sohrab Sepehri. Ruin Pakbaz remarks that his last work was made on his deathbed and explicitly illustrates the extent of his minimalist style.[98]

Nasrollah Afjei is another professional calligrapher who finished the Free Classes of Iranian Calligraphers course in 1963–4, but he later followed the trend of *Naqqashi-khatt*. The *Saqqa-khaneh* movement and related tendencies had a clear influence on Afjei too. According to his own interpretation, the atmosphere of those flourishing years of artistic activity during the 1960s, and the presence of each of the *Saqqa-khaneh* pioneers who were trying to benefit creatively from the traditional sources, were the main reason for the emergence of the *Naqqashi-khatt* movement.[99]

He asserts that the role of calligraphy in *Naqqashi-khatt* does not undermine the genuine reverence for calligraphic conventions and their roots. Afjei, being a professional calligrapher, holds this belief out of his deep respect for traditional calligraphy. Consequently, he has refrained from adopting the aesthetic standards of abstract imagery, as doing so would have contradicted calligraphic conventions.

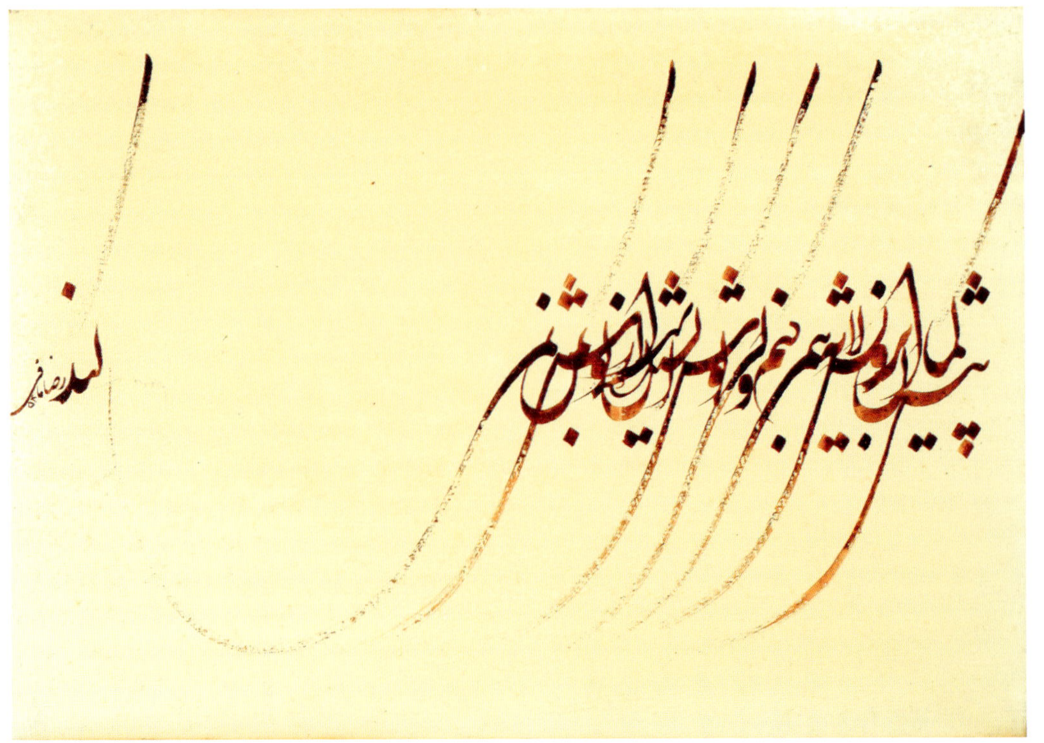

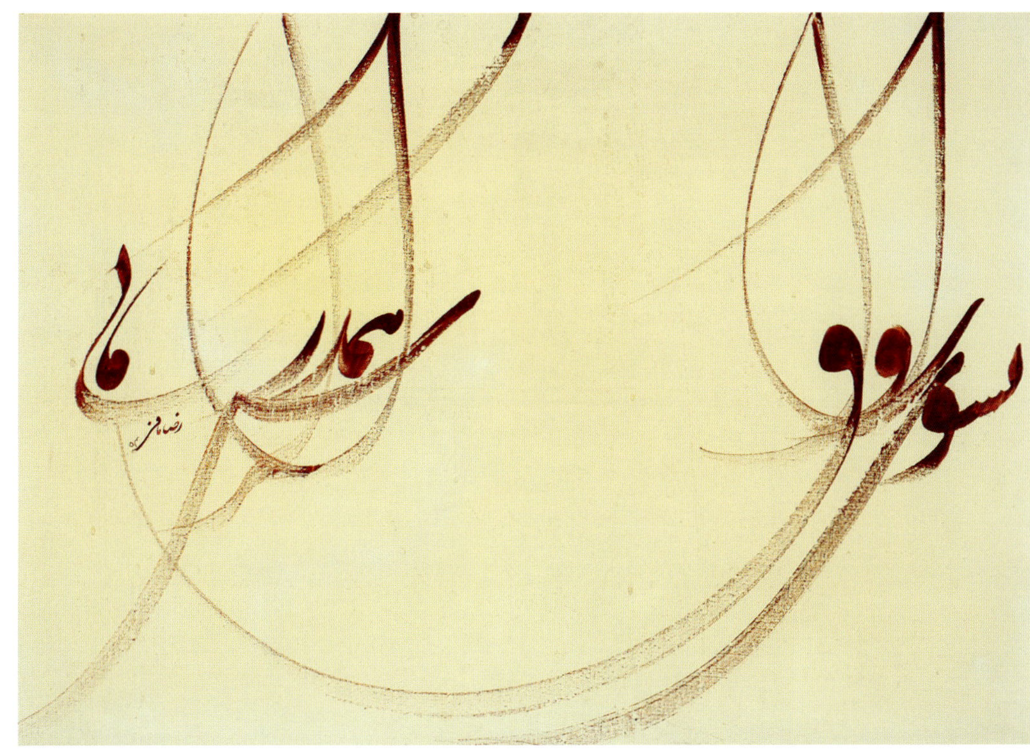

3.63
Reza Mafi, *Untitled*, 1975, oil on canvas, 60×85 cm, TMoCA

Afjei has used a variety of forms with diverse types of script including *Kufic*, *Mu'aqili*, *Thuluth*, *Nastaliq* and *Shikasteh*, in which the meaningful literary and religious content is the common feature. He began his *Naqqashi-khatt*s in 1972 with repetitive signature-like calligraphic writing shaped by rapid actions of the hand. In those works he followed the calligraphic style to produce rhythmical forms using the letters of the alphabet. Later, in 1973–6, he used the *Mu'aqili Kufic* and *Thuluth* scripts. (Figures 3.64–65) Regarding his reference to the traditional forms of calligraphic forms, Afjei states:

I was greatly influenced by Islamic architecture. I discovered that an Islamic structure lacked identity until adorned with calligraphy and decoration. It is through these inscriptions and embellishments that these buildings truly come to life. I was enamoured by these motifs and inscriptions; they shimmered like precious gems, gleaming in the sunlight for centuries, akin to flowers blossoming in the desert. Driven by these convictions, I made the decision to incorporate unique sources such as the *Mu'aqili* (*Banai*) script in my works.[100]

3.64
Nasrollah Afjei, *White Background*,
1975, oil on canvas, 63.5×63.5
cm, TMoCA

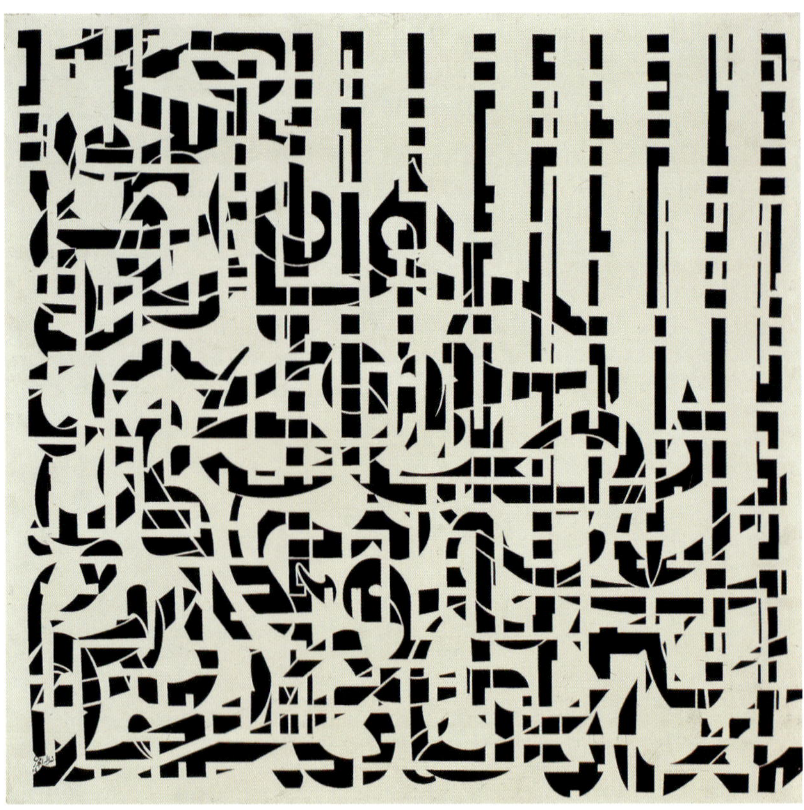

His play on the forms of classical calligraphy reminds us of the merging of the literary and the decorative function in the art, architecture and writing of Iranian-Islamic culture; and also of the narrative and formal quality of the decorated letter in medieval manuscripts, invariably the precursor to a verbal text.

After the use of precise principles of classical calligraphy, in his *Naqqashi-khatt*s, Afjei turned to construct illusionary perspectives in his canvases with a gradual change of calligraphic forms from thick to thin lines and vice versa. In some of his galaxy-like compositions, presented in the 1990s, the most important part of a Qur'anic or poetic verse was emphasised by increasing the size of the calligraphy, which was surrounded by countless tiny words. (Figure 3.66) The whole compositional atmosphere of these canvases was imbued with a constellation-like space.

Neo-calligraphy was continued as a popular genre by its pioneers and also by the newcomers in modern and contemporary Iranian art, as can be seen elsewhere in the Middle East.[101] Various approaches and forms have been created since the initial practices discussed above. Further developments in the post-revolutionary period will be discussed in the next chapter.

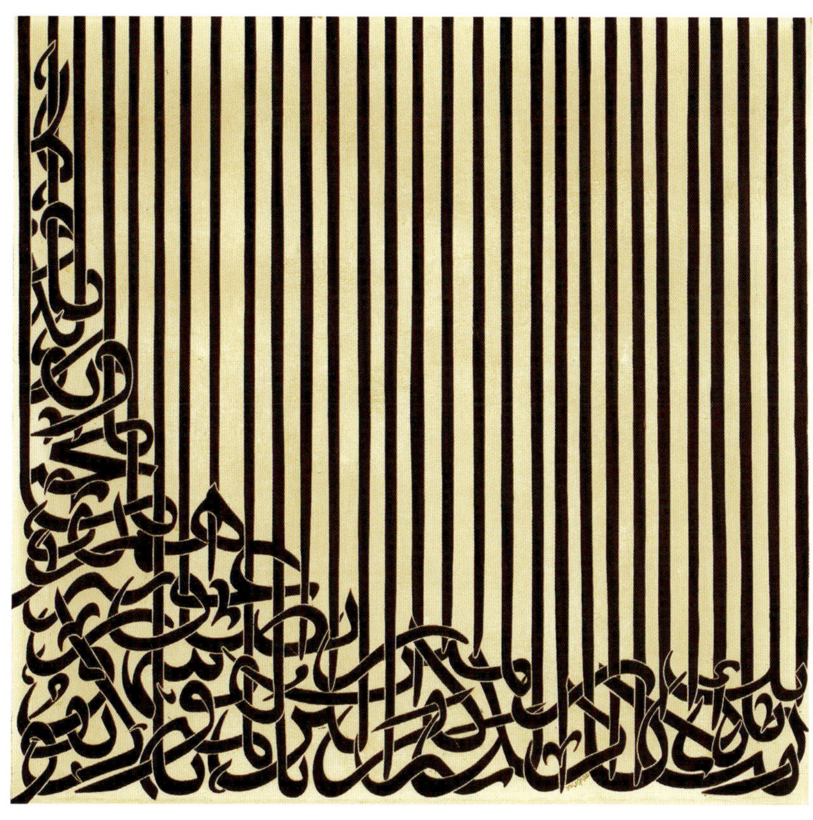

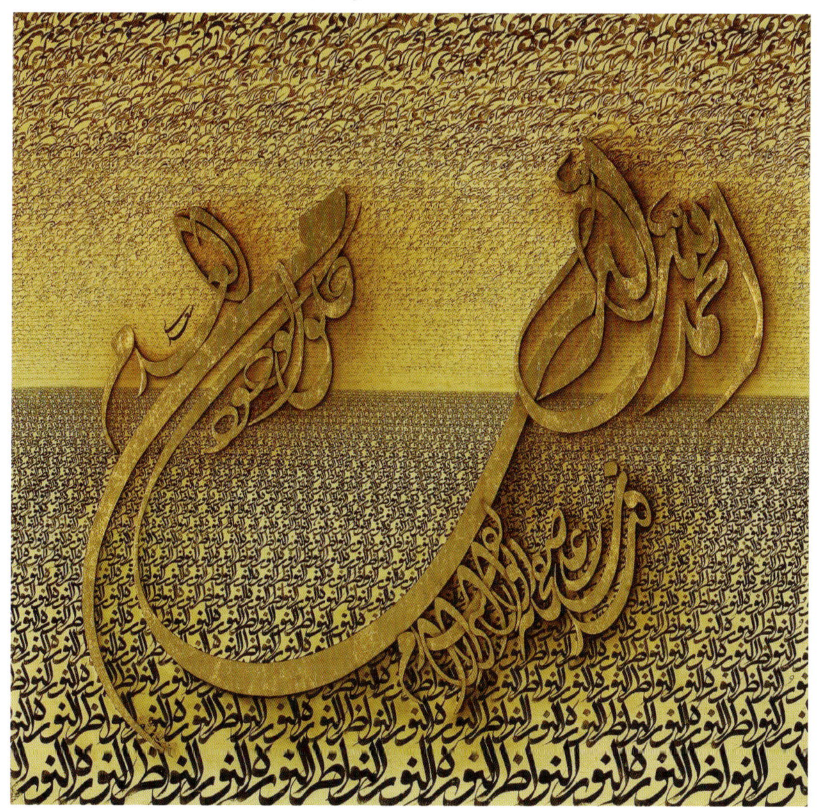

3.65
Nasrollah Afjei, *Untitled*, 1973, oil on canvas, 62×62 cm, TMoCA

3.66
Nasrollah Afjei, *First Majlis of Sa'di*, 1993, oil on canvas, 125×125 cm, TMoCA

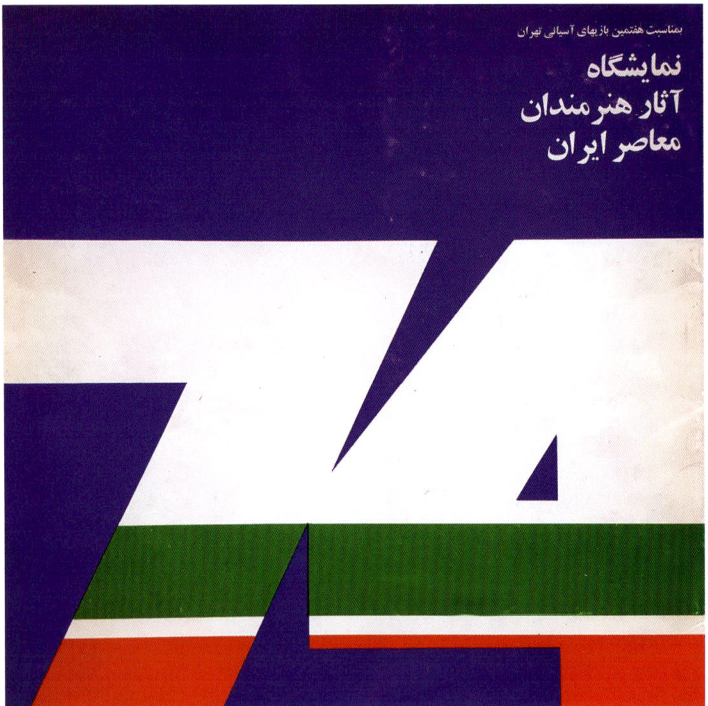
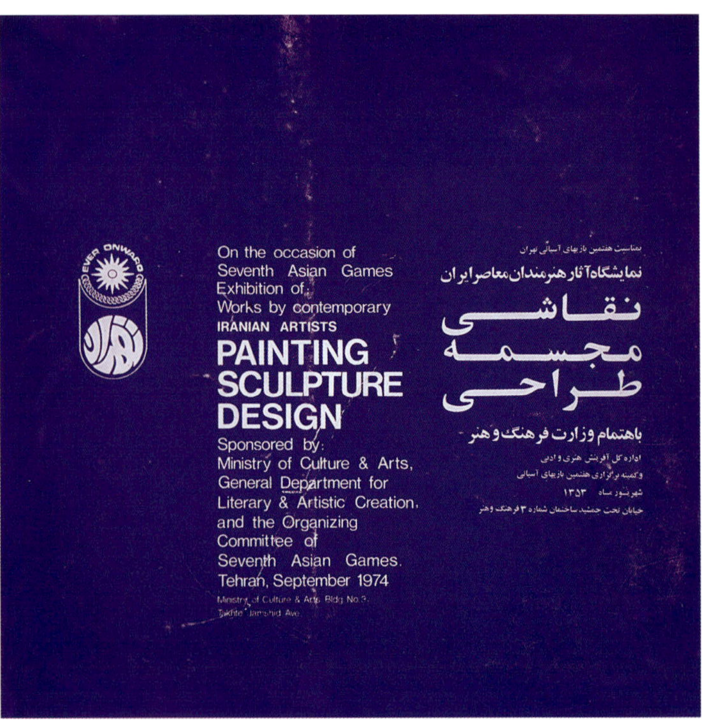

3.67
Cover of the catalogue for the
exhibition of contemporary Iranian
art on the occasion of the Seventh
Asian Games in 1974

2.2. Development of Various Modern Movements in the
1970s

We have seen how, after the mid-1960s, the Iranian art scene witnessed
the increasing development of art patronage. Also increasing was the
number of art activities and events (such as art festivals and biennials).
Like modern Persian poetry, modern art was generally considered an
urban art and limited to the middle classes. But in contrast to modern
poetry, art benefited from extensive state support. With the economic
boom in the 1960s, gradually, many government institutions and
private companies became patrons of modern art. Others, including
ministries, National Iranian Radio Television, banks, corporations
led by the Behshahr Industrial group, the Ladjevardi Foundation,
and the Prime Minister, Amir Abbas Hoveyda, were all effectively
patronising the visual arts and became the major supporters and
patrons of modern art. At the same time there were some foreign
cultural institutes and collectors of which the most important was the
American collector Abby Grey, who patronised modern Iranian art.

Public organisations such as the Iranian National Radio and
Television, together with daily newspapers and magazines, devoted
a considerable portion of their regular contents to art news and
sometimes criticism – an unprecedented development.

Against this backdrop, during the 1970s Iranian modern art reached a new peak. Grand cultural and artistic venues, festivals and exhibitions were established. Together with the development of the art market, spurred on mainly by the government but also by the private sector, all this injected a new lease of life into the cultural scene. National and international exhibitions were held in Tehran, including the exhibition of contemporary Iranian art on the occasion of the Seventh Asian Games in 1974, and the First International Art Fair in 1977, which presented contemporary European galleries. (Figure 3.67) The Cyrus Gallery in Paris actively exhibited works of Iranian artists. The participation of Iranian artists in other exhibitions in Europe and America, including Art Basel in Switzerland, was organised by the official cultural sections such as the Office of Empress Farah Pahlavi[102] n and the Ministry of Culture and Art.

Mainly through Queen Farah and her Office's patronage, many organisations were created and fostered to further the state's ambition of bringing historical and contemporary Iranian art to prominence both inside Iran and in the West. Along with her own efforts, she sought to achieve this goal with the assistance of various foundations and experts. Perhaps one of her most recognised endeavours to support the arts was her patronage of the Shiraz Arts Festival. This was held annually from 1967 until 1977 and featured performances and exhibitions by both Iranian and western artists. After the Tehran Biennial stopped in 1966, the Shiraz Arts Festival served as a form of replacement. This festival presented various art forms, including music, ballet, theatre, and the visual arts, although the latter was exhibited on a much smaller scale compared to the biennial. It was stated that the purpose of the Festival was to introduce Iran's culture and art; to encourage the people to extend and develop art and culture that could enforce national unity; and to familiarise them with international cultural values.[103]

This decade saw, in particular, the foundation of two cultural venues that would prove to be the key players in contemporary Iranian art. Both were established under the umbrella of the Farah Pahlavi Foundation and planned by the eminent architect Kamran Diba (b.1937), who was himself an artist and collector. Under the direction of Diba, the Tehran Museum of Contemporary Art was inaugurated in 1977 and quickly initiated a new phase of modern and contemporary Iranian art. (Figure 3.68) Its great collection (both in quality and quantity) combined important Western modern and contemporary art (from the late nineteenth century up to the 1970s) and major modern Iranian art. Using funds allocated from the government, the state took

3.68
Tehran Museum of Contemporary Art, view from the courtyard

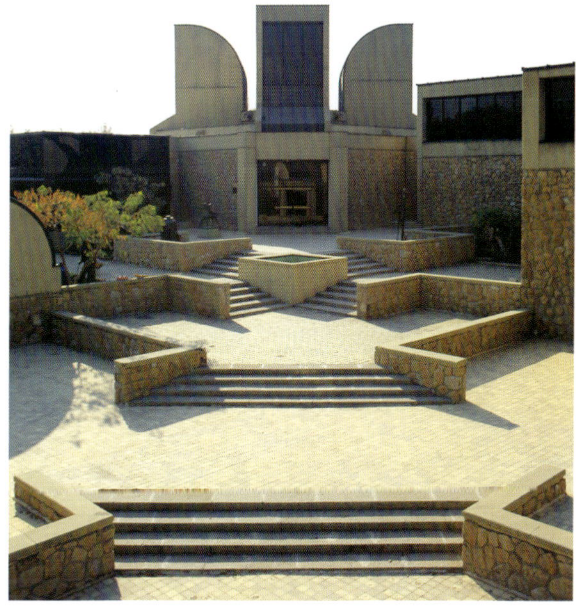

advantage of the somewhat depressed art market of the 1970s to buy a number of works by significant western artists. Under Kamran Diba's supervision, the Museum acquired nearly 150 great works by such prominent artists as Pablo Picasso, Georges Braque, George Grosz, Andy Warhol, Jackson Pollock and Roy Lichtenstein.[104] This period also saw the opening of the other major venue, the Niavaran Cultural Centre. A key role in its establishment was taken by Firooz Shirvanloo (1938–88), a scholar and translator who together with Lily Amir-Arjomand (b. 1938) had in 1965 supervised the founding of the Institute for Intellectual Development of Children and Young Adults (*Kanoon-i parvarish-i fikri-i kudakan va nowjavanan*) – another groundbreaking project under the Foundation. He was then Cultural Advisor to the Office of Empress Farah Pahlavi.

3.69
Ahmad Aali, *Self-portrait*, 1964,
mixed media, 214×76.8×61.6 cm,
courtesy the artist

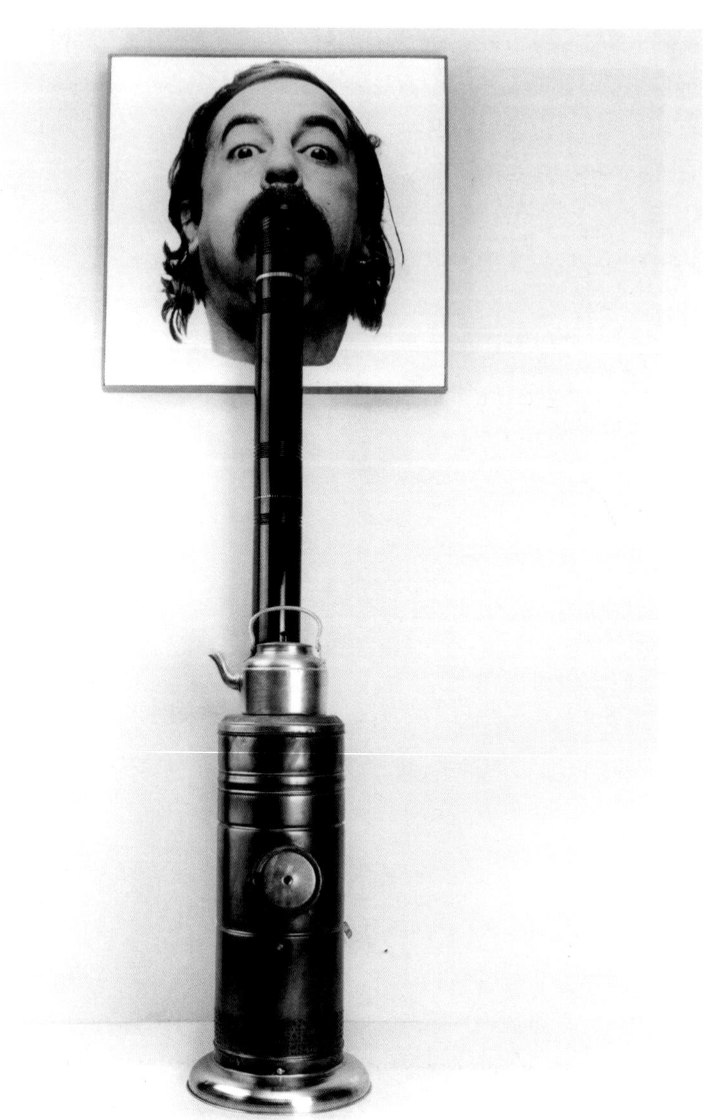

Iranian art in the 1970s was pluralistic, with the dominance of modernism and gradually contemporary art approaches. The decade saw a growth in the number of artists and groups rather than singular movements. A variety of modern approaches and styles emerged, highly affected by Euro-American contemporary art movements. Having a close relationship in terms of artistic exchanges and the presence of European and American artistic interests, Iranian art was rapidly informed by the most up-to-date currents across the international art scene. Such contemporary Western movements as Conceptual Art could be discerned in the Iranian art scene. (Figure 3.69) Artistic groups were shaped; many were short lived but a few continued for longer.

Founded in 1974, perhaps the most active and influential group of artists was the Independent Group of Painters and Sculptors (*Guruh-i azad-i naqqashan va mujassama-sazan*). It consisted of avant-garde artists of the time including Marcos Grigorian, Massoud Arabshahi, Gholamhossein Nami, Mir Abdolreza Daryabegi (1930–2012), Sirak Melkonian, Morteza Momayyez (1935–2005) and Faramarz Pilaram. This group was especially active in organising groundbreaking exhibitions, including the first examples of conceptual art, installations and performances in Iran, but its activities came to an abrupt end with the 1979 Islamic Revolution. (Figures 3.70–72)

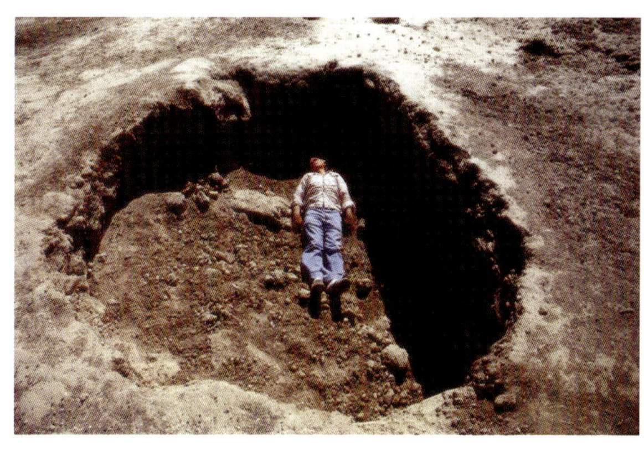

3.70
Marcos Grigorian, *A Place to Rest*, 1977, photo from the artist's performance

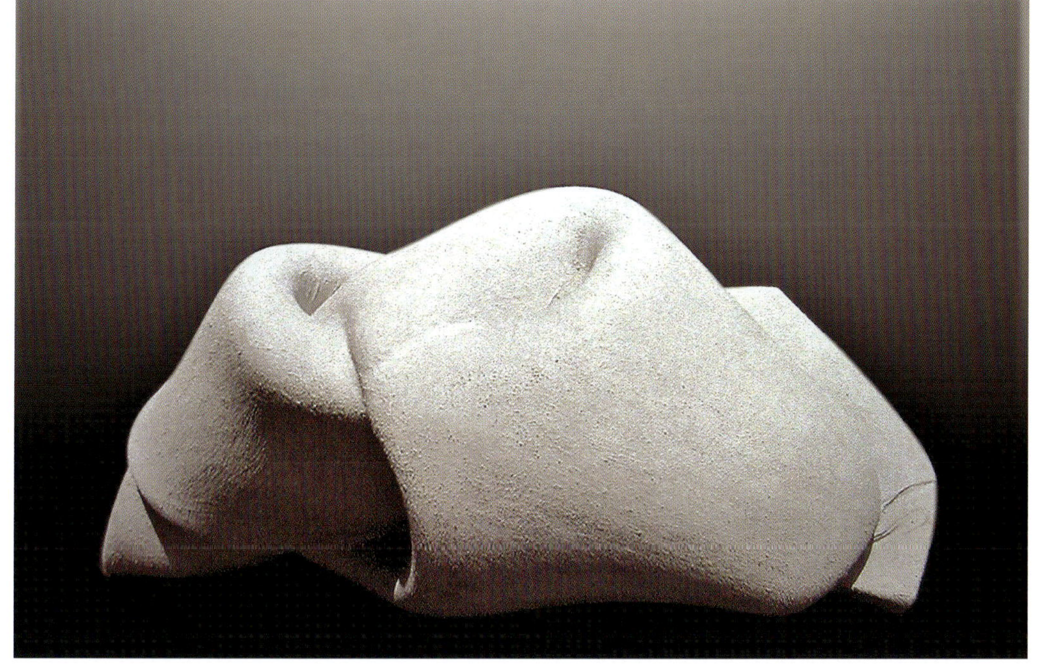

3.71
Gholamhossein Nami, *The Knot*, 1976, 280×100×100 cm, courtesy the artist

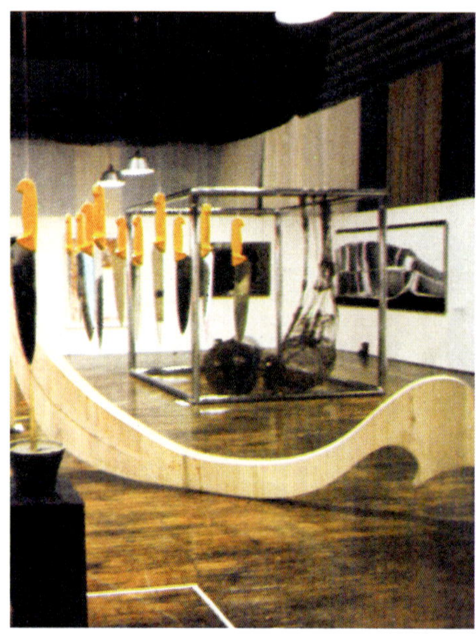

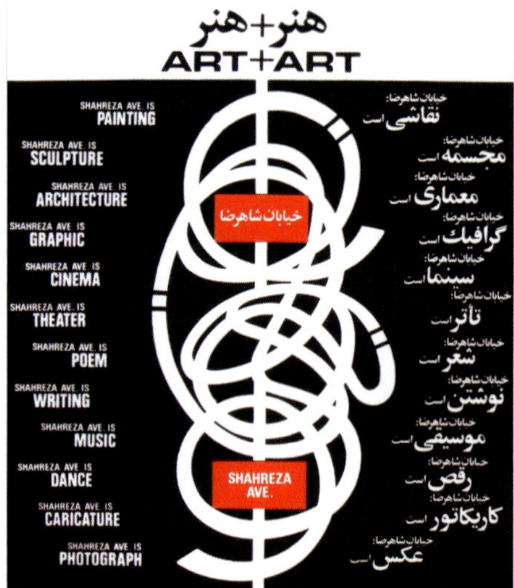

3.72
Morteza Momayyez, *Knife*
installation, 1977, Wash Art art fair,
Washington DC

3.73
Koorosh Shishegaran, *Art+Art,*
Shahreza is Art, 1977, silk screen
print on paper, 80×60 cm

In this context, artists such as Koorosh Shishegaran, a graduate of the Tehran Faculty of Decorative Arts, clearly used conceptual approaches in his works and garnered relative attention from the art community and publications. After his initial projects in the years 1973–75 including *Reproduction Art* and *Art of Appropriation,* where he explored the notions of reproduction and the authenticity of artistic work, making it accessible to the general public in some way, Shishegaran turned his attention to unconventional forms of artistic practices and reproduction that reflected clear influences from prevalent discourses in contemporary Euro-American art. Furthermore, in projects like *For Peace in Lebanon* (1976) and *Art+Art* (Koorosh Shishegaran Works: The Shahreza Street Itself) (1977), Shishegaran distinctly adopted an anti-establishment approach while also questioning the materiality of artwork – a stance that resonated with the prevailing paradigms of contemporary art in the 1970s Euro-American scene. (Figure 3.73)

In addition to these instances, the diverse art scene in Iran witnessed the continued innovation and presentation of works by established artists such as Sohrab Sepehri, Abolghassem Saidi, Behman Mohasses (1931–2010) and Mohsen Vaziri Moghaddam. Sepehri, who had established his artistic presence in the 1950s and 1960s, also experienced notable works in this decade, inspired by the aesthetic beauty of his favourite art, the Far East (especially Japan), combined with a modernist perspective – a crucial period in his artistic career and unique examples in the context of modern Iranian art. His series of tree trunks, stones, and landscapes around Kashan constitute some of the most significant works of this period. These examples are characterised by the depiction of contrasting filled and empty spaces, semi-figurative forms arranged within abstract compositions, all rendered in subdued tones. Sepehri's distinctive colour palette lacks strong contrasts, often featuring very subtle and neutral colours next to each other. In these paintings, much like his poetry, Sepehri demonstrates a simple serene in his compositions aimed at guiding the viewer's mind towards the world of lyrical beauty and spiritual contemplation. (Figures 3.74–75)

Abolghassem Saidi began his activity as a prolific artist in the 1950s. In ways that harmonise with Sepeheri's artistic mood, Saidi's art embodies the concept of immortality and presents an optimistic worldview. Despite residing and working in Paris, Saidi remained an active figure in the Iranian art scene. His works consistently feature colourful abstract elements intertwined with figurative forms, such as

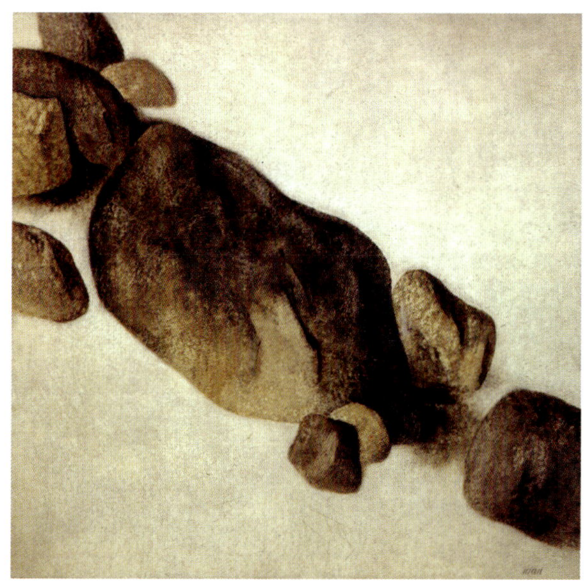

3.74
Sohrab Sepehri, *Stones*, early 1970s,
oil on canvas, 200×200 cm, TMoCA

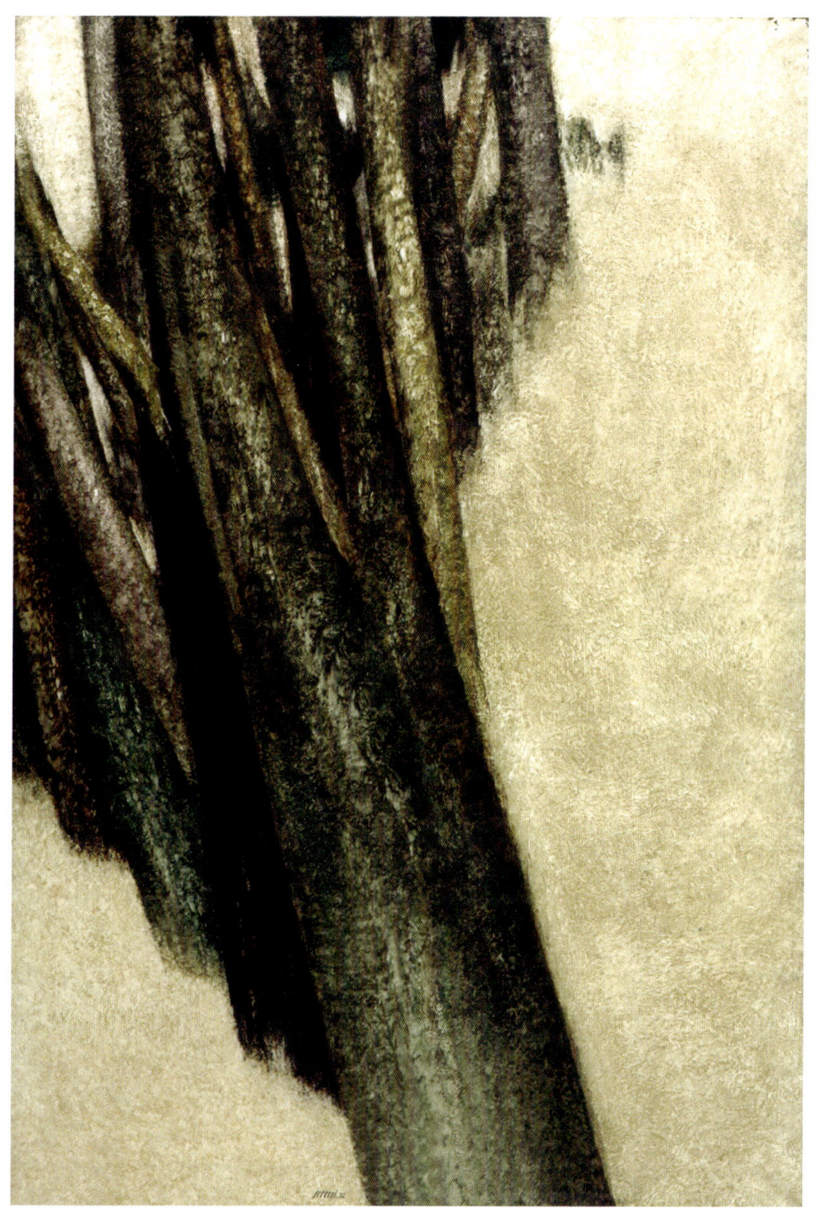

3.75
Sohrab Sepehri, *Untitled* (from the
Trees-Trunks series), 1972, oil on
canvas, 179×120 cm, TMoCA

trees or still life, imbued with poetic sensibility. Like Sepehri, Saidi shares a deep affinity for nature, often portraying dense and abundant trees or, in later periods, still-life subjects, within his abstract compositions, exhibiting a matured personal style. (Figures 3.76–77) His peaceful and symmetrical landscapes, adorned with mild colours, evoke a timeless sense of immortality.

3.76
Abolghassem Saidi, *Trees*, 1975, oil on cardboard, 99×70 cm, TMoCA

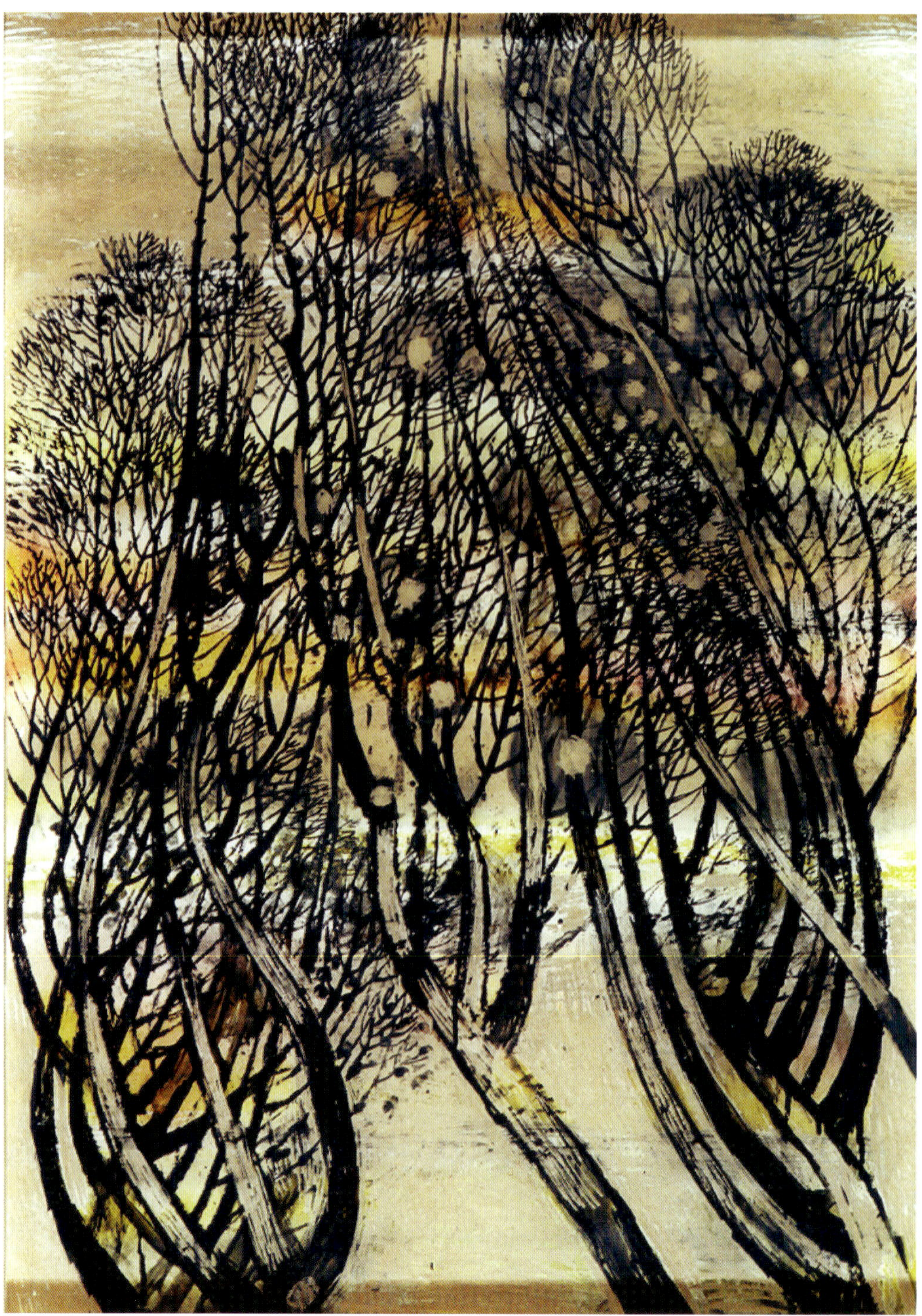

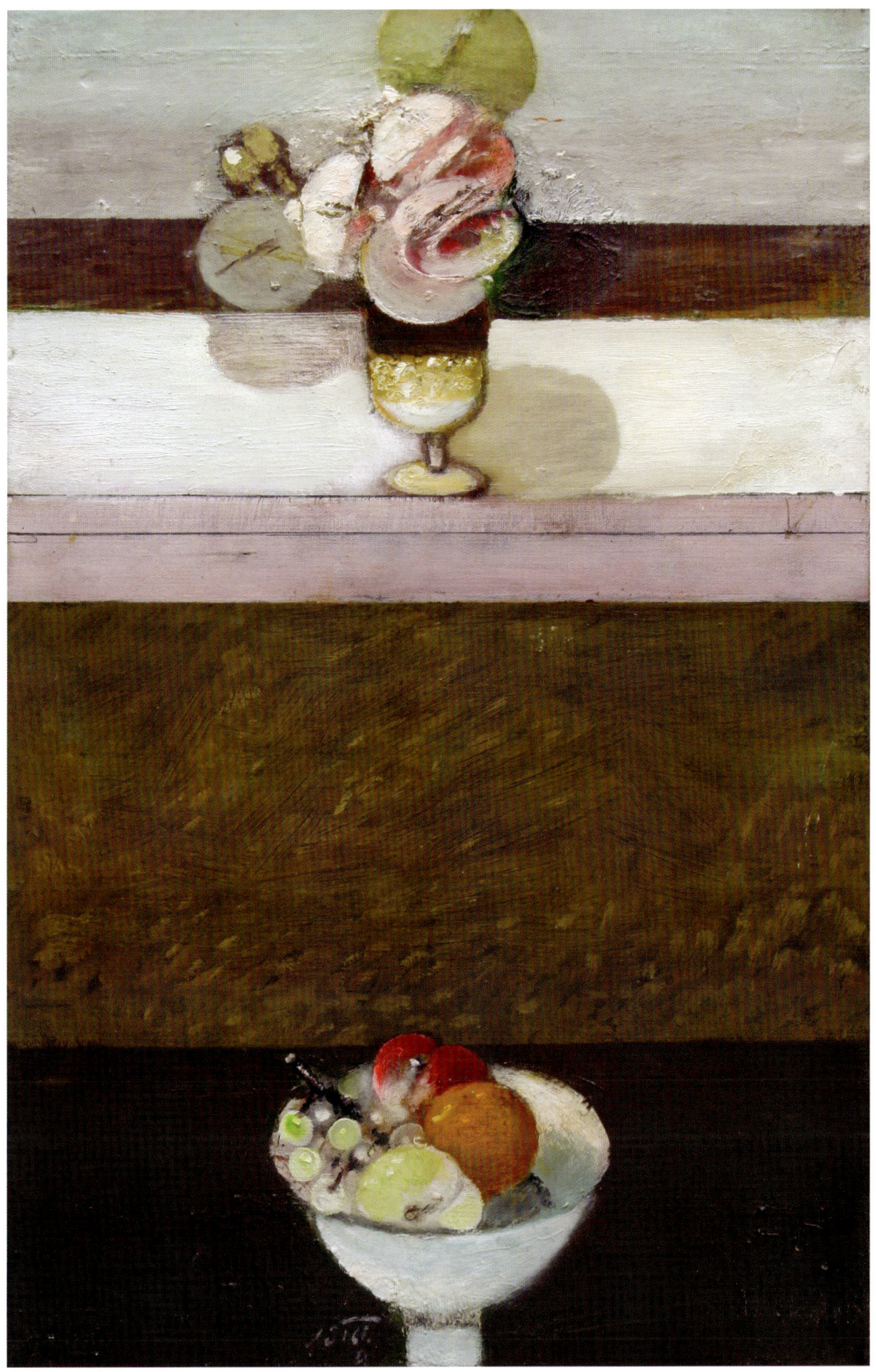

3.77
Abolghassem Saidi, *Untitled*, c. mid-
1970s, oil on canvas, 89×55 cm,
private collection, Tehran

In stark contrast to Sepehri and Saidi, who embraced themes of beauty, immortality, and eternity in their art, Bahman Mohasses (1931–2010) adopted a mode of expression characterised by a philosophical-critical and socially bitter perspective. Having studied in Italy, Mohasses developed a distinctive artistic ideology and approach, setting him apart as a prominent and unparalleled figure in Iranian art for several decades. His deep intellectual engagement with contemporary literary and social movements in Iran,[105] coupled with his years spent in post-war Italy, drew him towards European intellectual ideas. Unlike many of his peers, Mohasses showed no interest in referencing Iranian or Eastern traditions. His expressionist style, characterised by gruesome and grotesque content, often portrays the tragic realities of contemporary human existence. The harsh depiction of haunted creatures in anonymous wildernesses is a defining feature of Mohasses's paintings and sculptures, cementing his status as a uniquely distinctive figure in Iranian art. (Figures 3.78–80)

3.78
Bahman Mohasses, *Abstract of a Woman*, 1976, oil on canvas, 80×100 cm, TMoCA

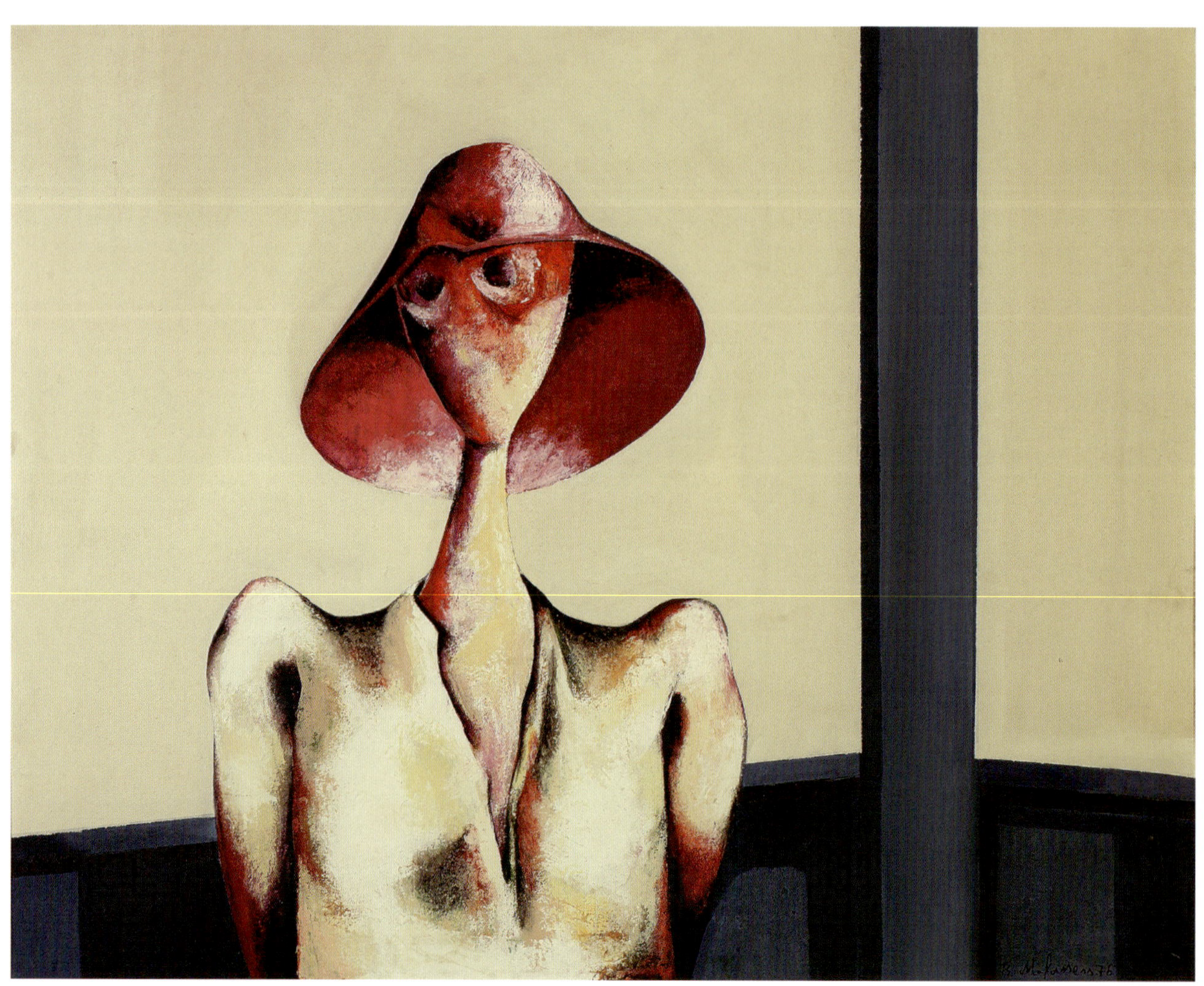

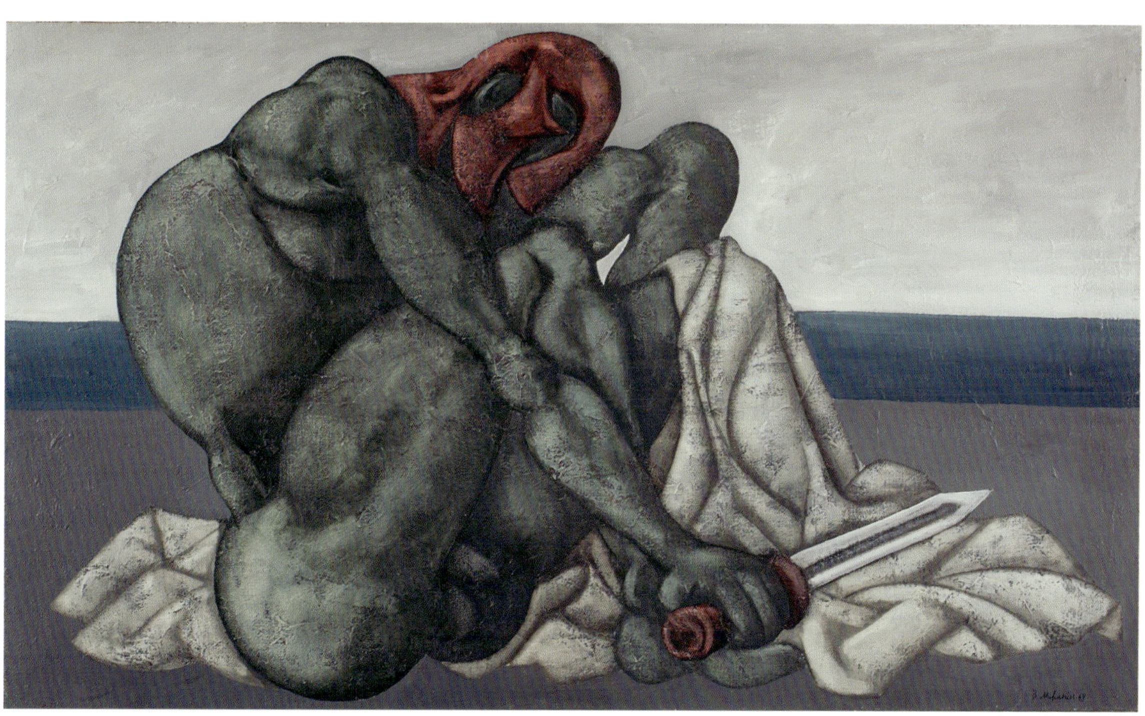

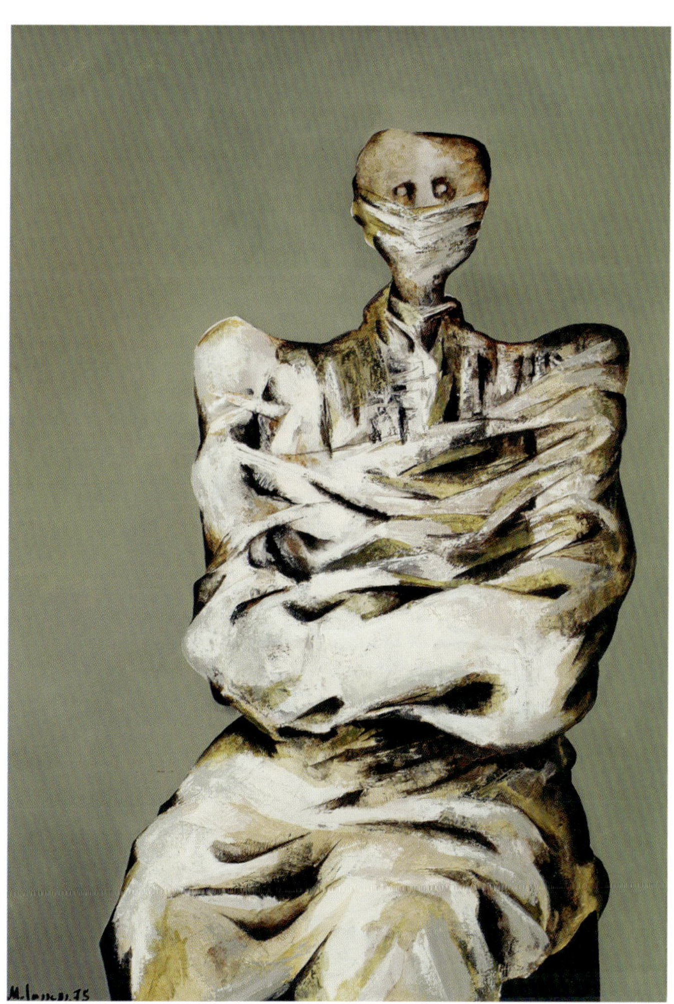

Above
3.79
Bahman Mohasses, *A Man Seated*,
1969, oil on canvas, 100×165 cm,
TMoCA

Left
3.80
Bahman Mohasses, *Untitled*, 1975,
oil on canvas, 100×70 cm, TMoCA

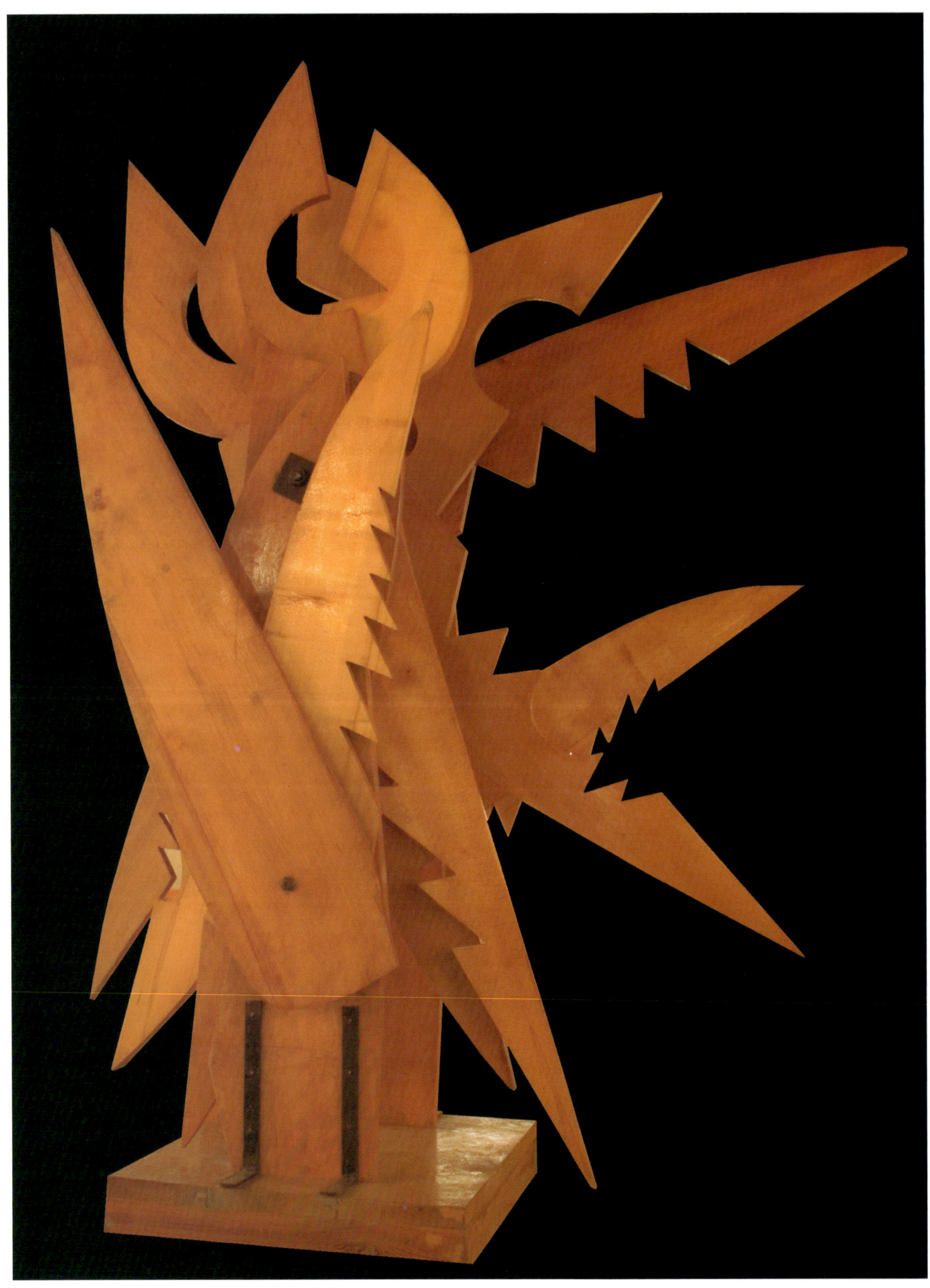

Mohsen Vaziri Moghaddam, a pioneer of Iranian modern and experimental art, continuously pursued new experiments throughout his artistic career while also contributing to art education in various faculties. His persistent interest in experimentation, particularly with unconventional materials, led him to create relief rhythmic patterns from aluminium sheets and metal foils starting in the late 1960s. Subsequently, he expanded this approach to develop a distinct series of articulated movable sculptures. (Figure 3.81) In the 1970s, he further refined this technique with the *Fear and Flight* series, featuring colourful versions of movable sculptures executed on two-dimensional platforms. Throughout these series, including both paintings and sculptures, Vaziri Moghaddam demonstrated a deep exploration of the essential concept of visual space.

As for the aforementioned neo-traditionalist approach, which was still alive among this younger group of artists, one can witness new styles and approaches. An example is the use of traditional materials as the foundational structure of the works of artists such as Monir Shahroudy Farmanfarmaian (1922–2019) and Parviz Kalantari (1931–2016). In the 1970s Farmanfarmaian developed an intuitive but meticulously crafted artistic practice in mirror mosaic and reverse-painted glass which would fuse the cosmic patterning of Iranian traditional architectural heritage with the rhythms of modern geometric abstraction. (Figures 3.82–83) The work of Parviz Kalantari provides an excellent example. He created paintings made by thatch from the early 1970s and exhibited the first series in the Seyhoon Gallery in 1972. His approach to this unconventional material was to an extent unprecedented, although one could cite the earlier works of the pioneer artist Marcos Grigurian, who used the same material. (Figures 3.84–85) Kalantari more or less continued this style throughout his career using a variety of approaches to the material. His subjects were Iranian old architecture and cityscapes, mainly scenes from cities such as Kashan, Yazd and Bam.

Mehdi Hosseini's (b.1943) works exemplify another instance of the diversity of new artistic experiences during this period. Influenced by American Pop Art, his semi-figurative paintings are characterised by minimalism, tranquillity, order, and fluidity. Often depicting scenes of interior settings and simple everyday objects, his works flatten and simplify landscapes and objects. The rhythm and order prevalent in these examples remain key features persisting throughout his works (Figure 3.86). In the following years, alongside his artistic experiments, Hosseini played a fundamental role in the Iranian art scene as a researcher, translator, writer, and art instructor.

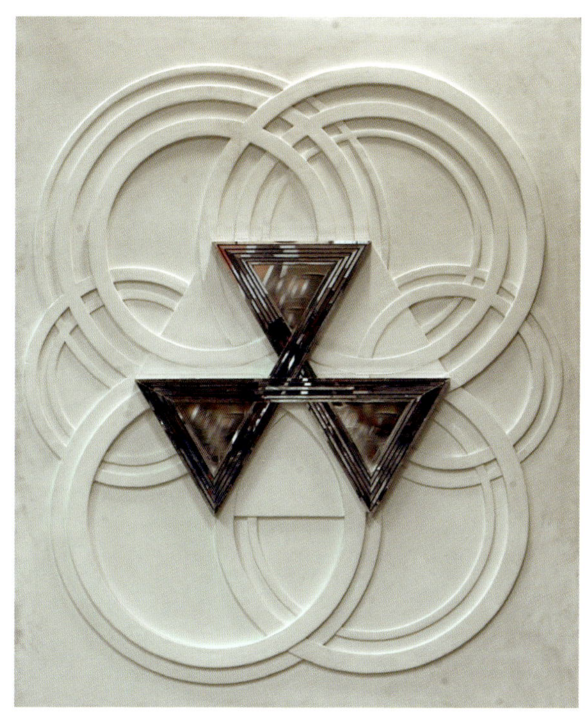

Facing page
3.81
Mohsen Vaziri Moghaddam, *Moving Form*, 1973, wood, 230×85×63 cm, TMoCA

Above
3.82
Monir Shahroudy Farmanfarmaian, *Untitled*, 1977, mirror-work and relief, 158×128 cm, TMoCA

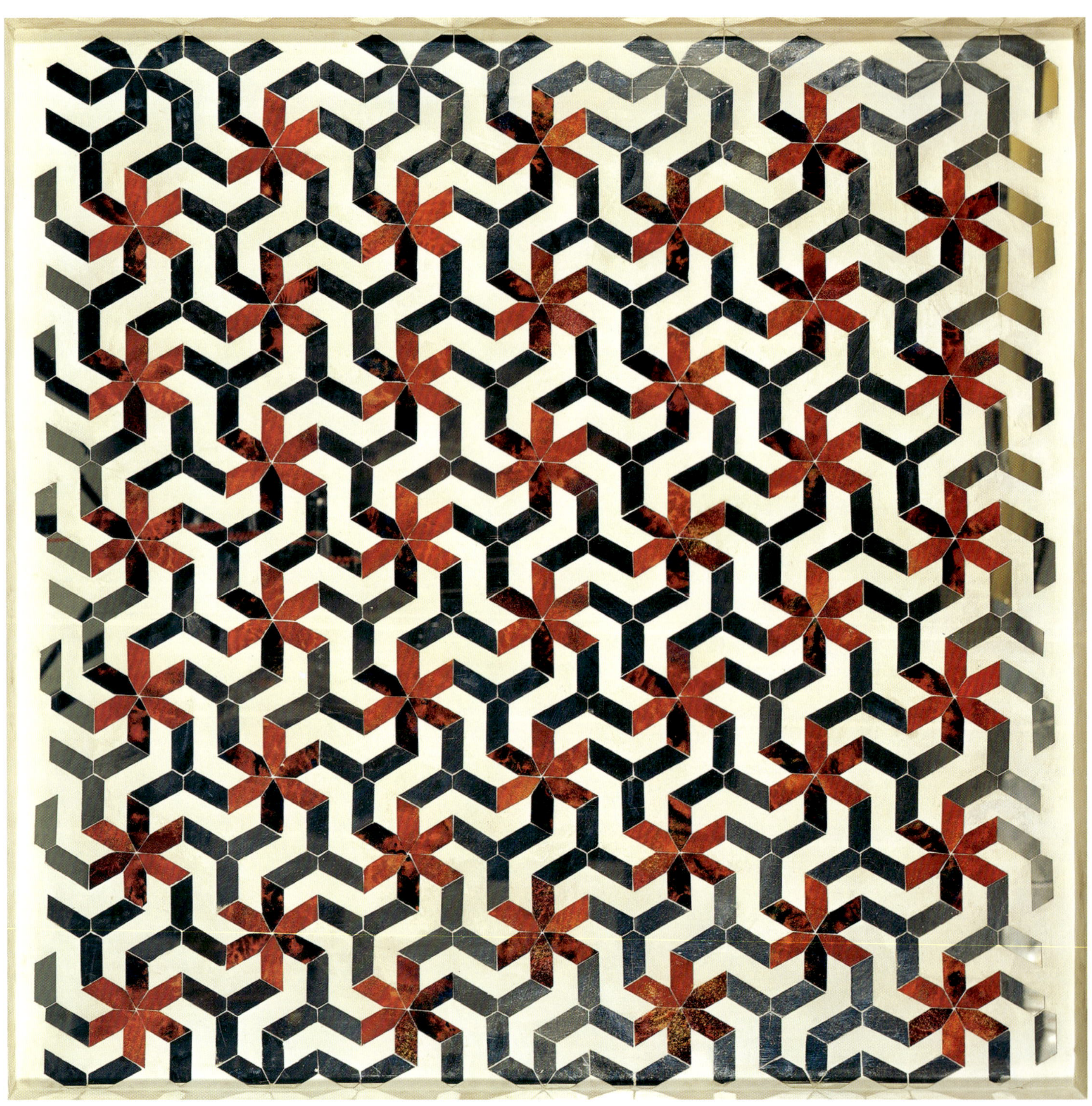

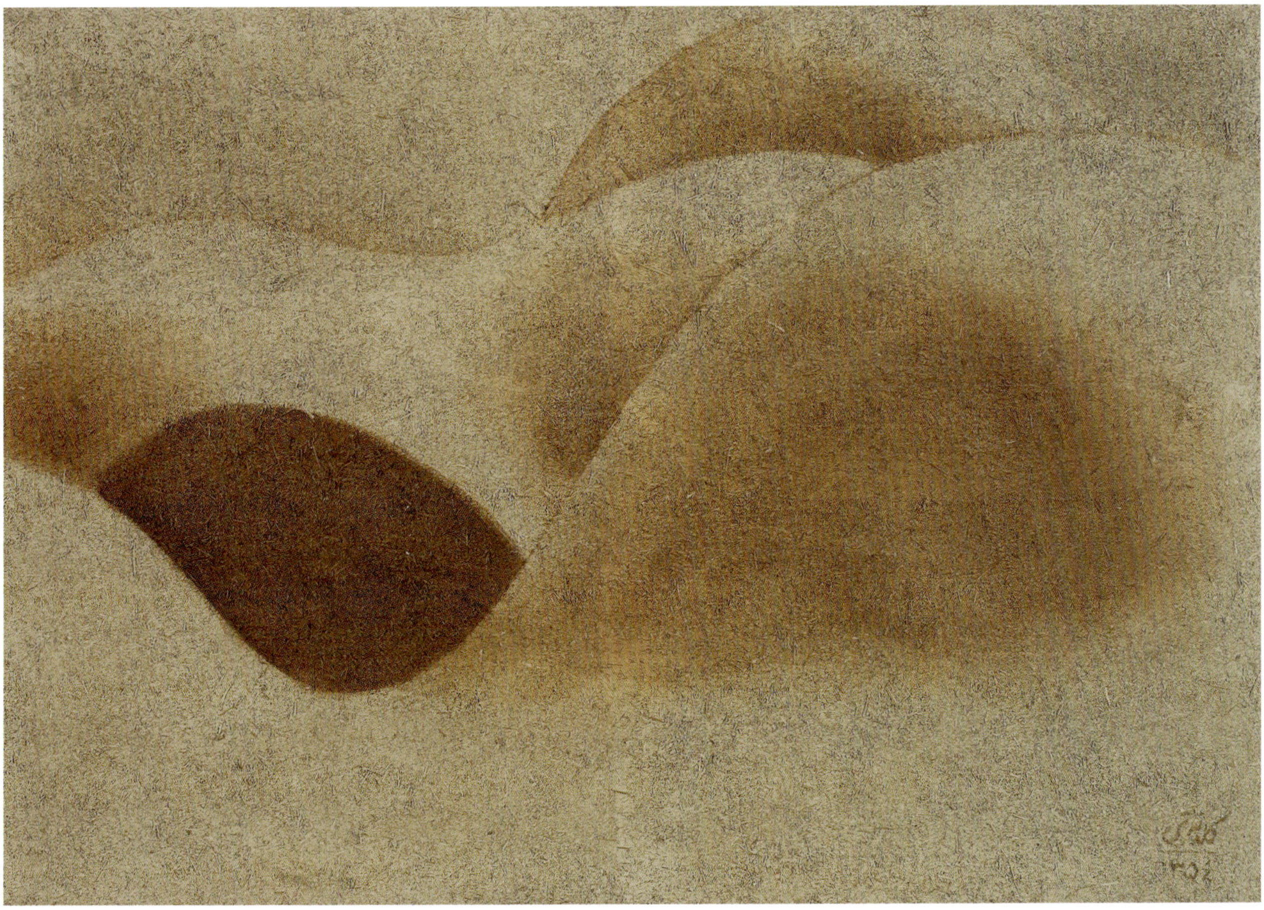

Facing page
3.83
Monir Shahroudy Farmanfarmaian, *Untitled*, 1975, mirror-work, 104×104 cm, TMoCA

Above
3.84
Parviz Kalantari, *Curved Roofs*, 1975, 100×140 cm, TMoCA

Right
3.85
Parviz Kalantari, *Village Houses*, 1975, 120×120 cm, TMoCA

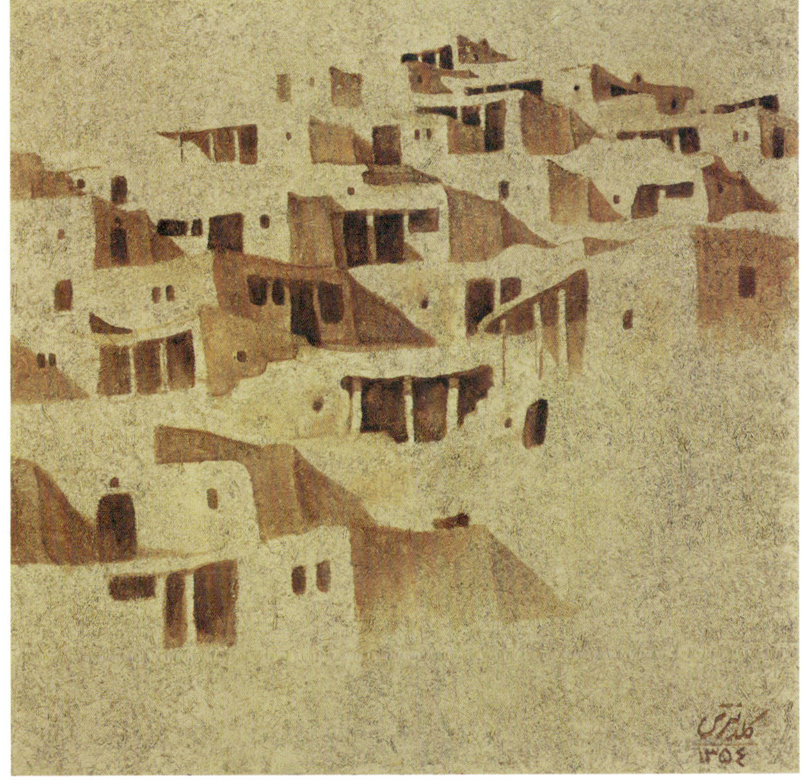

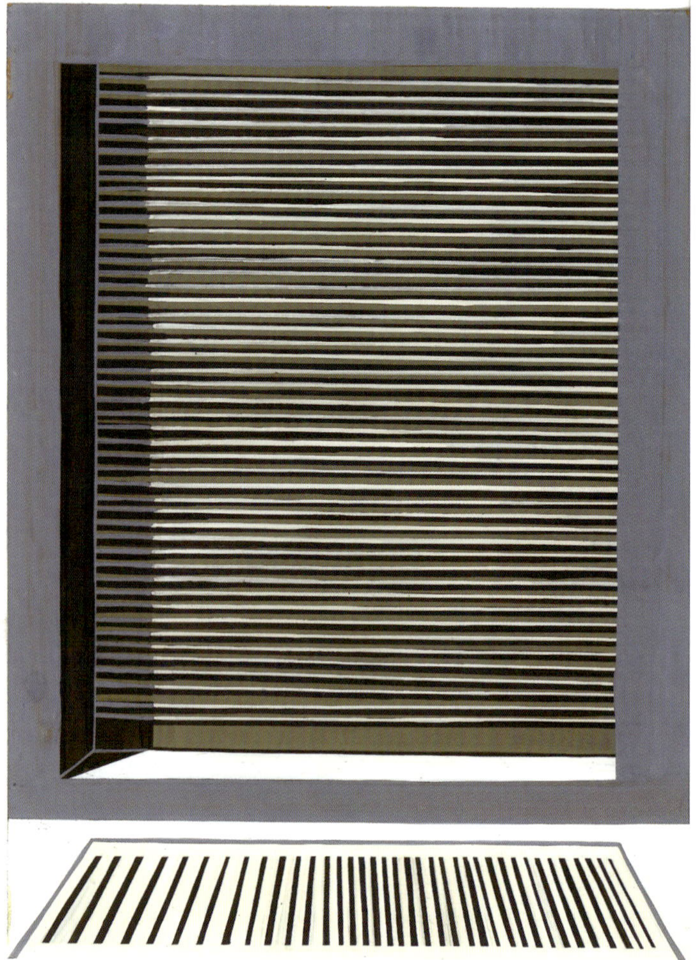

3.86
Mehdi Hosseini, *Snow in Tehran*,
1975, gouache on cardboard,
55×25 cm, courtesy the artist

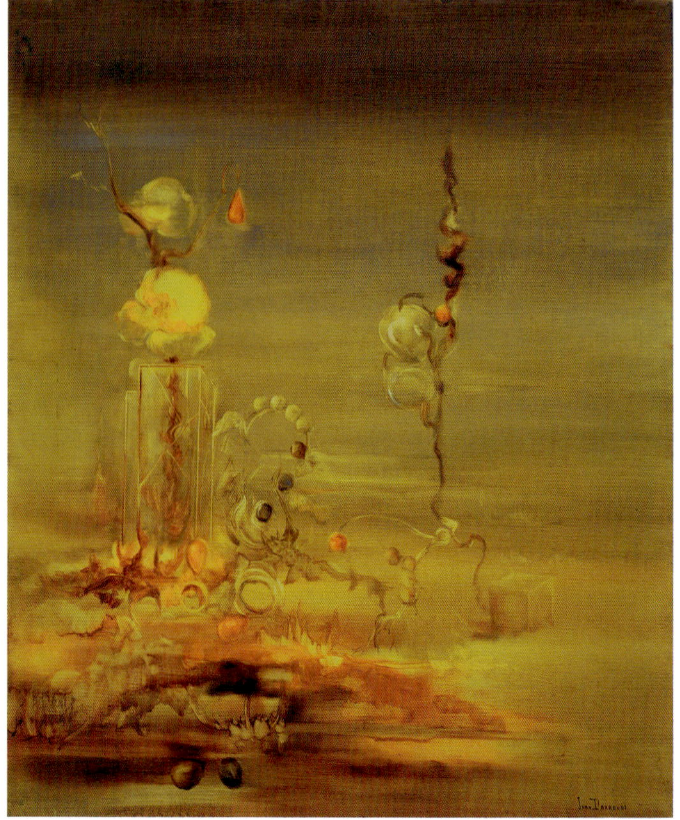

3.87
Iran Darroudi, *Untitled*, 1977, oil on
canvas, 100×80 cm, TMoCA

Among the most active figures in this decade, one can name Iran Darroudi (1936–2021), Hossein Mahjoubi (b.1930), Sadegh Barirani (b.1923), Nasser Assar (1928–2011), Leyly Matine-Daftary (1937–2007), Behjat Sadr (1924–2009) and Bahman Boroujeni (b.1942), as well as Ruin Pakbaz (b. 1939), Parvaneh Etemadi (b.1947), Morteza Momayyez, Sirak Melkonian, Mir Abdolreza Daryabegi, Gholamhossein Nami, Mohammad Ebrahim Jafari (1940–2018), Fereydoun Ave (b.1945), Jafar Rouhbakhsh, Changiz Shahvagh (1933–96), Mohammad (Michael) Radvand, Jamal Bakhshpour (1944–2015), Jalal Shabahangi (1940–2023), Ghasem Hajizadeh (b.1947), Ardeshir Mohasses (1938–2008), Reza Bangiz (b. 1937), Mahin Nourmah (b.1948), Kamran Diba (b. 1937), Habibollah Ayatollahi (b.1934), Behzad Golpayegani (1938–1985), Serge Avakian (1938–2020), Kamran Katouzian (b. 1941), Hojatollah Shakiba (b. 1949), Nahid Saliani (1936–2020) and Asghar Mohammadi (1938–84). (Figures 3.87–118)

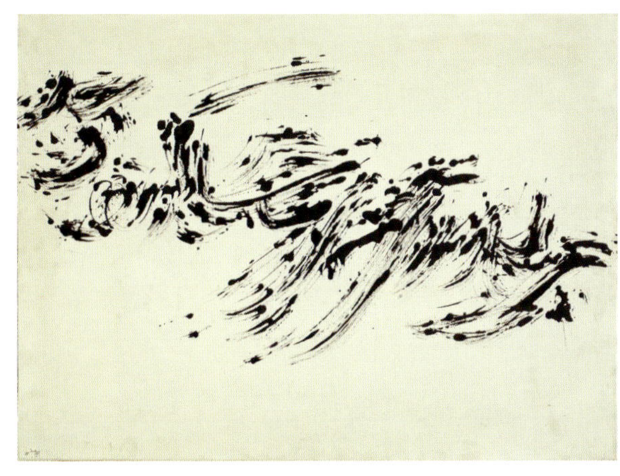

3.89
Sadegh Barirani, *Har bulbuli keh zimzimeh bar shakhsar kard* (*Every nightingale that whispered on the branch*), 1974, oil on canvas, 60×80 cm, TMoCA

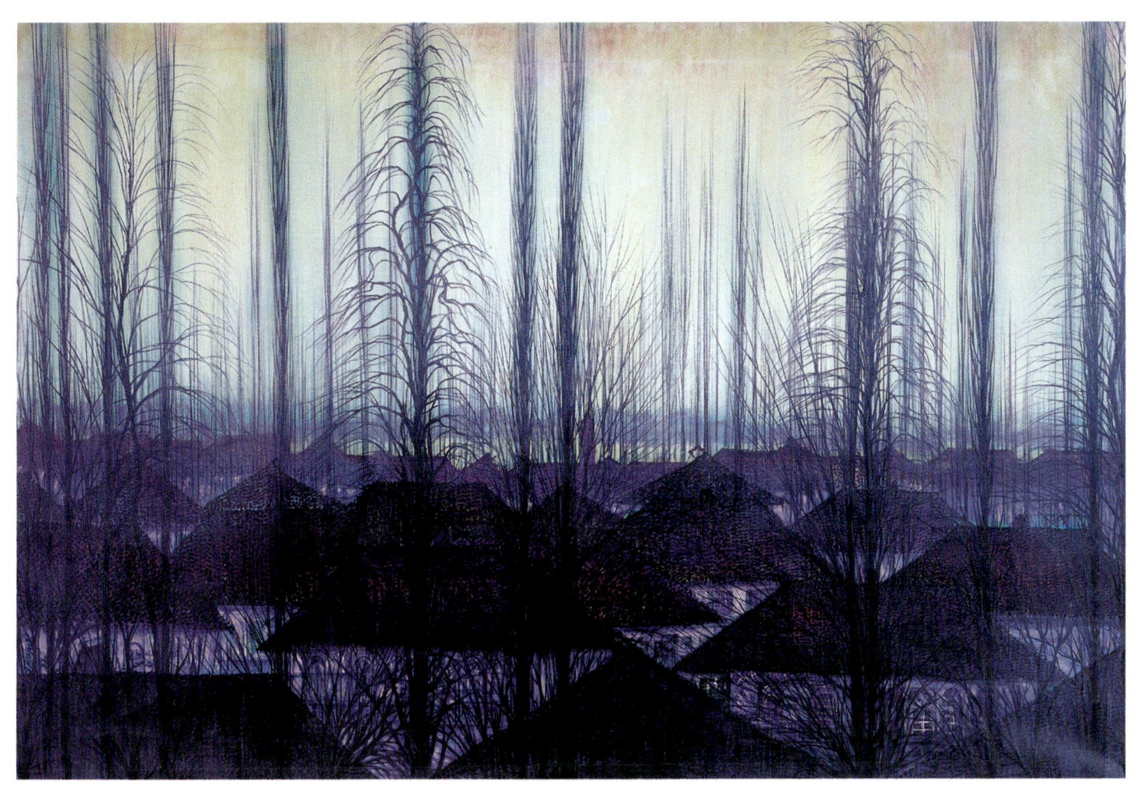

3.88
Hossein Mahjoubi, *City from the Distance*, 1977, oil on canvas, 80×120 cm, TMoCA

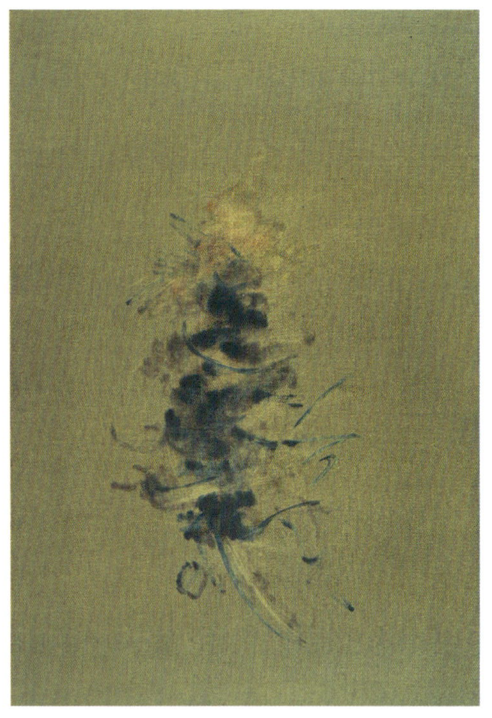

3.90
Nasser Assar, *Untitled*, 1963, oil on
canvas, 146×96 cm, TMoCA

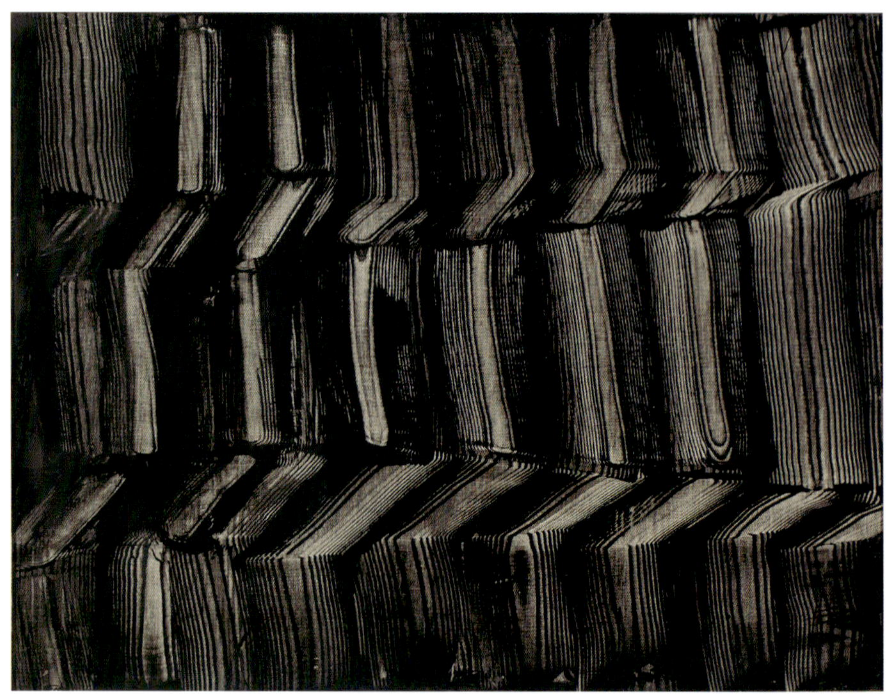

3.92
Behjat Sadr, *Untitled*, 1973, oil on
canvas, 96×122 cm, TMoCA

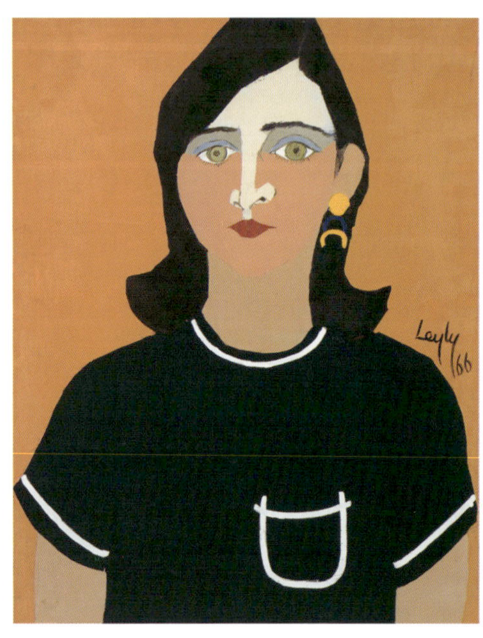

3.91
Leyly Matine-Daftary, *Portrait of
Nasrin*, 1966, oil and acrylic on
canvas, 90×70 cm, TMoCA

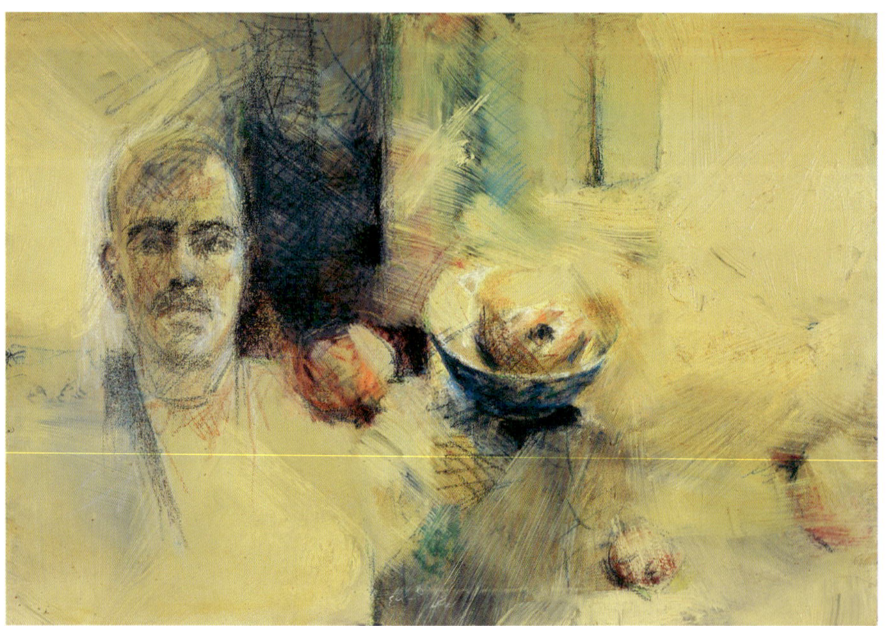

3.93
Bahman Boroujeni, *Untitled*, 1970, oil
and pastel on canvas, 70×100 cm,
TMoCA

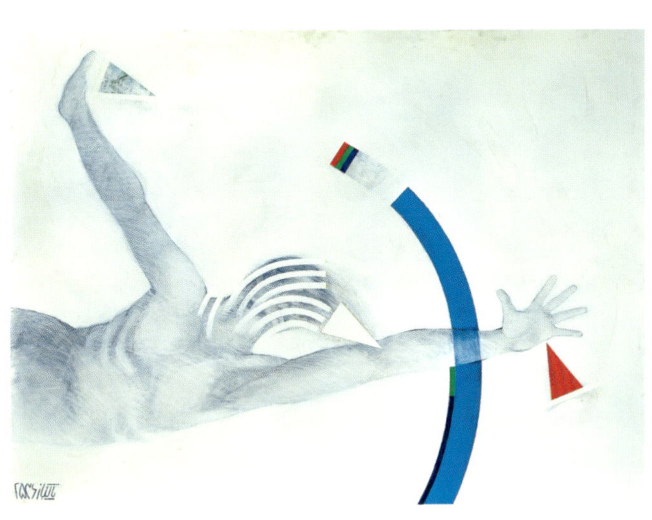

3.94
Ruin Pakbaz, *Untitled*, 1977, oil on board, 135×180 cm, TMoCA

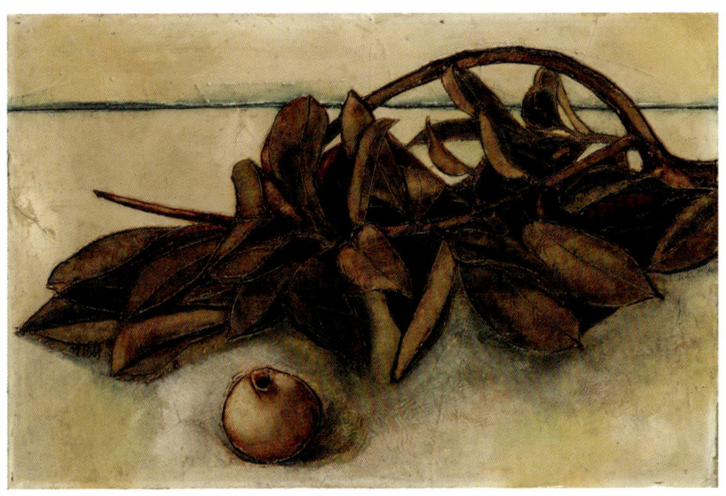

3.95
Parvaneh Etemadi, *Untitled*, 1980, oil and cement on plywood, 40×60 cm, private collection, Tehran

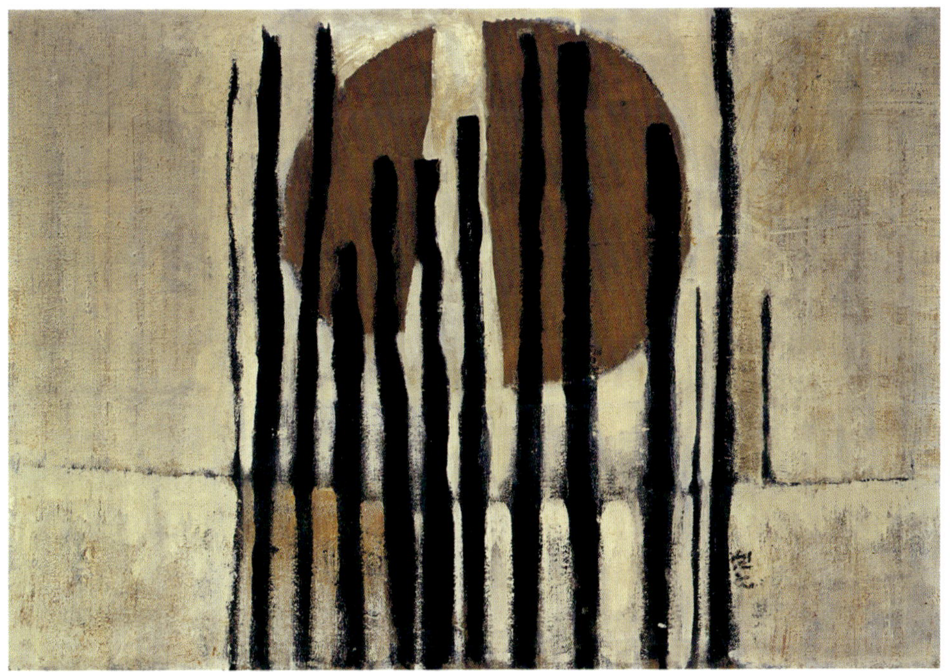

3.96
Morteza Momayyez, *Broken Sun*, 1963, oil on canvas, 70×100 cm, TMoCA

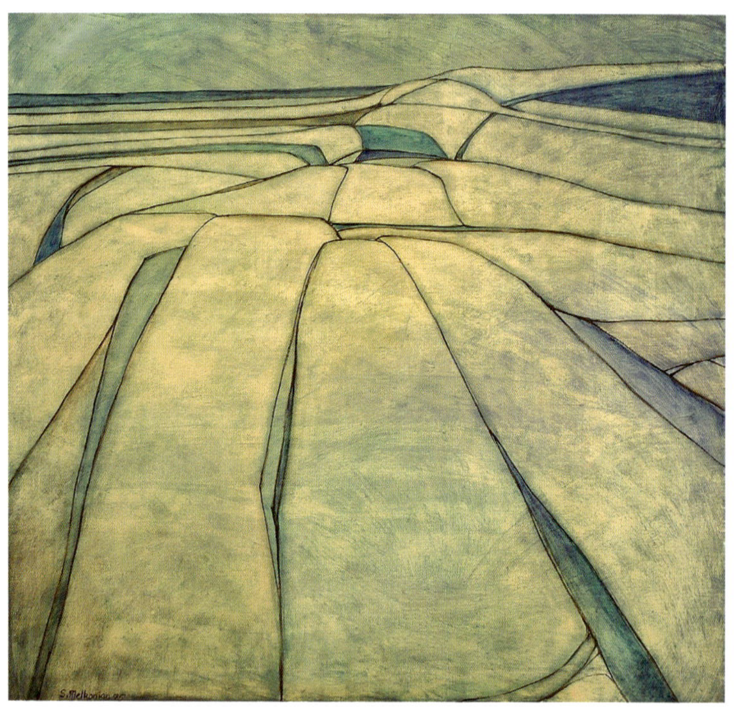

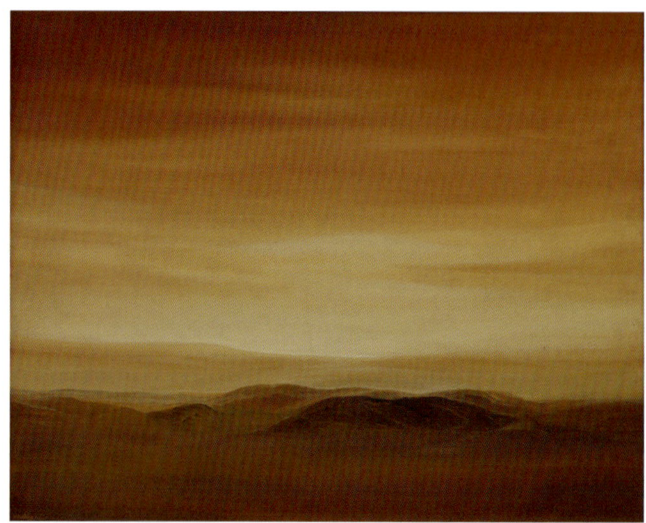

3.97
Sirak Melkonian, *Untitled*, 1975, oil
on canvas, 110×110 cm, private
collection, Tehran

3.98
Mir Abdolreza Daryabegi, *Desert*,
1976, oil on canvas, 130×160 cm,
private collection, Tehran

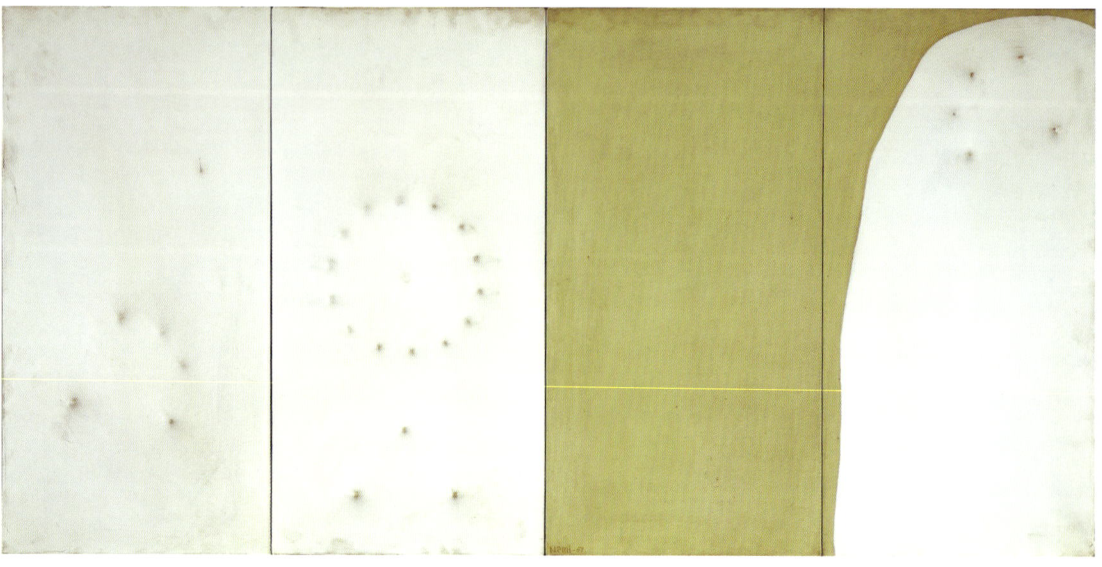

3.99
Gholamhossein Nami,
Traceless Grave, 1967, mixed
media and canvas, 80×160
cm, TMoCA

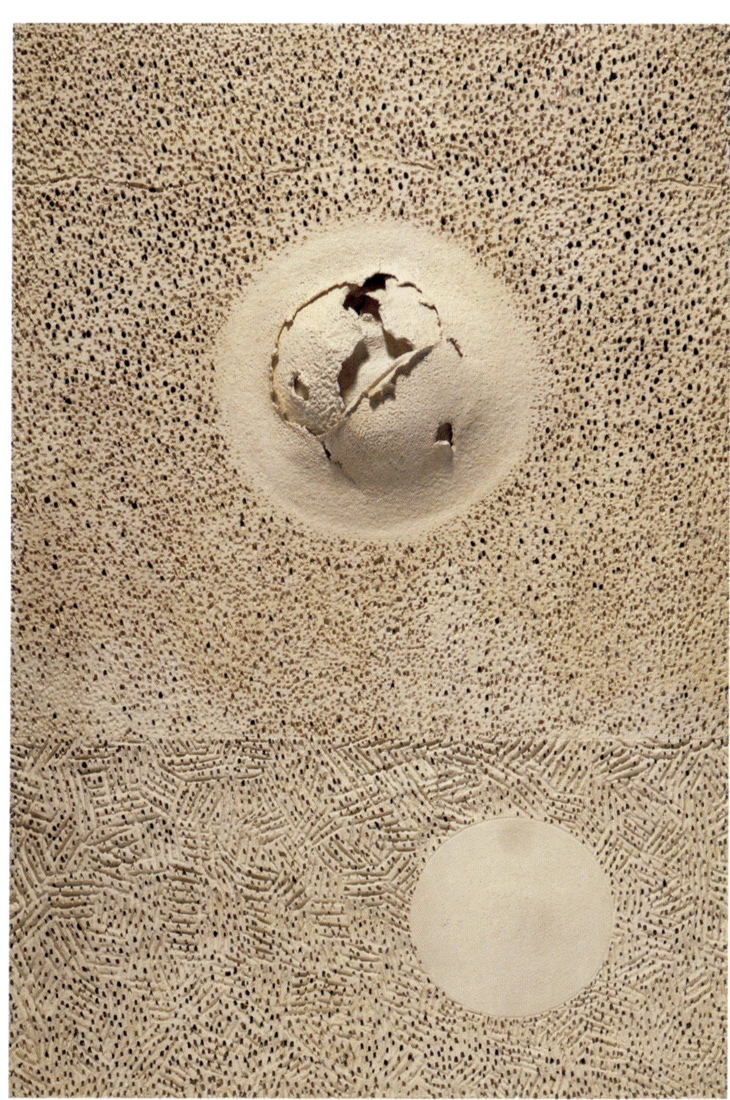

3.100
Mohammad Ebrahim Jafari, *Desert House*, 1973, plastic sponge, 150×100 cm, TMoCA

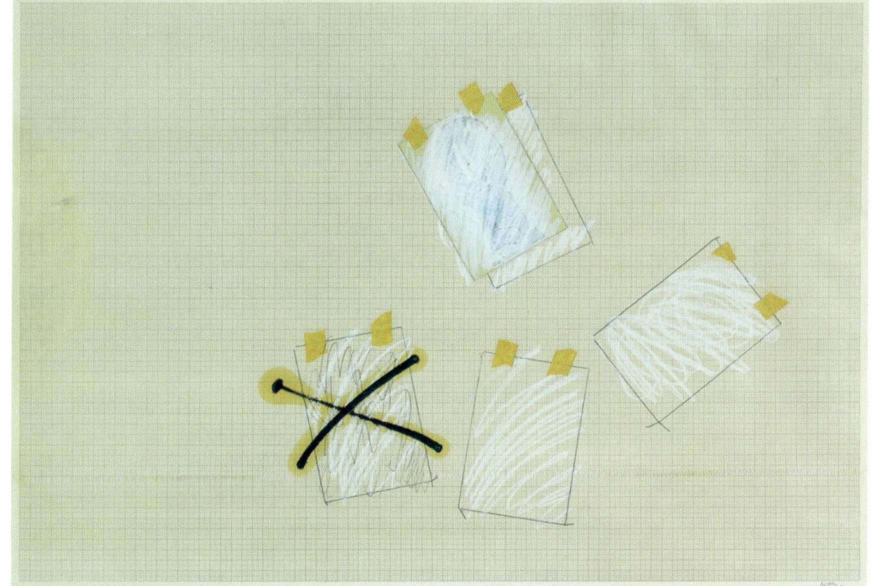

3.101
Fereydoun Ave, *Untitled*, 1977, oil and pastel on paper, 57×82 cm, TMoCA

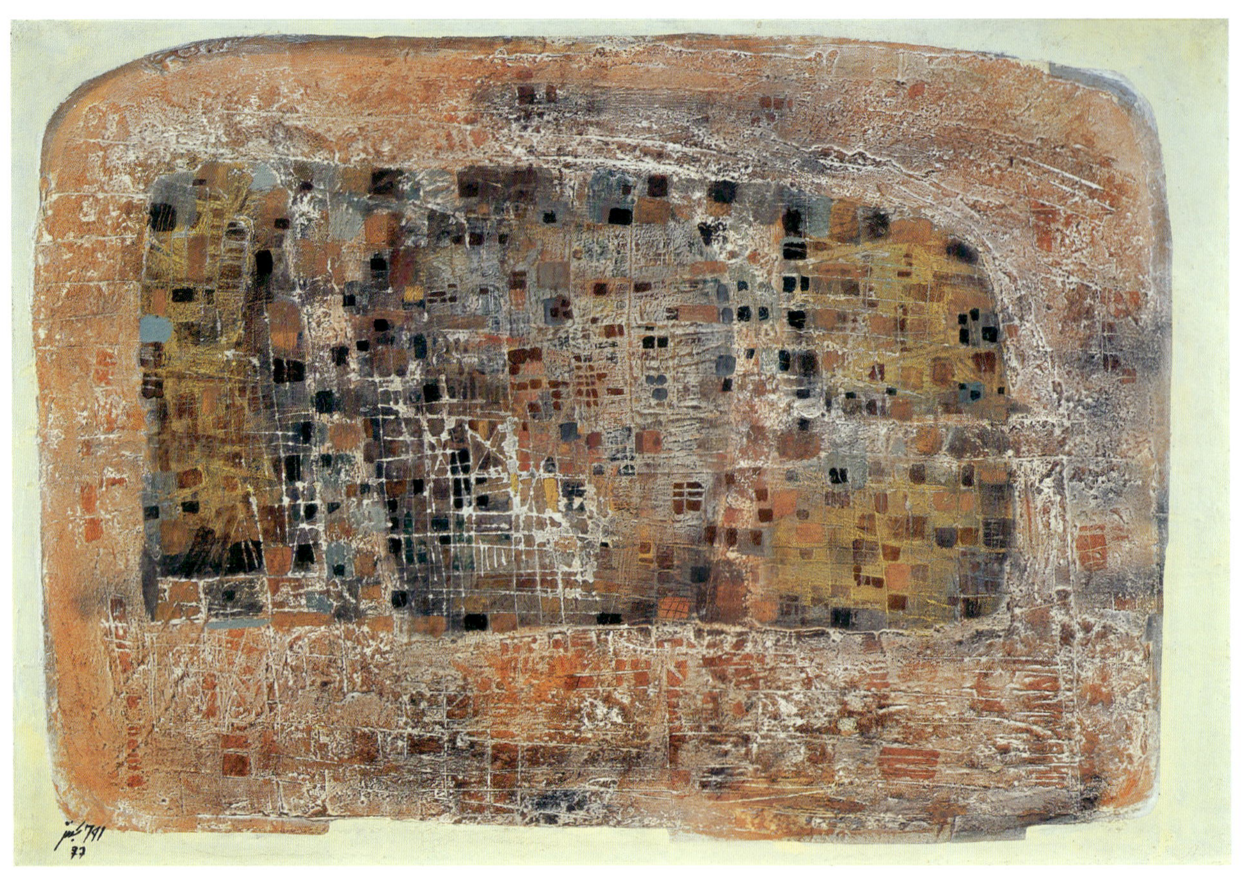

3.102
Jafar Rouhbakhsh, *Katiba*,
1977, mixed media on
canvas, 70×101 cm,
TMoCA

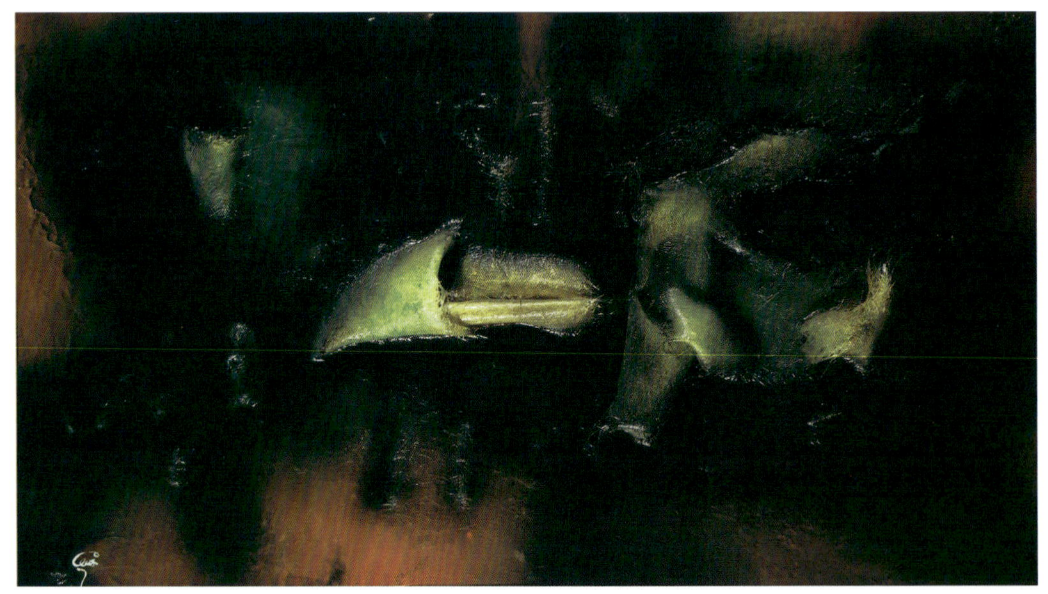

3.103
Changiz Shahvagh, *Untitled*, 1977,
mixed media, 72×135 cm, TMoCA

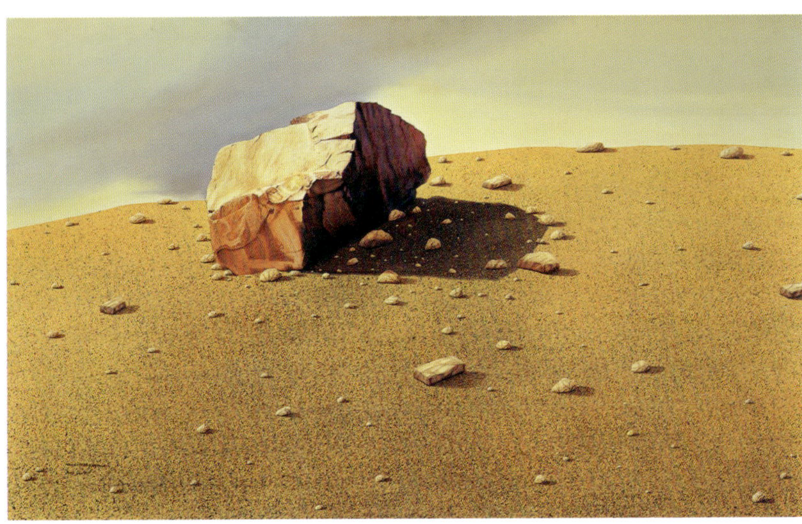

3.104
Mohammad Radvand, *Untitled*, 1977,
oil on canvas, 75×119 cm, TMoCA

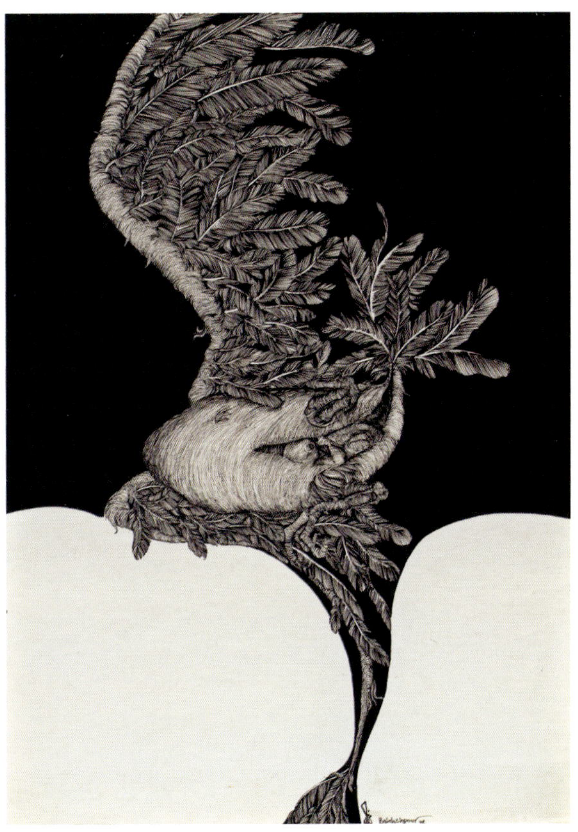

3.105
Jamal Bakhshpour, *Untitled*, 1972,
ink on cardboard, 70×50 cm, private
collection, Tehran

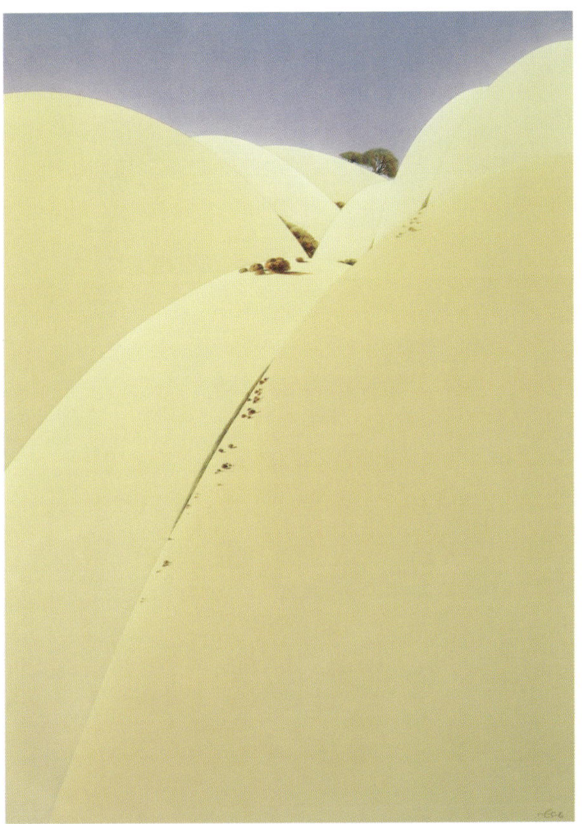

3.106
Jalal Shabahangi, *Landscape*,
1977, paint on paper, 85×60 cm,
TMoCA

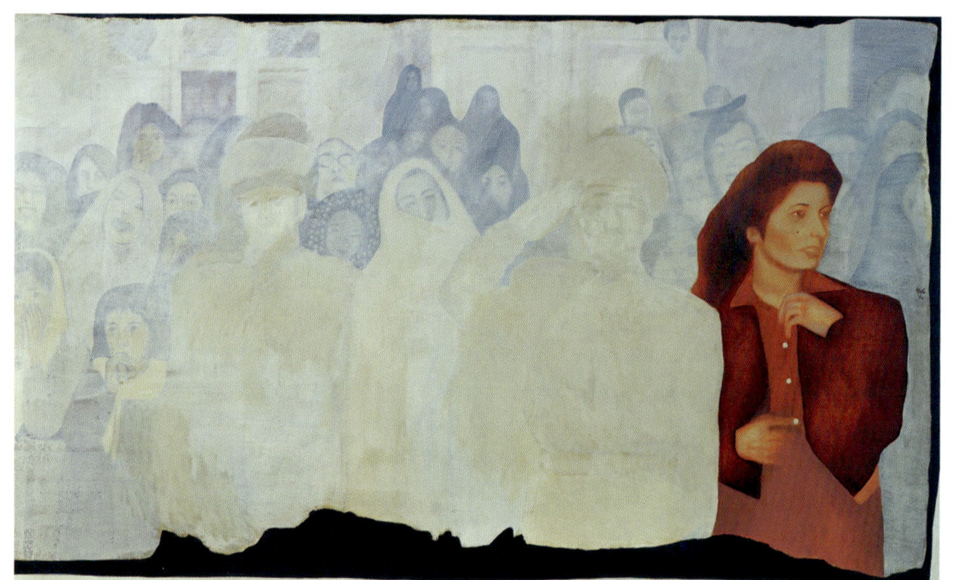

3.107
Ghasem Hajizadeh, *Unveiling*, 1976,
oil on canvas, 130×200 cm, TMoCA

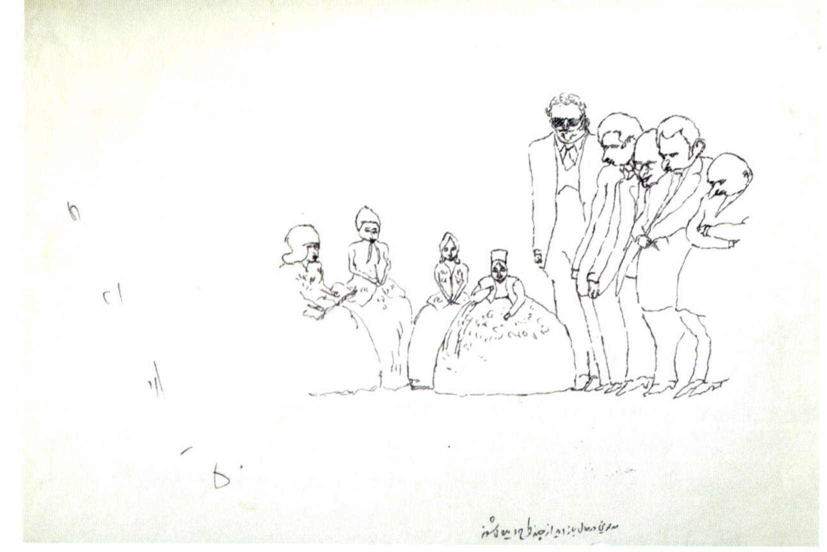

3.108
Ardeshir Mohassess, *Guests Are Seen
Visiting Several Projects*, from the
Vaqaye'-i ittifaqiyya series, 1971, ink
on paper, private collection, Tehran

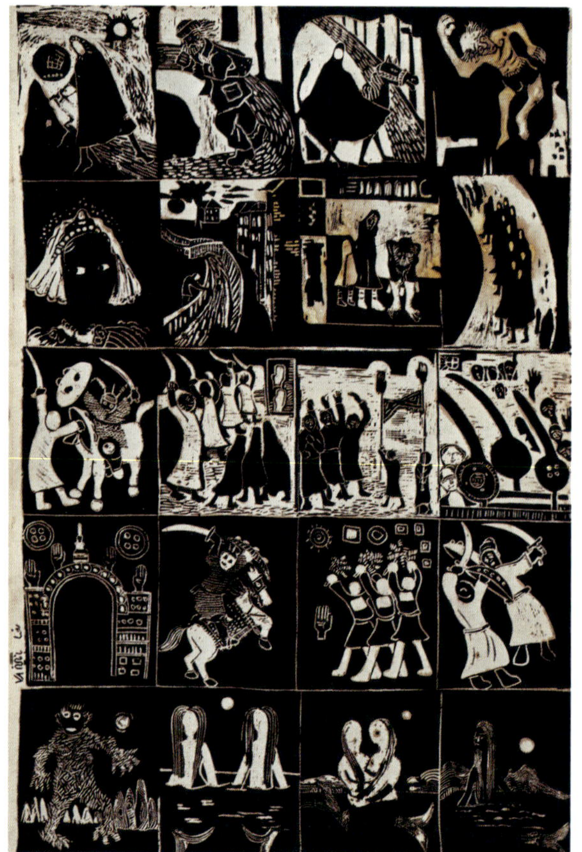

3.109
Reza Bangiz, *Life and
Imagination*, 1979, linocut,
151×100 cm, TMoCA

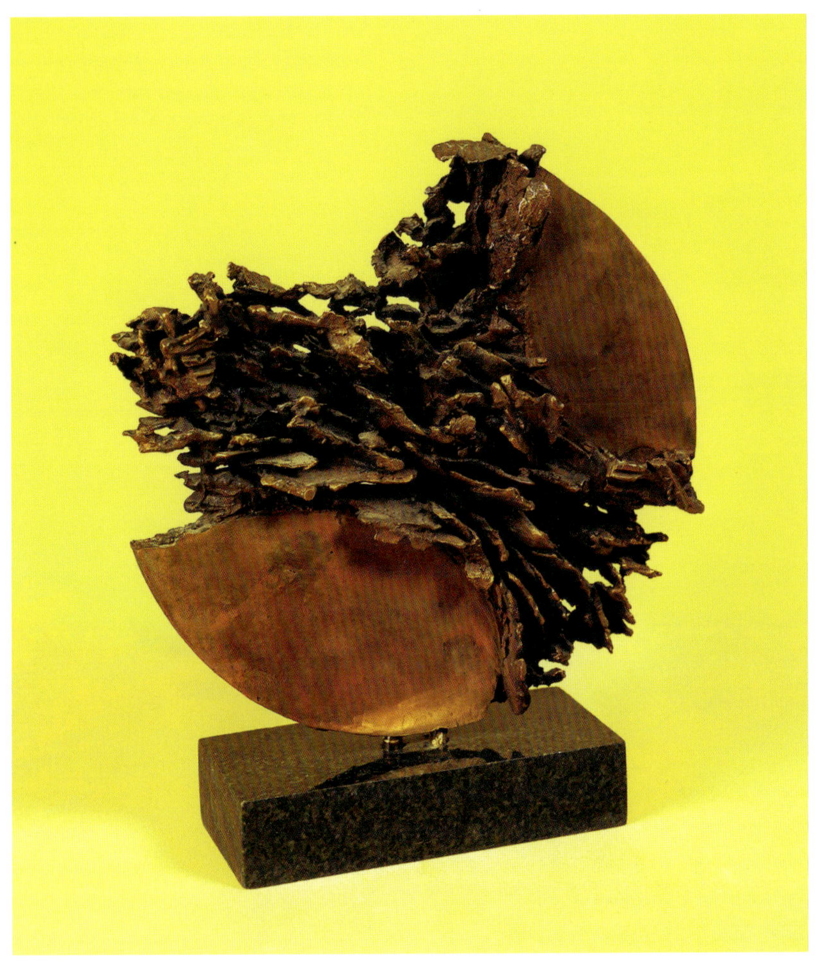

3.110
Mahin Nourmah, *Untitled*, 1996,
bronze, height: 32 cm, TMoCA

3.111
Kamran Diba, *Untitled*, 1961, oil on
canvas, 122×79 cm, TMoCA

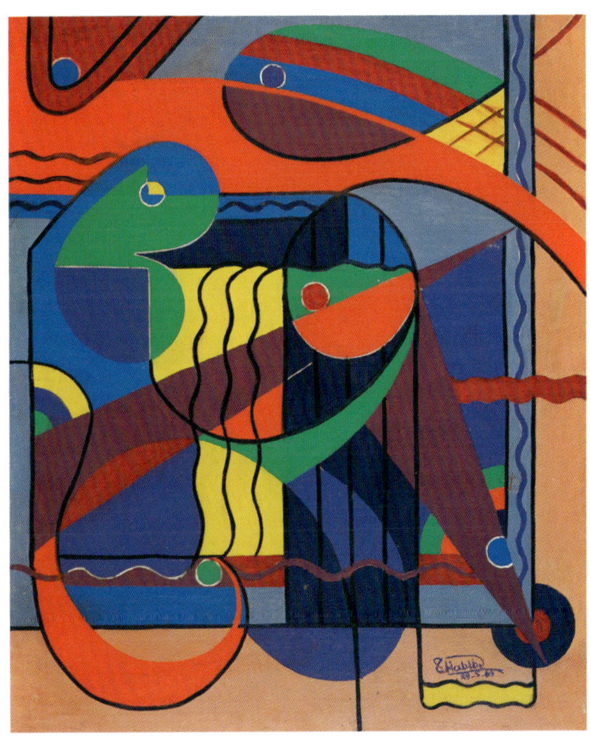

3.112
Habibollah Ayatollahi, *Untitled*,
1969, oil on canvas, 100×80 cm,
TMoCA

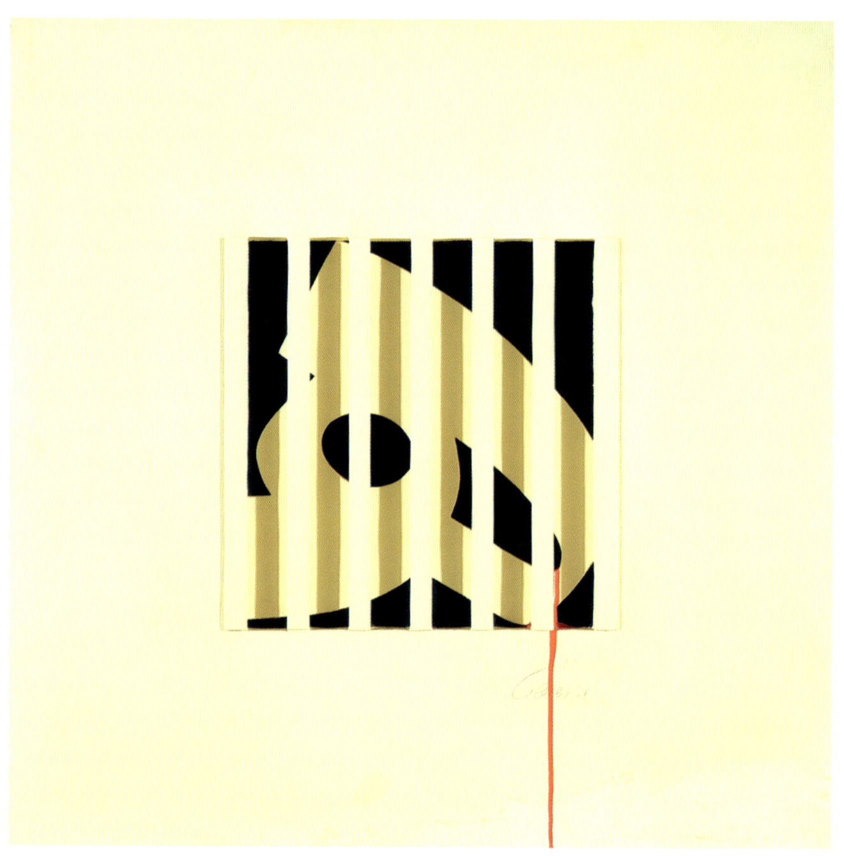

3.113
Behzad Golpayegani, *Heech in Prison*, 1975, relief on wood, 100×100 cm, TMoCA

3.114
Serge Avakian, *P-38*, 1975, oil on canvas, 125×125 cm, TMoCA

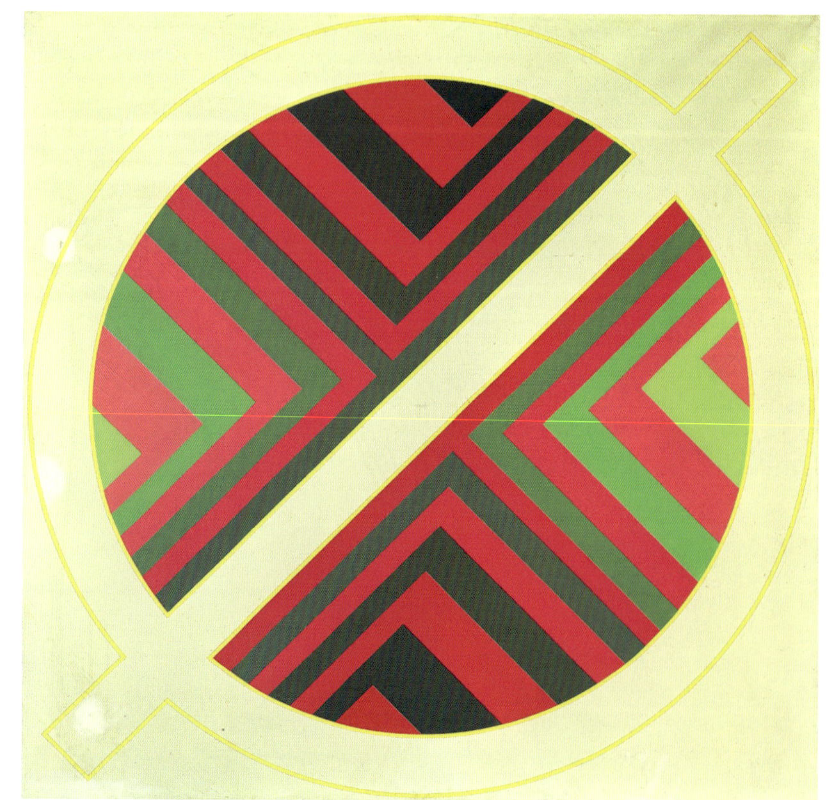

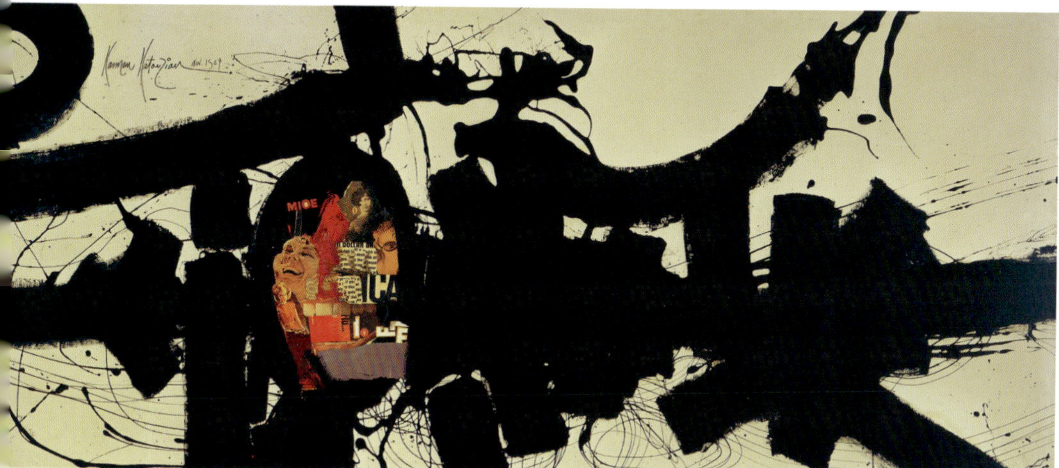

3.115
Kamran Katouzian, *Black and White*,
1964, mixed media on canvas,
121×283 cm, TMoCA

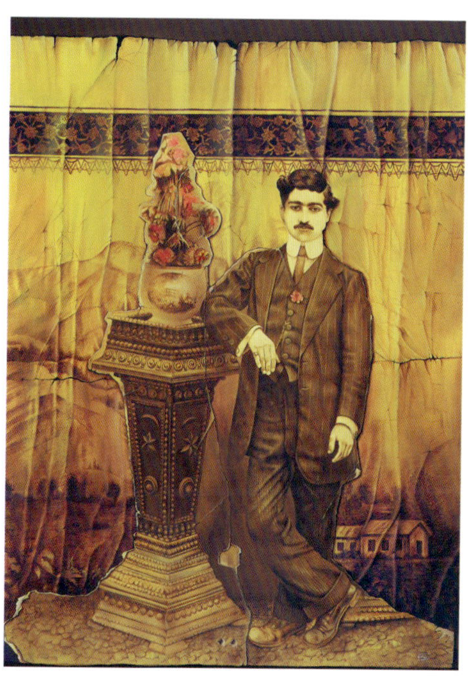

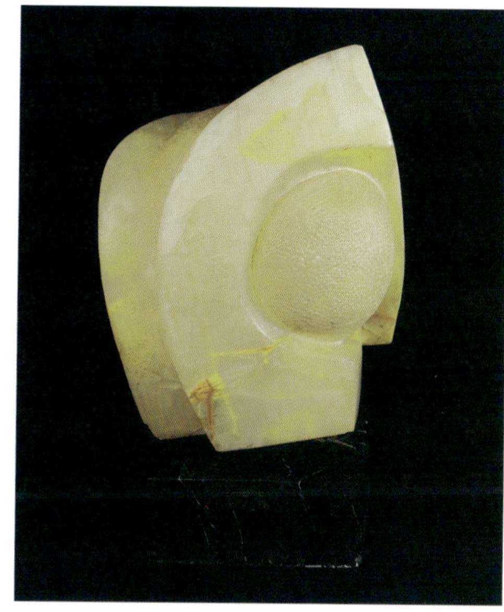

3.117
Nahid Saliani, *Untitled*, 1977,
marble, height:
59 cm, TMoCA

3.116
Hojatollah Shakiba, *Memorial
Photo*, 1977, oil on canvas,
70×100 cm, TMoCA

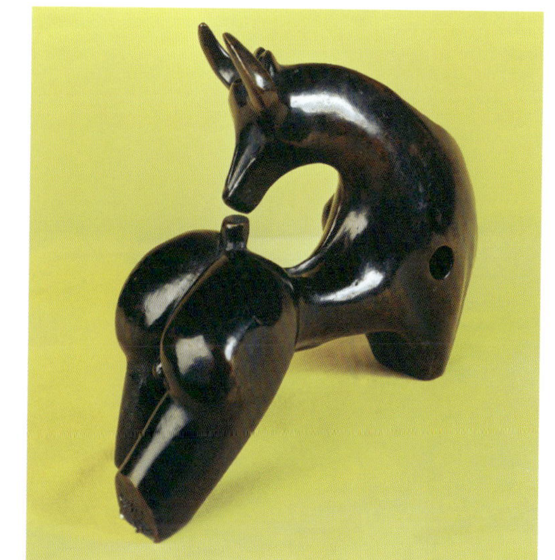

3.118
Asghar Mohammadi,
Transformation of a Bull, 1977,
bronze, height: 24 cm, TMoCA

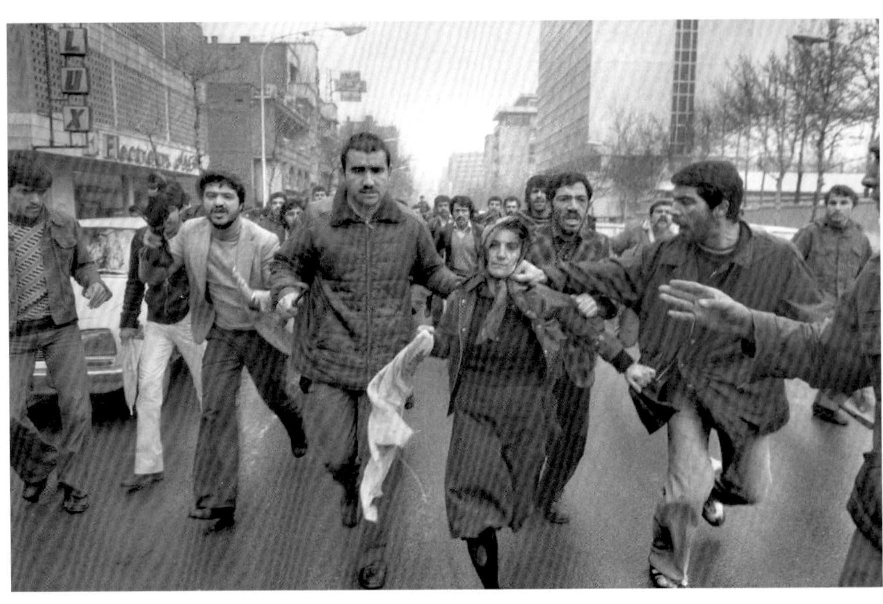

3.119
Abbas Attar, *Supporter of the Shah is Lynched*, 1979, black and white photograph, 50.8×61.2 cm

In the 1970s photography, particularly photojournalism, saw a considerable growth. In particular, the genres of social documentary and art photography can be seen in the works of artists such as Abbas Attar (1944–2018), Kaveh Golestan (1950–2003), Hengameh Golestan (b.1952), Bahman Jalali (1944–2009), Ahmad Aali (b.1935), Maryam Zandi (b. 1946) and Rana Javadi (b. 1953). (Figures 3.119–125)

Abbas Attar, better known as Abbas, was born in Iran and then moved to Algeria with his family when he was eight years old. He became a journalist in his adopted country and began his first documentary photographs during the Algerian war of independence. During the 1970s he made a number of trips back to Iran, taking several pictures of the extraordinary impact that the western petro-dollars had made on the country's society. Then, between 1978 and 1980, Abbas's focus was mainly on documentary photographs of the event of the Islamic Revolution and its aftermath. *Revolutions*, a part of a series of works later published in a book titled *Iran Diary* (1971–2002), presents a remarkable documentation of scenes of street demonstrations, including the murmuring street, the cortège of the collapsed regime and the insane stack of their cadavers at the morgue once the revolutionary spirit subsided. (Figure 3.119)

Kaveh Golestan began his professional career as a photojournalist in 1972. Over the following years he exhibited his documentary photographs in various galleries in Tehran, including his exhibition at the Seyhoun Gallery in 1975 showing the everyday lives of Iranian children. In 1977, Kaveh continued to work as a photojournalist and began working for the newspaper *Ayandegan*, for which he compiled many reports on the lives of Iranians; subjects included labourers, prostitutes and a mental hospital for children. (Figure 3.120) Golestan's wide-ranging works documenting the advent of the Islamic Revolution constitute another remarkable series.

Hengameh Golestan was another pioneer of Iranian photography. Her documentary photos taken in the 1970s mainly demonstrate everyday or ordinary life in Iran, recording the domestic life of women and children, instances of family life, and the traditional wedding. During the Revolution she also captured moments of rebellion. She photographed the last day for Iranian women without the veil, when groups of women from every profession took part in a massive demonstration that resulted in their being attacked and stabbed in the streets of Tehran. (Figure 3.121)

Behnam Jalali, who later became one of the most influential figures in contemporary Iranian photography, worked in various genres including social documentary photography and art photography. He began his artistic career in the 1970s and exhibited his works in numerous exhibitions in Iran and Britain. Following these successful experiences, Jalali, like his contemporaries, turned to social documentary photography, capturing scenes of the revolution in Iran. (Figure 3.122) Together with Karim Emami, he published the series *Days of Blood, Days of Fire* (1979). In the following years, in addition to his influential role in photography education, Jalali himself was an active and prolific photographer, recognised as one of the pioneers of art photography in Iran.

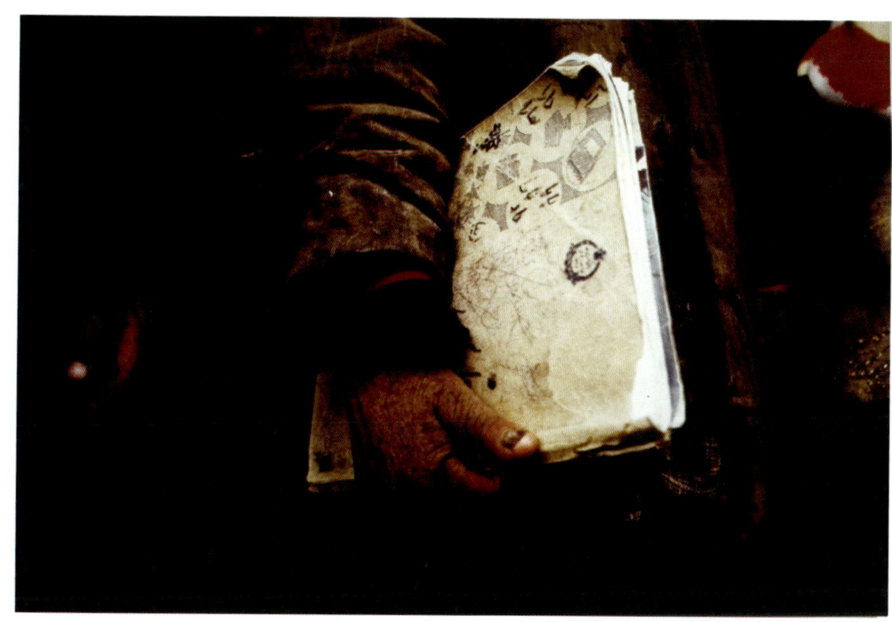

3.120
Kaveh Golestan, *School Book*, 1975,
colour photograph, 26×38 cm,
TMoCA

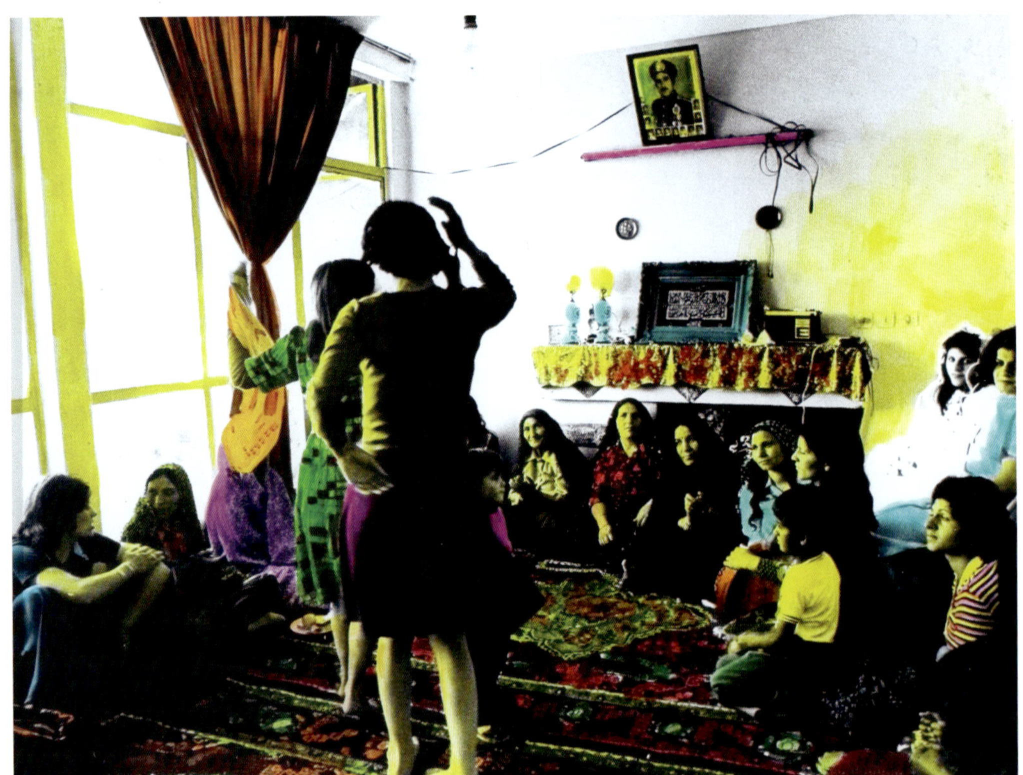

3.121
Hengameh Golestan, *Wedding*, 1977, colour photograph, 15×20 cm, TMoCA

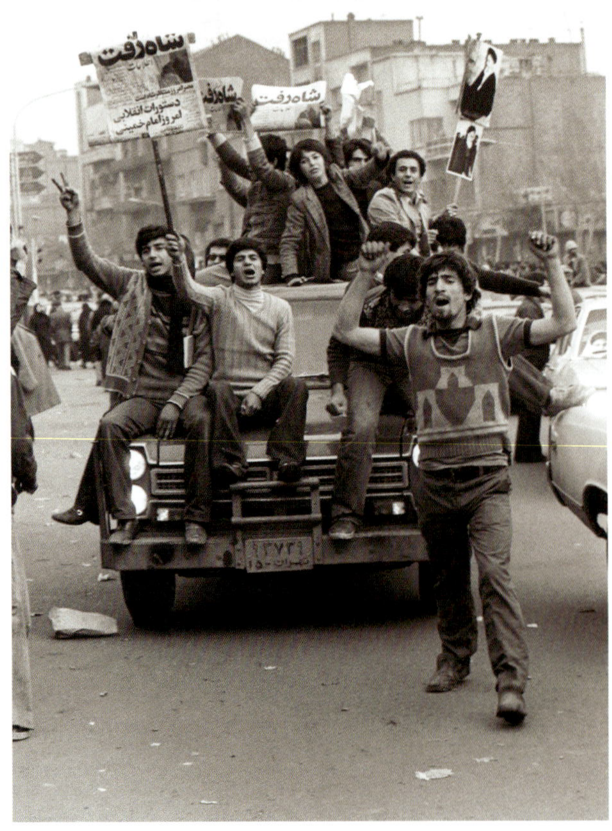

3.122
Bahman Jalali, *The day of Mohammad Reza Shah's departure* (16 January 1979), 1979, black and white photograph, size varies

Ahmad Aali, one of the pioneers of art photography in Iran, began his career in graphic design and painting before shifting his focus to photography. His solo exhibitions, starting in 1963, aimed to establish photography as an artistic medium alongside painting and sculpture. Throughout the following decade, he worked to solidify photography's place in the art scene, capturing traditional architecture, urban landscapes, and human presence with careful attention to form and composition. In the 1970s, he produced documentary photo series that, while touching on social themes, maintained a focus on formal values. Unlike many photographers of the era, Aali showed little interest in documenting the revolutionary events, preferring to capture the implications of those events through images of slogans and writings on city streets. While not direct documentation, these photographs reflected the atmosphere of the time. (Figure 3.123)

Amidst the multitude of developments in the 1970s, there were critiques and disapprovals regarding the new trends and currents in Iranian art. It was argued that there was a lack of determined criteria in artistic policies, resulting in a form of unhealthy artistic anarchism. During the later 1970s, when the Revolution of 1979 was fast approaching, criticism of the status quo steadily increased. At this juncture, while many artists opted to persist with their previous ambitions, a distinct group decided to reassess their artistic approach. Those who were critical of the mainstream modern art exhibited in formal Iranian art exhibitions chose to work in a figurative style, as a counterpoint. One could name Aydin Aghdashloo (b.1940), Alireza Espahbod (1952–2007), Nahid Haghighat (b.1943), Mohammad Hossein Shiddel (1939–2012), Rahim Najfar (b.1945) and Wahed Khakdan (b.1950) as prime examples. (Figures 3.126–131)

Aydin Aghdashloo is a writer, graphic designer and painter who was active both as an artist and an art advisor, in particular in the Office of Empress Farah Pahlavi.[106] An artist deeply engaged with the intellectual concerns of the era, his works during that period present a unique approach to figurative imagery by appropriating iconic paintings of Italian Old Masters. A good example is Aghdashloo's famous series *Memories of Destruction*. (Figure 3.126) Despite the overflowing anger and cruelty, a fervent commitment to painting and to praising its purity also underpins these works. With incredible passion, he sets himself up as a mirror to reflect the Old Masters – a broken mirror that tends to distort its images and disorder them all. This approach was initiated with the appropriation of the portraits

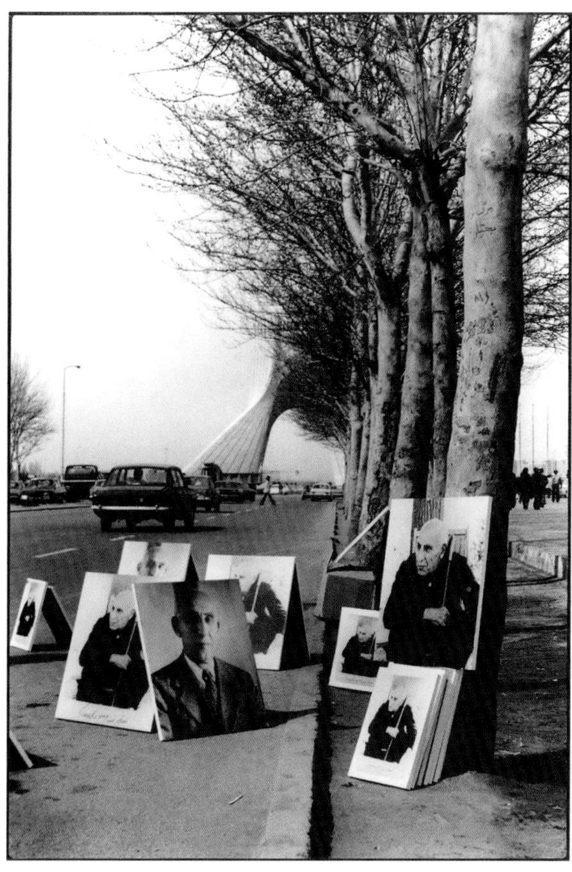

3.123
Ahmad Aali, *Tehran*, 1978, black and white photograph, no size

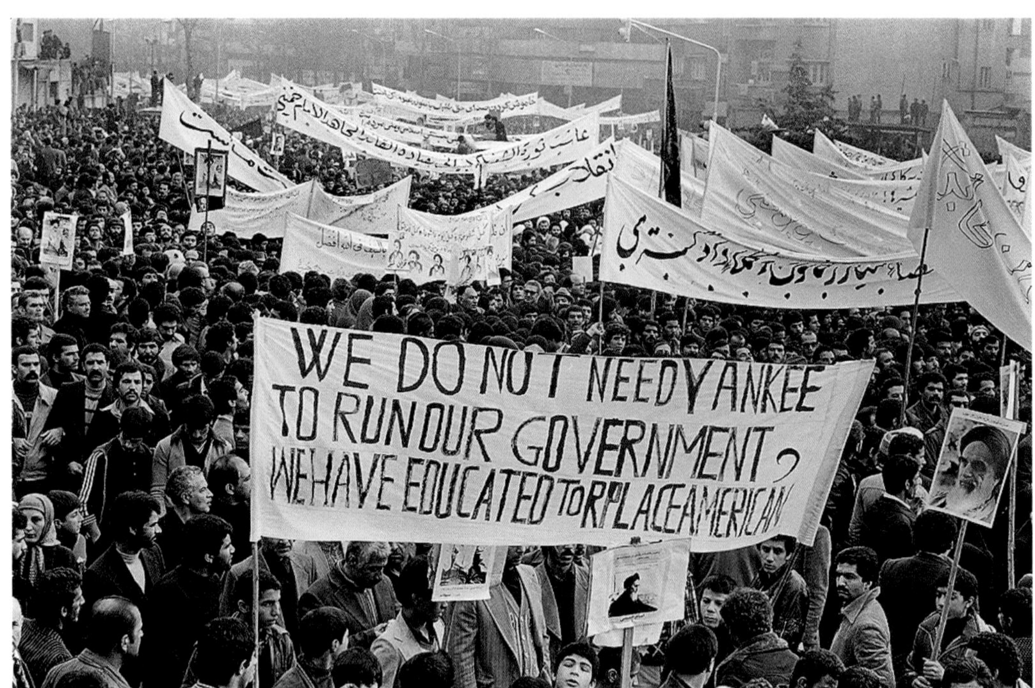

3.124
Maryam Zandi, from the *Revolution* series, 1978, black and white photograph, 24×29 cm

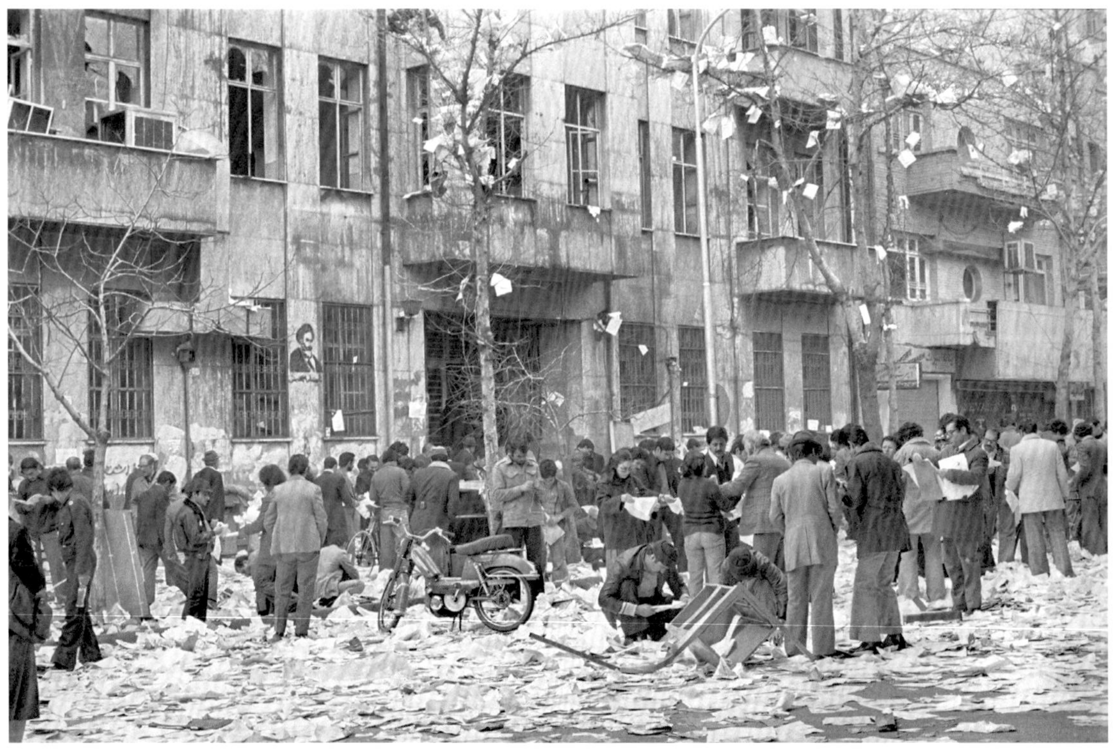

3.125
Rana Javadi, *Police Station on Shahreza Steet, February 1979*, from the *Days of Revolution*, 1979, black and white photograph, 45×60 cm, Smithsonian Museum

of Renaissance masters. Targeting the silent aristocracy that was ignorant of what might be a brewing storm, the *Years of Fire and Snow* series appears more like an anticipation of a change in the existing situation.[107]

In the 1970s, the upheaval of social order and the uprising of political activities mainly criticised the cultural and social policy of the Pahlavi regime. Following these crises, a group of artists including Hannibal Alkhas (1930–2010), Nikzad (Nicky) Nodjoumi (b.1942), Manouchehr Safarzadeh (1943–2023), Bahram Dabiri (b.1950), and Nosratollah Moslemian (b.1951) advocated for a form of social art and sought to promote it within the non-official art scene through private galleries. Influenced by practices from the Soviet Union and Mexican socialist art, a genre of painting emerged that conveyed figurative and propagandistic messages about social conditions and the plight of the poor. Typically executed on large-scale canvases, these artists also produced graphic works and murals to disseminate their socially directed messages. Indeed, these works, especially the public murals and graphic art, received admiration from so-called committed intellectuals as well as some members of the public who had access to them.

Hannibal Alkhas was one of the prominent figures of this movement. Educated in America, he returned to Iran in late 1959 and formed a close bond with the famous writer and thinker, Jalal Al-e Ahmad. He founded the Gilgamesh Gallery in Tehran and simultaneously promoted his ideas and artistic style through teaching at the Tehran Faculty of Fine Arts and other art institutions. Alkhas was generally known for his outspoken criticism, particularly in condemning some of the avant-garde movements of his time, such as conceptual art exhibitions and performances in the 1970s, by promoting his figurative narrative style. During this period, in addition to producing his own socially and politically engaged works, he was also highly influential in training a generation of artists who later joined the ranks of 'committed' artists before and after the revolution. (Figure 3.132)

Nikzad (Nicky) Nodjoumi who had also studied in the US, was one the first artists to join the group. A series of his drawings and paintings criticise the social condition of the masses in Iran, although he used indirect messages in the form of symbolic languages combined with images of horror. (Figure 3.133) Perhaps the first political posters in Iran were executed by Nodjoumi himself. In 1978 when he returned to Iran from the US he was making political posters

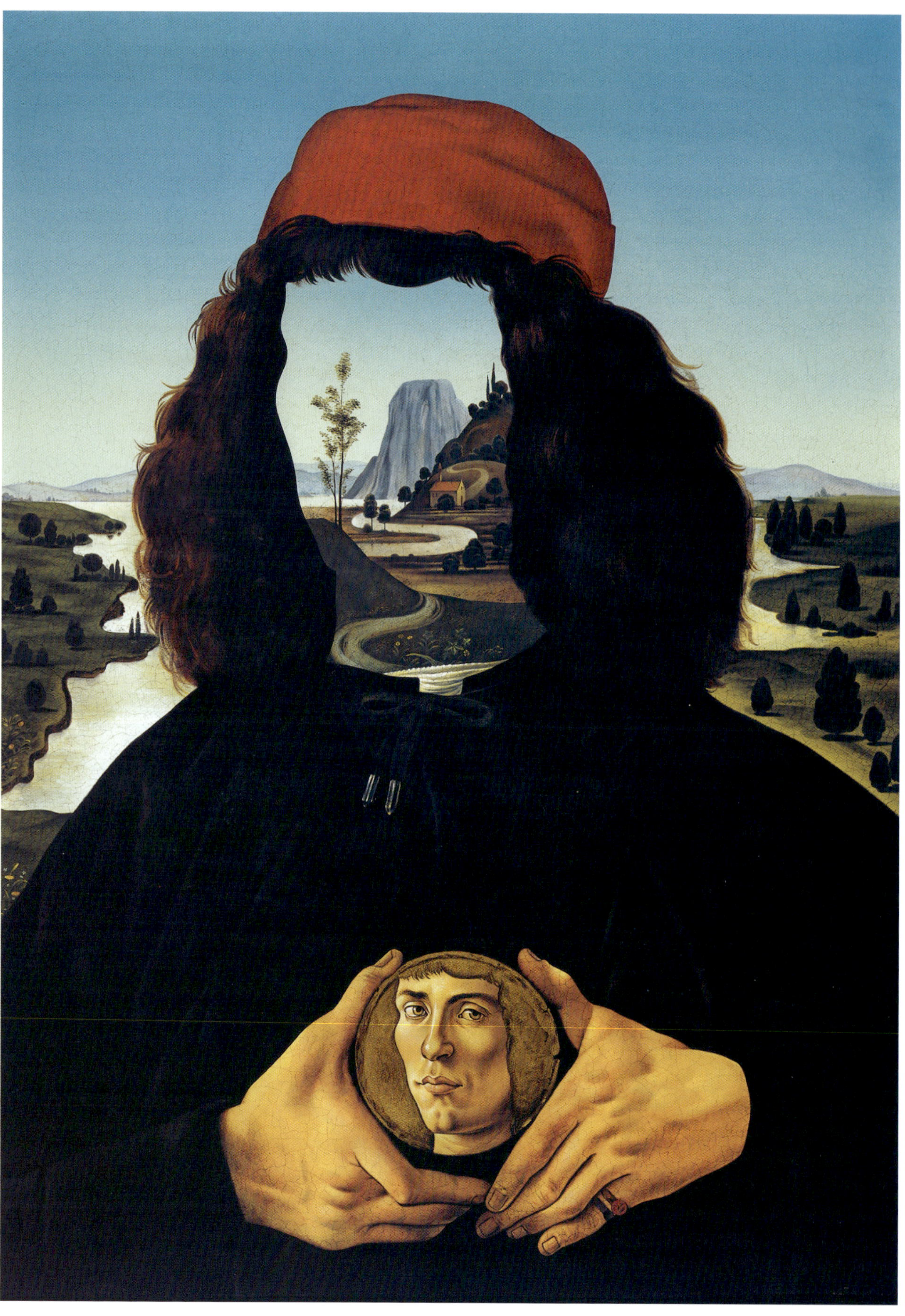

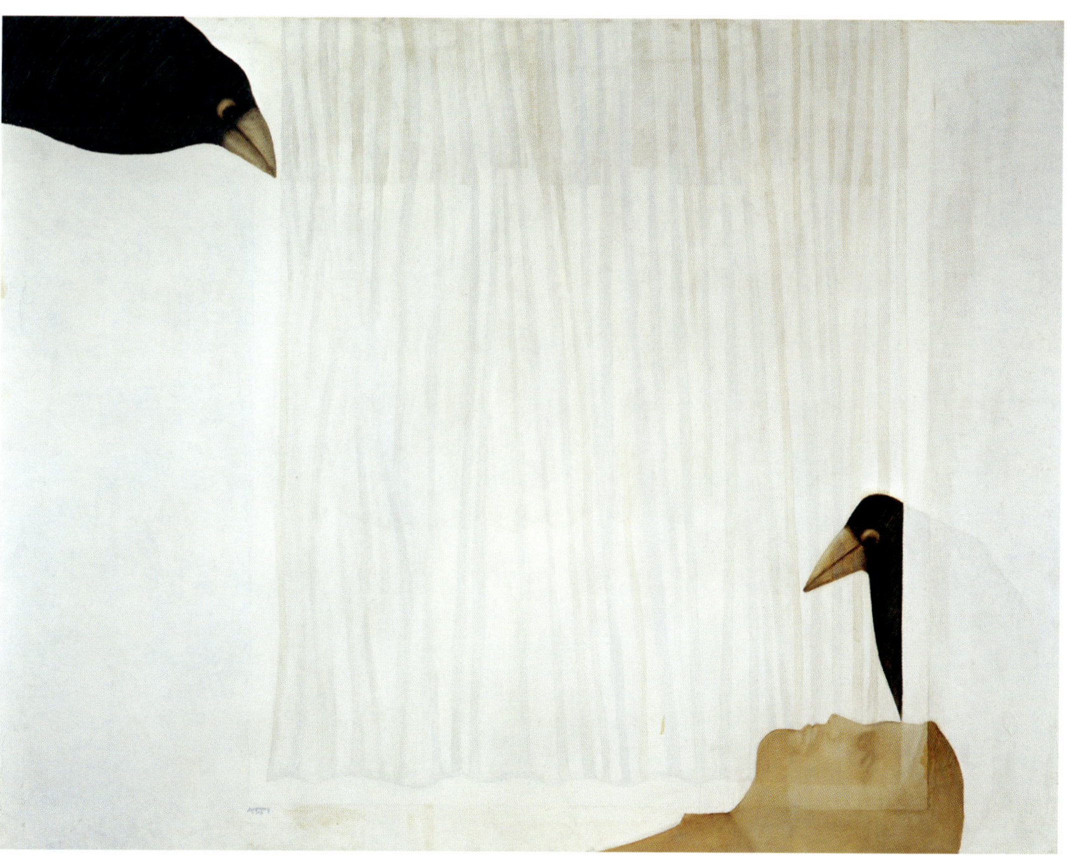

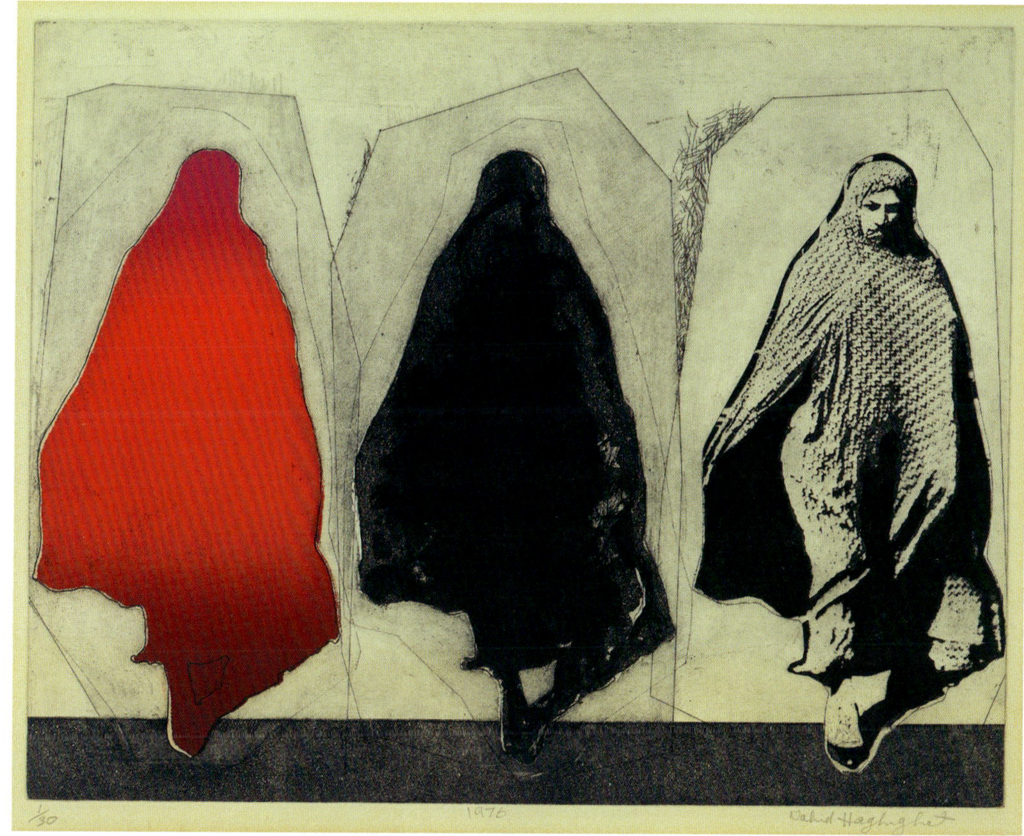

Facing page
3.126
Aydin Aghdashloo, *In Praise of Sandro Botticelli* (from *Memories of Destruction* Series), 1975, gouache on paper, 71×50 cm, TMoCA

Above
3.127
Alireza Espahbod, *Crows*, 1977, oil on canvas, 126×160 cm, TMoCA

Left
3.128
Nahid Haghighat, *Untitled*, 1976, etching, 32×39 cm, TMoCA

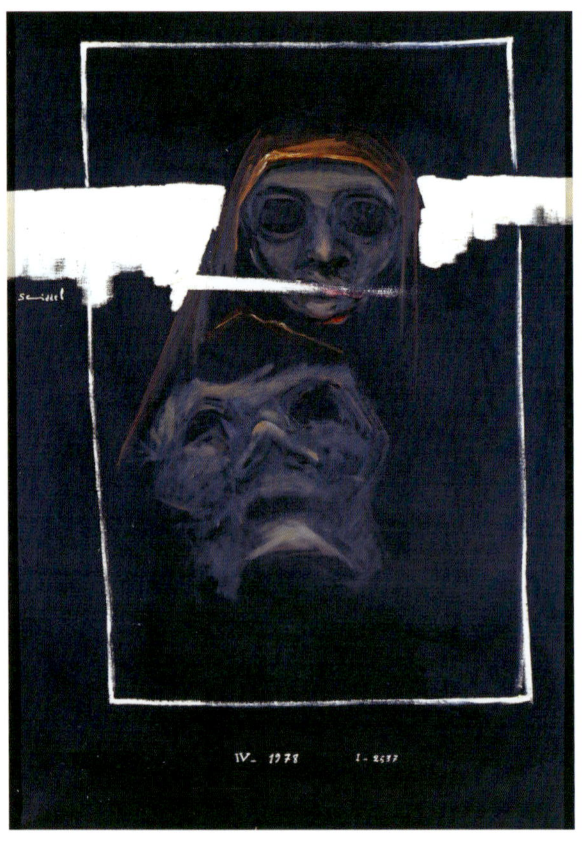

3.129
Mohammad Hossein Shiddel,
Untitled, 1978, oil on canvas,
101×70 cm, TMoCA

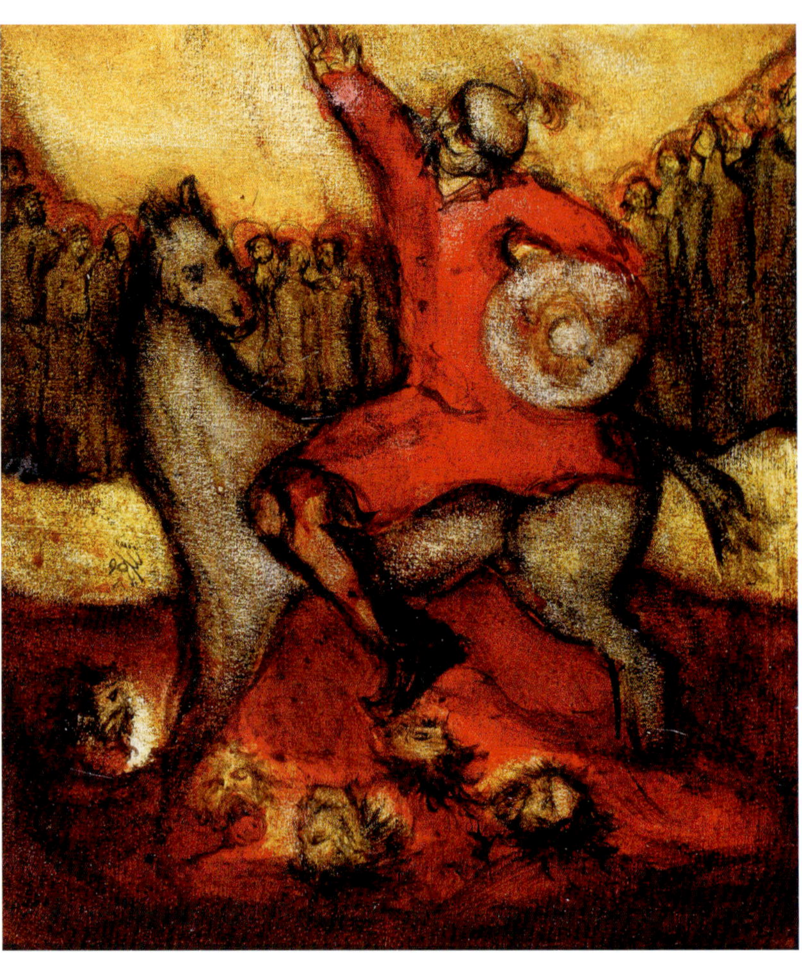

3.130
Rahim Najfar, *A Horseback-Rider Man
in Ta'ziyya*, 1974, gouache on paper,
29×25 cm, TMoCA

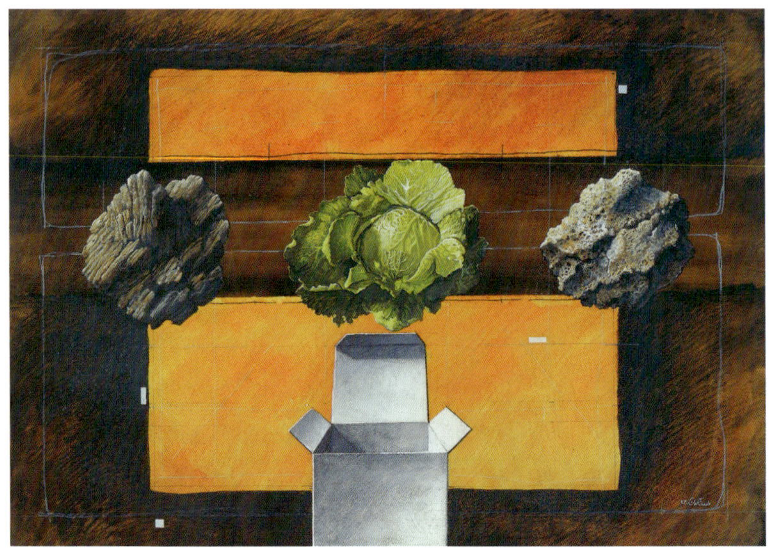

3.131
Wahed Khakdan, *Untitled*, 1977,
gouache on paper, 48×68 cm, TMoCA

and a large-scale series of paintings titled *Stories from the Revolution*. This series was later exhibited in one of the first post-revolutionary exhibitions held at the Tehran Museum of Contemporary Art.

The same notes of disapproval were sounded in many articles in magazines and newspapers. The core of this criticism was that many works of art were too repetitive and compliant with the artistic taste of the official cultural interest. Although the government's support (in a country where no art market funded private artistic sectors) had been able to establish a vibrant artistic atmosphere, it created an opposition faction that believed in other forms of cultural and political practices. The following years, however, saw a great change in cultural and artistic modes; these would fundamentally challenge the status quo.

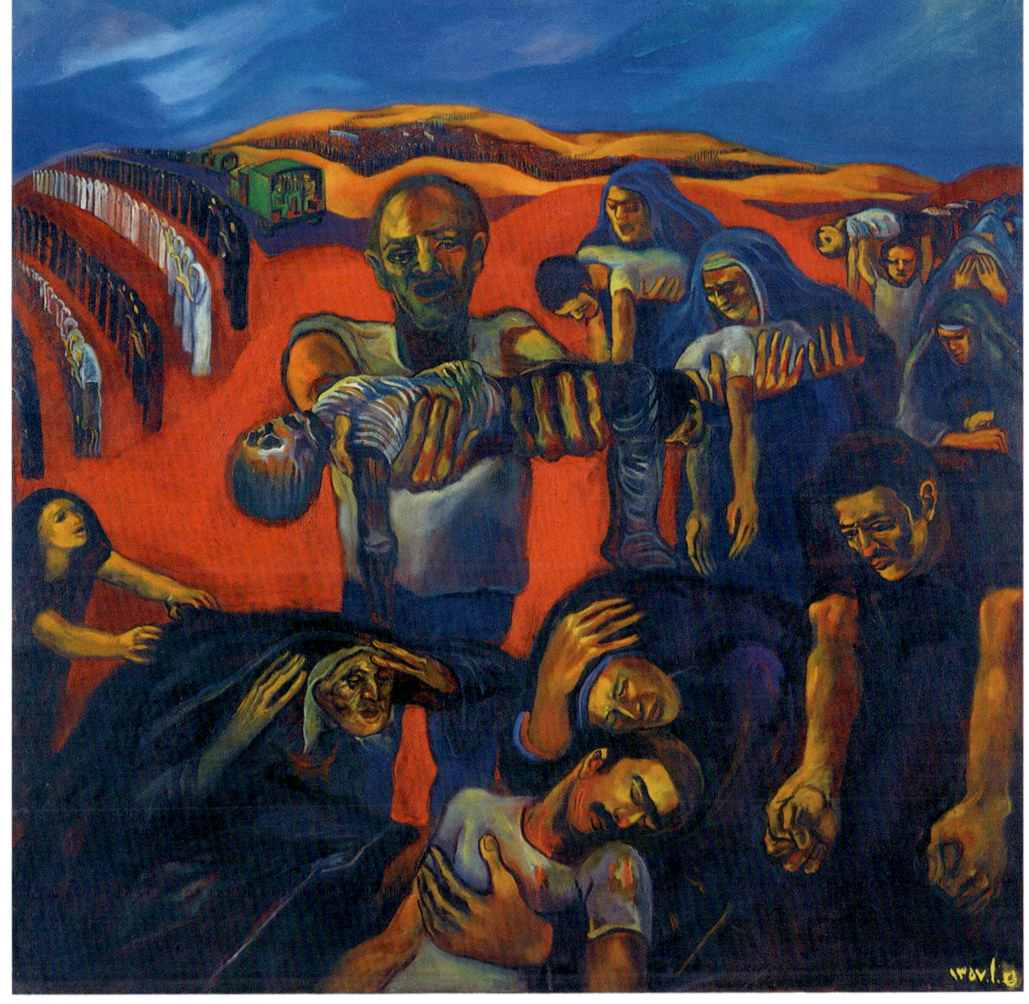

3.132
Hannibal Alkhas, *Revolution*, 1978, oil on canvas, 140×140 cm

3.133
Nikzad Nodjoumi, *Untitled*, 1977,
gouache and pastel on board,
95×69 cm, TMoCA

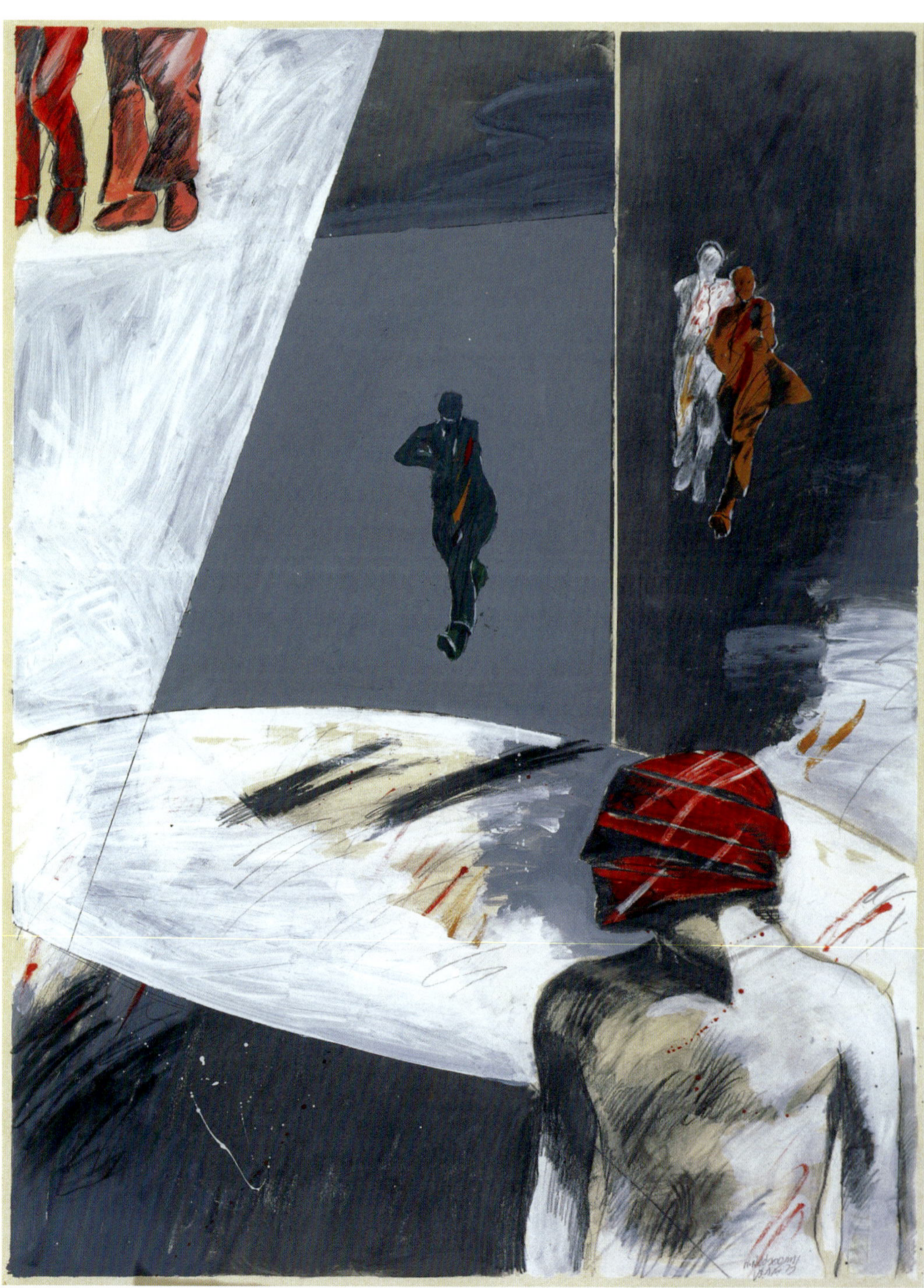

NOTES

1   Modernism here signifies the broad philosophical framework within which the modern art movement took place in the twentieth century, with all its diversity and disunity of forms and styles, and which also provides theoretical discourse for the evaluation and legitimisation of modern works of art.

2   It is worth noting that one might refer to Hobsbawm's theory of 'invented tradition' both for the artistic approach and the Iranian intellectual and political elites' milieu of the period. It is particularly useful when we see that the 1950s and 1960s are the 'times of rapid social transformation when "old" traditions were disappearing'. (Eric Hobsbawm, 'Inventing traditions' in Eric Hobsbawm and Terence Ranger, ed., *The Invention of Tradition*, Cambridge 1983, p.4.) It should, however, be stated that most of the traditional material found in the art, and perhaps literature, of this trend does not tend to be 'ancient' or 'reference to old situations' (Ibid, p.5–8), but rather from very recent history i.e. folk or native traditional productions.

3   A narrative quoted from Karim Emami describes the story in a different way, although Tanavoli himself contests the accuracy of the story. (Personal interview with Parviz Tanavoli, winter 2012) Emami narrates that one day in the late 1950s Tanavoli and Zenderoudi took a trip to the Shrine of Shah 'Abd al-'Azim (a shrine in the town of Shar-i Rey in the south of Tehran that today forms part of Greater Tehran). They found (and were fascinated by) some religious printed posters, talismanic seals and images. At that time, he declares, they were looking for local Iranian raw material to be used and developed in their works. Tanavoli believes that the first sketches Zenderoudi created on the basis of those materials were in fact the first examples of *Saqqa-khaneh* works. (See Karim Emami, 'Saqqakhaneh School Revisited', in *Saqqakhaneh* (exhibition catalogue), Tehran 1356S/1977, p.2.) Zenderoudi himself is quoted as saying that he was inspired by Shi'i religious stories circa 1958–59 after seeing a talismanic shirt with a prayer on it at the Iran-i Bastan Museum (Iran National Museum). (Ruin Pakbaz and Yaghoub Emdadian, *Charles Hossein Zenderoudi*, Ruin Pakbaz & Yaghoub Emdadian ed., Tehran 2001, p.33.) Yet although some artists affiliated to the movement have challenged Emami's account (Sadegh Tabrizi, 'Saqqa-khaneh az anja pa girift (interview with Artist)', *Hunar-hay-i tajassumi*, no. 6, 1377S/1998, p.93), undoubtedly a main branch of the movement owes its formation to the outcome of the friendship between these two artists and their joint research into Iranian folk culture.

4   Parviz Tanavoli, 'Atelier Kaboud', in David Golloway, ed., *Parviz Tanavoli: Sculpture, Writer & Collector*, Tehran 2000, p.69.

5   Karim Emami, 'Saqqakhaneh School Revisited', in *Saqqakhaneh* (exhibition catalogue), Tehran 1977, p.3.

6   Coffee-house (*Qahveh-khaneh*) refers to the works of mainly anonymous popular artists working in Iran during the early twentieth century. Their works were mainly shown in the public places like public coffee-houses. The principal aim of these artists was to express the respect of the religious and traditional beliefs of the ordinary people, who in turn expected their artists to depict their religious sagas and national epics, whether on canvases or in the form of mural paintings. Deeply affected by the early eclectic art of Qajar portraiture, these artists chose their subjects either from Shi'i narratives (Karbala tragedy in particular) or *Shahnameh*'s epics. Among the better-known Coffee-house painters, the names of Hossein Qollar Aghasi (1902–66), Mohammad Modabber (1890–1966), Abbas Boloukifar (1924–2000) and Hossein Esmaeilzadeh (1922–2007) are worthy of mention.

7   Reza Abbasi Hall was one of the few exhibition venues in Tehran that was running under the Dramatic Arts Administration (*Idareh-i hunar-hay-i diramatik*).

8   Meaning wall hanging, referring to the common expression for Coffee-house paintings.

9   One of the first of his works displayed in this exhibition, titled *K+L+32+H+4. Mon père et moi* (My Father and I), has been formally recognised as the first *Saqqa-khaneh* painting.

10 Karim Emami, 'Saqqakhaneh School Revisited', p. 2.

11 Ibid.

12 This description of *Saqqa-khaneh* is quoted from Ehsan Yarshater, 'Contemporary Persian Painting', in *Highlights of Persian Art*, New York 1979, p.368, and it refers mainly to the traditional form of *Saqqa-khaneh*. Today, the simple form of *Saqqa-khaneh* (not including the decorative or traditional elements) with the same origin still exists in most cities in Iran.

13 Within Muslim culture, Zamzam refers to the spring of eternal life believed to flow in paradise, hence it is considered blessed and holy.

14 Peter Lemborn Willson, 'The Saqqakhaneh', in *Saqqakhaneh* (exhibition catalogue), Tehran 1356S/1977, p.18.

15 John Anthony Clark, *Modern Asian Art*, North Ryde, N.S.W 1998, p.219.

16 Ruyin Pakbaz, *Encyclopedia of Art*, Tehran 1378S/1999, p.893. One of the main purposes of the establishment of the College of Decorative Arts was to emphasise applied and decorative art (something like the Paris École des Arts Déco that played the same role against the École des Beaux Arts). It should also be stated that the education system at the College of Decorative Arts was more progressive than at the Faculty of Fine Arts, Tehran University in terms of its updated system and method of education. The other reason for the establishment of the College was that the graduates of Fine Art High Schools could not easily enter the Faculty of Fine Arts at the University of Tehran. The system at the Faculty mainly preferred other secondary school graduates who were more successful in the Entrance Examination because they had a stronger theoretical background than art graduates.

17 Karim Emami, 'Art in Iran XI Post-Qajar', in Ehsan Yarshater, ed., *Encyclopaedia Iranica*, vol. II, London & New York 1987, p.642. Apart from Iranian instructors, the Faculty employed some foreigners. The Iranian instructors included avant-garde artists such as Hossein Kazemi and Mohsen Vaziri Moghaddam.

18 Karim Emami, 'Saqqakhaneh School Revisited', p.3.

19 It refers to the cut-hand-shape metalwork, usually used in Shi'i rituals and iconography. According to the Shi'i tradition,

the five fingers symbolise Prophet Muhammad, Fatemeh, Ali, Hassan, and Hossein as well as the severed hand of Abbas (Hossein's brother) when he struggled to bring water from the Euphrates for Imam Hussain and his companions.

20 Shiva Balaghi, 'Iranian Visual Arts in "The Century of Machinery, Speed and the Atom": Rethinking Modernity', in Shiva Balaghi, and Lynn Gumpert, ed., *Picturing Iran: Art, Society and Revolution*, London and New York 2002, p.25.

21 Ehsan Yarshater, 'Contemporary Persian Painting', p.356.

22 See Fereshteh Daftari, 'Another Modernism: An Iranian Perspective', in Shiva Balaghi and Lynn Gumpert, ed., *Picturing Iran: Art, Society and Revolution*, London and New York 2002, p.74.

23 Sadegh Tabrizi, 'Saqqa-khaneh az anja pa girift (interview with Artist)', p.93.

24 Kaboud Atelier was founded by Parviz Tanavoli in 1960 with some financial support from the General Administration of Fine Arts. Gradually, this Atelier became an artistic centre for modernist artists such as Zenderoudi, Grigorian, Melkonian, Sheybani, Saffari and Sepehri. The pioneer of *Saqqa-khaneh*, Charles Hossein Zenderoudi, held three exhibitions there (with the encouragement and support of Tanavoli). (Parviz Tanavoli, 'Atelier Kaboud', p.93.)

25 Sadegh Tabrizi, 'Saqqa-khaneh az anja pa girift (interview with Artist)', p.93.

26 Although he is preferably categorised as an abstract artist in his *Saqqa-khaneh* period, he himself and some critics considered him a figurative artist who looked at subjects in an abstract way. In fact, his name can be put between abstract and figurative artists among the other members of this genre. (Mansour Qandriz, 'Man beh suhulat-i bayan va azadi-i iradeh iman daram', *Firdowsi*, no. 714, 1344S/1965, p.16.)

27 This kind of viewpoint might have been influenced by the major concept of Abstract painting. According to Evans, 'one of the modernist characteristics in terms of artistic expression of the art work is that [. . .] modernist painting has, for example, sought to create nothing more than the "pure" self-referential image – abstract, non-verbal, free of representation, reference and narrative – although this interpretation of modernist works was fortified by elaborate verbal discourses of modernist art theory.' (Jessica Evans and Stuart Hall, *Visual Culture: The Reader*, London 1999, p.11.)

28 According to David Galloway, the first appearance of a *Heech* in Tanavoli's work was in an assemblage created in 1965 for a controversial show at the Borghese Gallery, Tehran. In the upper part of the composition was a plastic circle enclosing the word *heech*, also in plastic and rendered in a flowing Persian script. Below this emblem, a pair of plaster hands grasped a copper grille, as though pleading for help. (David Galloway, 'The Global Vision of Parviz Tanavoli', *Art Tomorrow*, no. 5, p.175.)

29 Parviz Tanavoli, 'Atelier Kaboud', in *Parviz Tanavoli: Sculpture, Writer & Collector*, Tehran 2001, p.97.

30 Abbas Daneshvari, 'Parviz Tanavoli of Existential Purity and Sophistication', *Art Tomorrow*, No. 5, p.183.

31 His works attracted critics when they were exhibited in the First Paris Biennale in 1959. A prize-winner of this Biennale in 1961, Zenderoudi settled in Paris in the same year. Immediately after his success in the Third Tehran Biennial in 1962, his works, selected as winners, were sent to the Venice Biennale and displayed there and then purchased by the MoMA, New York.

32 Karim Emami, 'Saqqakhaneh Revisited', p.3.

33 In 1970 he elaborated the periods of his development as follows: 'I divide my works into three periods. The period in which I was inspired by the occult and magic spells followed by another when I turned to calligraphy, and the current period that I am in – the third one. This period is marked by scripts that do not aim to create beauty; rather they maintain undefined space as in mathematics and seek movement like that of poetry and music.' (Anonymous, 'Man hichguneh qiyd va bandi ra baray-i hunarmand nimipaziram', *Firdowsi*, no. 984, Mihr 1349S/ October 1970, p.19.)

34 He was perhaps the first among members who used old seals in his paintings; this then became common in many other works of the movement.

35 In the later years, Pilaram participated in two exhibitions with the avant-garde Independent Group of Painters and Sculptors (*Guruh-e Azad Naqqashan va mujassameh-sazan*), titled *Abi* and *Gonj va Gustareh*, where he presented his calligraphic works.

36 Anonymous, 'Guft-u-gu-i ba naqqashan-i javan', *Sukhan*, no. 11, 12, Murdad & Shahrivar 1343 S/August 1964, p.1063.

37 Mansour Qandriz, 'Dowreh-i qajar', *Intighad-i Kitab*, no. 8, Isfand 1343S/March 1965, p.86.

38 Ruyin Pakbaz, *Contemporary Iranian Painting and Sculpture*, Tehran 1974, p.33.

39 Reza Baraheni, 'az aftabi beh aftab-i digar', in *Tarikh-i Muzakkar, Farhang-i hakim va mahkum*, Tehran 1363 S/ 1984, p.185.

40 He participated in the Third and Fourth Tehran Biennials in 1962 and 1964, São Paulo Biennial in 1963, and Paris Biennale in 1965.

41 Ruin Pakbaz, 'Chihreh-i az Qandriz', p.56.

42 One of the favourite subjects of Qajar royal painting was the representation of young female dancers, musicians and acrobats. The facial features of the females with joined eyebrows, almond-shaped eyes, puckered lips and flamboyant hairstyles depict the ideal form of beauty in that period.

43 Ibid.

44 See Karim Emami, 'Modern Persian Artists', in Ehsan Yarshater & Richard Ettinghausen, ed., *Iran Faces the Seventies*, New York 1971, p.357.

45 Talar-i Iran, one of the most active and intellectual artistic venues during the 1960s and 1970s, was the name of an independent gallery launched in Tehran in 1964. The gallery was established with three different missions: presentation (exhibition), writing, and lecture and discussions. (See Ruin Pakbaz and Mohammad Reza Jowdat, Fa'aliyyat-i ma keh dar Talar-i Iran shikl migirad, *Kitab-i sal-i Talar-i iran*, 1344S/1965, p.6.) With of the input of a group of young artists, in particular

Mohammad Reza Jowdat and Ruin Pakbaz, this gallery was established as an active cultural centre holding painting, graphic design, photography, architecture and sculpture exhibitions, introducing the young artists' works, translating and publishing various art and architecture books and artistic anthologies over a period of thirteen years until 1977. The publication included translations, books on modern art and architecture, from Impressionism, Fauvism and the Bauhaus movement to more critical writings on modern art such as the texts of Herbert Read. The Talar published several periodicals too, including the monthly *Guzarish* (twelve issues), quarterly *Fasli dar hunar* (four issues), *Kitab-i sal* (one issue), and exhibition critique on the occasion of each show in Talar. The aim was to make a ground for artistic communication with other artists and also with the general public and so create a connection between modern art and society. Such main debates as cultural and artistic identity, nationality in art, and the situation of Iranian art and the artist were examined through organising sessions of critical discussion, publication and critical writing which were unprecedented initiatives in those years. This Talar was first called Talar-i Iran after the death of Qandriz (1965), and in honour of his memory named Talar-i Qandriz. (See Ruin Pakbaz, *Encyclopedia of Art*, p.154.)

46 Ruin Pakbaz and Mohammad Reza Jowdat, 'Fa'aliyyat-i ma keh dar Talar-i Iran shikl migirad', *Kitab-i sal-i Talar-i iran*, no. 198, 1344S/1965, p.1.

47 Anonymous, Introduction to *Fasli dar hunar; dar bareh-y-i hunar-hay-i tajassumi, hunar-hay-i nimayishi va adabiyyat*, no. 4, summer 1350S/ 1971, no page number.

48 Apart from the oil revenues, the expansion of mining, almost exclusively on a small scale, continued rapidly to 1962. According to Julian Bharier, a national survey found that there were over 1,000 mines and quarries in operation, employing more than 15,000 workers. At the same time, nearly 600 mines of all types were idle. (Julian Bharier, *Economic Development in Iran 1900-1970*, London, New York, Toronto 1971, pp.152–153.) This period coincided with a time when state economic growth was pronounced. For example, according to Bharier: 'Within eighteen months of the start of the plan (The second Seven-Year Development Plan [1955–62]), the Plan Organisation obtained parliamentary approval to increase its total expenditure allocation by 20 per cent to 84 billion rials, and the total oil revenues started to grow much faster than anticipated.' (Ibid, p.91.) She also remarks: '[...] there is little doubt that Gross National Product (at current market prices) grew considerably during the 1960s, averaging 8–9 per cent annually. Moreover, there is some evidence that during 1955–60 an annual growth rate of about 7–8 per cent was achieved.' (Ibid, p.45.) Bharier, moreover, argues that although the overall effect of the White Revolution is hard to determine, since the real annual growth of the economy was running at about 10 per cent from 1964 to 1969, it is possible that, directly or indirectly, they helped to instil the type of confidence which would encourage the profit expectations of industrialists to rise. (Ibid, pp.96, 98)

49 Mehrdad Pahlbod, the Shah's brother-in-law, Director of the General Administration of Fine Arts and subsequently Minister of Culture and Art, had established a foundation attached to the court that funded the Tehran biennials.

50 Apart from the Cyrus Gallery, a number of gallery spaces were allocated for Iranian artist residencies at the Cité des Arts in Paris. Selected artists were awarded scholarships to reside there working with fellow artists in Paris, and to hold exhibitions of their works.

51 Before its establishment, there were Free Classes of Iranian calligraphers in which traditional calligraphy was taught. These started in 1950. In 1967, they developed into a society under the leadership of Hossein Mirkhani with the support of the Ministry of Culture and Art. It should be noted that the Society was mainly founded by two eminent proponents of contemporary Iranian calligraphy, Hassan and Hossein Mirkhani. Their style of calligraphy, especially that of Hossein Mirkhani, originated from that of a famous calligrapher of the Qajar period, Mirza Reza Kalhur.

52 Introduction to the Fourth Tehran Biennial (exhibition catalogue), Tehran 1343S/1964.

53 Under the influence of rising oil revenues, the public sector's share of consumption and investment expenditures rose more or less steadily throughout the period. (Hashem Pesaran, 'Economy IX in the Pahlavi Period', in Ehsan Yarshater, ed., *Encyclopaedia Iranica*, vol: VIII, Costa Mesa, California 1998, p.151.) Ervand Abrahamian remarks that 'hitting a new period of $555 million in 1963–1964, the oil income continued to climb reaching $958 million in 1968–1969.' (Ervand Abrahamian, *Iran Between Two Revolutions*, Princeton, New Jersey 1982, p.427)

54 The first Tehran Biennial was held with the recommendation and artistic advice of Marcos Grigorian in 1958. This was an influential event in introducing modern art to Iran. The first four biennials included the works of Iranian artists, which reflected official sanctioning of the modern artistic movements. The fifth Tehran Biennial was a regional exhibition in 1966, which included artists from Iran, Pakistan and Turkey.

55 Marcos Grigorian, Introduction to the First Tehran Biennial catalogue, p.6.

56 Anonymous, Introduction to the Second Tehran Biennial (exhibition catalogue), Tehran 1960, pp.14, 15.

57 The term 'global art', used in many written texts and also by artists in Iran, basically meant the majority of the idioms, artistic modes, approaches and happenings in both the European and American art scene.

58 In a more critical yet aligned stance, the manifesto of Talar-i Qandriz in spring 1969 declares: '...we uphold innovation (modernism) as an intrinsic trait of a "vibrant" human existence... However, we assert that it is not an unchecked concept. While we have unavoidably drawn from Western heritage and our techniques and ideologies have been shaped by this prevailing culture, we are focused on preservation. We deeply cherish our traditions and are dedicated to a deeper and more precise exploration of them.'(Anonymous, 'Bayaniyeh-i guruh-i naqqashan-i talar-i Qandriz', *Barrasi: mi'mari, naqqashi, mujjasameh-sazi, girafik...*, no. 6-7, 1944S/1965, p.1.

59 See illustrations in the previous chapter.

60 An example of this belief is a statement by Zenderoudi. Explaining the way in which he used the folk art, he declares: 'I took the inspiration from numbers, astrolabes, metal plates, prayer writing, etc. and came to know that these humble treasures of alleys and street, coloured by all civilizations, are the origin and basic essence of Iranian civilization. [. . .] Those treasures existed before. They are only materials, objects, places or cultural values in need of one who can summarise them and add polished elements.' (Zenderoudi, www.zenderoudi.com/eng/inter/html; accessed March 2002)

61 Mehrzad Boroujerdi, *Iranian Intellectuals and the West: The Tormented Triumph of Nativism*, p.132.

62 Ibid.

63 Patrick Williams and Laura Chrisman, *Colonial Discourse and Post-colonial Theory: A Reader*, New York 1994, p.174.

64 Kamran Diba, 'Iran', p.153.

65 Ibid.

66 Daryoush Shayegan believes that 'tourist is a modern pilgrim. A tourist always would like to know and basically wants to have a subject for dialogue [...]. A tourist wants to achieve everything fast and easily. He wants to see, use, and take anything as soon as possible, and come back home. Tourist is not patient enough to learn and watch the florescence, which is one of the conditions that a fruit bears in the silence of nature. A tourist is hasty, because he is worried; he is worried because he is a mist of contrary desires. A tourist wants to be given everything readily, everything is adjusted according to his understanding, and so he hates to waste his time. A tourist has money and likes to buy everything and as soon as possible benefit its maximum profit.' (Daryoush Shayegan, *Asiya dar barabar-i gharb* (Asia Facing the West), Tehran 1978, p.83.) According to the aforementioned definition, generally a tourist does not have time or does not want to be deep and profound when he is fascinated by something. Above all, a tourist is usually fascinated by something that cannot be found in his own region and would be novel there. There is no difference what it is, including its quality, or who produced it. The only criterion for him is its unique characteristics.

67 Anonymous, 'Bayaniyeh-i guruh-i naqqashan-i talar-i Qandriz', p.1.

68 Ibid, p.3.

69 The *Saqqa-khaneh* trend did not have an explicit doctrine; instead, the term 'doctrine' here refers to the core principles underlying the movement's objectives. These principles encompassed a focus on cultural and artistic identity, drawing from pictorial heritage while addressing the complexities of modern life through a neo-traditional approach.

70 The exhibition was curated by Nahid Mahdavi.

71 Mansour Qandriz, one of the major members of the movement, died in a car accident in 1965.

72 Karim Emami, 'Saqqakhaneh School Revisited', p.5.

73 Tanavoli's continuous interest in Persian poetry and mystical thought was formed in new media. His presentation in the exhibition *Gardens of Iran: Ancient Wisdom, New Vision* in the TMoCA in 2004 once again showed this essential interest. Tanavoli exhibited an installation titled *Bagh-i Simurgh* (The Garden of the Phoenix). In this work he extended metaphor to mysticism. The installation was composed of thirty small birds evoking the twelfth- and thirteenth-century Persian mystic poet Farid al-Din Attar's famous pun on the Simurgh – literally meaning 'thirty birds' – as being at the same time one bird and thirty birds. Tanavoli's installation evokes the challenge of entrapment and escape. The installation is therefore a multi-level reference to the mystical theme of the eternal garden. The colourful birds, with bright yellows, greens, blues and reds suggest the concept of a natural garden; at the same time birds refer to the concept of well-watered gardens of eternity. This work, however, is a metaphor for captivity and freedom. It implies that the bad birds in the cages can only see the 'flight' which is being shown on the screen, associated with freedom, but do not know what sin is and what the transgressions are for which they now have to be punished! (See Hamid Keshmirshekan, 'Reproducing Modernity: Post-revolutionary Art in Iran since the Late 1990s', in *Amidst Shadow and Light, Contemporary Iranian Art and Artists*, Hong Kong 2011, pp.54–56.)

74 Our usage of this word does not exactly refer to *Lettrism*, the Parisian avant-garde movement of the 1940s to 1970s. Rather, the important commonality of the Iranian neo-calligraphist artists of this group and *Lettriste*s is in their use of the letters as a main visual element through a fragmentary and unliterary approach. There was also no clear connection with the contemporary movements in Europe, in particular the English Art and Language movement. With regard to this highly conceptually orientated movement in the 1960s, a parallel cannot be found in the calligraphic oriented movement in Iran and the wider Islamic world.

75 This term consists of two words: *Naqqashi*, meaning painting, and *Khatt*, which means script. The combination of these two words is used to denote those paintings that have basically been produced by professional calligraphers as well as painters.

76 It is, however, worth noting that there are other terms used by such art historians as Wijdan Ali (1997). In her book *Modern Islamic Art*, she classifies different calligraphic schools in the contemporary Islamic world by using various terms such as 'The Neo-classical Style', 'Modern Classical Style' and 'Calligraphiti'. (See Wijdan Ali, *Modern Islamic Art: Development and Continuity,* Gainesville, 1997, pp.165–168) According to her definition, the last two styles can be similar to the two above-mentioned neo-calligraphic approaches, *Naqqashi-khatt* and Letterism, although not quite the same as in our definition. Therefore, here the use of the two mentioned terms is preferred.

77 To distinguish between the tendency and the works, I use the words 'movement', 'tendency' or 'trend' after the term when it refers to the movement.

78 For example, as Schimmel says, 'pious Arabic sentences, invocations of 'Ali, and short prayers are found on *nasta'liq* pages, but the major achievement of calligraphers was to copy classical Persian literature, particularly poetry ...' (Annemarie Schimmel, *Calligraphy and Islamic Culture*, London 1990, p.59.)

79   Ibid, p.45.

80   Anthony Welch, *Calligraphy in the Arts of the Muslim Wold,*
     Kent, 1979, p.38.

81   It is stated that *Siyah-mashq* is usually a variation of *Nasta'liq*
     script. *Naskh-i ta'liq, naskh-ta'liq, Nasta'liq* is said in the works
     on calligraphy to have been formed by joining *naskh* and
     ta'liq, and this compound gradually came to be pronounced as
     nasta'liq. Although it is said it was invented by Mir 'Ali Tabrizi
     (d.850/1446), the existing manuscripts contradict this view and
     show that the invention of this script goes back as far as the
     thirteenth century. (E. Van Donzel, B. Lewis, & Ch. Pellat, ed.,
     The Encyclopaedia of Islam (New Edition), vol. 4, Leiden 1978,
     p.1124)

82   There might be, as Ali argues, artists who had already practised
     calligraphic painting in the Islamic world. (see Ali Wijdan,
     Modern Islamic Art, pp.152–156) However, artists of *Saqqa-
     khaneh* were indeed pioneers in approaching calligraphy in a
     pure abstract form and with non-literary content.

83   Parviz Tanavoli, 'Atelier Kaboud', in David Golloway, ed.,
     Parviz Tanavoli: Sculpture, Writer & Collector, Tehran 2000,
     pp.96, 97. One of Tanavoli's close friends first influenced by
     the calligraphic movement in Iran was Siah Armajani (1939–
     2020; lived and worked in the US from 1960 until his death in
     2020). His initial works in this period which continued for just
     a short time showed similar characteristics to the works of such
     letterists as Zenderoudi. (Figure 3.56)

84   For examples of this category of neo-calligraphic works in the
     Islamic world, see Venetia Porter, *Word into Art: Artists of the
     Modern Middle East,* London 2006.

85   One of the major characteristics of traditional calligraphy is
     its dependence on the *Kalam* (word). It has been said that the
     emergence of calligraphy and its permanent presence in the
     Islamic world as a form of art is derived from its inseparable
     connection with sacred *Kalam* and later literature.

86   Later in Paris he was probably influenced by the *Lettriste*
     movement. However, he had already begun to use calligraphic
     handwriting and had invented pseudo-script even before his
     trip to Paris, in his initial *Saqqa-khaneh* works of the late 1950s
     and early 1960s.

87   In 1970, he explains his familiarity with this movement as
     follows: 'I am working with an artistic and literary group called
     Lettriste in Paris which is the most coherent group after the
     Dadaists and Surrealists. They are encouraging me [to work
     with them] because they want to have a visual artist among
     them.' (Anonymous, 'Man hichguneh qiyd va bandi ra baray-i
     hunarmand nimipaziram', *Firdowsi,* no. 984, Mihr 1349S/
     October 1970, p.19.) It seems that Zenderoudi exaggerates
     his role in this group. In none of the sources about the
     Lettriste movement can we find any mention of Zenderoudi.
     Furthermore, he never mentioned this point later and it cannot
     even be seen in his *curriculum vitae* or his 2001 book published
     by the Tehran Museum of Contemporary Arts. But it shows, at
     least, that he was well aware of this movement and its manifesto
     in Paris and definitely had close contact with them, although his
     description of that movement is not very clear.

88   Pierre Cabanne, 'Un Lettrisme Sacré', *Combat,* no.7987, Lundi
     23 Mars 1970, p.5.

89   Anonymous, 'Man hichguneh qiyd va bandi ra baray-i
     hunarmand nimipaziram', *Firdowsi,* no. 984, 1349S/1970, p.19.

90   One such work found its way to the Venice Biennale, where
     it was later bought for the New York Museum of Modern Art
     (MoMA). (Karim Emami, 'Modern Persian Artists', in Ehsan
     Yarshate, & Richard Ettinghausen, ed., *Iran Faces the Seventies,*
     New York, 1971, p.356.)

91   Jalaloddin Kashefi, 'Naqqashi-i mu'asir-i iran (3)' (contemporary
     Iran painting), *Faslnameh hunar,* no. 15, 1372S/ 1993, p.85.

92   The artist believes this trend had been practised earlier by him.
     However, there is no reliable document to show any of these
     works before that exhibition, at least from what we define as
     neo-calligraphy.

93   Mansoureh Hosseini, in *Huviyyat-i farhangi va hunari:
     majmu'eh bahs-hay-i kunfirans-i hunar-hay-i tajassumi*
     (Proceedings of the First Plastic Arts Conference), Tehran
     1372S/ 1993, p.127.

94   Interview with artist, 2001.

95   Ibid.

96   Ibid.

97   Ibid.

98   Ruin Pakbaz, 'Biographies of Artists', in Rose Issa, ed., *Iranian
     Contemporary Art,* London, 2001, p.132.

99   Zahra Zehtab, 'Guft-u-gu ba hunarmand-i naqqashi-khatt ustad
     Nasrollah Afjai', *Khabar-nameh-i hunar-hay-i tajassumi,* no. 26,
     Tehran, Farvardin 1376S/ March 1997, p.3.

100 Ibid.

101 Wijdan Ali in her book *Modern Islamic Art: development and
     Continuity* addresses the widespread interest in calligraphic
     forms in the Islamic world since the 1950s. Other developments
     have occurred since her book was published in 1997, in
     particular after the growing interest in the market for this kind
     of art. In addition to the renowned Arab artists who are living in
     diaspora, there are several emerging ones in Middle Eastern and
     North African countries, in particular Iraq, Sudan, Egypt and
     more recently Saudi Arabia.

102 It has been suggested that Queen Farah perceived the Ministry
     of Culture and Art as a formal organisation with rigid rules that
     did not fully facilitate the development and growth of artists,
     particularly those inclined towards modernism. As a result,
     she sought to bolster avant-garde art by founding the Office of
     Empress Farah Pahlavi (*Daftar-i makhsus-i shahbanu Farah*) in
     1967 and later in 1977 the Farah Pahlavi Foundation. The Office
     of Empress Farah Pahlavi was responsible for maintaining Iran's
     museums and for sponsoring a host of other cultural events.
     (See Mehrzad Boroujerdi, *Iranian Intellectuals and the West:
     The Tormented Triumph of Nativism,* New York 1996, p.43.) The
     former Director of the National Iranian Radio Television, Reza
     Qotbi was appointed as the first Director of the Foundation.

103 See Jalal Sattari, *Dar bi duwlati-i farhang: Nigahi beh fa'aliyyat-
     hay-i farhangi va hunari dar baz-pasin sal-hay-i nizam-i pishin,*
     Tehran 1379S/ 2000, p.201.

104 The collection of the Tehran Museum of Contemporary Art

is widely considered to be one of the finest twentieth-century Western art collections in the world, in addition to being the most significant outside of Europe and the United States.

105 For example, Mohasses drew inspiration from Jalal Al-e Ahmad's (1923–69) critical perspective on the social role of art, advocating for its commitment to societal inspirations. Al-e Ahmad's writings, in which he expressed admiration for Mohasses's works, serve as evidence of the sympathetic connection between the two.

106 He was in charge of the establishment of the Reza Abbasi Museum in 1977 under Farah Pahlavi Foundation.

107 See Alireza Sami Azar, 'An Investigation into Different Series of Works by Aydin Aghdashloo', *Art Tomorrow*, no.2, summer 2010, pp.163–167.

CHAPTER FOUR

Post-Revolutionary Art

1. Revolutionary art and artists: The Establishment of the Artistic Centre of Islamic Propaganda Organisation (*Howzeh-i Hunari-i Sazman-i Tablighat-i Islami*)

With the Revolution came profound transformations in much of Iranian life, particularly across politics and culture. However, it is difficult to discern any sort of comprehensive, organised state policy for the arts during the first decade after the Revolution. Nevertheless, those transformations had a significant effect on the development Iranian post-revolutionary art. Revolutionary sentiments and Islamicism influenced art and artistic practice in the immediate period after the 1979 Islamic Revolution. A deep transformation in cultural and artistic sentiments took place within Iran, along with fundamental changes in the formal nature of art during this period.

This section will consider both the major discourses on art and artistic production in Iran after the Islamic Revolution, tracking the emergence of neo-traditionalism in the art of the 1990s and the major artistic trends and discourses within the socio-cultural context of post-revolutionary Iran, including art exhibitions held in the country. We shall consider the impact of the Islamic Revolution on the formation of the discourse of *muta'ahhid*[1] ('committed', i.e. revolutionary) art, and analyse the intellectual and governmental discourses and their role in the development of new post-revolutionary artistic trends. Throughout this discussion, we shall explore the revival of intellectual and artistic preoccupations from the pre-revolutionary generation.

As Peter Chelkowski remarks, the Revolution in Iran held universal significance in the modern history of the Middle East.[2] It was not merely a regressive fundamentalist movement but also a modern one, albeit with a message deeply rooted in localised imagery, advocating for an idealised return to the past.[3]

'Modernism', transferred to a sort of art based on Islamic cultural traditions, was initially popular among the masses who were the main supporters of the Revolution. The 1979 event, however, brought a sudden end to the official artistic policies of the previous regime, which had been based on the promotion of modernism on the one hand and of nationalism on the other. Both of these were challenged by the Revolution as elements of Pahlavi policy.

The most problematic issue for artists working in Iran during the first years after the Revolution was their suddenly being prevented from interacting with the world outside the country: they were unable to show their works to an international audience or participate in the global discourse that dominated modern art. Nevertheless, a few of the most established artists, as well as a significant number of dynamic young ones, chose to stay in Iran. The activity of the pre-revolutionary artists of this group, however, was not legitimised in official coteries until the early 1990s. In that milieu, anything that could be associated with a monarchical system was condemned. Haggai Ram argues that: '...revolutions are [...] – perhaps principally – struggles over memory',[4] that is, they wage war upon memories of the old order. In the Iranian Revolution, as Ram maintains, 'the commitment to break with the past [the monarchical system] provided a foundation upon which to build a new society'.[5] Accordingly, the revolutionaries 'set out to eradicate the hegemonic historical narrative of the Pahlavi monarchy by creating a counter-historical narrative that was ideally structured to fit the new teleology of the Revolution.'[6]

Initially, the anti-Western nature of the Revolution and the slogan of political and cultural independence clashed with the promotion of modern art in Iran, halting its development. In the years following the Revolution, a new definition of 'modernism' was suggested. In the new terminology, 'modernism' mainly implied a kind of Western product consisting of different artistic forms, styles and movements easily associated with the mainstream practices of artists affiliated to the monarchy regime. Common to all of these 'modernist' works, it was believed, was their contrast with a kind of realistic and representational demotic art that could convey meaning to the public. 'Modern' art was not approved of in official circles; rather it was regarded negatively because it lacked any political, religious, social or ethical message to 'direct' the viewer. In those early years after the Revolution, not only was modern art not supported by the government and other sectors, including ministries, banks, private corporations, and the press (who had favoured it during the pre-revolutionary period), it was met with indifference or even active opposition. In its place, art officials eagerly proposed the creation of a kind of Irano-Islamic art that would possess its own characteristics distinct from those of Western art and that would convey revolutionary cultural values.

However, Islamic and revolutionary values remained largely uncodified during the transition period and were subject to local or expedient interpretations; no theoretical or practical principles or patterns were specified for   visual arts. This resulted in a situation that was, at best, uncertain for Iranian painting during the late 1970s. It lasted throughout the 1980s and well into the early 1990s. This uncertainty is clearly apparent when one looks at the formal exhibitions held in the period after the Revolution, even the First Iranian Painting Biennial in 1991.

The most significant artistic shift just after the Revolution focused attention on the production of a particular kind of popular painting: the term *hunar-i mardumi* (demotic/collective art) in revolutionary terminology referred to realist (and sometimes expressionistic) art that dealt mainly with political and revolutionary subjects in which lower-class and ordinary people played a primary role; and later to traditional Islamic art. The principle of demotic art lay in the belief that art was a tool for propaganda. Peter Chelkowski and Hamid Dabashi write:

> A particular delivery of the rhetorical images of convictions – the art of persuasion, the ability to move the individuals in a mass – is designed to make legitimate claims on political obedience, on measures of mass mobilization. To the degree that such rhetoricals [sic] of images are rooted in deep and surviving cultural paradigms, they expose a wide angle of vision on the dominant moral matters of a political culture. The purpose, whether or not self-conscious, of aesthetics in any art of persuasion is to transform the experience of rhyme and reason, shape and beauty, into elements of mobilizing conviction.[7]

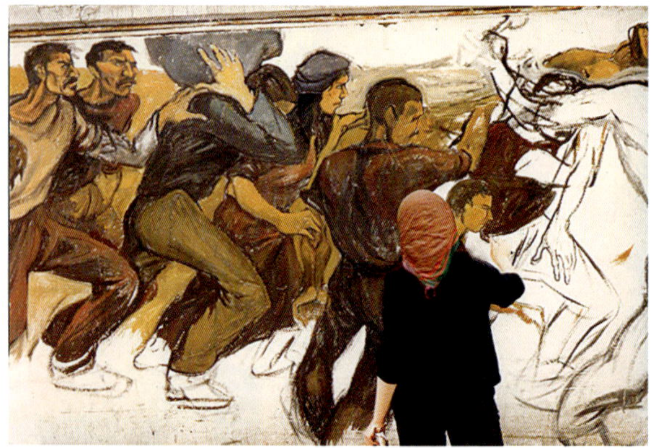
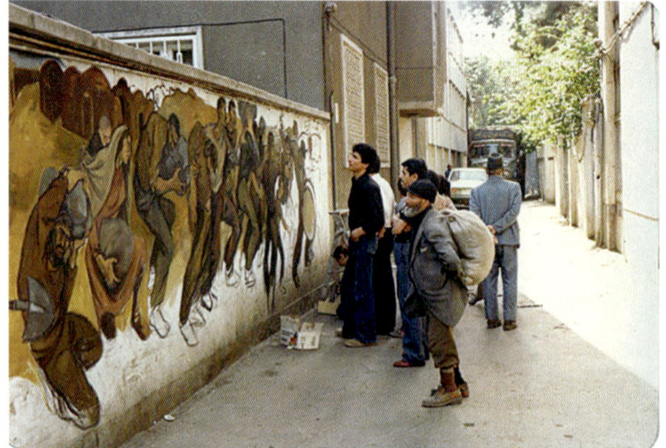
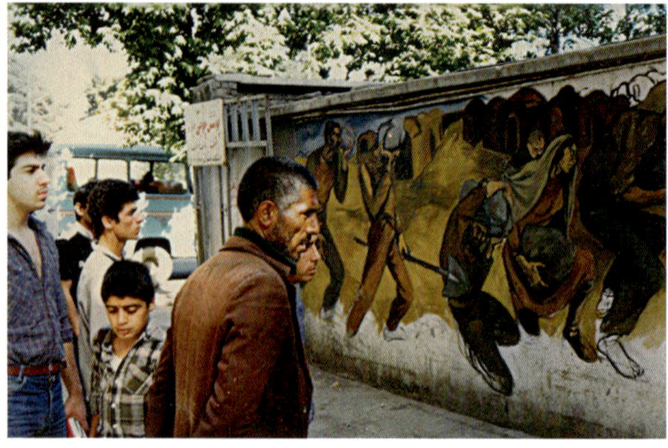

4.1
Niloofar Ghaderinejad, mural, 1978, Tehran,
courtesy the artist

Following the socialist trend already launched by a group of artists in the 1970s before the Revolution, other individuals attempted to participate in the grand social and cultural changes. In the period 1975–79 they focused on revolutionary works (though less on Islamic and more on Third World concerns), including murals, paintings and posters. (Figure 4.1) Among others, one can name Nosratollah Moslemian and Niloofar Ghaderinejad (b.1957). Moslemian was one of the pioneers of this trend; in works executed between 1975 and 1981, he showed vivid experimentation with revolutionary works. He was a true believer in a sort of 'committed art', although not in a religious way. He says: 'For me, painting was a kind of weapon, which could and had to change society. So my paintings automatically involved socio-political and ideological content.'[8] The use of large-scale canvases – because of the necessity of immediate and expansive communication with the audience – was one characteristic of the paintings of this period. Also recognisable is the influence of anti-Imperialist and anti-Capitalist ideology, the structure and content of such paintings as Soviet Union Socialist Realism and Mexican mural paintings, which dealt with social and human problems. (Figure 4.2) Of these independent artists, the Shishegaran brothers[9] also stand out for their creation of very popular posters on the theme of revolution, without any financial support or sponsor. (Figure 4.3–6)

However, much of this revolutionary art was produced by a group of young, mostly religious, ideologically minded artists who shared common socio-political, revolutionary and certain religious interests. These artists had had their first major show in the Ershad Assembly (Hussiyniyyeh-i Irshad) in Tehran in 1978, just before the Revolution. This marked the beginning of the Centre of Islamic Thought and Art (Howzeh-i andisha va hunar-i islami) later under the Centre of Islamic Propaganda Organisation (Sazman-i tablighat-i islami). A couple of years later in 1981, poets, filmmakers, writers and musicians joined the group and established the Artistic Centre of Islamic Propaganda Organisation (Howzeh-i hunari-i sazman-i tablighat-i islami). Scholars such as Christiane Gruber have commented on how the works produced by these artists were initially rather experimental and were only later appropriated and used as ideological weapons by officials.[10] However, most of these artists were happy to be considered members of the so-called Group of Revolutionary Artists. The most important figures of the Group (mainly art students at the Tehran Faculty of Fine Arts or the Tehran Faculty of Decorative Arts) include Kazem Chalipa (b.1957), Hossein Khosrowjerdi (b.1957), Habibollah Sadeghi

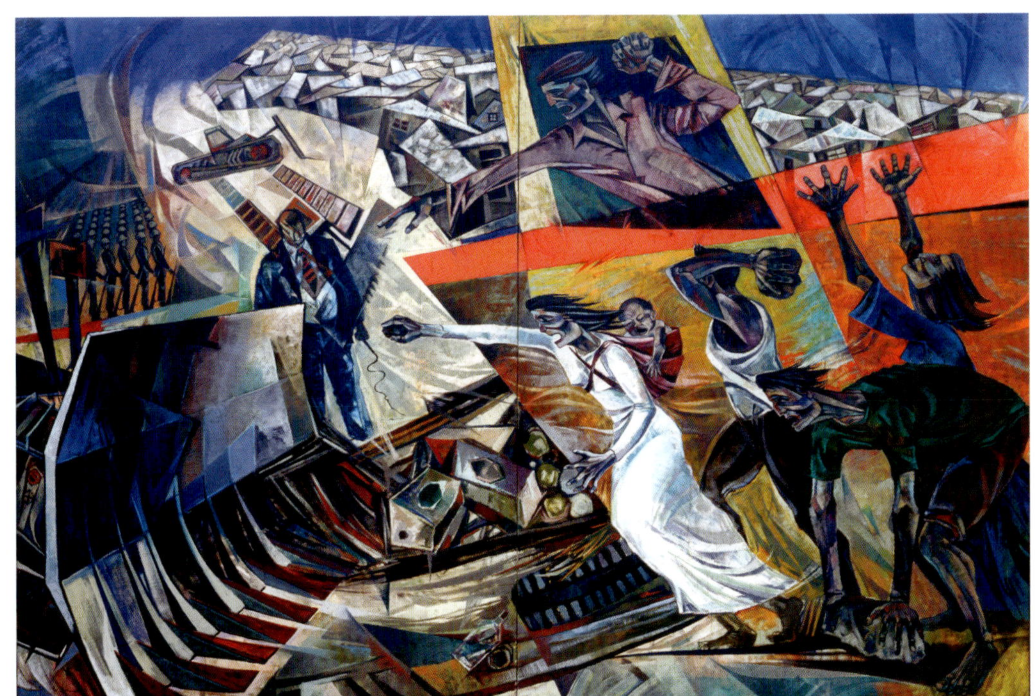

4.2
Nosratollah Moslemian, *Untitled*,
1977, oil on canvas, 210×300 cm,
courtesy the artist

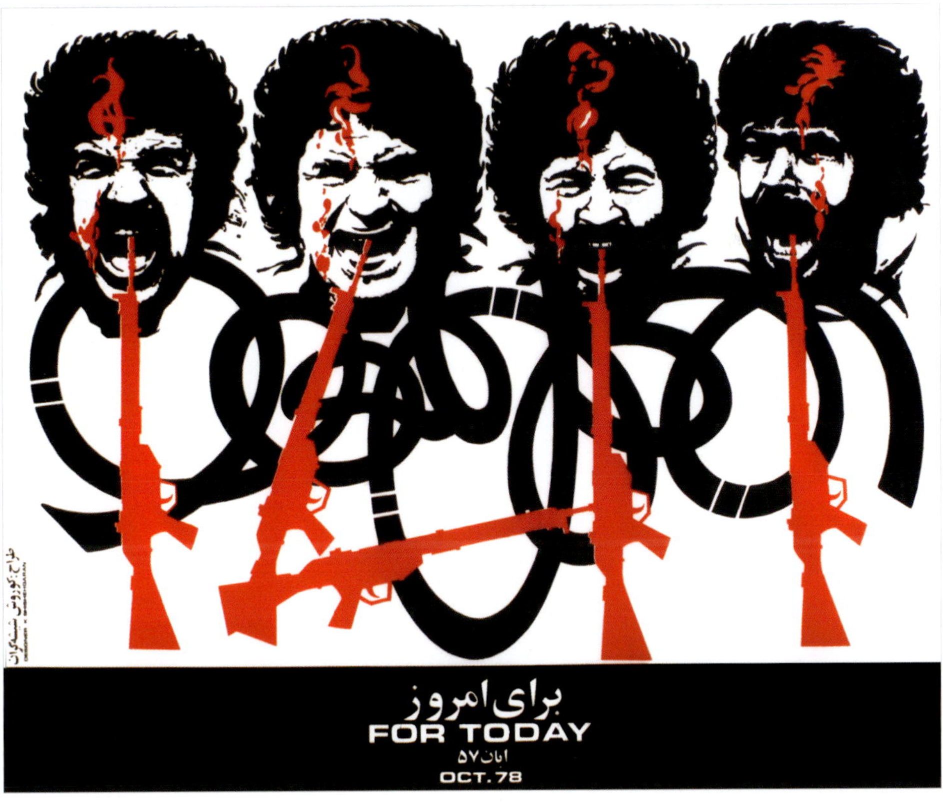

4.3
Koorosh Shishegaran, *For Today*, 1978,
poster, offset printing on paper, courtesy
the artist

(1957–2022), Nasser Palangi (b.1957), Iraj Eskandari (b.1956) and later Mostafa Goudarzi (b.1960), Ali Vazirian (b.1960), Abdolmajid Hosseini Rad (1959–2014), Abolfazl Aali (1955–87), Abdolhamid Ghadirian (b.1960) and Morteza Asadi (b. 1958).

It soon became obvious that these artists were formally supported by cultural officials. During this period, art centres were established in various ministries and militia units, including the Farabi Foundation in cinema, the Martyr and Veterans Affair Foundation (Bunyad-i shahid va janbazan) and the War Propaganda Army-Staff (Sitad-i tablighat-i jang) – all of which supported the revolutionary arts. The major official body of cultural and artistic affairs in post-revolutionary Iran, however, was the Ministry of Culture and Islamic Guidance, which had been established through the merger of two pre-revolutionary Ministries: of Culture and Art; and of Information and Tourism. This new body was first called the Ministry of Islamic Guidance, in 1980, and then in 1987 was renamed the Ministry of Culture and Islamic Guidance.[11] All of these establishments were there to support the so-called 'committed' or revolutionary art that then became a somewhat ideological art based on official interests.[12]

During this time young revolutionary artists filled exhibition halls, civic institutions and public spaces with large propaganda

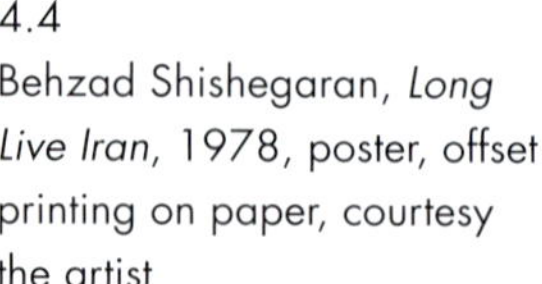

4.4
Behzad Shishegaran, *Long Live Iran*, 1978, poster, offset printing on paper, courtesy the artist

paintings, posters and murals commemorating the Islamic Revolution and revolutionary struggles. Furthermore, when the Cultural Revolution (*Inqilab-i farhangi*)[13] (1980–83) caused the temporary closing down of all universities (they were reopened in 1983), art institutions came under the absolute control of the ideological revolutionary agendas, and teachers were more often affiliated with the Artistic Centre of the Islamic Propaganda Organisation.

This situation remained almost unchallenged during the first decade after the Revolution. In 1983, the Minister of Islamic Guidance, Seyyed Mohammad Khatami (later in 1997 the reformist president), announced:

> We should recognise art as a significant branch of human culture and history, serving as a means to conceptualise and elevate the noble and profound spiritual essence inherent in humanity. Those who are emblematic embodiments of these values, have their characters intertwined with the ideals and aspirations of the Islamic Revolution. Presenting art in any other manner would betray both the essence of art itself and the dignity of human beings...[14]

The idea that modern art could not connect with ordinary people's beliefs seemed to be the other main reason for ignoring any form of it. It was argued that modern Iranian painting, despite its expanding growth in the 1960s and 1970s, had lost the public.[15] The post-revolutionaries also criticised the situation of Iranian artists and intellectuals working simply for themselves, and they found fault with pre-revolutionary artists because of their preference for formalism over content and meaning in their works. One of the theoreticians of the Group of Revolutionary Artists, Abdolmajid Hosseini Rad, claims:

> In the years preceding the Revolution, formalism reigned as the primary aspect of Iranian painting, captivating the focus of modernist painters. During that era, formalism held such sway that even attempts to develop a new visual language in alignment with national and local requisites were profoundly influenced by a formalistic viewpoint.[16]

Although revolutionary art first condemned or repudiated all kinds of pre-revolutionary art, careful consideration of some works by the

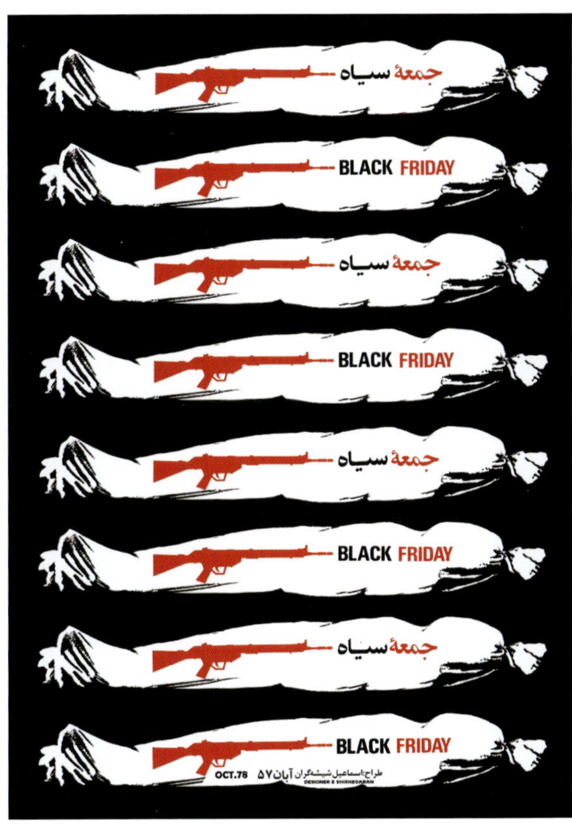

4.5
Esmail Shishegaran, Black Friday, 1978, poster, offset printing on paper, courtesy the artist

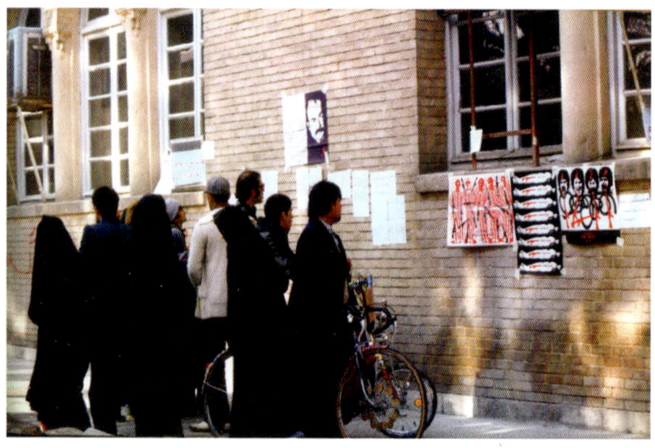

4.6
Posters by Shishegaran brothers in public during the 1978–9 Revolution

Facing page
4.7
Hossein Khosrowjerdi, *Hayyi 'alal-Falah*, 1977, oil on canvas, triptych, total size 200×500 cm, *Howzeh-i hunari*

Group of Revolutionary Artists reveals a measure of resemblance to the 1960s works by artists of the *Saqqa-khaneh* movement. This applies at least to their use of popular religious pictorial elements and motifs even in formalist constructions. In the varied forms of revolutionary art (especially posters, stamps and murals), calligraphic forms and Shi'i iconography were dominant features. These were mixed with a propagandist quality and figuration inspired by other twentieth-century revolutionary art, especially that from the Soviet Union, Mexico and Cuba. There was a clear and fundamental difference between the Islamic Revolution of Iran and other major revolutions of the twentieth century – the latter were future-orientated and based mainly on socialist beliefs and aspirations, while the Islamic Revolution focused on the Islamic past in order to redefine the future. Yet despite this, the formal characteristics of artistic production based on revolutionary and propagandist ideas were similar. In their use of symbolic elements, the Iranian revolutionary artists tried to reflect such concepts as the Revolution, the Iran-Iraq war, martyrdom and Gnosticism by a form of realistic expression that was a familiar language in other revolutionary art. Social commitment and storytelling that conveyed a religious or political message were among the most important features of these works. (Figures 4.7–12) This further increased their popularity and acceptance among the masses, since they were simple and understandable in both form and execution.

In terms of theory, however, the frequent use of such pompous expressions as 'spiritual identity' and 'elevation of forms' for Iran's post-revolutionary art, along with the absence of principles and accurate methods for its analysis, only intensified problems of its definition. For example, a message that Ayatollah Khomeini addressed to artists in September 1988 urged that revolutionary art be conceived as 'the gnosis of challenge', 'the rejection of uncommitted art and art for art's sake', 'the revolt against violence', 'the illustration of martyrdom', and the 'dedication to Islamic values'.

What proved to be one of the major official post-revolutionary exhibitions was held in 1983 at the Tehran Museum of Contemporary Art on the occasion of the fifth anniversary of the victory of the Revolution. Its aim was explained as follows:

> We should esteem the impulse to organise these exhibitions as an earnest and meaningful attempt, because the main reason for holding them is clearly to enshrine the spiritual as well as the committed content, the sincere and eloquent

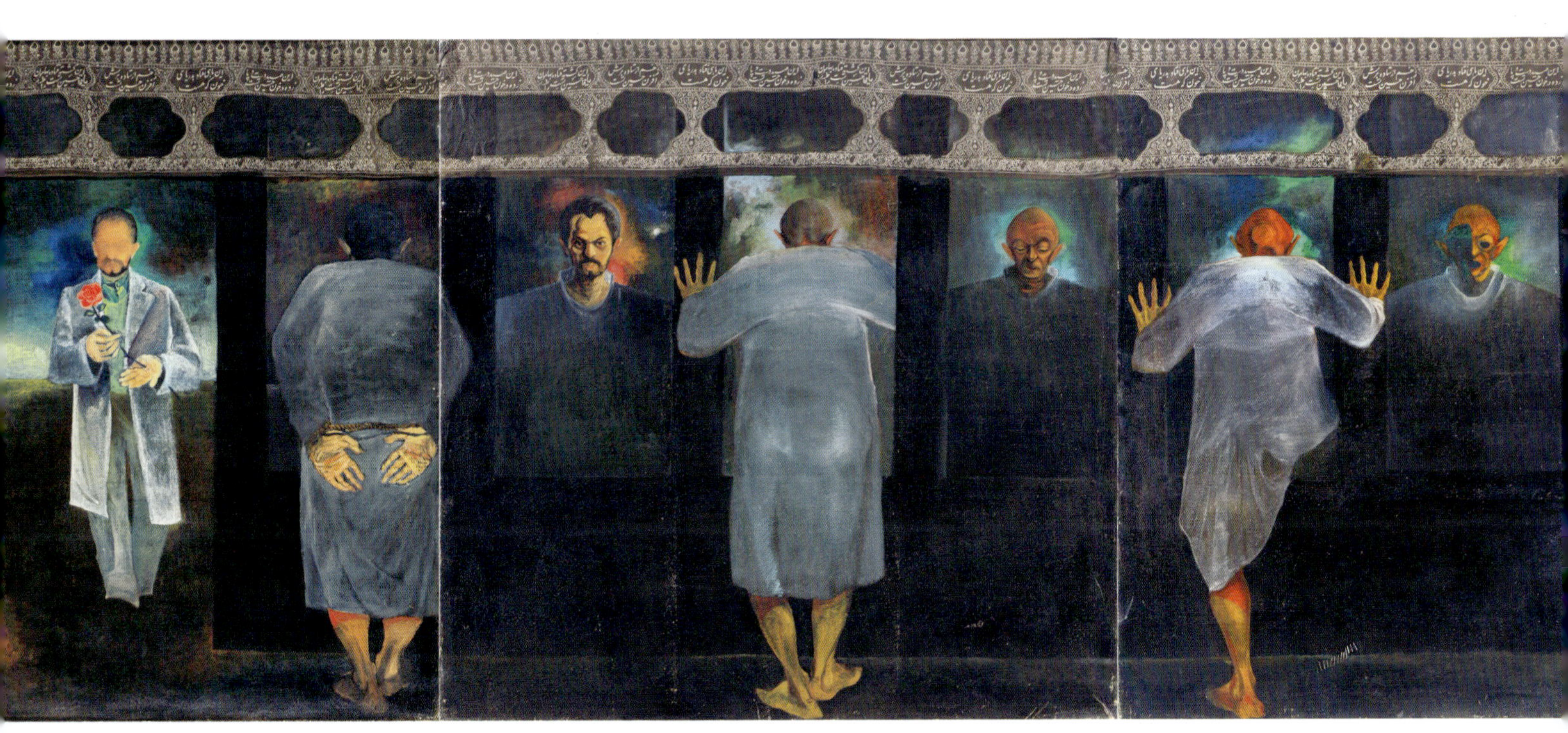

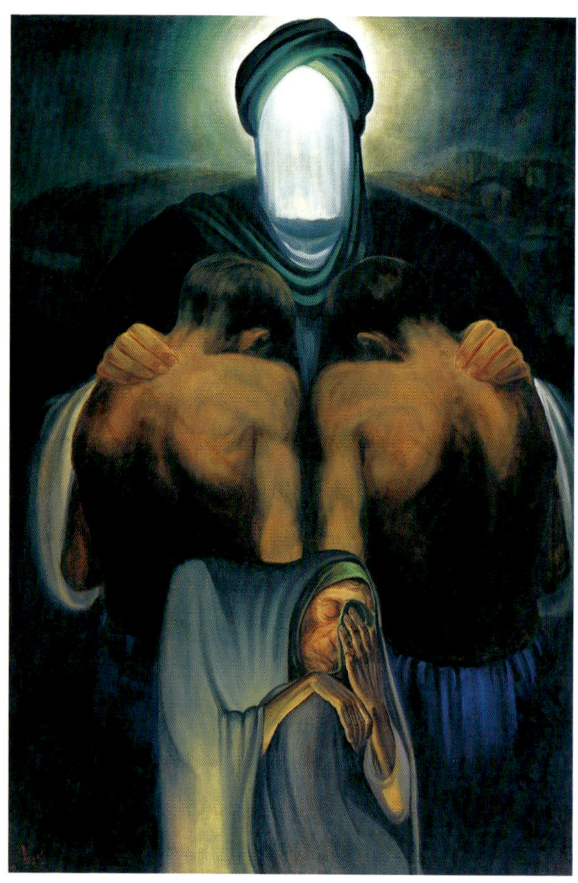

4.8
Kazem Chalipa, *Yaqin*, 1981, oil
on canvas, 150×100 cm, *Howzeh-i
hunari*

Facing page
4.9
Kazem Chalipa, *The Great Day*,
1984, oil on canvas, 160×115 cm,
Howzeh-i hunari

language of artists. [...] The dominant atmosphere of the
works shows a united message of artists who have created
their art with sincerity, faith, and seriousness in accordance
with principles of the Islamic Revolution, posing the
messages of the Revolution and, more important, creating
a committed, eloquent art. We should believe that after an
interval of doldrums in the formation of post-revolutionary
art, especially   visual arts, caused by the initial conflicts of
the Revolution, we can now see in these exhibitions the
flowering and growth of talent; [these are] artists whose
art does not originate in dilettantism but is full of message,
faith, and sincerity.[17]

This situation persisted and was further accentuated during the Iran-
Iraq war (1980–88): wall paintings, panel drawings and poster designs
centred on epic, religious, and political themes thrived. Popular beliefs
and rituals found expression in various forms such as stamps, banknotes,
and even chewing gum wrappers, all aimed at mobilising the masses in
support of the Revolution and the war effort.[18] The eight-year war with
Iraq was to create crucial problems in Iran for several more years, but it
led to an increasing sense of nationalism throughout the country. In this
period, the earlier Islamic universalist inclination, evident in themes like
pan-Islamism reflected in notions such as exporting the revolution and
criticising nationalism, had left Islamists vulnerable in terms of patriotic
values. However, managing a complex modern state and grappling with
a myriad of domestic and foreign challenges, notably the war, bolstered
the Islamic Republic's nationalist inclinations. Consequently, the state
progressively tailored its universalist Islamic ideology to better fit
within the national context. Chelkowski and Dabashi write of "'the
Museum of Furious Art" that is the Iran of the 1980s, a nation engaged
in revolution and war, relentlessly remaking itself in images and forms,
shapes and colors, frames of angers and anxieties'.[19] This situation lasted
throughout the 1980s, although things began to change after the end
of the war: in 1988 the production of art as propaganda significantly
diminished. After the war, wartime murals and posters on the untended
walls of Iran were gradually fading away, while others were whitewashed
outright. From the end of the 1980s and increasingly during the 1990s,
a post-revolutionary modernism started to develop among artists.
However, one can find in the works of the new generation a quest for a
mode of modern artistic expression that might achieve an equilibrium
between the past and modernism.

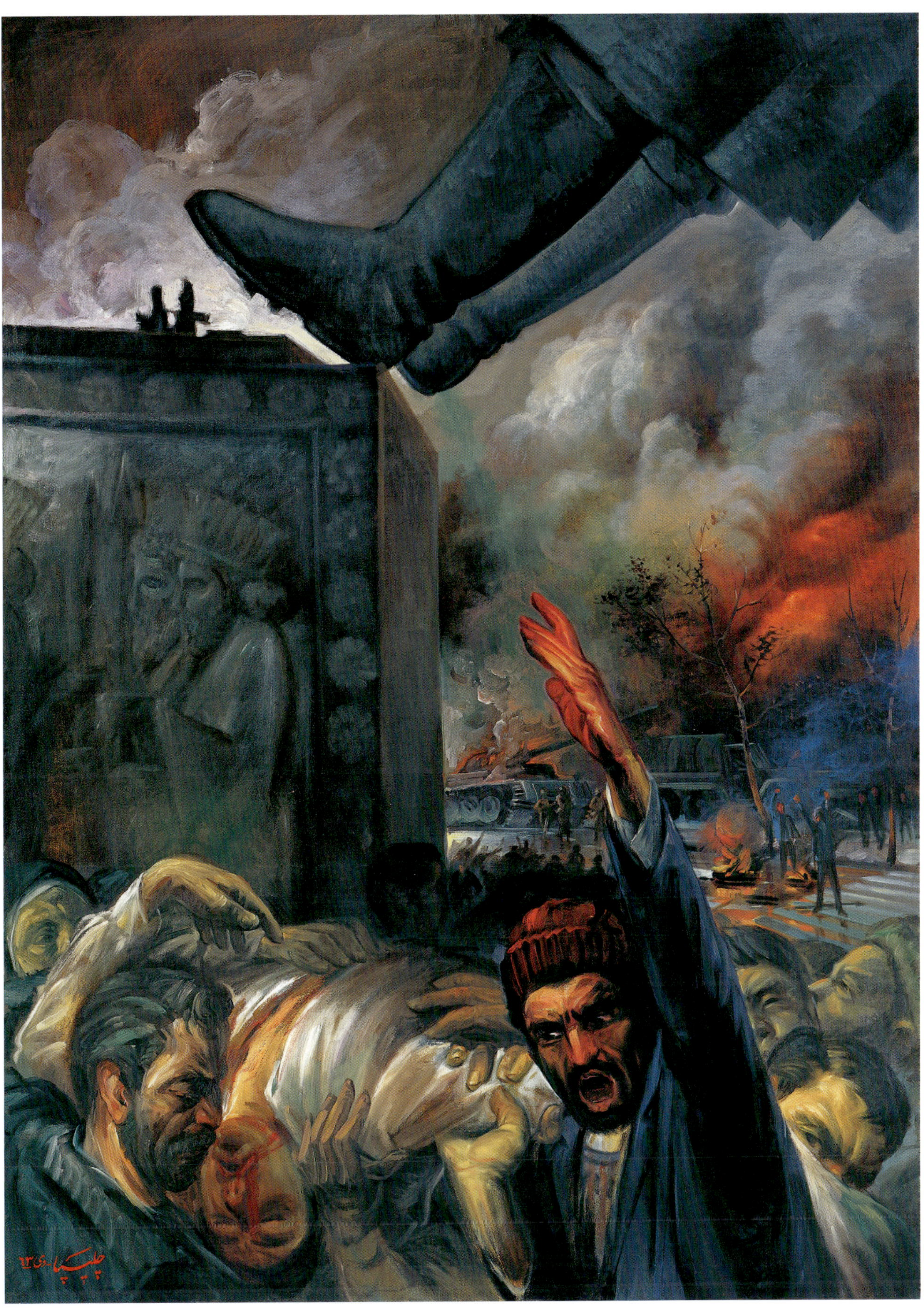

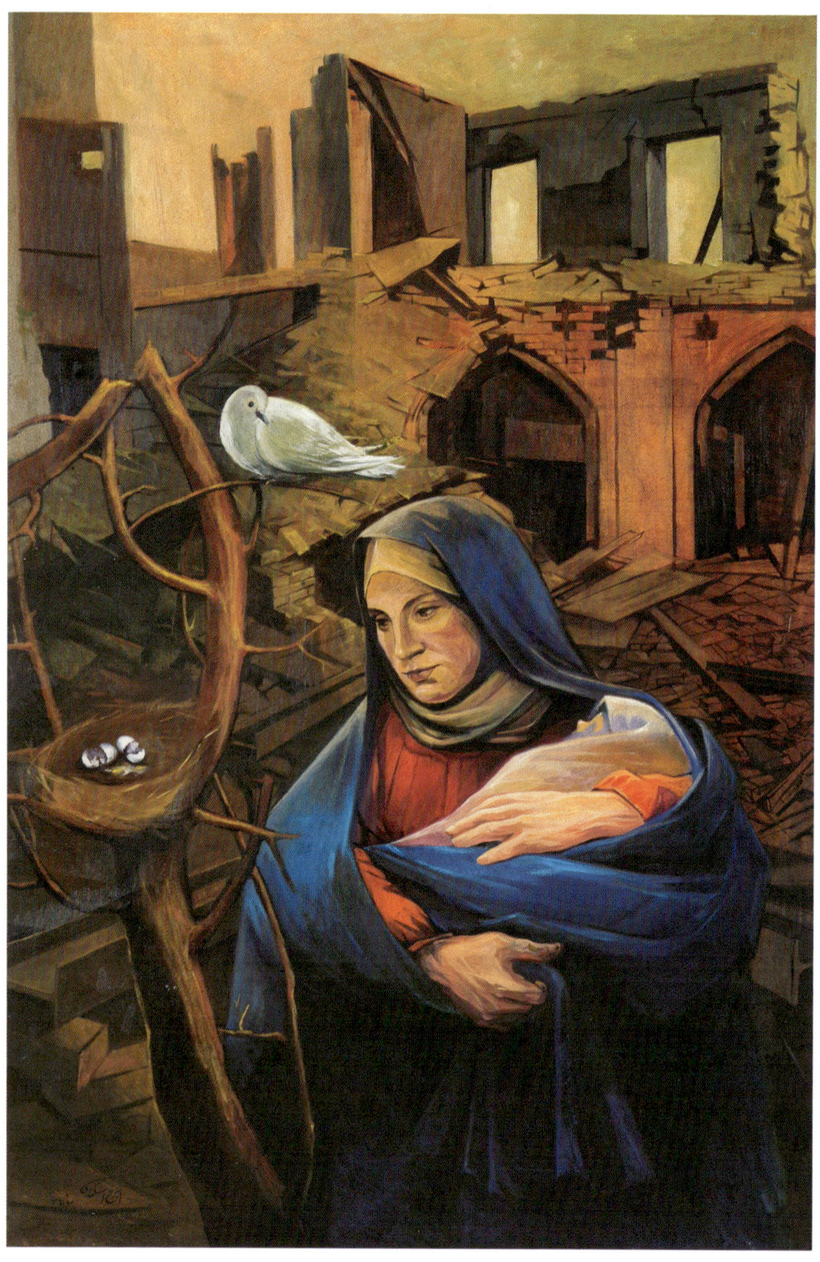

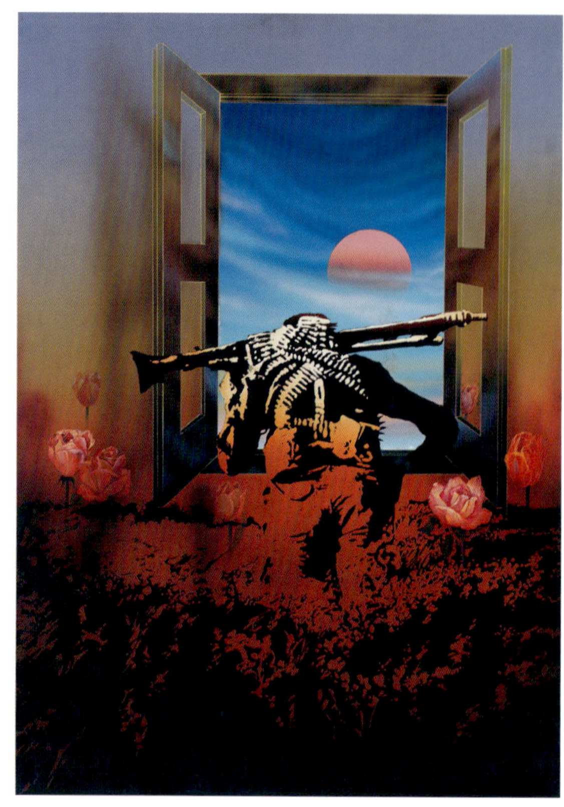

4.12
Mostafa Goudarzi, *Ila al-Nur*, 1985,
airbrush on paper, 100×70 cm,
Howzeh-i hunari

4.10
Iraj Eskandari, *Bombardment,*
1984, 150×100 cm, oil on canvas,
Howzeh-i hunari collection

Facing page
4.11
Habibollah Sadeghi, *Rami Jamarat,*
1985, oil on canvas, 200×150 cm,
Howzeh-i hunari collection

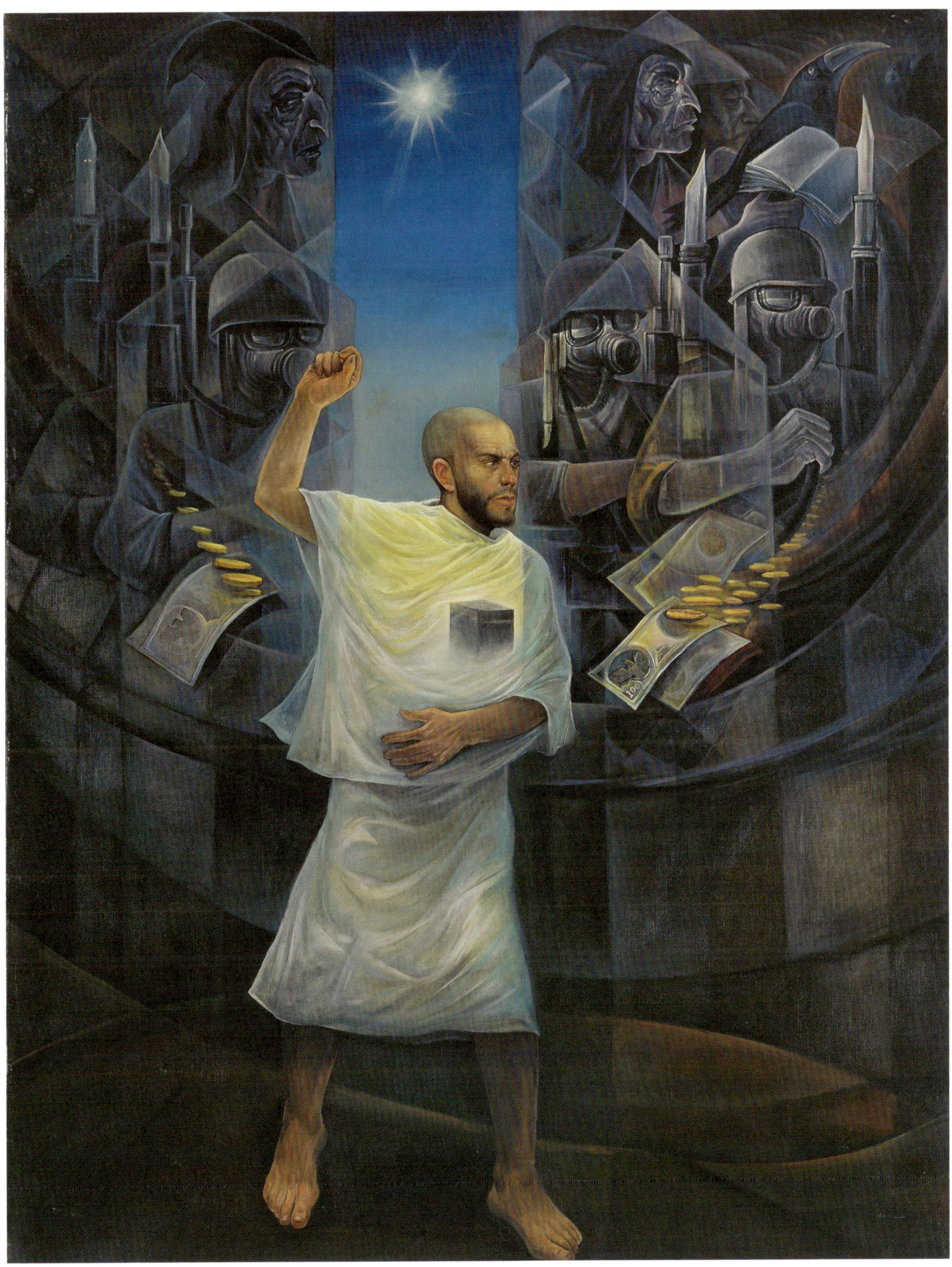

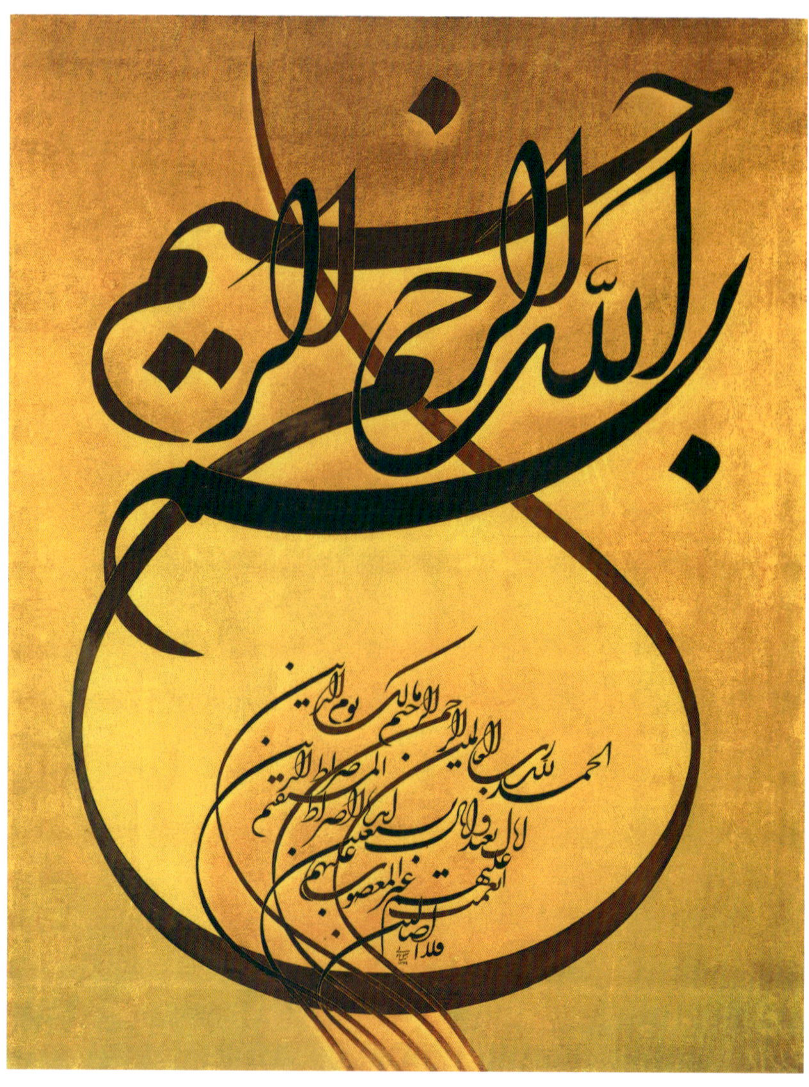

4.13
Jalil Rasouli, *Sura al-Hamd*, 1985,
oil on canvas, 122×91 cm, TMoCA

2. The development of traditionalist trends: calligraphic tendencies and miniature painting

After a few years, the state and its cultural and artistic organisations started to encourage mainly so-called traditional Islamic arts. The issue of cultural and artistic identity again posed itself through the artistic coteries. In the early post-revolutionary era, most traditional arts such as miniature painting, Coffee-house (*Qahveh-khaneh*) painting and classical poetry flourished. Among other artists, the traditional calligraphers at the Society of Iranian Calligraphers also began to develop their activities throughout the country. Interestingly, at this juncture, artists affiliated with the *Naqqashi-khatt* tendency,[20] in particular figures, such as Mohammad Ehsai and Nasrollah Afjei, were able to sustain their artistic careers following the Revolution. Their artistic practice already encompassed religious or literary narratives directly tied to the Islamic tradition emphasised by the new regime. In this post-revolutionary milieu, *Naqqashi-khatt* artists asserted that their inspiration stemmed from the Islamic calligraphic forms of the Iranian-Islamic traditions, rather than any association with the earlier *Saqqa-khaneh* movement.[21] In contrast, artists aligned with the neo-traditionalist *Saqqa-khaneh* movement did not have the opportunity to exhibit their works. Pilaram died three years after the Revolution, during a period when he, like Tanavoli and other modernists, was prohibited from being active in the art scene. Zenderoudi's absence from the Iranian art scene during the post-Revolution period already rendered him ineffectual within the country's artistic community. Their perceived lack of commitment to the Islamic Revolution and its ideals, coupled with the modernistic elements in their art, had garnered significant support from the pre-revolutionary state.

Two of the eminent artists who emerged in this period are Jalil Rasouli (b.1947) and Gholam Ali Ajali (b.1939). Although Rasouli started his professional career in the mid-1970s, he became better known in the post-revolutionary period, specifically during the 1980s and 1990s. Rasouli demonstrated a keen interest in experimental techniques on his canvases. In his early *Naqqashi-khatt* works from the late 1970s and early 1980s, he explored figurative shapes composed of religious or predominantly Qur'anic verses in *Thuluth* script, reminiscent of a particular calligraphic practice in nineteenth-century Iran. This practice involved arranging letters in such a way that they formed shapes of animals, more commonly birds. Rasouli's approach, which incorporated chiaroscuro within the words, bore resemblance to some of Ehsai's earlier canvases. (Figure 4.13) His steadfast commitment to classical calligraphy principles, such as imbuing text with meaning, stands as testimony to his choice to remain an established calligrapher.

Among other calligraphers who sought new functions and techniques of calligraphy in calligraphic composition is Gholam Ali Ajali. Ajali's experiences in *Naqqashi-khatt* while not extensive, have paved the way for him to pursue his career with a focus on his distinctive style, *Gulgasht*.[22] In the first series of *Gulgasht*, an accumulation of thousands of letters varying from thick to minute are used to construct a figurative shape from nature or a portrait. In his later *Naqqashi-khatt*s in the late 1990s and 2000s, this is not the case; rather, here the monochrome letters of the *Nasta'liq* and *Thuluth* scripts cover most of a monotone background. (Figure 4.14)

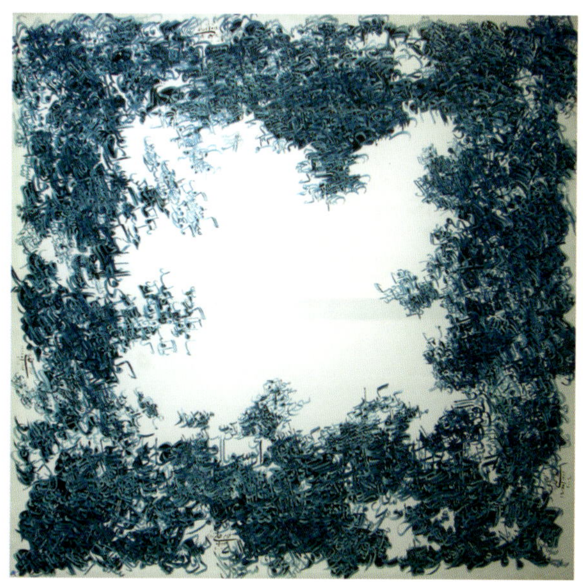

4.14
Gholam Ali Ajali, *Untitled*, 2004, acrylic on canvas, 150×150 cm, private collection, Tehran

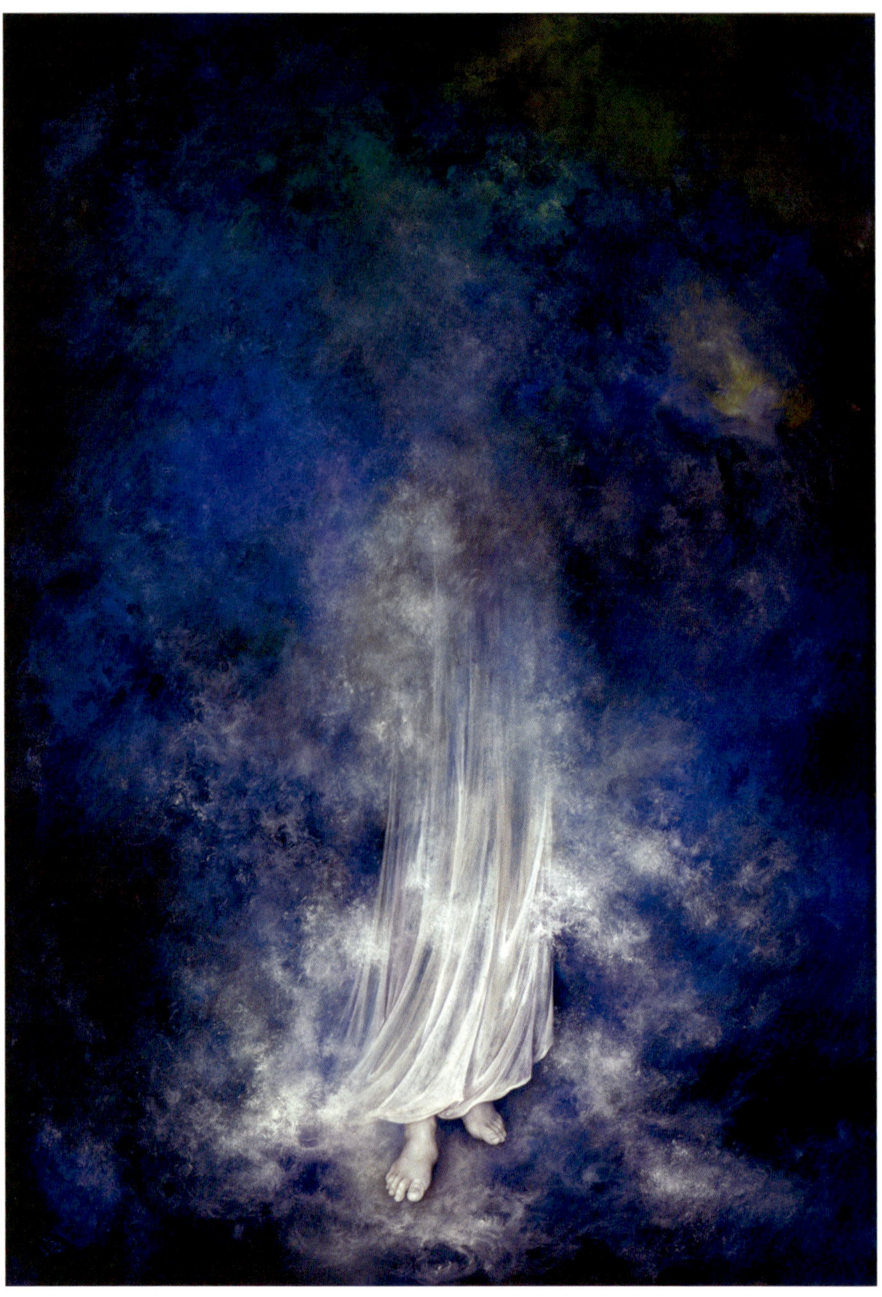

4.15
Mahmoud Farshchian, *Birth of Hope*, 1990, gouache and watercolour on paper, 81.28×55.88 cm, TMoCA

The 1980s marked a resurgence in the second and third generations of miniaturist artists, following the establishment of Madrasa Sanayi'-i Qadima in 1929.[23] They are now referred to as *nigar-garan*, with their works being termed *Nigar-gari*. The term emerged because of the perception that 'miniature' was a Western term inadequate to capture the distinct essence of Persian painting. Like the *Naqqashi-khatt* artists, supported by the new ideological and cultural atmosphere of post-revolution, these artists also emphasised Iranian-Islamic traditions as the basis of their inspiration. They also named themselves the heirs of traditional Muslim artists. Trained under masters in the field either in Tehran or in Isfahan, they have followed the same pattern, while becoming more interested in social, mystical and poetical themes, and keener to incorporate contemporary subject matters. These include such artists as Mahmoud Farshchian, Houshang Jazizadeh, Majid Mehregan (b.1945), Mohammad Bagher Aghamiri (b.1950) and Ardeshir Mojarrad Takestani (b.1949). (Figures 4.15–18) The growth and importance of this genre expanded to such an extent that in 1993, the post-revolutionary art officials decided to hold a separate national biennial dedicated exclusively to the works of *nigar-garan*.

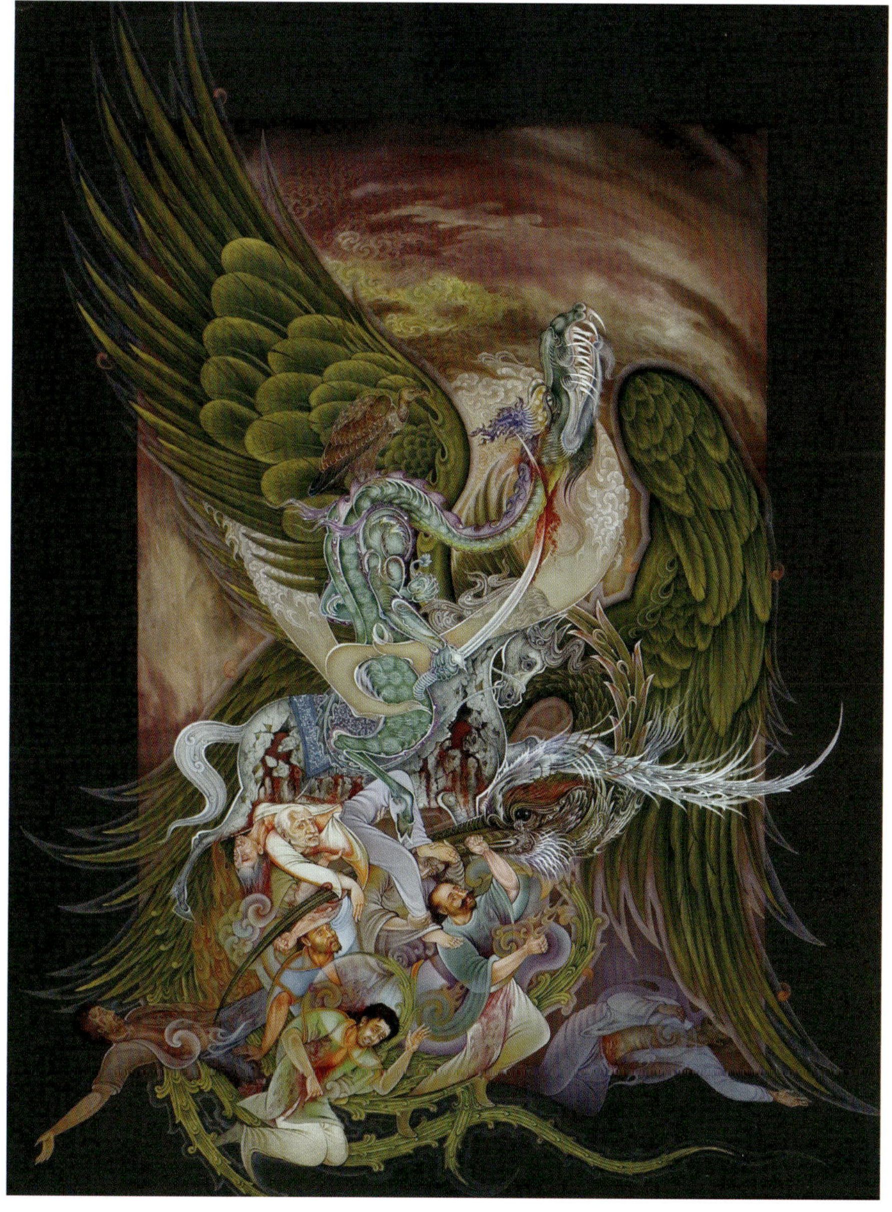

4.16
Majid Mehregan, *The Phoenix of the Revolution*, 1983, gouache and watercolour on paper, 94×67 cm, TMoCA

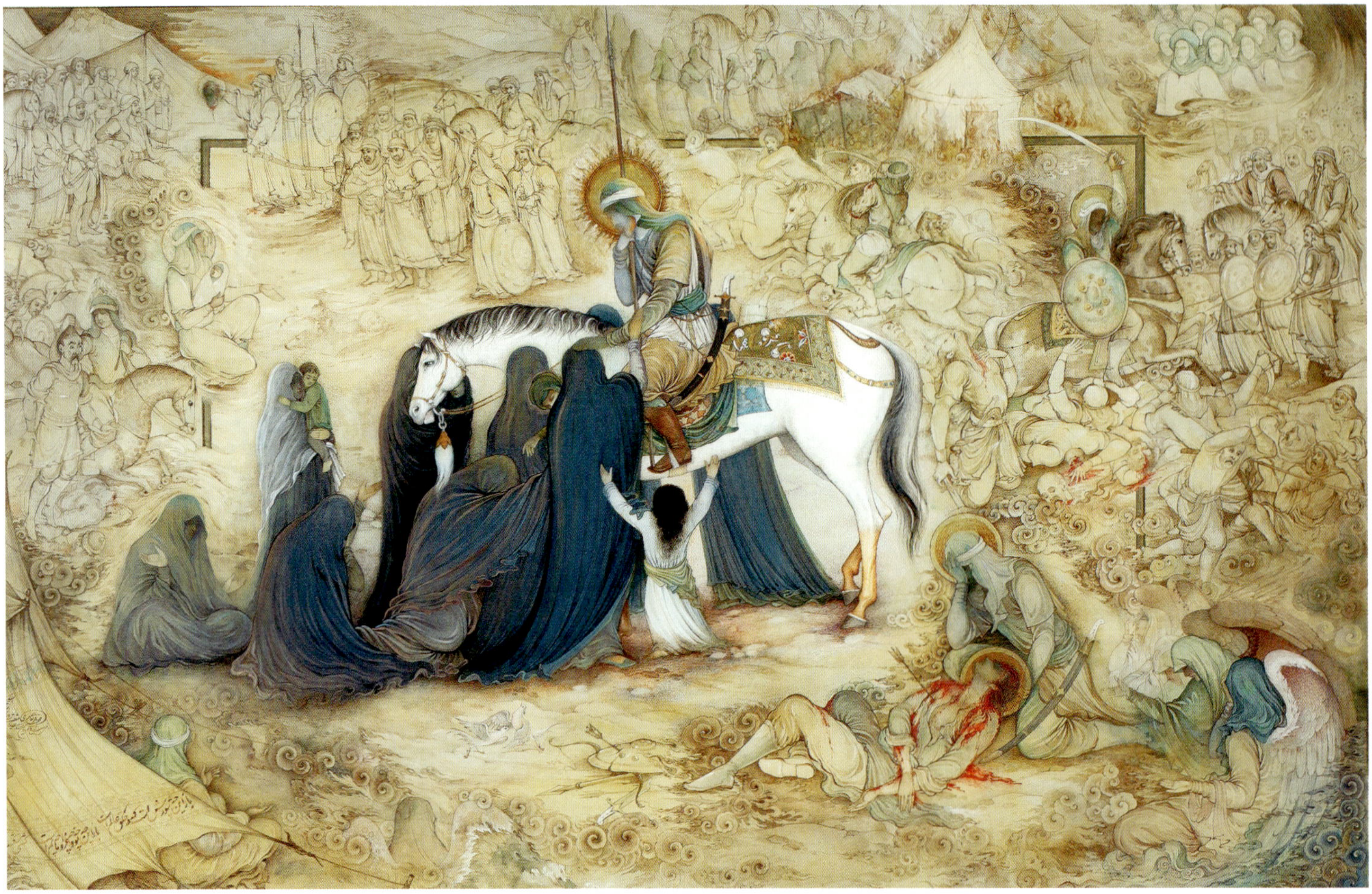

Above
4.17
Mohammad Bagher Aghamiri,
'Ashura Noon, 1986, gouache and
watercolour on paper, 55×84 cm,
TMoCA

Right
4.18
Ardeshir Mojarrad Takestani,
Wise Old Man, 1995, gouache
and watercolour on paper, private
collection, Tehran

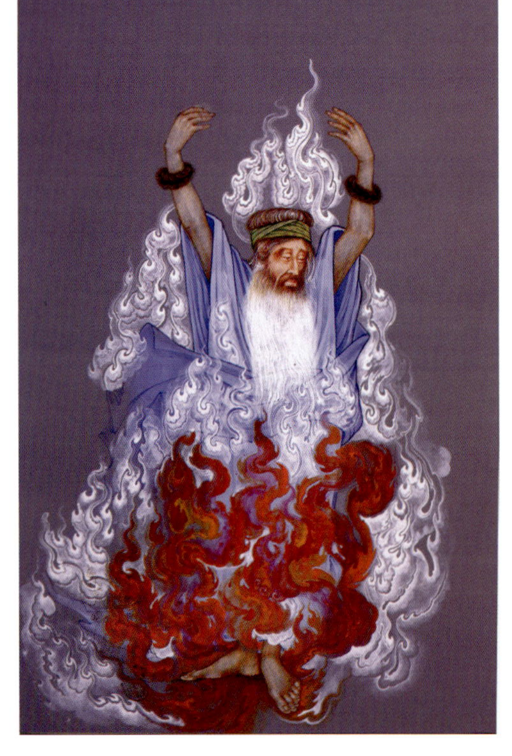

3. Post-revolutionary Modernism; Post-revolutionary national art biennials, the state and cultural policy: cultural identity in question

The late 1980s and early 1990s saw the second phase of post-revolutionary art and culture. If the first decade of the era provoked widespread opposition to the doctrine of the Pahlavis, this second period saw the issue of national artistic identity and an art informed by national-Islamic characteristics as an underlying precept. Still influential were the ontological and political underpinnings of *gharb-zadegi* ('Westoxification'), addressed through a critical interpretation of works by the Iranian intellectuals of the 1960s and 1970s. The distinguishing features of this era, wherein the leaders were now political elites, remained rooted in anti-colonialism, anti-Westernism, and a quest for an authentic culture. More specifically, there persisted a deep-seated concern regarding 'the West' as an overarching global paradigm overshadowing a troubled Iranian 'self'; coupled with a steadfast resistance against what was perceived as Western imperialism.

The formulated interest of officials within the country clearly promoted particular values such as resistance against the 'cultural aggression' (*Tahajum-i farhangi*) of cultural globalisation. Much of what was, for example, considered local – that is, with reference to tradition or having the nature of a localised culture and therefore being worthy of preservation in the face of Westernisation – was said to be based on 'cultural essentialism.'[24] In official cultural and artistic events, clear encouragement was given to 'taking refuge' in cultural authenticity, historical specificities and traditional values, particularly of Islam or the so-called Irano-Islamic Shi'i traditions.[25] A large body of art works created in this era – continuing for almost a decade – shows the characteristic uncertainty of a transitional episode.

By the beginning of the 1990s, the Iranian artistic scene seemingly required a comprehensive exhibition in which various post-revolutionary artistic activities and tendencies would be showcased. After the destruction of the war, Iranian society had begun its task of reconstruction in various domains, including socio-cultural and economic life. During the period after the Revolution, the population had greatly increased, the majority consisted of young people. At the same time a new middle-class and technically educated stratum of the Iranian population was being formed. A large number of these people gravitated towards the arts, especially visual arts. Hence, the number of artists, art lovers and applicants to study or practice art increased tenfold during this time, by comparison with the 1970s. This decade gradually witnessed the expansion of art faculties in the capital, Tehran, and most other cities, primarily through Azad University branches. Among various fields, visual arts were more popular and chosen by the applicants and also better approved by the officials compared to others, such as performing arts such as music and cinema.[26] By the end of the 1980s, private galleries that had hitherto been inactive or closed were reactivated; while many new ones were opened, which began to exhibit non-political and non-propagandising art. In addition to the Barg Gallery and other major official galleries affiliated with the Tehran Municipality, more galleries in Tehran and in other Iranian provinces were launched.

The pervasive influence of the government in dictating art should not be overlooked. Governmental cultural sections played a significant role in enforcing a sort of sanctioned art scene, dictated and bolstered by state cultural policies. In the initial post-revolutionary years, different exhibitions – held in particular on anniversaries of the Islamic Revolution – had been mounted in various public spaces, especially the Tehran Museum of Contemporary Art (TMoCA). At the time the museum was the most active artistic venue in the post-revolutionary era. These exhibitions were affected by the politicised and propagandising atmosphere of the time. The core of these exhibitions comprised the works – both paintings and posters – of revolutionary or 'committed' artists, and a range of traditional arts including calligraphy (both classical calligraphy and *Naqqashi-khatt*, now with a clear religious or political message) and miniature painting (*Nigar-gari*).

Following several years of haphazard activity, the TMoCA began organising regular biennials and triennials, among which the painting biennials were the largest and seemingly the most controversial.[27] The First Iranian Painting Biennial opened in the autumn of 1991, twelve years after the victory of the Revolution.[28]

The catalogue of the First Iranian Painting Biennial, organised by the Artistic Deputy of the Ministry of Culture and Islamic Guidance, announced a clear and very ambitious goal: it was intended to 'improve the art of painting in both quantity and quality, establish a true atmosphere of competition among artists, and explore and support young talent.'[29] The 1991 biennial was in actuality the sixth, since there had been five others held in Tehran before the Revolution; the organisers justified its title with the logic that, due to deep transformations in different aspects of Iranian life including politics, society and culture, this post-revolutionary Biennial could not have many affiliations with pre-revolutionary ones! And since it was the first official comprehensive exhibition in the period after the Revolution, it had to be called 'The First Iranian Painting Biennial.'[30]

In the words of the manifesto presented at the First Biennial:

After the establishment of the Islamic Republic, there has been a notable development in the art of painting. Influenced by the social and political dynamics of their society, today's vanguard 'committed' and independent artists are determined to reclaim the religious and national identity eroded by imitation. They seek to let the unpolluted, pure, independent, and dynamic atmosphere invigorate the talents of the youth.[31]

4.19
Kazem Chalipa, *Didar* (*Visit*), 1985, oil on canvas, 180×200 cm, TMoCA

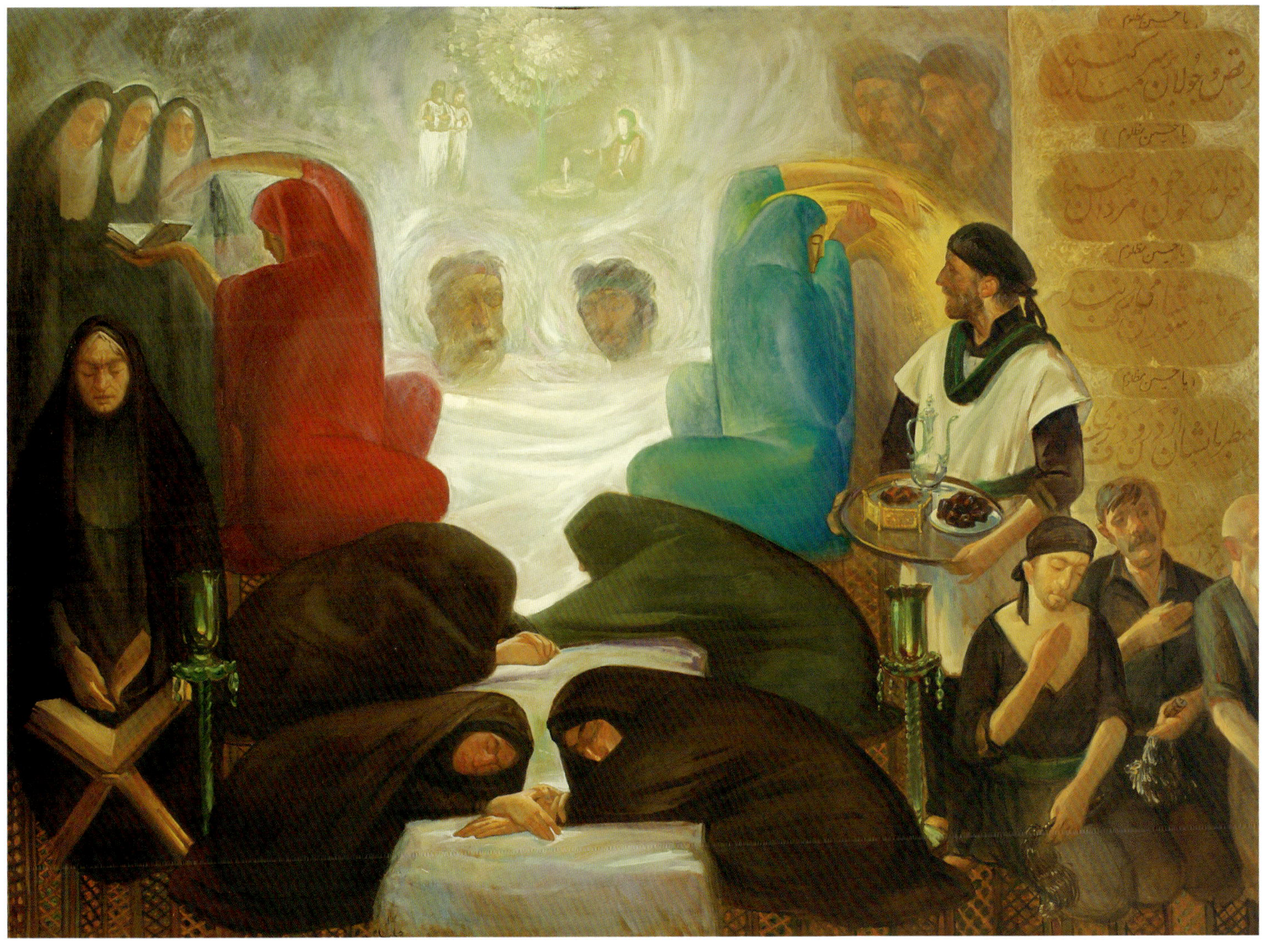

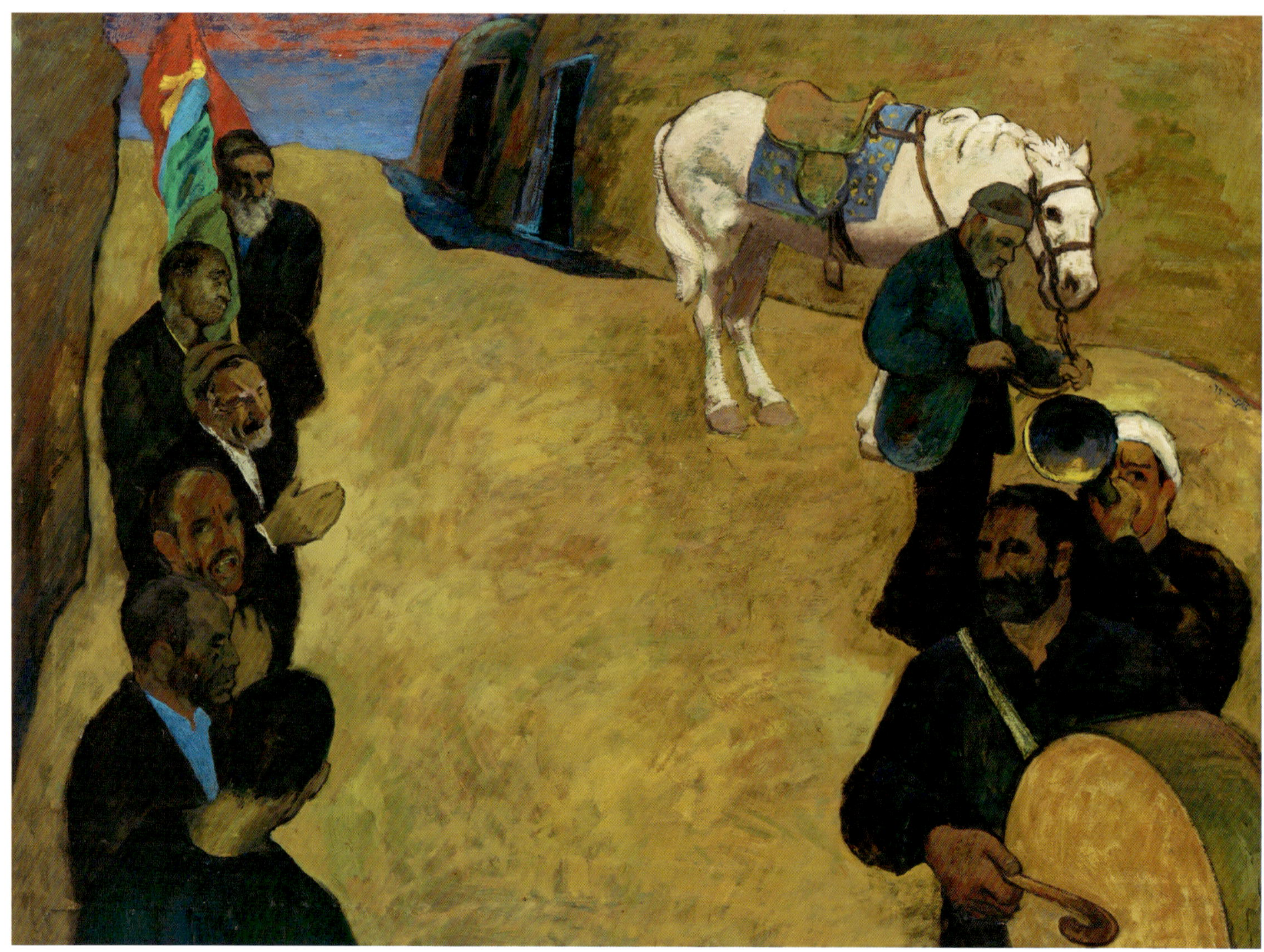

4.20
Ali Zakeri, *Dar sug* (*Mourning*),
1990, oil on canvas, 89×116,
courtesy the artist

A small yet bold section of the exhibition was dedicated to the works of the *muta'ahhid* artists. However, the majority of the exhibition showcased works that demonstrated a tendency to incorporate pre-Islamic Persian forms, traditional motifs, and elements of folkloristic art as references. Some works aimed to establish an 'artistic identity' by incorporating musical instruments, scenes of Sufi dancing, details of traditional architecture, and other similar features, which were now evident in the works of many young artists.

It is evident from the prize-winning works in the Biennial that a primary criterion for their selection was their resemblance, both formally and aesthetically, to what was commonly referred to as Irano-Islamic art. This includes their use of decorative motifs and calligraphy, as well as their representation of religious traditions and rituals.[32] (Figures 4.19–20)

The First Biennial also featured different traditional genres, including Coffee-house (*Qahveh-khaneh*) and miniature painting. (Figure 4.21) Works of some prominent *Naqqashi-khatt* artists were also exhibited.

One of the key issues put forward during the First Biennial was the question of cultural identity. It is important to note that during this period, there was no standardised definition or literature regarding the term 'cultural identity'. Instead, it was primarily used as a rhetorical device, often referencing Irano-Islamic culture, with a particular emphasis on Shi'i identity. As the introduction to the Biennial catalogue put it:

> Revision of values and authenticities is neither an artistic and mental reaction nor a weakness regarding modernism. Rather it is a strong attempt to achieve an artistic identity that is appropriate and understood based on visual and subjective frameworks originating from our cultural authenticity. [...] Drawing upon the unique characteristics of Iranian revolutionary society, and with the aim of fostering a dynamic and meaningful artistic model, the Centre of Plastic Arts under the Ministry of Culture and Islamic Guidance is committed to use all its resources to enhance the burgeoning and inclusive art of the Islamic Revolution.[33]

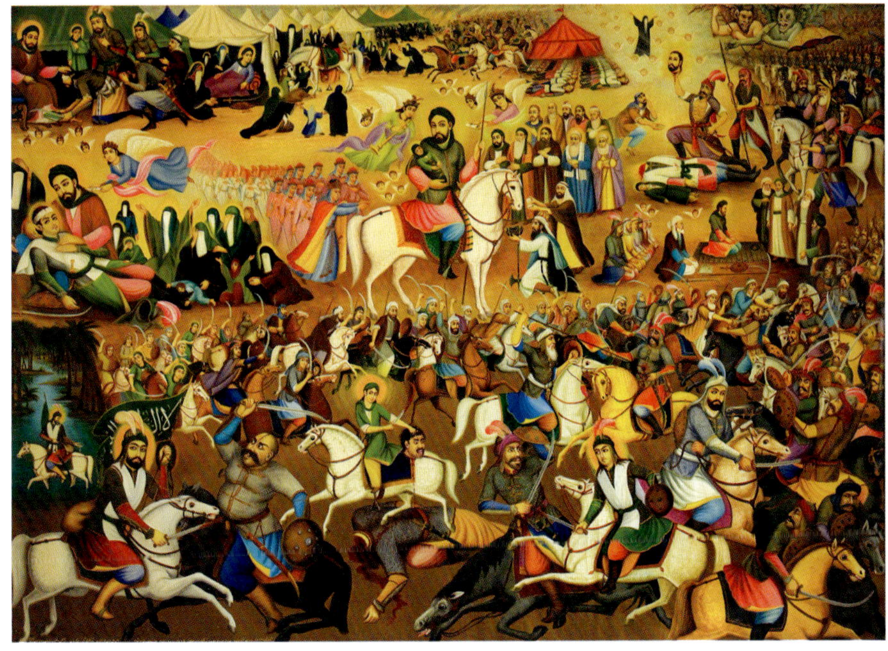

4.21
Abbas Bolokifar, *Karbala Epic*, 1985, oil on canvas, 325×420 cm, TMoCA

Here 'meaningful artistic model' refers to the section of the biennial titled *Palestine*. It seems that the organisers felt the need to include a political element to justify the independent and non-political components of the exhibition.[34]

Alongside the exhibition the TMoCA held a conference, which, common in the early 1990s at least, considered issues of 'cultural and artistic identity' and how such identity could be preserved against the 'mighty storm of Western culture'.[35] At the same time there was a growing ambition to participate in the international art scene. A review of exhibition catalogues and conference proceedings from that period reveals a growing interest in 'contemporary international art movements', although there is no explicit advocacy for such art forms. The formal stance of Iran's officials still clearly promoted resistance against 'other cultural norms' of 'cultural globalisation' or so-called 'Westernism'.

In the 1991 First Conference of Iranian Plastic Arts, hosted by the TMoCA, the main issue addressed was 'national identity' in art and how it could be preserved[36] – as is suggested by the title of the conference proceedings: Cultural and Artistic Identity (*Huviyyat-i farhangi va hunari*). The introduction to the publication of the proceedings frames the issues thus:

> What response have we contrived against the mighty storm of recent centuries that has blown from the West and has assumed different shape and emphasis in every period? Is there any way to preserve our culture and art [from that storm] – What is the responsibility of the young generation of revolutionary artists? These questions and tens of similar questions were the motivations for holding this Conference.[37]

Considered carefully, the contents of the debates and arguments of the conference bear a close resemblance to the major artistic and intellectual preoccupations in the period before the Revolution, in particular during the 1960s. 'Cultural and artistic identity' were topics that had already been advocated, but which now showed particular emphasis on the revolutionary aspect of Iranian culture and on Islam as an integral part of that culture. Generally speaking, however, the new discourse did not essentially differ from what had been advocated before the Revolution, although the main emphasis was now on the content of traditional values.

In this period, it appears that a myriad of old questions resurfaced, albeit in a different guise. The Revolution, like many other revolutions, created a divide between the new and older generations. Perhaps it is due to this rift that many works from the previous generation were being revisited in the official exhibitions of the post-revolutionary era.[38] Thus, we observe a revival of various romanticised traditional scenes depicted with realistic styles, characterised by the recurring use of symbolic motifs and the manipulation of coloured elements. These elements encompassed various features, including tilework designs adorned with gold, lapis lazuli, green, and various shades of blue; frequent use of seals; repetitive incorporation of arabesque patterns; calligraphic forms reminiscent of the works of certain *Saqqa-khaneh* artists; illumination (*Tazhib*) and Persian painting; as well as portraits of Qajar women with distinctive joined eyebrows, adapted to modern artistic styles.

In 1991, twelve years after the Revolution, the subject of the 'identity crisis' in Iranian art emerged once again;[39] this time it was primarily emphasised by the officials. They seem to have hoped that the First Biennial could represent in both form and content a kind of new 'national Islamic art', or a so-called 'independent art' (which seemed not to be achievable easily). Also discussed were topics including spiritualism in art, religious art, Gnostic art, Islamic art and its theoretical principles, artistic traditions and traditional art as well as the reflection of tradition in Iranian art.

The Second Iranian Painting Biennial, held in 1993, had a similar atmosphere, but with more flexibility: this time there was no particular restriction regarding subject matter or content. Although the selection criteria bore similarities to those of the previous biennials and earlier exhibitions, it was clear that the nature of Iranian art was now tending towards modernism. The judging panel announced its criteria for selecting works as follows:

> After considering valuable subjects (such as the Islamic Revolution, spiritual thought, mystical subjects, as well as social, political, and cultural issues) [...] the formal aspect of works [...] should draw inspiration from the Irano-Islamic cultural and artistic heritage, while demonstrating an innovative and creative approach.[40]

Thus it was surprising that the dominant approach was the attempted synthesis of traditional and modern. (Figures 4.22–23) In this

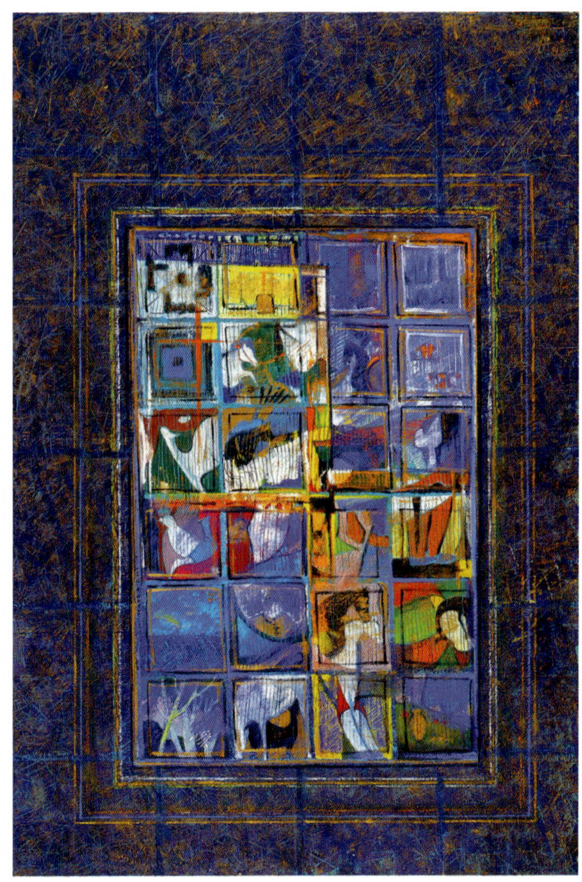

4.22
Mohammad Memarzadeh, *Legacy*, 1995, oil on canvas, 120×80 cm, TMoCA

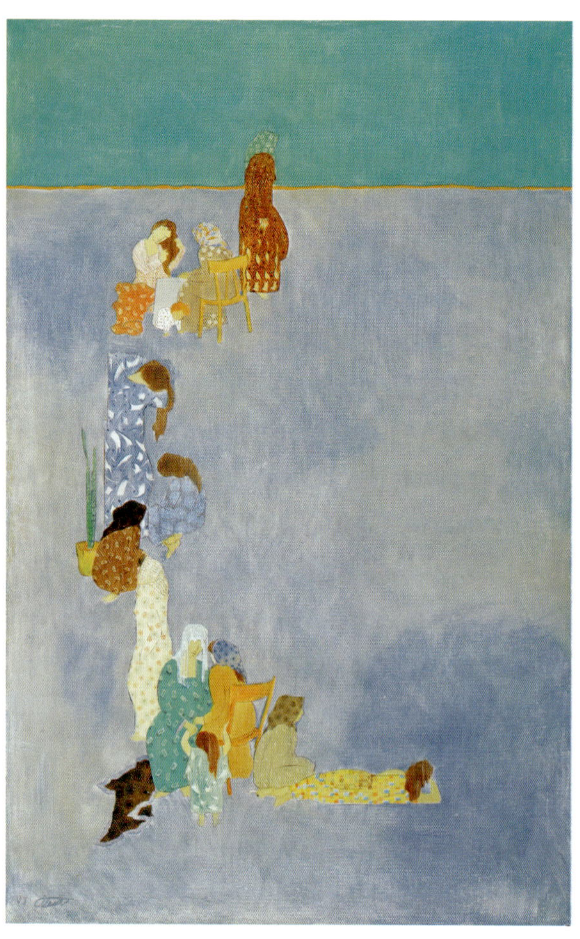

4.23
Rezvan Sadeghzadeh, *Woman's
Dignity*, 1997, oil on canvas,
149×93 cm, TMoCA

Second Biennial, most of the existing trends in Iranian painting were represented, with the exception of miniature painting (*Nigar-gari*), which as of 1993 was given a separate biennial exhibition.

As for the 'artistic identity crisis', organisers of the Second Biennial again suggested that more attention should be directed to national and Islamic arts, although a 'national school of art' was not proposed. As one member of the selection panel suggested, 'The essence of new thought exists in our national and Islamic art, but it has covered itself over. We must find it and expand it into other artistic and cultural domains.'[41] Since it was difficult to find any comprehensive tendency in the works exhibited in the first two biennials, the crisis of 'artistic identity' was still the main topic for debate in the Second Conference of Plastic Arts, held during the 1993 biennial. One of the proposed solutions was that artworks refer to the 'principal structures' of past Iranian art – a reference that should not be formal, however, but that should instead concern the content and meaning of the traditional arts. At this second conference Mohammad Ali Rajabi, an artist and writer, suggested,

> In our country, we encounter various discourses such as identity and cultural aggression, which are unprecedented and different from what we have encountered before. It is crucial that we do not approach these discourses superficially. In this year's biennial, different groups of artists have attempted to express a sense of identity in their works, and their efforts should be acknowledged. However, we also witnessed a group advocating for a simplistic approach, believing that using colours like lapis lazuli and gold or creating flat works [devoid of perspective] would establish identity in their art. This mentality has become increasingly prevalent. Another group asserts that any work by an Iranian is inherently Iranian [and there is no need to worry about lacking identity in it]. [...] The reality is that we are stagnant, spinning in circles. [...] I call this a counterfeit identity.[42]

Another important ambition (or intention) stated at both biennial conferences was participation in the international art scene,[43] which would later become a preoccupation of both artists and art officials. As an anonymous author in a leading official art quarterly wrote, 'We must actively engage in the contemporary international art scene. However, this presence should be guided by well-thought-out principles.'[44] Many suggestions and arguments were put forward with regard to inviting foreign judges[45] or turning the Iranian biennial into an international biennial[46] and exhibiting Iranian art in other international exhibitions, perhaps on the model of the Fifth Tehran Biennial in 1966 and other pre-revolutionary exhibitions of the 1960s and 1970s.[47] The sponsoring of international exhibitions was also considered even by the art officials as one of the programmes on the agenda of the Artistic Deputy of the Ministry of Culture and Islamic Guidance.[48]

Discernable in the introduction to the catalogue of the Second Biennial is a theme similar to that of the pre-revolutionary biennials, particularly of the 1960s: the necessity of paying more attention to contemporary art movements. Following the statement of purpose of holding the Second Biennial, it is also suggested that:

> Exploring the innovative perspectives of Iranian art elites, fostering interaction among artists, introducing the contemporary language of art and various movements to the public, nurturing creative and authentic artists, evaluating their endeavours, and selecting works based on cultural identity...[49]

At the same time, the deliberate and careful survey of traditional Iranian art with a view to its resuscitation and reconstruction was recommended to artists who wanted to use the 'contemporary language of art'.[50] The preservation of artistic identity as one of the main conditions for a successful presence on the international scene was also suggested. For example, at the Second Conference of Plastic Arts, Zahra Rahnavard, an artist and activist, commented:

> How can we address global realities in our works without compromising our identity? There is a continual sense of concern for our ancient culture, which boasts a rich heritage. We are always wary of either remaining stagnant and outdated or rushing forward recklessly, without any guiding principles or frameworks, risking the loss of our identity entirely. For our art to maintain its identity and engage in a dialogue with the international art scene, it must uphold its unique aesthetic quality.[51]

Another lecturer at the conference, Ruin Pakbaz, emphasised the language that Iranian art should employ to convey its characteristics:

> It seems that our only defence against cultural aggression is to seek refuge in tradition. However, the concept of 'tradition' often seems limited to a few clichés and patterns. We witness our young talents increasingly turning to miniature and naturalistic painting, which, at their finest, tend to be repetitive. [...] We expect the message conveyed by our artists [in their art] to be both spiritual, defending values, and political, protesting against the absence of values. Therefore, it is imperative that this message be presented in a modern form.[52]

Also discernable among the intellectuals of the time were similar signs of sensitivity to the issue of identity, both artistic and cultural, and to the situation of Iranian society in a fast-changing world. This sensibility was usually accompanied by criticism of the structure of Iranian society and reflections on the conjunction of modernity and tradition. In an essay titled 'On the Mental Distortions Afflicting Those Civilizations That Have Remained on the Sidelines of History and Played No Part in the Festival of Changes,'[53] Daryoush Shayegan underlines how enriching the situation can be if one accepts the ambivalent challenge consciously, lucidly, and without resentment. But Faraj Sarkouhi, a famous Iranian writer and intellectual activist, maintains that,

> Since the period of the Constitutional Revolution [1906–11], and especially since September 1941,[54] our ancestors and we have inhabited a society where all the economic, political, social, and cultural events from various historical periods coexist simultaneously, creating a complex and interconnected fabric. In our society, one can encounter everything from primitive ideologies to ultramodern interpretations, from ancient social structures to the most advanced ways of life. Furthermore, we are not isolated from the global trends and transformations occurring in economic, technological, social, and cultural domains worldwide. Our situation can be likened to that of a 'man of the border zones' – someone who carries with them the entirety of their ancient past, yet remains entangled in the unresolved inconsistencies and challenges of societal life,

both in terms of thought and aesthetic expression. He carries with him the weight of his past and present, with all their contradictions and contrasts.[55]

Sarkouhi's conclusion, nevertheless, traces an approach towards modernism that, as he remarks, is to be seen in Iranian vanguard art and literature:

> In a society where primitive tribalism coexists with modern industrialisation, and superstition and magic persist alongside modernity, where traditional problems remain unresolved amid advanced forms of technology and telecommunications, it is natural to witness a variety of artistic and literary styles and structures. This diversity stems from the fact that the different layers of our society have not developed simultaneously or within a single framework. [...] Consequently, our vanguard art and literature, mindful of this historical context, have endeavoured to break free from the confines of this situation, to transcend the 'border zone' in which they find themselves confined, and to bridge the gap between the past and the present.[56]

These intellectuals now discussed more ardently the use of modernity both in art and culture. They maintained that, through an organic approach to contemporary life, artists could creatively combine the modern language of art with any traditional materials that were still functional in contemporary time. Nevertheless, from their point of view, contemporary culture, life and interests had to play the main role in this kind of art. At the same time, these intellectuals criticised the insufficiently informed imitation and acceptance of modernism, which might result in a superficial modishness. They also opposed a meaningless return to the past by the mere reproduction of the traditional image.[57]

At this time, the phrase 'creating a modern Iranian visual language'[58] was used to explain the approach of the modernist artists, whose goal was described as an effort to establish an 'independent identity' for Iranian art that took into account the efforts of the previous generation. In art the final answer is always present during the process of creation. Therefore, any kind of question – including the connection between past and present, or between pictorial tradition and the modern language of art – was supposed to be answered in the 'form' and 'structure' of the work of art itself. In this art, then, the question of 'form' or 'visual language' could be considered the most important issue.

The regeneration of modern Iranian art occurred at the beginning of the 1990s, about a decade into the post-revolutionary period. It coincided with the art biennials in which various modernistic approaches were exhibited and rapidly developed. During the late 1970s and 1980s, as Sarkouhi maintains,

> It has been demonstrated that traditionalism and rigid adherence to tradition in art, as well as in other cultural and social domains, do not yield positive results. The two forms of traditionalism – reproduction of traditional images and revolutionary social realism – affected by the politicised atmosphere of the early years of the Revolution, exacerbated the crisis in contemporary Iranian art. Instead of progress, these tendencies only highlighted their limitations and led to self-negation.[59]

It was believed that, for the first time in twentieth-century Iranian art, a generation had the opportunity to experience two pivotal periods of Iranian history – both pre- and post-Revolution – and they were able to intellectually and practically assimilate the positive and negative aspects of these experiences. Consequently, this generation could potentially play a pivotal role in guiding the subsequent one, which, due to the abrupt upheaval of the Revolution and its aftermaths, lacked awareness of the achievements made by the pre-revolutionary generation across various aspects of Iranian culture and life.

To summarise, Iranian art during the late 1980s and 1990s can be generally classified in three main groups: traditionalists (*nigar-garan* and calligraphers), modernists (mainly practising artists of the pre-revolution) and the neo-traditionalists. Simultaneously, there was also a trend toward realism, with artists depicting local scenes and rituals. (Figure 4.24) Among these, it could be argued, the neo-traditionalists were dominant. The situation is similar for Iranian poetry and fiction, which, in 1990, Sarkouhi believed to be flourishing more than at any time in the recent past.[60]

Owing to their variety it is difficult to characterise the neo-traditional genres in the 1990s; however, their main characteristics can be distinguished. During this period, neo-traditional artists

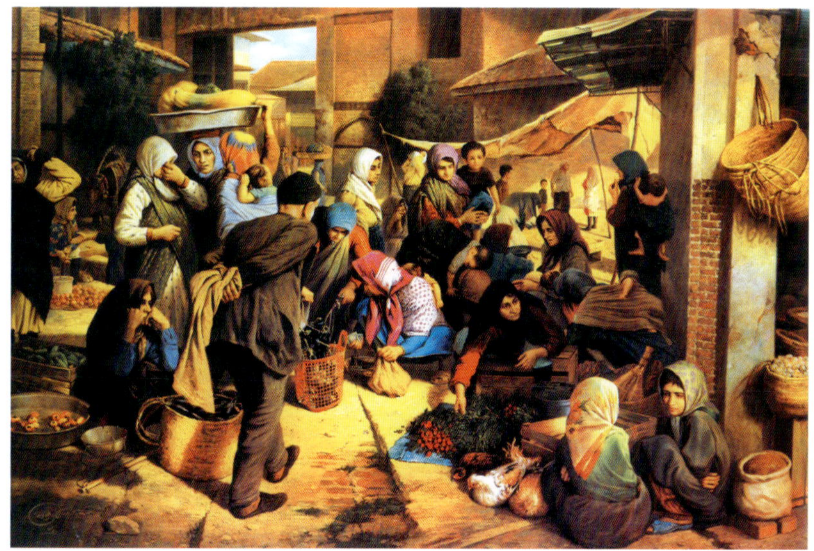

4.24
Mehdi Mohammad Alizadeh, *Bazaar*, 1995, oil on canvas, 110×160 cm, TMoCA

absorbed influences from Western art trends, trying to blend them with traditional iconographies and forms. While some artists focused on exploring local Iranian folk art traditions, others delved into concepts derived from ancient Iranian mythology and mysticism. However, unlike the predominantly decorative approach adopted by *Saqqa-khaneh* artists in the pre-revolutionary period, these artists aimed to transform traditional motifs into highly emotive metaphors. In contrast to the pre-revolutionary neo-traditionalists' emphasis on formal aspects of the pictorial past, post-revolutionary artists displayed a greater interest in the content and message conveyed by traditional forms and pictorial traditions. They tried to explore the meanings and concepts underlying these forms, moving beyond their mere visual representations.

The majority of their works were characterised by several key features, including the use of forms derived from classical Persian painting, such as the depiction of natural phenomena, as well as the creation of a sense of simultaneous dynamism and unity across the two-dimensional space of the painting. Additionally, symbolism permeated their works, manifesting in both figurative and abstract forms. Ancient Iranian myths, legends, and literary works frequently appeared as subject matter, their forms showing a tendency towards symbolic and allegorical expression.

During that period, these artists deliberately emphasised the use of a modernist language, believing that the past could be revisited, reassessed, and rejuvenated through innovative interpretations. The figurative neo-traditionalists were primarily interested in contemporary social and philosophical concepts, attempting to

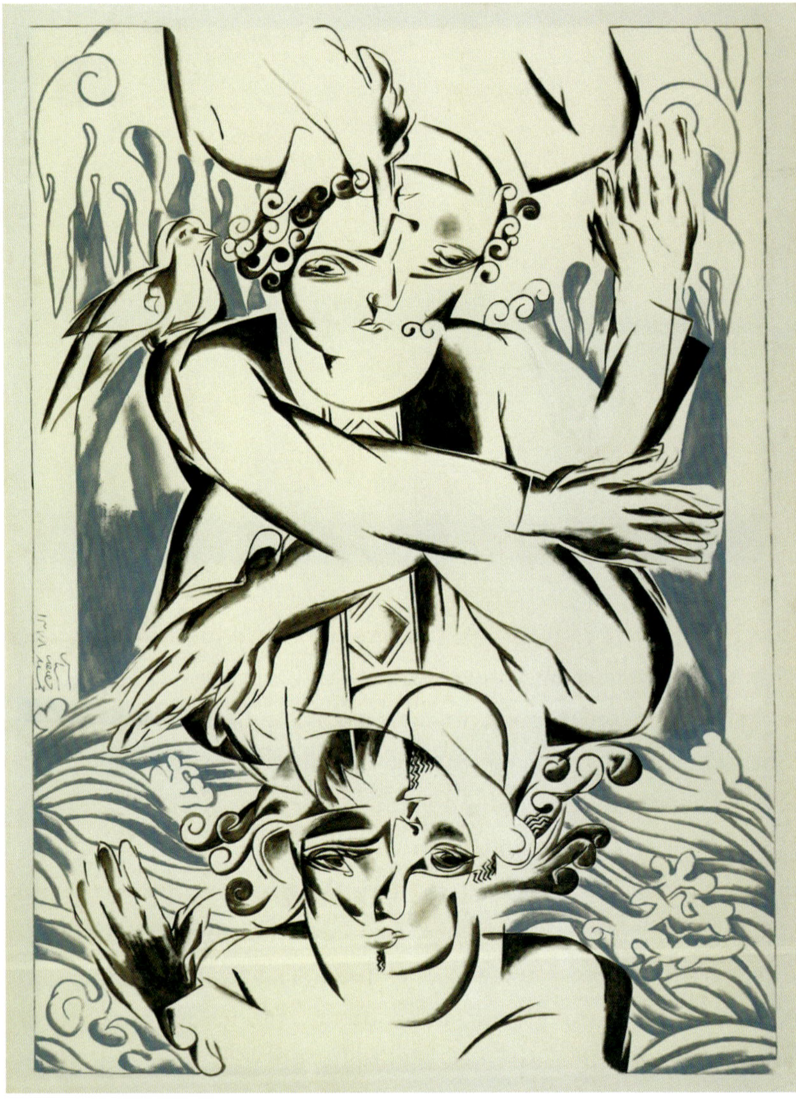

4.25
Jamshid Haghighatshenas, *Black and White*, 1999, oil on canvas, 140×100 cm, TMoCA

represent these concepts within the specific context in which they found themselves as artists. Possessing a modernist attitude, they drew inspiration from both the conceptual and pictorial aspects of their heritage, integrating them with the vocabulary of modern art. Their use of the pictorial characteristics of classical Persian painting is evident in various aspects of their work, including their colour schemes, spatial compositions, two-dimensional image structures, and the incorporation of symbolic elements and concepts.

Experimentation with different modern styles enabled them to express their sentiments, particularly through movements such as Symbolism and Expressionism, which was supposed to be resonated with the prevailing atmosphere of Iranian society, shaped by events like the Revolution and the war. Additionally, they explored ancient Iranian myths and Islamic mysticism, often representing mythological and epic subjects sourced from traditional texts like the *Shahnameh* of Ferdowsi.[61]

Among the most active and distinguished figures of the group were Nosratollah Moslemian, Ahmad Amin-Nazar (b.1950) and Jamshid Haghighatshenas (b.1963). (Figure 4.25) Unlike previous generations, they have been significantly engaged in addressing the profound challenges of cultural engagement and intellectual inquiry. This engagement, a perennial preoccupation of Iranian intellectuals, now occupies the minds of these artists as well.

The work of Moslemian provides a good example of the characteristics of post-revolutionary Iranian painting. Although his work was initially rooted in radical social or political ideologies, it then developed to convey a more poetic expression. However, what is identifiable in the artist's works, across his life and career, is that the personal is always political. Indeed, for Moslemian, the *process* of painting encompasses all aspects of his life and work. His work reveals social confrontations and elicits a wide variety of emotional responses and interpretations, as if to him the process of creating means discovering contradictions and connections, continuity and disruption, and exploring the idea of beauty versus reality.

His striking canvases, for instance, reflect the ambiguity and doubt that engulf contemporary Iranian society. Within a continual re-examination and re-interpretation of traditional artistic genres, Moslemian's art has been concerned with contemporary socio-cultural realities, especially those in his own society. He maintains:

When national modernity is tailored to fit within the cultural essence and context of Iran, it can be argued that we have assimilated modernism into our society. This results in a national modernity with distinct characteristics, although incorporating essential elements of Western modernity such as individuality and rationality. It is natural for this national or native modernity to be influenced by specific characteristics and elements of Iran's socio-cultural background, and even by its geographical conditions.[62]

Moslemian, like the preceding generation of neo-traditionalist artists, shares the belief that if an artist intends to depict shapes in accordance with contemporary culture and thought, it is natural for that artist to scrutinise his own background while grappling with the complex realities of his surrounding world. In reacting to the world,

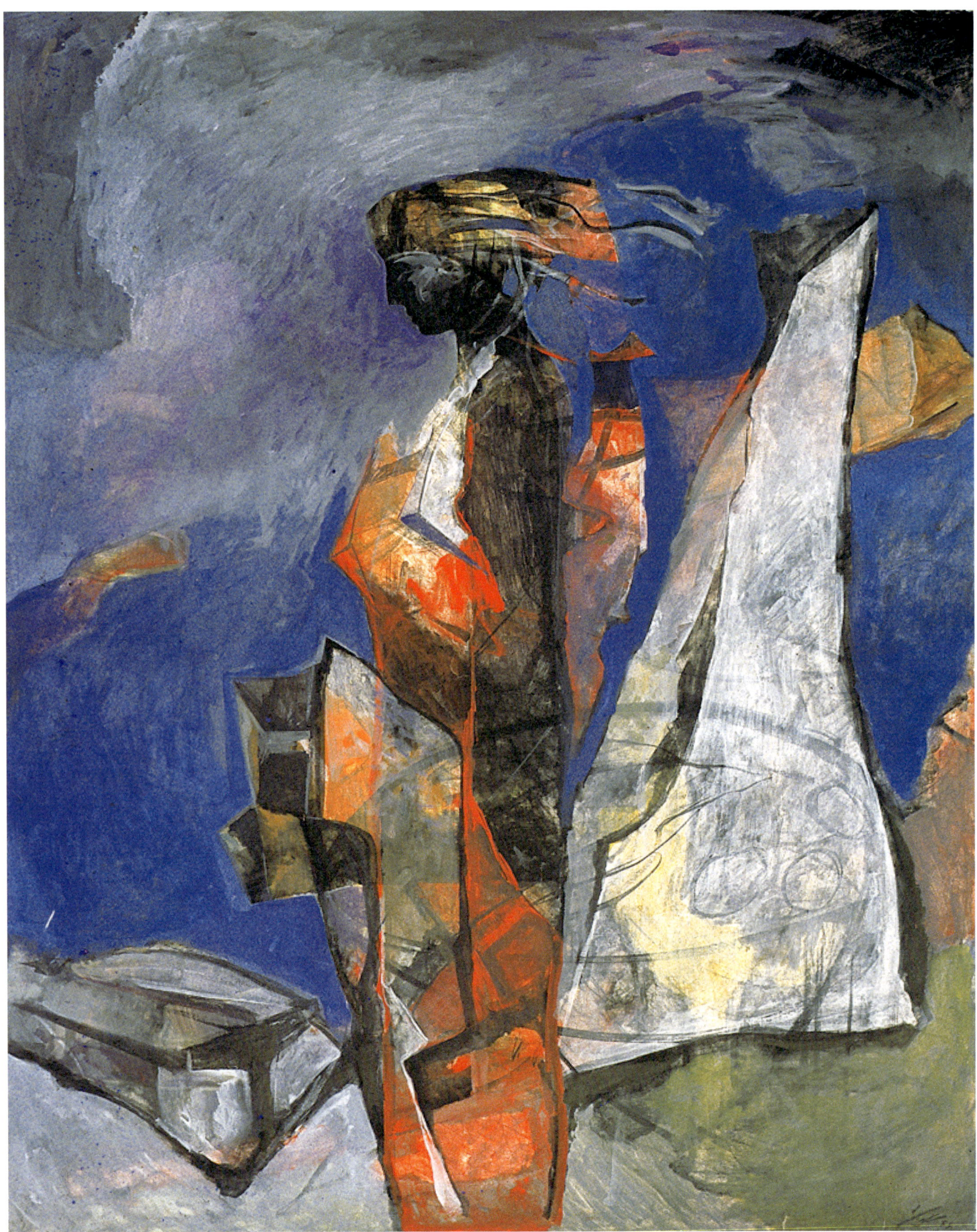

the artist draws upon elements from his own experiences as well as those of others.

In his *War* series, created in essence between 1981 and 1988, he dealt extensively with the problem of war, both intellectually and artistically. His paintings in this period are like acts of personal defiance against the state of war, sanction and misery. (Figure 4.26) In a later stage of his career, Moslemian's art gradually distanced itself from that of the war period and instead confronted the issue of identity politics and its representation in art and culture. Simultaneously, his works began to adopt a more lyrical approach to social subjects, while retaining their critical confrontation. Like enduring monuments, his figures speak not of individual identity but as symbols of a collective cultural lineage and a human presence that cannot be erased. These images, with their forms, existences, and characters, owe much to the artist's contemplation and represent independent visual worlds, which are not inherently narrative. For example, his large-format lyrical canvas portraits depict faces that look urgently at the viewer, challenging them directly.

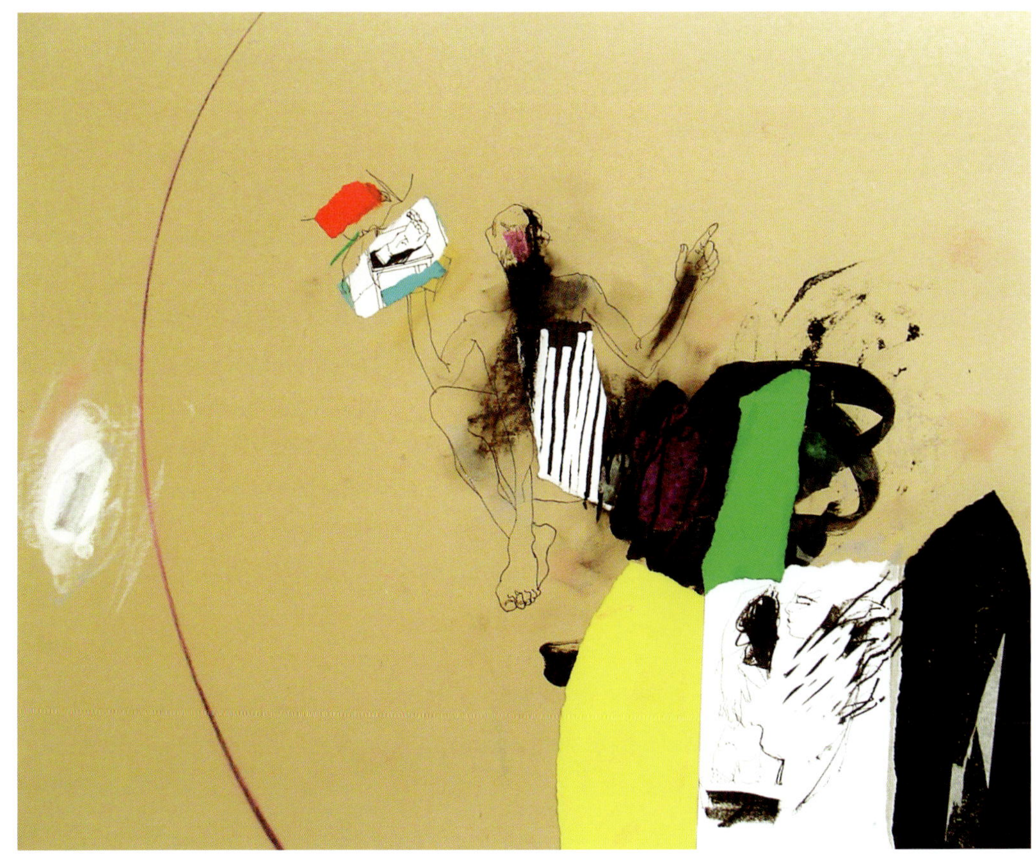

Facing page
4.26
Nosratollah Moslemian, *Untitled,* from the *War* series, 1987, acrylic and oil on canvas, 170×135 cm, courtesy the artist

Left
4.27
Nosratollah Moslemian, *Untitled,* 2006, acrylic on canvas, mixed media on canvas, 46.5×56.5 cm, courtesy the artist

If contemporary art is characterised by pluralism, relativity and eclecticism, Moslemian's art stands as a clear and typical example. In his latest works during the 1990s, one can observe a juxtaposition of everyday life with traditional or even mythical elements, a fusion of figuration with abstraction, and the integration of contradictory-textured and technical strategies. The more recent series essentially confront viewers with issues of violence and gender in a patriarchal society. (Figure 4.27) While the works principally address social issues such as gender inequality and identity politics, they are aesthetically juxtaposed with careful formal considerations. In a series of portrait paintings from the 1990s and 2000s, Moslemian aims to transgress representational conventions. (Figure 4.28) A preoccupation with tragedy and despair runs through the entire period of his works and is expressed in the choice of ironic and bitter representational forms.

In this context, some of the active figures in the artistic scene from the pre-revolution era, primarily associated with modernist figurative tendencies, maintained their presence during this period by adapting their approaches within the framework of the new

4.28
Nosratollah Moslemian, *Untitled*, 2007, acrylic on canvas, 100×100 cm, courtesy the artist

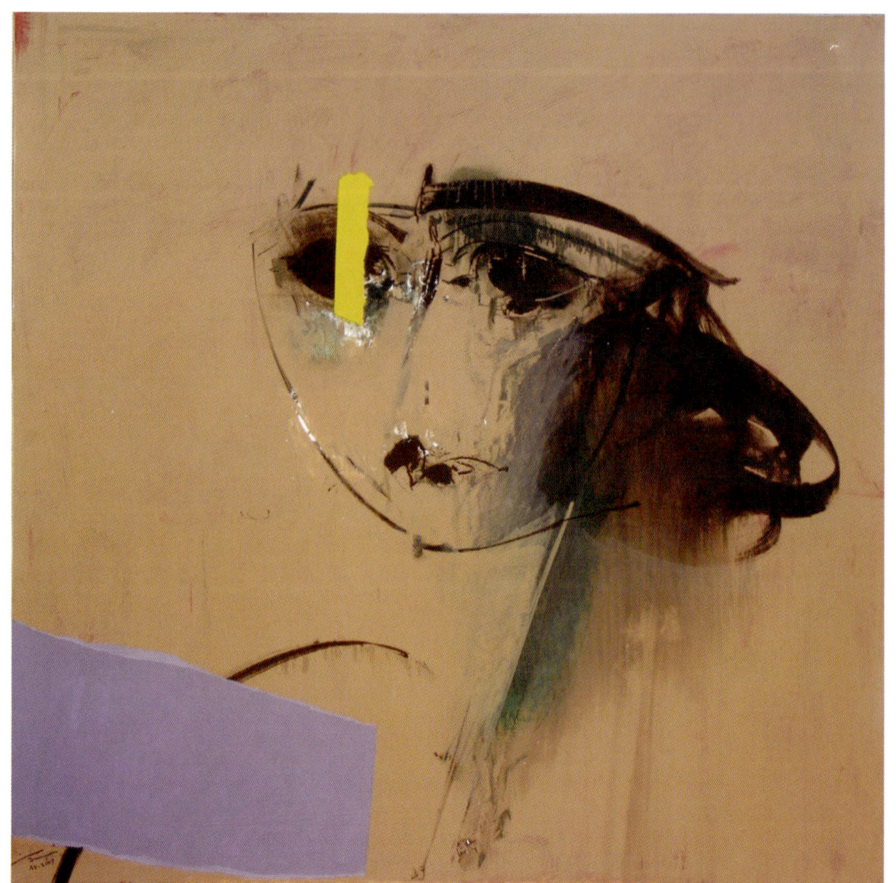

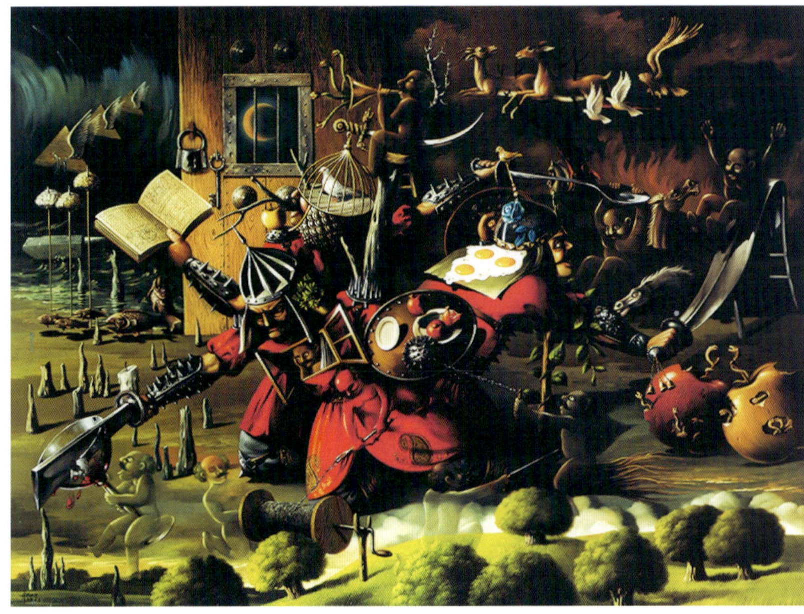

4.30
Ali Akbar Sadeghi, *Shahnameh*,
1985, oil on canvas

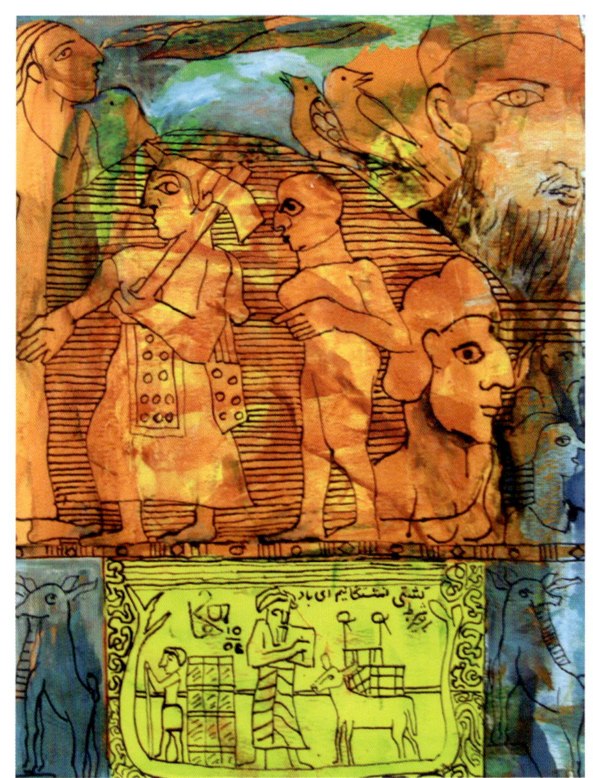

4.29
Hannibal Alkhas, *The Ship of our
Stters, O Wind, Rise up* (a verse
from Hafiz), 1999, acrylic and ink
on paper, 30×22 cm

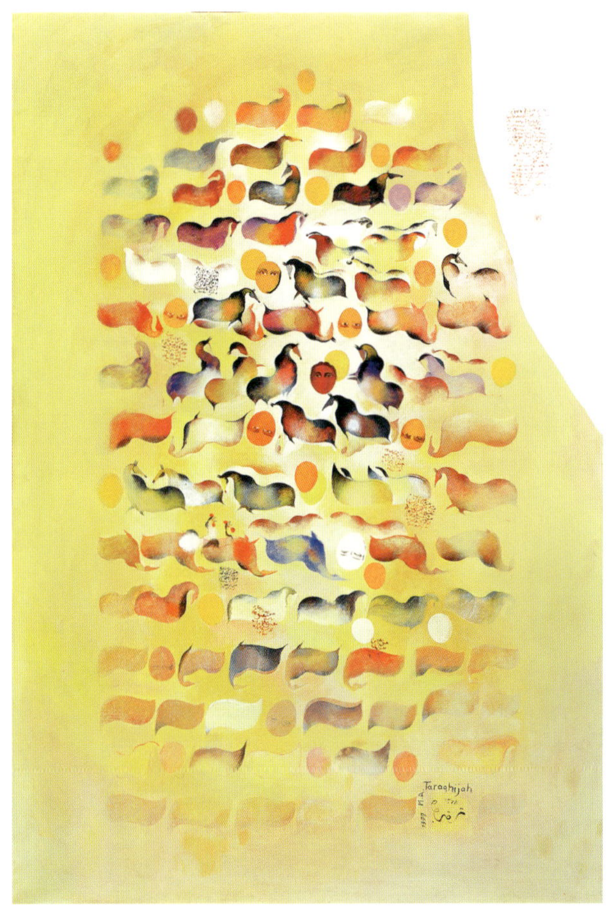

4.31
Mohammad Ali Taraghijah, *Quest 7*,
1999, acrylic on paper, 180×120
cm, TMoCA

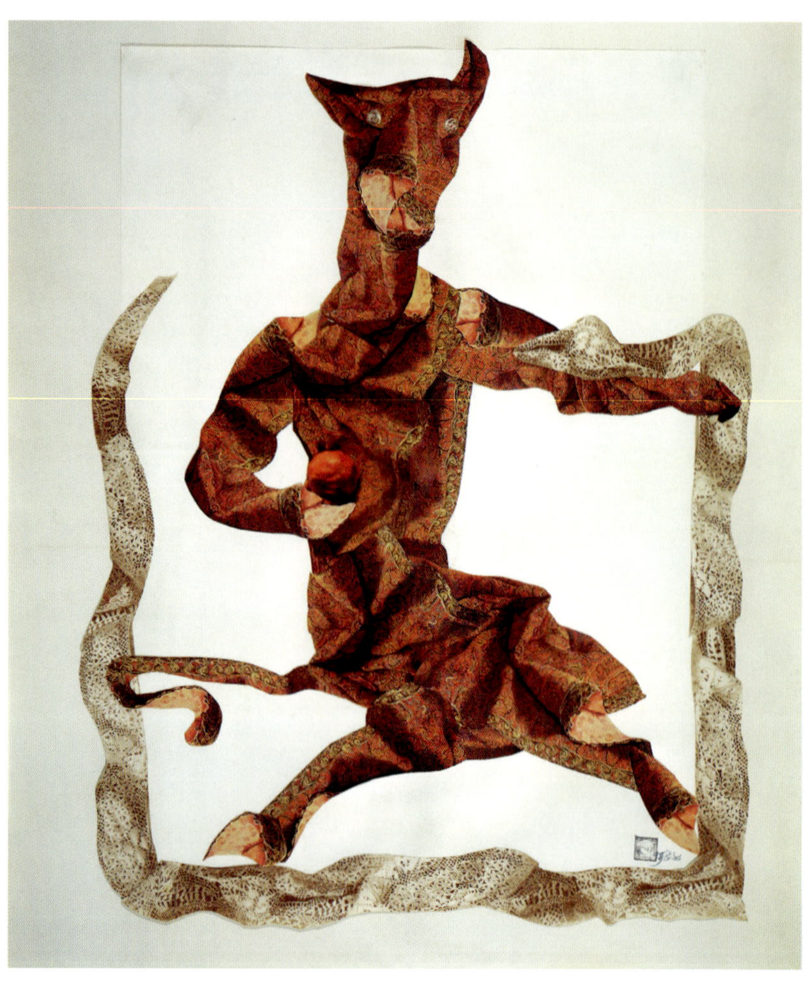

4.32
Parvaneh Etemadi, *Magician*, 1998,
colour pencil on paper, 133×107 cm

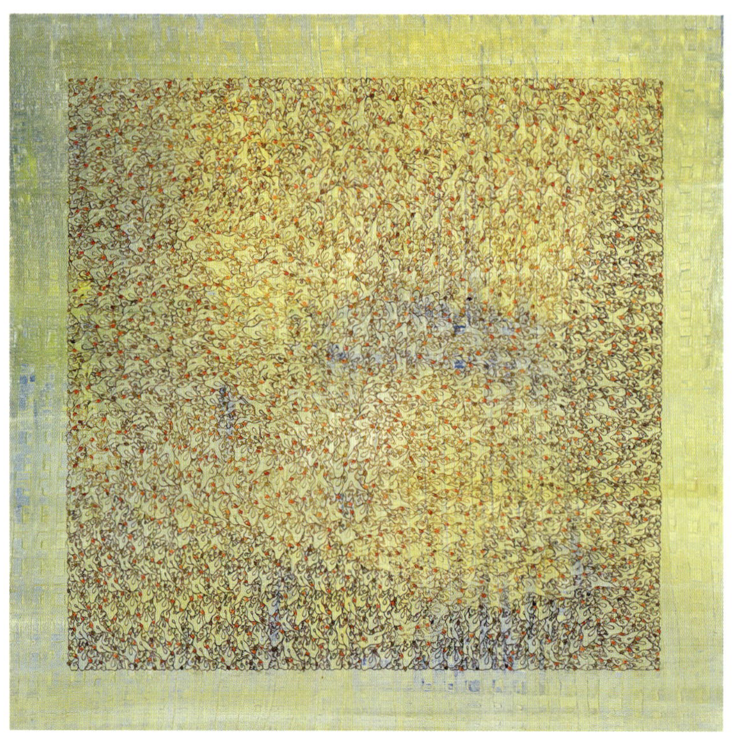

4.33
Shahla Habibi, *Abstract Celebration
2*, 1987, oil on canvas, 99×99 cm,
TMoCA

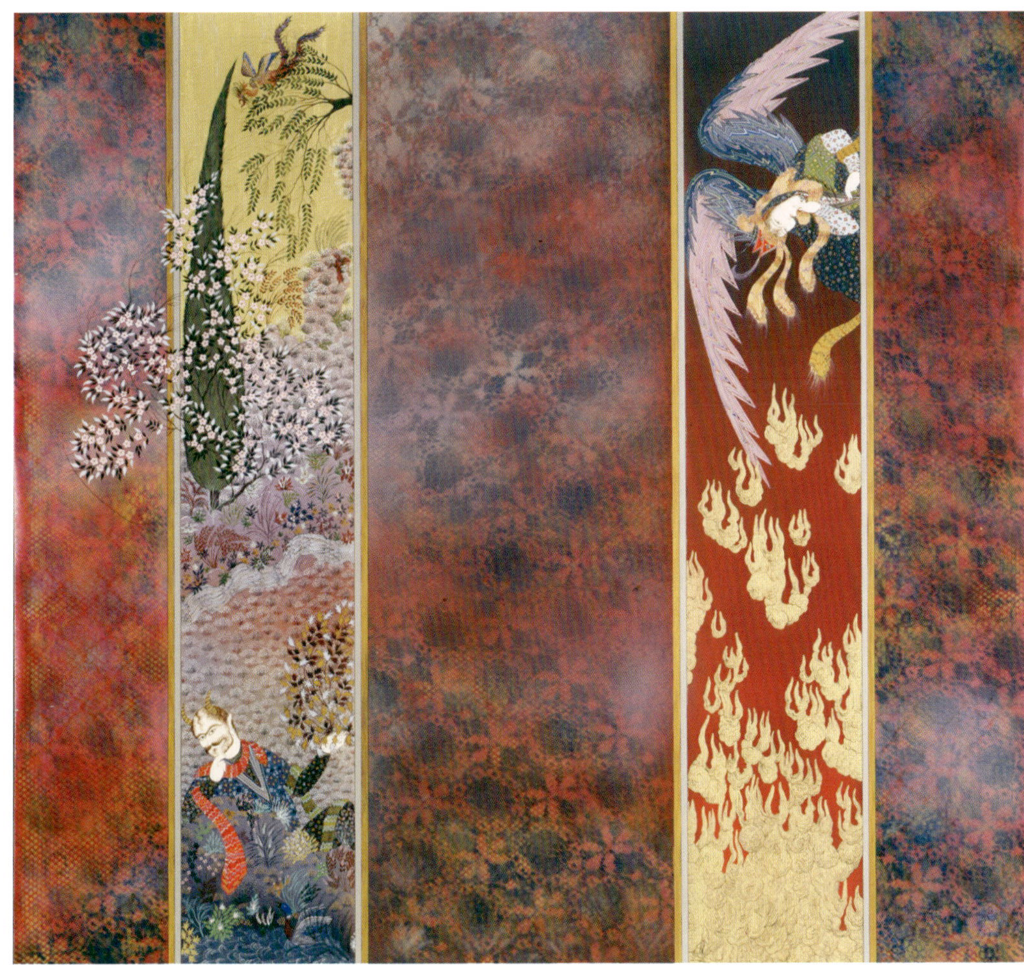

4.34
Farah Ossouli, *Paradise and Hell*,
1992, gouache on paper, 70×70 cm

cultural milieu. These artists drew inspiration from various aspects
of Iranian art, historical themes, or traditional crafts in diverse ways.
Figures such as Hannibal Alkhas, Aydin Aghdashloo, Ali Akbar
Sadeghi (b.1937), Mohammad Ali Taraghijah (1943–2010), Shahla
Habibi (b.1945), Parvaneh Etemadi, Farah Ossouli (b.1953), and
Gizilla Varga Sinai (b.1944) can be categorised within this group.
(Figures 4.29–34)

In contrast to the neo-traditionalists practising figurative art, a
second group of artists during this period worked with abstraction.
In many of their works the decorative quality manifest in *Saqqa-
khaneh* art appears to have been eliminated; they rely instead
on the abstract characteristics, favouring mystical and spiritual
concepts such as mysticism and Gnosticism, over overt social
issues. Distinguished members of this group are Jafar Rouhbakhsh,
Ziaoddin Emami (1922 2008) and Homayoun Salimi (b.1948).
Calligraphic trends were also actively developed in this period.
(Figures 4.35–37)

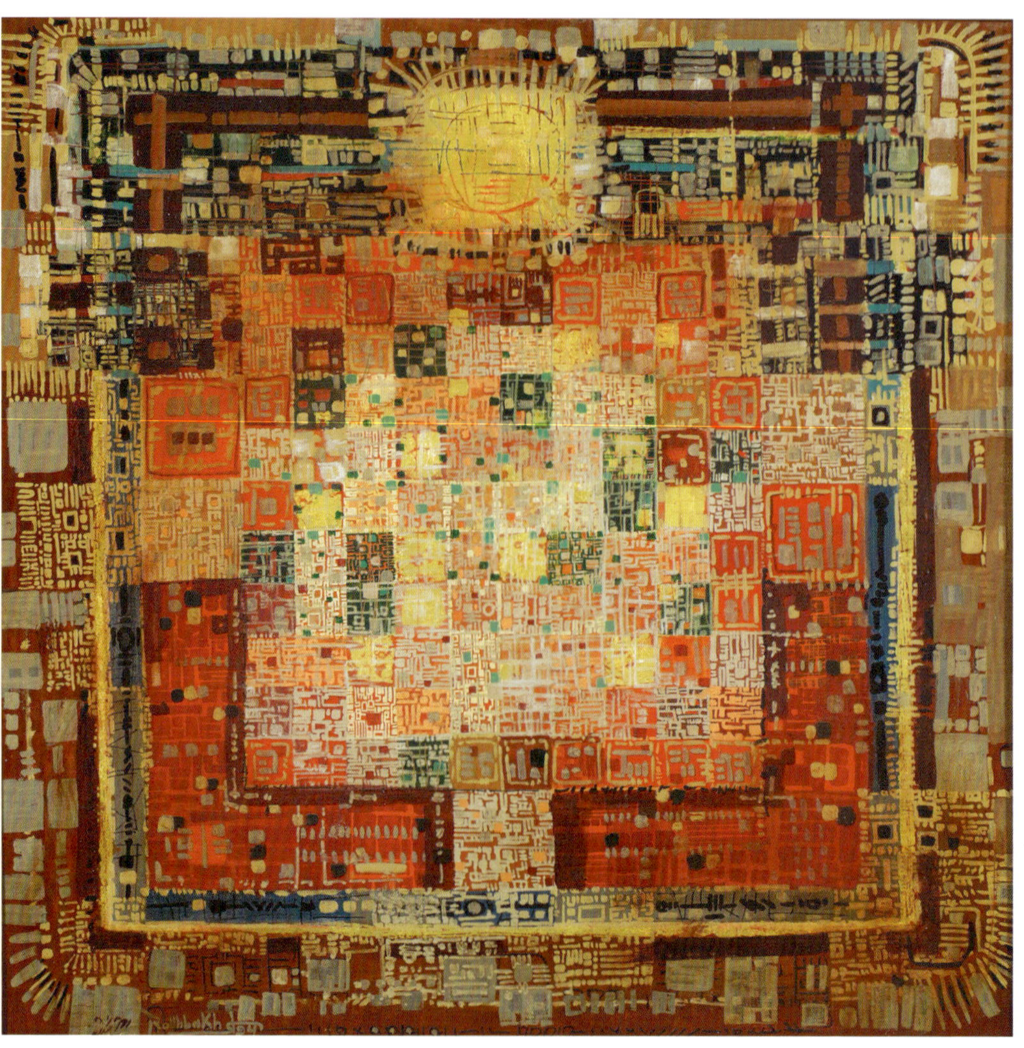

4.35
Jafar Rouhbakhsh, *Composition*,
1994, oil on canvas, 100×100 cm,
TMoCA

Rouhbakhsh can be regarded as representative of this group. Although he embarked on his professional career in the years before the Revolution, his most prolific artistic period unfolded in the post-revolutionary years, particularly during the 1990s, when he emerged as an active and influential artist. A graduate of the Tehran Faculty of Decorative Arts in 1969, his paintings from the late 1980s and 1990s exhibit close ties to early *Saqqa-khaneh* works. However, he goes beyond mere replication of traditional motifs and patterns, instead innovatively employing the geometric structure of Islamic art and architecture. In his paintings, forms are not thematic; rather, they exist as purely formal and independent entities, devoid of any narrative or symbolic meaning. The composition of the works is established through abstraction, resulting in pictorial metaphor and poetic sentiment without reliance on literary texts. His most distinguished works, executed primarily between 1985 and 1995, feature structural frameworks based on various rectangular

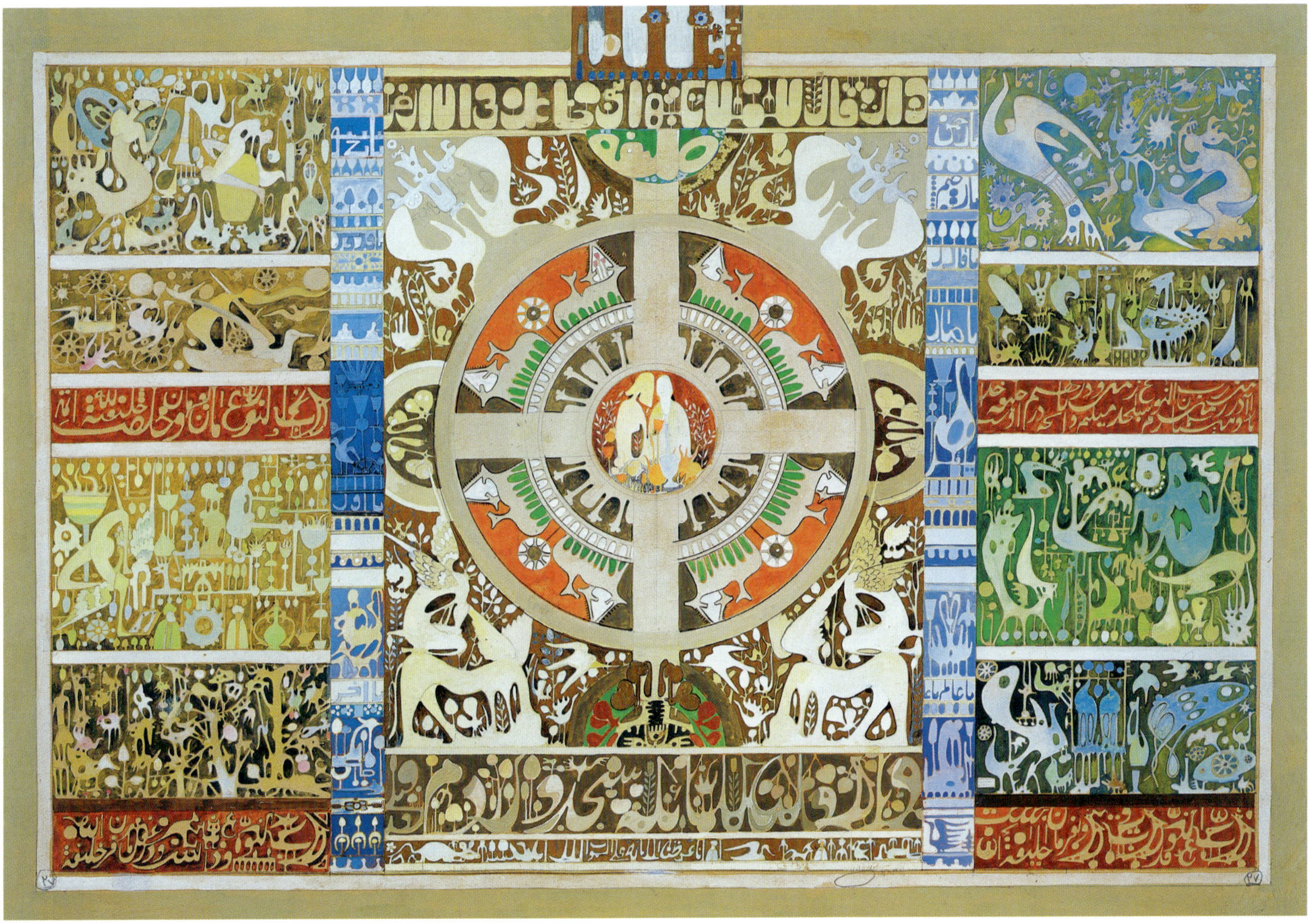

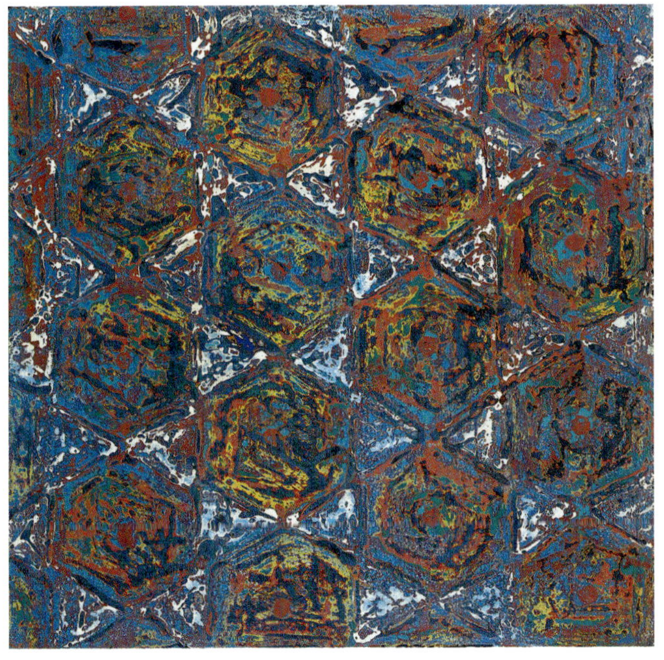

4.36
Ziaoddin Emami, *Adam's Creation*, 1988, watercolour on paper, 50×74 cm, TMoCA

4.37
Homayoun Salimi, *My Mother was from Kashan*, 1998, mixed media on canvas, 90×90 cm, TMoCA

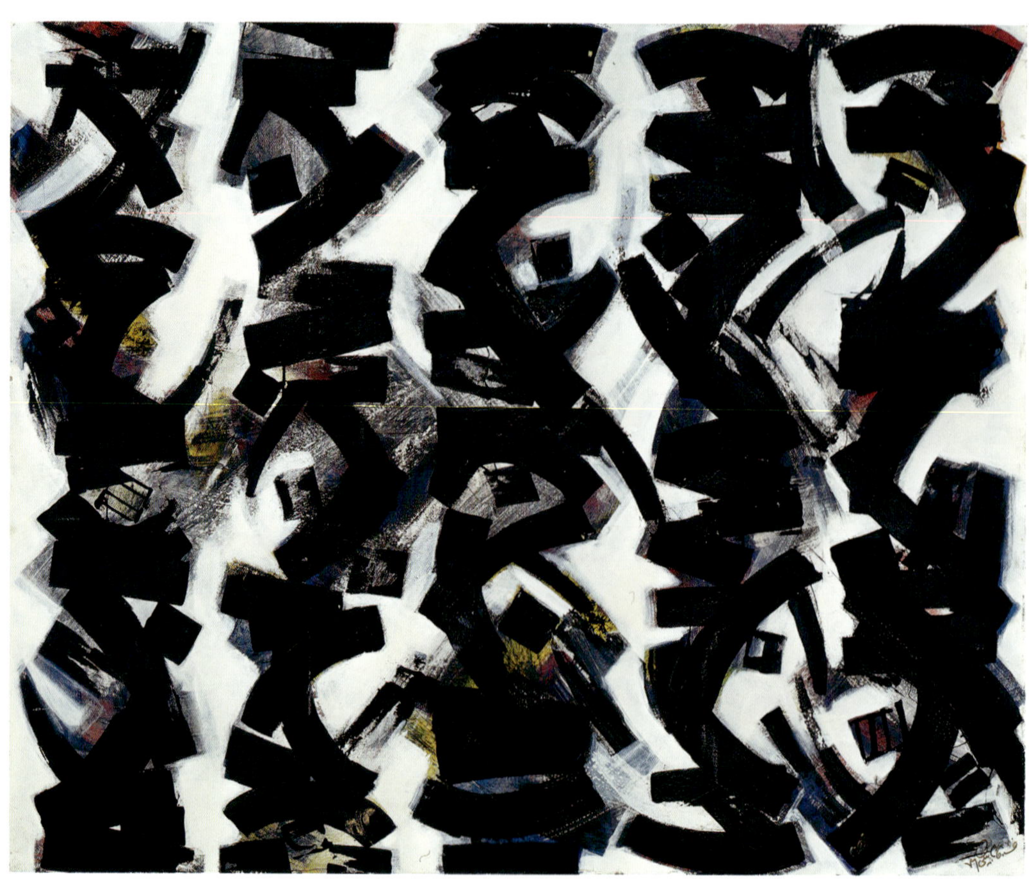

4.38
Fereydoon Mambeigi, *White Spaceship*, 1997, mixed media on canvas, 110×120 cm, TMoCA

forms filled with countless visual elements, often with modifications to their strict geometrical shapes. (Figure 4.35)

During this period Iranian Letterism did not continue under its founders. However, the continuation of this approach can be observed in the works of a new generation of artists seen in Iranian post-revolutionary national biennials and other major exhibitions, both inside and outside the country, throughout the 1980s and 1990s. During these decades, several younger artists – painters, photographers or even those practising other means of media – produced works that paralleled those of the pioneers.

A ceramicist, sculptor and painter, Fereydoon Mambeigi (1940–2009) established his career, mainly as a painter, in the post-revolutionary period. A graduate of both the Tehran Faculty of Decorative Arts and then Rome's Accademia di Belle Arti, his works are part of the same trend as those of Letterists; however, they make clear reference to Far Eastern art, in particular calligraphy. Featuring a variety of calligraphic methods, Mambeigi's canvases of the 1990s show him to be a devotee of modernist abstraction, particularly through his obvious interest in American Abstract Expressionism.

Mambeigi's mixed media canvases incorporate basic calligraphic forms in concert with a modernistic reference. (Figure 4.38)

Rafat Negarandeh (b.1947), active mainly during the 1980s and 1990s, was another key figure of this genre. In his colourful *Shikasteh*-like calligraphic canvases, the ornamental forms do not depict literary or narrative content. Instead, they serve as two-dimensional elements of calligraphy and colour, amalgamating to evoke a mystical atmosphere reminiscent of mystical words. Some of his works feature geometric and silhouette-like coloured forms that craft a mysterious background, evoking expressions of a magical and ambiguous space. (Figure 4.39)

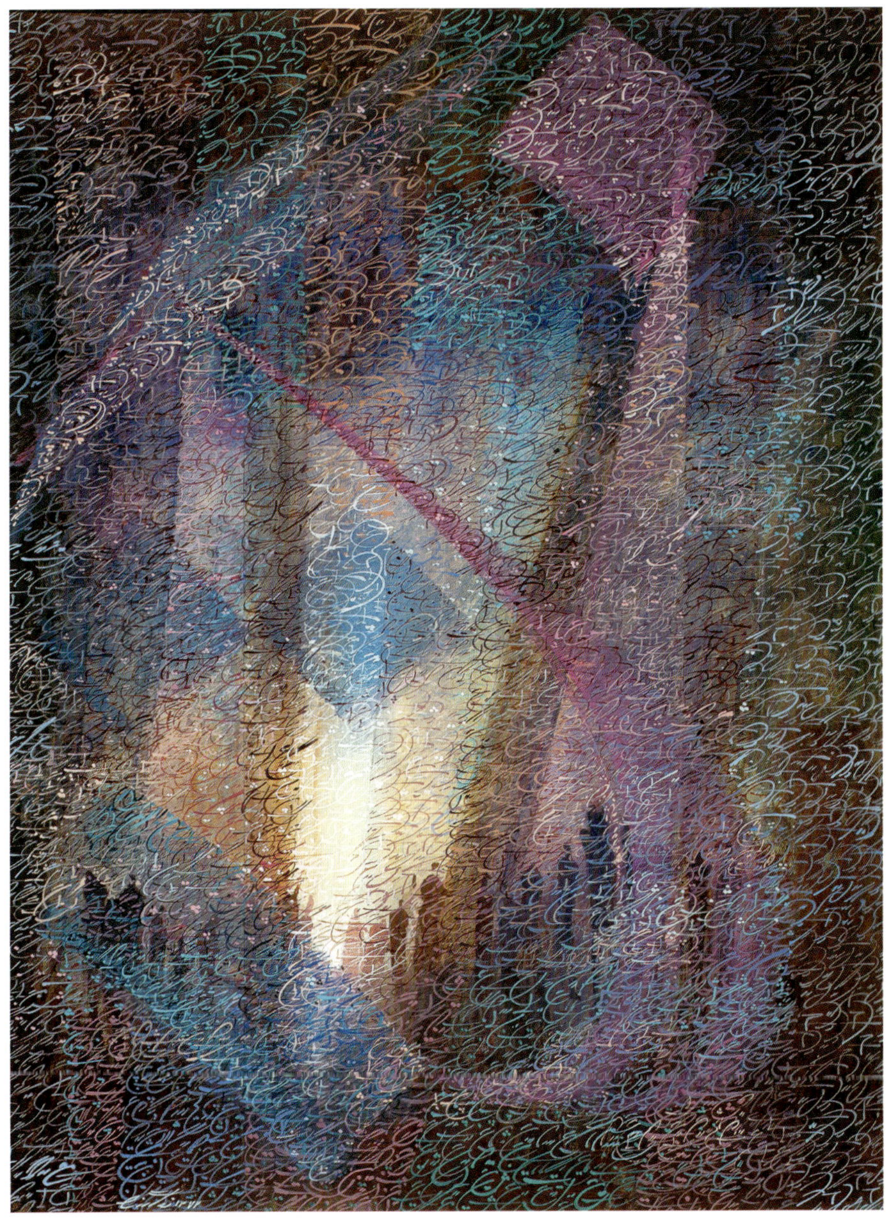

4.39
Rafat Negarandeh, *In la'l-i sukhan*, 1993, acrylic on canvas, 91×61.5 cm, TMoCA

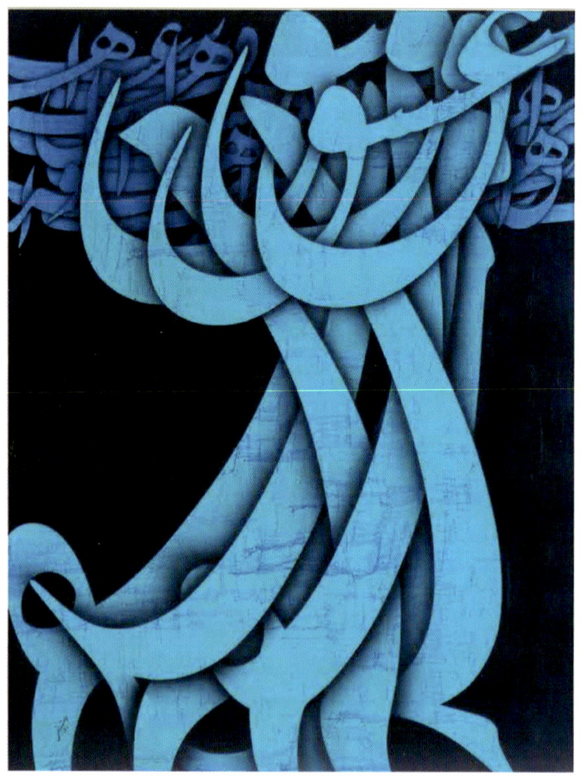

4.40
Ali Shirazi, *Untitled*, 2011, oil on
canvas, 200×150 cm

During this period, other professional calligraphers demonstrated a similar level of consideration and respect for traditional calligraphic conventions, mirroring the approach taken by the pioneers of *Naqqashi-khatt*. One can mention names such as Asadollah Kiani (b.1946), Alireza Karami (b.1949), Ali Shirazi (b. 1960), Einoddin Sadeghzadeh (b.1965), Hamid Ajami (b.1962) and Sedaghat Jabbari (b.1961). (Figure 4.40)

Sedaghat Jabbari, who joined during the group's later years, started practising his neo-calligraphic paintings in the 1990s and was first influenced by the works of his teacher Ehsai. Articulating the forms and words with reference to standard calligraphic scripts, Jabbari then shifted into a more abstract orientation. Having been trained in both traditional calligraphic lessons and the field of graphic design, he tried to fuse these two in his works. In his latest artistic phase, he shows a drastic departure from traditional calligraphy through experimenting with different techniques and compositions. The words and characters in these works are no longer identifiable or clear, and so do not communicate their precise import to viewers; instead, they display themselves as mere visual elements wrapped in colours and textures. (Figure 4.41)

In addition to the aforementioned groups, other artists from different generations that what joined them was their modernist approaches that now seemed to be legitimate. Among the most active and prolific, working in painting, sculpture and photography, one can name Alireza Espahbod, Mirhossein Mousavi (b. 1941), Bahram Dabiri, Iraj Karimkhan Zand (1952–2006), Farideh Lashai (1944–2013), Samila Amir Ebrahimi (b.1950), Mehdi Hosseini, Mohammad Ebrahim Jafari, Mehdi Sahabi (1944–2009), Koorosh Shishegaran (b.1944), Behzad Shishegaran (b.1952), Manouchehr Motabar (b. 1936), Yaqub Ammamehpich (b. 1946), Niloofar Ghaderinejad, Saeed Shahlapour (b.1944), Pariyoush Ganji (b.1945), Rana Farnoud (b.1953), Hosseinali Zabehi (b.1945), Fatemeh Emdadian (b.1955), Karim Nasr (b.1952), Mohammad Hossein Maher (b. 1957), Babak Etminani (b.1946) and Mostafa Dashti (b.1960) (Figures 4.42–53)

Emphasis on Iranian artistic heritage, even in its interaction with the contemporary art scene, continued into the new millennium. For instance, with regard to the Fifth Iranian Painting Biennial, held in 2000, we read:

It appears that nurturing the national, artistic, and social heritage is essential for the advancement of Iranian art. Even if there is a desire to align with global contemporary art movements, maintaining a distinct character rooted in the unique values and traits of Iranian art is crucial for success. Otherwise, within the broader contemporary art landscape still influenced by modernism, contemporary Iranian art might appear inferior.[63]

The themes of 'Iranian mysticism' and the Shi'i pictorial tradition were actively applied in the first exhibition of conceptual art held at the TMoCA in 2001. However, in the ensuing years, the art scene would undergo more significant shifts in approach, characterised by a more critical stance toward the prevailing status quo.

The 1990s witnessed numerous developments in the Iranian art scene. This era marked the emergence of a new generation of artists whose work challenged established trends and norms with innovative approaches. These artists explored various media, including sculpture, art photography, video, performance and installation, contributing to the diversification and evolution of contemporary Iranian art.

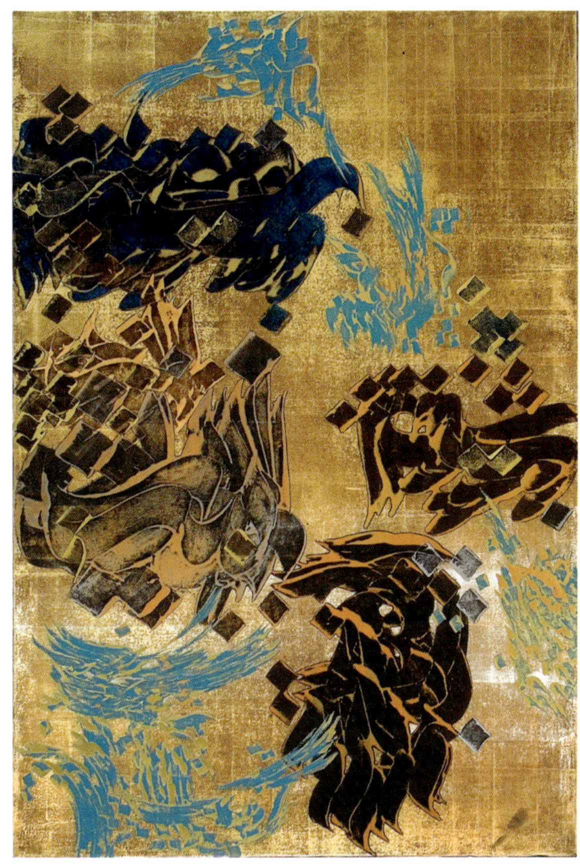

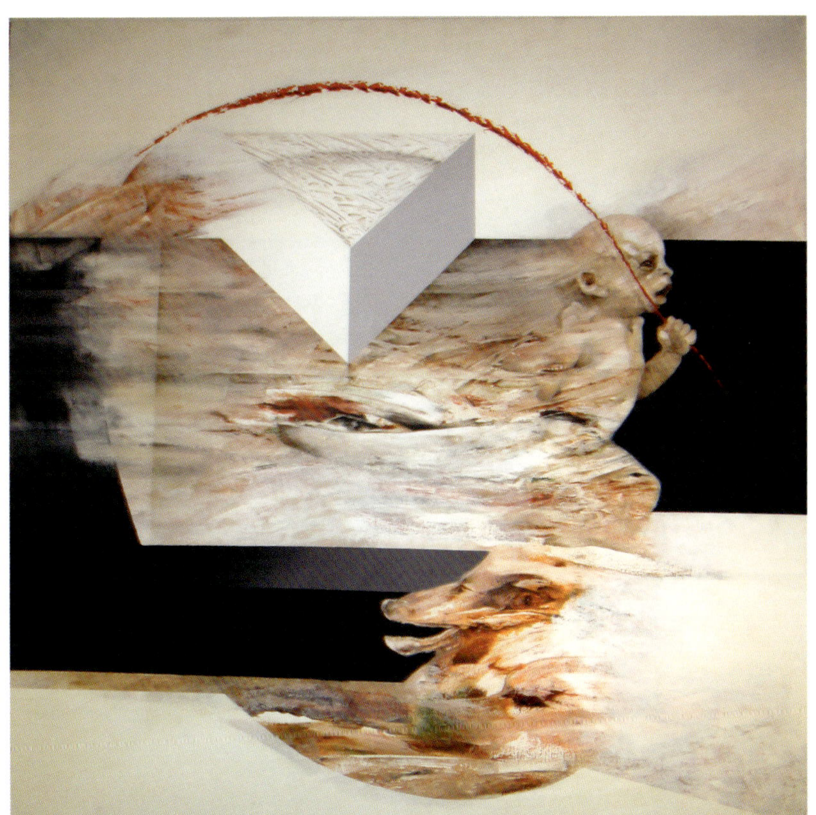

4.41
Sedaghat Jabbari, *The Sound of Rain*, 2005, oil and acrylic on canvas, 142×99.5 cm

4.42
Alireza Espahbod, *Untitled*, 1998, acrylic and oil on canvas, 110×110 cm

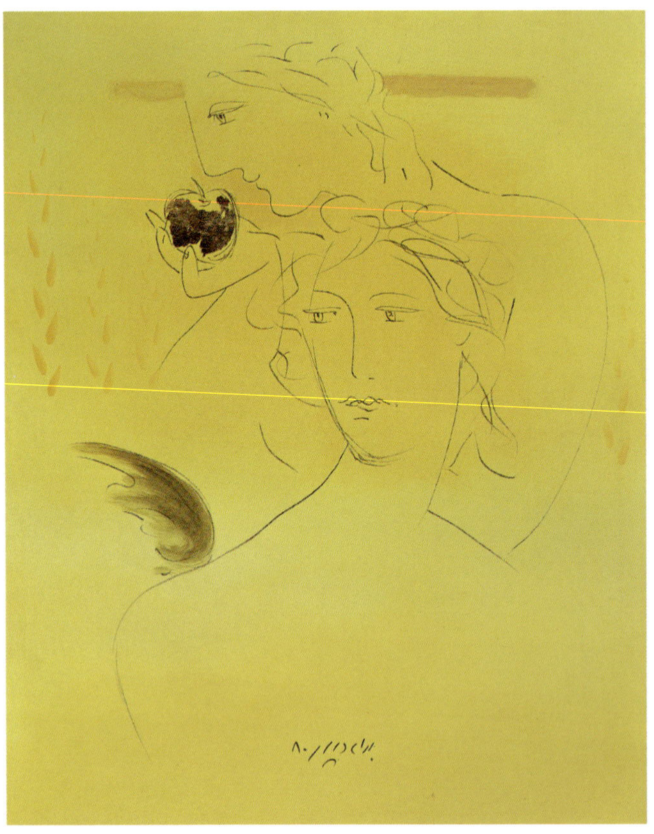

4.43
Bhram Dabiri, *Gold of Apple*, 2001,
acrylic on canvas, 120×80 cm,
TMoCA

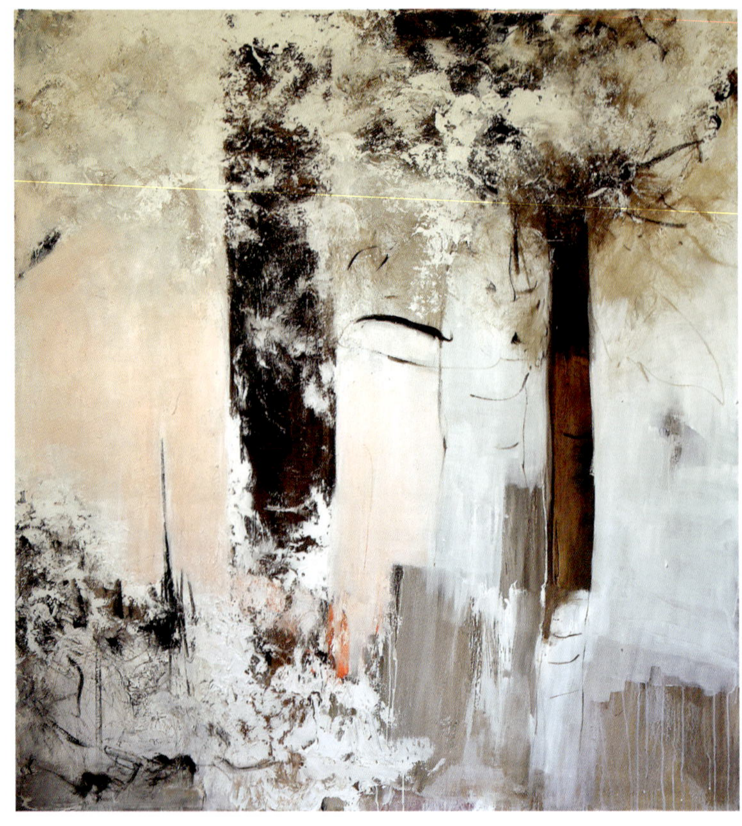

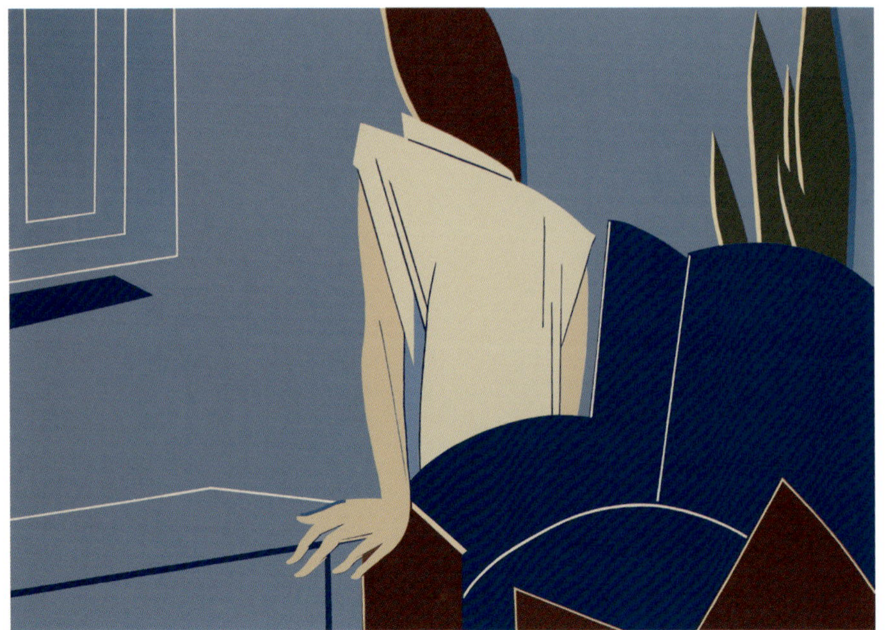

Above
4.44
Farideh Lashai, *Untitled,* from the
Trees series, 2011, oil, acrylic and
pencil on canvas, 170×150 cm

Left
4.45
Mehdi Hosseini, *Untitled*, 2000,
acrylic on canvas, 150×100 cm,
courtesy the artist

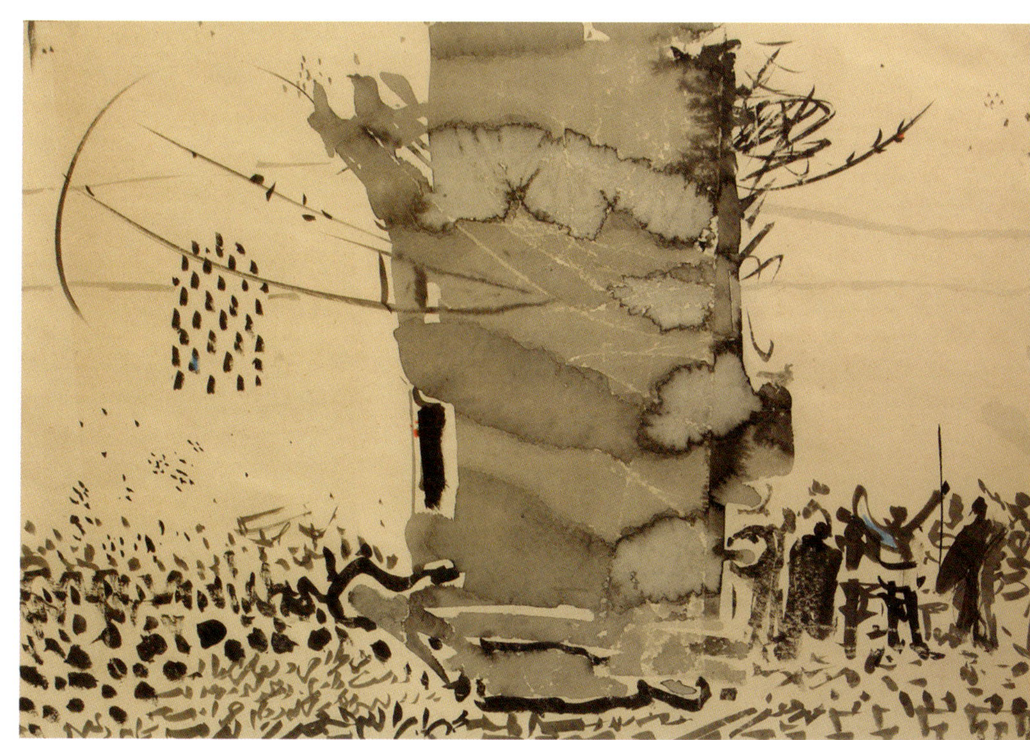

4.46
Mohammad Ebrahim Jafari, *Untitled*, 1990s, ink on paper, 48×62 cm

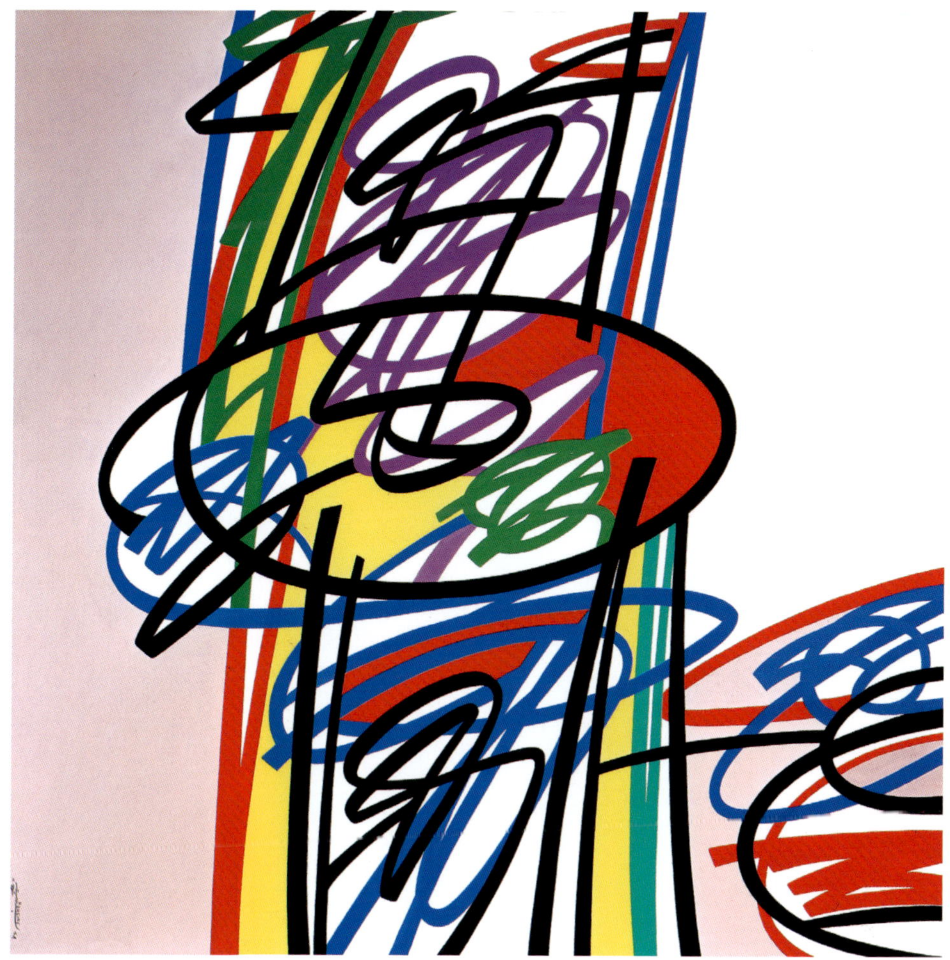

4.47
Koorosh Shishegaran, *Untitled*, 1997, oil on canvas, 120×120 cm, TMoCA

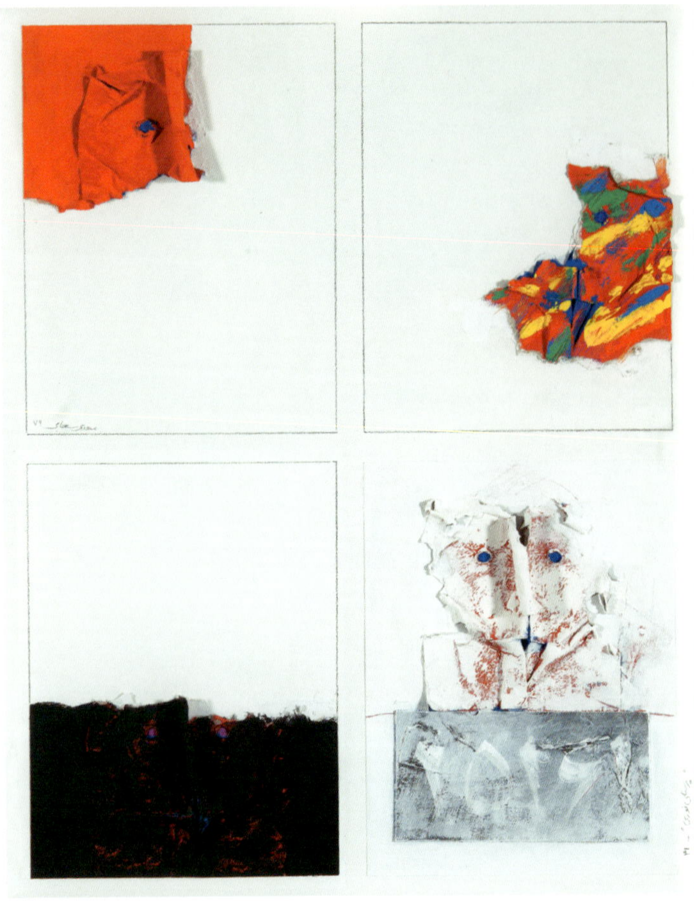

4.48
Mehdi Sahabi, *Instant Personal Photo*, 2000, 100×80 cm, TMoCA

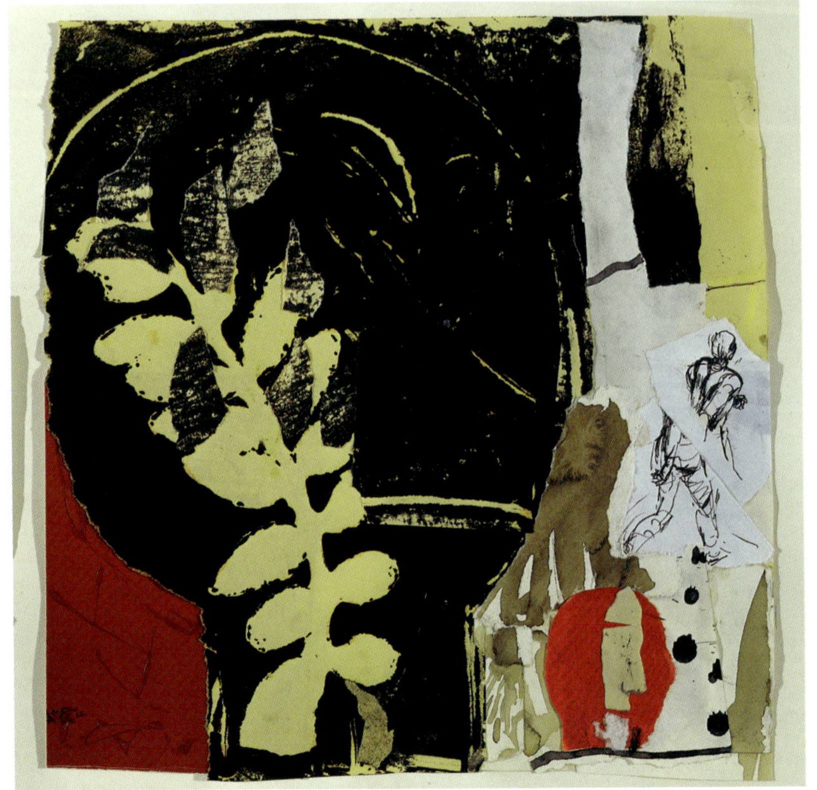

4.49
Ya'qub Ammamehpich, *Untitled*, 1984, collage, 34×32 cm, TMoCA

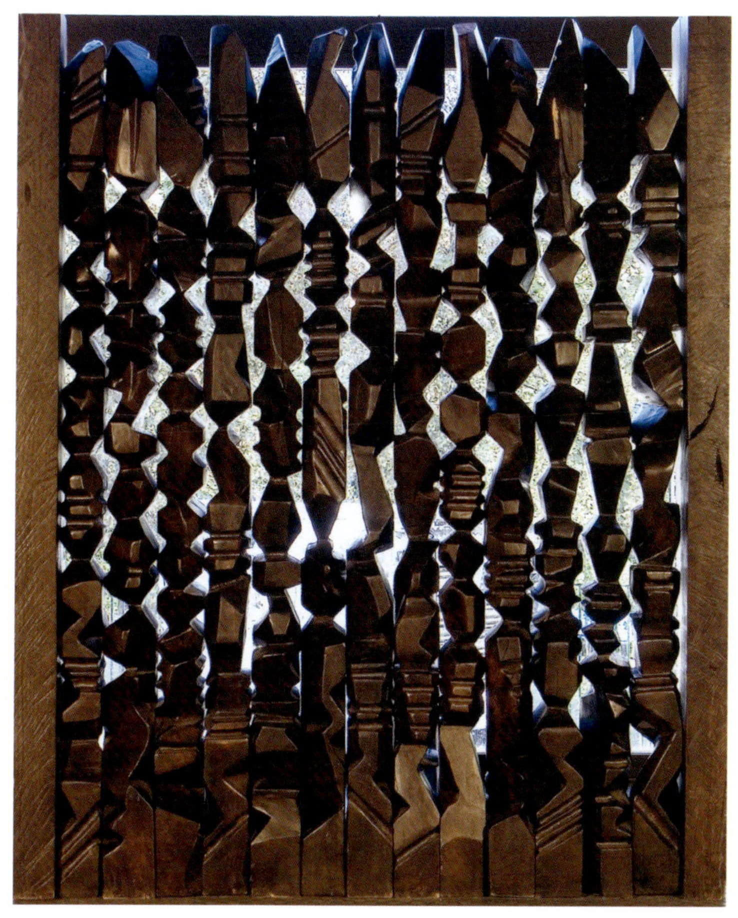

4.50
Saeed Shahlapour, *Untitled*, 2001,
wood, 197×158×30 cm, TMoCA

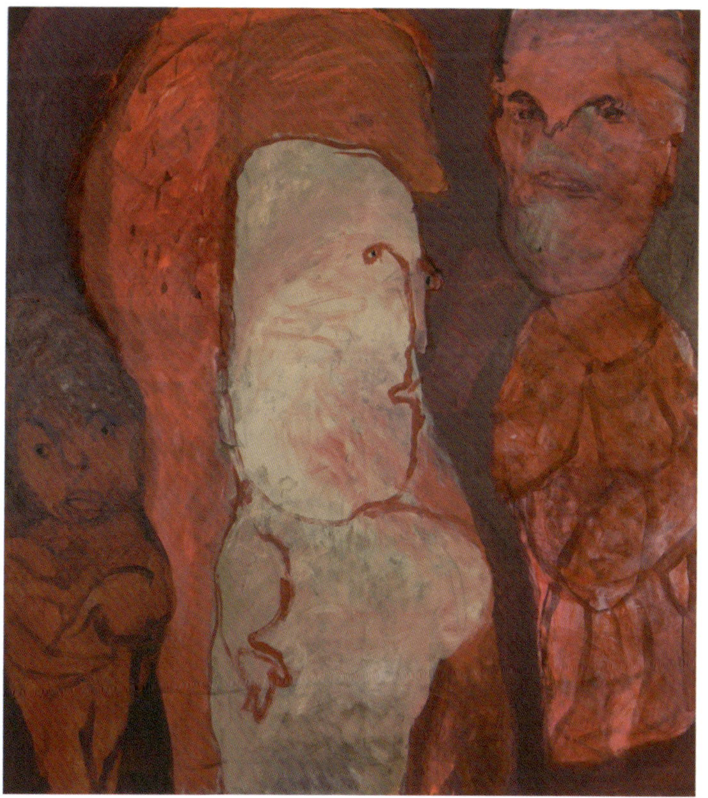

4.51
Raana Farnoud, *Untitled*, 2012,
acrylic on canvas, 168×148 cm

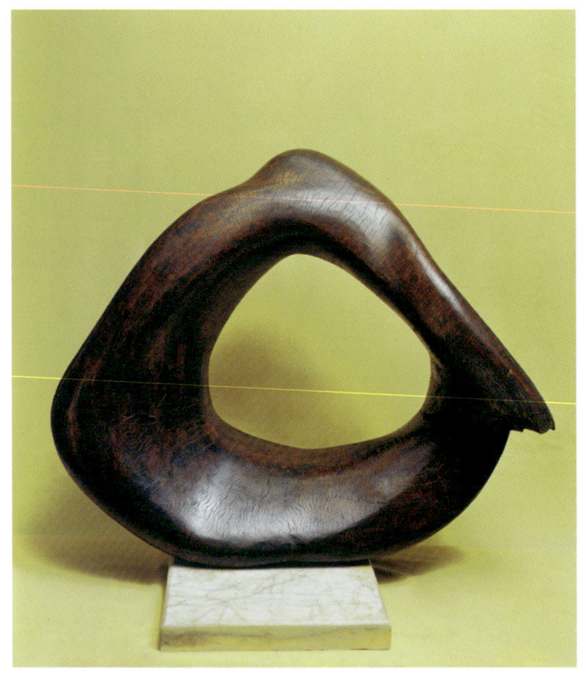

4.52
Fatemeh Emdadian, *Untitled*, 2000,
wood, height: 90 cm, TMoCA

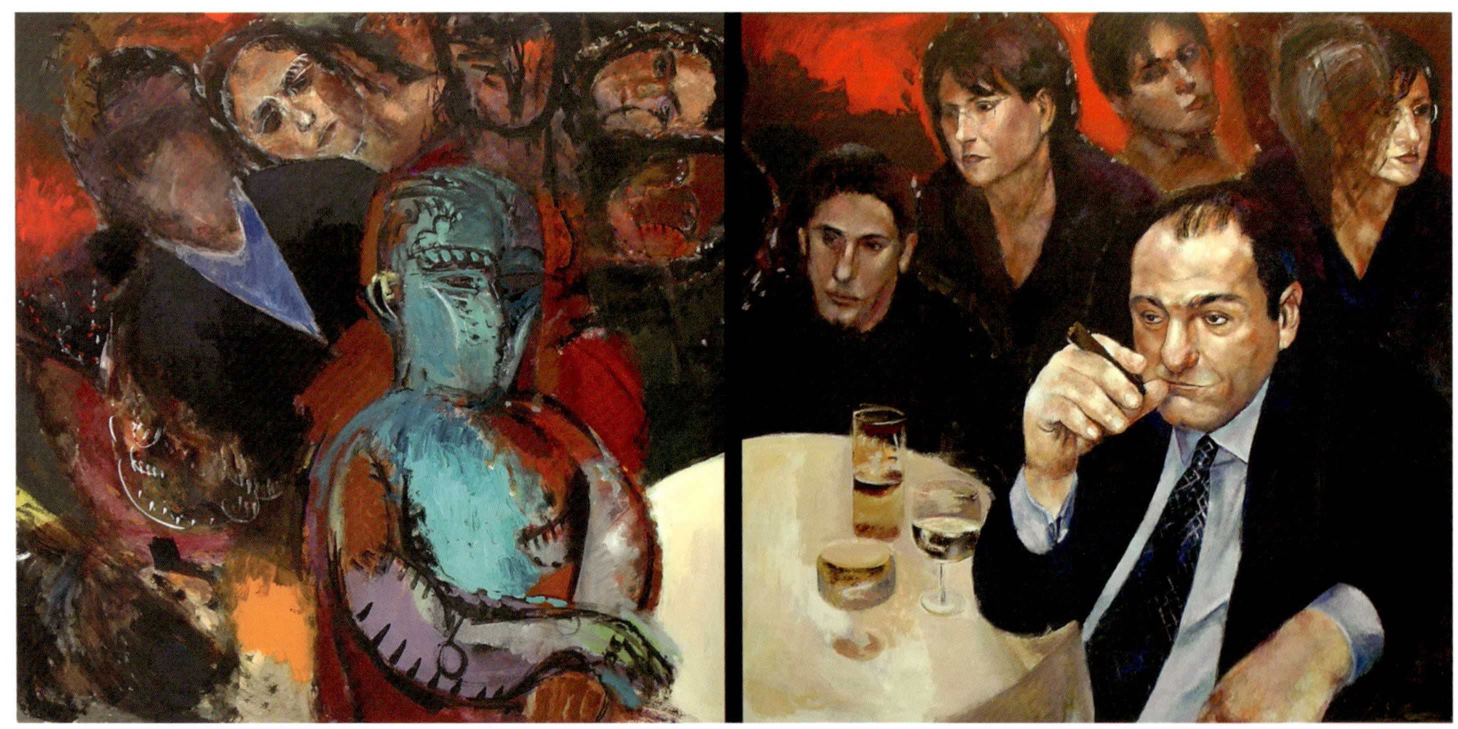

4.53
Karim Nasr, *Dialogue*, 2006, acrylic
on canvas, 160×320 cm, courtesy
the artist

NOTES

1 As with the term 'committed art', this term emphasises the responsibility of art to society. Here, the content of the artwork holds more significance than its aesthetic aspect. This approach to art is closely aligned with socialist beliefs that reject the notion of 'art for the sake of art'.

2 Peter Chelkowski, 'The Art of Revolution and War: The Role of the Graphic Arts in Iran', in Shiva Balaghi and Lynn Gumpert, ed., *Picturing Iran: Art, Society and Revolution*, London and New York 2002, p.22.

3 See Lynn Gumpert, 'Introduction', in Shiva Balaghi and Lynn Gumpert, ed., *Picturing Iran: Art, Society and Revolution*, London and New York 2002, p.11.

4 Haggai Ram, 'Multiple Iconographies: Political Posters in the Iranian Revolution', in Shiva Balaghi and Lynn Gumpert, ed., *Picturing Iran: Art, Society and Revolution*, London and New York 2002, p.98.

5 Ibid.

6 Ibid.

7 Peter Chelkowski and Hamid Dabashi, *Staging a Revolution: The Art of Persuasion in the Islamic Republic of Iran*, London 2000, p.32.

8 Interview with the artist, 2001.

9 Koorosh (b.1944), Behzad (b.1952) and Esmail (1955–2020) Shishegaran.

10 For further exploration of *Howzeh*, see Christiane Gruber, 'Media/ting Conflict: Iranian Posters from the Iran-Iraq War (1980–88)', in Jaynie Anderson, ed., *Crossing Cultures: Conflict, Migration. Convergence*, Proceedings of the 32nd Congress of the International Committee of the History of Art, Melbourne 2009, pp.710–715.

11 This ministry essentially carried out similar functions to those of the Pahlavi-era Ministry of Culture and Art, although with an explicit ideological emphasis.

12 Here, works by prominent figures like Kamal al-Mulk and his artistic school, which had diminished in significance within the Iranian art scene since the emergence of modernist trends in the 1940s, saw a revival in official exhibitions, largely because of their emphasis on direct representational modes. As a result, Kamal al-Mulk's paintings were published and were even attributed with a remarkable revolutionary and anti-monarchical spirit, both in terms of his artistic output and his personal character.

13 It was directed by the Cultural Revolutionary Headquarters and later by the Supreme Cultural Revolution Council. The main aim of the Revolution was purification of the education system of Western influences as well as from staff who were non-Islamic – being secular or leftist (the main force against the regimes' theocratic ideology). After the reopening of the universities many books were banned and many of students and professors were purged from the universities. The process of purification was not without sacrifice. In addition to interrupting the education and professional livelihood of many, and striking a major blow to Iran's cultural and intellectual life and achievement, it contributed to the emigration of many professors and technocrats. (see Nikki R. Keddie, ed., *Modern Iran: Roots and Results of the Revolution*, New Heaven 2006, p.250.)

14 Seyyed Mohammad Khatami, 'Hunar-i risheh-yafteh az adyan', *Faslnameh-i hunar*, no. 3, 1362S/ 1983, p.16.

15 Mostafa Goudarzi, 'Dar-amadi bar naqqashi-i mu'asir-i iran', *Faslnameh-i hunarhd-yi tajassumi*, no. 2, 1377S/ 1998, p.66.

16 Abdolmajid Hosseini Rad, *Ru'ya-y-i firishtigan: Bayan-i tamsili dar naqqashi i now-gira-y-i iran* (Symbolic Expression in Iranian Modernist Painting), exhibition catalogue, Tehran 2000, p.7.

17 Anonymous, 'Siyri kutah dar nimayishgah-hay-i buzurgdasht-i ayyam-i daheh-i fajr', *Faslnameh-i hunar*, no. 3, 1362S/ 1983, p.335.

18 See Chelkowski and Dabashi, *Staging a Revolution*, p.6.

19 Chelkowski and Dabashi, *Staging a Revolution*, p.10.

20 It is worth noting that during this period, the term *Naqqashi-khatt* was used even more frequently and occasionally ambiguously, encompassing both trends of neo-calligraphy explored in Chapter Three. However, based on our classification and the aforementioned fundamental distinctions, it was possible to distinctly differentiate between the works of *Naqqashi-khatt* and those of letterists.

21 However, as mentioned in Chapter Three, such eminent *Naqqashi-khatt* artists as Afjei confirm the leading role of the *Saqqa-khaneh* movement and its popular artists in the formation of their trend.

22 *Gulgasht* literally means sightseeing; and refers to the formal naturalisation of traditional calligraphy and its contents.

23 See Chapter One.

24 An explanation in terms of cultural specificities sliding into cultural essentialism is provided in the work of Bertrand Badie, *Les deux etats: pouvoir et societe en Occident et en terre d' Islam*, Paris 1986, which presents a detailed argument for the historical and ideational distinction and contrast between the 'two states', the Western and the Islamic.

25 See Hamid Keshmirshekan, 'Discourses on Postrevolutionary Iranian Art', *Muqarnas*, vol. 23, 2006, pp.131–157.

26 Faculty of Radio and Television (Danishkadeh-i sida va sima) was also established under the Islamic Republic Radio and Television (Seda va Sima).

27 Other biennials and triennials included works created by graphic designers, illustrators, photographers, cartoonists, ceramicists, and sculptors.

28 Before that exhibition, as previously mentioned, numerous exhibitions were held by the TMoCA and other public artistic centres, including the Reza Abbasi Museum, and the Niavaran and Azadi Cultural Centres. However, these exhibitions had minimal impact on Iranian art scene, largely due to their lack of organisation and comprehensiveness. None of these exhibitions covered a wide range of existing Iranian art or adhered to established principles and rules. The most comprehensive exhibition at the time was perhaps *Views of Contemporary Iranian Art*, held in 1990 at the TMoCA.

29 *First Iranian Painters Biannual: 19 Nov.-19 Dec, 1991, Tehran, Tehran Museum of Contemporary Art, Niavaran Cultural Centre, Azadi Cultural Centre* (exhibition brochure), Tehran 1370S/ 1991, p.1.

30 M. Mohajer, 'Avvalin nimayishgah-i dusalaneh-i naqqashan-i iran', *Hunar-hay-i tajassumi*, no.2, summer 1377S/ 1998, p.119.

31 *First Iranian Painters' Biannual*, p. 1.

32 See *Avvalin nimdyishgah-i dusdlaneh-i naqqashdn-i iran* (First Iranian Painters' Biennial) (exhibition catalogue), Tehran 1370S/ 1991. The use of such motifs continued in the two subsequent biennials, in 1993 and 1995.

33 *Guzideh'i az asar-i avvalin nimdyishgah-i dusdlaneh-i naqqashan-i iran* (Selection of Works of the First Iranian Painters' Biennial), Tehran 1371S/ 1992, p.3.

34 The First Biennial consisted of two sections: the main part was titled 'The Free Subject', and the second part 'In Advocacy of the Palestinian Islamic Revolution'. By this, as M. Mohajer later (1998) noted, the biennial secretariat wished to emphasise its allegiance to the revolutionary aspirations and struggles of the Islamic world. See M. Mohajer, 'Avvalin nimayishgah-i dusalaneh-i naqqashan-i Iran', p.120.

35 See *Huviyyat-i farhangi va hunari: majmu'eh bahs-hay-i kunfirans-i hunar-hay-i tajassumi* (Proceedings of the First Plastic Arts Conference), Tehran 1372S/ 1993.

36 Seyyed Mohammad Sohofi, 'Introduction to the First Plastic Art Conference of Iran', in *Huviyyat-i farhangi va hunari*, Tehran 1372S/ 1993, p.5.

37 Ibid.

38 In addition to the national biennials which continued, although intermittently, other national exhibitions such as the Manifestation of Feeling (*Tajalli-i ihsas*) biennial exhibition, featuring works by Iranian women artists, were also organized by the Artistic Deputy of the Ministry of Culture and Islamic Guidance. These exhibitions exhibited a striking similarity in terms of artistic approach.

39 See Habibollah Ayatollahi, 'Buhran dar hunar-i imruz-i iran',in *Huviyyat-i farhangi va hunari*, p. 96.

40 See Anonymous, 'Duwumin nimayishgah-i du-salaneh-i naqqashi-i iran', *Mah-nameh-i hunar-hay-i tajassumi*, no. 4, 1372S/ 1993, p.1.

41 Kazem Chalipa, 'Now-avari va tanawu'-talabi', *Naqsh* (a special magazine series published on the occasion of each Iranian Painting Biennial, commencing with the second), no. 1, 1372S/ 1993, p.5.

42 Mohammad Ali Rajabi, 'Huviyyat va haqiqat-i naqqashi-i imruz', *Hunar-i mu'asir*, no. 3, 1372S/ 1993, p.68.

43 The first Iranian arts and crafts comprehensive exhibition, called A Festival of Iranian Art, was held from 12 September 1991 to 13 October 1991, in Dusseldorf, Germany. Launched to introduce Iranian art in the West, this exhibition comprised 150 works, most of them by traditional Iranian artists and craftsmen, including miniature paintings, carpets, calligraphy, Coffee-house paintings, ceramics and tiles.

44 Anonymous, 'Barr va bahr farakh ast va adami bisyar', *Faslnameh-i hunar*, p.19, 1369S/ 1990, p.7.

45 During the biennials, a number of foreign artists and art critics (most of them from France or Russia) were invited by the TMoCA, although their presence played no role in the biennial judging process.

46 To be noted is that the Iranian Cartoon Biennial and Illustration Biennial had already become international exhibitions that included works both executed and selected by Iranians and international artists.

47 These suggestions primarily originated from artists of the pre-revolutionary generation. Examples of such opinions are evident in the articles or interviews published in the editions of *Naqsh* dedicated to the Second Biennial exhibition and conferences.

48 Abolghasem Khoshroo, 'Sukhanrani-i aghay-i muhandis Abulghasim Khoshroo dar marasim-i iftitahiyyeh-i duwumin kunfirans-i hunarhay-i tajassumi dar muzeh-i Hunar-hay-i Mu'asir', in *Hunar-i qudsi majmu'eh sukhanrani-hay-i duvumin kunfirans-i hunar-hay-i tajassumi* (Proceedings of the Second Plastic Arts Conference), Tehran 1373S/ 1994, p.32.

49 *Naqqashi-i muc'sir-i iran* (Iran Contemporary Painting, catalogue of the Second Iranian Painting Biennial), Tehran 1373S/ 1994, p.2.

50 See *Hunar-i qudsi*, Tehran 1373S/ 1994.

51 Zahra Rahnavard, 'Huviyyat-i gumshudeh va dayalug-i jahani', *Hunar-i mu'asir*, no. 3, 1372S/ 1993, p.65.

52 Ruin Pakbaz, 'Taqabul ba tahajum-i farhangi', *Hunar-i mu'dsir*, no. 3, 1372S/ 1993, p.72.

53 Daryoush Shayegan, *Cultural Schizophrenia: Islamic Society Confronting the West*, translated from French by John How, London 1992, p.vii.

54 The year that Reza Shah, the first Pahlavi shah, was dethroned and exiled and his son Mohammad Reza came to power. In 1941, during the Second World War, British military forces occupied Iran, leaving shortly after Iran officially joined the Allies in the war against Germany in 1943. During these years Iran was essentially governed by Allied troops, which brought about more contact between Iranians and the West and a period of greater self-expression in Iranian literature, art and the press.

55 Faraj Sarkouhi, 'Daheh-i shast: Adabiyyat va hunar dar gir va guriz', *Adineh*, no. 75, 1369S/ 1990, p.67.

56 Ibid.

57 Ibid., pp.67–68.

58 Ibid.

59 Faraj Sarkouhi, 'Aya tahavuli dar rah ast?', *Gardun*, *vizheh nameh-i hunar-i naqqashi*, Bahar1370S/ spring 1991, p. 66.

60 Faraj Sarkouhi, 'Daha-i shast', p.69.

61 One of the successful group exhibitions, *The Epic of Kings (Shahnameh) and the Contemporary Iranian Artist*, was held in 1990 to honour the thousandth anniversary of Ferdowsi's *Shahnameh*. Participating artists included Nosratollah Moslemian, Mir Ya'qoub Ammamehpich, Sara Irvani, Massoumeh Mozaffari, Soghra Zareh, Abbas Saranj, Touran Ghadiri, Hossein Ghara-Gozlou, Parastou Frouhar, Arya Eghbal, Amin Nourani, Fatemeh Etemadi, and Davood Mozaffari.

62 Interview with the artist, 2001.

63 Abdolmajid Hosseini Rad, 'Naqqashi-i now-giray-i Iran dar hich kuja-yi In jahan-i pahnavar na-istada ast', *Naqsh* (series for the Fifth Painting Biennial), no. 25, 1379/ 2000, p.8.

CHAPTER FIVE

Development of Contemporary Discourses: the Mid-1990s Onward

I. The Emergence of Contemporary Art

During the late 1990s, the intellectual preoccupation with a 'return' to an 'authentic' and glorified Iranian and Islamic 'self' that had dominated the 1960s and 1970s had developed into a more critical attitude towards national culture and character. Here, the validity of the question of cultural identity, which had preoccupied artists and the intelligentsia for years, was revisited.

The post-revolutionary intellectual discourse inclined to conform to the West was a phenomenon of the late 1990s. Unlike their intellectual predecessors, thinkers in the 1990s generally tended not favouring ideological views that emphasised one factor as a solution to Iran's problems.[1] Maintaining the cultural ideals informing the works of those previous generations had become problematic.

Towards the end of the 1990s, new artistic trends, attitudes and methods unfolded. Several factors contributed to this transformation and the dynamic new developments in Iranian art. First, more artists entered the art scene during this period than at any time in the past. Perhaps one of the most striking changes was the appearance of an energetic group of young artists among whom the presence of women was quite noticeable. Second, public institutions supporting artistic activities (such as art faculties, museums, non-governmental societies of Iranian artists and art journals) were established or expanded.

At the same time, the arrival of the information age and means of mass communication exposed Iranian artists to the predominant contemporary artistic discourses of the international art scene.

The third phase of post-revolutionary art began with the election of the moderate president Seyyed Mohammad Khatami (the former Minister of Culture and Art, 1983–92)[2] in 1997. Strongly popular among both the public and cultural elites, he came to power with a more liberal view of Islam and the Islamic Republic. He brought promises of more freedom and a relaxation of the press, among other political and cultural reforms. His administration, in particular in the cultural sections, encouraged communication with the outside world, something that had for long been strongly opposed by officials. It certainly was a turning point in contemporary Iranian culture and art, both in terms of theory and approach; visual arts assumed a significance not seen since the Islamic Revolution.

The Tehran Museum of Contemporary Art, the main focus of contemporary Iranian art, began to include non-political or ideological art in group exhibitions. The Museum, and in particular the Centre of Plastic Arts of Iran (Markaz-i hunar-hay-i tajassumi-i kishvar), played a key role in promoting various forms of contemporary Iranian art. The Centre, which came under the control of the Deputy of the Ministry of Culture and Islamic Guidance for Artistic Affairs, had been established in 1983; it was directed by the head of the TMoCA.[3] The Society of Painters (Anjuman-i hunarmandan-i naqqash) and the Society of Sculptors (Anjuman-i mujassameh-sazan) were both established in 1999 as independent cultural-artistic associations funded exclusively by the membership fees they receive from their members. They have, however, benefited from the support of the Centre of Plastic Arts.[4] The directorship of Alireza Sami Azar, between 1998 and 2005, saw a relaxation of the controls placed on visual arts and its associated activities, including those in major public and commercial galleries. The Centre also began to support commercial galleries in Tehran and other cities through funding and collaborations, while private galleries were freed of the requirement that they should gain the Centre's approval for each show they planned to mount. In this context, it was a significant development against those restrictions on art and artistic affairs imposed by the governmental section and marked a decisive reduction in government regulation of artistic affairs.[5]

The Museum and the Centre also bolstered support for visual arts by implementing organised programmes, which included broadening the scope of biennials with more comprehensive objectives. They also directly engaged with newly established artists' societies. Thematic exhibitions were curated, showcasing both contemporary Iranian art and works from European and American contemporary art scenes (for example, of 20th-century British sculpture in 2004 and contemporary Japanese art in 2005). (Figure 5.1) National and international gatherings and academic discussions on different aspects of contemporary art and culture were also organised. The number of art publications and public places exhibiting visual arts grew considerably.[6]

Now, the TMoCA served not only as the primary venue for exhibiting contemporary art but also played a crucial educational role in advancing contemporary art practices in Iran. This was a notable development, particularly considering the absence of robust artistic discourses within existing art education, including faculties and institutions. In fact the Museum had begun these programmes as early as 1990–1, by organising different national (and sometimes international) biennials, but they were now more systematic and determined. This period of liberalisation also saw the exhibition of many works by both prominent pre-Revolution Iranian artists and Euro-American artists represented in the Museum's rich collection. Eminent Iranian artists such as Charles Hossein Zenderoudi, who had left Iran and severed all links with the art scene after the Revolution, were now invited to participate in solo or group exhibitions. Particularly important in this context was the 'Pioneers of Iranian Modern Art' series of exhibitions. Curated by Ruin Pakbaz,[7] these included works by pre-Revolution Iranian modernist artists such as Sohrab Sepehri, Hossein Kazemi, Houshang Pezeshknia, Zenderoudi, Massoud Arabshahi, Parviz Tanavoli, Mansoureh Hosseini, Behjat Sadr and Mohsen Vaziri Moghaddam. There were even exhibitions in which works of diasporic Iranian artists such as Shirin Neshat and Shirazeh Houshiary were included – a strategy that was completely unprecedented.

The TMoCA also increased its international activities by establishing links with other international art institutions and museums, by lending works from the Western collection of the Museum (many of which had been unseen for years) and through a number of exhibitions of Iranian artists in Europe, America and Asia.

The year 1998 also saw the establishment of the more conservative Iranian Academy of the Arts (Farhangistan-i hunar).[8] According to the Academy's charter, its activities are intended to focus mainly on

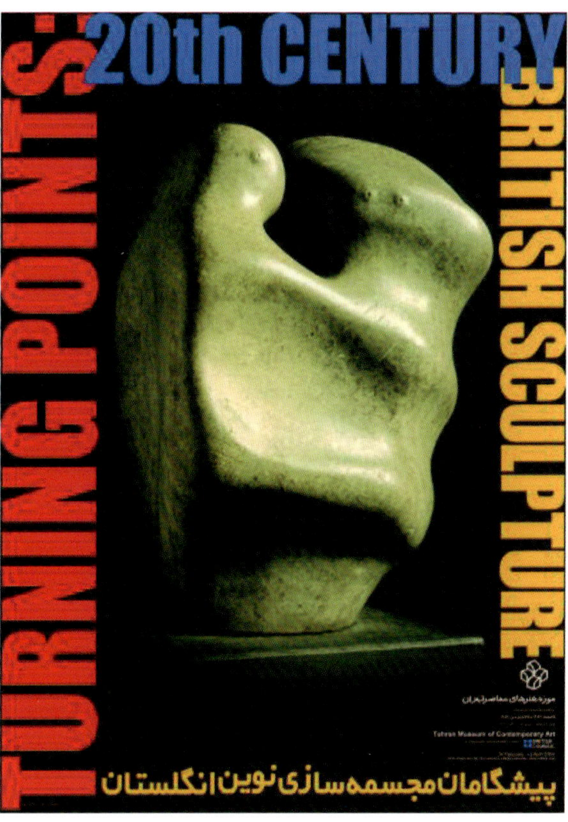

5.1
Poster of the exhibition *Twentieth Century British Sculpture*, 2004, TMoCA

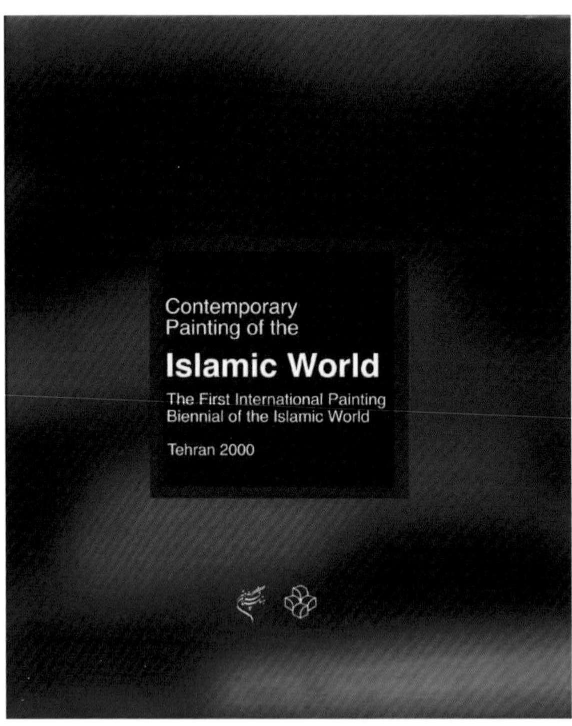

5.2
Poster of the exhibition *Contemporary Painting of the Islamic World*, 2000, Iranian Academy of Arts

'Islamic art' – both traditional and contemporary.[9] Its main focus is Iranian art (with a tendency towards 'Irano-Islamic art'), as well as Islamic and Eastern art. 'International' or Western art was considered less important. Established as a centre for artistic policy-making, the Academy did not have a mandate to get involved in artistic activities. During Mir Hossein Mousavi's[10] directorship (1998–2009) it nevertheless continued to organise various exhibitions from the Islamic world including calligraphy, posters and painting, mainly in the Academy's newly established gallery, the Saba Cultural and Artistic Centre.[11] The gallery was founded in 2004 and contemporary Islamic art biennials were all held there, including: Painting Biennial from the Islamic world, Poster Biennial from the Islamic world, and the Calligraphy Biennial from the Islamic world (on some occasions with the collaboration of TMoCA). (Figure 5.2) The Academy also held various conferences on broad subjects including the philosophy of art, traditional art, and art and globalisation. The Academy, however, became largely inactive after Mousavi was dismissed as director in 2009 following the controversial presidential election, in which Mousavi was the main opposition candidate.

During the third phase (1997–2005), post-revolutionary Iran experienced a period of cultural thaw. The relaxation of restrictions led to the emergence of a generation of artists whose main preoccupation was the idea of contemporaneity. Although no comprehensive study is available, the majority of the emergent artists were young, educated and middle class, and were mostly from central Iranian cities, in particular the capital, Tehran. They also belonged mostly to the 'third generation'[12] born after the 1979 Islamic Revolution (already a majority in Iranian society). The term, third generation, was also used in the press and political conversation during the 1997 General Election and throughout the reformist mottos to express an emphasis on the importance of this generation who came to be the main supporters of the Reform movement during the late 1990s and early 2000s.

The third phase of post-revolutionary Iranian art also saw the development of new means of visual expression, such as video, performance, installation and art photography. The new generation of artists showed less concern for the affirmation of collective identity than with their own biography within a society undergoing radical change. To summarise, this period was defined by the artists' eagerness for experimenting with new idioms and a new willingness from official channels to promote and support these new languages. This

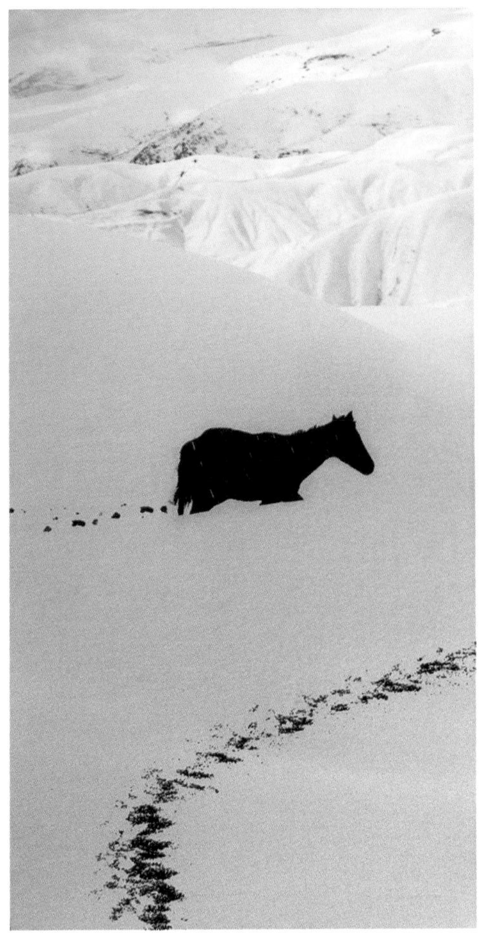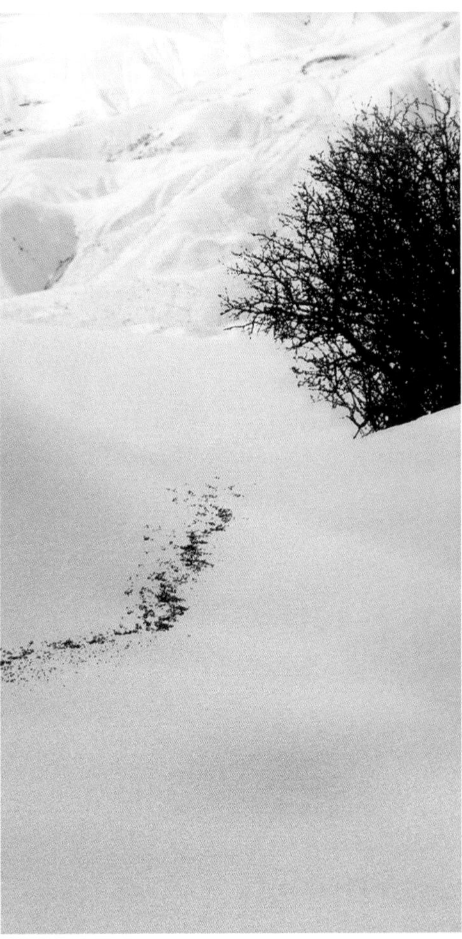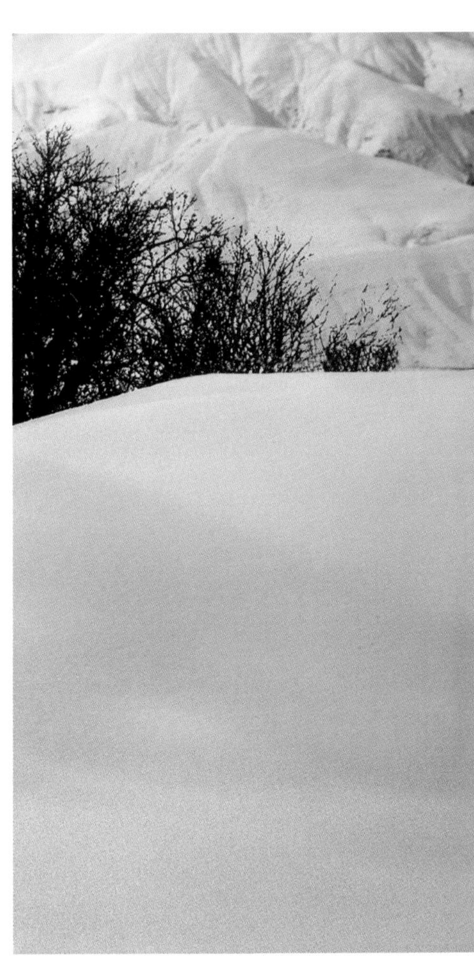

5.3
Abbas Kiarostami, *Untitled*, from the *Snow White* series, 2009, triptych, total size 164×257 cm, digital photograph printed on canvas

combination created fertile ground for the development of what is termed New Art in Iran. The term that was used since the conceptual art exhibition in the TMoCA and Tehran Gallery (attached to the Faculty of Fine Arts, University of Tehran) in 2002. Here it was used to distinguish the new art media, including video art, installation, performance and photo art, from the other genres such as painting, sculpture, photography, etc., which had their own biennials and exhibitions.[13]

Artists now had the opportunity to secure funding for their projects, which required more and more resources, space and other equipment. As a result, many artists who had previously worked in media such as painting, sculpture, cinema or theatre switched to the new fine art media. These artists range from emerging young talents to older, more established artists, filmmakers or performers such as Abbas Kiarostami (1940–2016), Daryoush Mehrjoui (1939–2023), Seyfollah Samadian (b.1953) and Atila Pesyani (1957–2023). (Figures 5.3–4) Some of the artists who came to be the most prolific and active during this phase are Bahman Jalali, Behrouz Daresh

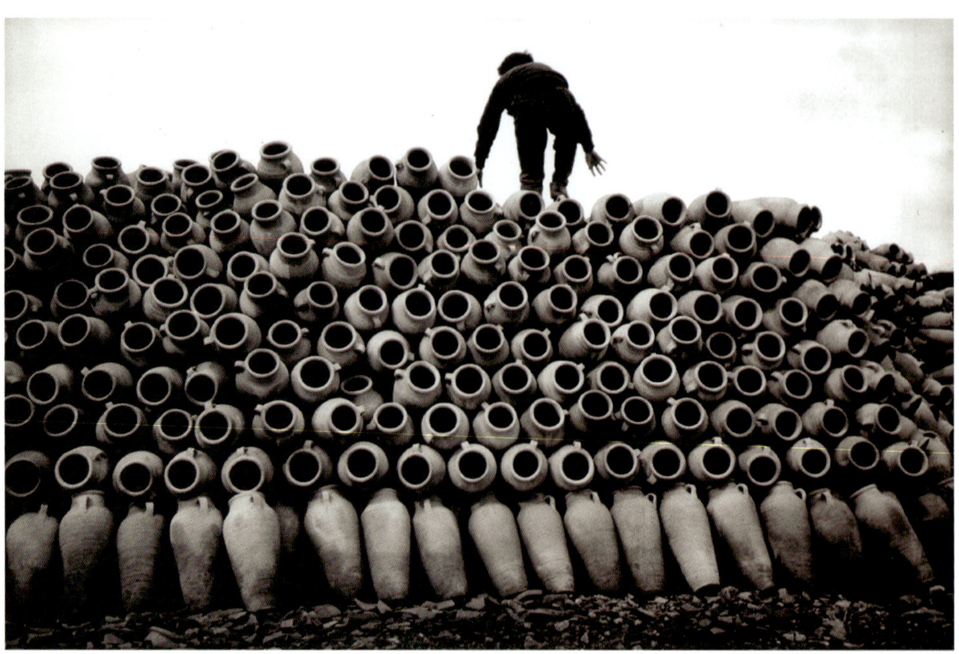

5.4
Seyfollah Samadian, *Jugs*, 2001,
black and white photograph,
100×150 cm, TMoCA

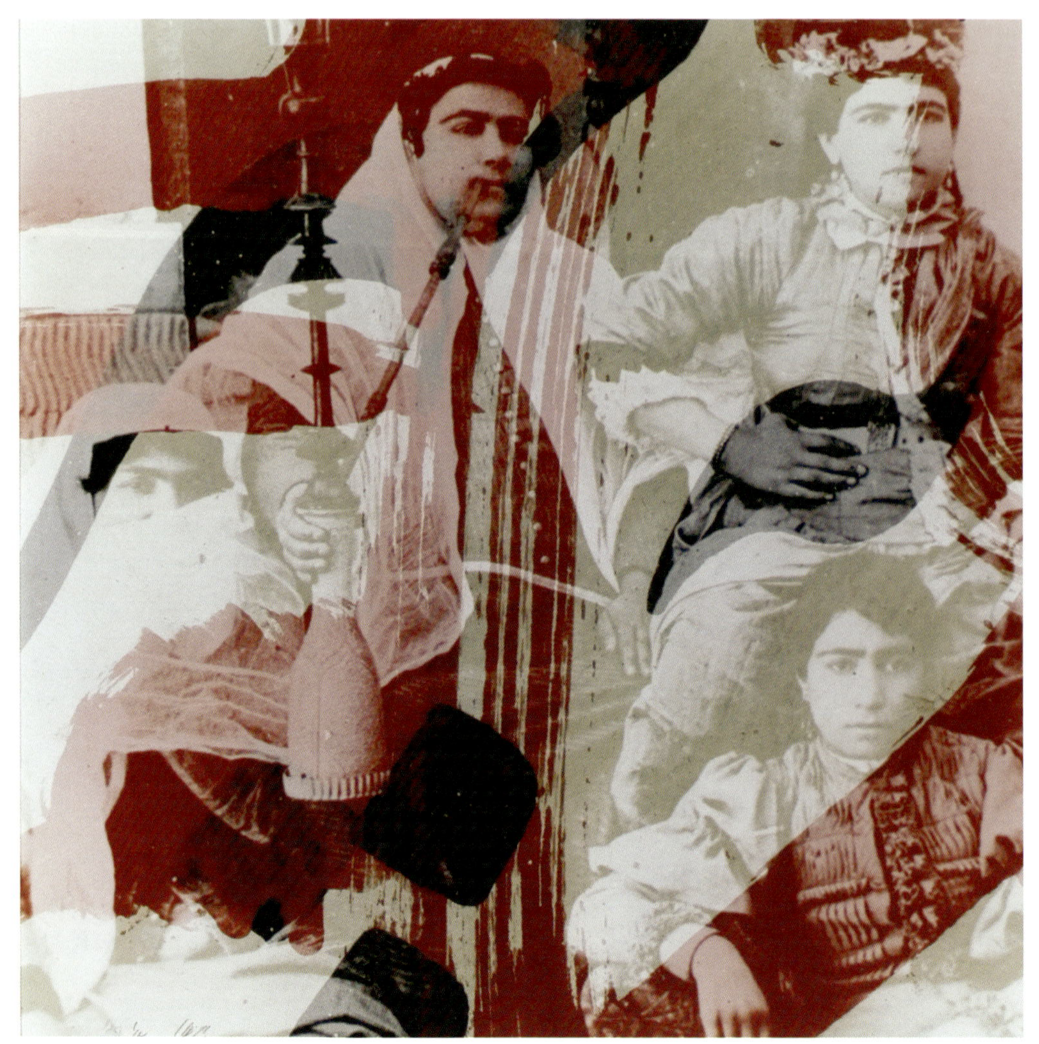

5.5
Bahman Jalali, *Untitled*, from the
Image of Imagination series, 2002,
digital print on coated paper

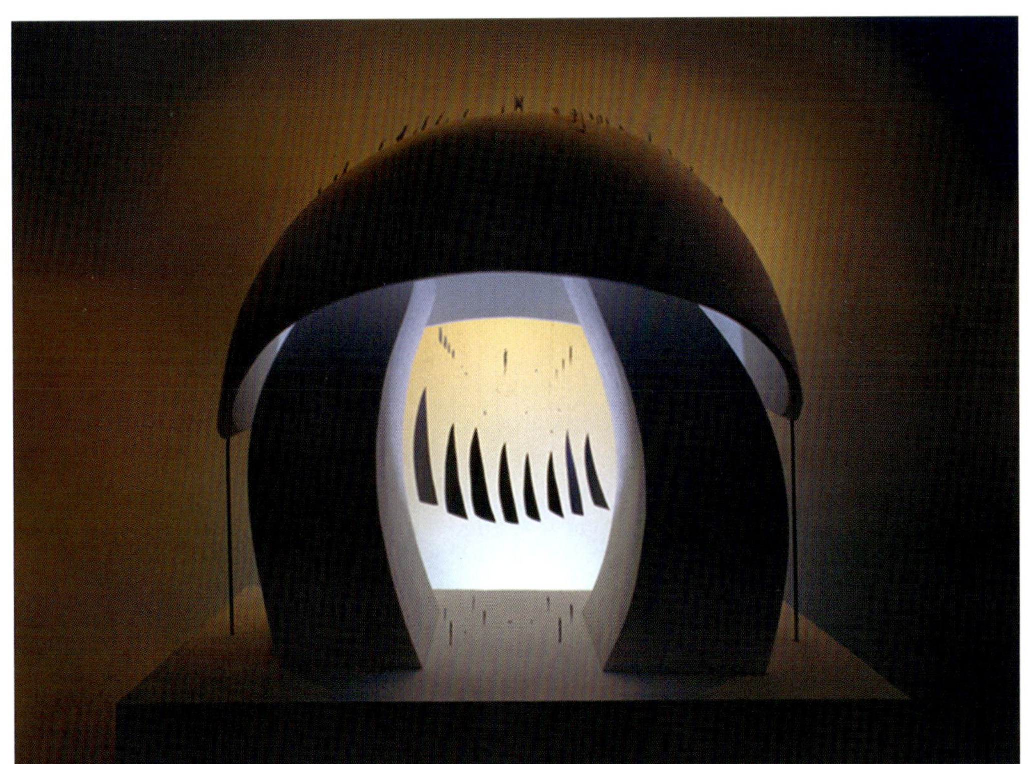

5.6
Behrouz Daresh, *Entitled*, 2005, aluminum, iron, Styrofoam, light and space installation, 200×100×200 cm, courtesy the artist

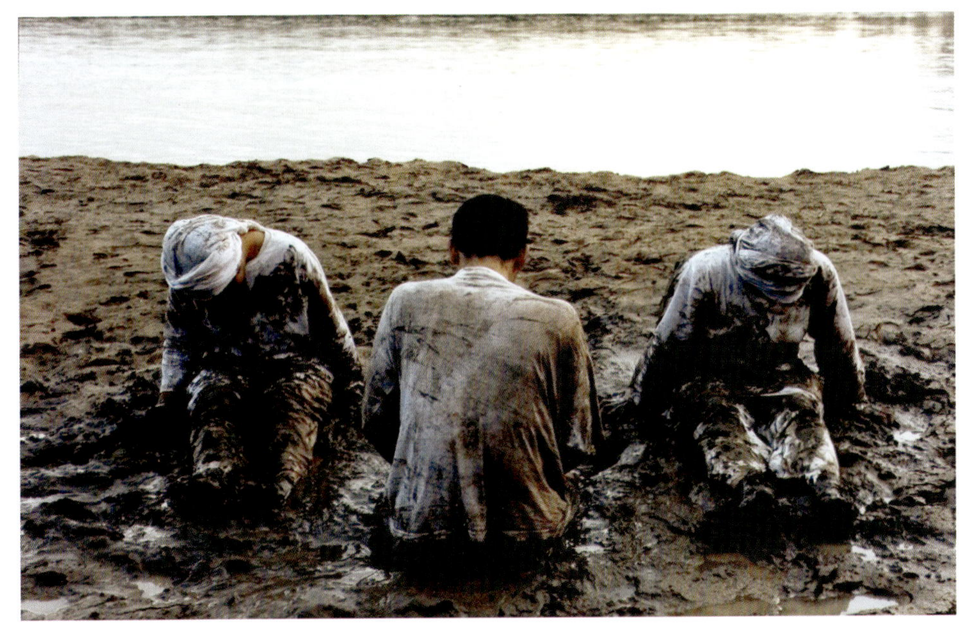

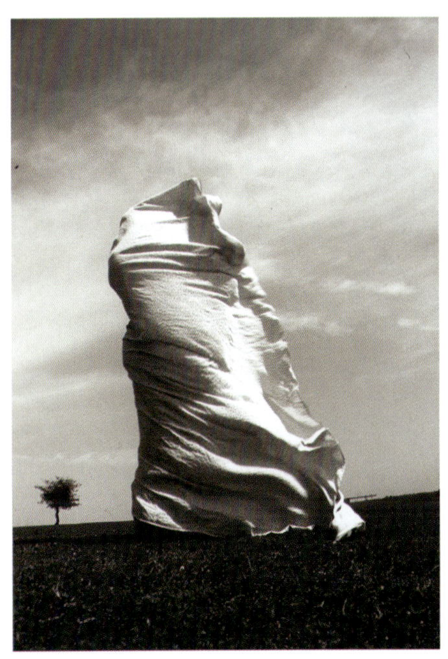

5.8
Koorosh Adim, from the *Dreamy Woman* series, 1996, 150×100 cm, courtesy the artist

5.7
Sadegh Tirafkan, *Untitled*, 2001, colour photograph, 40×60 cm, TMoCA

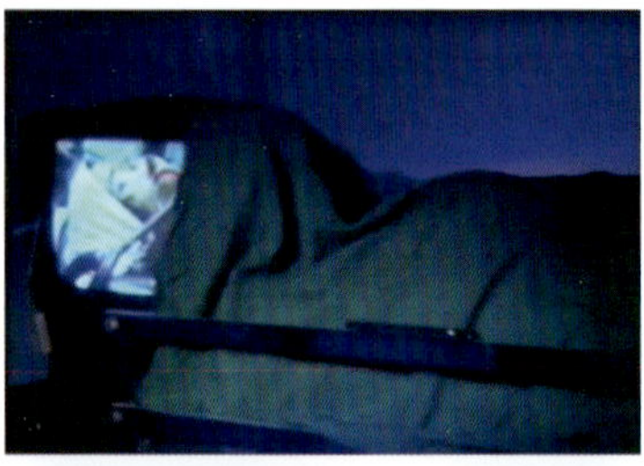
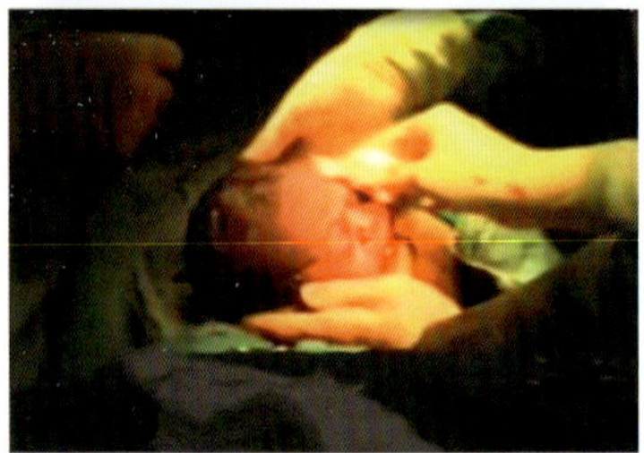
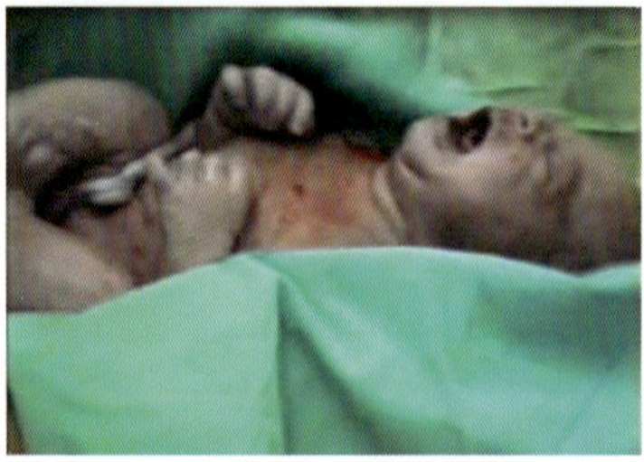
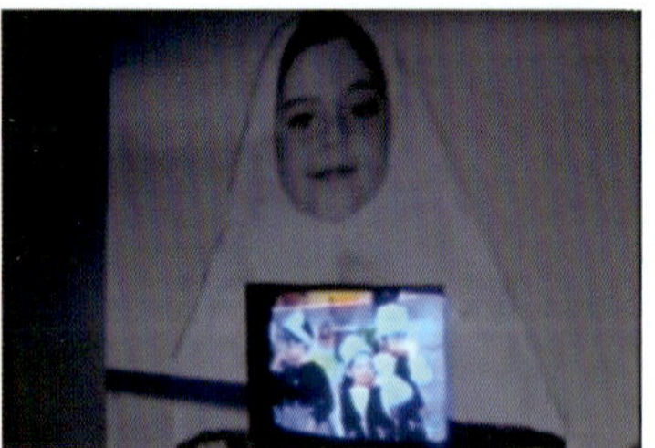
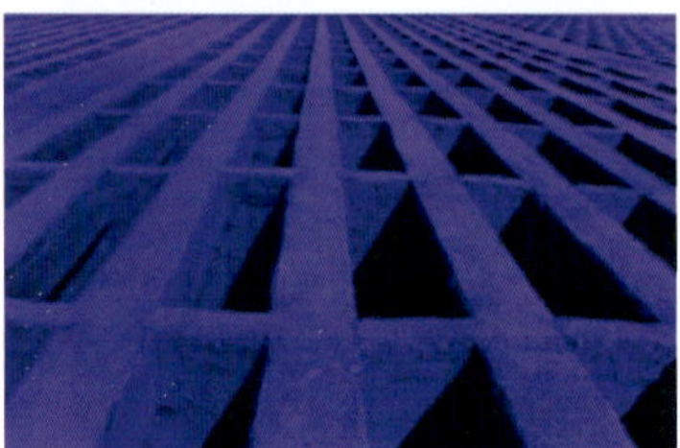
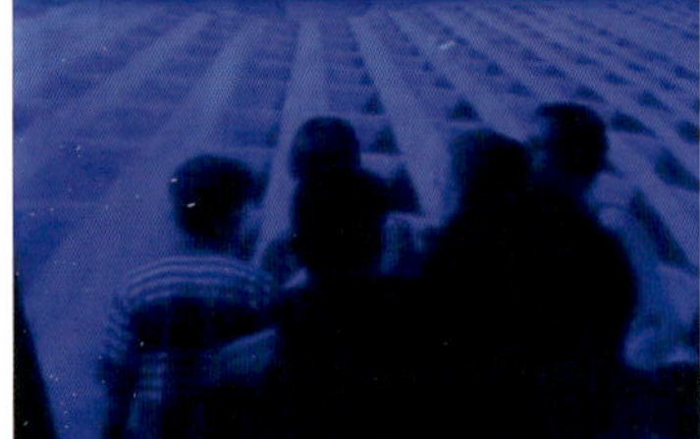
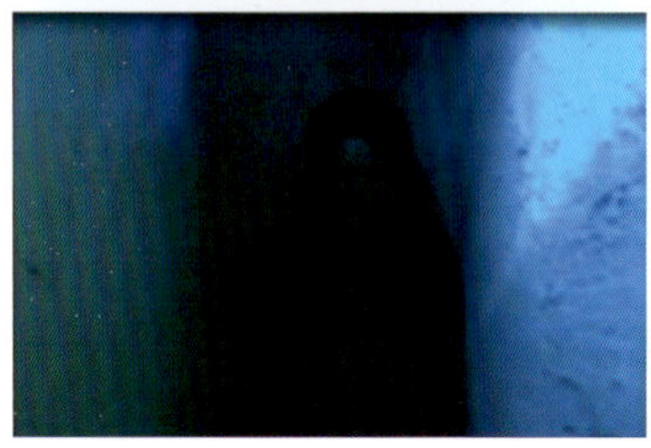

(b.1942), Ahmad Nadalian (b.1963), Hossein Khosrowjerdi, Bita Fayyazi (b.1962), Ali Zakeri (b.1959), Mostafa Dashti, Masoumeh Mozaffari (b.1958), Khosro Khosravi (b.1965), Rozita Sharafjahan (b.1962), Behnam Kamrani (b.1968), Koorosh Adim (b. 1971), Shahab Fotouhi (b.1980), Neda Razavipour (b.1969), Pooya Aryanpour (b.1971), Farhad Moshiri (1963–2024), Farshid Azarang (b.1972), Simin Keramati (b.1970), Shadi Ghadirian (b.1974), Khosrow Hassanzadeh (1963–2023), Mohsen Rastani (b.1958), Arash Hanaei (b.1978), Mehraneh Atashi (b.1980), Afshan Ketabchi (b.1966), Rokni Haerizadeh (b.1978), Afshin Pirhashemi (b.1974), Amir Mobed (b.1974), Sadegh Tirafkan (1965–2013), Ghazaleh Hedayat (b.1979), Farhad Fozouni (b.1979), Shahriar Ahmadi (b.1980), Hamed Sahihi (b.1980), Behrang Samadzadegan (b.1979), Samira Eskandarfar (b.1980), Peyman Hooshmandzadeh (b.1969), Majid Koorang Beheshti (b.1967), Amirali Ghasemi (b.1980), Mostafa Darehbaghi (b.1966), Morteza Darehbaghi (b.1969) and Mehdi Moghimnejad (b.1976). (Figures 5.5–10)

Although on a few occasions Iranian artists had already practised forms of New Art (mainly in the form of site-specific works) on a limited scale,[14] the first comprehensive exhibition was held at the TMoCA in the summer of 2001. A recurring event, it proved to be a turning point. While the sense of experiment attached to New Art was intense during this heady period, successive exhibitions at the TMoCA were also rewarded with increasing, and full, attendance. (Figure 5.11) Major exhibitions from 1998 to 2005 included the *First Conceptual Art* exhibition (2001), *New Art 1* exhibition (2002), *New Art 2* exhibition (2003). The two later thematic exhibitions, *Spiritual Vision* and *Gardens of Iran: Ancient Wisdom, New Vision*, were also held, both in 2004, during that period.[15] New Art flourished during this period, with artists experiencing similar levels of enthusiasm as some successfully exhibited abroad. The increasing frequency of exhibitions reflected a growing interest in experimenting with emerging forms of artistic expression. There was an appetite for the new, unconventional, and, in a word, contemporary. Artists sought to break down barriers that may have previously prevented them from exploring subjects, materials, methods of working, and modes of exhibition.

Many artists believed that the imperative task was to become internationally acknowledged. Moreover, there were certain themes that artists considered as representative of important issues of their time; among these are environmental and ecological issues, the gender issues in society, and themes relating to religion and spirituality.

Even private commercial galleries operated with more confidence. Following a long period during which Iranian artists had little communication with other countries, contact between artists and the outside world increased. At the same time, Iranian visual arts began to be integrated with that of the international scene. For a brief period, contemporary Iranian art acquired a new cosmopolitan veneer.

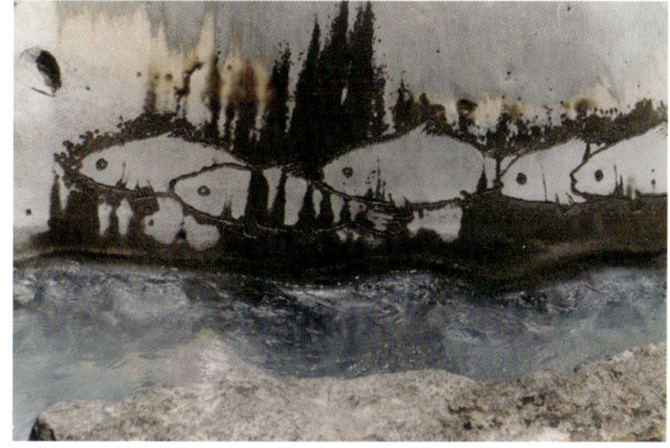

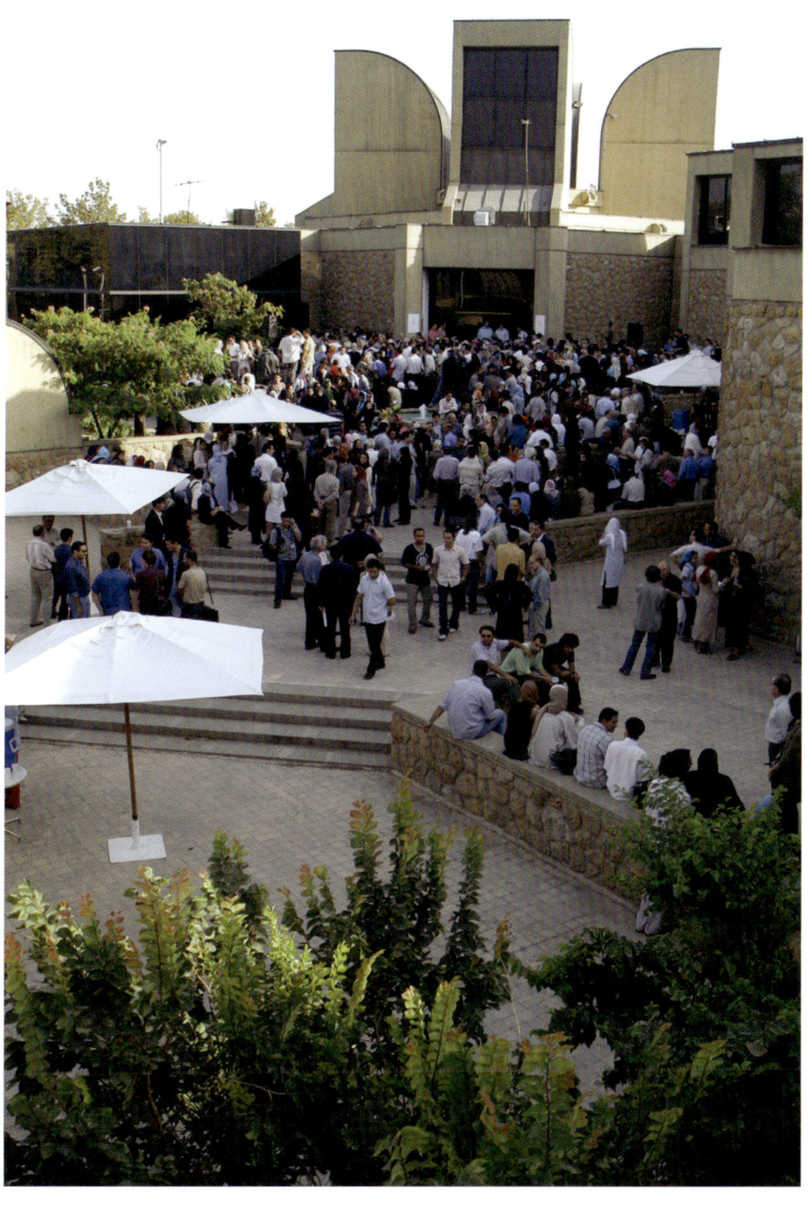

Facing page
5.9
Afshan Ketabchi, *What I have Common with Roudabeh*, 2001, video installation, image courtesy the artist

Above
5.10
Ahmad Nadalian, *The River Still Has Fish*, 2000, Iran- Haraz River, photo by the artist, image courtesy the artist

Left
5.11
A view of the TMoCA opening exhibition in 2004

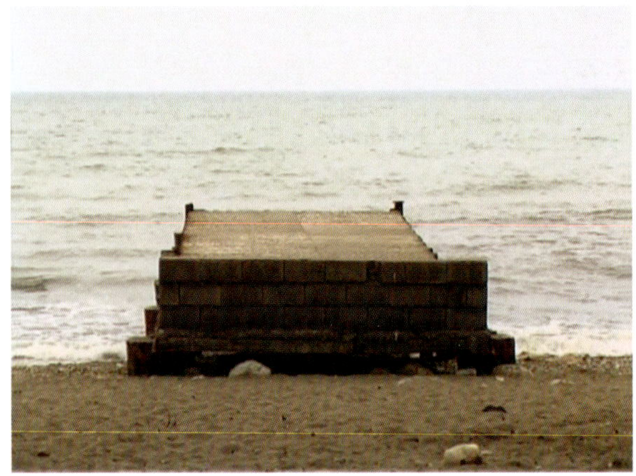

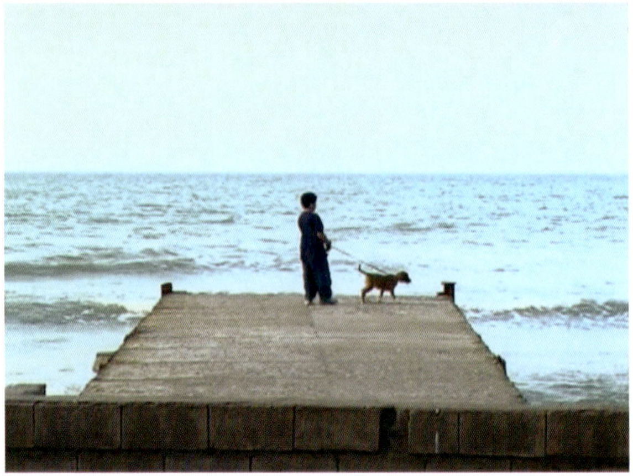

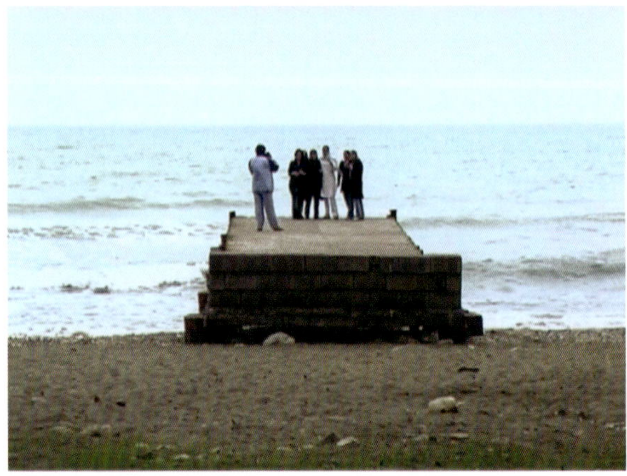

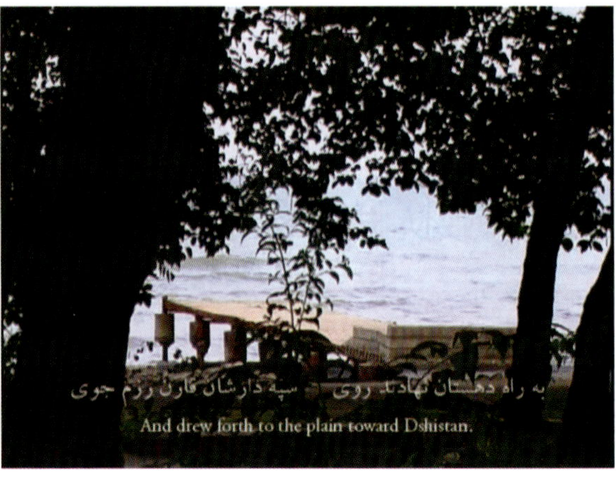

The presence of Iranian artists at international artistic events and exhibitions such as the Venice Biennale[16] was a direct result of this opening of cultural boundaries. Moreover, Iranian artists were now continually exposed to other cultural values through electronic media, magazines, and books. The idea of being 'up to date' and imbued with the 'spirit of the time' was an obsession for younger artists. They created works that moved against the grain of the educational art system of the time, although some institutions started paying more attention to so-called unconventional or New Art. Finding appreciation and credibility outside Iran was another aim supported by the country's artistic officials.

During this period, exhibitions in several venues outside the country showcased art through which Iranian artists gained success.[17] The earlier recognition of Iranian cinema at international level was perhaps one of the reasons for this success, in particular for those artists working in the field of moving image and video. The other reason, as can also be seen in Iranian cinema, was the artists' attention to the human condition in their works and the presentation of issues such as gender, psychological challenges and forms of poetic expression – narrated from a highly personal point of view. (Figures 5.12–13) Many works were inspired by mystical, poetic and literary sources (such as Rumi and Attar), or even modern poetry, while others shared a critical interest in the social, political and aesthetic history of Iran. (Figures 5.14–16)

The dynamic situation of contemporary Iranian art did not remain unchallenged, however. There were arguments from different factions saying that movements such as conceptual art were a Western production, in essence incompatible with definitions of Iranian art.[18] However, these factions failed to articulate why such work was incompatible with Western art. Instead, they reiterated the argument that there was a fundamental disparity between Iranian and Western cultures, and consequently, between their artistic expressions, including contemporary approaches and styles. They denounced the works of Iranian artists as 'adventures' pursued by a 'group of adventurers'.[19] Another criticism of this group was that all forms of New Art – exhibited in different venues and supported by the artistic officials, mainly of the TMoCA, and even by the wider Iranian audience – followed a sort of 'social modishness' or 'cultural pretension' and did not pose a real cultural challenge.[20]

During Khatami's presidency from the late 1990s until 2005, a cultural and intellectual explosion facilitated the emergence of many

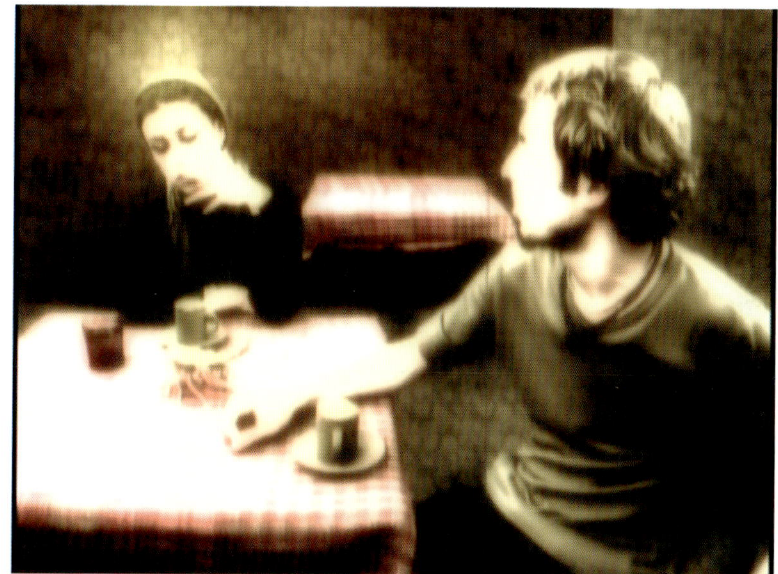

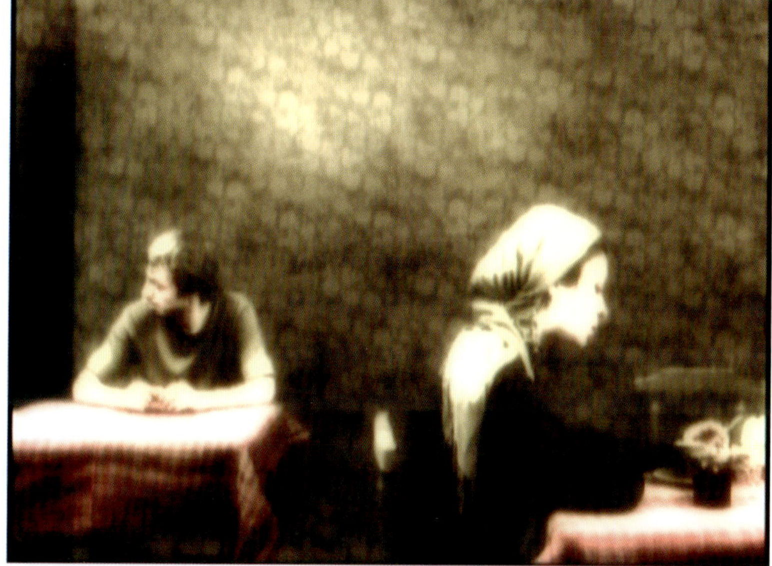

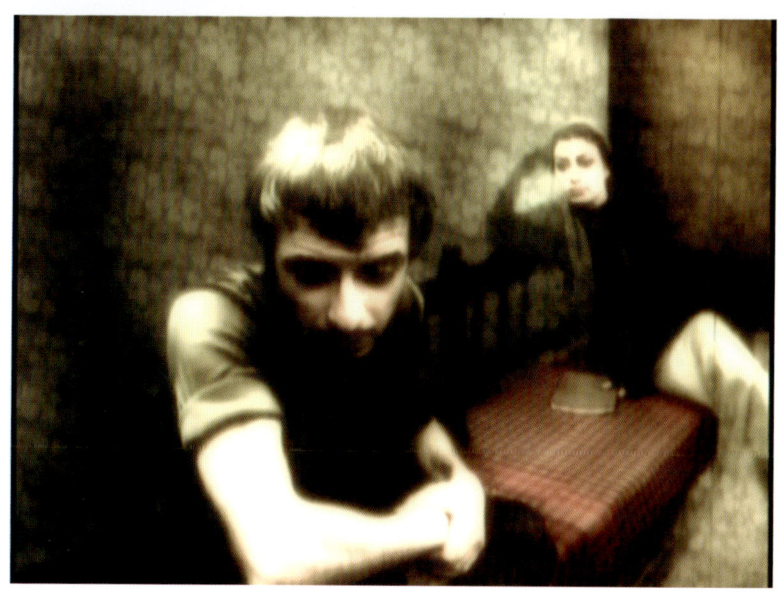

Facing page
5.12
Khosro Khosravi, *Port*, 2001, stills from the video, image courtesy the artist

Left
5.13
Samira Eskandarfar, *Monologue under White Light*, 2005, still from video, image courtesy the artist

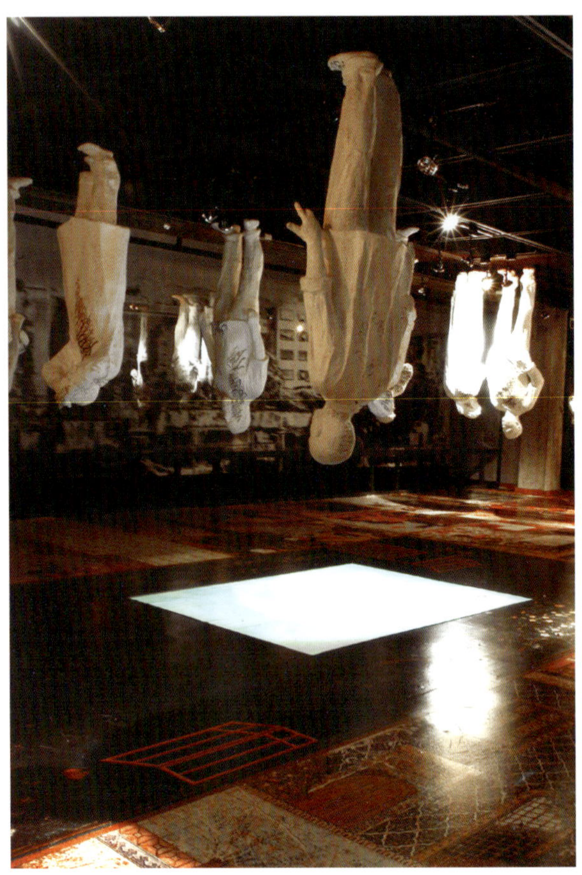

5.14
Group +30, *Iranian Garden*,
installation view at the TMoCA,
2004

new ideas in art, paralleling the dynamic shifts in social and political discourse. This period encapsulated Iran's multifaceted experiences and conflicting social processes: the Islamicisation enforced by authoritarians, the rationalisation advocated by intellectuals, the modernisation pursued by pragmatists, and the resistance to inevitable globalisation by certain factions within the political landscape. These diverse processes posed significant challenges for Iranian society as a whole, profoundly influencing the art scene and its associated discourses.

After 2005, with the end of the Reform period marked by the election of the radical conservative Mahmoud Ahmadinejad, official support for new forms of contemporary art practices underwent a shift. In this fourth phase, artists continued the pursuits initiated in the preceding period, albeit increasingly through private channels and, notably, via foreign networks, forums, and exhibitions. While contemporary Iranian expressions encountered limited distribution outlets within Iran, they found a more receptive reception in the international art scene. This trend may be attributed to the growing interest of the global art market in non-European or American art forms, alongside an increase in exhibitions showcasing such art in international cultural venues. Additionally, the affluent Persian Gulf states began to play a significant role as a market for artists from various countries in the region, including Iran, through the

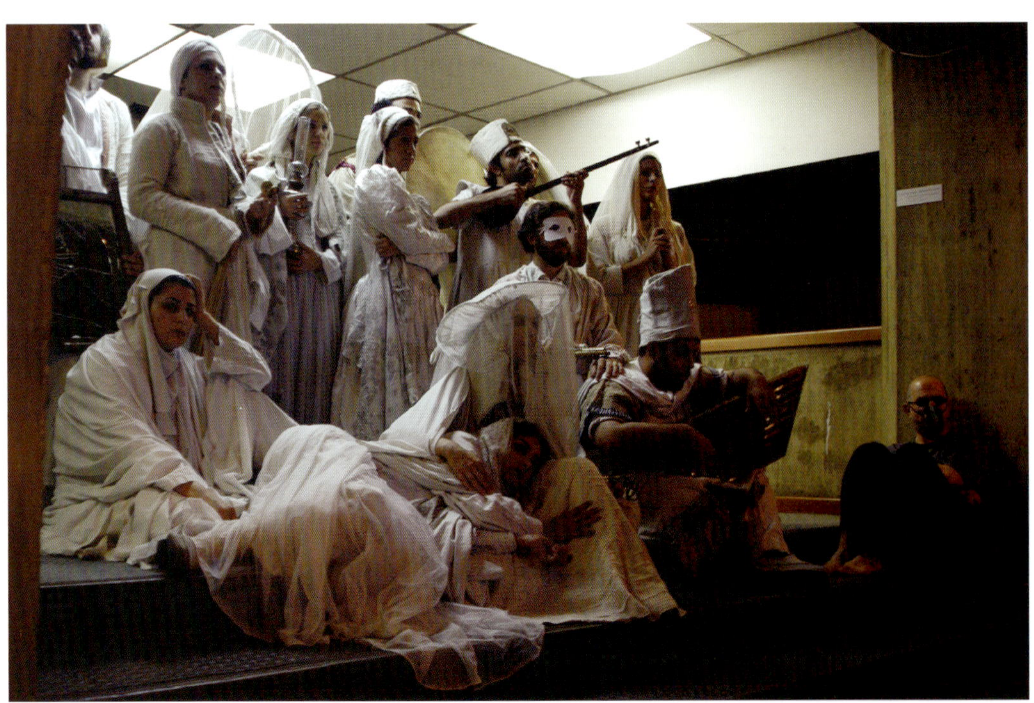

5.15
Performance group on the occasion
of the exhibition *Gardens of Iran:
Ancient Wisdom, New Vision*,
TMoCA, 2004

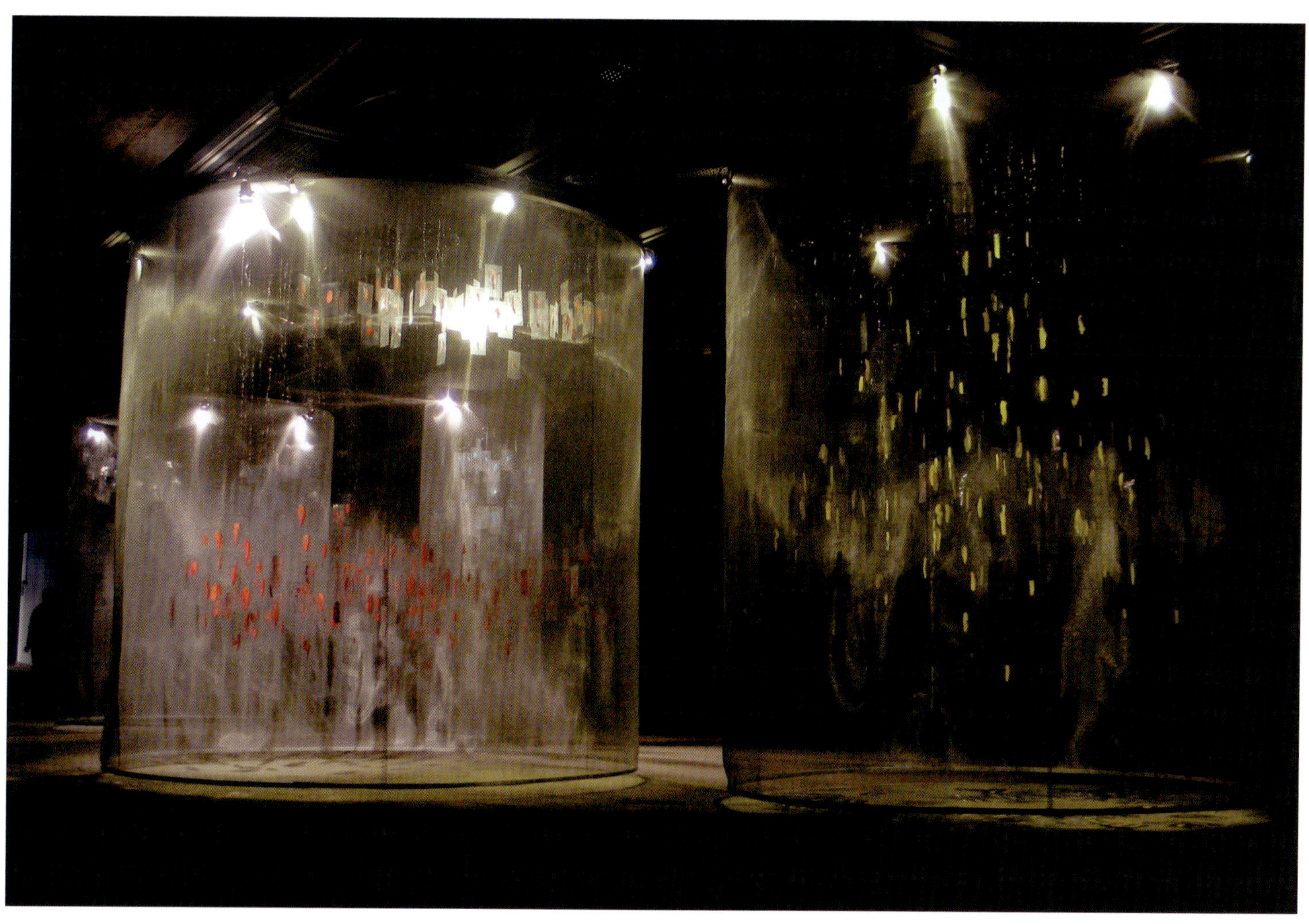

5.16
Farideh Lashai, *Not Every Tree Should Bear the Pressure of Autumn*, 2004, net installation, TMoCA

establishment of new museums, events, and exhibition spaces. Examples include Art Dubai and Christie's auction house in Dubai.[21]

This increasing interest has inevitably played an influential role in defining the art market's expectations. Indeed, there has been criticism in the intellectual domain that this type of art is now subject to such a great deal more 'visibility' (rather than 'invisibility' or marginalisation) that non-European or non-American artists are somehow expected to produce either 'ethnic' or 'political' art. This heightened degree of 'visibility' has proved problematic for these artists in terms of providing the necessary conditions for the independent speaking subject: they would be confined to representing only that which is expected to be seen as 'Iranian' or 'Middle Eastern'. This has led to concern in certain areas of artistic community that artists will end up producing work solely for international art festivals and exhibitions.

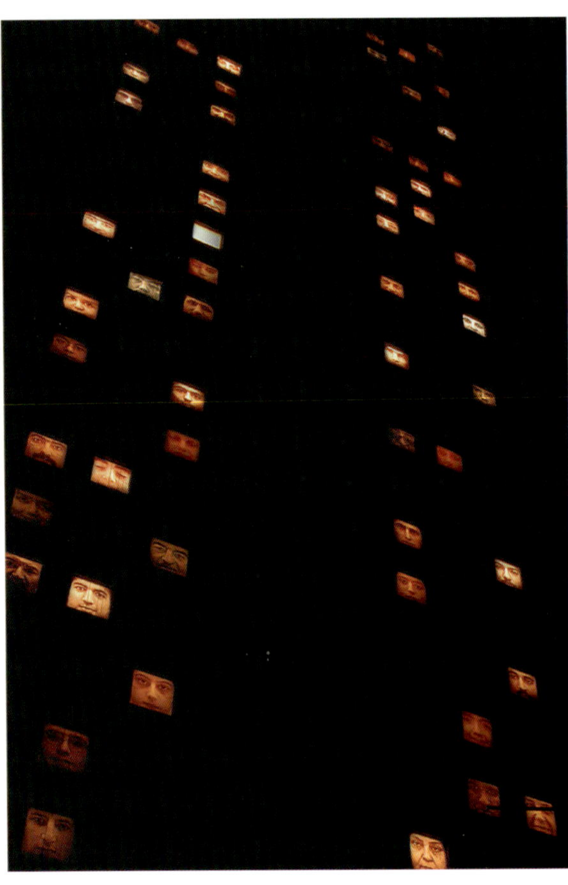

5.17
Shahab Fotouhi and Neda Razavipour, *Census*, 2003, Ati-Saz Buildings, Tehran

2. Perspectives on Contemporary Iranian Art: Navigating New Horizons

The first question we need to ask is what does contemporary mean? As the art historian and critic Terry Smith explains it, 'in the etymological sense, the word "contemporary" means "with it" which can be with any time; replay any past time and any imagined future in any combination.'[22] The term 'contemporary' could also imply a state of timelessness, suspended beyond historical bounds, signifying a condition of perpetual existence solely in the present moment.[23]

Similarly, we need to ask is meant by 'contemporaneity'.[24] We can agree with Smith's definition, which holds that contemporaneity is basically a concept that 'captures the frictions of the present while denying the inevitability of all currently competing universalisms', new ways of conceiving the present, as well as 'important questions about temporality and change'.[25] Indeed, art emerging from the complexities of contemporaneity resists easy categorisation.[26] It is formed from the deepest impulses of its time, bearing the marks of diverse influences, from the forward-looking to the paradoxical, from stark dichotomies to subtle nuances. Truly contemporary art, then, arises organically from the conditions of its era.[27]

By the 1990s Iranian art had witnessed a gradual change, departing from the frame of the newly emerging, post-revolutionary artistic modernism,[28] and incorporating new viewpoints of existing realities such as social disorders. The impetus for this shift stemmed partly from international influences and partly from internal circumstances. In a transitional era marked by shifting realities, there arose a compelling need to document and register these changes. However, before discussing the implications of these shifts, it is crucial to examine the debates that have emerged surrounding the driving force of the contemporary art scene in Iran over the past decades.

The 2000s and 2010s saw the emergence of a generation of artists whose main preoccupation has been the notion of contemporaneity,[29] a passion for being always and only in the present time and one of the most significant currents in contemporary Iran. It seemed, that initially any art practised in these new media was glibly seen as 'contemporary', especially when set in contrast to traditional media like painting. The artists' enthusiasm for experimenting with new idioms paved the way for the development of the so-called New Art. Yet gradually they began to show less or no media preference. This shift was characterised by a particular focus on the *idea* in their art rather than on the formalism inherent in earlier modernism. It is important, however, to note that such a comparison between Iranian and European modernism can be somewhat problematic. Post-revolutionary modernist practices did not seek to adopt or co-opt the discursive framework of European modernism. Instead, it offered an alternative discourse that did not strive for the definitive establishment of utopian meanings or the realisation of itself as a purely 'formalistic object'. Its focus was on its own method, one that resonated with the artists' concerns about navigating the rapidly changing landscape of post-revolutionary Iran, especially during the nascent stages of alternative modernism. There also developed a desire to work with others and experience globalised internationalism. Here contemporaneity maps the diverse ways in which artists use visual means to record, define and interrogate their time. They seek to identify with and represent what it is to live in the contemporary moment, justifying the cross-cultural nature of contemporary art as being relevant to the globalising era. Enjoying government patronage, during the third phase, it was possible for practitioners of contemporary art to perform or make their works with the support of the TMoCA. The official centre came to be a supportive, encouraging space, and to exhibit their works – both inside and outside the

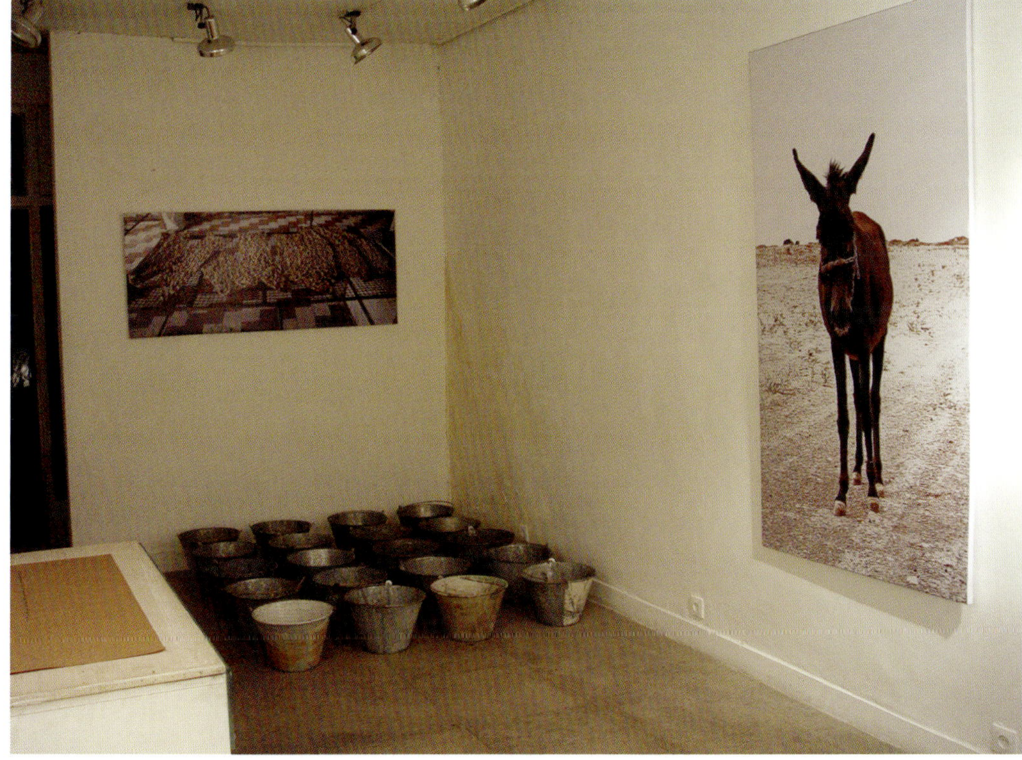

5.18
Homayoun Askari Sirizi, *Buridan's Society*, 2007, installation, image courtesy the artist

country – with much more flexibility. However, there was an obvious and essential dissimilarity between the development of New Art in Iran and what had already been practiced in the West. Ironically, just as art acquired an avant-garde status – precisely at the juncture when it went outside the institution of art and connected with the more radical political movements of its time or, at any rate, with the subversive aspects of the cultures in opposition – in Iran, it basically appeared to be an institutionally supported art.[30]

An increasing number of exhibitions testified to the rapidly developing interest in the New Art movement in Iran. The designation 'Conceptual Art' applied to any art that was neither painting nor sculpture – or which, if it was painting or sculpture of a sort, owed nothing to material tradition or memory. The exhibition of such art could, therefore, encourage younger artists of the same generation to broaden their view of contemporary art within the context of a globalised world.

The cultural policymakers were deeply fixated on 'updating' the Iranian art scene, likely due to nearly two decades of limited connectivity with the global art community, stemming from restricted international exhibitions and publications. The emergence of a new generation of artists, driven by a passion for contemporary art, was not merely a response to these restrictions but also to the recognition that prior artistic approaches had reached a stalemate. Consequently, the inaugural Conceptual Art exhibition at the TMoCA stood as a direct challenge to entrenched artistic norms and what was named 'outdated artistic approaches'.[31] Furthermore, certain curators and advisors associated with these events held the

5.19
Farideh Shahsavarani, *I Wrote You Read*, 2006, video and installation in the old Ettela'at Newspaper office, Tehran, courtesy the artist

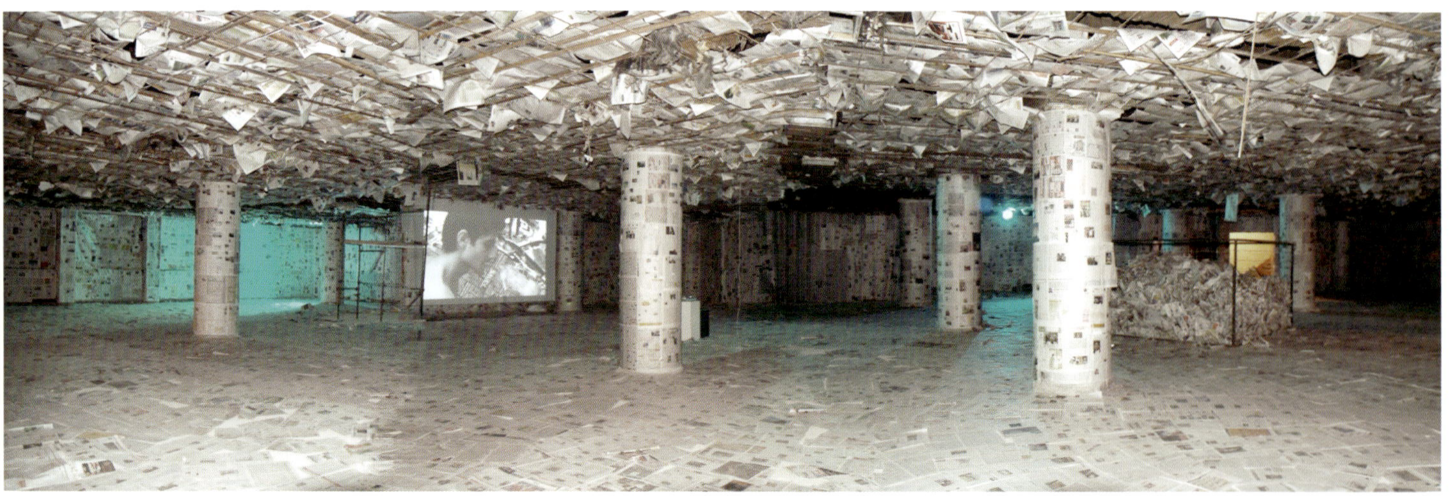

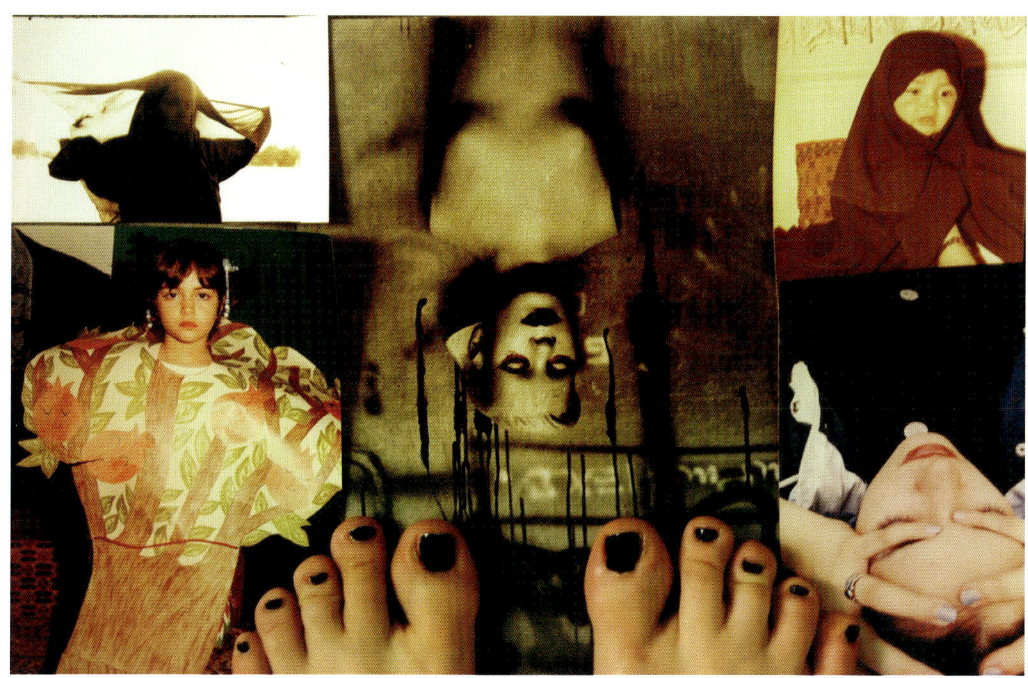

5.20
Mehraneh Atashi, *Self-Portrait*, 2005, light box, 30×45×5 cm, courtesy the artist

belief that New Art, in contrast to 'elitist formalism', should embody meaningful themes, preferably with religious or spiritual undertones. Consequently, efforts were made to infuse exhibitions with specific themes aimed at shaping their distinctive characteristics. For instance, the introduction of themes like 'spiritual art', prominently featured in the third New Art exhibition, can be attributed to this perspective. This underscores the ongoing official concern regarding issues such as Iranian and Islamic identity, which continue to serve as criteria for evaluating artworks.[32]

The New Art exhibitions attracted unprecedented numbers, many of whom were perhaps visiting the museum or an art exhibition for the first time. The fruitful political and cultural atmosphere was very much in line with Khatami's administration, specifically the doctrine defined as 'Dialogue between Civilisations'; the new cultural strategy found the chance to relatively end Iran's cultural isolation from the rest of the world.[33] As a result, a firm ground was provided for Iranian art to see more of contemporary art practices even after the reformers were out of power.

The political failure of the Reform movement highlighted that socio-political changes cannot be attributed solely to the movement itself. Since the post-Reform period (2005 onward), the official cultural stance has reverted to pre-1997 attitudes. During the fourth phase, starting with the Ahmadinejad presidency, officials

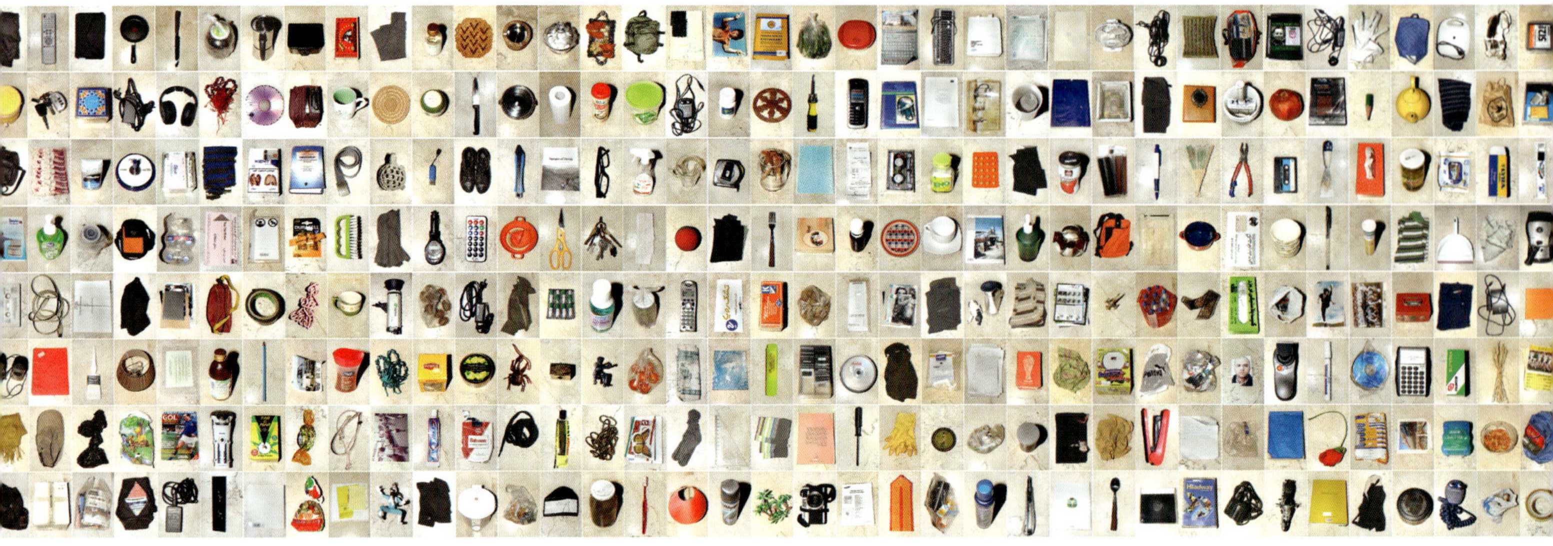

5.21
Arash Hanaei, *320 Pieces from Personal Belongings*, 2010, C-Print on photo paper, 120×400 cm, courtesy the artist

began to promote traditional Islamic and revolutionary values while expressing xenophobia toward the West. For eight years, political and cultural institutions were under conservative control, promising to revive the 'roots' and 'values' of the Revolution. All pre-Reform regulations, including the pre-show licensing requirements before each exhibition, were reintroduced, extending to all other art forms such as theatre and music. This trend began to shift after the 2013 election with the inauguration of the more moderate President Hassan Rouhani's administration, although significant changes were not immediately evident. Despite some re-evaluations in cultural policies and relative efforts to engage artistic participation and foster international connections, prevailing artistic attitudes did not witness substantial changes following the end of that eight-year period. The 2021 election and the beginning of hard-line President Ebrahim Raisi within the existing Islamic Republic marked the onset of a new wave of political and cultural extremism.[34] This transition has resulted in heightened restrictions and increased control over cultural practices. All such activities are now slated to be even more monopolised under the 'unified' governance (*hakimiyyat*), extending oversight to the other two branches of government – the parliament and judiciary – ultimately falling under the authority of the Supreme Leader Ayatollah Ali Khamenei and his directives. This unified authority aims to 'rectify' perceived 'untidiness' in cultural and artistic practices, addressing what is considered 'failures' in previous administrations' approaches to art and culture. However, this centralised control fosters an ideologically defined cultural sphere that fails to capture the diverse and dynamic nature of recent developments in Iran. This polarisation resulted in a division between ideological adherents, often referred to as 'insiders' or *Khudi*, and those who challenge or do not conform to the official master narrative and formulated 'values', commonly known as 'outsiders' or *Ghiyr-i khudi*, comprising the majority of the artistic community. However, this sparked a lukewarm response from the artistic community. Many of the new generation of artists see debates about 'authentic identity' or 'revolutionary values' as relics of history, no longer relevant or interesting. To these artists, contemporary art transcends national boundaries, and attempts to confine it within ideological frameworks contradict the artist's perception of their 'autonomous' subjectivity. In current circumstances, efforts toward socio-cultural change do not rely solely on institutional politics; instead, artists seek autonomy through private channels or outside Iranian borders.

For artists working in such a climate, contemporaneity is not merely about the present moment; it is an intentional artistic or theoretical construct that asserts a specific temporality and spatiality. Their works reflect an awareness of the psychic, philosophical, autobiographical, social, cultural, and political environments in which they are created. These artists recognise the demands necessitated by these conditions on their practice, often making them central themes of their work. Some artists employing this approach focus on questions of time and place, addressing wide-ranging concerns. However, the most compelling works of this nature qualify as contemporary art not solely because of their use of new media or marketing strategies, but because they address one of the most pressing personal, social, and political needs of our time: the imperative to communicate effectively and constructively, while also acknowledging the complexities of contemporary Iranian culture. (Figures 5.17–28)

If self-criticism and reflection are integral to contemporary thought and art, these elements are evident in the recent works of Iranian artists, which consistently intertwine with political and social aspirations. Meanwhile, some artists have become increasingly text-based. The work of these text-based artists explores the visual potential of language politics, which is one of the dynamics of global contemporary art. Accordingly, their work questions the limits of visual representation – what cannot be represented solely through images can be evoked through the traces of language. Textual forms

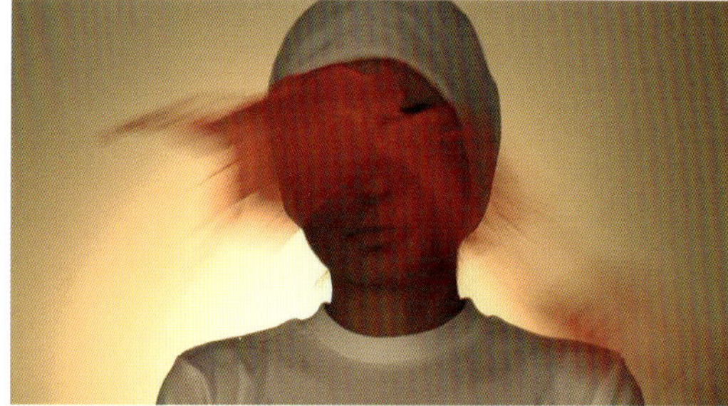
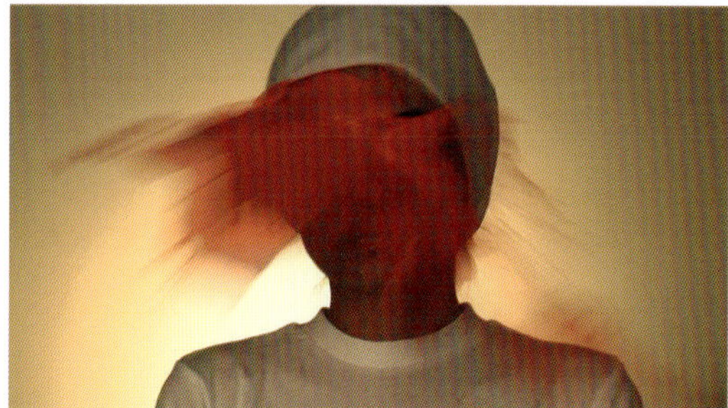
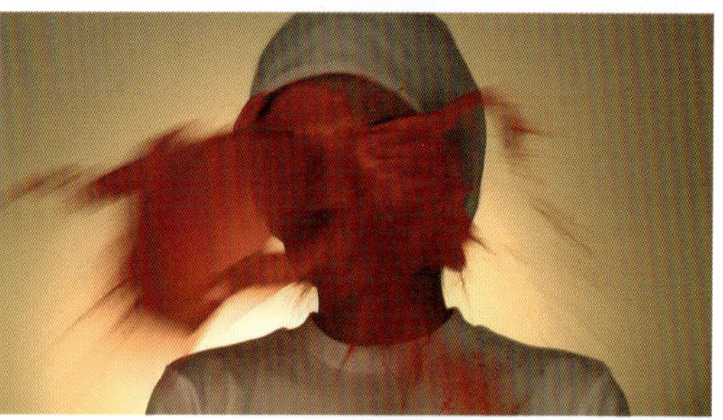
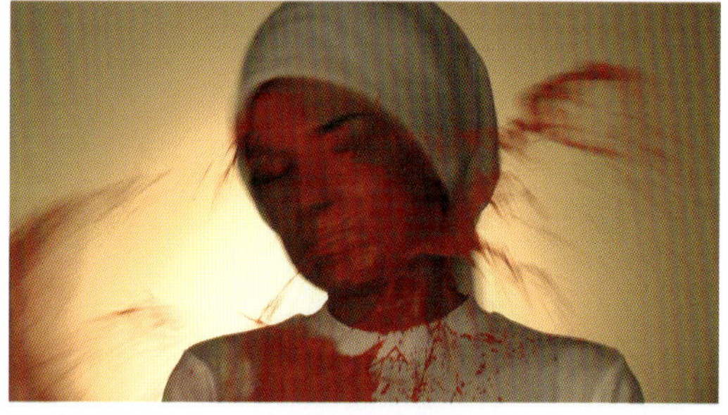
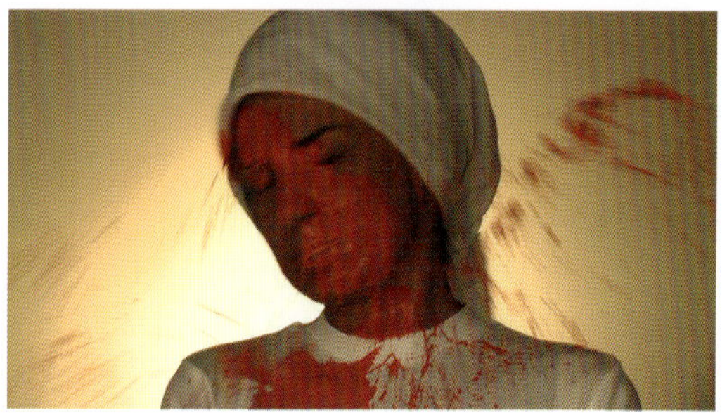

5.22
Simin Keramati, *Biopsy*, 2012, stills from the video, courtesy the artist

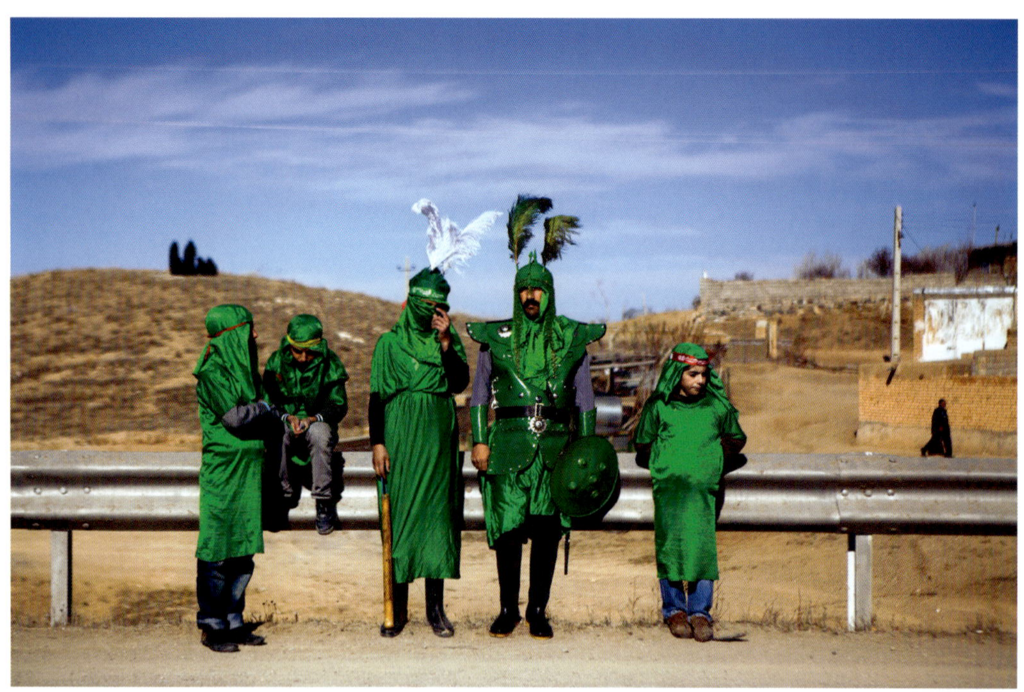

5.23
Abbas Kowsari, *Untitled*, from the
Reds and Greens series, 2012–14,
digital photography, C-Print on
metallic photo paper, 70×105 cm,
courtesy the artist

Right
5.24
Behnam Sedighi, *Hadi*, from *The
Reminder* series, 2014, C-Print,
120×150 cm, courtesy the artist

Facing page
5.25
Shadi Ghadirian, *Untitled*, from the
Nil, Nil series, 2008, 76×76 cm,
C-Print, courtesy the artist

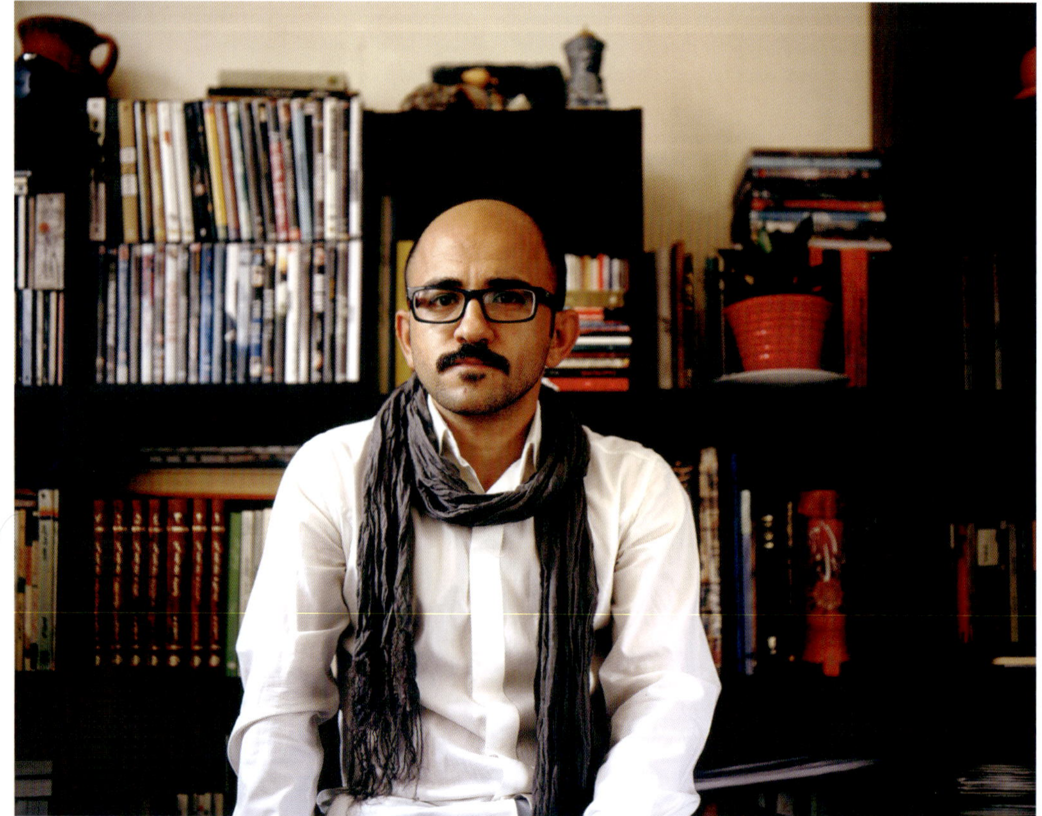

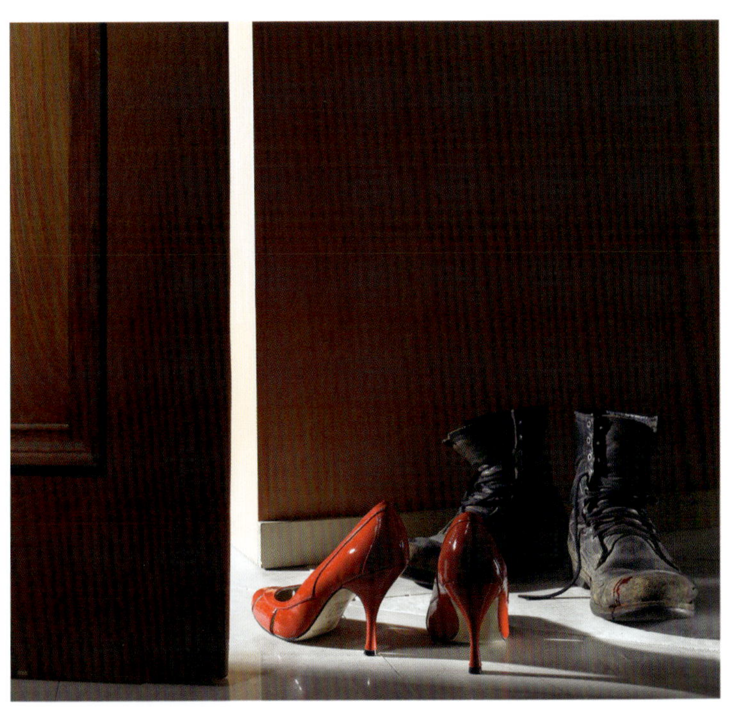
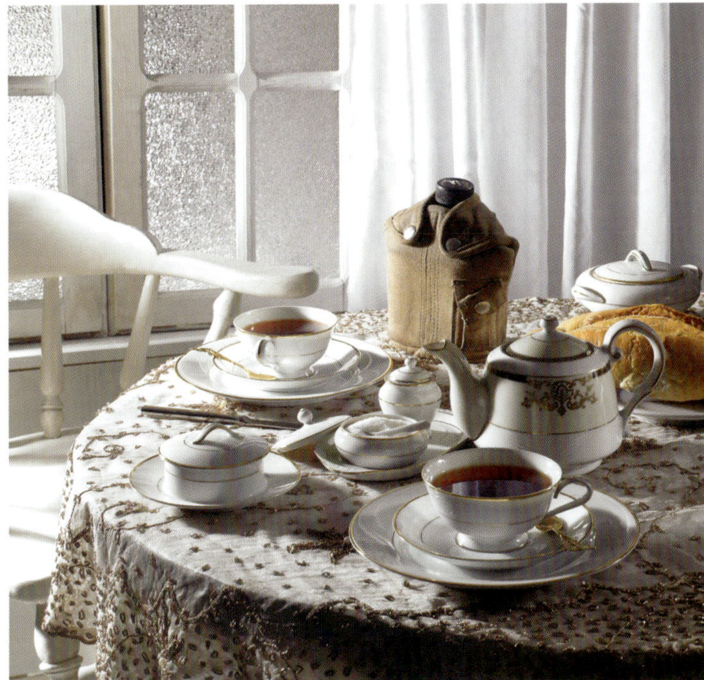
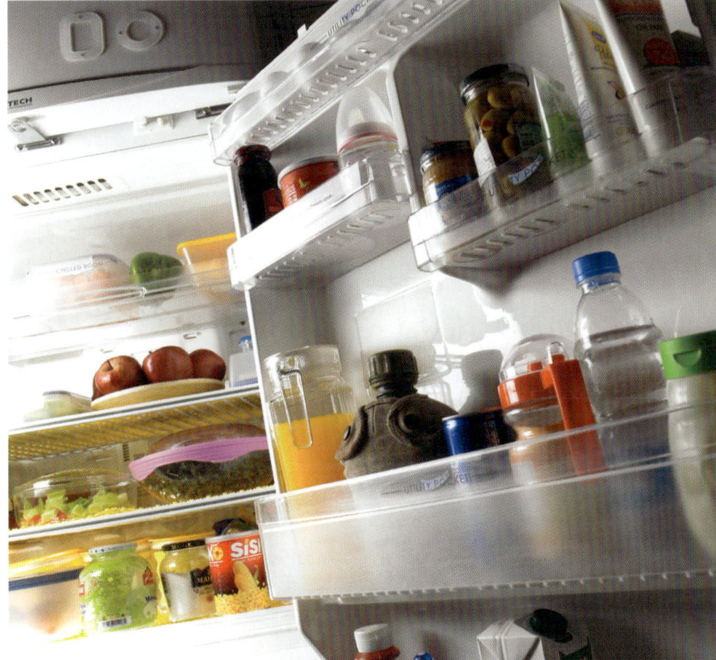
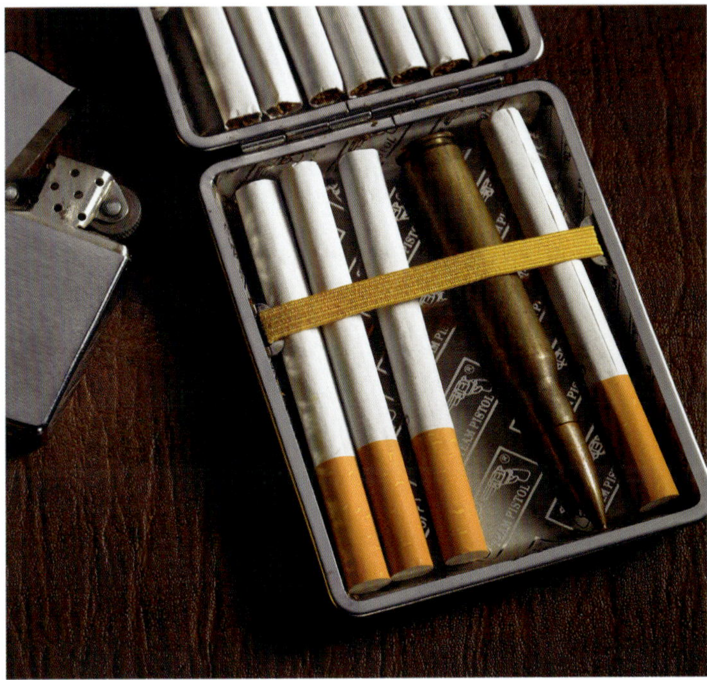

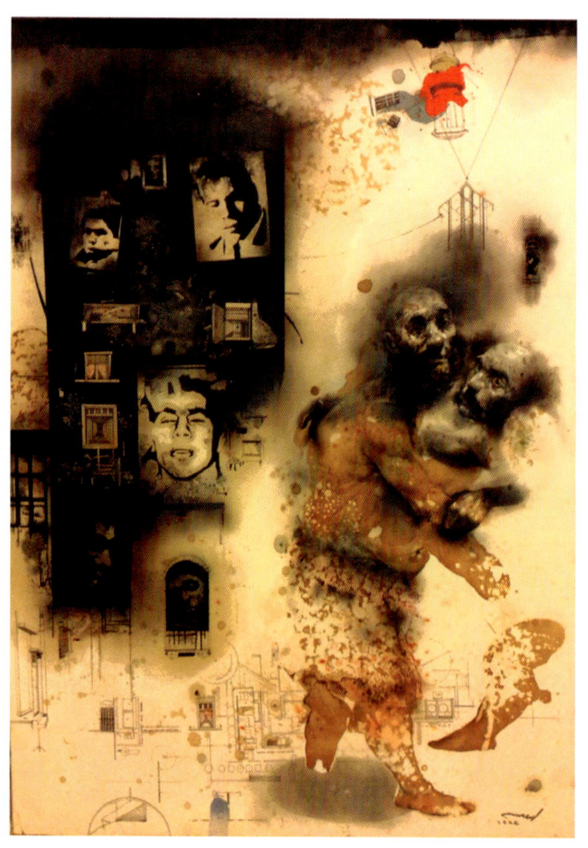

5.26
Mehrdad Khataei, Untitled, 2014,
mixed media on paper laid on MDF,
100×70 cm

5.27
Jamshid Haghighatshenas, *Untitled*,
2014, mixed media on canvas, ns,
courtesy the artist

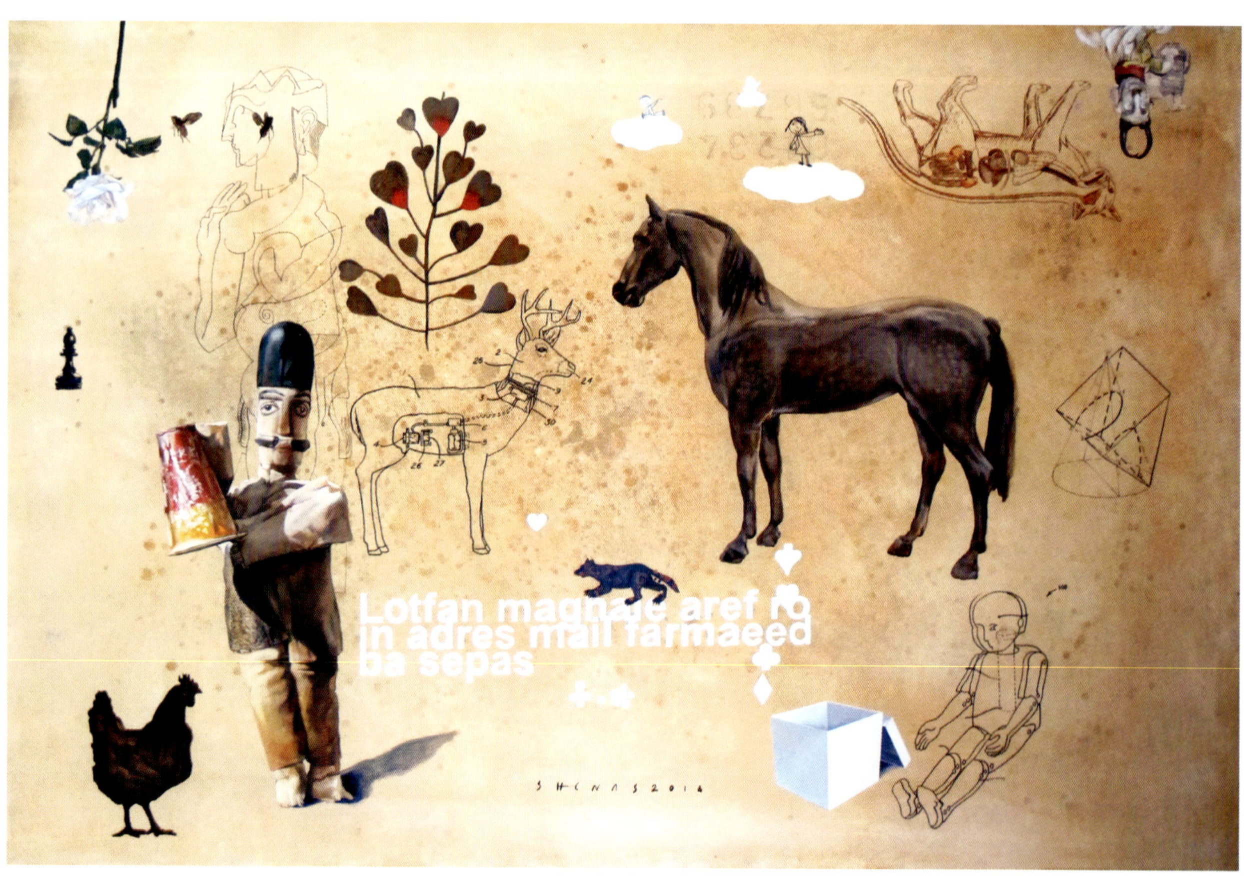

are used with a variety of approaches – ranging from addressing identity question, to social concerns, to employing critical and subversive approaches towards the use of calligraphic forms and critiquing its exoticism,[35] while also incorporating linguistic and (post-)structuralist thought into artistic expression. One can name artists as diverse as Reza Derakshani (b.1952), Sadegh Tirafkan, Farhad Moshiri, Barbad Golshiri (b.1982) and Mahmoud Bakhshi Moakhar (b.1977). (Figure 5.29)

Addressing contradictions and demonstrating critical messages through biographical exposition, depictions of everyday life, and lived experiences are among the dominant approaches in the art of this period. Barbad Golshiri uses his own voice in expressing the infinite cultural aspects that he grapples with. Golshiri's artistic thought reveals and questions social limitations, transforming repression into creation, and testing the possibilities of critically addressing social realities. His works extend from photographic works to sculpture, installations, digital media, videos, performances, critical writings and more recently site-specific graves. As an artist, Golshiri embodies a coded protest against socio-philosophical dilemmas, intertwining a sense of despair and irony within his creations. His oeuvre reflects a deep engagement with critical thought, drawing inspiration from diverse disciplines such as language, literature, art history and theory, philosophical discourse, and socio-political issues. Golshiri selects themes from a myriad of sources, ranging from Samuel Beckett to James Joyce, from Suhrawardi's wisdom to Nizami's poetry, and from Hieronymus Bosch to Francis Bacon, synthesising them with his own contextual concerns and critical reflections on contemporary issues, even if some of these matters have been previously explored and resolved elsewhere.

We can see these concerns in his early works: his video-performance, for example, *What Has Befallen Us, Barbad?*[36] (2002) or *Bahram Does Not See Any Right Wing* (2003). Using English is a typical act in Golshiri works. He explains that he employs Persian script only when he intends for it to be readable, using it as both a language and a pictorial signifier. That is why his 2010 work *Quod* (slang for prison), for example, is only for audiences who could experience the nauseating effect of reading when seeing the text – meaning only the ones who could read Persian.[37] Since reading *Quod* (slang for prison) stimulates nausea, it is deeply rooted in the unique experience of reading it and, hence, 'only available to those who read Persian.'[38] Golshiri's work, when criticising modern calligraphic

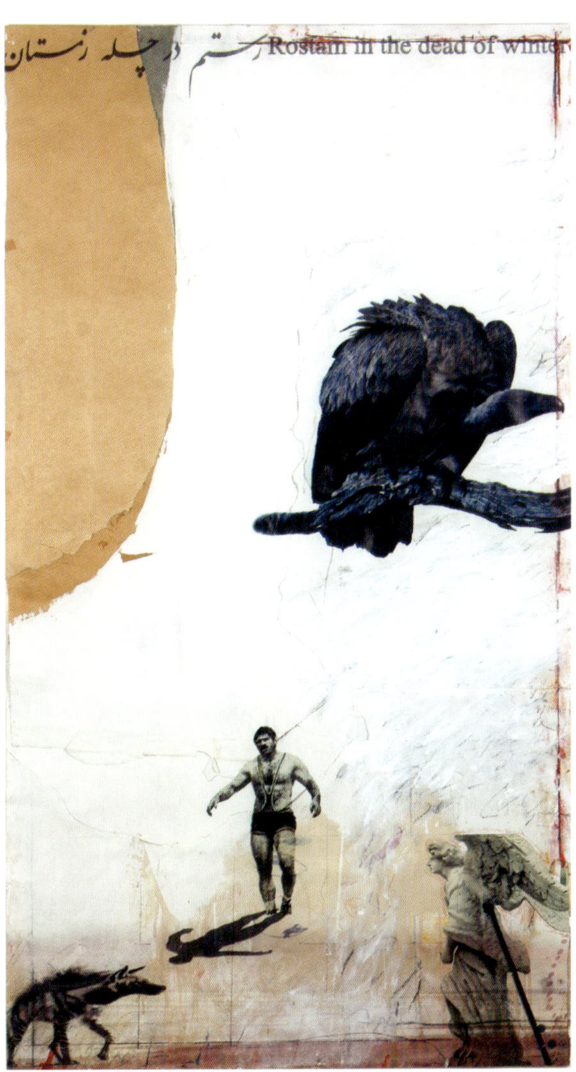

5.28
Fereydoun Ave, *Rustam in the Dead of Winter*, 2009, mixed media and digital print on paper, 129×68 cm

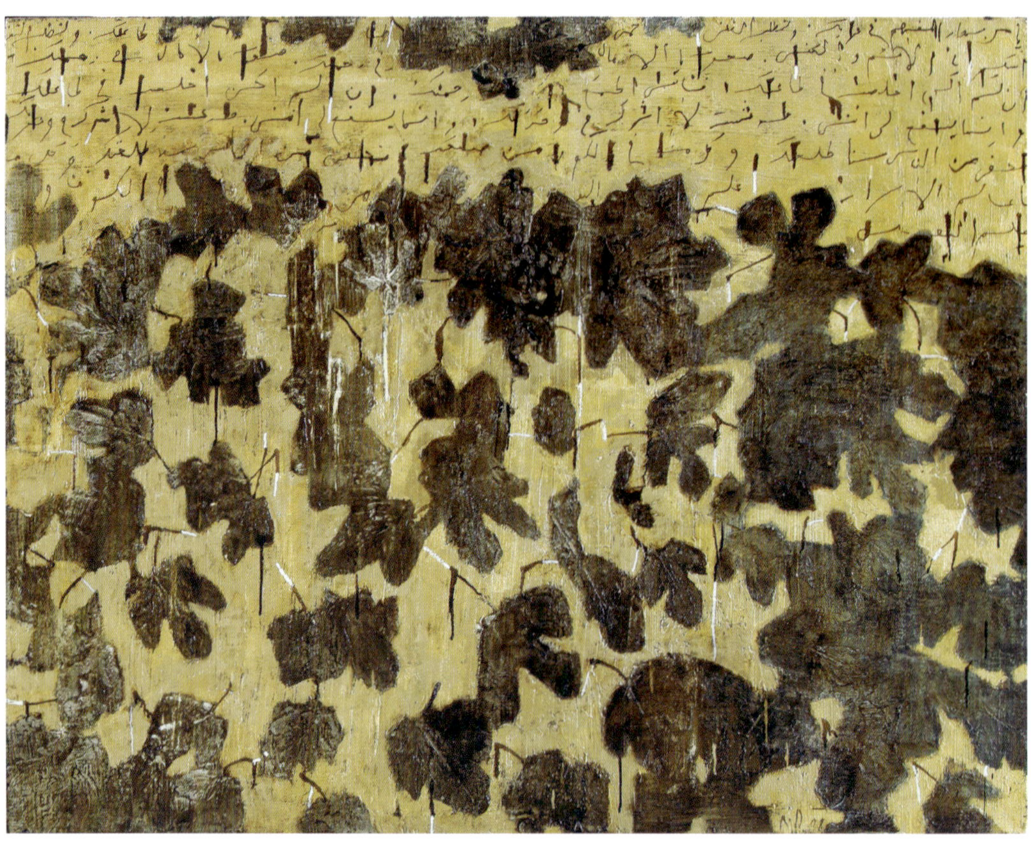

works, concerns itself with that perception in this way. By emphasising the availability of the work 'only to those who read Persian' (for anyone who wants to view or purchase it), he criticises the ambiguity of written materials and Persian calligraphy and suggests that for non-Persian readers it becomes merely a decorative piece. (Figure 5.30)

The necessity for constant repositioning has led to a dynamic development in new forms of expression encompassing mainly symbolic, metaphorical and poetic traits.[39] Usually the metaphors and allegories of the artwork, offering political irony, are acknowledged to go beyond recognisable forms of cultural representation. (Figures 5.31–38) It is because the artists feel an urgent need to respond to the changing cultural climate of their country by creating works that critically make political and cultural statements.

The works of Mahmoud Bakhshi Moakhar exude an ambiguous presence, delicately poised between the concepts of faith and devotion on one hand, and the realm of official propaganda on the other.[40] Bakhshi has integrated everyday objects from his country into his work, objects that have acquired a political character beyond their banal everyday use. The *Anonymous Martyr* series (2005), for example, derived from an official term broadly used to refer to the

چیزی پیدا کنم بالاخره یک سنجاق

هیچ جوری نمیتوانم توضیح بدهم

یعنی چی یک دو سه چهار نمیدانم

میکردم ذهنم داشت با این یک دو

یک چار گوش دیگر توش میکشیدم

با یک سنجاق زنگ زده چار خانه

کوچک بعد میدیدم ظهر شده

من هی هر روز به محض

دیگری من عاشق چار گوش

وقتی محدوده تنگ شود

عمق که بروم نقطه می شود

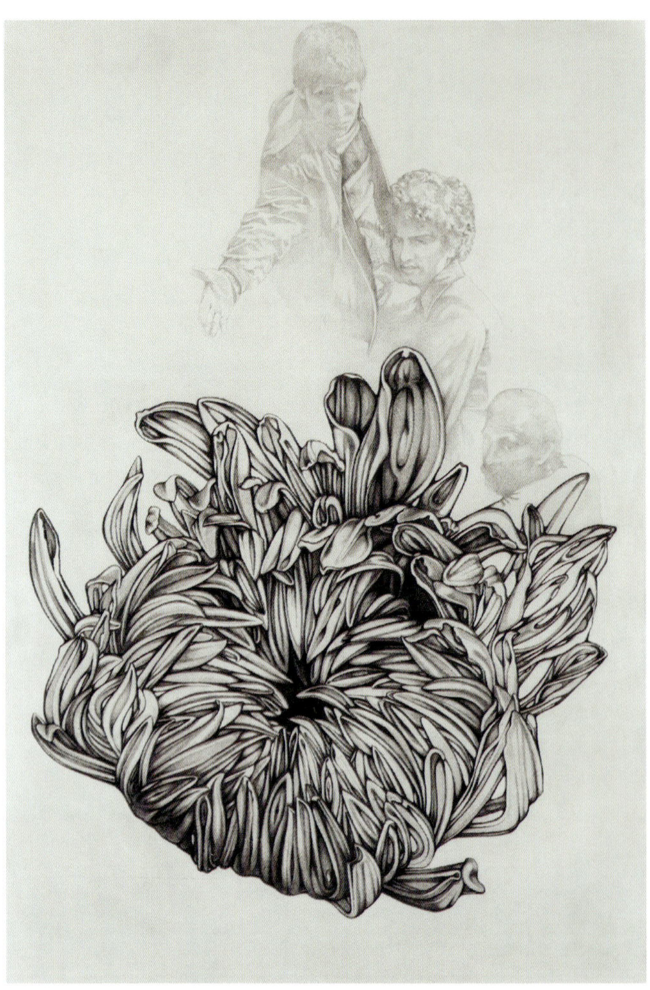

5.31
Mojgun Bakhtiary, *No.5*, from the
Dispiriting Perspectives series, 2017,
pencil on canvas, 150×100 cm,
courtesy the artist

5.32
Amirhossein Bayani, *The Long
Sunset*, from the *Fidelity III, 'We' to
the Extent of Politics* series, 2022, oil
on canvas, 180×150 cm, courtesy
the artist

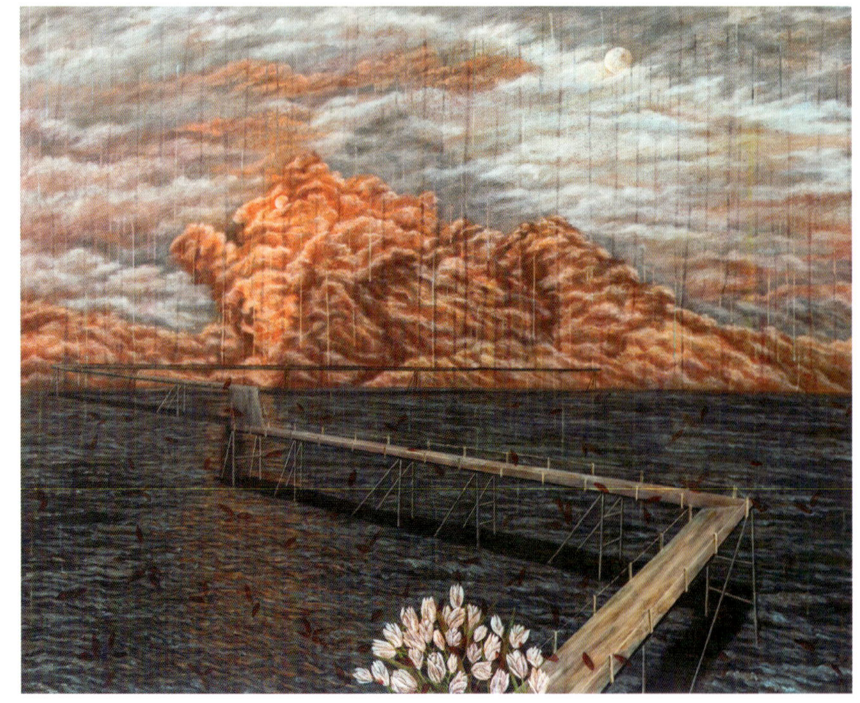

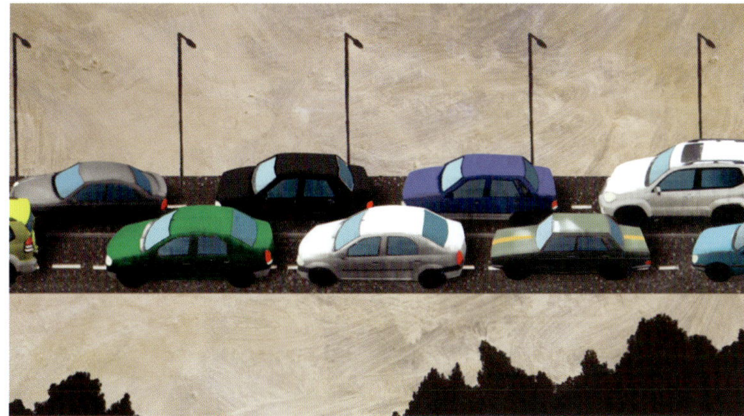

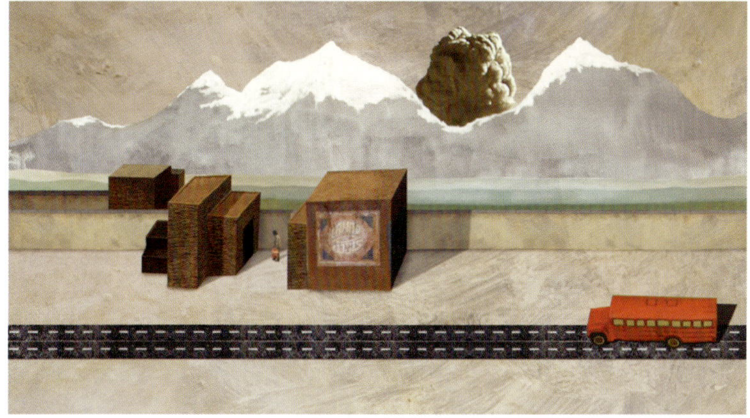

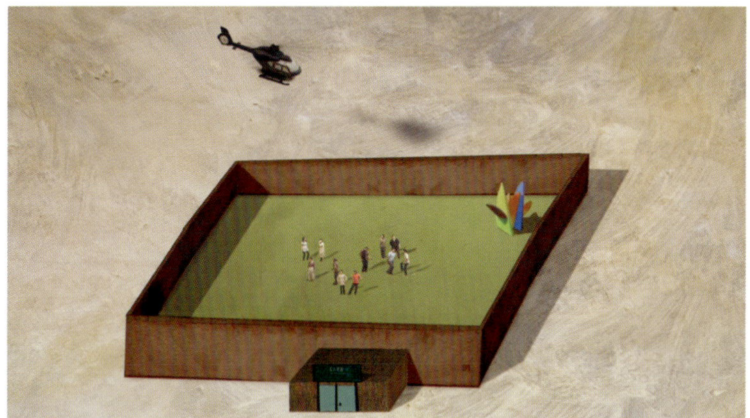

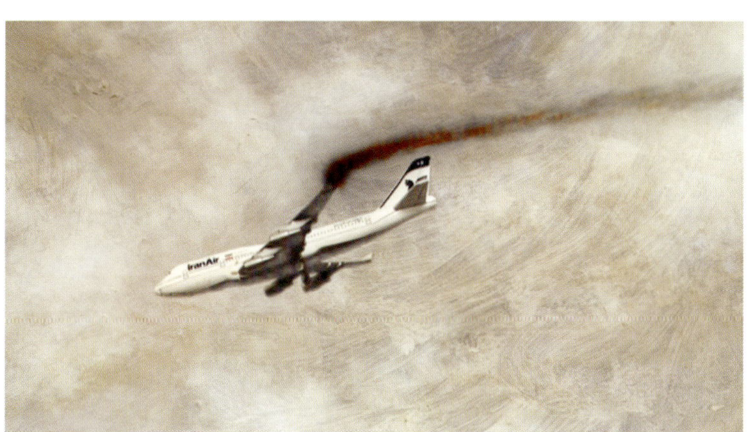

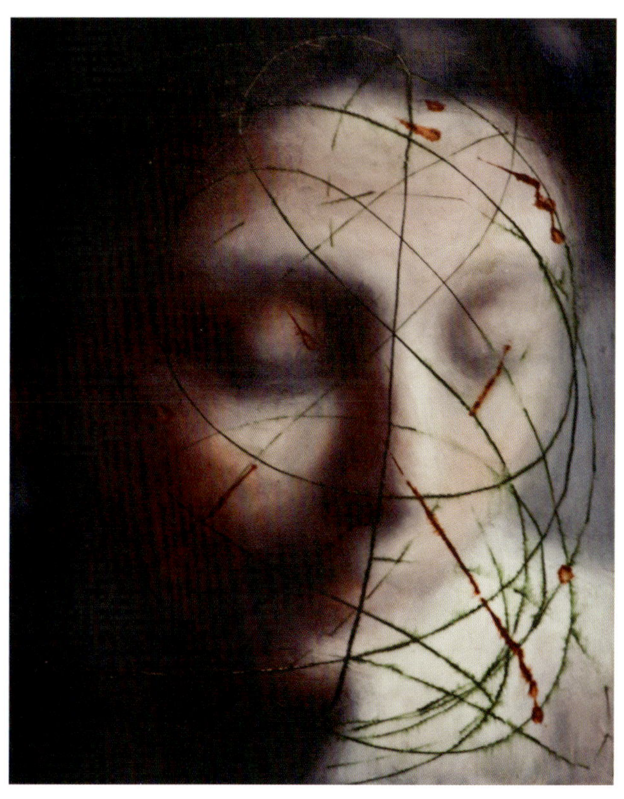

Left
5.33
Hamed Sahihi, *But in Your Head Baby, I'm Afraid You Don't Know Where It Is*, 2010, 1 min. Loop, each screen, stills from different video screens of the whole project, courtesy the artist

Above
5.34
Mojtaba Tabatabaei, from the *Interior, Exterior* series, 2021, oil on canvas, 27×20 cm, courtesy the artist

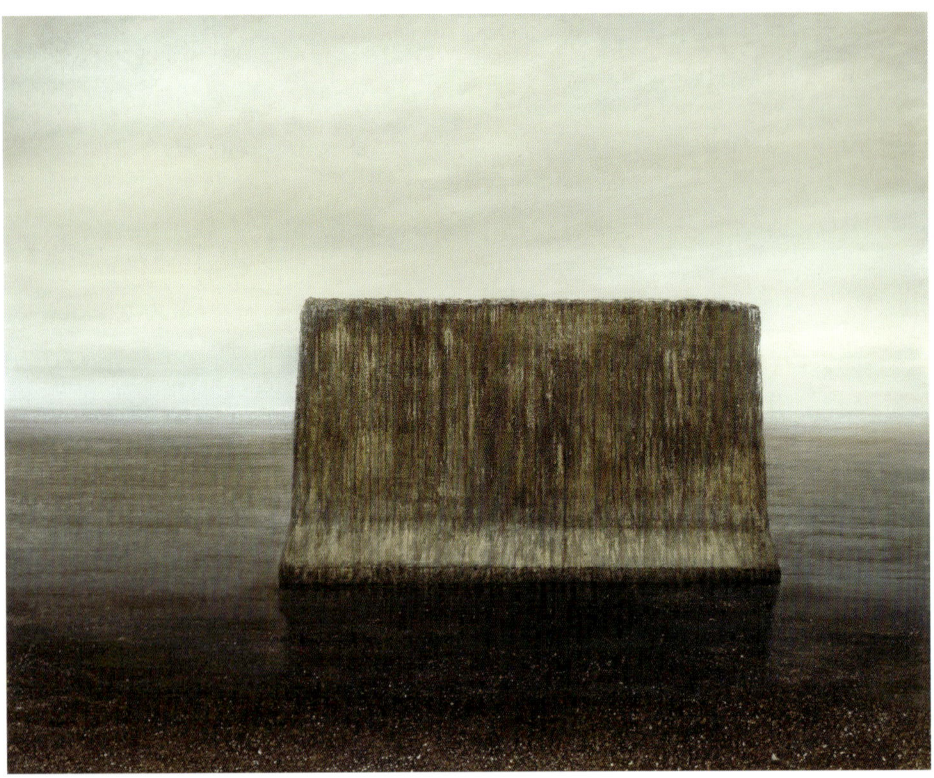

5.35
Mohammad Khalili, *Untitled*,
2020, oil and acrylic on canvas,
160×195 cm, courtesy the artist

5.36
Mohsen Ahmadvand, *Wanted*,
2011, colour pencil and ink
on paper, 41×30 cm, courtesy
the artist

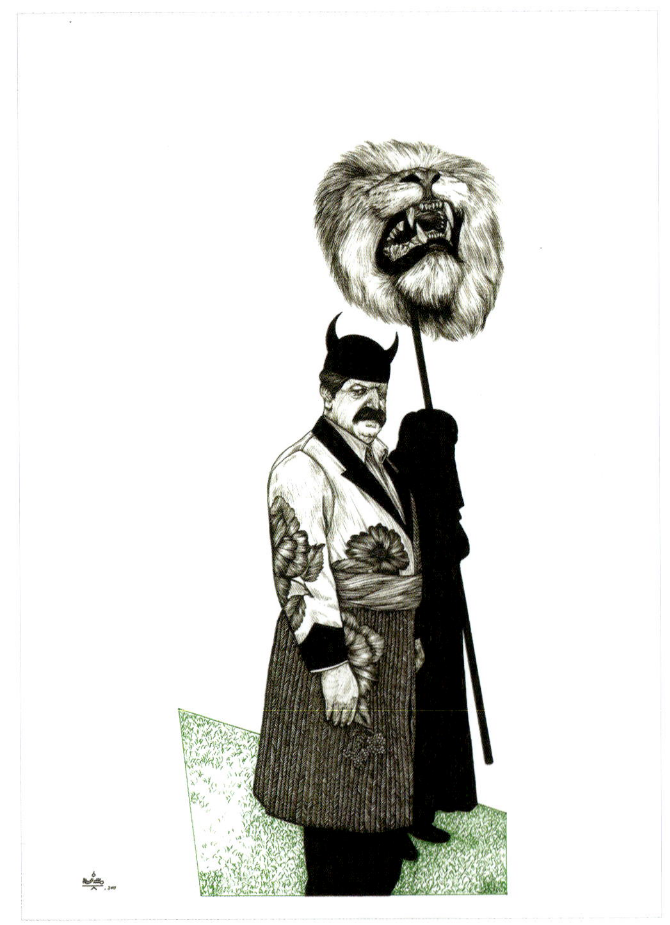

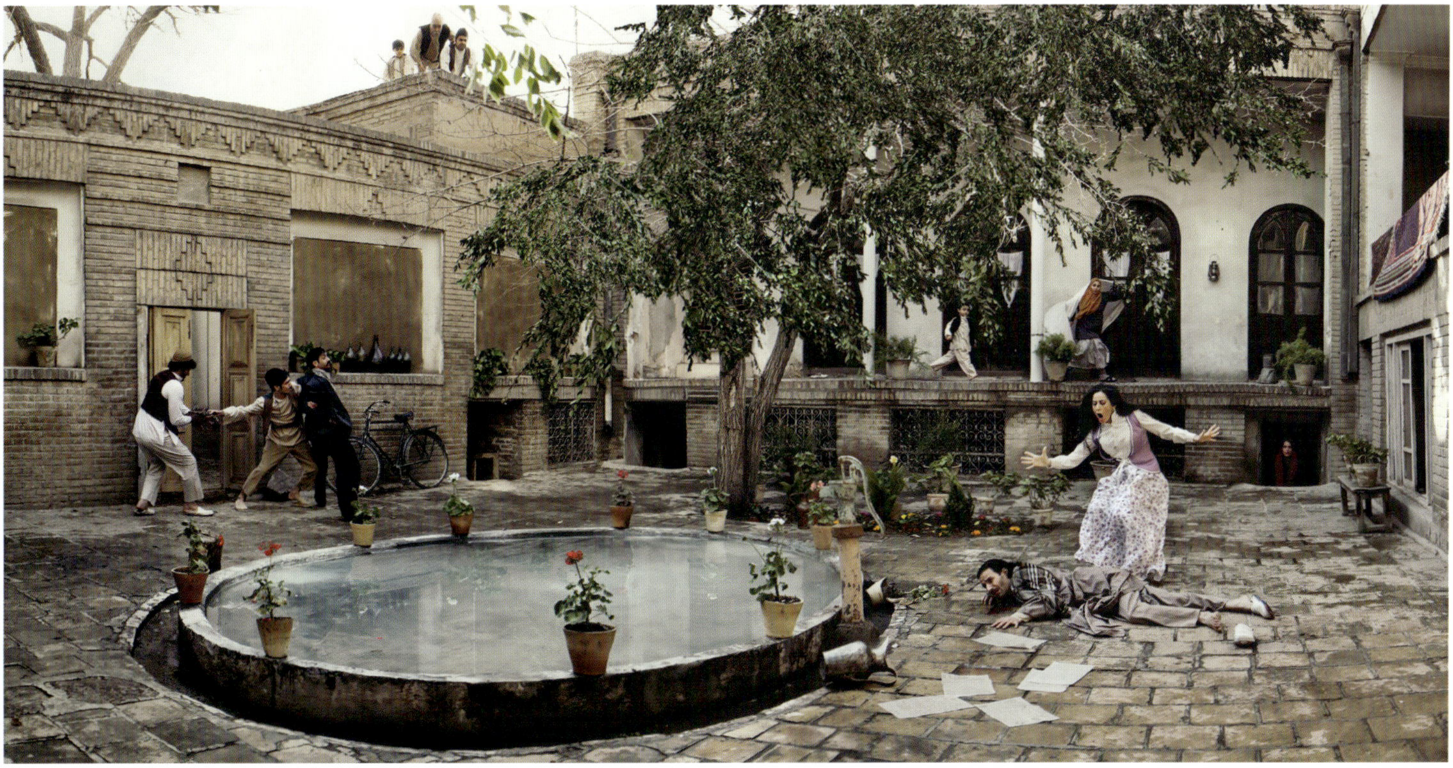

Above
5.37
Azadeh Akhlaghi, *Tehran, Mirzadeh Eshghi, 3 July 1924*, 2012, digital print on photo paper, 110×209 cm, courtesy the artist

Right
5.38
Parham Taghioff, from the *Asymmetrical Authority* series, 2018, photographs, HD inkjet print on Archival acid free paper, 50×50 cm, courtesy the artist

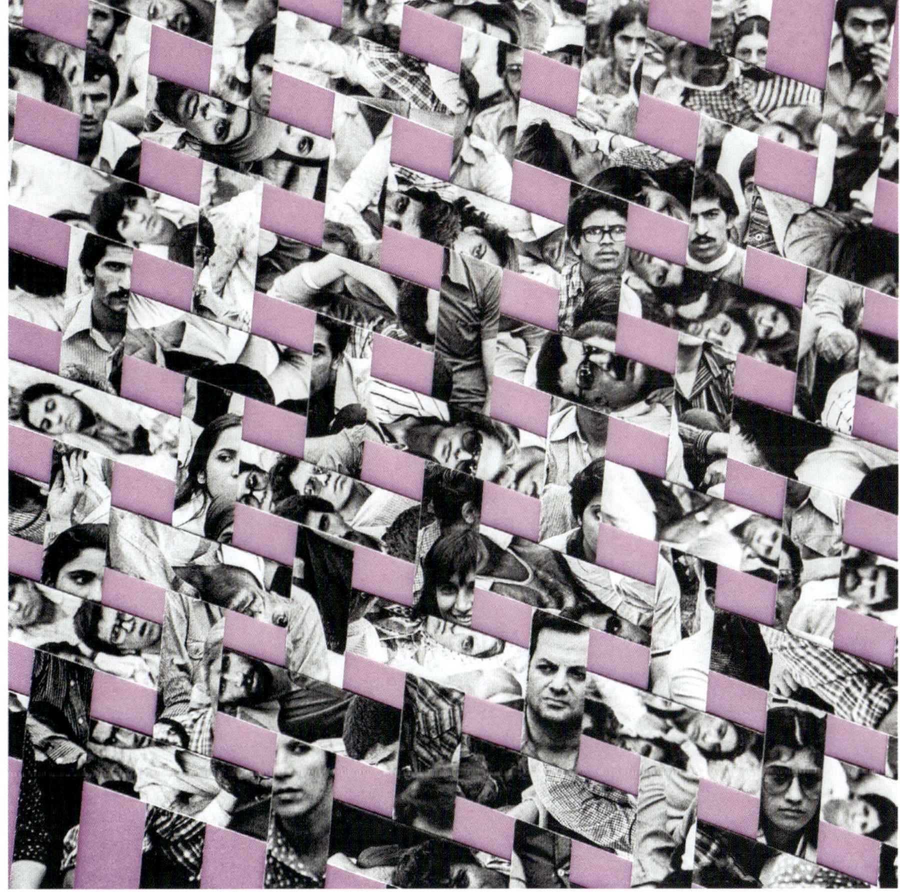

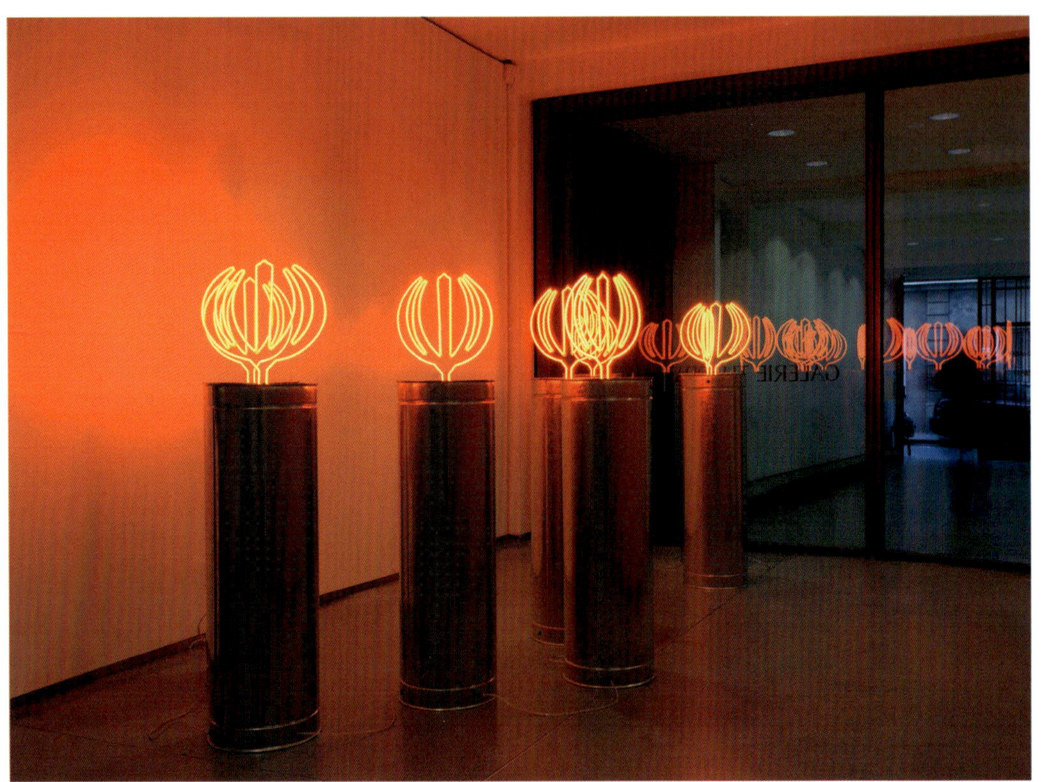

5.39
Mahmoud Bakhshi Moakhar, *Tulip*,
from *The Industrial Revolution* series,
installation view, courtesy the artist

unidentified bodies of the soldiers of the Iran-Iraq war, is in fact challenging the significance of the words; it is applying the term to the executed opposition and political prisoners in 1988 by the Islamic Republic. The installation is made up of eight framed Iran national flags – referring to the war years. These were the actual flags that had hung from official buildings for several months. Old and dirty, they appear to have become a visual suggestion of the severity of Tehran's air pollution. The work then suggests multi-layered meanings: signifying not only air pollution but also conveying the depth of corruption and violence. It also carries subversive content by manipulating the symbolism of the flag and the representation of anonymous martyrs.

The artist's series *The Industrial Revolution* (2010) comprises various pieces of complex, interactive machinery running either by electricity or by hand. The pieces each address several layers of issues inherent in Iranian culture, politics and everyday life. (Figure 5.39)

In the series *Talk Cloud* (2013), Bakhshi uses famous quotes from political leaders, social activists, or popular artistic figures from recent decades in ironic ways. These quotes are presented in lightboxes or executed in three-dimensional forms, drawing attention to the multifaceted and layered relationships of power systems and the concepts they impose. Furthermore, the series critically examines other issues such as the dynamics of economic and cultural power relations, as well as the processes and struggles of authority and ideology construction within power structures. (Figure 5.40)

Common discourses in contemporary art, such as criticism of 'originality', serve as familiar strategies for engaging with these themes. This criticism becomes even more pronounced when engaging with collective memories, often manifesting through humorous commentary on these ideals instead of their mere commemoration, as demonstrated by artists of previous generations. The painting of Rokni Haerizadeh is a good example. His works ironically criticise the hypocritical aspects of Iranian culture. His main inspiration comes from Iran's rich literature – such as

5.40
Mahmoud Bakhshi Moakhar, *Halal*, from the *Talk Cloud* series, 2013, galvanised iron and fluorescent lamp, 117x132x20 cm

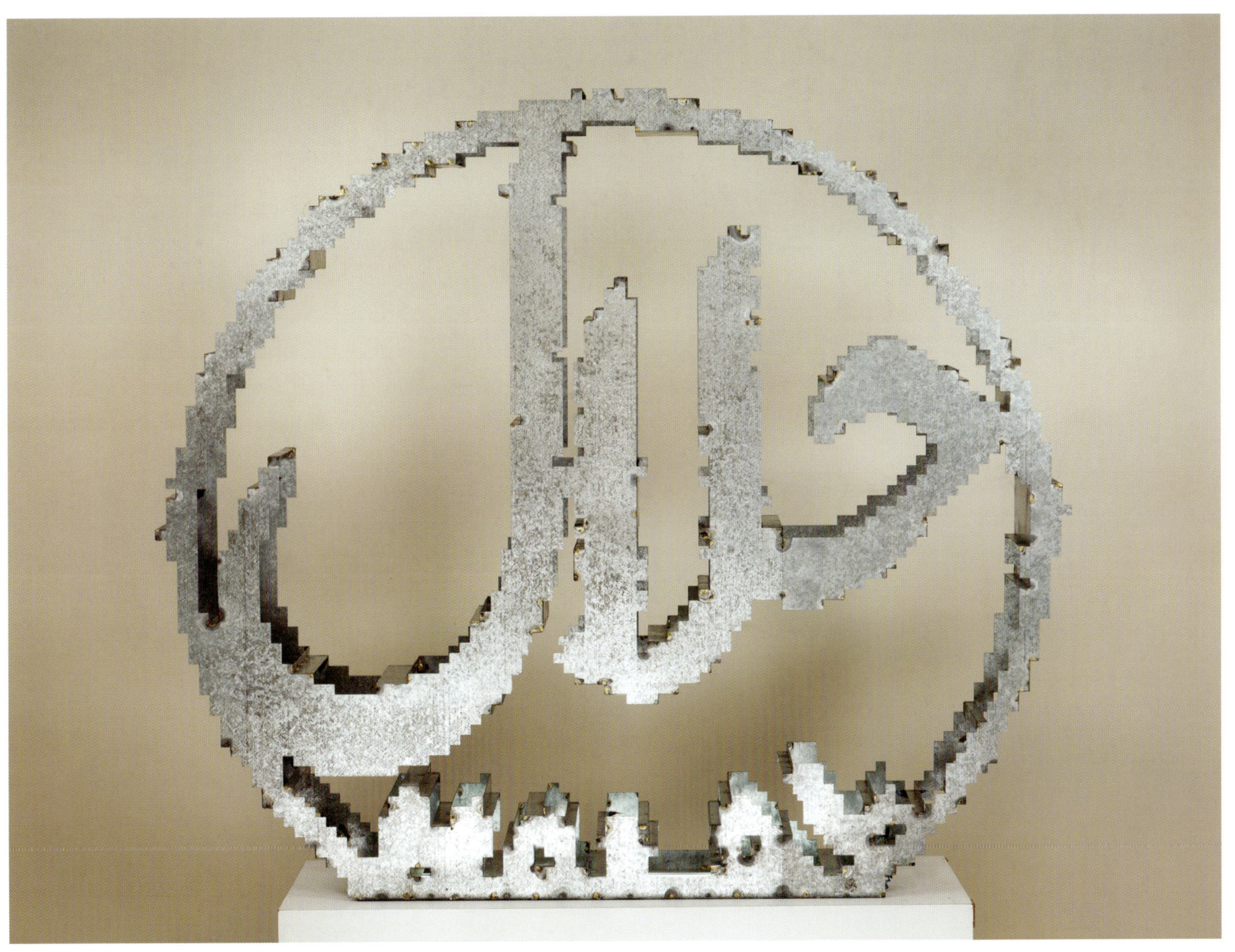

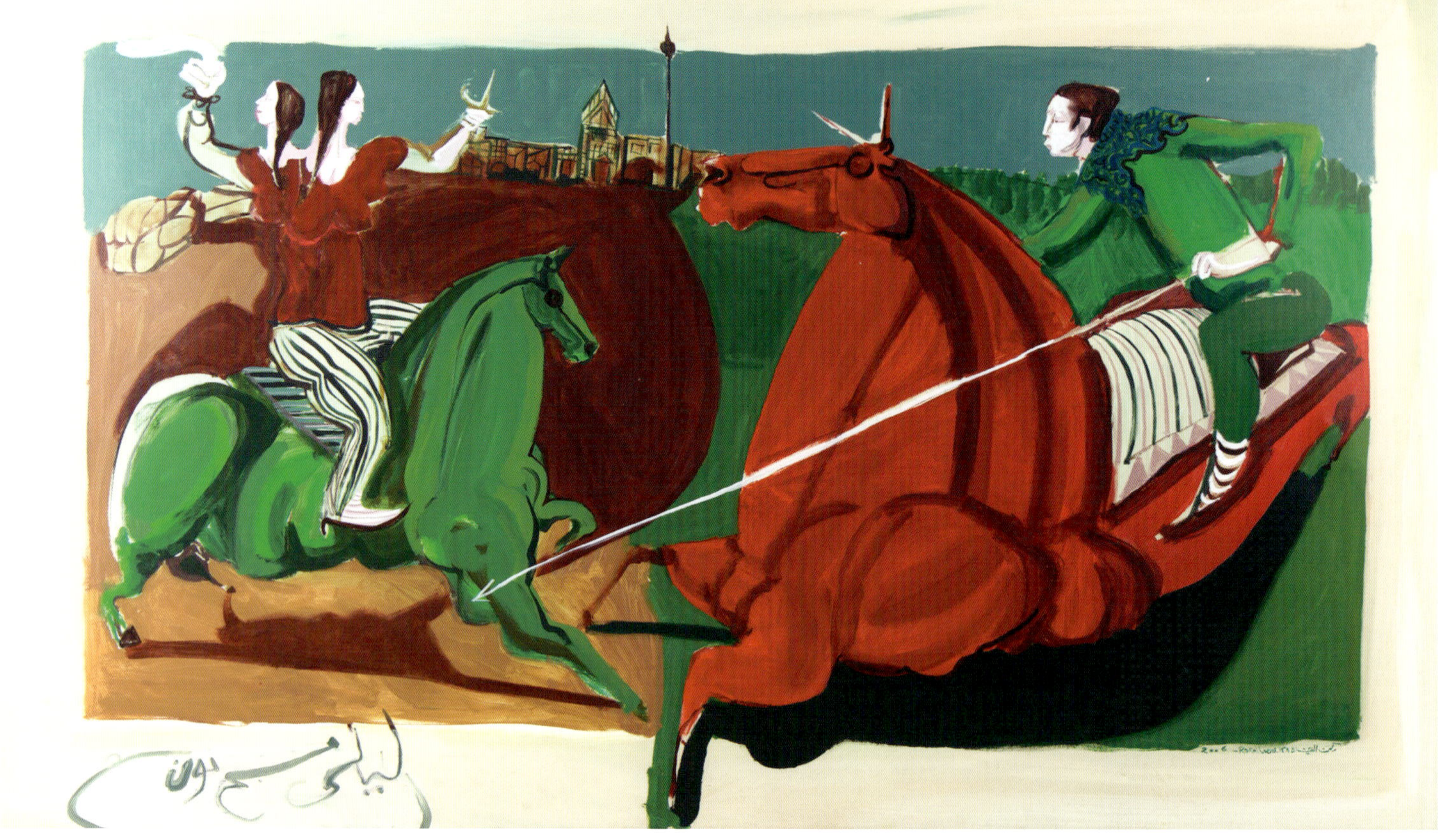

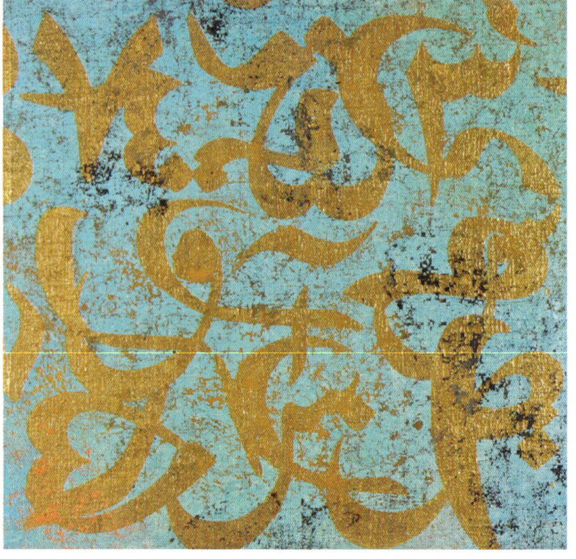

Ferdowsi's *Shahnameh*, Nizami or Rumi's poetry – using their grand themes as allegories for contemporary Iranian social issues. Haerizadeh renders these scenes with a satirical taste and caricature-like qualities. (Figure 5.41) Farhad Moshiri is also well known for his ironic interpretations of hybrids of traditional Iranian forms and those of the consumerist and globalised popular culture widespread in Iran. These include his painted jars in the early 2000s, bursting with popular foods, drinks and desserts with elegant popular scripts written on the body of the large vessels. In his later period, the artist has experimented with incorporating textual elements and calligraphic letters and numbers in various ways. (Figure 5.42) Similarly, by mixing elements both from consumerist and traditional culture, the works of Behnam Kamrani address the contradictory situation of a culture. They aim at capturing the aesthetic nuances that shape, reshape and reinvent the identity of the new Iranian culture. These works explore how modernism has permeated Iranian culture and how it has been influenced by local struggles. Through nostalgic memories of the recent past, they evoke a sense of both attainability and unattainability. (Figure 5.43)

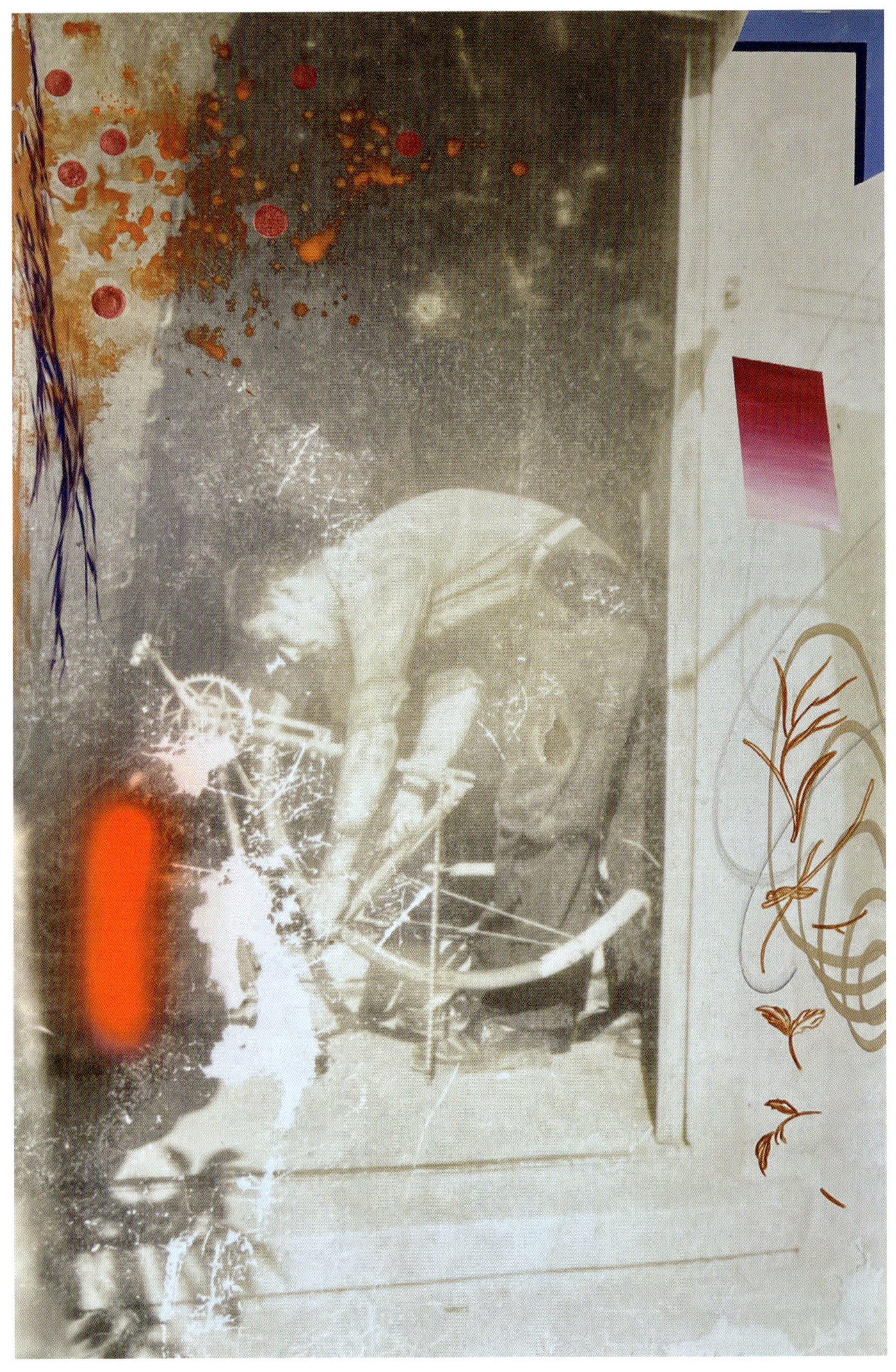

Facing page: above
5.41
Rokni Haerizadeh, *Leyli va Majnoon*,
acrylic on paper, 2006, 167×270 cm

Facing page: below
5.42
Farhad Moshiri, *Untitled*, 2005,
mixed media on canvas,
170x170 cm

Left
5.43
Behnam Kamrani, *Bicycle 1*, from
the *Familiar Shadows* series, 2023,
mix media on canvas, 172×112 cm,
courtesy the artist

Social critiques occasionally manifest through the presentation of pop culture and an exploration of fashionable currents experienced in Iran. Jinoos Taghizadeh (b.1971), an artist working with various media, interrogates her own identity while critiquing what is termed as definitive collective memory. She employs autobiographical imagery to address both gender and cultural disorders. (Figure 5.44) Central to her art and life is a strong emphasis on protest and resistance.

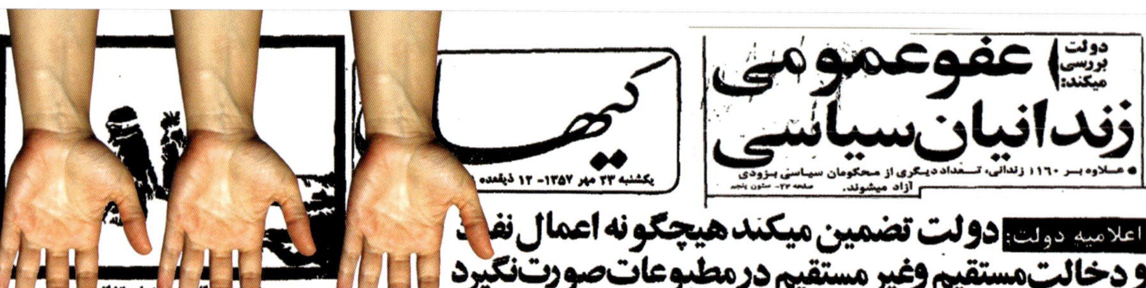

کیهان

یکشنبه ۲۳ مهر ۱۳۵۷ - ۱۲ ذیقعده

دولت بررسی میکند: عفو عمومی زندانیان سیاسی

● علاوه بر ۱۶۰۰ زندانی، تعداد دیگری از محکومان سیاسی پژوهی آزاد میشوند.

اعلامیه دولت: دولت تضمین میکند هیچگونه اعمال نفوذ و دخالت مستقیم و غیر مستقیم در مطبوعات صورت نگیرد

پایان یک قرن سانسور

مطبوعات آزادی خود را پس گرفت

گفت و گوی نویسندگان و نخست‌وزیر و وزرا:

در ۷۰ سال مشروطه ۷۰ روز هم آزادی مطبوعات نداشتیم

آزمون وزیر مشاور: آزادی کامل مطبوعات ممکنست ضرباتی بما وارد سازد.. باید این ضربات را تحمل کنیم

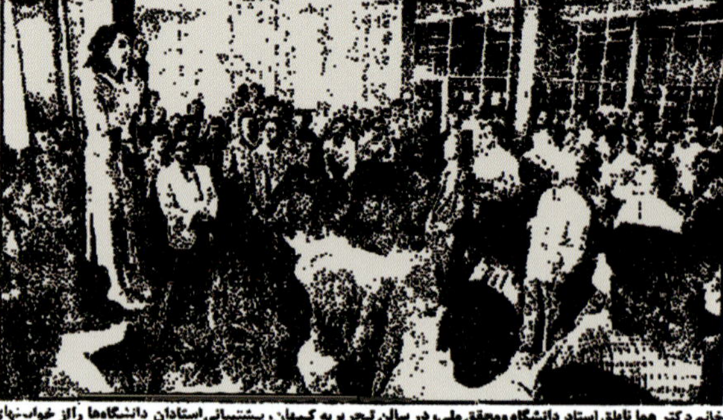

خانم دکتر هما ناطق استاد دانشگاه و محقق ملی، در سالن تحریریه کیهان، پشتیبانی استادان دانشگاه‌ها را از خواسته‌های حق‌طلبانه مطبوعات اعلام میکند.

دبیر سندیکای نویسندگان و خبرنگاران مطبوعات:

اعتصاب مطبوعات صد در صد سیاسی بود

میلاد فرخنده حضرت امام رضا(ع) صفحه ۲ - ستون هشتم

اعلامیه آیات عظام درباره تعطیل فردا

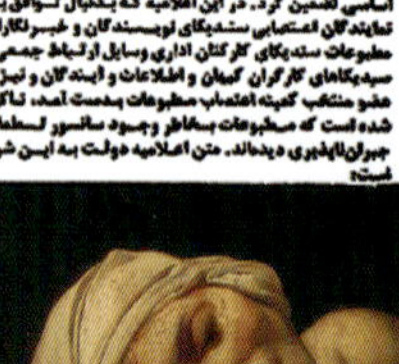

در تهران شیراز و اعتصابات ادامه دارد صفحه ۲۲

کریم سنجابی رئیس جبهه ملی شد

داریوش فروهر عضو هیات اجرائی جبهه ملی ایران از طرف جبهه ملی اعلام کرد.

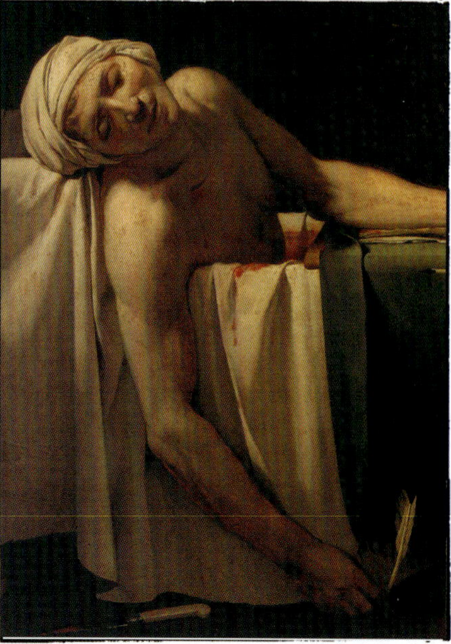

دکتر کریم سنجابی

طی بیانیه‌ای کانون نویسندگان ایران:

آزادی نویسندگان زندانی ایران درخواست شد

کانون نویسندگان ایران طی بیانیه‌ای خواستار آزادی نویسندگان و هنرمندان اسیر زندانی شده است...

دانشجویان مسلمان دانشگاه تربیت معلم: برخورد غیردموکراتیک را محکوم می‌کنیم

دولت آزادی مطبوعات را تضمین میکند

اعلامیه دولت: برابر قانون اساسی

مینویسم، پس هستم...

Through her works, she satirically challenges various forms of authority, addressing issues such as resistance against institutionalised patriarchy and questioning prevailing norms in the art market. Mehran Mohajer's (b.1964) photographs depict a world of silent contemplation while engaging with social sensitivities, criticising power relations, and highlighting the apparent homogenisation of life. Cultural aspects of life serve as the primary content of his works, a subject he attempts to approach impartially. His works often explore the concept of expression through visual implications and transcendentalism, all the while focusing on the everyday life in Iran. (Figure 5.45)

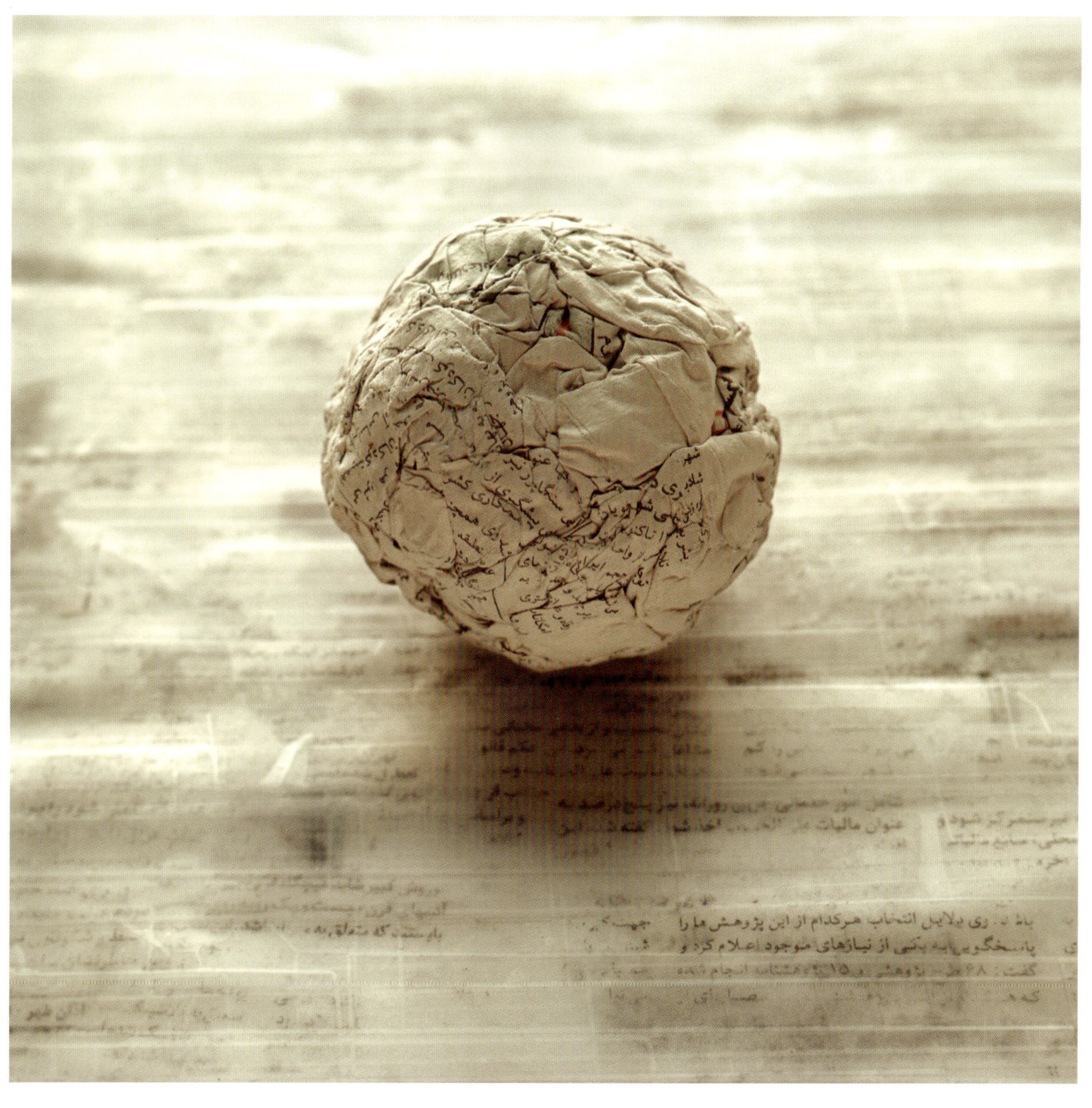

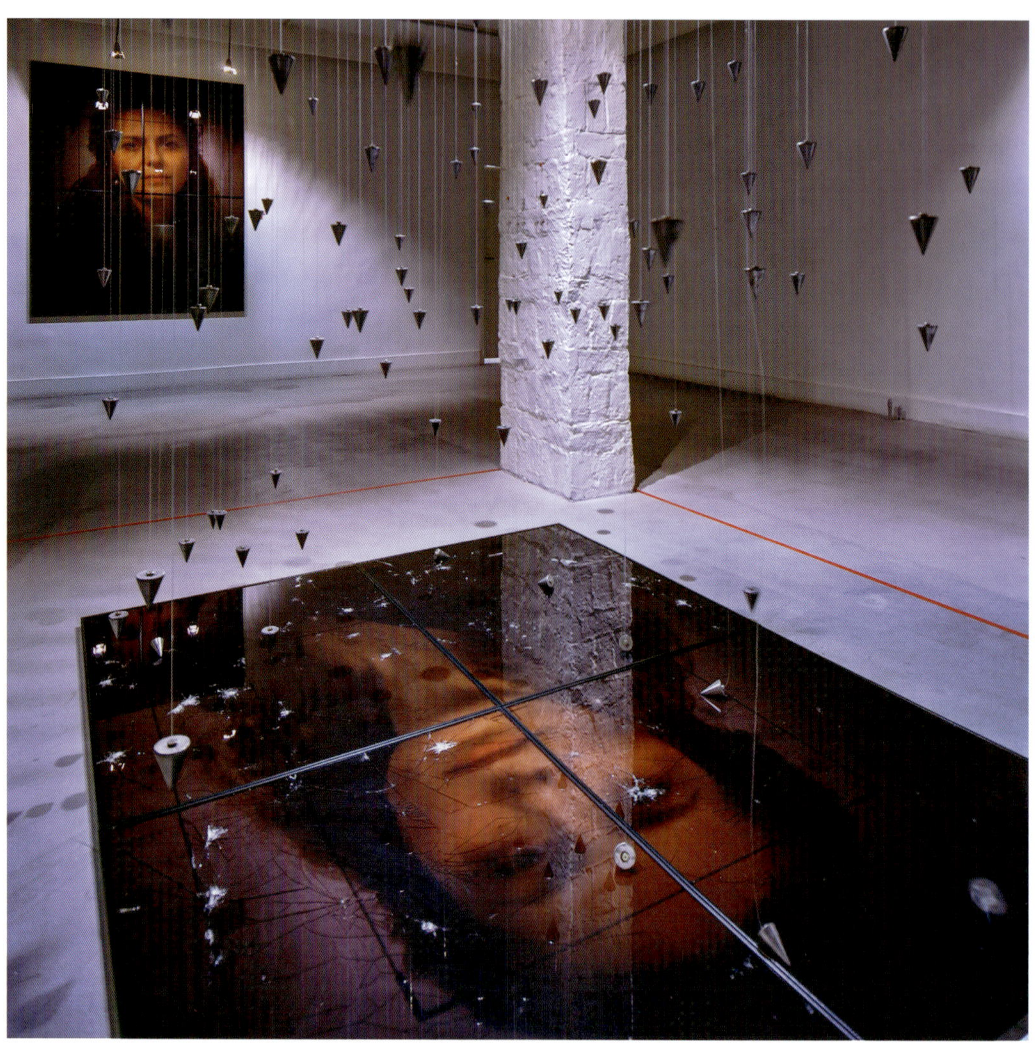

5.46
Katayoun Karami, *Have a Break*,
2012, installation, Azad Gallery,
Tehran, image courtesy the artist

Many artists strive to distance themselves from the nationalist agenda that has traditionally dominated discussions of Iranian art, instead positioning their work firmly within the global art scene. This is particularly notable in works by artists working in unconventional media. Some have taken a critical approach to social and political issues, such as the exploration of highly gendered notions of public space and tradition. For example, through various series, Katyoun Karami (b.1967) portrays gender debates, censorship, and issues that her generation have grappled with. (Figure 5.46) Questions of gender in a patriarchal society are also prominent themes in the works of Rozita Sahrafjahan, approached through the lens of her personal life experiences. Her works depict despair and depression within the context of her politically charged narratives, while others explore social boundaries and the restrictions she has personally encountered. (Figure 5.47) In an intriguing multimedia project within the same thematic vein, Mohammad Parvizi (b.1972) executed a multimedia (video performance) work titled *Come Closer, Closer than This?* (2013), addressing harsh political issues and social ignorance. This sophisticated piece engaged the audience directly through a combination of performance and multimedia elements. As the audience navigated through labyrinthine corridors, they were enveloped by the sounds of a personal dialogue performed by Pegah Ahangarani (b.1984, a renowned Iranian actress), recounting fragmented memories of a loving relationship and a prison interrogation. The labyrinth, with scaffolding reminiscent of a prison, gradually guided the audience closer to the main scene: a large LED screen displaying a close-up view of performer Athena Eshtiaghi's face, atop which, in a glass cubicle, Eshtiaghi played Gabriel Fauré's *Elegy*. The music was intended to drown out the audible monologue. The final segment of the piece, titled *Even Closer than This*, featured five cubicles showcasing Ahangarani's face. Seated in the middle, she engaged in a dialogue with herself, largely reconstructing scenes from her own experiences during interrogations while detained for seventeen days in Evin prison in July 2011.[41] (Figure 5.48)

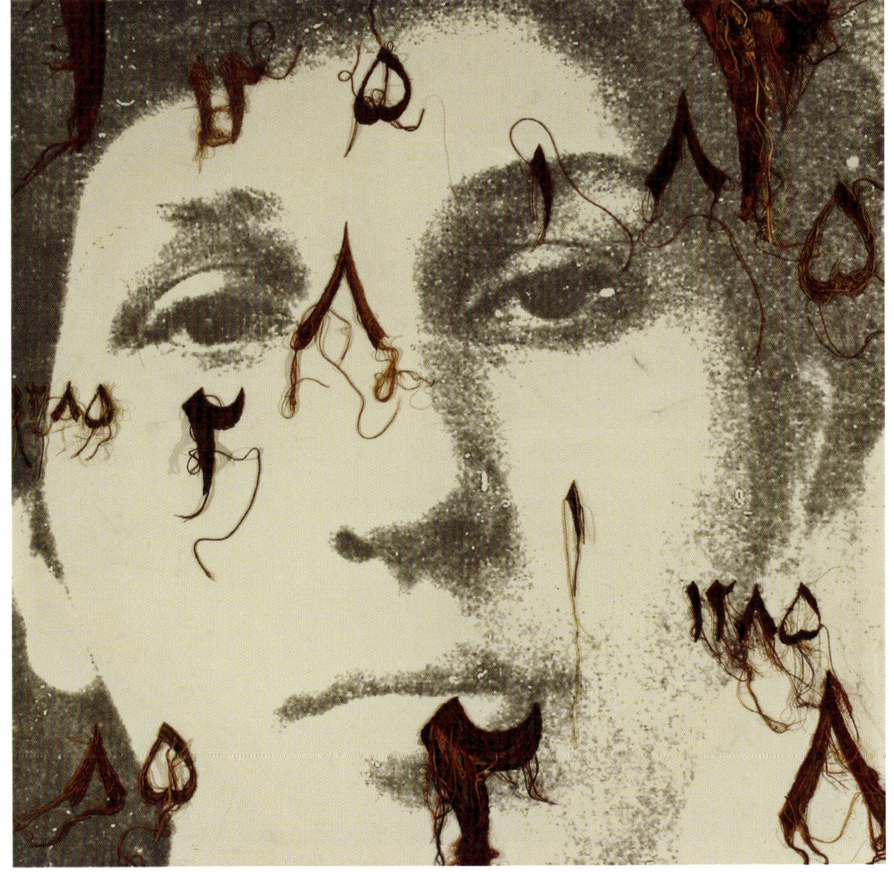

5.47
Rozita Sharafjahan, *The 1360s*, 2009, mixed media and collage on canvas, 160×160cm

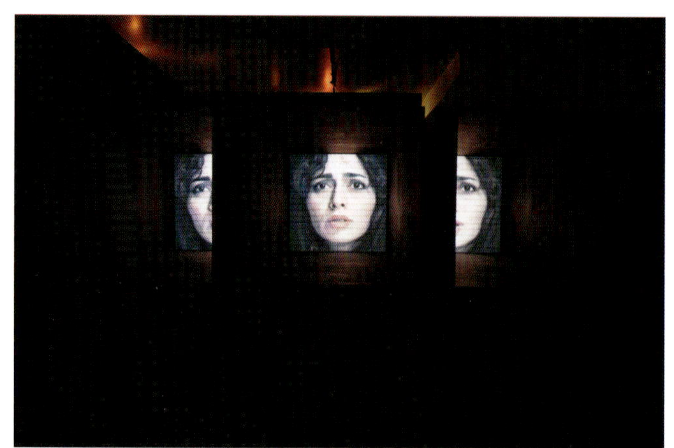

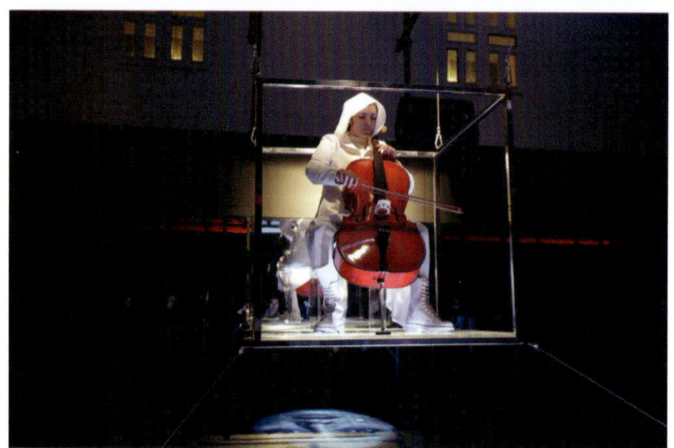

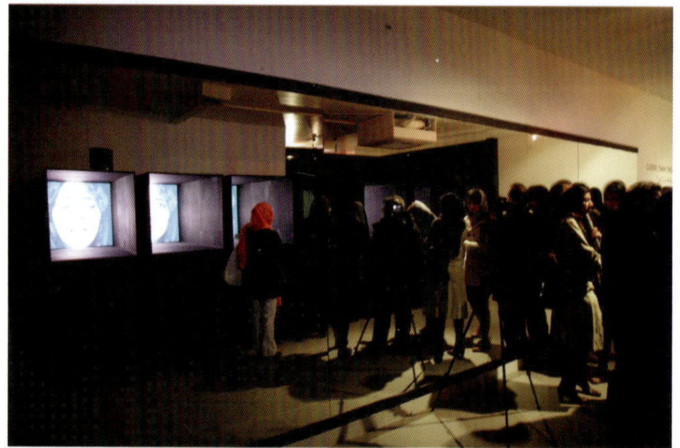

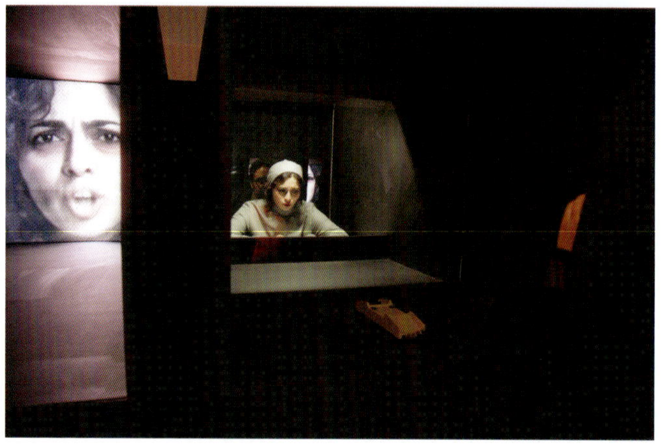

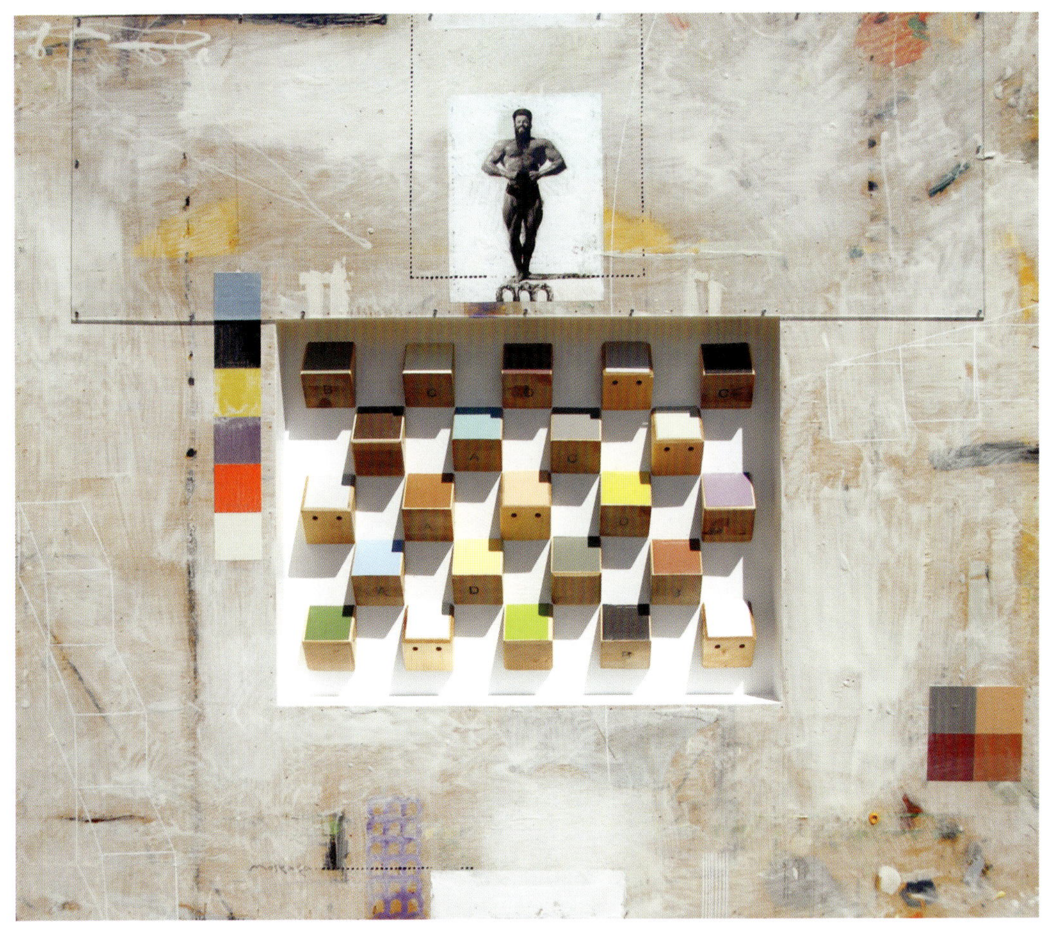

The works of Mostafa Darehbaghi (b.1966) define and celebrate different possibilities for mapping contemporary Iranian culture. These possibilities are addressed through several overlapping themes such as the politics of gender, and personal narratives revolving around isolation, memory and nostalgia. (Figure 5.49) Nostalgic commentary on domestic life is also addressed in the large canvases of Masoumeh Mozaffari. In an exploration of domestic civic life, objects and even human figures are relegated to a silenced world. The depicted individuals go about their ordinary actions without exhibiting notable emotions or involvement in significant events. Through this approach, Mozafari transforms the mundane into a multifaceted web of significance. (Figure 5.50) Samira Eskandarfar's videos often feature subjects with mostly unsympathetic faces, reflecting on a long, unknown grief. Using enigmatic language and ironic visual elements, she often explores the challenging situations confronting women in Iranian society. Through metaphor and occasional explicit expression, her art delivers a critical commentary on these issues. (Figure 5.13)

Facing page
5.48
Mohammad Parvizi, *Come Closer*, 2013, interactive performance, stills from the performance, Shrirn Art Gallery, Tehran, courtesy the artist

Above
5.49
Mostafa Darehbaghi, *I Am in Good Shape*, 2008, mixed media on panel, 120×145 cm, courtesy the artist

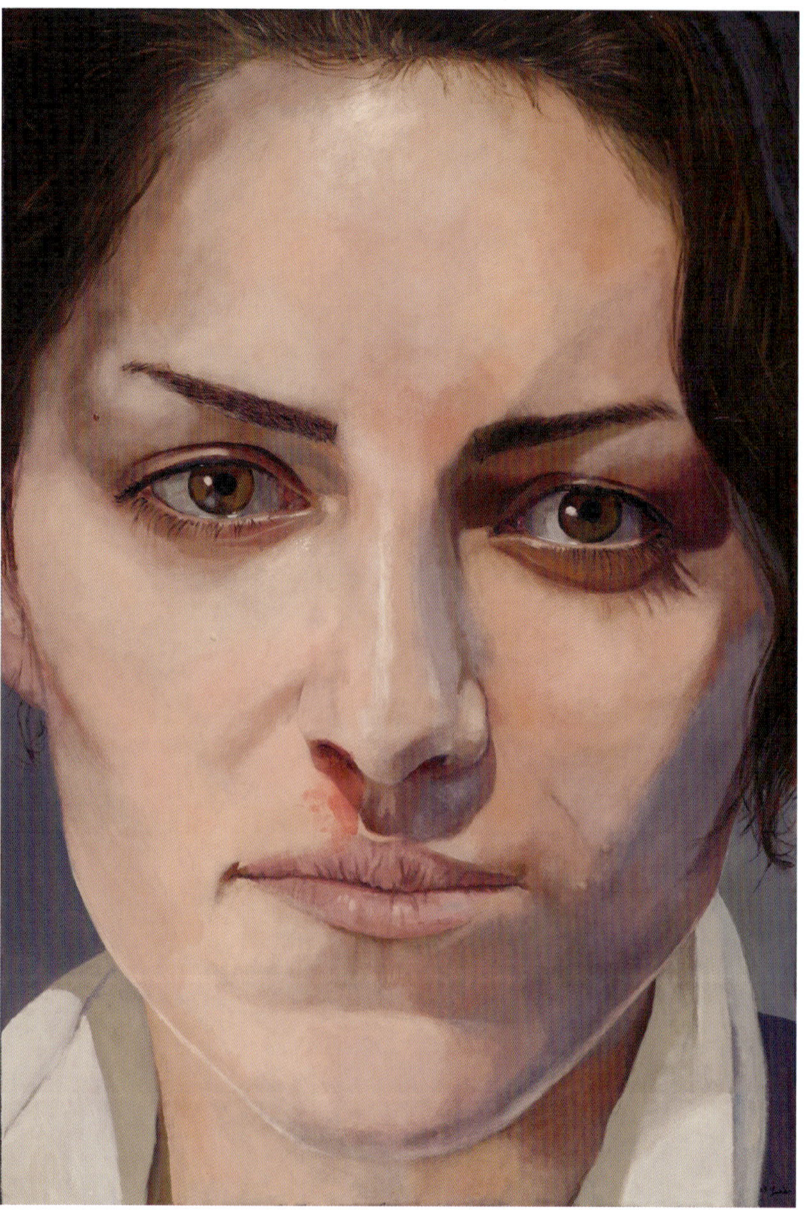

5.50
Masoumeh Mozaffari, *Heat Stroke*, 2010, acrylic on canvas, 150×100 cm, courtesy the artist

Mehdi Farhadian (b.1980) predominantly selects unconventional themes from Iran's recent history, portraying images of the recent past in his paintings. He focuses on elements that symbolise grandeur and glory, often associated with the late Pahlavi period (1941-79). On the other hand, Farhadian's depiction of these motifs surpasses a romantic and nostalgic fascination with the past. Instead, they function as conduits for critiquing and engaging with concepts such as grandeur, authority, national pride, and national history. (Figure 5.51) In contrast, Ahmad Morshedloo (b.1973) provides a personal commentary through his work, focusing on themes of obsession, bitterness, contradictions, and the contemporary realities of his society. His highly detailed depictions, often portraying unpleasant faces, convey emotions of indifference, alienation, and isolation alongside suffering, perhaps reflective of the living conditions. At times, these figures, seemingly absorbed in their personal worlds, stare blankly at the audience. (Figure 5.52)

Indeed, the sense of contemporaneity poses options and challenges for Iranian society and will continue to influence art and artistic representations. The aforementioned works serve as a repository of historical and social commentary, often rooted in the experiences and explorations of the artists themselves.

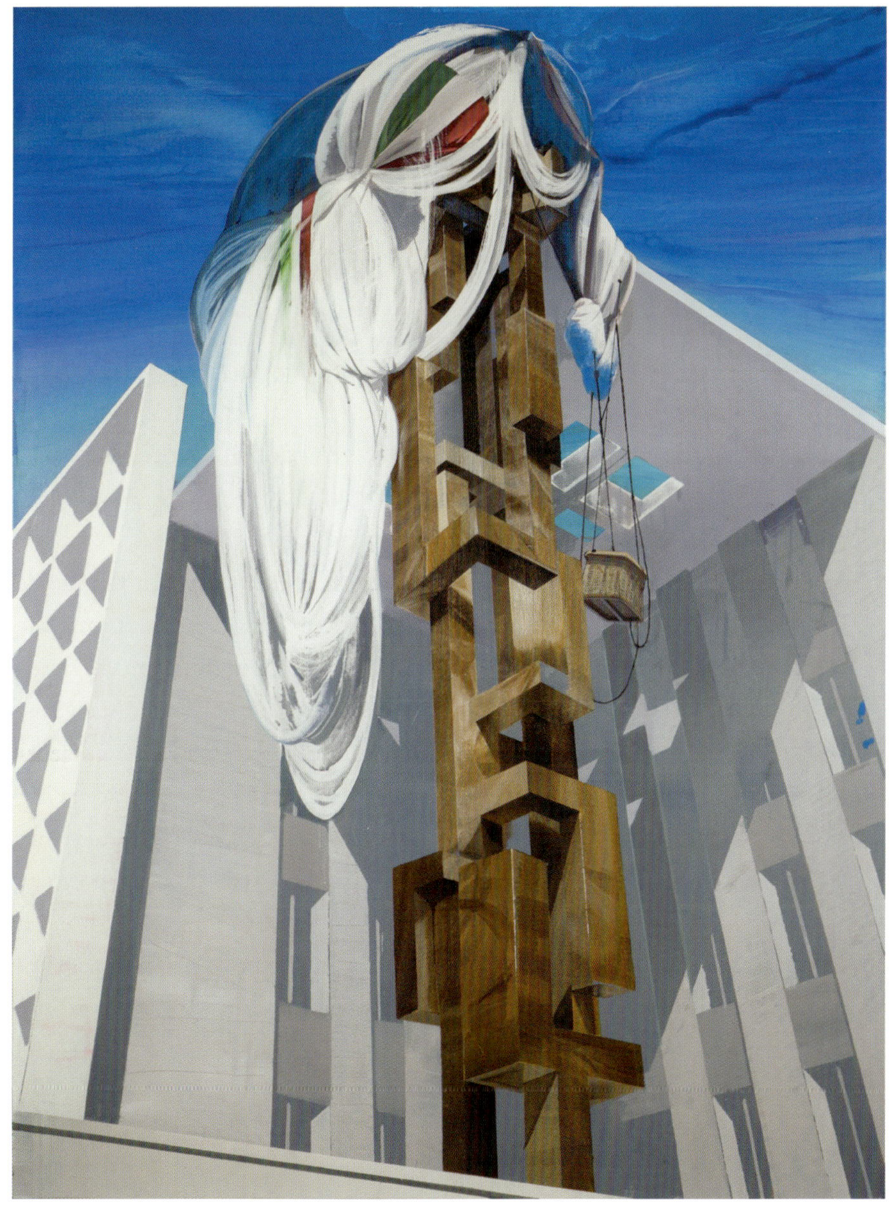

5.51
Mehdi Farhadian, *Technical Defect*, 2018, acrylic on canvas, 180×130 cm, courtesy the artist

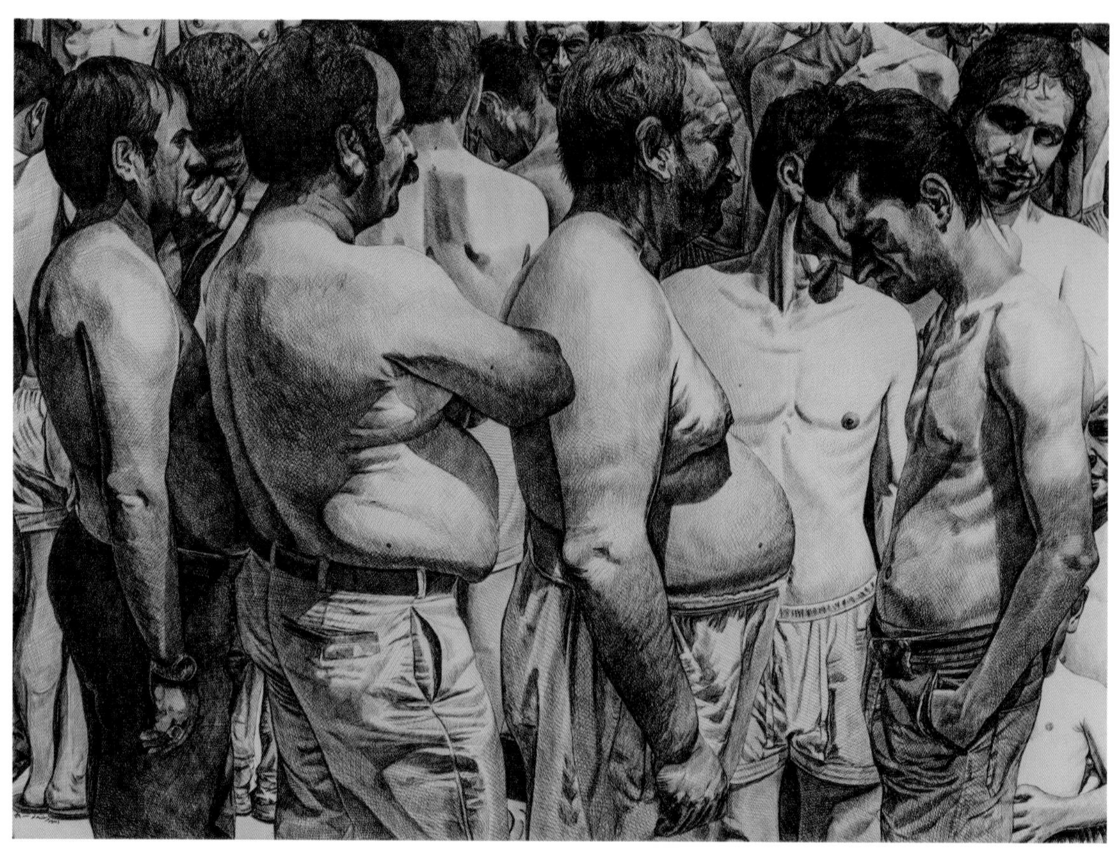

5.52
Ahmad Morshedloo, *Untitled*, 2010,
black pen and acrylic on board,
90×120 cm, courtesy the artist

When the concept of contemporaneity suggests that a multiplicity of identities and the boundaries between history and present are blurred, fixity is replaced by relativity. The result is that some 'contemporary arts practices are not historically or materially "specific", as [...] they do not rely very much on "context" for their embedded meaning'.[42] This may lead to the belief that a consequence of contemporaneity will soon emerge in the manner of an unhealthy homogenisation.[43] There are concerns that contemporary Euro-American art and its associated institutional networks are not merely observers of globalised cultural currents, but function as mediators or 'gatekeepers' actively shaping discourse.[44] However, addressing this hegemonic structure may heavily rely on intellectual and artistic strategies employed to navigate it.[45] Moreover, just as cultures worldwide visually construct their presentness, the works of Iranian artists depicting contemporaneity are influenced by various aspects of this condition. From a broader perspective, recent developments in contemporary Iranian art suggest an inevitable demand for this new condition of contemporaneity.

3. Contemporary Tensions: Cultural Particularity in Flux

This section navigates the divide between contemporary relevance and cultural distinctiveness within artistic discourse, a recurring challenge faced by Iranian artists. These artists find themselves grappling with the dual demands of embracing 'specificity', particularly concerning local cultural nuances, and addressing other pertinent 'particularities' such as social, ideological, religious, and political issues. The latter aspect underscores the phenomenon of regionalising art, or its classification within specific local contexts, a dilemma that inherently suggests the necessity of adopting strategies of resistance against the perceived homogenising effects of globalisation. However, such resistance carries the risk of misinterpretation or co-option by commercial or political forces. Central to this discourse are fundamental questions: Can artists effectively advocate for local and specific cultural differences within the constraints of this seemingly irresolvable dilemma? How can locally rooted artistic languages evolve to engage with broader, globalised artistic discourse? Moreover, what impacts do hegemonic artistic languages have on artists whose primary language differs from these dominant discourses? Therefore, it becomes imperative to address the complexities of identity politics, including its intersection with the cultural strategies of the state, external expectations regarding predefined identities, and the aesthetic responses of artists to these external pressures.

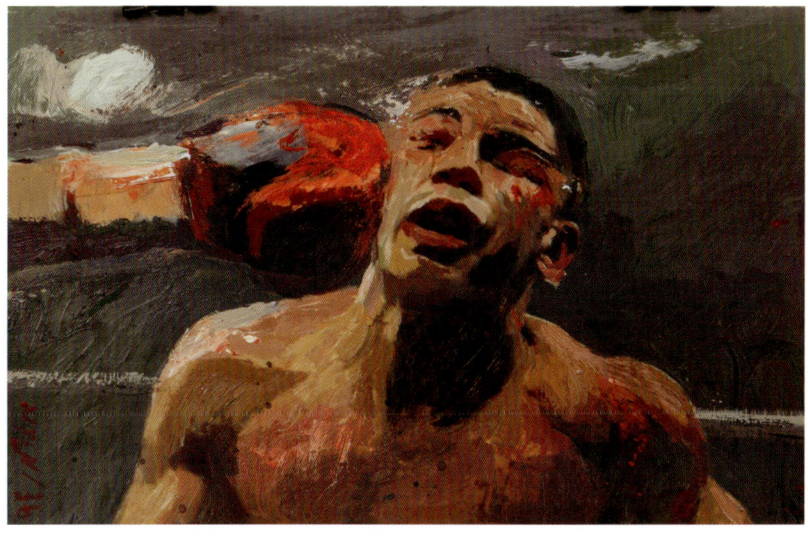

5.53
Ali Zakeri, *No 15*, from the *Eliminate, The Sons of God* series, 2016, acrylic on canvas, 29×40.5 cm, courtesy the artist

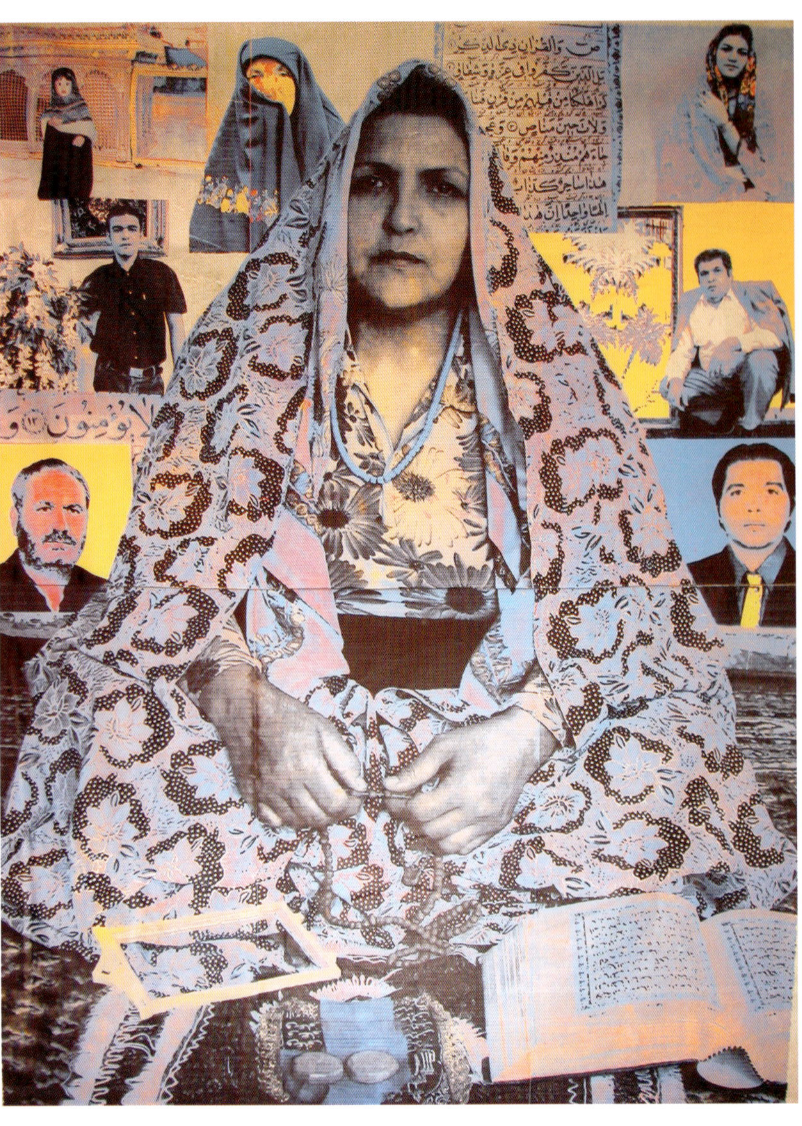

5.54
Khosro Hassanzadeh, *Azimeh 5*,
from the *Terrorist* series, 2004,
screen print on canvas, courtesy the
artist

Contemporary Iranian artists' beliefs about social relations and cultural essentialism have found tangible expression in their artwork through the employment of creative strategies. This is an issue in particular for artists and art activists concerned with rethinking notions of embodiment and performativity, in tension with the Iranian political context. It is in the course of unfolding new dialectics of global culture in contemporary Iran that the artists attempt to produce or transfer different subject positions[46] in their art.

In contemporary Iranian cultural life, including artistic activities, one can discern the continual presence of the state and its role in standardising the conventional paradigms in all cultural and artistic dispositions. Shireen Hunter convincingly posits that alongside efforts to Islamicise Iran's cultural life, the state actively attempted to imbue it with a revolutionary ethos. Undoubtedly, a cornerstone of the Islamic Republic's cultural doctrine has been the insistence that art must serve Islam and the Revolution. In other words, artistic expressions were deemed valuable only insofar as they contributed to the objectives of the Revolution, which included fostering an Islamic and revolutionary fervour among the populace.[47]

The state has sought to construct a definition of an 'authentic' identity, portraying itself as a unified entity. This centralised, monopolistic, and ideological stance adopted by the post-revolutionary state necessitates that any alternative response be inherently 'political-cultural' in nature. Consequently, the Islamic Republic, assuming a hegemonic role in state governance, has placed significant emphasis on cultural transformation and the institutionalisation of an Islamic political culture. Central to this effort is the Ministry of Culture and Islamic Guidance, which exercises comprehensive control over cultural production. Operating within the framework of the state's ideologically structured principles, the Ministry has instituted regulations governing various artistic expressions, including exhibitions, films, music, and other forms of artistic expressions. According to the state, ideology is employed to

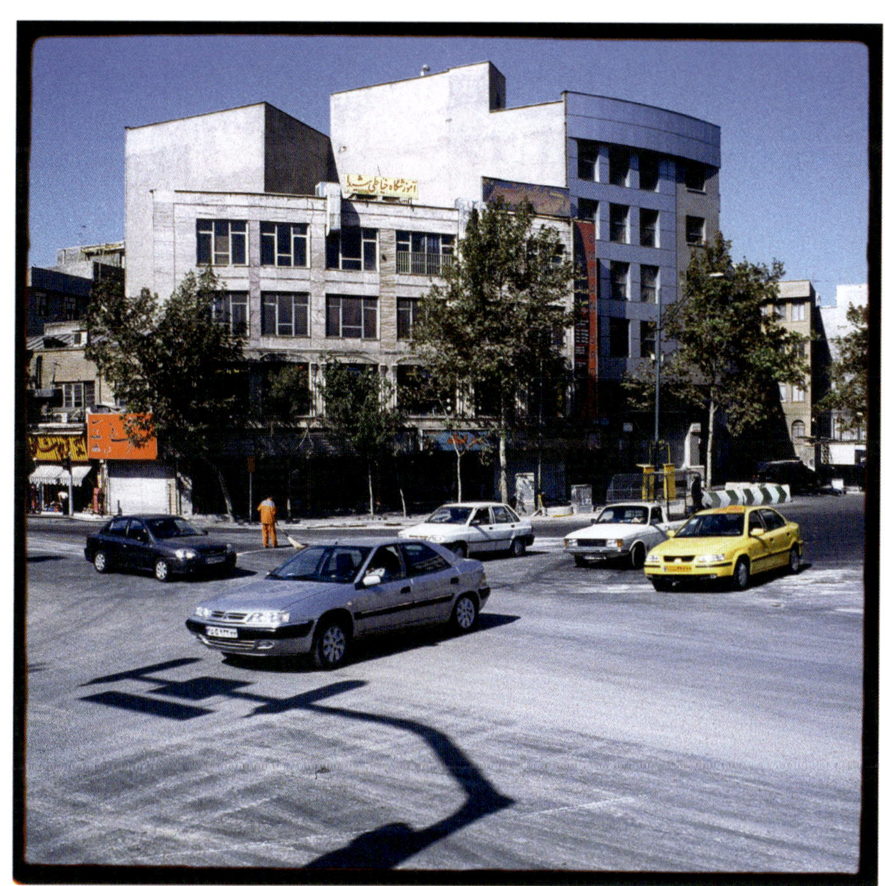

5.55
Mohammad Ghazali, *Abu Saeeid Abul-Khayr*, from the *Where the Heads of the Renowned Rest (Jay-i sar-i khouan)* series, 2009, digital print on paper, 112×134 cm, courtesy the artist

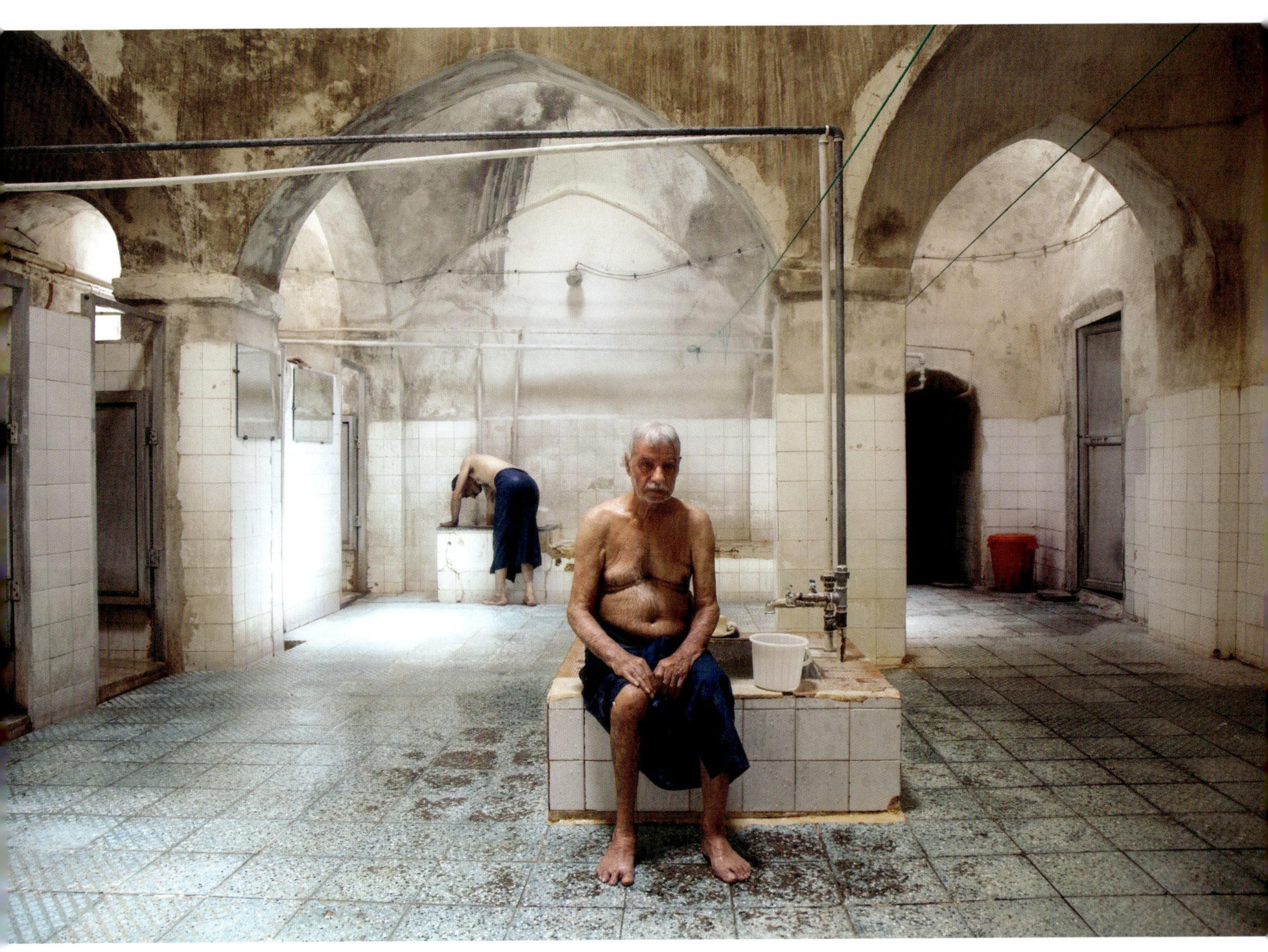

remedy social, psychological, and cultural maladjustments, such as moral and political strains.[48] But, as Ramin Jahanbegloo maintains, the very notion of 'ideology' gradually lost much of its coherence in the later years among the new generation of Iranian intellectuals and art activists. This accompanied the crisis of political legitimacy in Iran.[49] Thus, it is not surprising that for the majority of artists of the new generation, this formulation of culture does not seem, in the current phase in an increasingly globalised world, to be any longer plausible. One then witnesses an artistic and intellectual reaction against these stereotypes. Jahanbegloo further argues, '[T]oday, a democratic notion of identity, emphasizing the formation

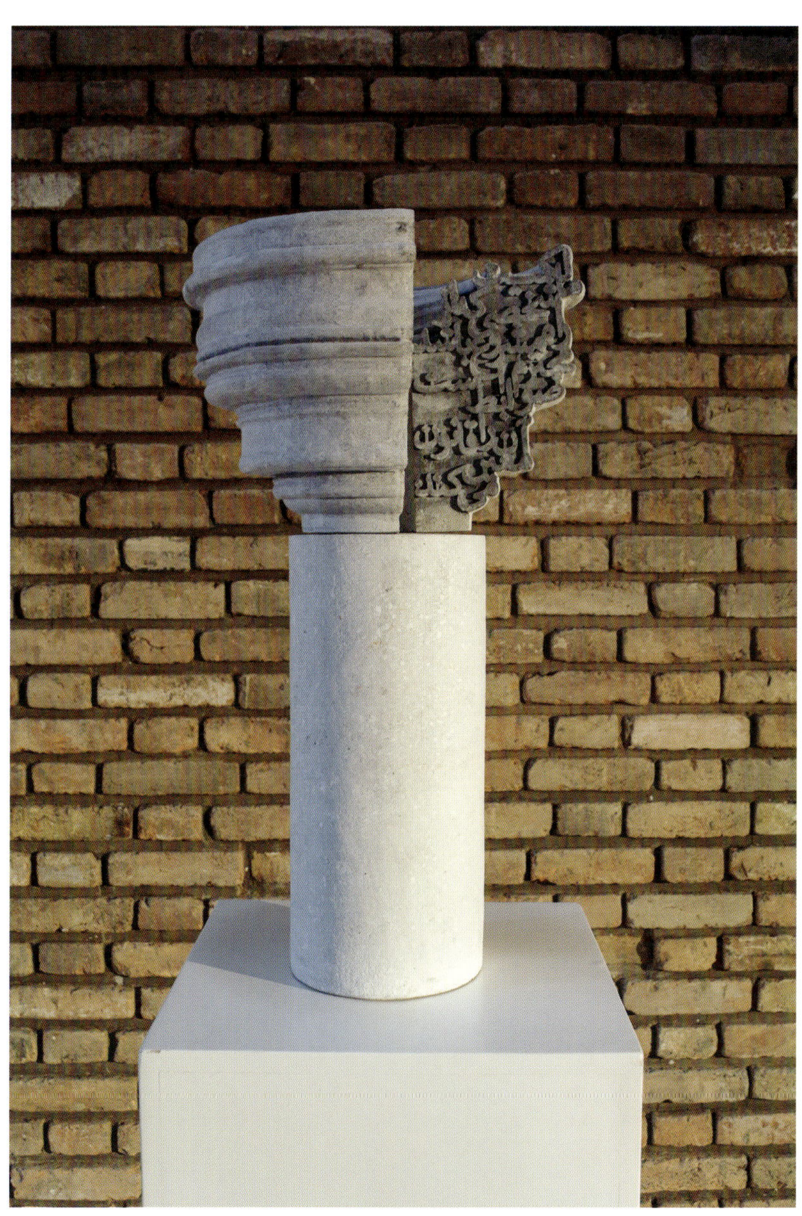

Facing page
5.56
Peyman Hooshmandzadeh, *Untitled*, from the *Dry!* series, 2011–17, digital photography, inkjet print on Epson Traditional Photo Paper, size varies, courtesy the artist

Above
5.57
Nazgol Ansarinia, *Article 47*, from the *Pillars* series, 2015, paper paste and cardboard, 65h×35w×35d cm

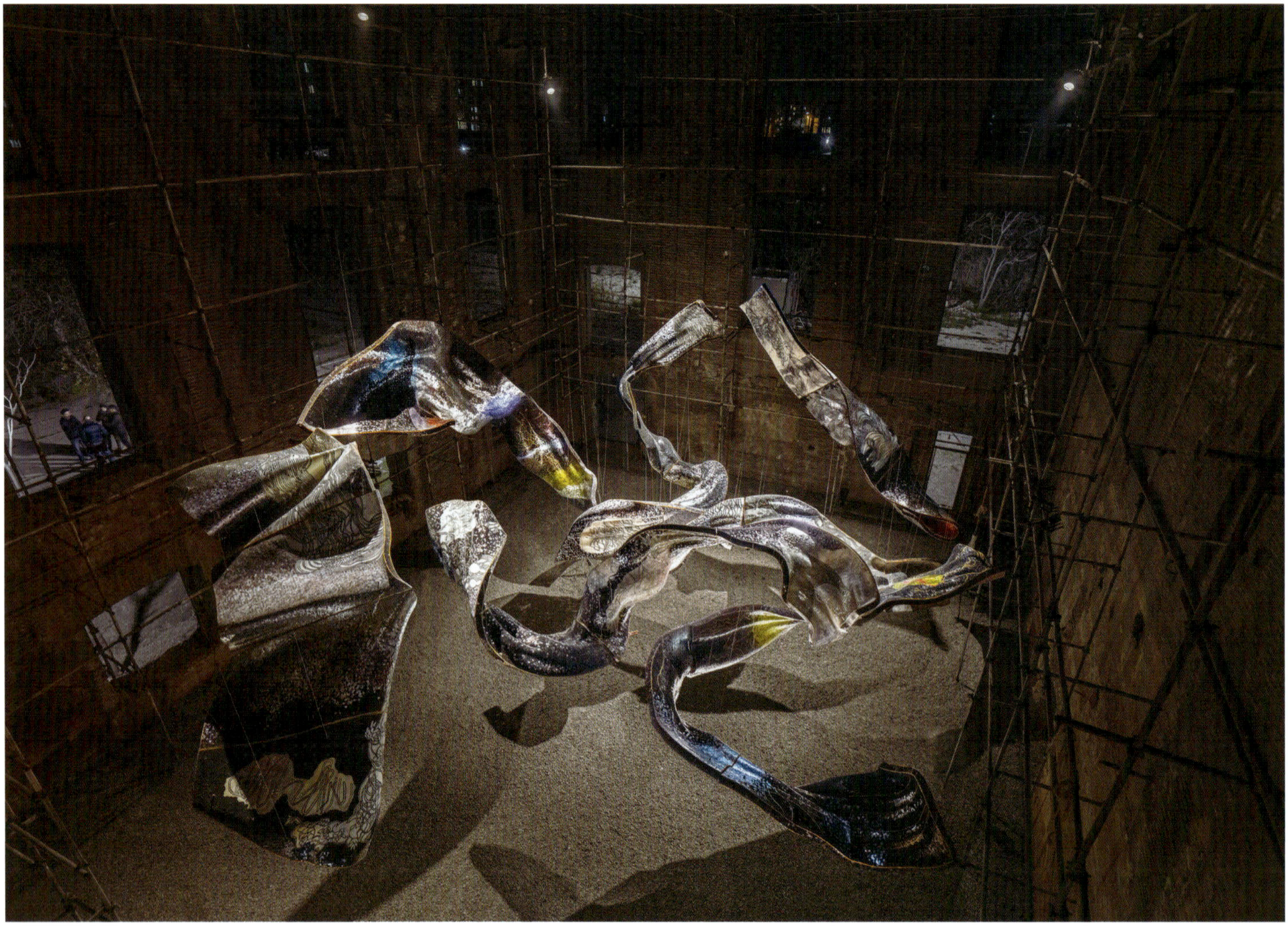

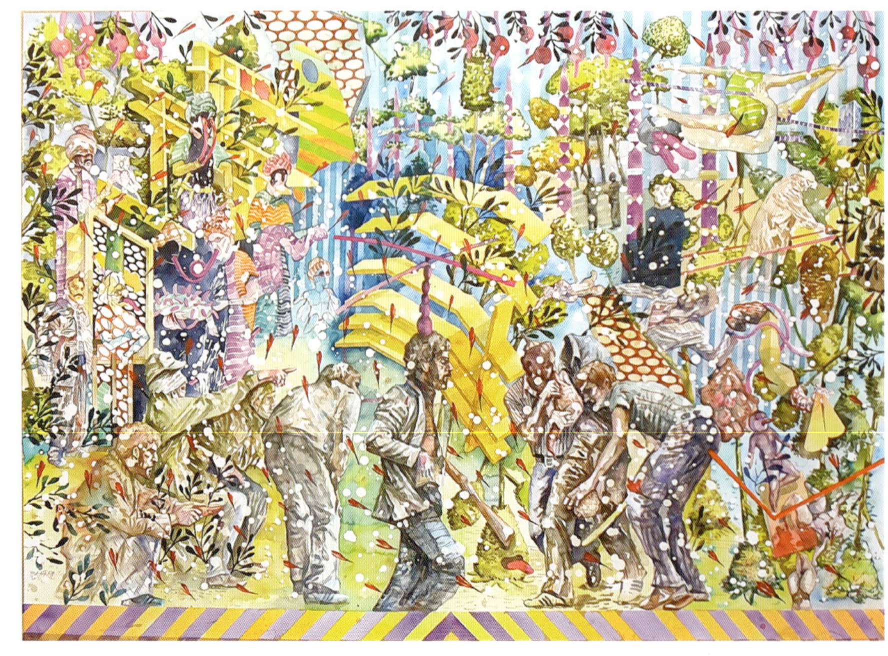

Above
5.58
Pooya Aryanpour, *Gone with the Wind*, 2022, installation view, Kahrizak Sugar Factory, Tehran suburb

Right
5.59
Behrang Samadzadegan, *Depart the World, Meet Me in Istanbul*, 2021, watercolour on paper, 131×182 cm, courtesy the artist

of a pluralistic civil society in Iran, is more welcomed among the new generation of Iranian elites than romantic or traditionalist notions of Iranian identity.'[50]

However, through the institutionalisation of a cultural collective identity, the state is still attempting to formulate these identities.[51] The definitions of collective identities are essentially ideological constructs, imposed from above and used to divide and control populations. Both political and cultural critics argue that efforts should be directed towards eliminating the imposition of identity in everyday life rather than institutionalising it.[52] It is now recognised that the uncertainties surrounding collective identity reveal more about the processes and power dynamics involved in identity constructions than the apparent certainties do; these uncertainties underscore the socially constructed nature of collective identities rather than their essentialist character.[53] This realisation is increasingly evident in Iranian cultural life, where artists are actively challenging essentialist political dictates while reclaiming their cultural spaces and asserting self-defined identities.[54] Their fundamental belief aligns with the theory, asserting that identity is commonly perceived as experienced and envisioned in ways that challenge its association with a specific geographic locale.[55]

We may concur with Vikki Bell, who posits that one does not inherently or ontologically 'belong' to the world or to any

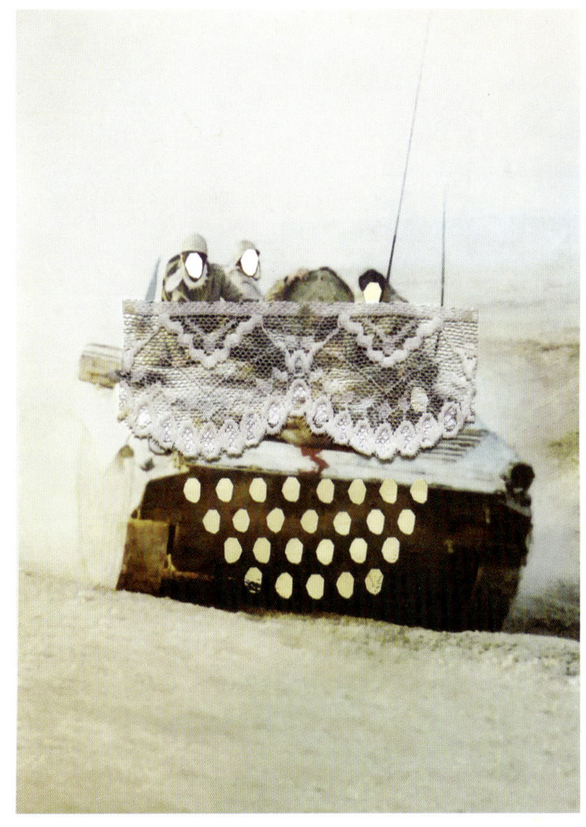

5.60
Saeed Ensafi, *Forgotten Superheroes*, from the *Smile Brother* series, 2014, assemblage on a photo Iran-Iraq war, 16×9 cm, courtesy the artist

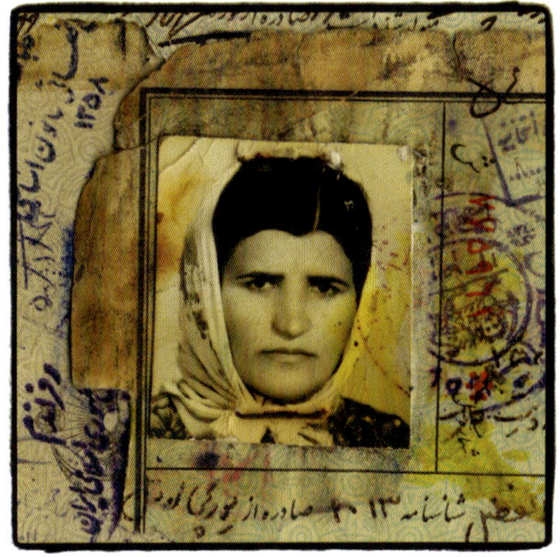
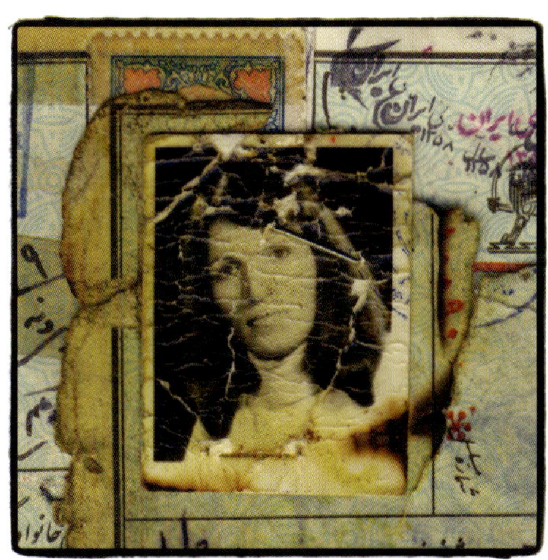
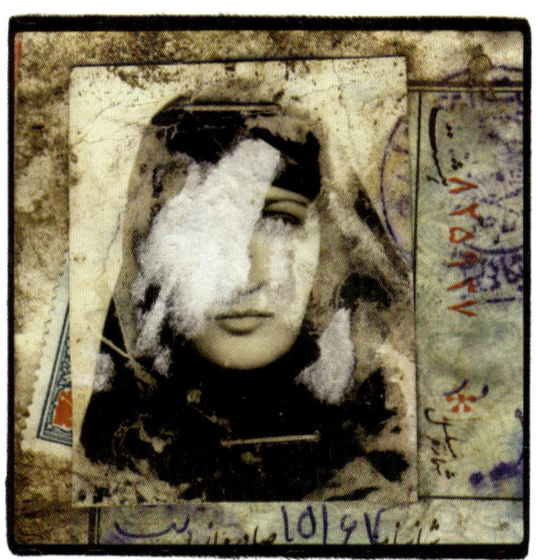

5.61
Najaf Shokri, from the *Irandokht* series, 2016, sonography, digital print on paper, each frame 20×20 cm, courtesy the artist

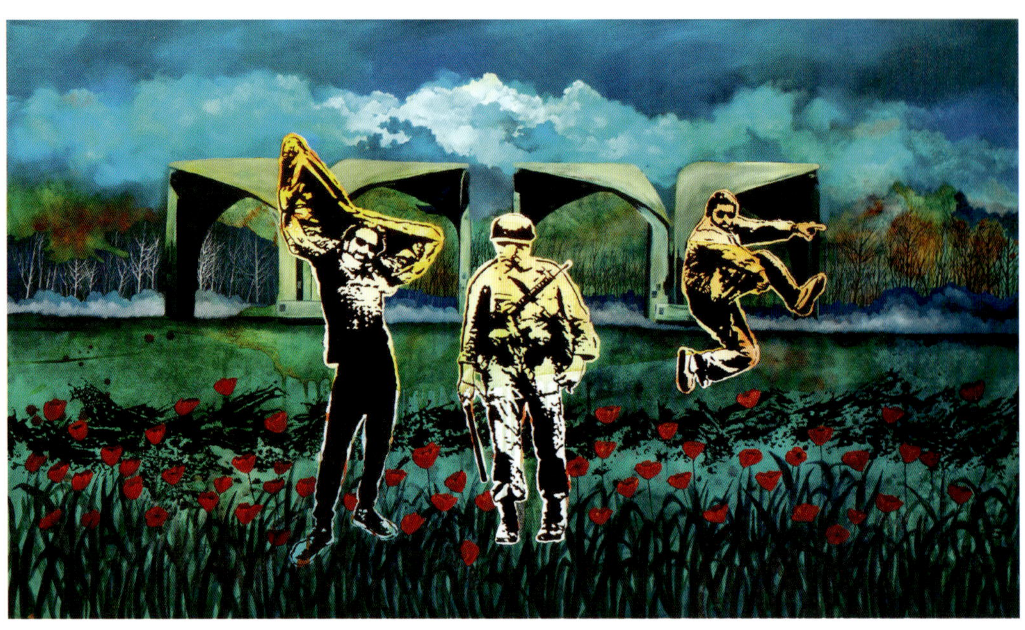

5.62
Mohammad Eskandari, *Tehran University*, 2015, oil on canvas, 130×220 cm, courtesy the artist

specific group within it.[56] She suggests that belonging is instead an accomplishment that operates on multiple levels of abstraction. In this context, it is crucial to emphasise the significance of performative processes in shaping experience and identity, including elaboration, and construction.

This concept of performativity has prompted many Iranian cultural activists and artists to deeply consider the formative moments and methods of identity. Regarding identity as performative implies that identities are shaped by the very actions and expressions that are considered their outcomes.[57] Therefore, identity transcends mere definition of an individual or a larger group, but rather emphasises the subjective experiences, particularly experiences of oppression, and the potential for a collectively imagined alternative – an alternative that may not necessarily align with the framework imposed by the state.

These meanings of identity are clearly in contrast with those of the Iranian state. The emphasis on being or becoming, rather than the framed fixity of identity, is the main challenge here, along with the subject position of identity and construction rather than institutionalisation. One can detect the new interpretations of national culture and counter-narratives of the state's hegemonic narrative, particularly in artistic strategies and representations in Iran.

The formulated interests of the state clearly promote particular values as a resistance against the secular cultural norms of cultural globalisation, or, as the authorities put it, 'Westernisation'. This general cultural attitude explains why it has been perfectly clear in official cultural and artistic events that encouragement is given to taking refuge in clichés of cultural authenticity, historical specificities and traditional 'values', particularly Islamic or the so-called Irano–Islamic Shi'i traditions. Any other kinds of approach would formally be sentenced to marginalisation. However, it is said that the sense of being marginalised or threatened, through which identity-

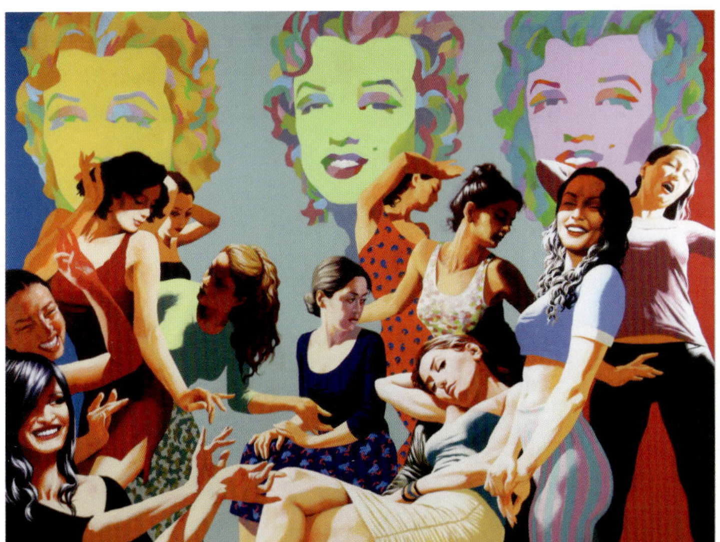
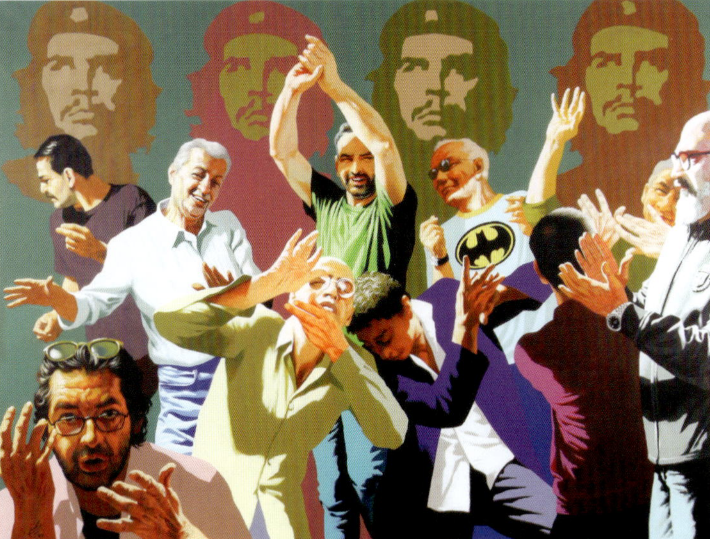

5.63
Mehrdad Mohebali, *Marilyn vs Che*, 2021, acrylic on canvas, 150×360 cm, courtesy the artist

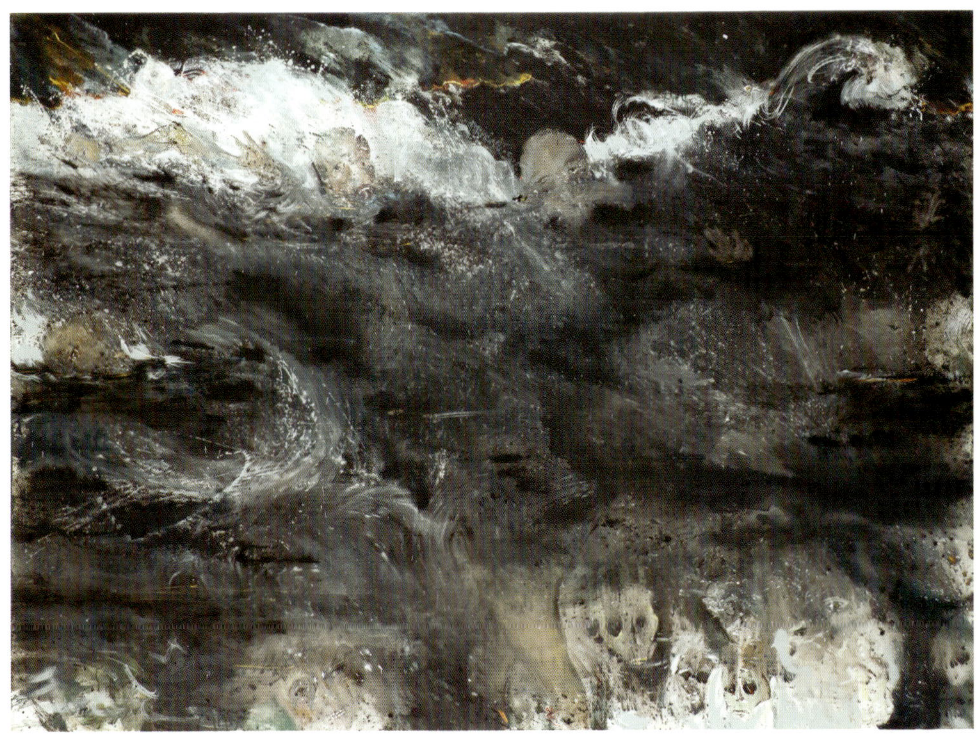

5.64
Alireza Adambakan, *Whatever Waves Throw out of the Sea*, from the *Haftad-o-Du-Tan-Ha* series-ink, 2017, pencil, acrylic and chalk pastel on canvas, 150×200 cm, courtesy the artist

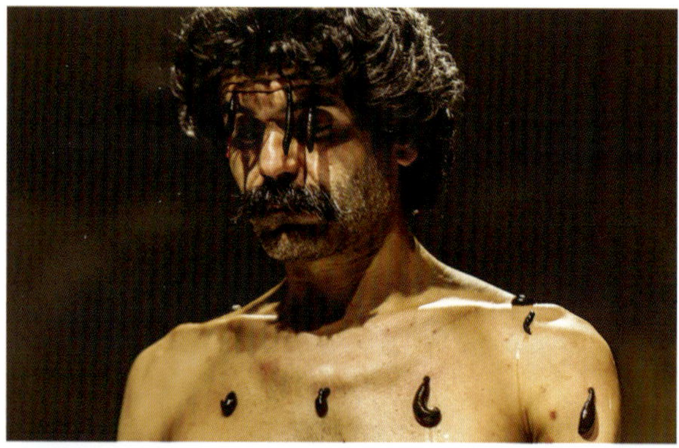

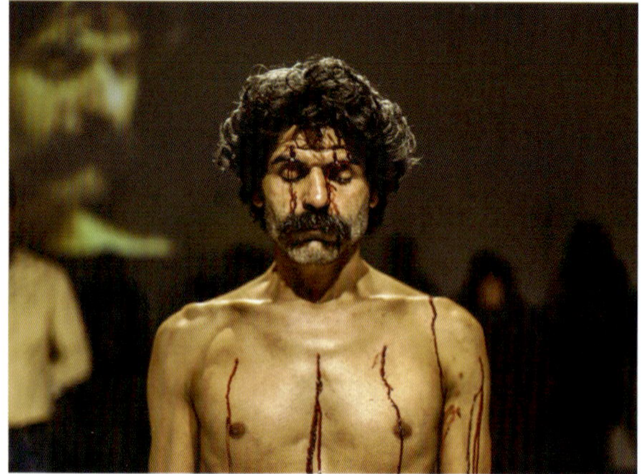

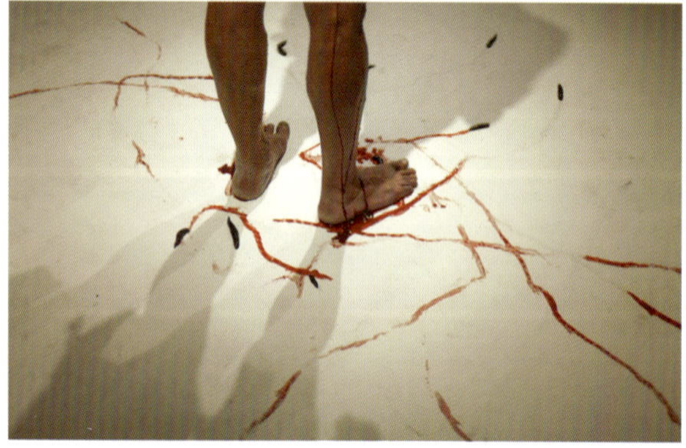

Above
5.65
Amir Mobed, *Upon Us Is What Is Inside Us*, 2017, stills from the performance, Iranshahr Gallery, Tehran, courtesy the artist

Facing page
5.66
Barbad Golshiri, *Memorial of Jina (Mahsa) Amini and the Victims of the Women, Life, Freedom Revolution in Iran*, 2022, digitally created image, courtesy the artist

based political positions consolidate themselves, naturally pulls the subject in contrary directions. An identity-based political position that is consolidated through marginalisation pits itself against the dominant establishment wherein marginalisation occurs. As cultural historian Suman Gupta contends, 'working against marginalization is an emancipatory step, equivalent to striving for an egalitarian prospect.' [58] Therefore, artists who oppose the state's prioritisation typically advocate for their own cultural spaces and alternatives. They often convey meanings, especially through representations of the human body as a cultural medium in their artistic expression, which imbues their work with ideological and political significance within an Iranian context. Consequently, addressing social problems and issues critically becomes a method for artists to campaign against the state's ideological objectives. (Figure 5.53–64) These artists have embraced fluid identities and self-definitions, which take centre stage while hegemonic identities fade into the background. Unlike their modernist predecessors, it seems they are less inclined to approach the question of identity through a 'self-other' binary opposition, as the concept of the 'other' is no longer perceived as homogeneous.

This notion is exemplified in the artist's use of his or her body. The body holds fundamental significance, serving as a central site of interaction between the Self and the world. Through self-representation, many artists use their bodies as a means of challenging cultural constraints, political impositions, and entrenched stereotypes. In this sense, the body serves as a locus where artists and interpreters interact, engaging in processes of meaning-making together.[59] This interaction extends to various forms of two-dimensional artwork, including paintings, photographs, graphic works, and frequently, performances. It becomes evident that challenging representations occurs through the body, and the artists' attempts to reclaim cultural space begin to manifest.

Using a range of unconventional materials, particularly notable in his controversial performance projects, Amir Mobed has focused on addressing social and psycho-political issues. He frequently employs his own body, often assuming tortured positions, while the audience typically plays an active role in his torment or remains as indifferent observers. His provocative performances confront issues of social and political violence – both domestic and institutionalised – agony, human pain and suffering, and totalitarianism as a whole. *Come Caress Me* (2010), *50% Off* (2011) and *Virus* (2013) are among the most distinguished performances that epitomise his exploration of these themes. *The Field* (2011) addresses issues of execution and hanging, as well as terror and depression. Here the artist takes his body to extremes of hurt and damage, to make reference to the institutionalised and internalised violence. In his performance *Upon Us, Is What Is Inside Us*, (2017), Mobed revolved around similar themes. Once more, he pushed his body to its physical extremes to offer commentary on personal and political tensions and pressures. Through techniques of 're-enactment' and 'displacement', the artist exposes the extent of violence that has often been normalised or overlooked. (Figure 5.65)

Another rich example of the kind is the work of Barbad Golshiri. His series of tombstones, titled *Curriculum Mortis* (2013–15), explores the theme of death. Throughout his artistic practice, this theme remains a central focus, with *Curriculum Mortis* emerging as a culmination of this exploration. In this series, Golshiri portrays death through the designation of various tombstones. Instead of cantering on physical bodies, these tombstones serve as memorials commemorating the lives of political activists and young demonstrators who fell victim to institutionalised brutality. Through this portrayal, Golshiri's work epitomises the tragic losses and sacrifices linked to their deaths.

In his (unrealised) *Memorial of Jina Mahsa Amini and the victims of the Women, Life, Freedom Revolution in Iran* (2022), the artist responds to the uprising movement in Iran against compulsory hijab and the state's brutality towards the movement. The work is primarily dedicated to Jina (Mahsa) Amini, a 22-year-old woman whose tragic death at the hands of the 'morality police' sparked nationwide protests, leading to the emergence of the Women, Life, Freedom movement. The memorial features a cement block inscribed with poignant words in Kurdish, prophesying Jina's enduring legacy as a symbol of resistance. Reproduced in weathered bronze, the original cement block serves as the foundation for a dynamic structure signifying both emergence and decline. Each victim of the movement is symbolised by braids of hair transformed into ropes, tethered to sickles in the earth. Multilingual inscriptions of the movement's rallying cry adorn the monument, alongside a polished stone bearing a bronze ear – a chilling reminder of Jina's tragic fate. Visitors to the memorial can immerse themselves in the narratives of resistance, reclining upon the sloping stone and listening to chants, melodies, and the life stories of those lost. The surrounding pavement, meticulously adorned with brass inscriptions detailing victims'

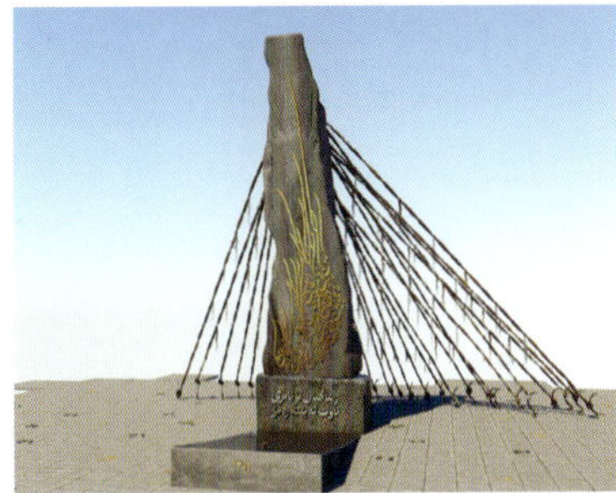
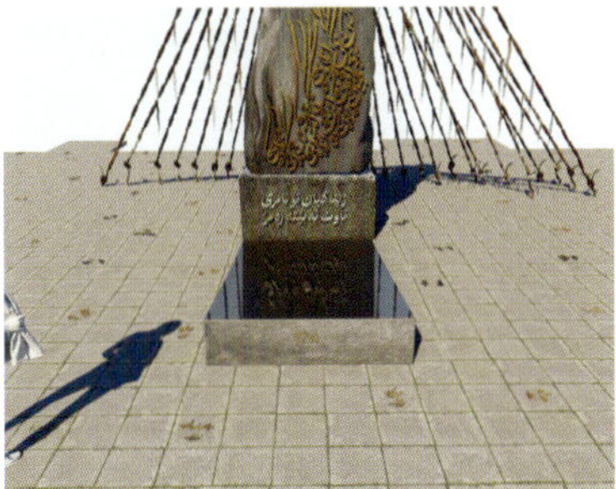
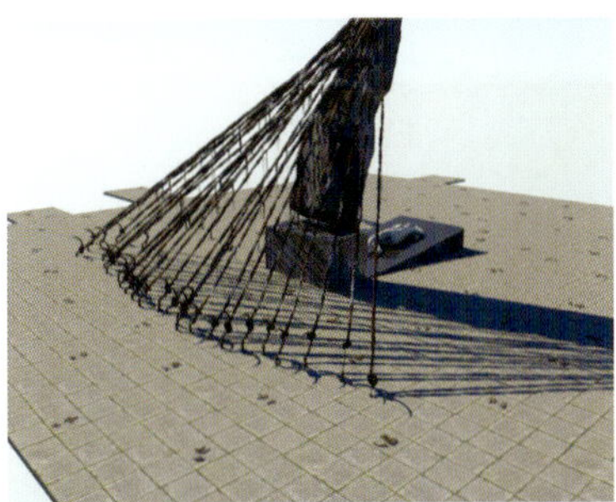
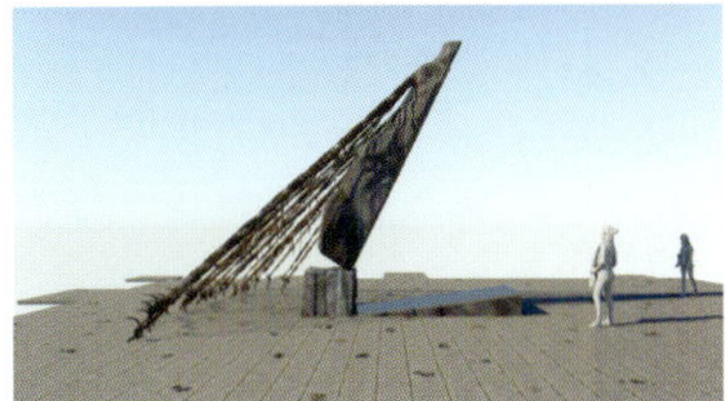
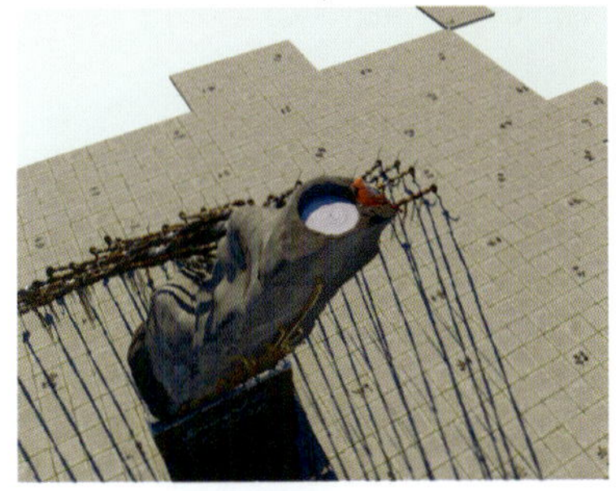
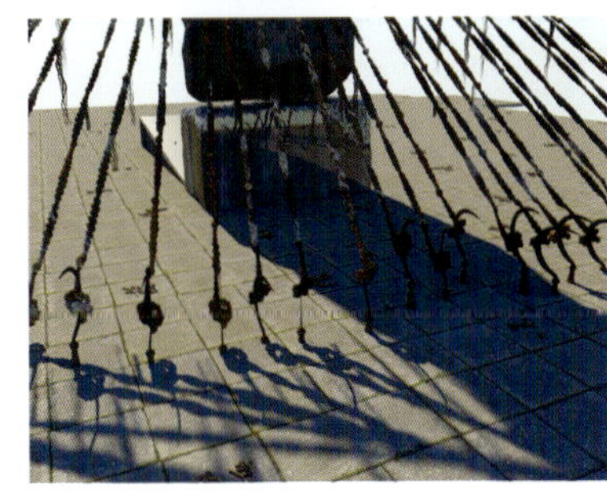

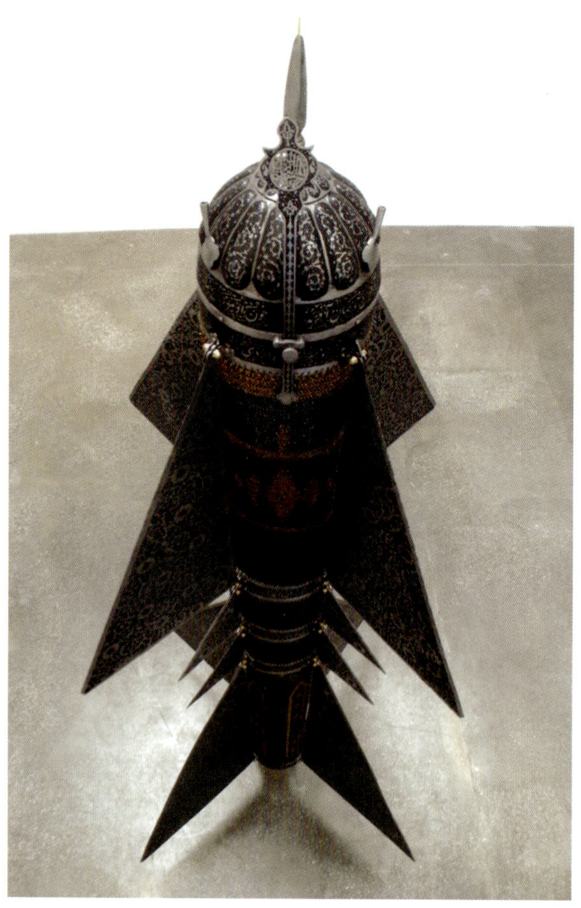

5.67
Shapour Pooyan, *Projectile 7b*,
2012, brass, iron, and steal,
200×86×86 cm

5.68
Iman Safaei, *Abji Khak Andaz*,
2013, iron, 115×120×15 cm,
courtesy the artist

names and locations of their demise, serves as a respectful passage for collective remembrance amidst Iran's tumultuous socio-political landscape. (Figure 5.66)

The ideological authorities often seem very distant from these aspirations and interests, yet have tried to characterise this opposition as excessively alien, socially exclusive and without 'real roots' in the local culture.

Parallel to the state's insistence on the formulation of a specific cultural life, another challenge faced by artists in general is with the so-called 'given identity' connoted by foreign expectations. In the pursuit of uniqueness, artists are usually expected to portray their given identities as safe havens. However, a group of artists have rebelled against this notion, contending that striving to produce art that ensures their uniqueness and sets them apart from their Western counterparts has, in many instances, led to artistic stagnation, resulting in the creation of monolithic art. These artists recognise that institutions tend to rely on narrow analytical frameworks influenced by stereotyping and ethnocentrism, emphasising the visual distinctions between Western and non-Western art.[60] This dilemma poses a significant challenge concerning the politics of visual representation, which revolves around how specific identities are rendered visible. This intricate dynamic highlights the complex interplay between artistic expression, identity politics, and institutional frameworks.

Many artists have never contemplated what is 'Islamic' or specifically 'Iranian' in their artwork, as these labels are often formulated or stereotyped. Even when addressing such themes in their

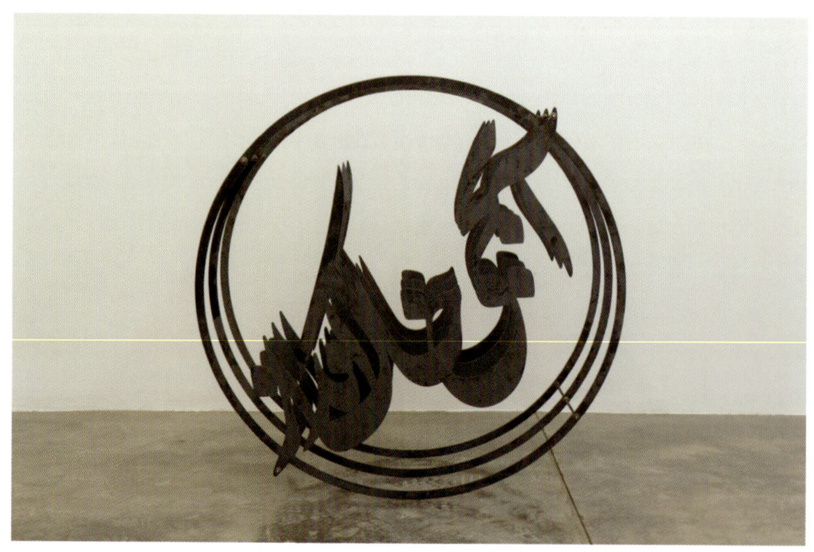

work, their primary concern is not to conform to these preconceived notions, but rather to challenge formulated demands. In other words, when faced with disapproval of stereotyping, artists prioritise depicting their lived experiences and genuine self-expression rather than responding to external expectations. This highlights the tension between artistic autonomy and external expectations, particularly in contexts where cultural and religious identities are highly politicised and stereotyped.

A number of artists reacted sharply against this idea of cultural specificity and indigenous expression in artwork, which usually reminded them of venerable clichés. Artists, particularly those from the new generation born from the 1990s onward, have been critical of the Perso-Islamic stereotypical label. Their critique stems from the notion that while Orientalism is rooted in how the West constructs the East, Neo-Orientalism is based on how the cultural East grapples with an orientalised version of itself.[61] The term 'self-exoticisation' is employed to elucidate this phenomenon. In a radical sense, this could lead to the internal rationale and aesthetic choices of an artist being directed towards an unrealistic and derivative product shaped solely by global hegemonic powers, purportedly for the best interests of the 'Other'.

Even as recent works by Iranian artists have gained exposure in auctions or overseas exhibitions, cultural confrontations have emerged. These issues stem from a subjective and exoticised expectation of what is deemed 'Iranian' and 'contemporary'. While it can be argued that objectivity in such matters is elusive, these judgments often rely on a limited understanding of the realities within contemporary Iran. Themes such as gender relations, the status of Islamic women, and Third World feminist elements have inadvertently become stereotypes, overshadowing the multifaceted nature of Iranian art and society.

This criticism argues that the dominant discourse in the cultural domain has been significantly influenced by the relation between art from non-European artists and the Western art system – encompassing its historiography, market dynamics, aesthetic standards, and critical values. It posits that the more a work is visibly linked to radical or ethnic contexts, the less it is able to express itself as an individual artistic statement.[62] In response to demands to address cultural marginalisation, galleries and museums in the West have increased the exhibition of non-European artists, albeit in a selective and representative manner, often contingent upon the demonstration of culturally distinctive attributes.

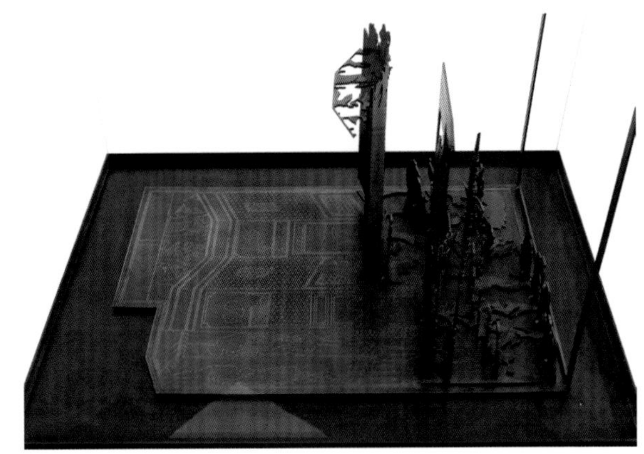

5.69
Shahryar Hatami, *After Sultan Mohammad*, from *The Concealed over the Revealed* series, 2021, iron, glass, 54.6×42.4×128 cm, courtesy the artist

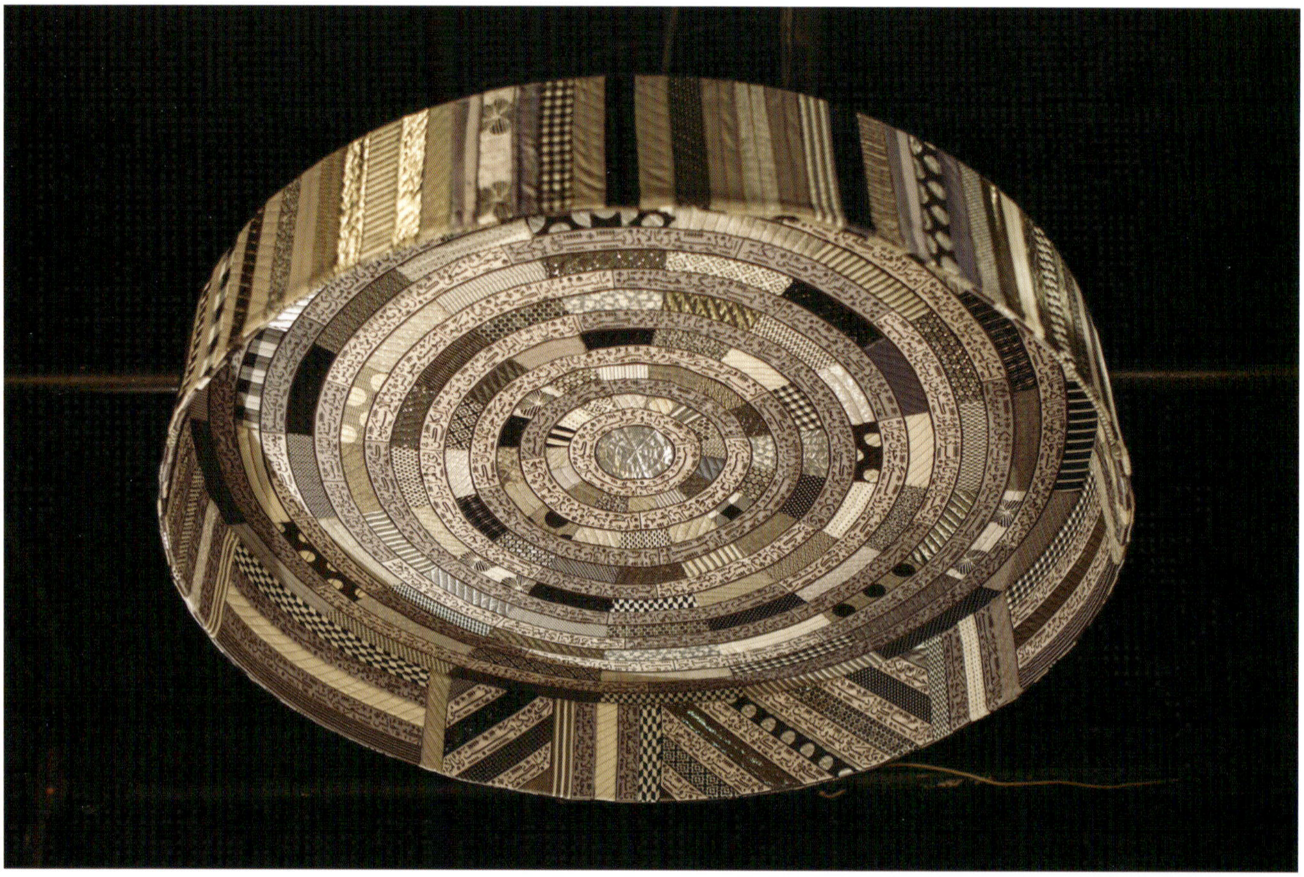

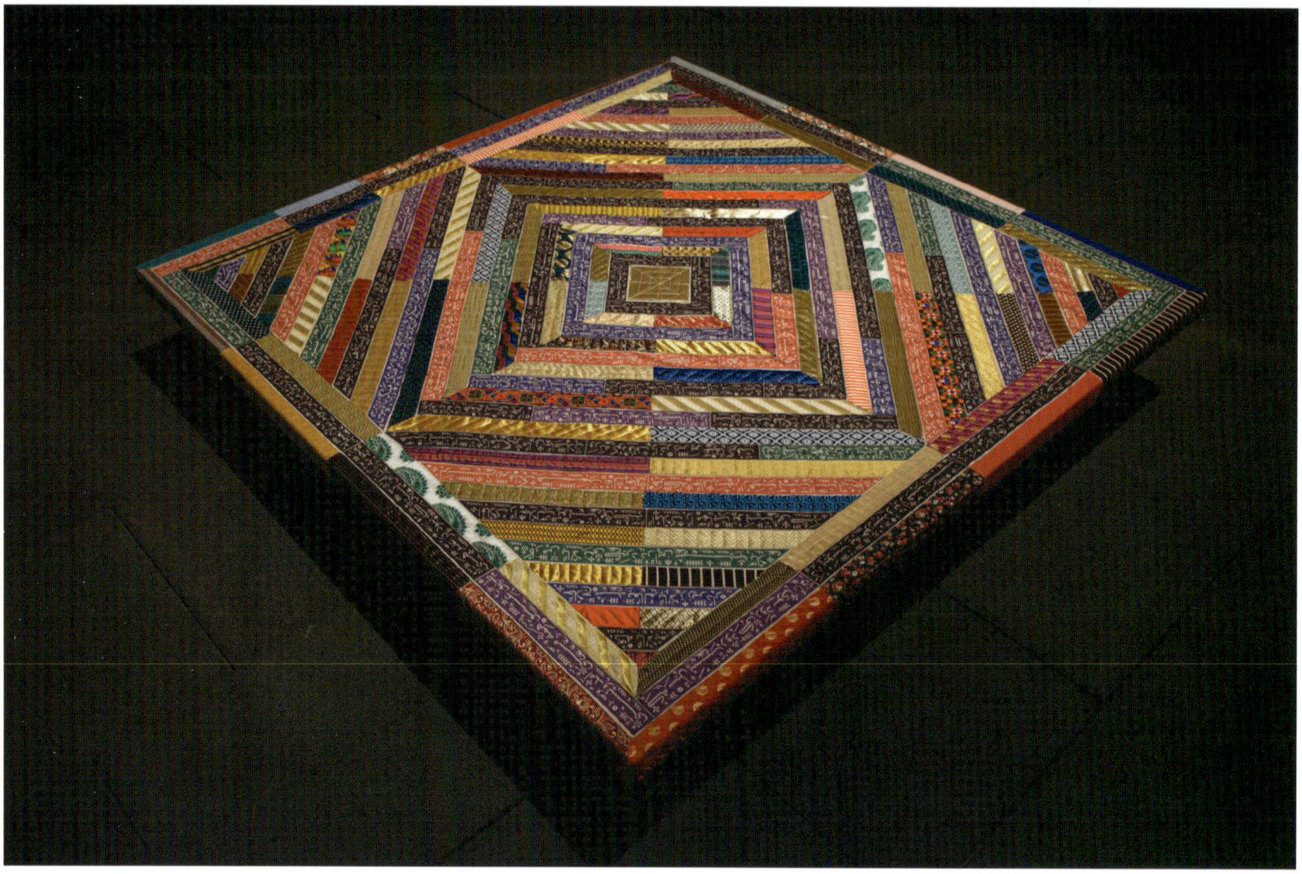

It is at the same time worth considering whether, in advocating for pluralism, non-Western artists might unintentionally be relegated to the role of mere showcases for the 'Other', resembling a kind of ethnic museum. Thus, the carnivalesque aspect of multiculturalism cannot be overlooked and warrants closer examination. What was once termed 'local taste' in relation to an established 'international standard' is now evolving into the concept of pluralism. However, the emergence of a global art scene highlights a notable shift in how the politics of identity are negotiated between the local and the global. Without acknowledging this ongoing concern, artists may be driven towards a pathological production of art tailored for international festivals and exhibitions, ultimately leading to art devoid of intrinsic significance, merely catering to a global audience.

For intellectuals, artists, and cultural activists, embracing the local – meaning imagining and representing the here and now – presents a dual challenge. Firstly, there is the issue of repetition, grappling with how to maintain contemporaneity in what feels like a recurring cycle. Secondly, there is what we can term the 'anxiety of tradition', navigating how to assert local, regional, national, or otherwise culturally distinctive identities without constantly rehashing or rewriting specific traditions or localities. The most

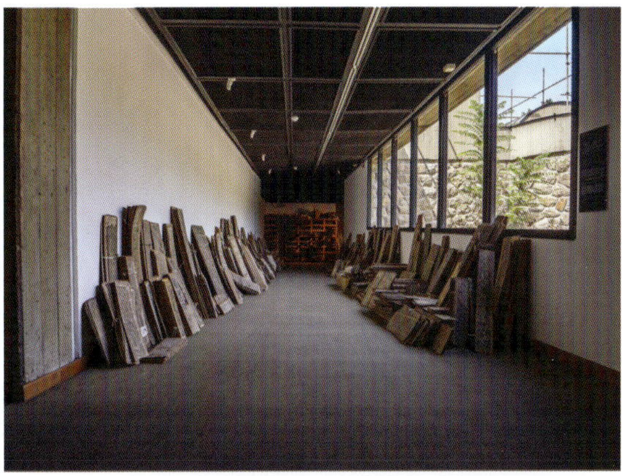

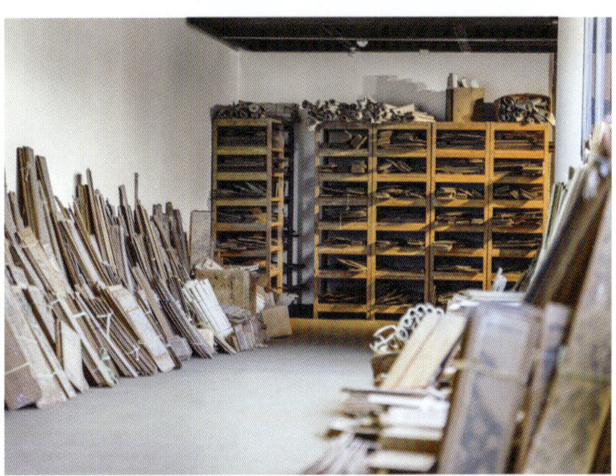

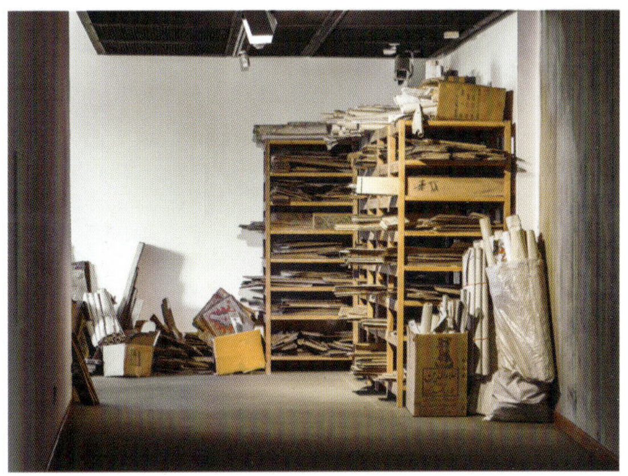

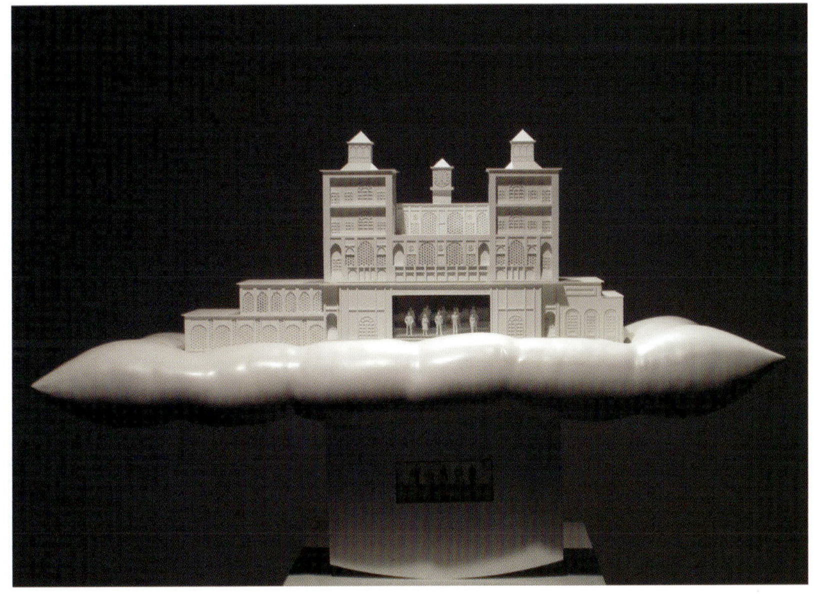

5.72

Kambiz Sabri, *To The Best of My Memory*, 2012, fiberglass, 70×110×40 cm, courtesy the artist

Facing page
5.70
Homa Delvaray, *Neither Up nor Down*, 2020, installation view, fabric, digital printing on fabric, wood, courtesy the artist

Above
5.71
Peyman Shafieezadeh, *Vagireh*, 2017, installation view, found object (original handmade rugs pattern), wood, paper, dust, cardboard, 800×400×300 cm, courtesy the artist

effective imaginative endeavours to alleviate this anxiety and redefine this burden are inherently both cultural and political.

Several artists have explored traditions and the evolving modes of social life, as reflected in the Iranian visual culture or through deeply personal expression. Through their artistic representations, these artists navigate the complex interplay between the sacred and the commercial imaginary. Employing ironic and sometimes satirical language has become a prevalent method to criticise homogenisation and exoticism[63] – an aspect of cultural tourism – and to metaphorically push back against rigid definitions of specificity. (Figures 5.67–72)

Similarly, a significant portion of the artistic community rejects the notion of a fixed, unified identity, instead advocating for a fluid and negotiable identity. They oppose particularism, which entails imposing standardised modes of identity or conforming to singular viewpoints, whether imposed by the Iranian state or external systems, affecting both domestic and international spheres. Instead, they advocate for a conception of identity that embraces multiplicity and fluidity. Recent criticisms appear to address the dissolution of nationalistic boundaries and advocate for an inclusive approach, as artists draw inspiration from a diverse array of sources.

Contemporary artists exhibit a keen critical engagement with the social and political realities, as well as the aesthetic heritage, of Iran. (Figures 5.73–76) Through their works, they employ a language that is often critical, satirical, and ironic, reflecting on various aspects of contemporary life, including the fashionable lifestyles prevalent among the youth and broader elements of popular culture. Moreover, their art explores philosophical questions and themes, such as human existence, identity, and the nature of reality, through the application of visual aesthetics. (Figures 5.77–105)

Amidst a backdrop of entrenched religious ideology and state-mandated revolutionary fervour, the younger generation – representing the majority of Iran's populace – assumes a nuanced stance, displaying neither fervent revolutionary zeal nor overt ideological fervency. Many artists of this generation aim to break away from the older identity-centric discourse that had long dominated discussions of Iranian art. Instead, they explore diverse interpretations of contemporary Iranian cultural life. Through politically astute creations, these artists tackle themes such as generational dynamics, gender politics, social corruption, and personal narratives encompassing isolation, discrimination, and women's rights within the current patriarchal ideological system. This artistic movement has spurred a new trend that critically examines the socio-political and cultural forces shaping Iranian society. The diversity in contemporary Iranian art mirrors the complexity of Iranian society itself – its multifaceted nature, varied expressions, and insightful responses to ongoing socio-political crises.

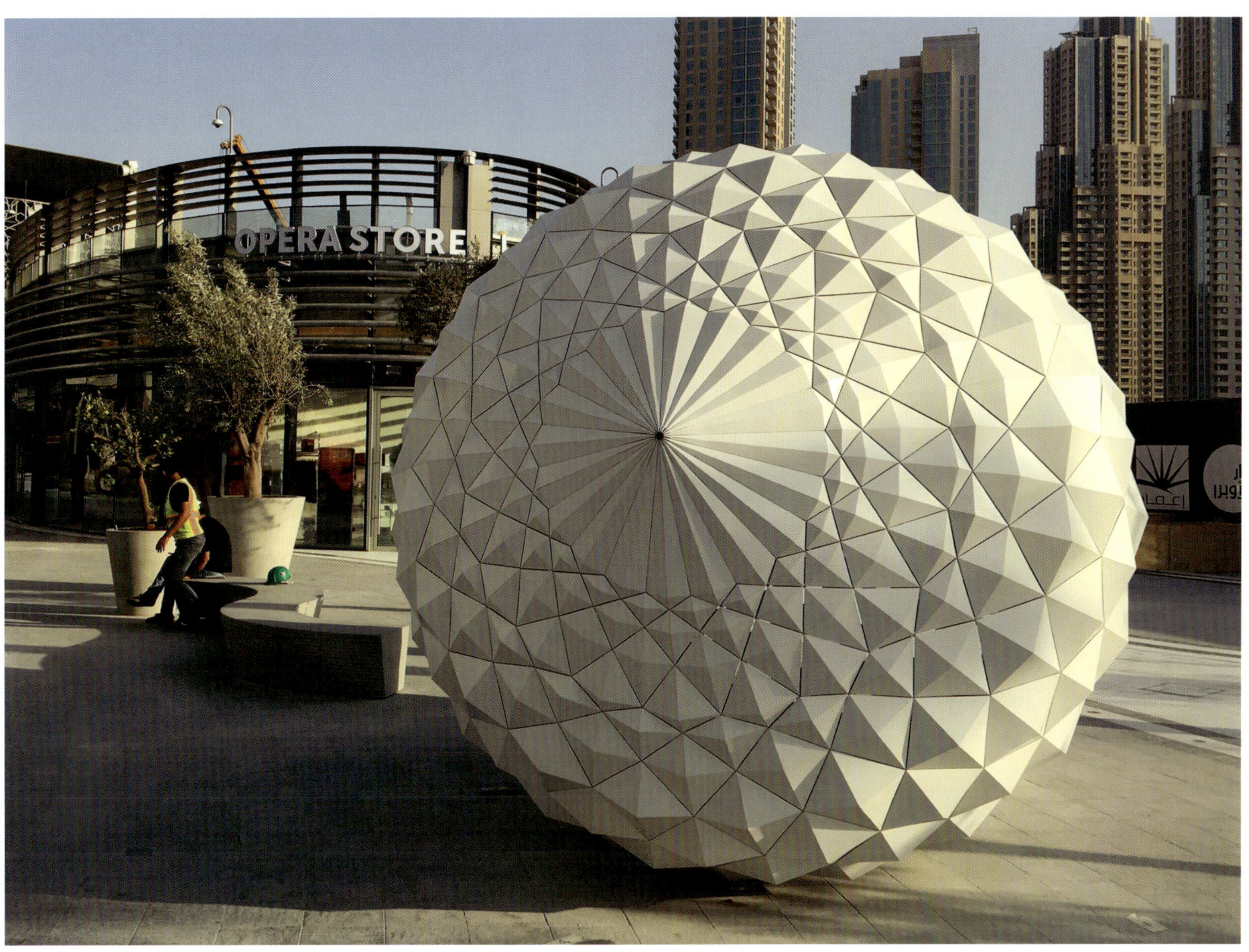

5.73
Sahand Hesamiyan, *Khalvat*,
2014, stainless steel, gold leaf, and
electrostatic powder paint, courtesy
the artist

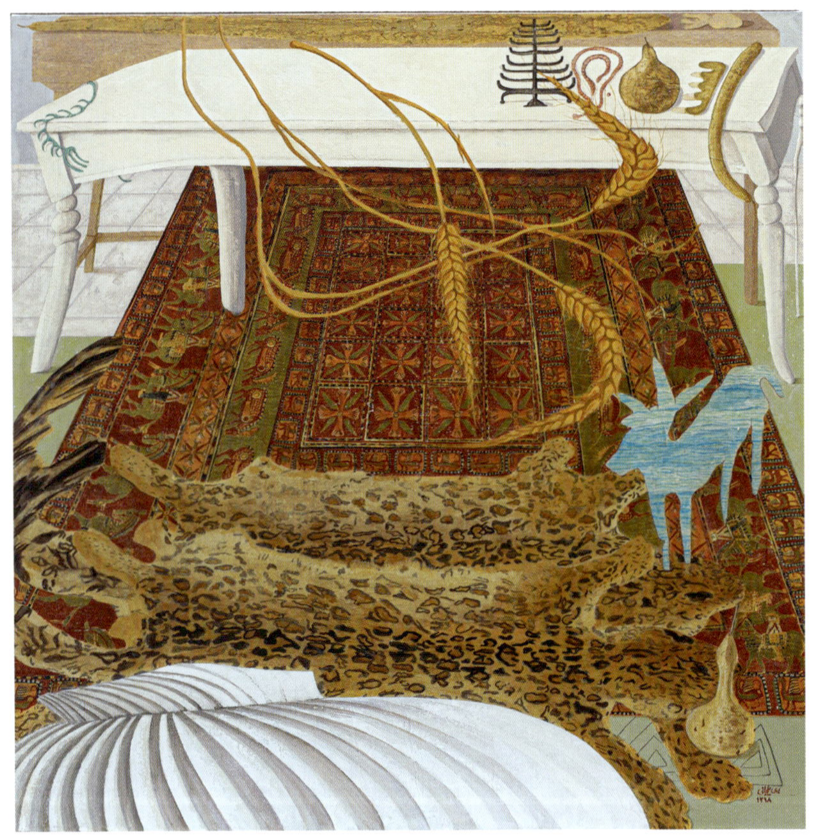

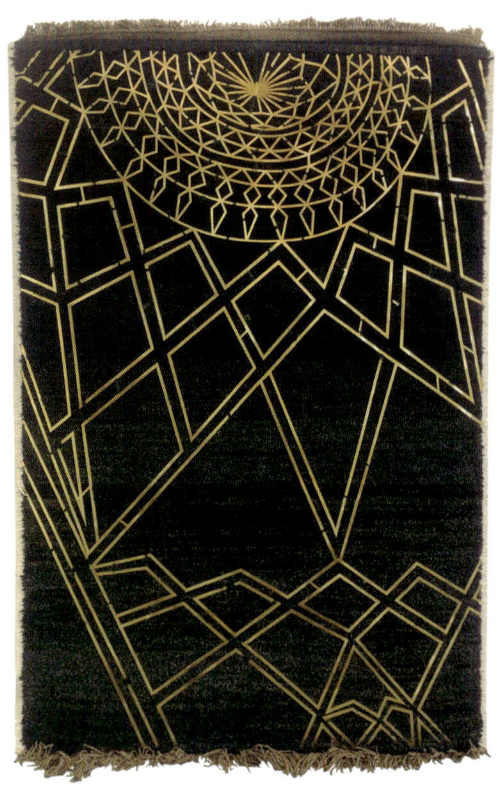

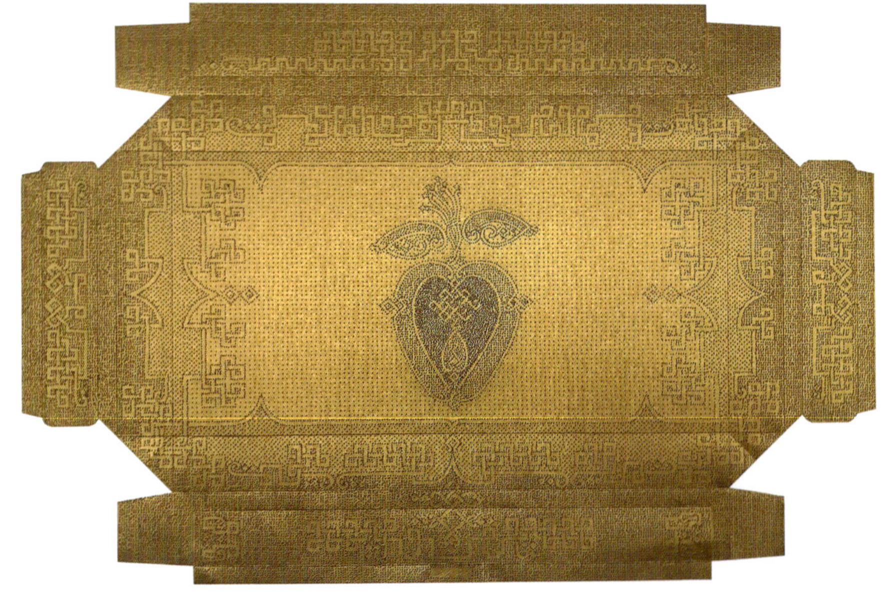

Above: left
5.74
Hadi Alijani, From the *In Search of Lost Space* series, 2019, acrylic on canvas, 170×175 cm, courtesy the artist

Above: right
5.75
Morteza Ahmadvand, *Untitled*, 2022, mixed media, brass alloy and woven wool, 165×108 cm, courtesy the artist

Right
5.76
Reza Lavassani, *Untitled*, 2018, 91.4×62.5 cm, courtesy the artist

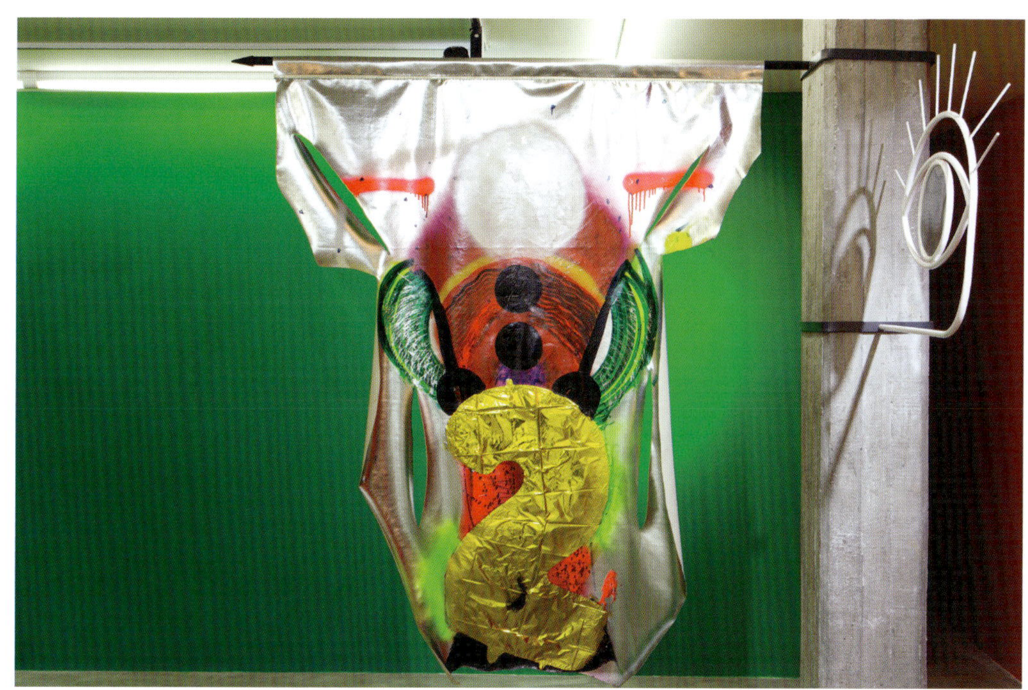

5.77
Maryam (Mimi) Amini, *Self-studies in Flight Methods*, 2019, exhibition view, flag, animal skin, courtesy the artist

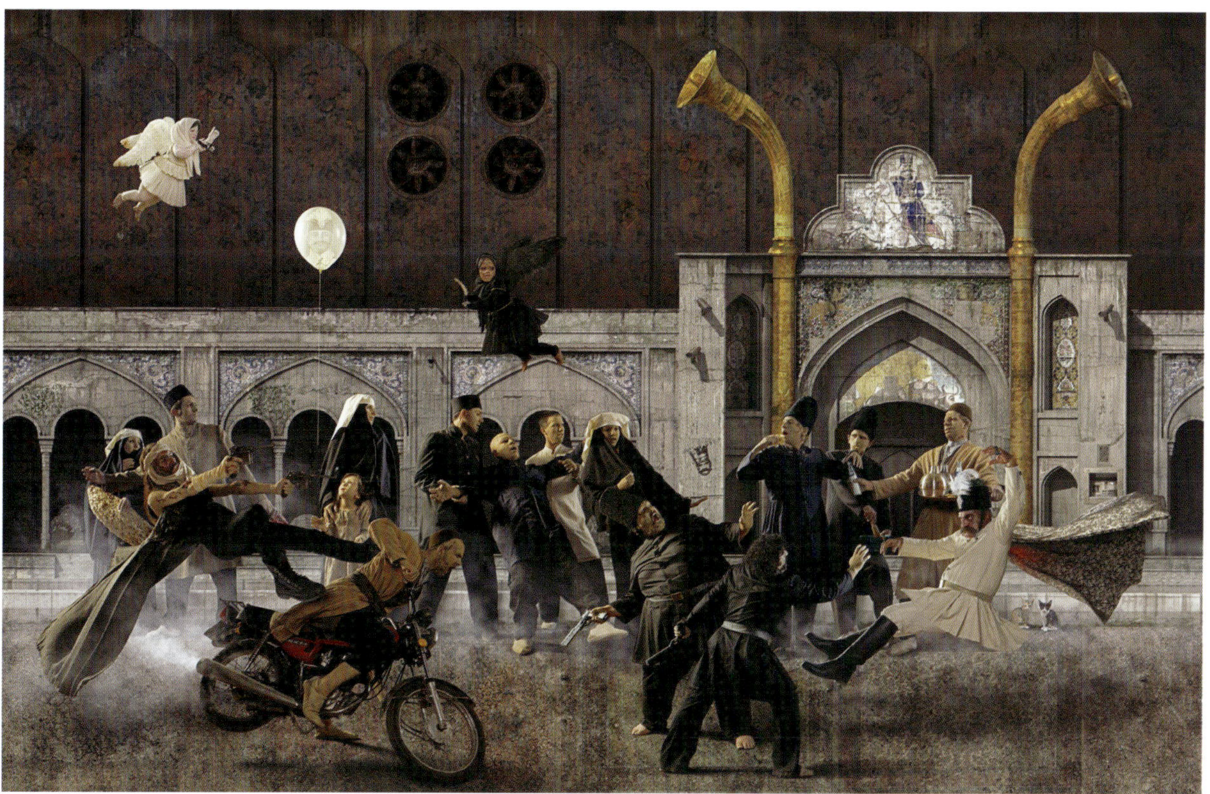

5.78
Siamak Filizadeh, *Assassination*, from the *Underground* series, 2014, 140×215 cm, courtesy the artist

Right
5.79
Bita Fayyazi, *Lenore; Nevermore*, (inspired from Edgar Alan Poe's *The Raven*), 2022, resin and acrylic paint, 35×27×26 cm, courtesy the artist

Below
5.80
Mahsa Aleph, *The Container Made of the Contained*, 2019, installation view, plates made of bread dough, wooden shelves, chair, sulphur, courtesy the artist

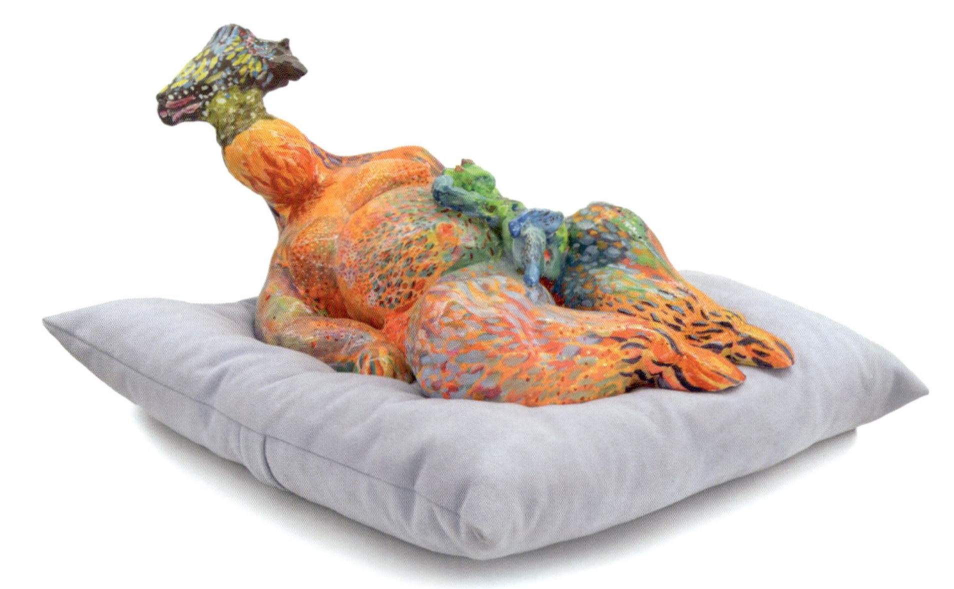

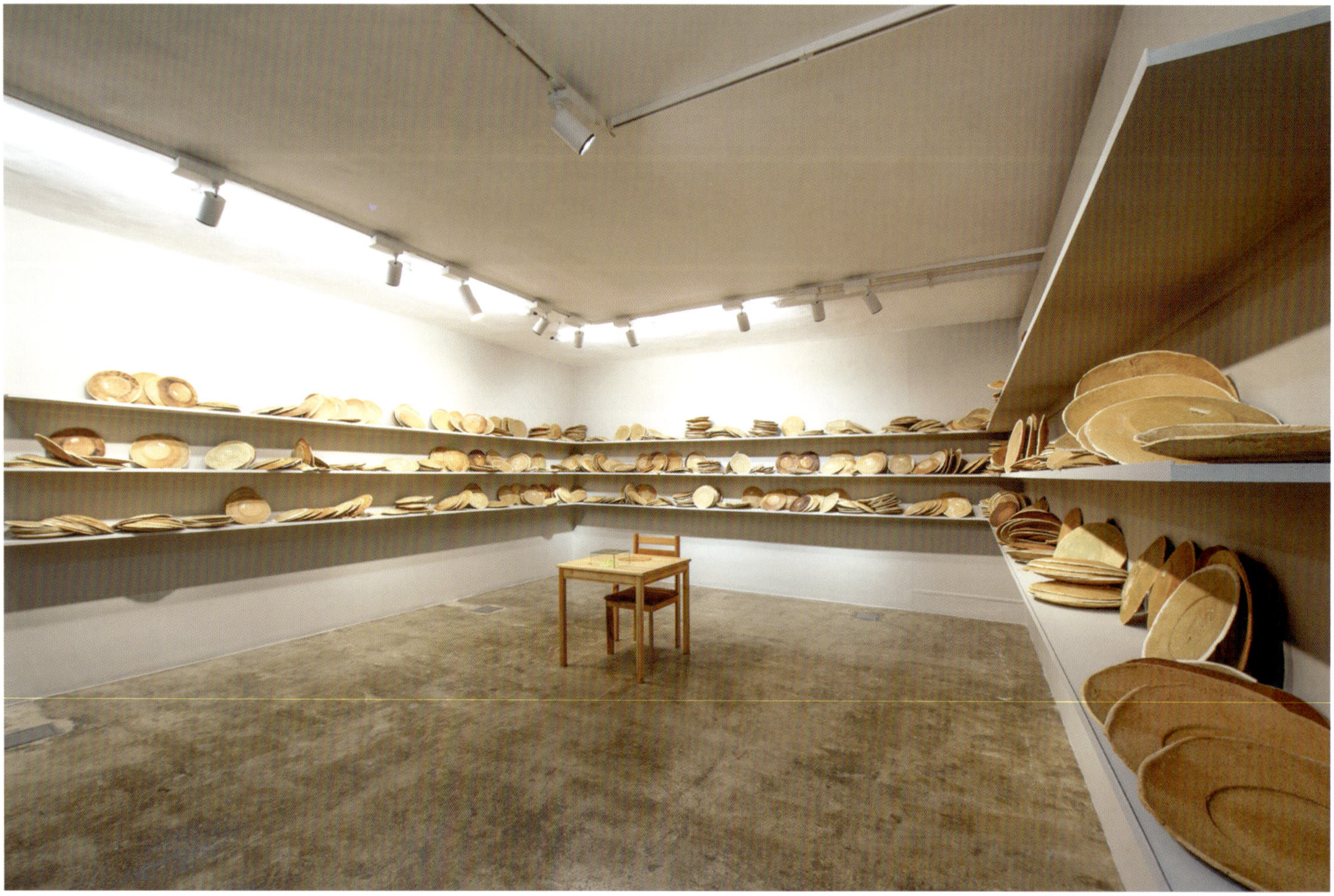

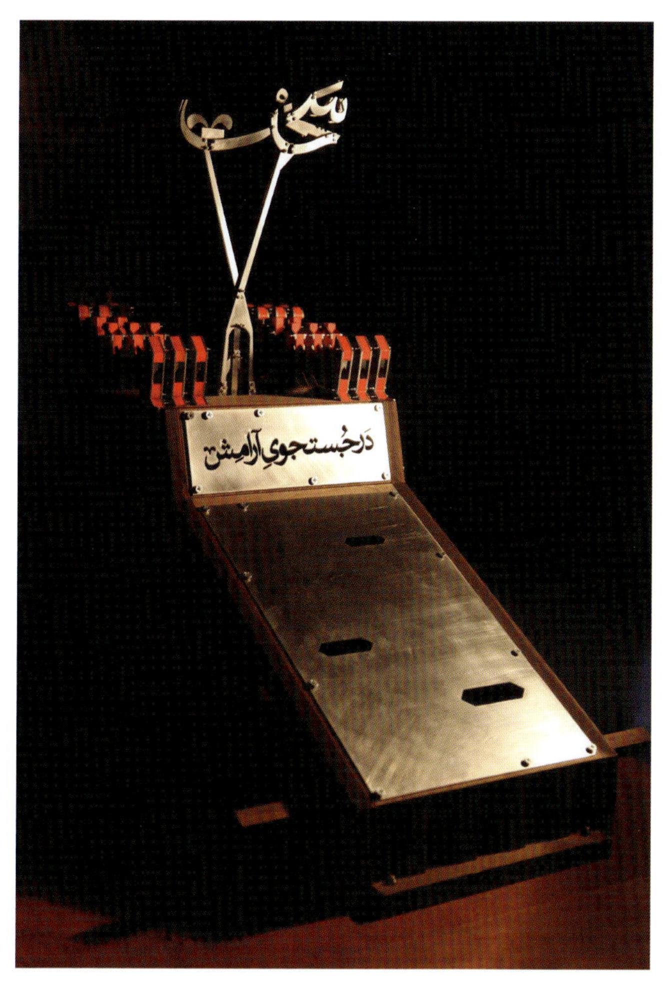

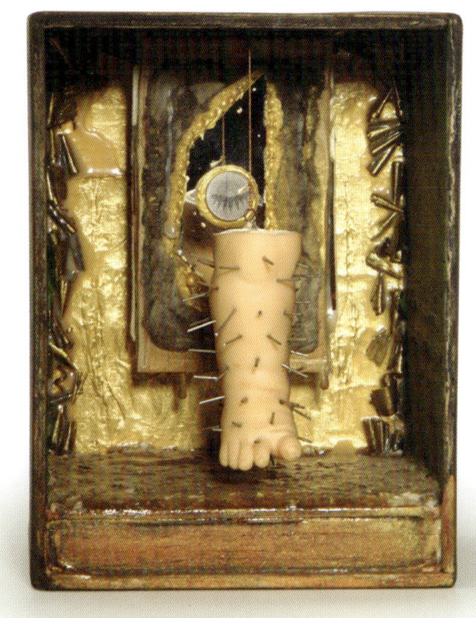

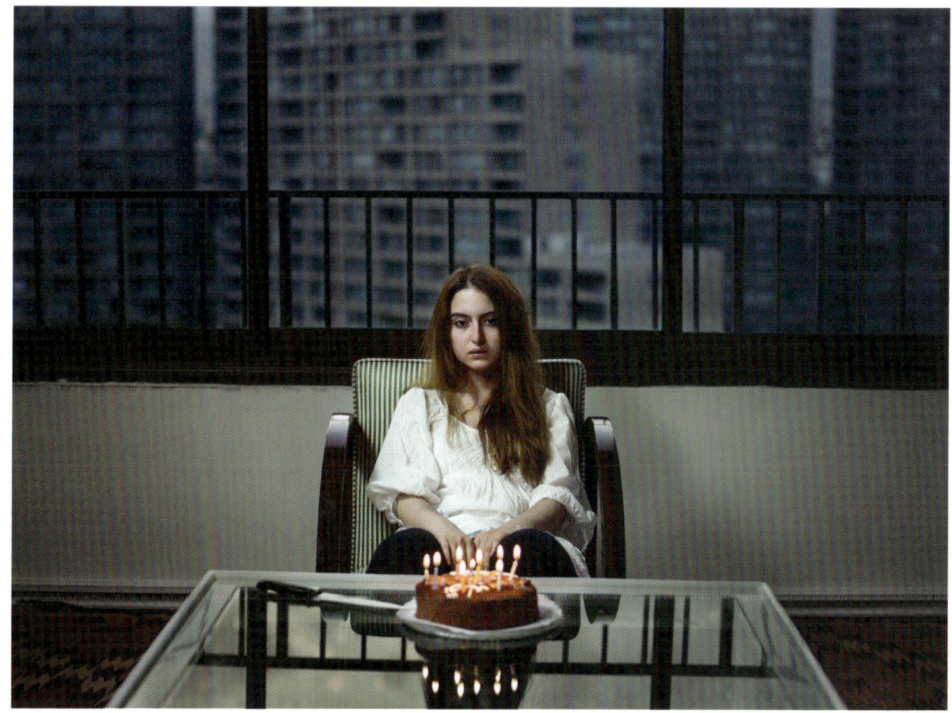

Above left
5.81
Farhad Fozouni, *Mushaddad*, 2011,
66. 5× 43×71 cm, ed. of 1/5,
courtesy the artist

Above right
5.82
Houman Mortazavi, *Untitled*, from the
Stranger series, 1998, mixed media
(found objects, magnets), 11×15×11
cm, courtesy the artist

Right
5.83
Newsha Tavakolian, *Look*, 2012,
C-Print, 105×140 cm, courtesy the
artist

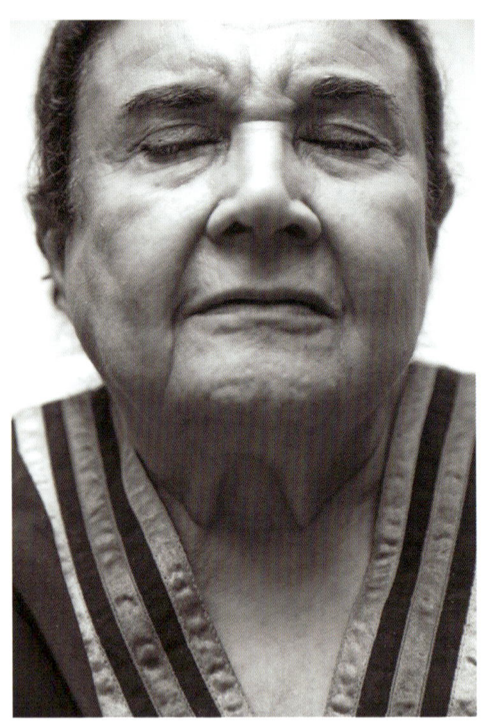
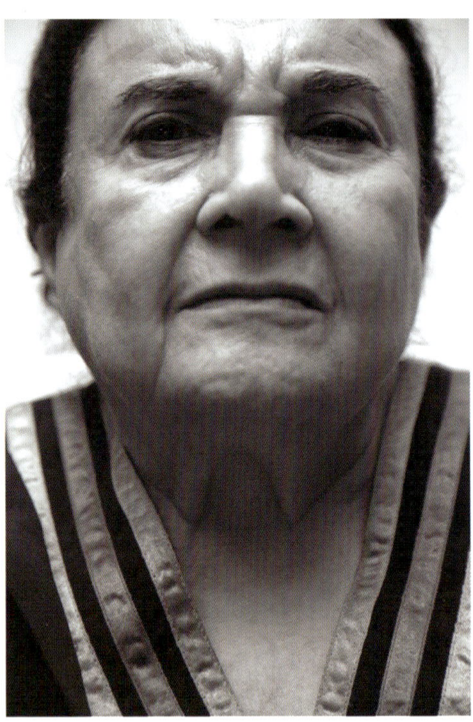

Left
5.84
Mahdyar Jamshidi, *Pooran Farrokhzad*, from the *Ecology of Pain* series, 2016, black and white inkjet photograph, each frame 116×82.5 cm, courtesy the artist

Below left
5.85
Morteza Niknahad, *Untitled*, from the *Big Fish* series, 2017, digital photography, sizes vary, courtesy the artist

Below
5.86
Samira Alikhanzadeh, *No. 9*, from the *Glorious Decay* series, 2020, digital print on fibreboard, acrylic paint, acrylic mirror, wood glue, marble dust and cardboard, 120×90 cm, courtesy the artist

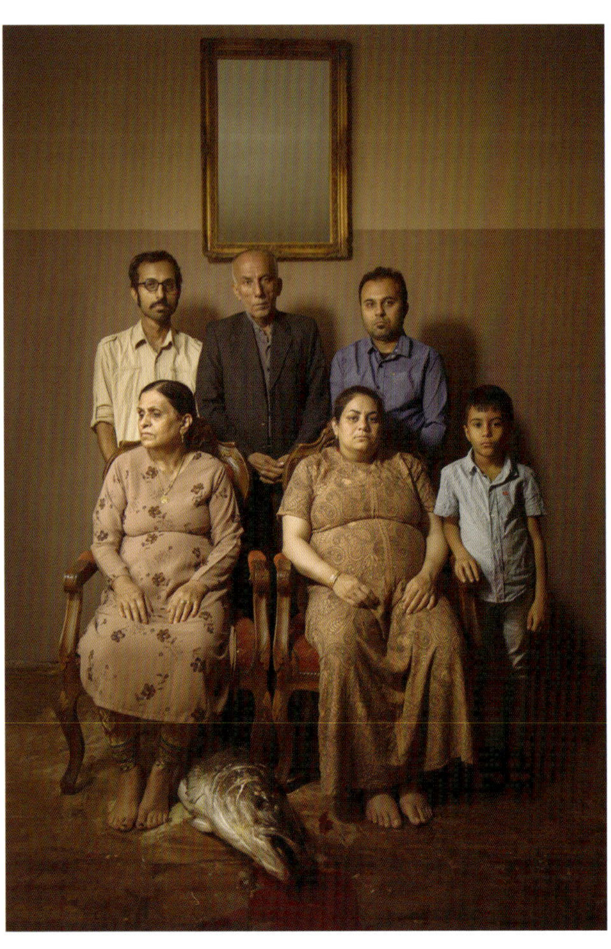

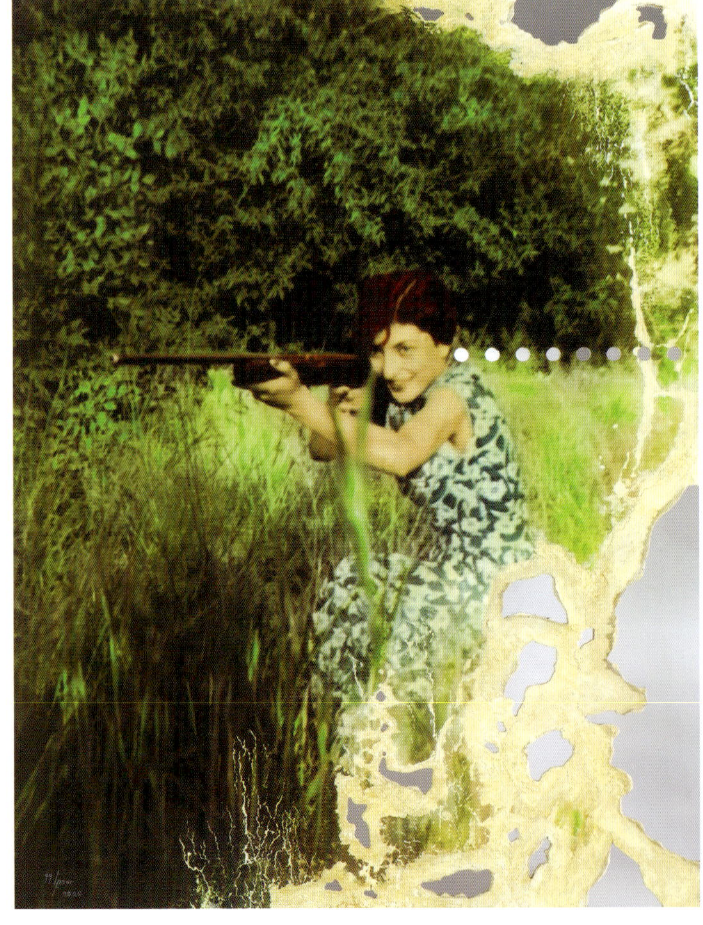

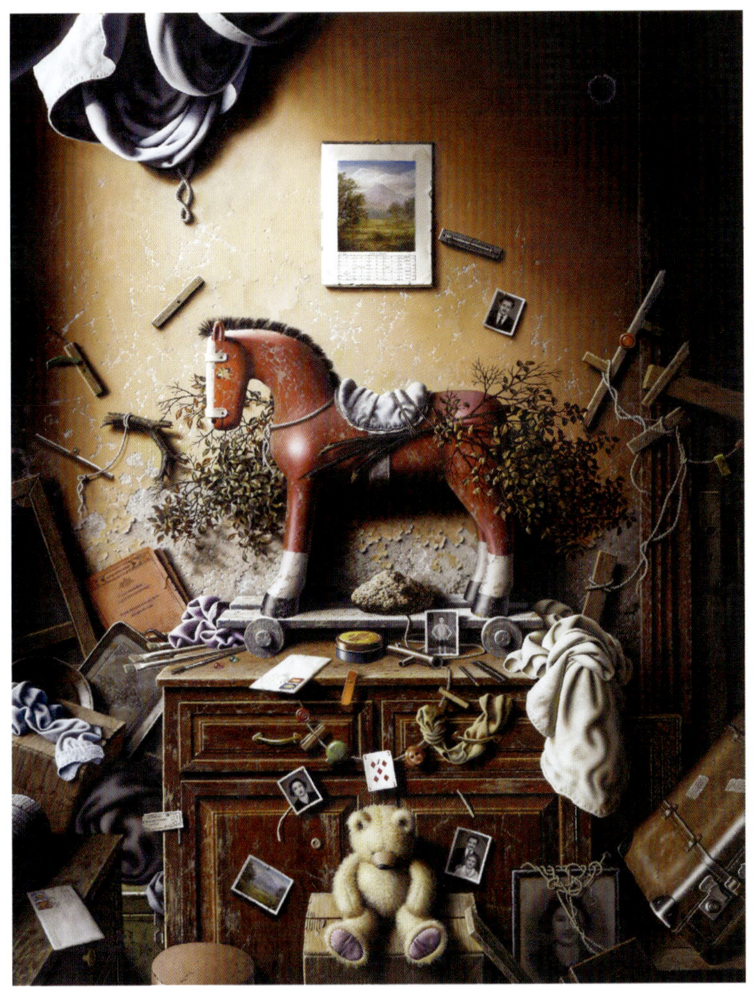

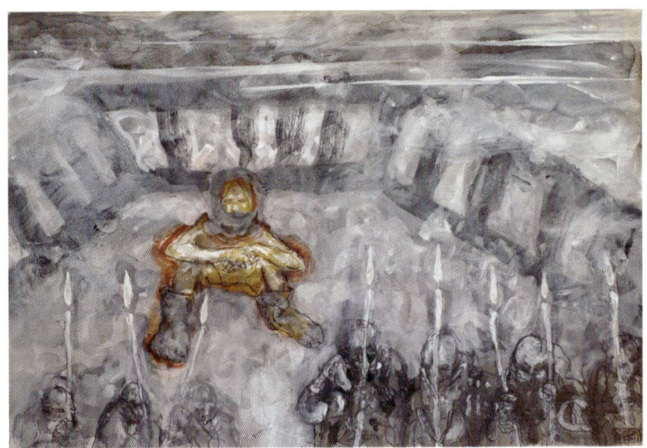

Left
5.87
Wahed Khakdan, *Poker Horse*, 2021, oil on canvas, 160×120 cm, courtesy the artist

Above
5.88
Majid Fathizadeh, *Untitled*, 2020, ink and watercolour on paper, 28×39 cm

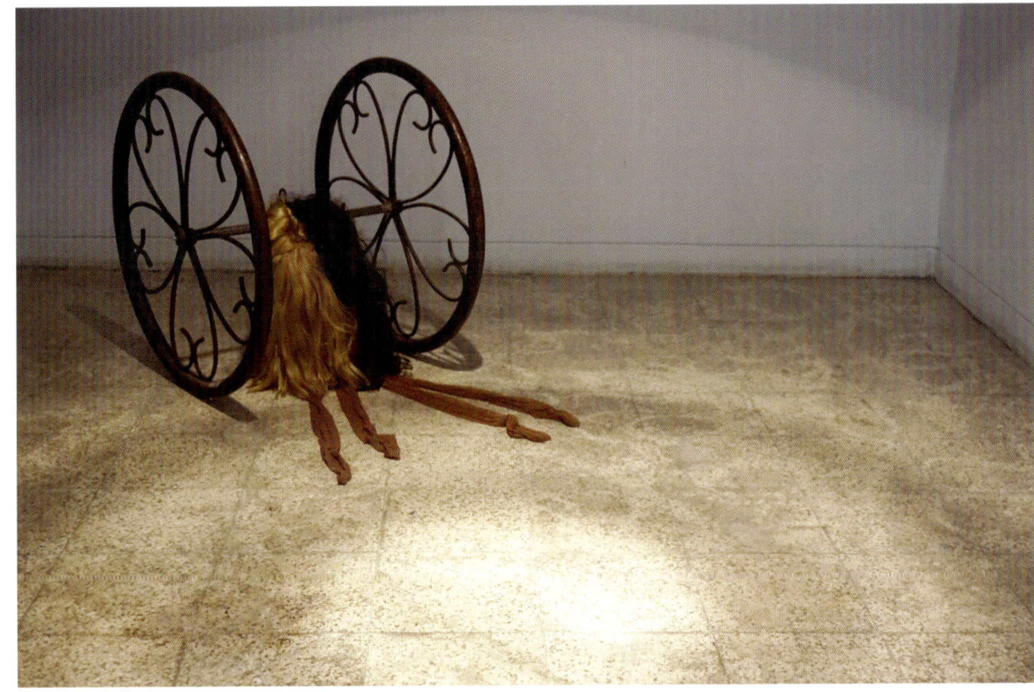

5.89
Nastaran Safaei, *This is What We Are*, 2017, hair extension, bronze, pantyhose, 63×80×140 cm, courtesy the artist

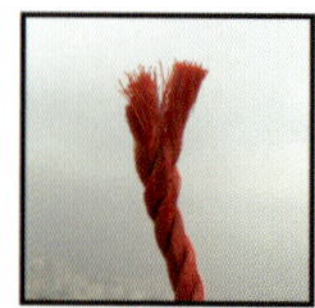
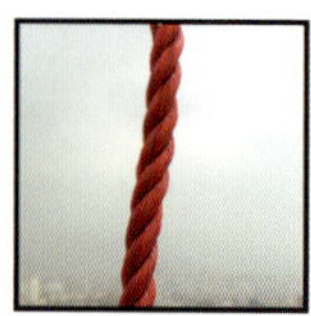
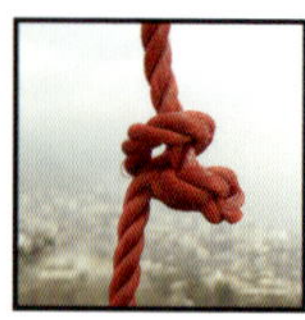
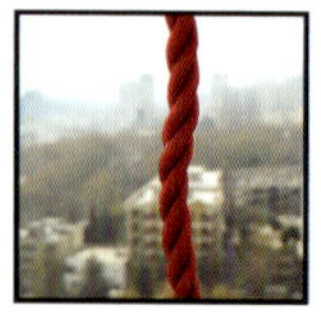
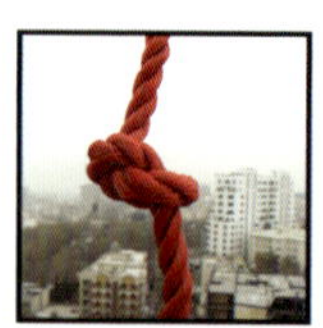
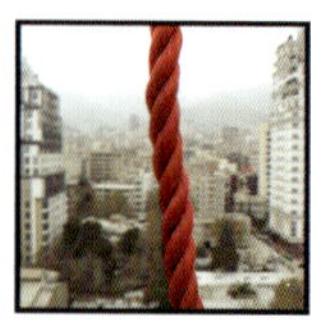
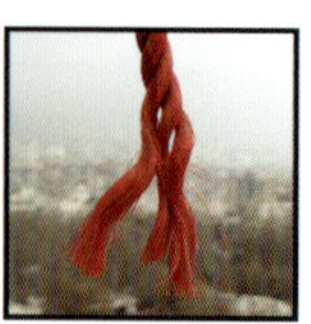
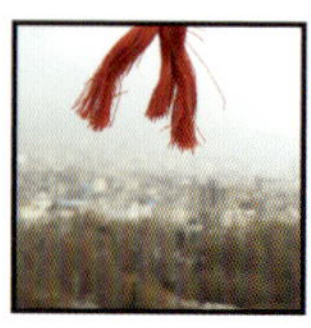

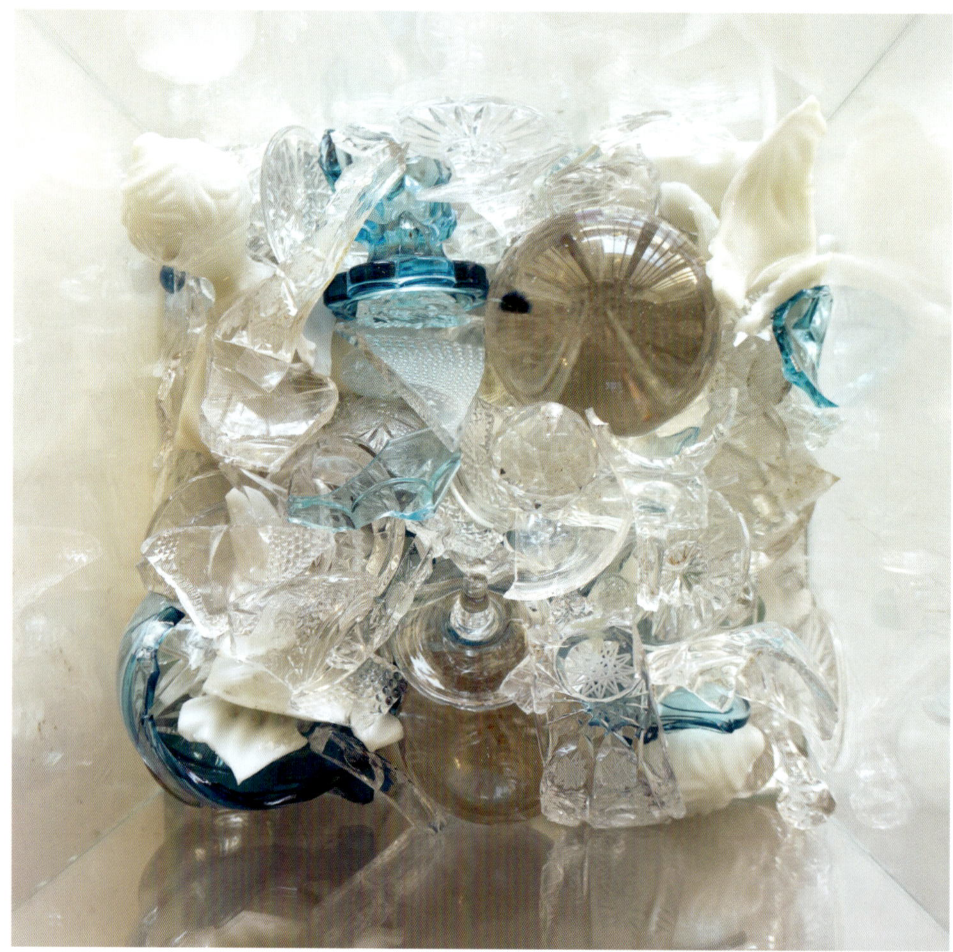

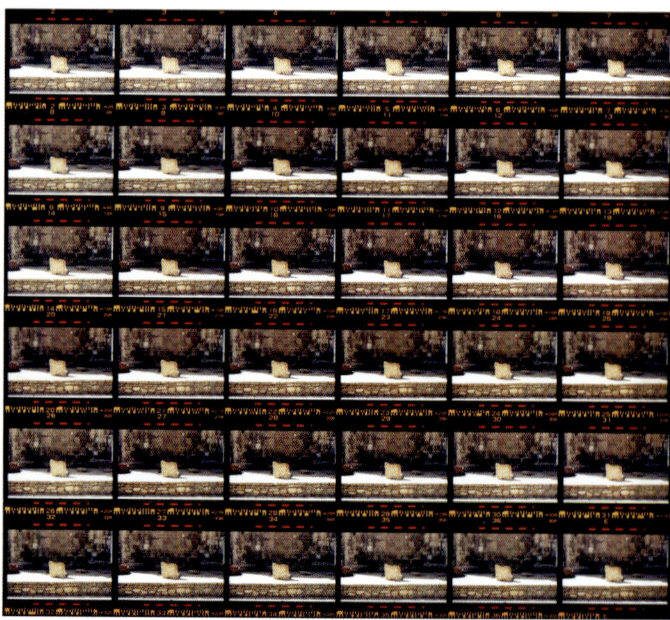

Left
5.90
Ghazaleh Hedayat, *Maar-o-pelleh*,
2012, photo installation, courtesy
the artist

Above
5.91
Neda Razavipour, *Edge of Chaos*,
2015, light box, 120×120 cm,
courtesy the artist

Right
5.92
Mehrdad Afsari, from the *Gradual
Disappearance of Things*, 2012,
analogue photography, inkjet print
on archival paper, 26×28 cm,
courtesy the artist

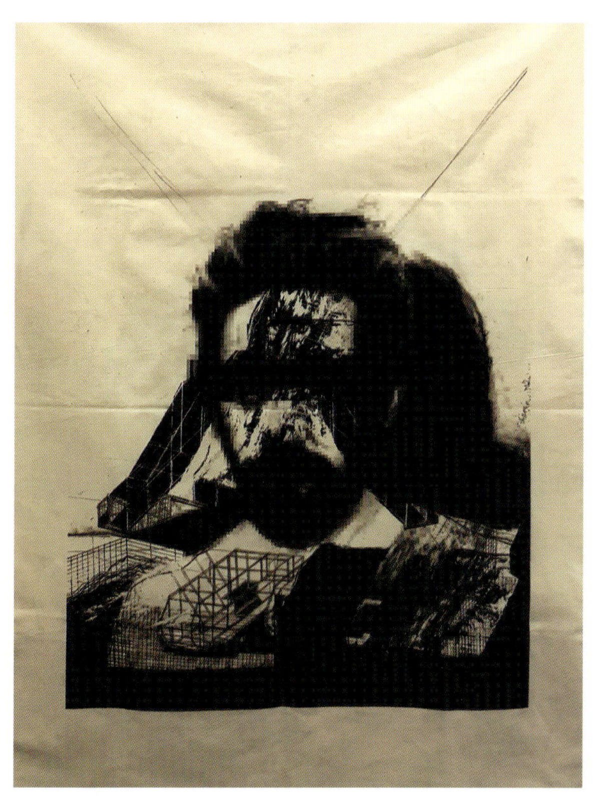

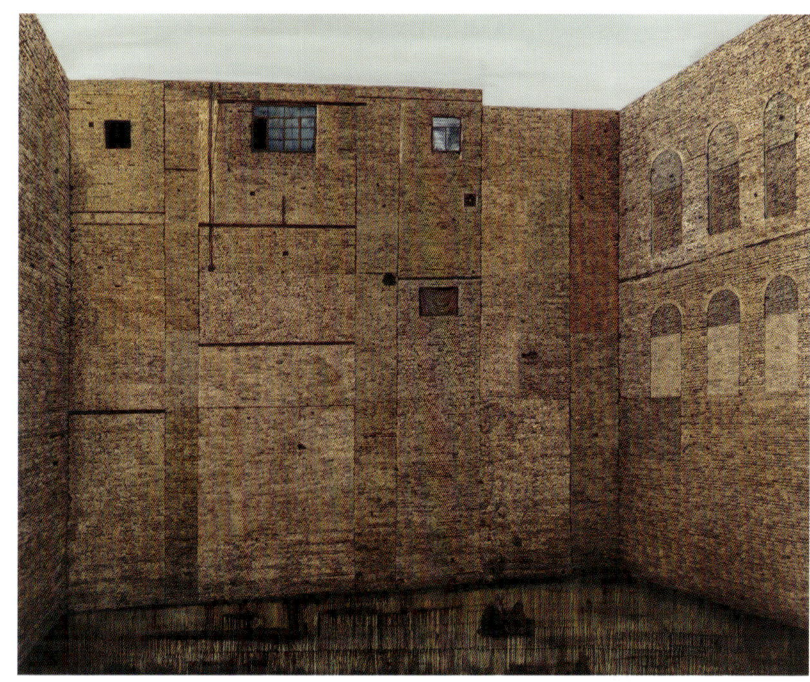

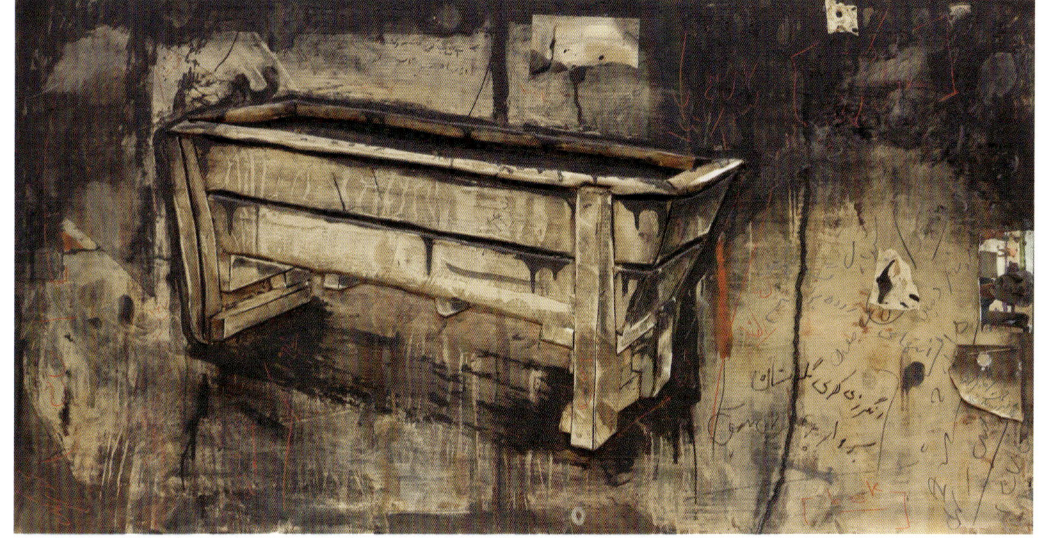

Above left
5.93
Baktash Sarang Javanbakht, *Self-portrait*, 2018, Digital printing on cotton fabric, UV Flatbed Printer, 134×98 cm, courtesy the artist

Right
5.94
Mojtaba Amini, *The Chronicles of Intermingled Masses*, 2018, paper, wood and organic glue on canvas, each piece 71×131 cm, courtesy the artist

Above right
5.95
Javad Modaresi, *The Day Off*, 2020, oil on canvas, 150×180 cm, courtesy the artist

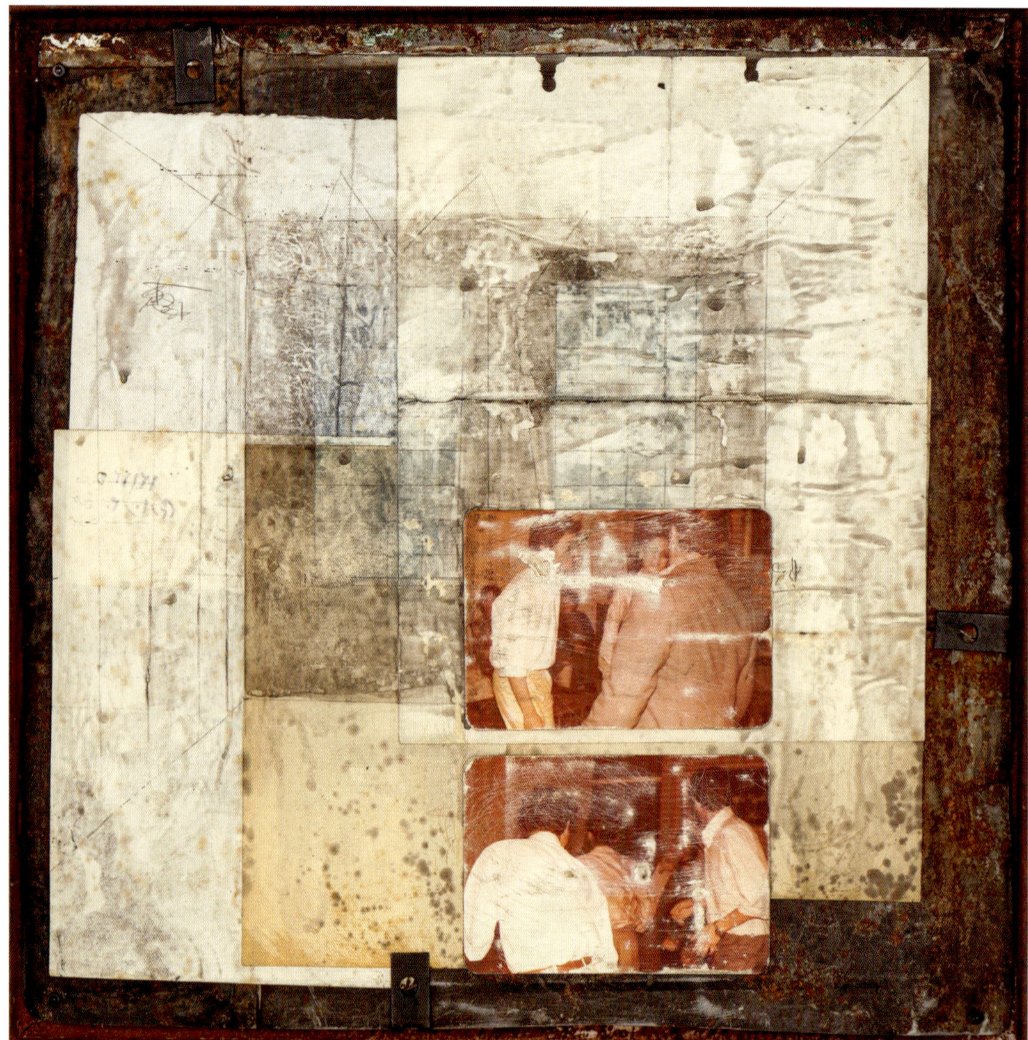

5.96
Majid Biglari, *Imaginary Friends*, from the *Soot, Fog, Soil* series, 2021, mixed media: tin, paper, letters, photographs, watercolour, water-based paint, pencil, 42×41 cm, courtesy the artist

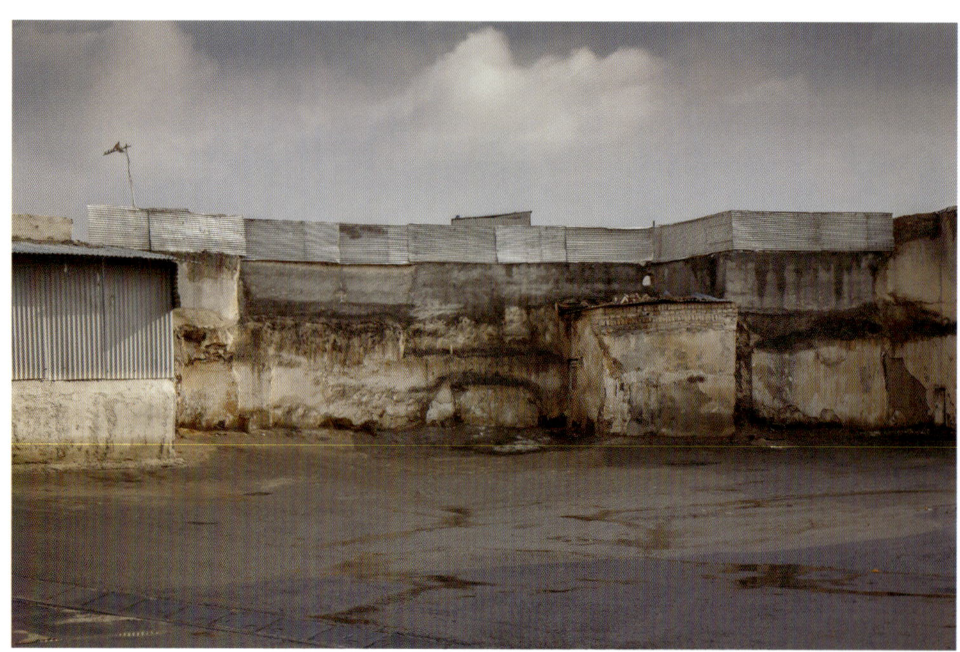

5.97
Mehdi Vosoughnia, *Untitled*, from the *Pamenar* series, 2013, digital print on chemical print, 24×36 cm, courtesy the artist

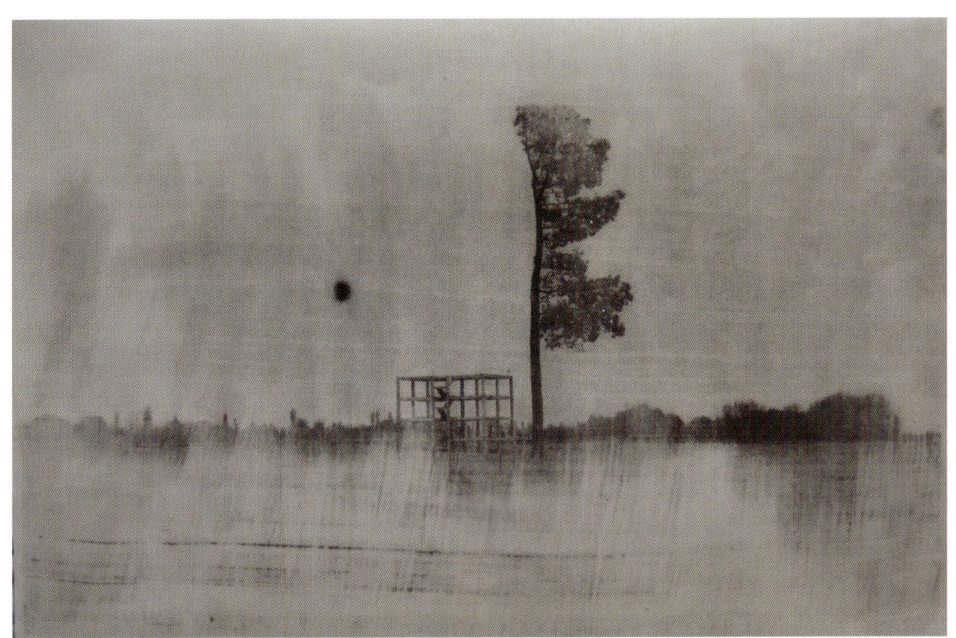

5.98
Babak Kazemi, from the *Captives* series, 2020, gum print on photographic paper, 35×50 cm, courtesy the artist

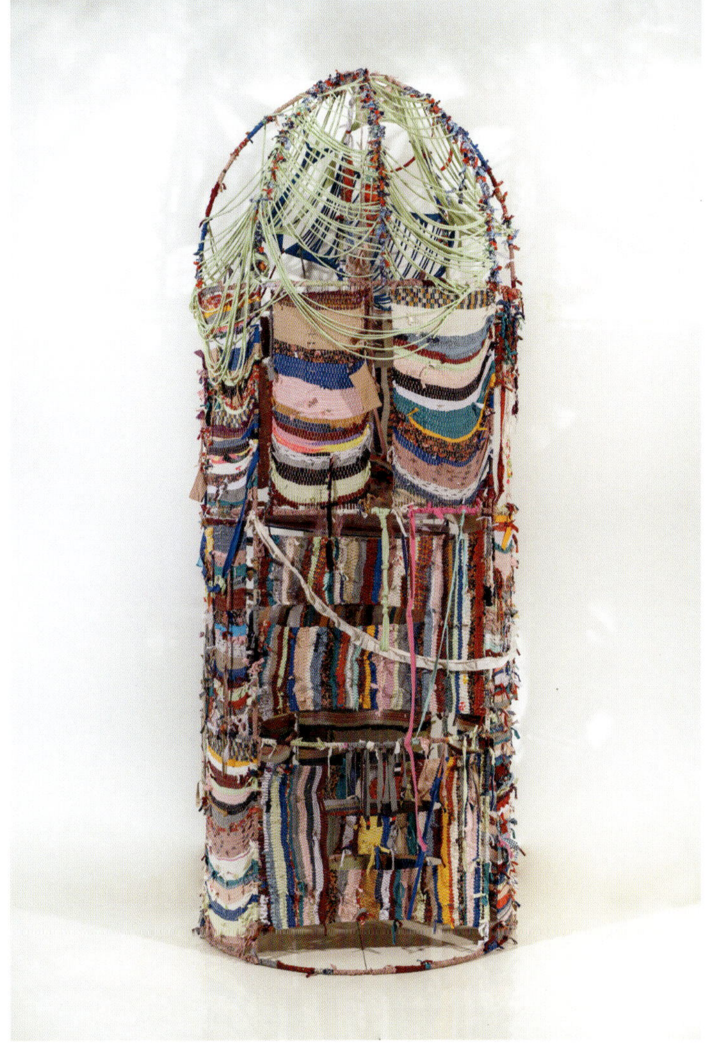

Above
5.99
Mehrdad Naraghi, *Untitled,* from *The City* series, Tehran, 2014, 20×30 cm, courtesy the artist

Right
5.100
Shirin Mellatgohar, from the *Relics* series, 2021, mixed media discarded clothes and metal, 240×90×90 cm, courtesy the artist

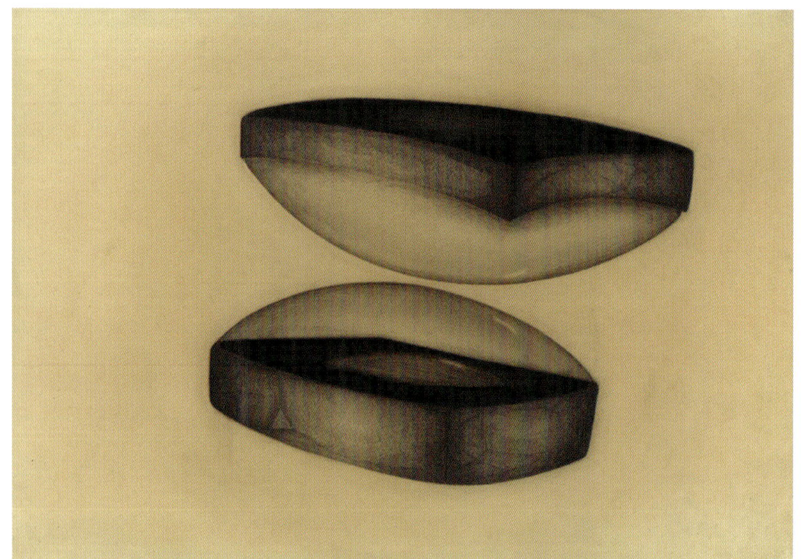

5.101
Arash Fesharaki, *Untitled*, 2020,
pencil on paper, 30×40 cm,
courtesy the artist

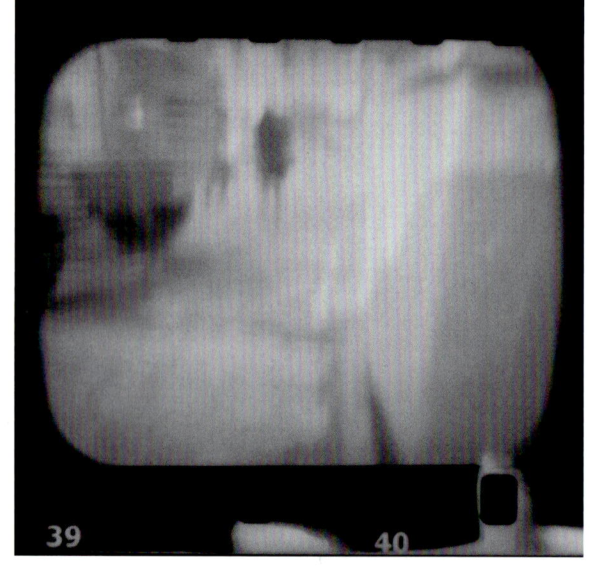

5.102
Sina Boroumandi, *Untitled*, 2019,
inkjet print, 250×260 cm, courtesy
the artist

5.103
Mohammad Hossein Emad, *Inhale*,
2017, fabric, tarpaulin and wood,
36×26×45 cm, courtesy the artist

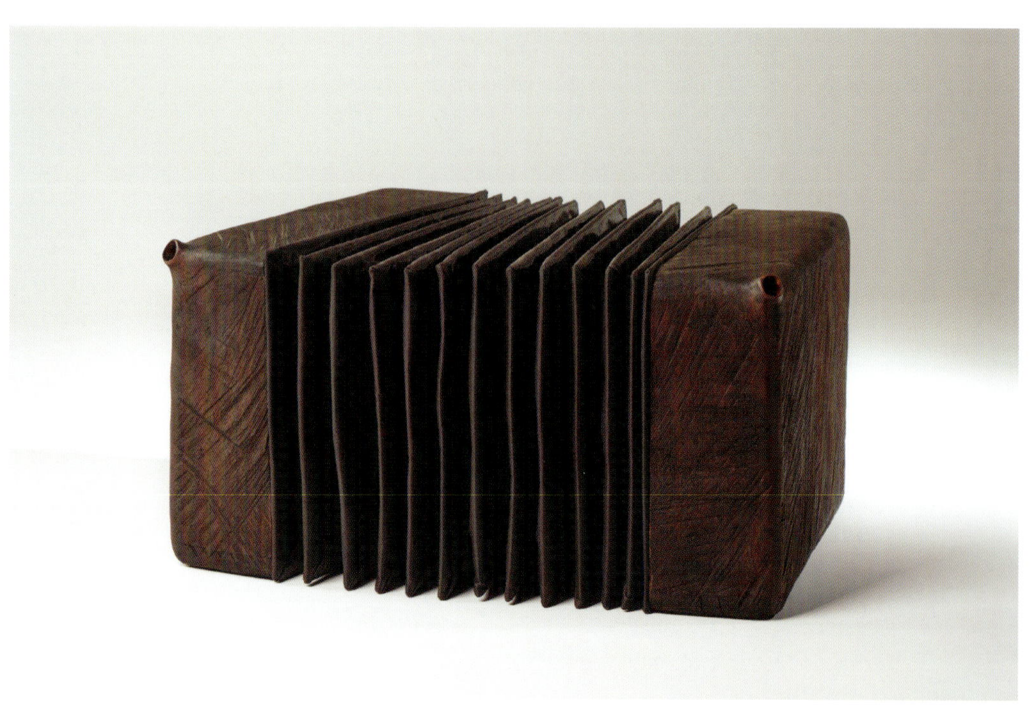

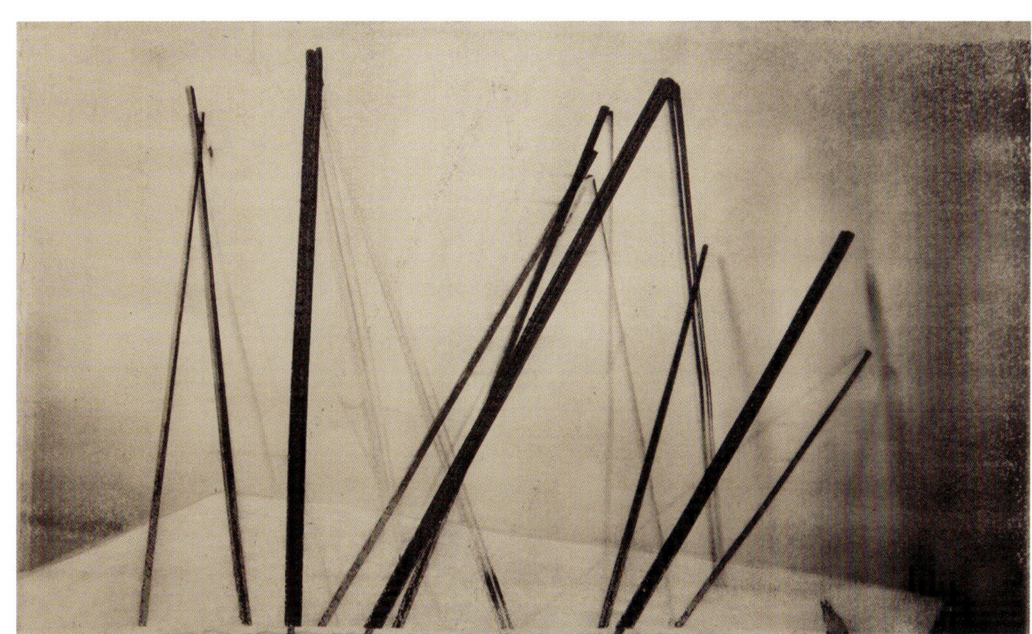

5.104
Ali Beheshti, *Untitled*, from the
Ta'vil series. 2018, transfer print,
automobile paint and charcoal on
cardboard, 22×37 cm, courtesy the
artist

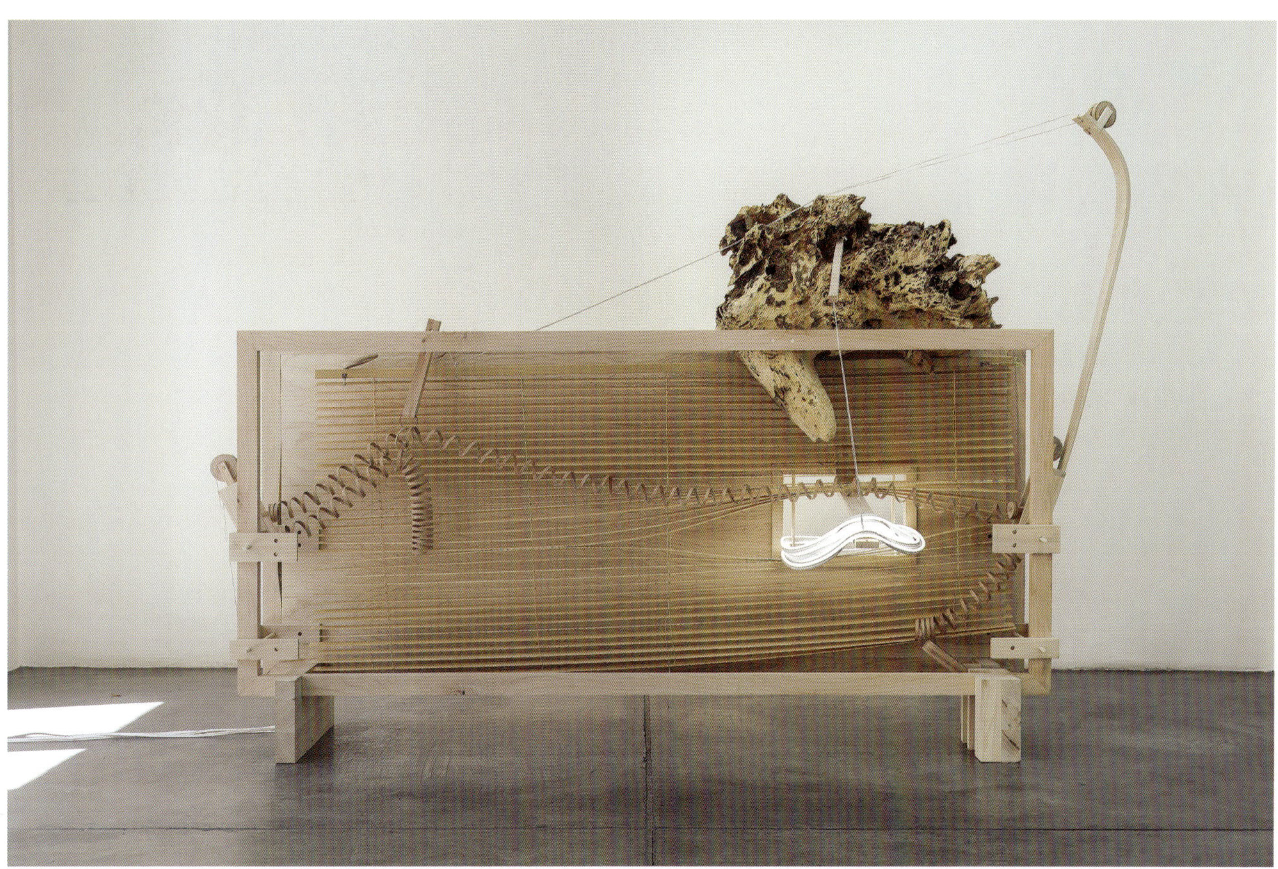

5.105
Ali Meer Azimi, *Untitled*, 2016,
mixed media, sizes vary

NOTES

1   See Nikki R. Keddie, *Modern Iran: Roots and Results of Revolution*, New Heaven & London 2003, p.304.

2   Khatami earned a positive reputation for his high appreciation of art during his tenure as the Minister of Culture and Islamic Guidance. The Iranian artistic community, recalling Khatami's favourable policies during his ministerial term, held high expectations of benefiting from his presidential leadership.

3   This routine changed during 2012 when the Deputy Office decided to appoint two posts, one for the TMoCA and the other for the Centre.

4   They were housed in the newly established House of Iranian Artists' Forum (Khaneh-i hunarmandan-i iran) in Tehran.

5   However, it was short-lived, as under Mahmoud Ahmadinajad's cultural administration, the requirement for approval before each exhibition was once again implemented.

6   In my interview with Sami Azar in 2006, he emphasised that 'this need really existed and the Museum provided the opportunity for it to happen and for this generation of artists to be seen!'

7   A major number of these exhibitions were curated by Pakbaz, the renowned art historian, researcher and curator.

8   Although it was established in 1998, its main activities, including exhibitions, started in the early 2000s.

9   Reza Jalali, 'guft-u-gu ba ductur Namvar Motlagh dabir-i farhangistan-i hunar: tafakkuri khas nisbat beh jahan-i islam', *Sharq Newspaper*, no. 382, 1383S/ 2004, p.14.

10   He was the former Prime Minister of Iran, 1981–89.

11   The gallery was founded in 2004 and hosted several contemporary Islamic art biennials, including the Painting Biennial from the Islamic world, Poster Biennial from the Islamic world, and the Calligraphy Biennial from the Islamic world. These events, on some occasions, were held in collaboration with TMoCA.

12   This term was also prevalent in the press and political discourse during the 1997 General Election and throughout the reformist slogans. It was used to highlight the significance of the younger generation, who emerged as the primary supporters of the Reform movement in the late 1990s and early 2000s.

13   See Anonymous, 'Guft-u-gu ba Hamid Severi; agar istifadeh nakunim, 'aqab mimanim' (If we don't use it, we shall straggle), *Hirfeh hunrmand*, no. 2, 1381S/ 2002, p.131.

14   One of the apparent examples of this emergence came in the exhibitions of Iranian artists in the period just before the revolution in the late 1970s, in particular by the Independent Group of Painters and Sculptors (Guruh-i azad-i naqqashan va mujassameh-sazan). In these exhibitions, works by Morteza Momayyez (1935–2005) and Marcos Grigorian (1925–2007) were exhibited in the form of installations or performances. After about two decades, however, in the post-revolutionary period (1992/3), a conceptual experience took shape in Tehran. In this project, a group of young artists, including Ali Dashti, Shahrokh Ghiyasi, Sasan Nasiri, Farid Jahangir and Mostafa Dashti, worked with a variety of materials on different floors of an old house which was slated for demolition shortly after the completion of the project.. The most important event after this was the 1998 project titled *Tajrobeh-i 77* (Experience of 98) by Contemporary Art Workshop consisting of Sasan Nasiri, Bita Fayyazi, Farid Jahangir, Khsrow Hassanzadeh and Ata Hasheminejad. This group exhibition was held in a shabby house in Tehran with the co-operation of most of the artists who were involved in the previous show. In the following year Bita Fyyazi, Mazyar Bahari, Sadegh Tirafkan and Khosrow Hassanzadeh held a multimedia show titled *Kudakan-i abi* (Blue Children) in an old house in central Tehran with the theme of pollution in Tehran.

15   The next comprehensive one was supposed to be titled *One and Thousand Nights*; it never realised owing to the radical transformation in cultural and artistic policy of the post-2005 Presidential Election and above all administrative alteration in the TMCoA. (Interview with Alireza Sami Azar, 2006) There were other minor exhibitions during 1997 to 2005 by new media artists held in various venues both inside and outside the country. These were also supported mainly by the Museum.

16   The first presence of contemporary Iranian art in the post-revolutionary period was in the 50th Venice Biennale in 2002.

17   During this time, apart from a very active presence in several Euro-American exhibitions, Iranian artists were able to receive recognition and also prizes from other prestigious Asian exhibitions, including the Asian Art Biennale Bangladesh, the Beijing International Art Biennale in China, and the Sharjah Art Biennial.

18   Mostafa Goudarzi, 'rah-i chuharum', *Hunar-hay-i tajassumi*, no. 2, 1377S/ 1998, p.10.

19   Iman Afsarian, 'Huviyyat an chizi ast keh beh ijra dar mi-ayad: guft-u-gu ba Mansour Barahimi', *Hirfeh Hunarmand*, no. 5, 1382S/ 2003, p.125.

20   This criticism echoed similar critiques from the period just before the Revolution, particularly during the 1960s and 1970s when modern Iranian art reached its peak. Artists attempting to blend traditional themes with modern styles faced accusations of formalism and a lack of meaningful integration between various forms of Iranian folk traditions and modern Western art. The motivation of Iranian modernist artists in the 1960s to establish a national modern art school was criticised as an attempt to gain recognition through the approval of Western critics who assessed national exhibitions like the Tehran biennials. Critics also targeted foreign cultural institutions actively involved during that period, accusing them of imposing a 'tourist-oriented' trend on Iranian art. See Chapter Three for further details.

21   In May 2006 Christie's held its first auction of International Modern and Contemporary Art in the Middle East. The sale was first named Modern and Contemporary Arab, Iranian and Turkish Art and then changed to Modern and Contemporary Middle Eastern Art. Christie's sales in Dubai continued until 2018, typically taking place twice a year in April and October. Eventually, it was decided that the auction would be held once a year in Dubai and once in London.

22 Terry Smith, 'What is Contemporary Art? Contemporaneity and Art to Come', *Konsthistorisk Tidskrift*, vol. 71, no. 1–2, 2002, p.8.

23 Ibid, p.7.

24 It is argued that 'postmodernism' has long vanished as a descriptor of current art. Hence, 'postmodernity' cannot be the right concept for the social and cultural conditions of this art's production any more. Contemporaneity then could not match, let alone replace modernity and postmodernity as a definition of the state of things.

25 Terry Smith, 'Contemporary Art and Contemporaneity', p.703.

26 See Donald Kuspit, 'The Contemporary and the Historical', *Artnet*, 13 Apr. 2005, www.artnet.com/Magazine/features/kuspit/kuspit4-14-05.asp. These views are given fuller treatment in Donald Kuspit, *The End of Art*, New York 2004, pp.696–7.

27 See Terry Smith, 'What is Contemporary Art? Contemporaneity and Art to Come', *Konsthistorisk Tidskrift*, vol. 71, no. 1–2, pp.11–13.

28 See Chapter Four and Hamid Keshmirshekan, 'Discourses on Postrevolutionary Iranian Art: Neotraditionalism during the 1990s', *Muqarnas*, vol. 23, 2006, pp.131–157.

29 See Hamid Keshmirshekan, 'Contemporary Iranian Art: the Emergence of New Artistic Discourses', pp.335–366.

30 See Hamid Keshmirshekan, 'Contemporary or Specific: the Dichotomous Desires in the Art of Early 21st Century Iran', *Middle East Journal of Culture and Communication*, p.47.

31 Ibid. In response to the question 'Was this movement being promoted by you and the Museum?' Sami Azar replied: 'Yes; undoubtedly this movement was supported and even promoted by the Museum for three main reasons. First, the necessity of updating Iranian art, which (since the Revolution) was about twenty years "behind" the contemporary art scene. The second reason was that "modern art" was forfeiting its audiences, with many intellectuals recognising its elitism as a significant issue. This problem, already evident in the West, was becoming increasingly apparent. Consequently, the third reason for promoting the movement was that the Museum was experiencing a decline in its spectatorship.' (Interview with Alireza Sami Azar, 2006.)

32 Hamid Severi, who served as the Head of the Research Section at the TMoCA, (Interview with Hamid Severi, 2006).

33 Sami Azar further told me that 'The reformist government actively encouraged us to enhance our global connections, particularly with the West and other regions. We were urged to engage proactively in cultural endeavours as a means to alleviate Iran's political isolation.' (Ibid.)

34 While this edition was in final stage of preparation, Raisi was killed in a helicopter crash in May 2024. The new presidential election was scheduled for June 2024. Although the results are still unknown at this time, it does not appear that there will be any fundamental changes in the state's political direction, and consequently, no shift in cultural policy is expected.

35 See Hamid Keshmirshekan, 'Contemporary Iranian Art: the Emergence of New Artistic Discourses', pp.335–366, and also 'The Question of Identity vis-à-vis Exoticism in Contemporary Iranian Art', *Iranian Studies*, 43, no. 4, 2010, pp.489–512.

36 See Hamid Keshmirshekan, 'Reproducing Modernity: Post-Revolutionary Art in Iran Since The Late 1990s', in Hamid Keshmirshekan, ed., *Amidst Shadow and Light: Contemporary Iranian Art and Artist*, Hong Kong 2011, pp.44–63, and also Hamid Keshmirshekan, 'The Concealed Layers of Meaning: Barbad Golshiri's Art', *Art Tomorrow*, no. 5, summer 2011, pp.92–95.

37 Golshiri's statement, in Barbad Golshiri, *And I Regurgitate And I Gulp It Down* (exhibition catalogue), 2011.

38 Golshiri, Barbad, *And I Regurgitate And I Gulp It Down*, p.13.

39 Examples of this approach towards the self were the exhibitions *Deep Depression* (*Afsurdigi-i 'amiq*) in 2005 and *Deeper Depression* (*Afsurdigi-i 'amiq-tar*) in 2006, both curated by Amirali Ghasemi.

40 For further study of Mahmoud Bakhshi Makhar's works, see Helia Darabi, 'Mahmoud Bakhshi Makhar', *Art Press*, no. 17, May/June/July 2010, pp.72–74.

41 I am grateful to Helia Darabi for providing comments on this work.

42 See Irit Rogoff, 'The Where of Now', *Art Tomorrow*, no. 3, 2011, p.153.

43 See Hamid Keshmirshekan, 'Globalisation and the Question of Identity: Discourses on Contemporary Iranian Art During Past Two Decades', in Hamid Keshmirhsekan, ed., *Amidst Shadow and Light: Contemporary Iranian Art and Artists*, Hong Kong, 2011, pp.64–81.

44 See John Clark 'Asian Modernism,' in Yashodhara Dalmia, ed., *Contemporary Indian Art, Other Realities*, Mumbai 2002, p.109

45 See Tirdad Zolghadr, 'Ethnic Marketing: An Introduction', in *Ethnic Marketing* (exhibition catalogue), Tehran 2006, p.12. In the same catalogue, Michaela Kehrer also points out the same issue in the broader context of marketing. She argues: 'It is often assumed that the proximate cause for worldwide cultural assimilation is grounded in the particularities of a global relationship between western centres and non-western peripheries. Mainly, we recognise symbols pertaining to the "triad" (Europe, America, and East Asia) infiltrating other cultures – be it in terms of consumerism or marketing strategies. Here, a cultural superiority seems explicitly located in the uniforming power of the western capitalist system, strongly supported and pushed forward by the activities of western transnational corporations'. (Michaela Kehrer 'How Culture Sells: Examples from National and International Marketing Perspectives', in *Ethnic Marketing* (exhibition catalogue), Tehran 2006, p.19.)

46 For an interesting definition of resistance and power see Michel Foucault, 'The Subject and Power', in Hubert L. Dreyfus, ed., *Michel Foucault: Beyond Structuralism and Hermeneutics*, Chicago 1983.

47 See Shireen T. Hunter, *Iran After Khomeini*, New York 1992, p.92.

48 See Rasool Najafi, 'Education and the Culture of Politics in the Islamic Republic of Iran', in Samih K. Farsoun and Mehrdad Mashayekhi, ed., *Iran: Political Culture in the Islamic Republic*, London 1992, p.161.

49 Ramin Jahanbegloo, ed., *Iran Between Tradition and Modernity*, Lanham, Md 2004, p.xx.

50 Ibid., p.xxii.

51 See Hamid Keshmirshekan, 'Reclaiming Cultural Space: Artist's Performativity versus State's Expectations in Contemporary Iran', in Staci Gem Scheiwiller, ed., *Performing the Iranian State: Cultural Representations of Identity and Nation*, London, New York 2013.

52 See Linda Martín Alcoff and Satya P. Mohanty, *Identity Politics Reconsidered*, New York 2006, p.3.

53 Suman Gupta, *Social Constructionist Identity Politics and Literary Studies*, New York 2007, p. 12.

54 Talking about his own views on the two issues of contemporaneity and specificity, Barbad Golshiri maintains: 'I think one should not look for the concept of contemporaneity in time or age. It is, rather, an ontological question. I do not limit myself to choosing the technique or theme. I may choose my theme from Dante or Beckett or anyone else. [...] Yet I never try to ensure my work depicts a local characteristic; I would rather avoid it. When I use narration from Descartes or the Bible, I write in English, which is to me a kind of self-denial. I am against the unity of the self and a fixed identity. I am talking about hybrid, schizophrenic identity, and one which is lost in intertextuality. I think being aware of the schizophrenic situation or identity is not a negative thing. I think even being other is not bad.' (Interview with the artist, 2010.)

55 Anne-Marie Fortier, 'Re-Membering Places and the Performance of Belonging(s)', in Vikki Bell, ed., *Performativity and Belonging*, London 1999, p.41. Paula M. L. Moya argues that the other aspect of the dialectical concept of identity is called the subjective identity or simply 'subjectivity'. Subjectivity refers to one's individual sense of Self, interior existence and lived experience of being a more-or-less coherent Self across time. The term also implies one's various acts of self-identification and thus necessarily incorporates one's understanding of oneself in relation to others. (Paula M. L. Moya, 'What's Identity Got to Do with It?' in Linda Martín Alcoff et al., ed., *Identity Politics Reconsidered*, New York 2006, p. 98.)

56 Vikki Bell, *Performativity and Belonging*, London 1999, p.3.

57 Judith Butler, *Bodies That Matter: On the Discursive Limits of "Sex"*, London 1993, p. 45. See also Anne-Marie Fortier, 'Re-Membering Places and the Performance of Belonging(s)', p. 43.

58 Suman Gupta, *Social Constructionist Identity Politics and Literary Studies*, p.18.

59 See Amelia Jones, 'Body', in Robert S. Nelson and Richard Shiff, ed., *Critical Terms for Art History*, Chicago 2003, p.255.

60 See Khaled D. Ramadan, 'Introduction', in Khaled D. Ramadan, ed., *Peripheral Insider: Perspectives on Contemporary Internationalism in Visual Culture*, Copenhagen 2007, p.27; and Hamid Keshmirshekan, 'The Question of Identity vis-à-vis Exoticism in Contemporary Iranian Art', *Iranian Studies* 43 (2010), pp.489–512, and 'Contemporary or Specific: the Dichotomous Desires in the Art of Early 21st Century Iran', *Middle East Journal of Culture and Communication*, pp.44–71.

61 See Hamid Keshmirshekan, 'The Question of Identity vis-à-vis Exoticism in Contemporary Iranian Art'.

62 Jean Fisher, 'The Syncretic Turn, Cross-cultural Practices in the Age of Multiculturalism', in Zoya Kocur and Simon Leung, ed., *Theory in Contemporary Art since 1985*, Oxford 2005, p.234. Fisher argues that this trend amounts to exoticisation. The popular curatorial practice of 'globetrotting' has resulted in what she terms 'geo-ethnic entertainment', perpetuating unequal intellectual hierarchies between European and non-European art practices while masking their disparate economic and power relations. Above all, such practices evade the necessary complex negotiations between European aesthetic language and those of the rest of the world. Framing and evaluating all cultural productions through Western criteria and stereotypes of otherness reduces them to spectacles of essentialist radical or ethnic typologies, disregarding their individual insights and human values – a treatment not applied to the work of white European artists. (Ibid., pp. 234–235.) She further elaborates on the reasons why non-Euro-American artists have felt compelled to adhere to this system. She argues that, for the sake of artistic and economic survival, non-Euro-American artists have had to acquiesce to 'promotion through the commodified signs of ethnicity,' aligning themselves with the Western desire for the 'exotic other' against which it can assert its own superiority. As a result, the 'exoticized' artist is not recognised as a 'thinking subject' and individual innovator in their own right, but rather as a conveyor of prescribed and homogenised cultural symbols and meanings. (Ibid.)

63 See Hamid Keshmirshekan, 'The Question of Identity vis-à-vis Exoticism in Contemporary Iranian Art'.

CHAPTER SIX

Iranian Art in Diaspora

1. In-betweenness and the Ongoing Dialogue between the Past and Present

The chapter focuses on the artistic practices of Iranian expatriate artists, exploring their engagement with issues such as identity, the state of 'in-betweenness' vis-à-vis the cultural dichotomies between their homeland and their adopted contexts. Alongside the significant transformations within Iran outlined in preceding chapters, the post-revolutionary period saw the emergence of extensive migration and varied artistic communities dispersed across the diaspora. The sense of dual existence and perpetual negotiation between past and present profoundly shapes the artistic productions of Iranians residing outside their homeland. Many of these artists have gained prominence within the global art scene. Their works grapple with questions concerning geographical displacement, the fluidity of identity, the critical analysis of the 'self' and the 'other', and the preservation of cultural memory.

Donald Winnicott, a prominent psychoanalyst known for his work on object-relations theory, highlights the distress that accompanies the loss of identity, as individuals often tether their sense of self to their possessions and surroundings. Therefore, emigrating from one's native land entails more than a mere change in geographical location; it also involves severing ties with familiar relationships, fostering a feeling of estrangement from one's accustomed social milieu.[1] Consequently, individuals may find themselves defining their identity in contrast to the people and groups in their new surroundings. Host countries introduce entirely different cultural norms and geographical landscapes compared to the country of origin, further accentuating the sense of displacement.

It is not surprising that one prevalent approach in diasporic art involves socio-political commentary filtered through personal narratives. Stuart Hall's definition of the diaspora experience emphasises heterogeneity and diversity rather than essence or purity. He views identity as something that thrives within difference, embracing hybridity rather than seeking to erase it.[2] In this framework, diaspora identities are in a constant state of flux, continually reinventing themselves through transformation and difference.[3] This conception of identity challenges the essentialist notions often associated with discussions of ethnic and cultural identities.

When it comes to art, this viewpoint often leads to remarkable artistic expressions. Multiculturalism and the blending of cultural influences in art naturally give rise to hybrid forms where the boundaries of identity become fluid. Thus, displacement emerges as a central theme in contemporary culture, and diasporic art often serves as a testament to this experience. These artworks, mostly anonymous and self-sufficient, can transcend specific locales, evoking a sense of familiarity while also defying categorisation within any single cultural context. Hybridity, then, appears as an antidote to essentialist notions of identity and ethnicity.[4] With respect to cultural forms, hybridisation refers to the process by which existing forms break away from their original contexts and merge with new forms in novel practices.[5] This continuous process of recombination and reinvention reflects the dynamic nature of cultural phenomena in today's globalised world.

In his exploration of Iranian cinema, Hamid Naficy highlights the significant influence of 'in-betweenness' on the work of Iranian artists living in exile. Drawing upon Arnold van Gennep's concept of 'liminality' from the early twentieth century, Naficy applies it to the contemporary context of migration and exilic culture that he examines.[6] According to Naficy, liminality and incorporation entail a state of ambiguity, resistance, fluidity, disguise, and even rebellion against the cultural norms of both the homeland and the host societies.[7] Furthermore, Naficy contends that this condition liberates the exiled artist from the constraints of both their past and present circumstances. Being 'de-territorialized' emerges as a potent source of creativity and vitality, infusing the artists' works with a rich tapestry of iconographic blends, duplications, and fractures. These tensions and ambivalences give rise to the complexity and multidimensionality that are remarkable features of such art.[8]

Diasporic artists also confront another significant challenge: nostalgia, which could be seen as a defining aspect of the exile experience, has evolved into a cultural practice and a mode of representation in recent years.[9] According to Frederic Jameson, this dislocation lead individuals to perceive time differently; they come to view the present as a type of absence, or as Jean Baudrillard suggests, as a phenomenon devoid of origin and reality, experienced as 'hyper-reality'.[10] Moreover, the longing for one's homeland is fundamentally a psychological experience, expressed in the metaphor of an eternal desire to return – a return that is structurally unattainable. The same inability to capture an image of homeland resonates in exilic discourse; devoid of distance and separation, the nostalgic longing prevalent in exile would cease to exist, as Susan Stewart articulates: 'It is in this gap between resemblance and identity that nostalgic desire arises. The nostalgia is enamoured of distance, not of the referent itself.'[11]

Studies on the Iranian diaspora also investigate how political events and socio-cultural dynamics, both within Iran and their host countries, impact the artistic production and subject matter of diaspora artists. These studies explore how experiences of exile, discrimination, and marginalisation shape the themes and approaches chosen by these artists.

Indeed, these characteristics are evident in the works of a number of Iranian artists living and working across the diaspora. Their art serves as a reflection of the complex interplay between personal experiences and broader socio-political contexts. While I have chosen to highlight specific examples of diaspora artists and their works, it is important to acknowledge that this selection is not exhaustive nor fully representative of the current state of the genre. These examples merely scratch the surface of the diverse and multifaceted artistic expressions found within the Iranian diaspora community.

2. Exploring the Artistic Diaspora

Perhaps the first generation of self-exiled artists left Iran during the period between the 1940s and the 1990s. This can include figures such as Charles Hossein Zenderoudi, Abolghassem Saidi, Nasser Assar,

Siah Armajani, Abbas Attar, Nikzad (Nicky) Nodjoumi, Ali Nassir (b.1951) and Ghasem Hajizadeh.

Chapter Three explored the significant contributions of some of these figures within the Iranian art scene, particularly during the 1960s and 1970s. However, it did not specifically discuss their artistic activities within diasporic contexts. One such figure is Siah Armajani, a renowned artist known for his prolific projects of public art, who spent most of his life in the US. Armajani's sculptural installations for public spaces often examine themes of 'social expansion', philosophical-cultural concepts, and the societal role of art. Rooted in his philosophical background, his works consistently reflect this influence. This is evident in his architectural creations that pay homage to literature and culture. Armajani's extensive body of work is characterised by a diverse range of formal appearances complexly intertwined with philosophy and politics. In some of his projects, Armajani explicitly criticises fraudulent and belligerent policies, incorporating layers of broader ethical concepts into his art. (Figure 6.1)

Nikzad (Nicky) Nodjoumi's art explores themes of political oppression, social injustice, and personal afflictions, revealing their complex and multi-layered nature. Through deliberate deformations in figurative art, Nodjoumi portrays characters, at times exaggerating them into caricature-like figures. The recurring presence of suit-wearing figures in Nodjoumi's works serves as a pointed reference

6.1
Siah Armajani, *Emerson's Parlor*, 2005, laminated maple, mattress, plywood, mirror, coat, hat and cane, 25.4h×55.88w×53.34l

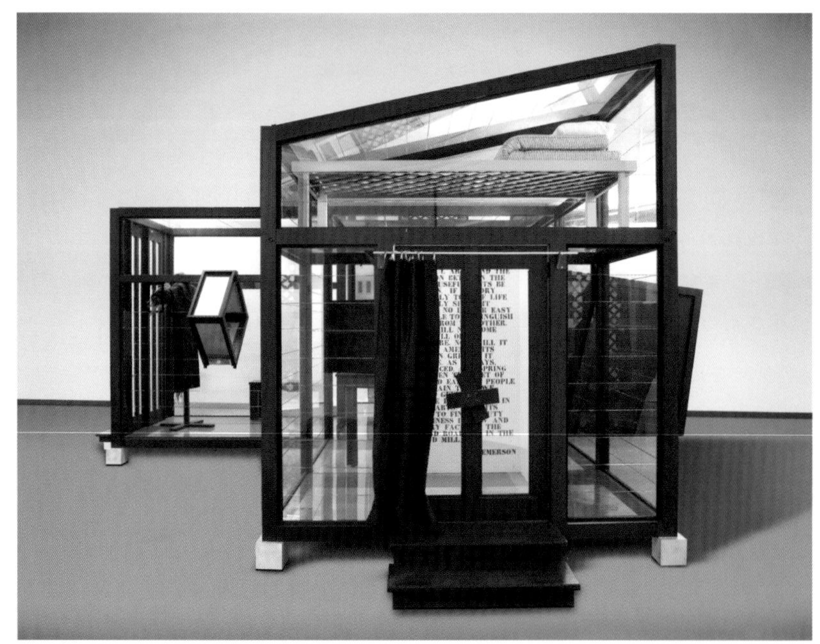

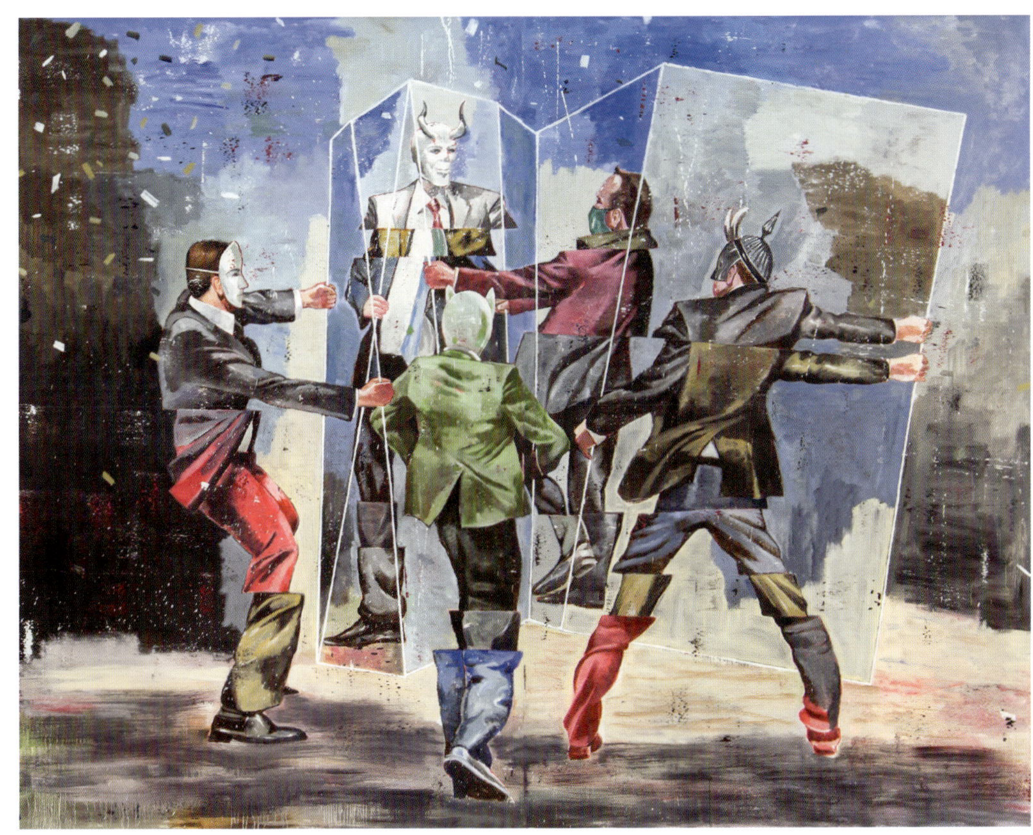

6.2
Nikzad (Nicky) Nodjoumi, *The Oaths of Infidels*, 2017, oil on canvas, 243x304 cm, courtesy the artist and Third Line

to politicians and businessmen whom the artist views as hypocrites, bearing partial responsibility for the troubling issues in the contemporary world. (Figure 6.2) Similarly, but less vividly, Ali Nassir's paintings show the concealed layers behind ordinary life while addressing broader concepts of contemporary human life such as loneliness, life and death. (Figure 6.3) Ghasem Hajizadeh, who left Iran for Paris in 1986, is famous for his use of old photographs, which have become the main source of his imagery and suggest a nostalgic return to the recent past and memories. (Figure 3.107)

Shirin Neshat (b. 1957), perhaps more widely recognised in the West, has been a resident of New York since 1974, where she lives and works. The core of her artistic exploration revolves around the concept of binary oppositions: men and women, exile and belonging, sacred and profane. Neshat has received significant attention for her explicit examination of gender relationships, particularly concerning the situation of Muslim women and, more recently, men. Notably, her series of photographs, *Women of Allah* (1993–7) challenges prevailing perceptions of Iran's social, political, and religious norms by portraying militant Muslim women infused with the concept of martyrdom. (Figure 6.4) In her series of split-screen video

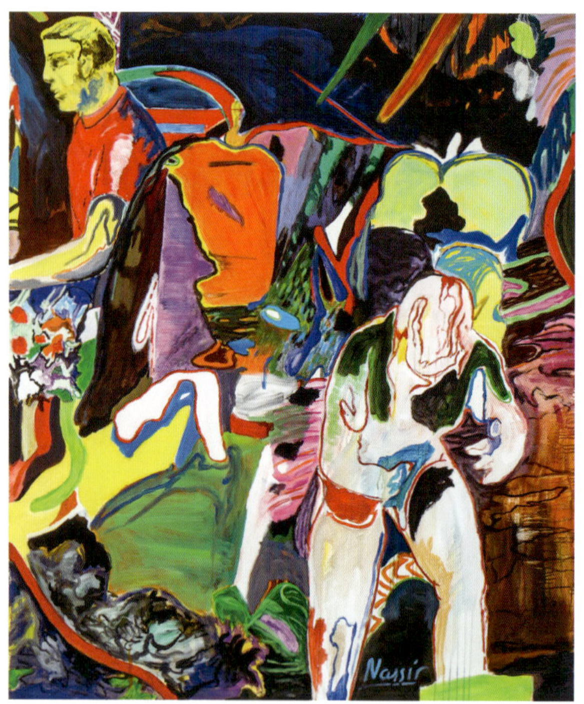

Above
6.3
Ali Nassir, *Untitled, 2013,* acrylic
on canvas, 195x160 cm, courtesy
the artist

Right
6.4
Shirin Neshat, *Speechless*, from the
Women of Allah series, 1996, RC
print and ink, 118.7×86 cm

installations, *Women without Men* (2002–9), inspired by Shahrnush Parsipur's novel of the same name, Neshat continues to explore these themes. More recently in her two-channel video *The Fury* (2022) Neshat explores the experiences of female political prisoners within the Islamic Republic, shedding light on the torture, sexual assaults, and political trauma they endure. Beyond her visual arts, she has also directed a number of feature-length films, including *Looking for Oum Kulthum* (2017) and *Land of Dreams* (2021), expanding her exploration of complex socio-political themes across different media.

The artist and filmmaker Shoja Azari (b. 1958) has collaborated with Neshat since 1997 on projects that include short films and video installations. Azari has also collaborated with the painter Shahram Karimi (b. 1957) in a series of projects called 'video paintings'. One of the best-known series, *Oil* (2009), refers to the First Gulf War and depicts deserts aflame with scorched skies and billowing smoke. More recently, Azari's work has re-examined various aspects of Iranian

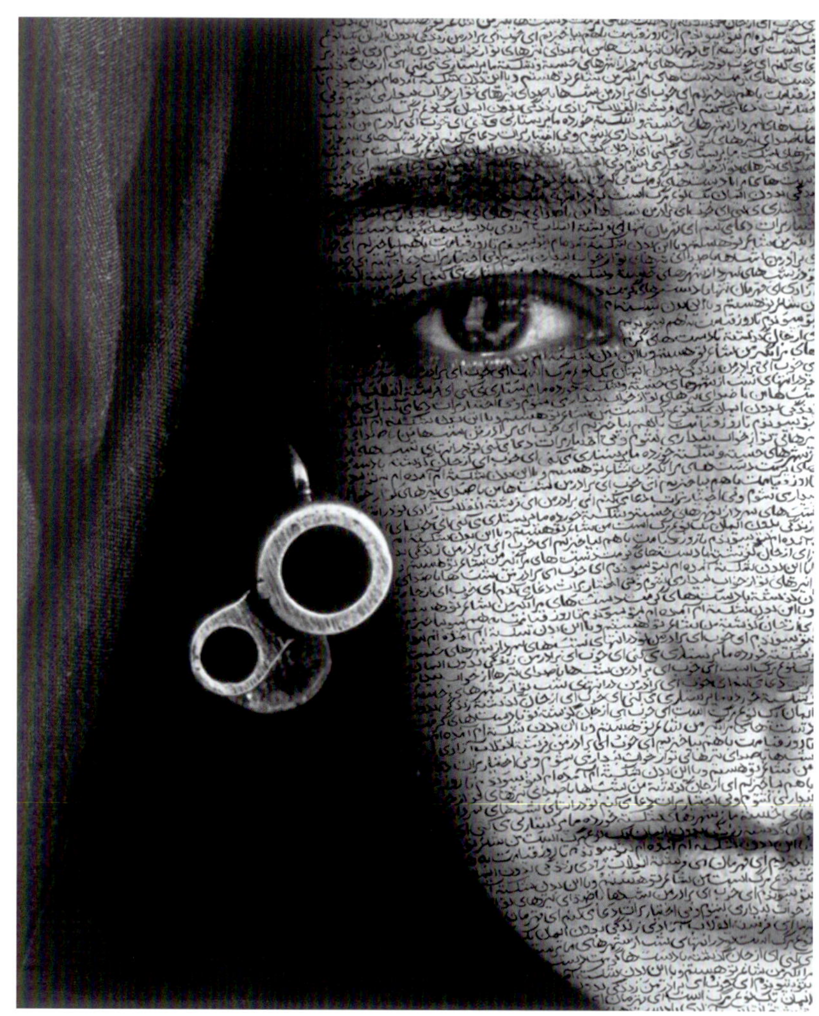

vernacular material culture. In these works, the artist is inspired by Iranian popular imagery, such as Coffee-house (*Qahveh-khaneh*) painting and mass-produced posters featuring Shiʻi Imams and martyrs. *Coffee House Painting* (2009) and *Icons* (2010) are hybrid works, incorporating different concepts and methods.[12] Azari re-contextualises these sources with irony, so that they signify political and religious practice both with reference to their original sources and to the more contemporary ideological use of the themes within the Iranian socio-political domain. (Figure 6.5)

The Iranian–British photographer and film director Mitra Tabrizian (b.1959)[13] examines contemporary themes and issues such as idea of homeland, immigration, nomadism and consumer culture. Employing a range of techniques from documentary and stage photography to film, she weaves together narratives that reflect contemporary contradictions. Tabrizian's work is particularly influenced by theories such as post-colonialism, post-feminism, and the portrayal of late capitalism in Britain, which she visually explores in her art. Her photographic project *Border* (2005–06) captures real immigrants lost in contemplation, seemingly carrying a psychological border with them. These images evoke a state of limbo, where immigrants find themselves suspended between a yearning for their homeland and their new surroundings. A number of Tabrizian's series tackle the ever-evolving realities of life in post-revolutionary Iran. For example, *Untitled* (2009), features large panoramic photographs of the area around Tehran. Drawing on the genre of documentary photography, Tabrizian addresses the notion of political and cultural displacement, portraying individuals who are simultaneously part of a city yet excluded from it. (Figure 6.6)

Hossein Valamanesh (1949–2022), who immigrated to Australia in 1973, is a visual artist who works across various media, including installation, sculpture, painting, and collage. His works evoke a constant dialogue between past and present, homeland and country of residence, imagination and reality, dreaming and wakefulness, and the interplay of inescapable destiny and ambiguous future. Ordinary objects in his art, such as stone and rope, serve as signifiers for both local and global existential questions. Despite their simplicity, his works convey complex concepts, inviting the audience to imagine the artist's fragments of memory and his dialogue with the world. Importantly Valamanesh's works avoid exaggerating or exoticising Persian or Australian motifs, nor do they imagine a global homeland. Instead, they subtly hint at notions of 'becoming',

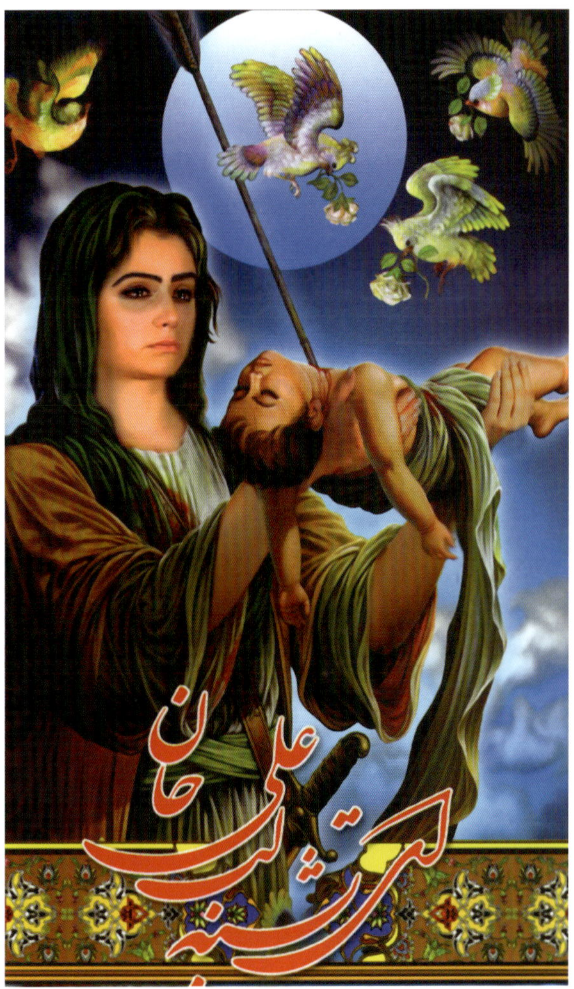

6.5
Shoja Azari, Shoja Azari, *Icon #5*, 2010, still from video, video portrait, loop on Blu-ray, ca. 4 minutes

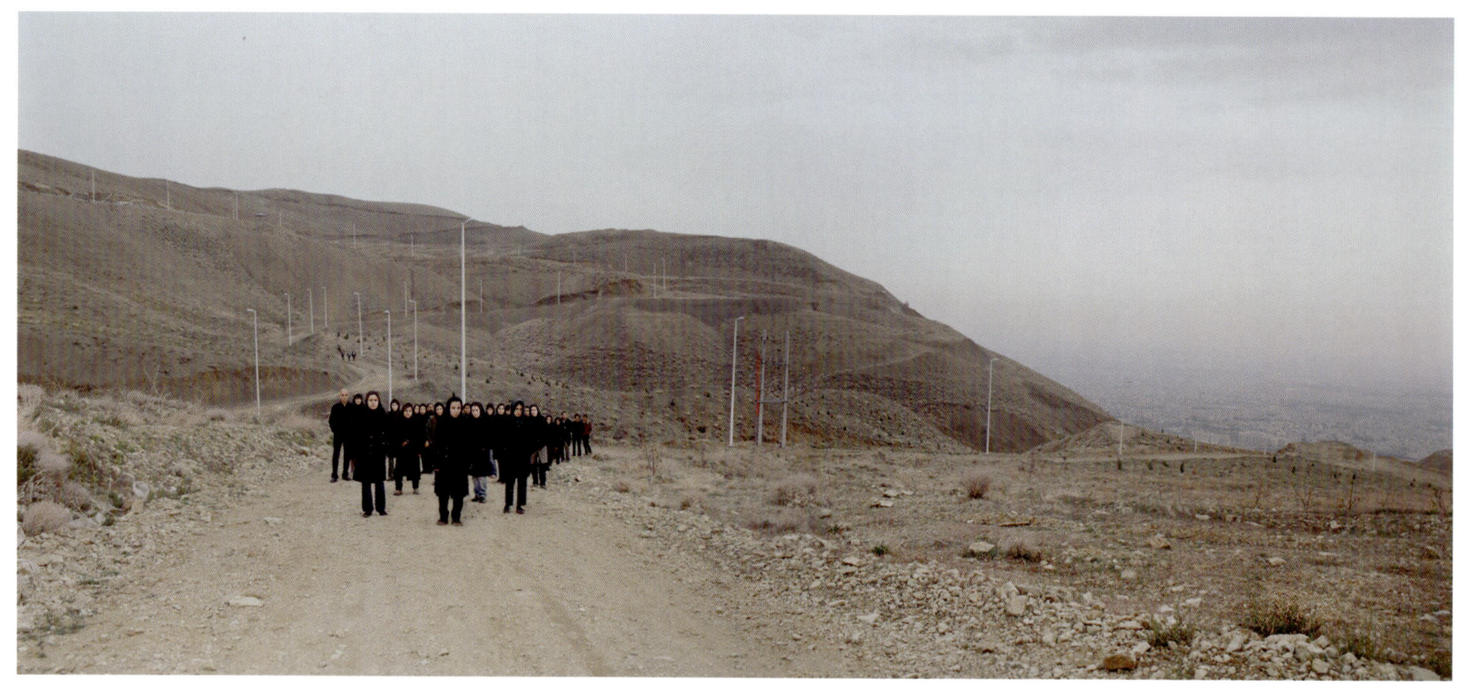

6.6
Mitra Tabrizian, *Untitled*, 2009,
C-Print, 121.9×152.4 cm, sizes
vary, courtesy the artist

'journey' and 'relocation', rather than 'being', 'settlement' and 'home'. Through his art, Valamanesh encourages viewers to ponder the fluidity and complexity of identity and belonging in an increasingly interconnected world. (Figure 6.7)

Shirazeh Houshiary has established herself in London as one of the foremost sculptors of her generation. She was nominated for the Turner Prize in 1994. Houshiary's diverse body of work encompasses paintings, prints, and installations, often referencing Islamic geometry and formal traditions. Her artistic inspiration extends to Iranian literary sources, particularly drawing from the poetry of the thirteenth-century Sufi mystic Rumi. This influence infuses her work with a sense of spiritual depth and philosophical inquiry, enriching her exploration of themes related to identity, existence, and transcendence. (Figure 6.8)

The painter Y. Z. Kami's most striking works are his large, silent and meditative frontal portraits of ordinary people. Depicting the inward and contemplative world of their subjects, these fresco-like paintings merge the traditional genre of portraiture with contemporary psychology. Another very different set of artworks by the New York-based artist include a series of works on paper titled *Endless Prayers*. (Figure 6.9) These follow the structure and forms of Islamic architecture, especially domes. Created by attaching numerous brick-shaped patterns selected from prayer texts or Persian poetry to the canvas, the works invoke the whirling Sufi rituals that signify

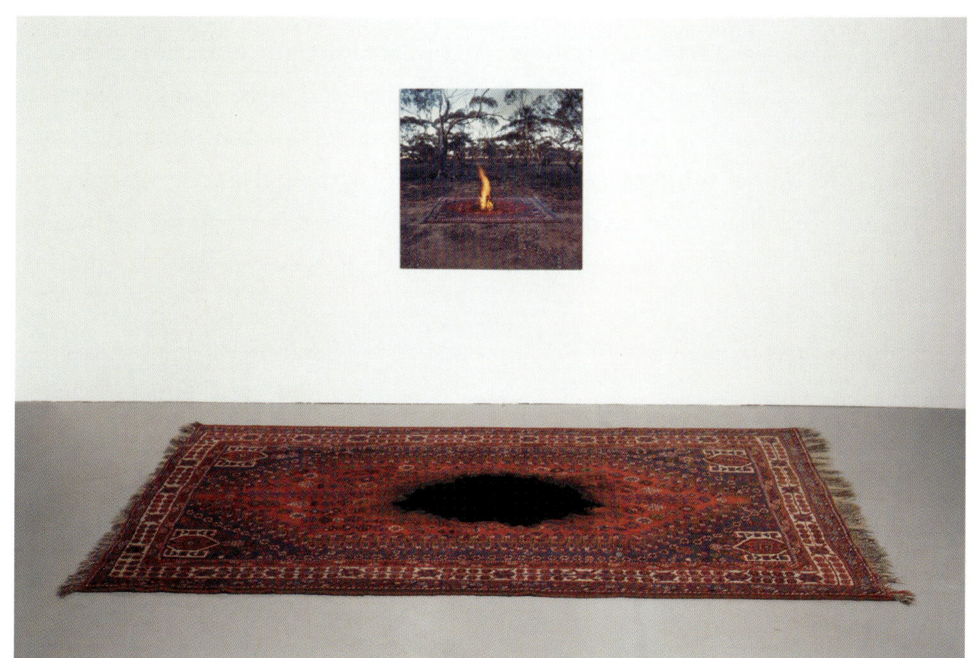

6.7
Hossein Valamanesh, *Longing
Belonging*, 1997, colour photograph,
99×99 cm, Persian carpet, black
velvet, 215×305 cm, courtesy the
artist

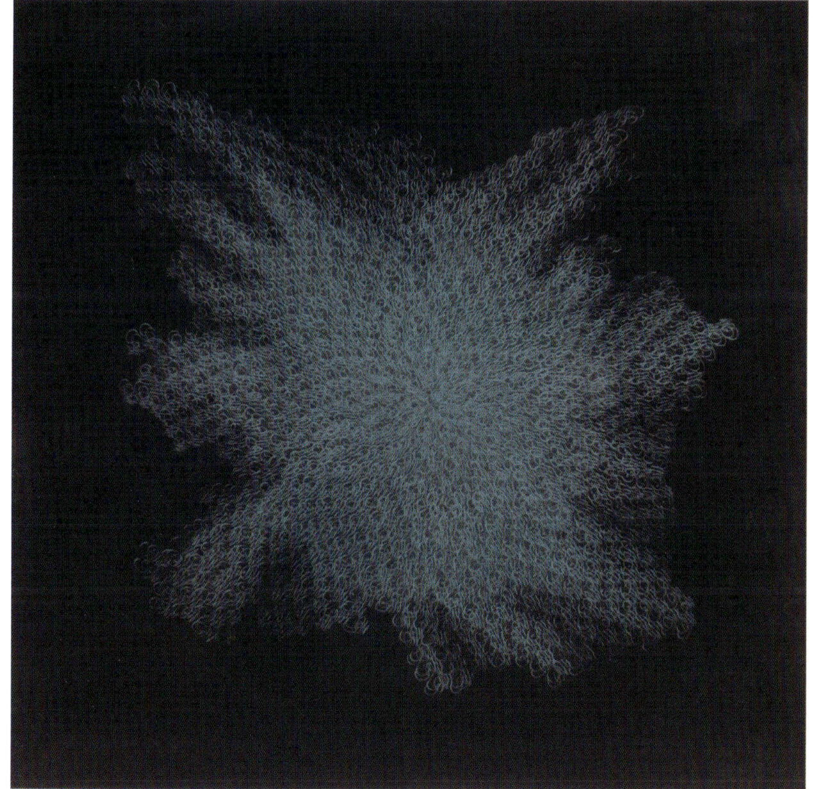

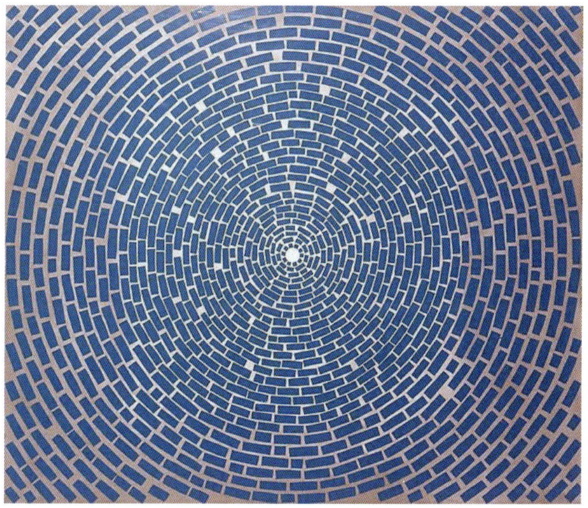

6.9
Y. Z. Kami, *Blue Dome 2*, 2007,
144.7×124.4 cm

6.8
Shirazeh Houshiary, *Untitled*, 2007,
etching and mixed media, 40x40 cm

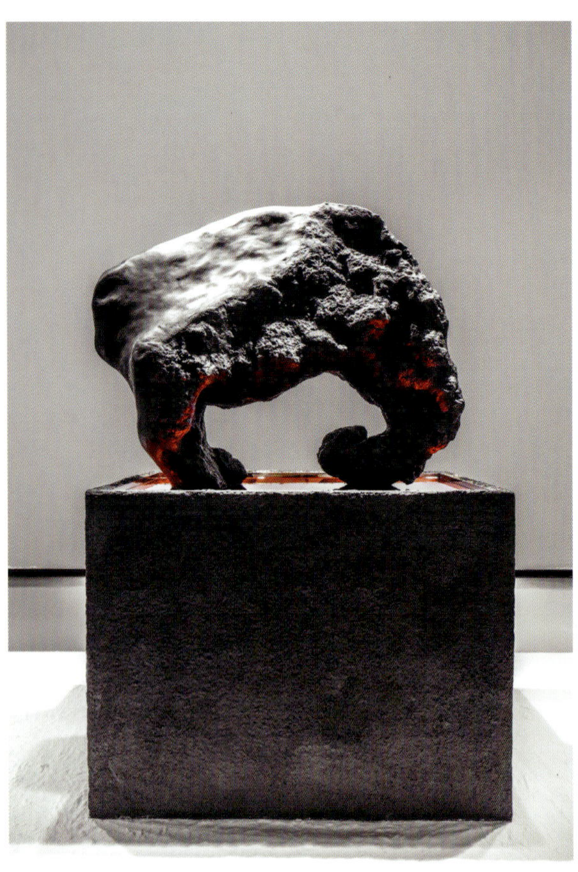

Above
6.10
Bizhan Bassiri, *Beast*, 2008, black
glossy bronze, steel and hydraulic
red oil, 260×160×100 cm, courtesy
the artist

Facing page
6.11
Shirana Shahbazi, *Halek*,
2019, lithography (four-coloured
lithography on cotton paper),
courtesy the artist

purification of selflessness and finding unity in bodily movement.

Bizhan Bassiri's (b. 1954) works cannot be easily categorised within a single artistic trend. Among his most prominent works are his sculptures, often installed within classical museums or religious sites such as churches. In these pieces, Basiri focuses on the continuous interaction and dialogue between classical (ancient) and contemporary elements. For Bassiri, structure, corporeality, and even the materiality of the artwork hold significant importance – a characteristic that can be associated with post-conceptual aesthetics, although often the 'concept' resonates with this 'visuality'. Here, the conventional dualities or normative contradictions unfold: tradition or classical versus the contemporary order. Therefore, Basiri's works, alongside pre-existing examples in these classical spaces, engage in a mutual dialogue. He believes his *Celestial Stones* series (1390–1387) embodies cosmic energy; much like a heavenly stone of art that emerges suddenly and randomly from the cosmos and manifests itself only in this world. This very characteristic he ascribes to these sculptures resembles archetypical forms that all humans are collectively connected in their subconscious. (Figure 6.10)

Shirana Shahbazi (b.1974) is an Iranian-born photographer, trained in Switzerland and currently resident there. Her work comprises images of everyday events, people and objects in still-life. Shahbazi's innovative analogue photography challenges our perception of time and space, reimagining traditional genres like landscapes and portraits across diverse media such as hand-made carpets and photorealistic billboards. Her polished style, reminiscent of commercial studio photography, is achieved without digital manipulation, showcasing a captivating blend of representation and abstraction. Through her precise technique, Shahbazi captures ephemeral moments, while her exhibition strategies explore themes of disassembling, superimposing, and recombining surfaces and motifs, resulting in multi-layered works that transcend traditional boundaries. (Figure 6.11)

Living and working in Gothenburg, Mandana Moghaddam (b.1962) explores themes such as femininity, memories of her homeland, and the dynamics of power. Beyond personal reflections, her work also delves into global issues like migration, dislocation, and reconciliation. Her personal experiences, notably her exposure to unrest, violence, and instability during the 1979 Revolution and its aftermaths, profoundly shape her artistic practice. Through her art, Moghaddam seeks to address and reconcile the fractured sense of self

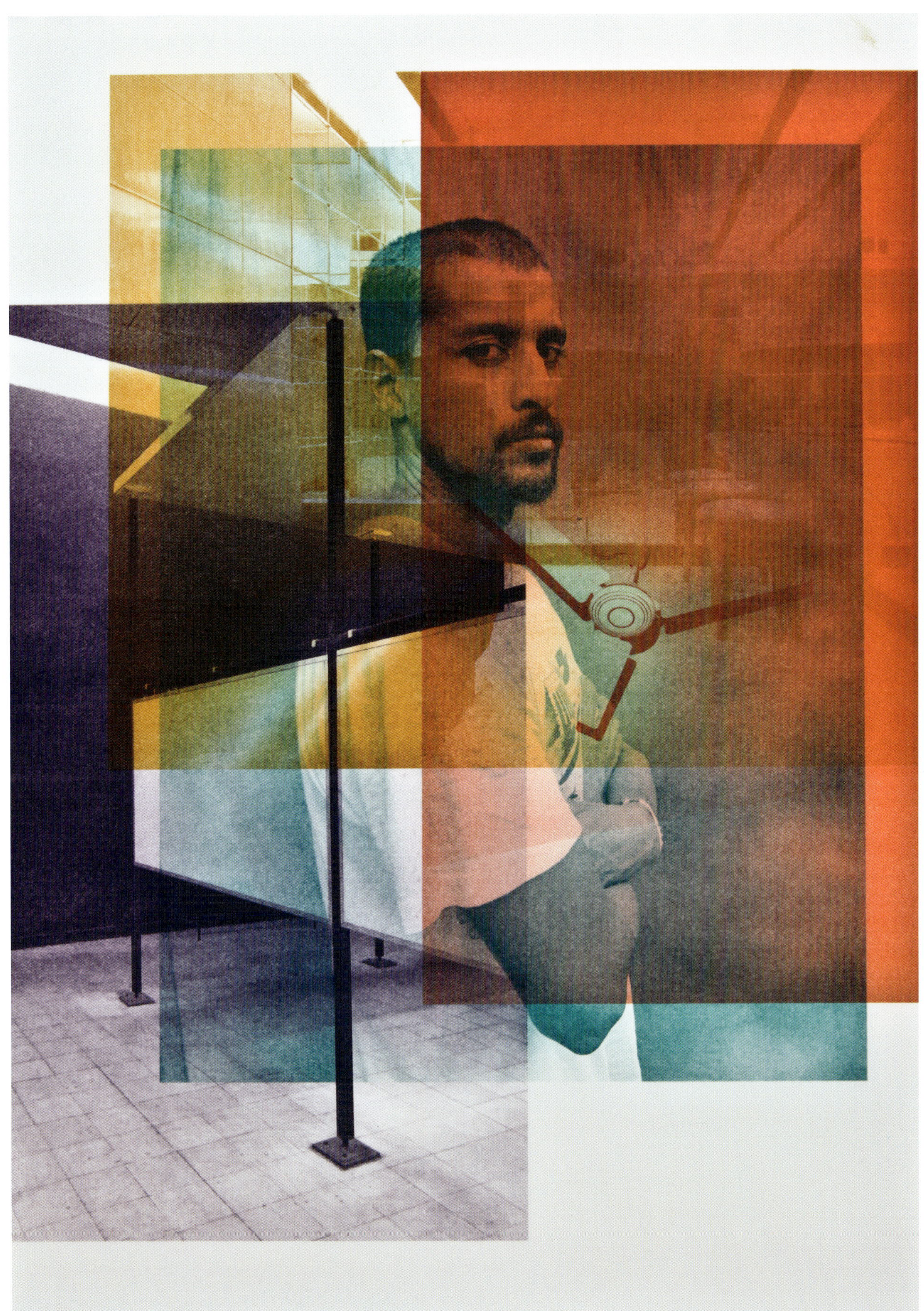

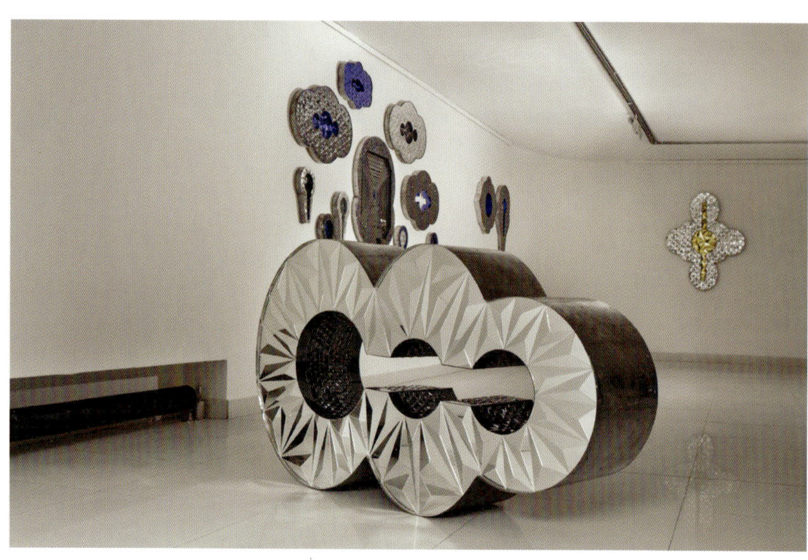

6.12
Mandana Moghaddam, *Untitled*,
from the *Wonderland* series,
2014, 149 W×88.5 L×31 D cm,
installation view, courtesy the artist

Facing page
6.13
Parastou Forouhar, from the *Butterfly*
series, 2010, each frame 50×50
cm, digital print on paper, courtesy
the artist.

and identity that she encountered during her formative years. Her art serves as a means of reclaiming and reconstructing narratives of personal and collective identity in the face of tumultuous historical events. Her works offer examples of the artist's interest in the complex situation of women in society in general, and in Iran in particular, for example, depicted in works such as *Chelgis* series and *Manije* (2008). Her work transcends the confines of particular cultural identities, breaking down borders and exploring their inevitable impact. In *Underlandet* (2014) project, Moghaddam employs subversive and ironic expressions, disrupting traditional methods like mirror-works to blur the boundary between specific cultural identities and their tangible manifestations. (Figure 6.12)

Parastou Forouhar (b.1962), who relocated to Germany in 1991, currently resides and practices her art in Frankfurt. Her multimedia art encompasses prints, installations, performances, and photographs. The trajectory of her work took a markedly poignant turn following a tragic incident in 1998, wherein her parents were brutally murdered in Iran by the Iranian Intelligence Service. In Forouhar's art, recurring motifs, notably the butterfly, hold profound symbolism. Traditionally, the butterfly signifies beauty, freedom, and the transient essence of life in Persian literature and culture. However, in her works, the butterfly assumes a darker significance, emblematic of the deceitful facade of power and the concealed suffering entrenched within oppressive regimes. Forouhar juxtaposes the delicate allure of the butterfly form with imagery depicting pain, torture, and death, creating a striking contrast that explores the coexistence of beauty and brutality. (Figure 6.13)

Marjane Satrapi (b.1969) employs graphic imagery and writing

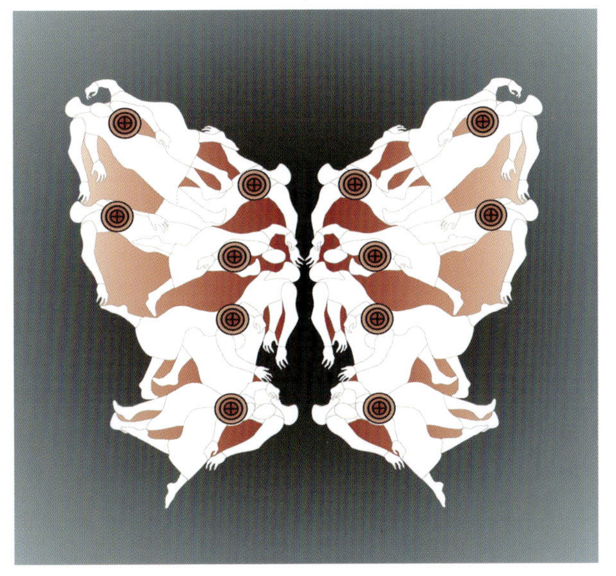 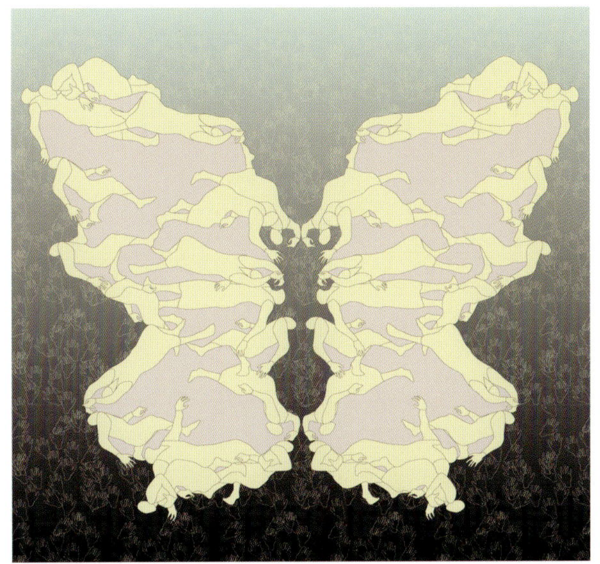

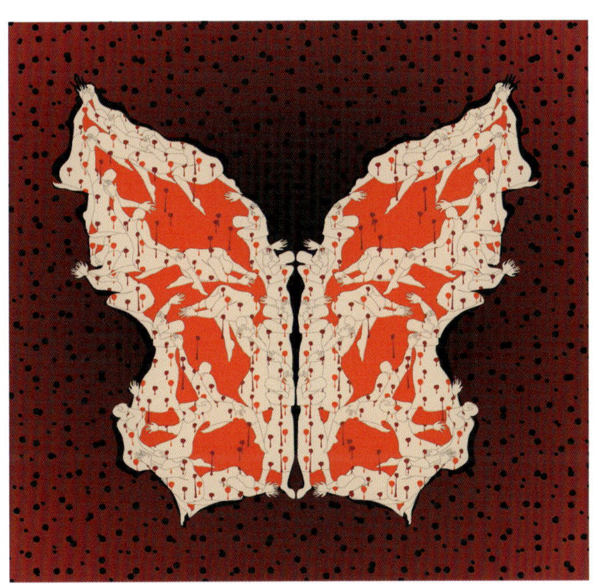 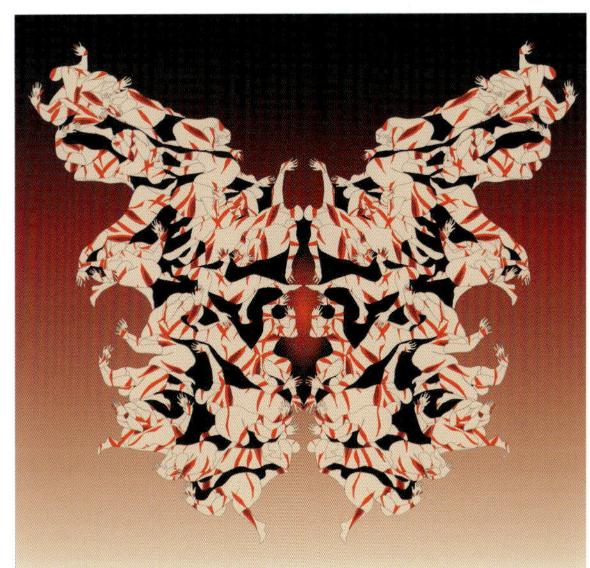

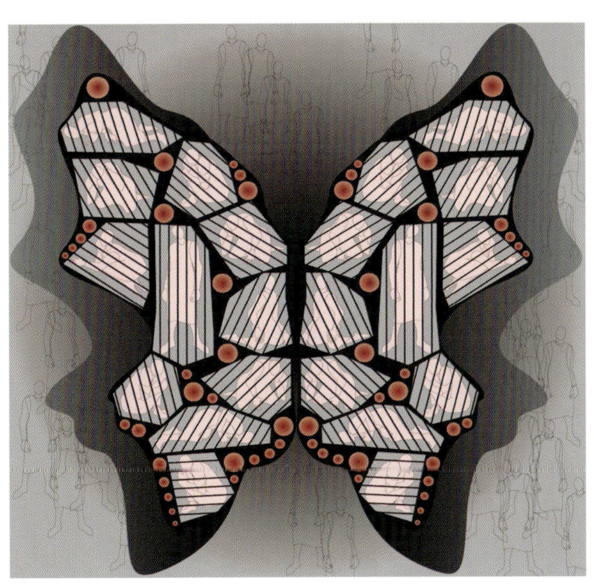 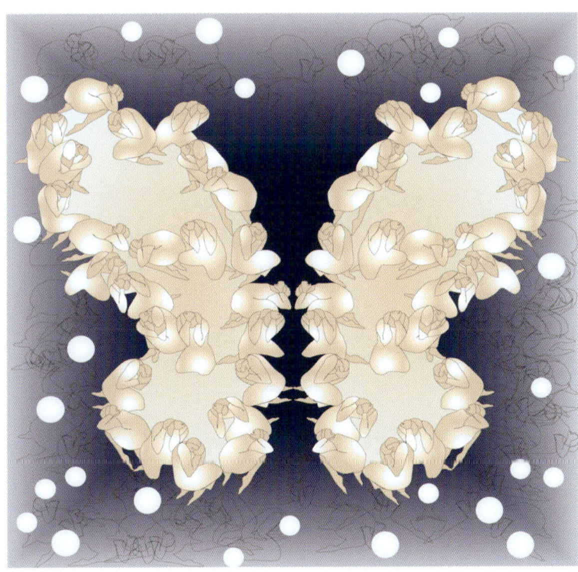

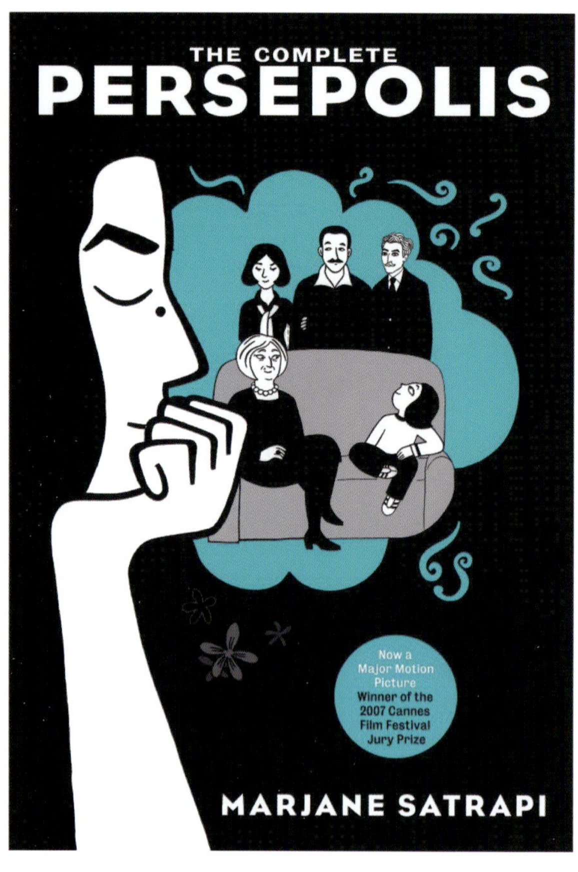

6.14
Marjane Satrapi, cover of the
book *Persepolis*, 2007

to address complex and controversial narratives, offering a raw depiction of her personal encounters with the politics of identity. Residing in Paris, Satrapi is a multifaceted artist, serving as an author, graphic novelist, director, and illustrator. Her striking cartoon illustrations predominantly draw from autobiographical narratives or tales rooted in her homeland. She is perhaps best known for her graphic novels *Persepolis 1* (2003) and *Persepolis 2* (2004) – detailing her experiences growing up following the 1979 Revolution. (Figure 6.14) The dynamic work was adapted into an award-winning film made in collaboration with Vincent Parronaud in 2007, which featured the same stories.

The London-based artist Reza Aramesh (b. 1970) employs a diverse range of media including photography, sculpture, video, installation, and performance. His works examine themes of war, violence, gender, and the inequalities present in contemporary culture. Aramesh's artistic practice is deeply influenced by his interest in the history of painting, film and literature, as well as contemporary sociology and politics. This diverse range of interests informs his choice of media, with a particular emphasis on photography and sculpture. His works, often referred to as 'actions' by the artist,

6.15
Reza Aramesh, *Action 97* (Algerian civilians suspected of being terrorists are searched and put on trucks to be taken to the inter-rogation cells, Algiers 1956), 2010, silver gelatine print on aluminium, total size 190×245.4 cm, courtesy the artist.

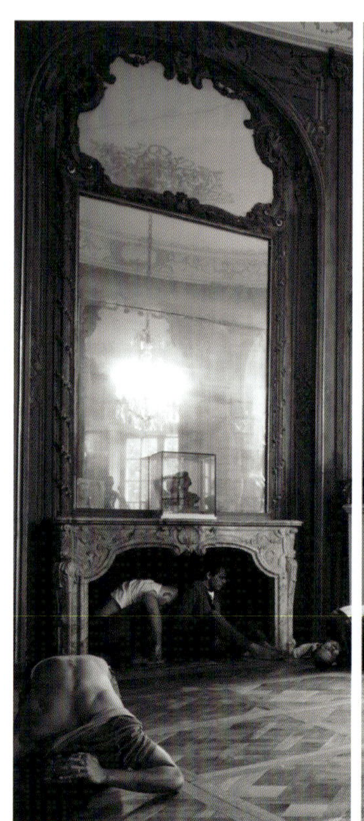
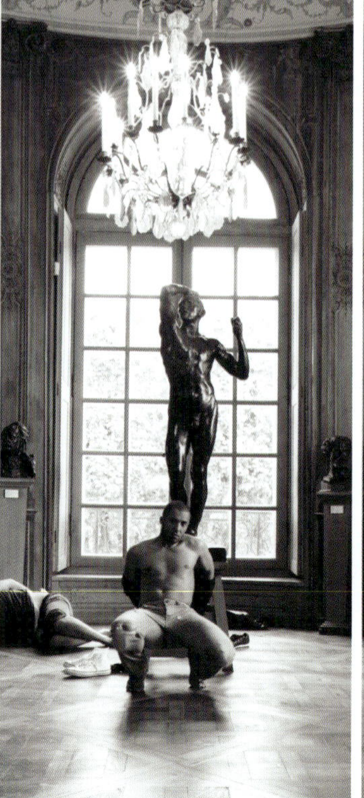
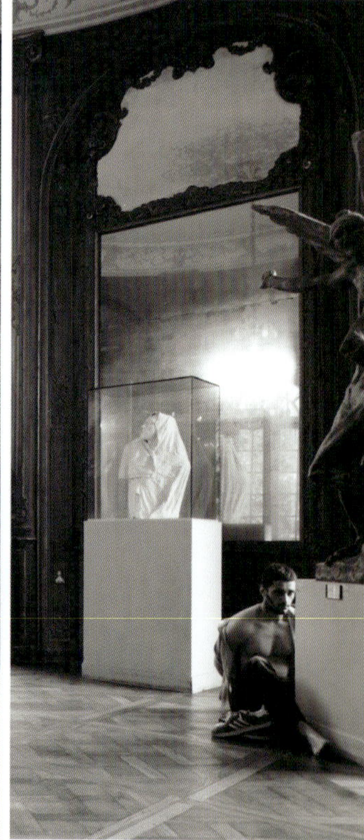

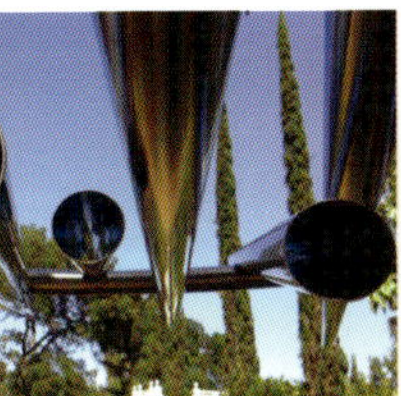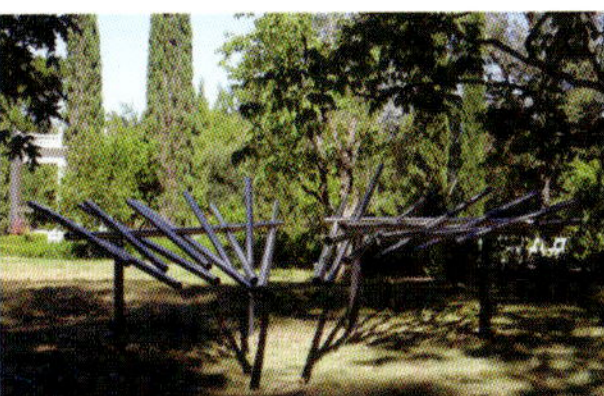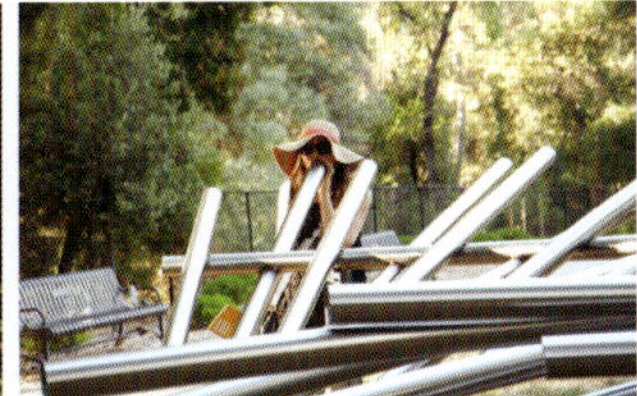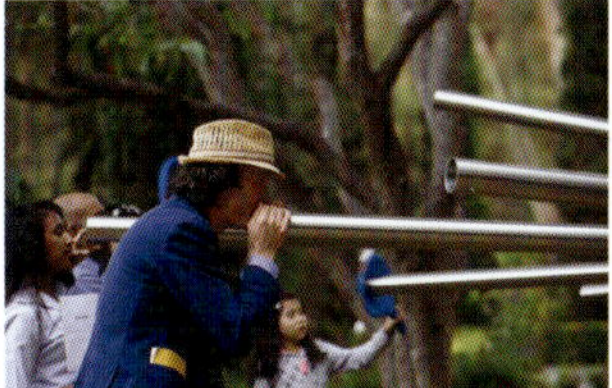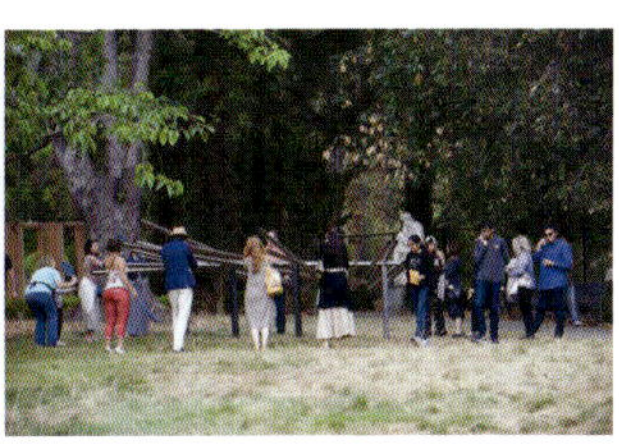

6.16
Taraneh Hemami, *One Voice*
(*Yekseda*), 2017–18, interactive
installation, sound sculpture, Montalvo
Arts Center

involve restating and reframing narratives. The source material for these actions is frequently drawn from conflict zones worldwide, intersecting with the imagery prevalent in mainstream print and televisual media.[14] His numbered *Action* series, initiated in 2008 comprises black-and-white photographs and sculptures that subvert traditional notions of space and time. The classic and dramatic scenes depicted in these works are juxtaposed against the opulent settings of British homes and historical museums, creating a sense of surrealism and tension. (Figure 6.15)

The Iranian-American artist Taraneh Hemami's (b.1960) narrative works penetrate the silence surrounding the Iranian diaspora experience; displacement and belonging are also prominent themes. In *One Voice* (*Yekseda*) (2017–18), inspired by the Iranian feminist poet Forough Farokhzad's poem *It is only Voice that Remains*, the artist presents a modular sculptural installation that serves as a conduit for connecting voices and transmitting messages, stories, lullabies, whispers, and shouts from one person to another. The installation comprises polished stainless-steel structures, resembling basic tube-like shapes clustered together. The installation invites visitors to engage in dialogue and exchange, encouraging them to both listen to others and make their own voices heard. It serves as a platform for individuals to express what is in their hearts and minds, bridging the gap between spoken words and unspoken thoughts. (Figure 6.16)

The works of another Iranian-American artist Tala Madani (b.1981), including both paintings and animations, focus on discourses surrounding cultural and sexual identities. Madani often approaches these themes in a satirical and challenging manner. Her art confronts notions of ugliness and abomination, typically infused with irony and humour. Madani's imagery frequently features middle-aged, naked men engaged in actions that push their bodies to extreme limits. In her work, slapstick humour intertwines with themes of violence, where creation becomes synonymous with destruction. This amalgamation reflects a complex and visceral vision of contemporary power

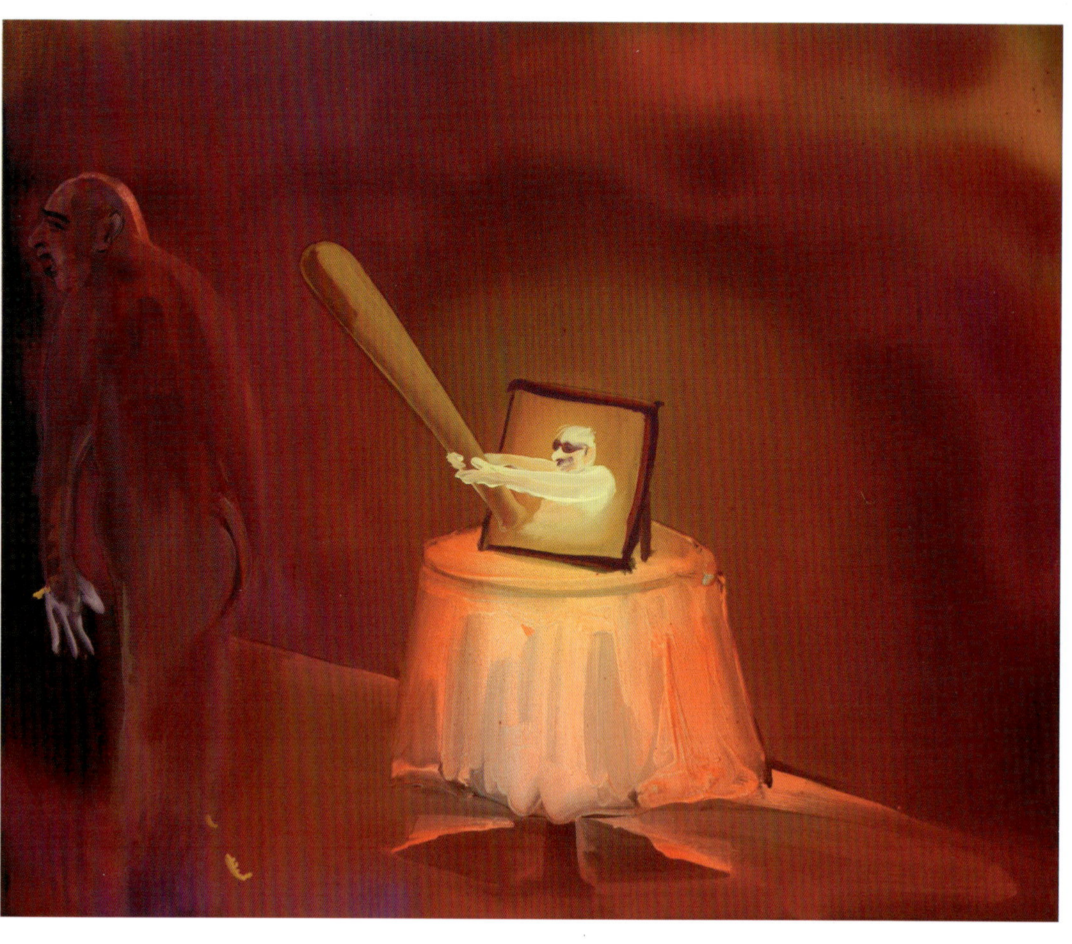

6.17
Tala Madani, *The Bruise*, 2016, oil
on linen, 43.2x50.8x2.5 cm

imbalances across various spectrums. Madani's bizarre and somewhat surreal world serves as an extension of her fantasies, where violence, crime, idiocy, deception, and superstition hold sway. (Figure 6.17)

On the other hand, Shahram Entekhabi, a Berlin-based artist, focuses on themes where the crux of his intellectual engagement lies in grappling with the establishment of laws in urban spaces and the complexity of self-perception from the perspective of an immigrant. His satirical interpretations of cultural norms in Iran and on a broader global scale manifest in symbolic representations of personal experiences within his works. His series *My Superheroes*, which explores whimsical issues of this nature, draws attention to the struggle over the creation of a new world and the presentation of possible alternatives for leadership in an impossible void that can only be filled by the sudden appearance of a hero; a hero who is expected to confront threats and adversities and demonstrate courage and determination for 'self-transcendence'. (Figure 6.18)

Sara Rahbar (b.1976) resides in New York, where her multidisciplinary work explores the conflicts and intersections within culture. Spanning photography, sculpture, collage, assemblage and installation, her art is primarily autobiographical. In her renowned series *Flag* (2005–17), Rahbar reimagines traditional objects like fabrics and embroideries. Through collage, she juxtaposes elements such as old paintings, motifs, and everyday objects. This mixture creates a striking visual that disrupts the original function of the flags. These works explore notions of belonging, nationalism, and the political while representing the ideological conflicts stemming from the artist's dual nationalities. By juxtaposing these objects, Rahbar establishes connections to cultural backgrounds and fragmented aspects of identity, offering insights into her personal journey of self-discovery. (Figure 6.19)

Bahar Behbahani's (b. 1973) art revolves around a dialogue with geography and space, focusing on Iran's history through painting,

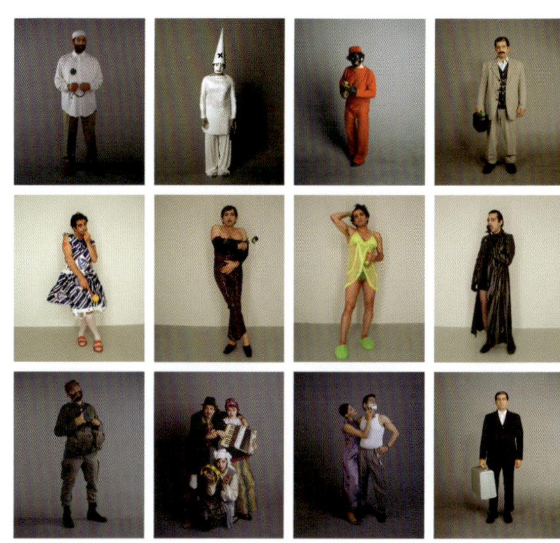

6.18
Shahram Entekhabi, *My Super Heroes*, 2005-2010, C-Print, 70×90 cm, each, image courtesy the artist

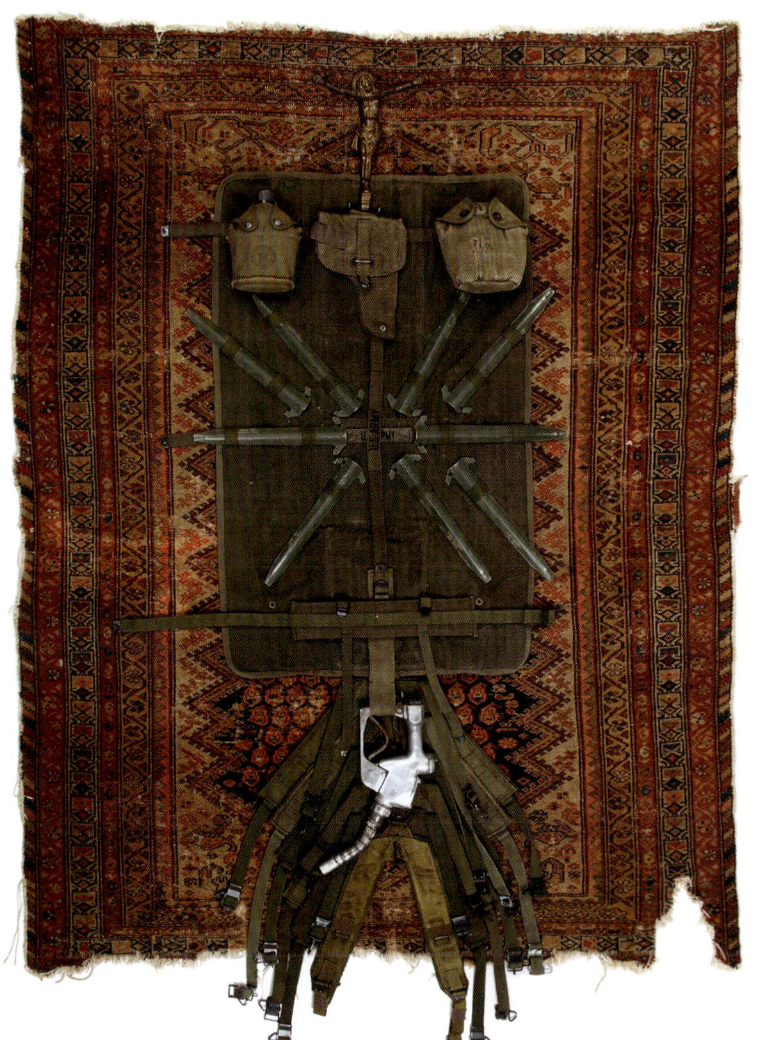

6.19
Sara Rahbar, *The Sun Grew Cold; Our Lands Soaked in Blood; Donkeys Became Gods; Prostitutes Nuns*, from the *War* series, 2010, mixed media, 213.4×147.3 cm, image courtesy the artist

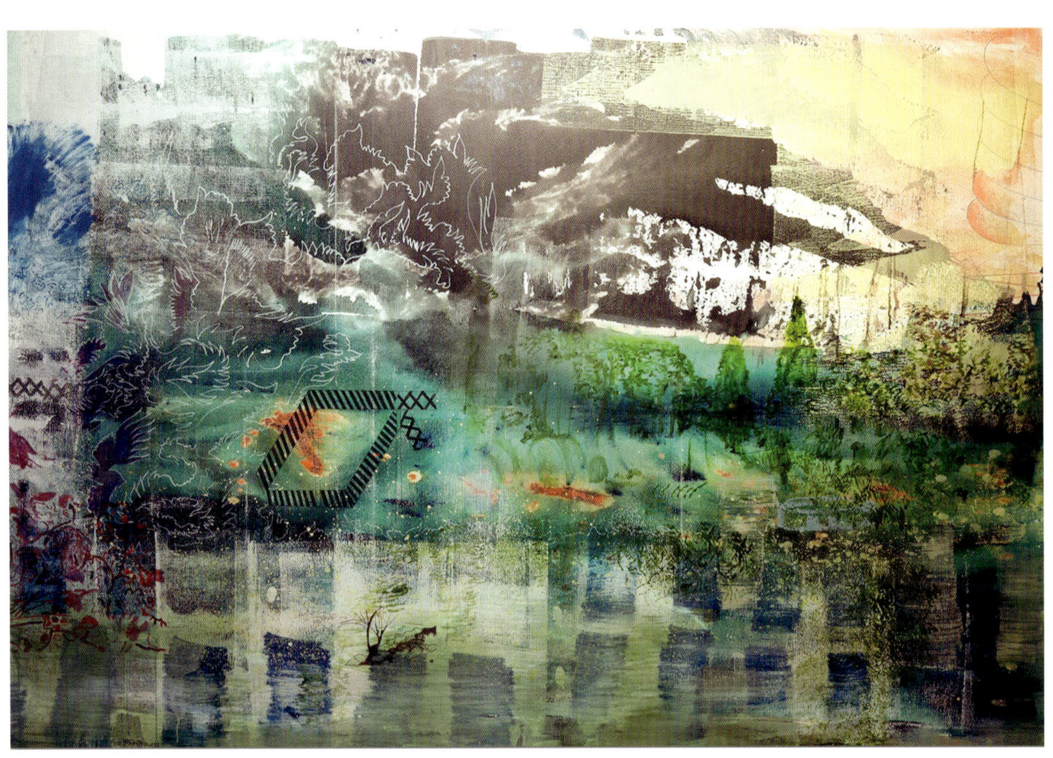

6.20
Bahar Behbahani, *Unwalled*,
2020, mixed media on canvas,
178x254 cm

photography, installation, video, and performance. While her earlier work had a dreamy, poetic quality with occasional political and social themes, her recent pieces predominantly feature plants, flowers, water, rivers, space, and architecture. Inspired by the Persian garden's form and concept, she connects Iran's socio-political history with global environmental issues. *Eram* (2019) is part of her *Liquid River* series, depicting a traditional Persian garden's partial pattern. It features water, plants, and simplified architectural elements, evoking a dreamlike atmosphere. The central stream holds particular significance, signifying the importance of water in Persian gardens. (Figure 6.20)

The work of the German-Iranian artist, Timo Nasseri (b. 1972), is influenced by archetypes derived from mathematics and language, as well as the intrinsic truths found within form and rhythm. His drawings and sculptures draw inspiration from the aesthetic connections between diverse subjects, such as the geometric precision of mathematics and the ornate complexities of Islamic ornamentation, notably *muqarnas* – decorative element commonly found in the entrances of Iranian/Islamic buildings, particularly mosques. Nasseri's works also explores a multitude of concepts surrounding *muqarnas*, including the obsessive nature inherent in their design process, the emphasis on repetition, and their symbolic representation of the infinite.[15] Through his art, he invites viewers to observe the complex relationships between mathematics, and culture. (Figure 6.21)

Iman Raad (b.1979) currently residing and working in New York City, is an artist known for his diverse approach to media and materials. His artistic repertoire encompasses a wide range, from grandiose wall paintings to meticulously embroidered flags. Human figures rarely occupy the focal point in his creations. Instead, Raad draws inspiration from a myriad of sources, including birds, flowers, and still-life compositions, evoking echoes of the traditional *Gol-o-Morgh* (Rose and Nightingale) paintings – a cherished genre in classical Persian art and literature that flourished during the late Safavid era (later seventeenth-early eighteenth century). Raad's art reflects a fusion of diverse visual cultures, with a pronounced nod to Ira's rich artistic legacy. In his *The Table the Night Has Left Behind* series, inspired by the Qajar *Gol-o-Morgh* paintings, he embarks on an exploration of meaning conveyed through repetitive patterns in varying colour palettes. In doing so, he not only pays homage to tradition but also challenges the notion of mechanical mass production by infusing each piece with meticulous craftsmanship. (Figure 6.22)

Babak Golkar (b.1977), a multidisciplinary artist based in Vancouver, approaches his artistic practice with the aim of fundamentally re-contextualising, deconstructing, and rearranging perceptions of the surrounding world. Characterised by an intellectual iconoclasm and an unbridled philosophical spirit of inquiry, Golkar's works playfully challenge the notion that the fixity of meaning is anything more than an illusion, which he systematically disassembles and exposes.[16] Central to his artistic inquiry is the idea of truth and its nature. His project *The Longer You Can Look Back, The Farther You Can Look Forward* (2020), which encompasses paintings, prints, installations and videos, offers a playful perspective on the complex ideas of contemporary manipulation. Drawing on his research into historical and contemporary propaganda theories and practices, along with the pervasive impact of imagery in our everyday lives, Golkar investigates the influence of Internet markets, social networks and the resulting culture of images that profoundly saturates our existence. Within his exhibition, Golkar scrutinises the concept of perpetual manipulation stemming from our constrained perception, underscoring the potent influence of imagery on shaping our perceptions of reality. Through his inquiry, Golkar highlights the imperative of maintaining a critical scepticism toward the visual

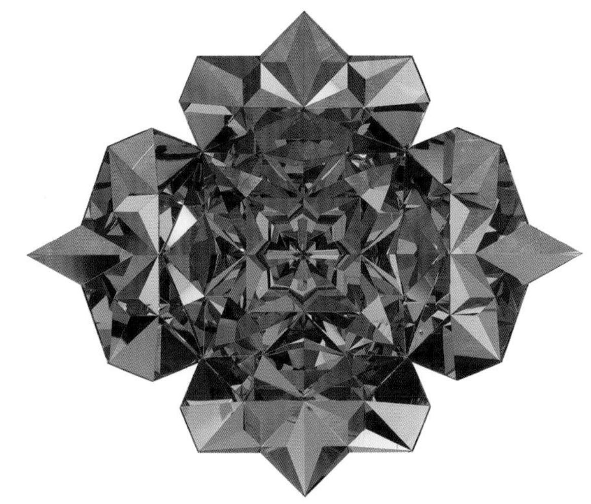

6.21
Timo Nasseri, *Epistrophy VI*, 2012, sculpture embedded in wall, polished stainless steel, 100×150×150 cm

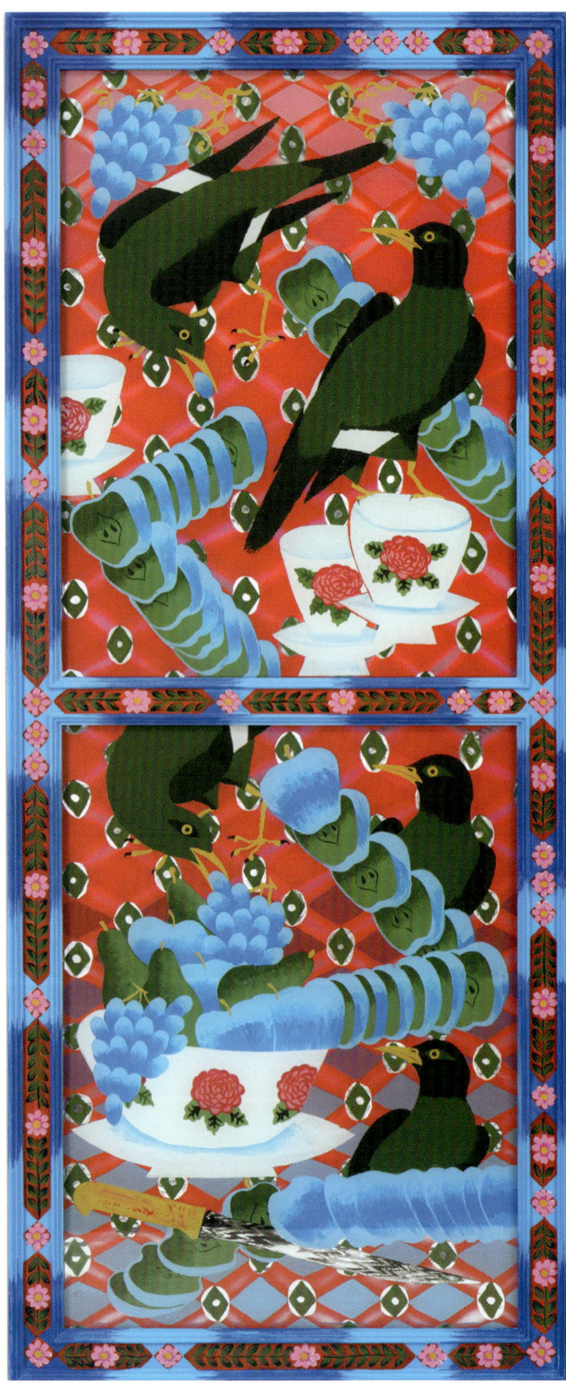

6.22
Iman Raad, *Still Life with Blue Apples, Cuts, a Knife, And Cups*, 2022, reverse glass painting in artist's painted frame, acrylic gouache on tempered glass, aluminium foil, and acrylic on wood, 134.5×55.5×3.8 cm

domain, urging us to question the authenticity and manipulation inherent in our mediated encounters. (Figure 6.23)

Using various media such as painting, drawing, photography, sculpture and installation, the work of Navid Azimi Sajadi (b. 1982) examines the cultural traditions of Islamic lands and revisits many of the symbols and elements of these past traditions together with those found in European ones. Sajadi's recent interactive installations explore mythology and cultural history in spaces like museums and cathedrals. He examines the connections between Eastern and Western traditions, challenging notions of cultural differences by highlighting shared roots. His installation *East and West: Allegories and Symbols of the Mediterranean Tradition* (2020) connects Sicilian Arab-Norman buildings, blending Greek funerary masks with *muqarnas* structures. Glazed ceramic vessels depict Eastern origin stories, incorporating elements from both Mediterranean and Middle Eastern traditions. (Figure 6.24)

In addition to the aforementioned examples, a great number of other Iranian artists living and working across diaspora, including Davoud Zandian (b.1954), Afsoon (b.1971), Pouran Jinchi (b.1959), Nooshin Farhid, Yari Ostovany (b.1962), Avish Kheberehzadeh (b.1969), Farkhondeh Shahroudi (b.1962), Simin Keramati, Mahmood Sabzi (b.1955), Leila Pazooki (b.1977), Ali Banisadr (b.1976), Ala Ebtekar (b.1978), Farhad Ahrarnia (b.1971), Mamali Shafahi (b.1982), Arash Hanaei, Mehraneh Atashi, Bijan Moosavi (b.1983), Sam Samiee (b.1988), Mehdi Ghadyanloo (b.1980), Abdolreza Aminlari (b.1979), Kamrooz Aram (b.1978), Ghazaleh Avarzamani (b.1980), Ali Ahadi (b.1984), Sepand Danesh (b.1984), Gohar Dashti (b.1980), Taha Heydari (b.1986), Mohammad Barrangi (b.1988) and Yasi Alipour (b.1989), among others. (Figures 6.25–31) Their works, although using different methods and approaches, address the issues and discourses explored in the above cases. It is worth concluding this section by saying that these artists all share a preoccupation with 'liminality',[17] which allows them to assimilate and modify Western approaches, and to use their works as a means of commenting upon issues of nostalgia, alienation, memory and loss. Similarly, the experience of marginality – or living between borderlines – provides an important and productive context for artists, in which they can be active spectators in another culture, while exploring their roots and pasts.

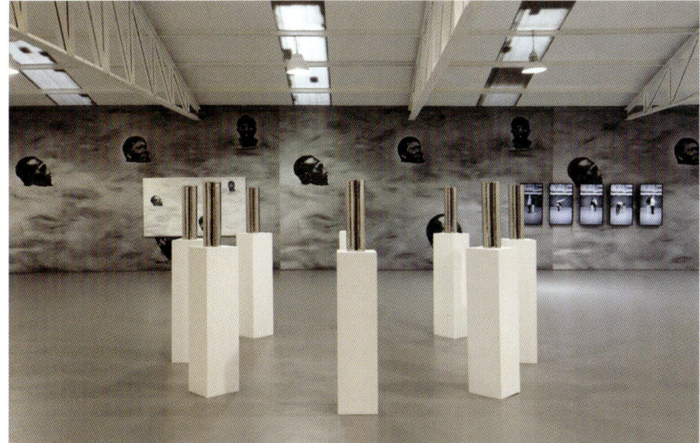

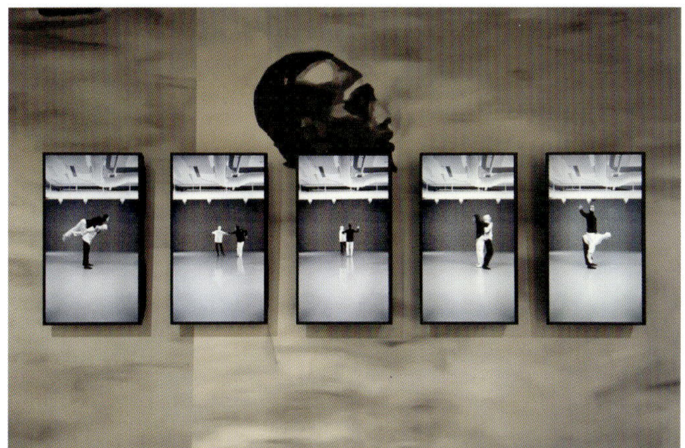

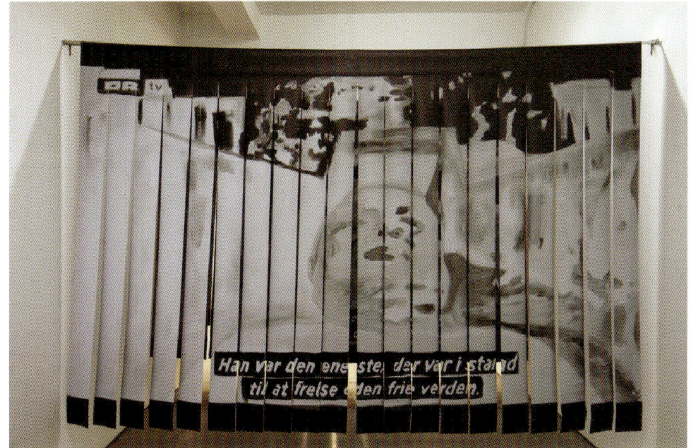

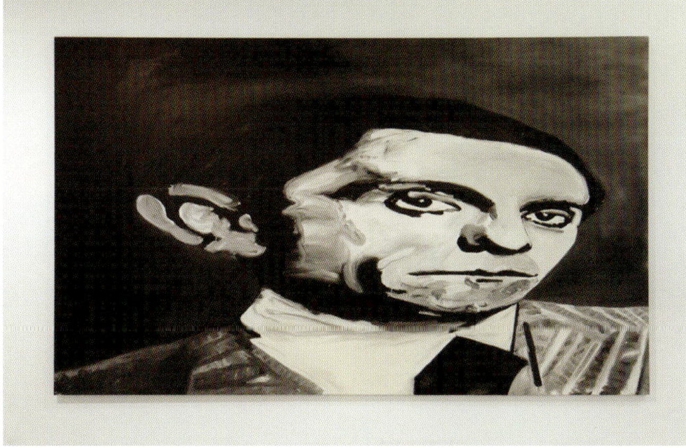

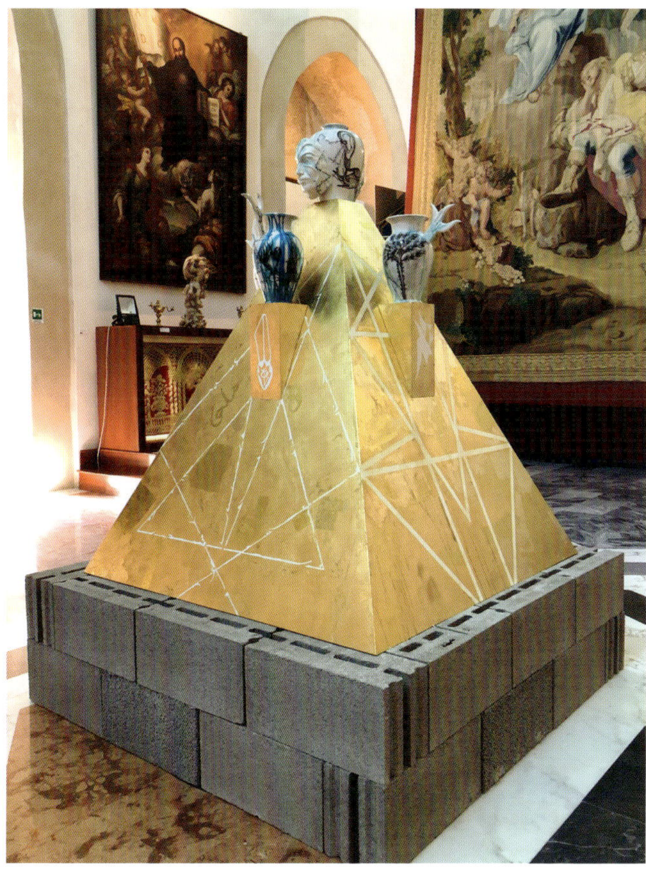

6.24
Navid Azimi Sajadi, *Lucid dream
fountain*, 2020, under-glazed painted
ceramics, each jar 35×18×21cm

6.23
Babak Golkar, *The Longer You Can
Look Back, The Farther You Can Look
Forward*, 2020, exhibition view,
Sabrina Amrani Gallery, Madrid,
Spain

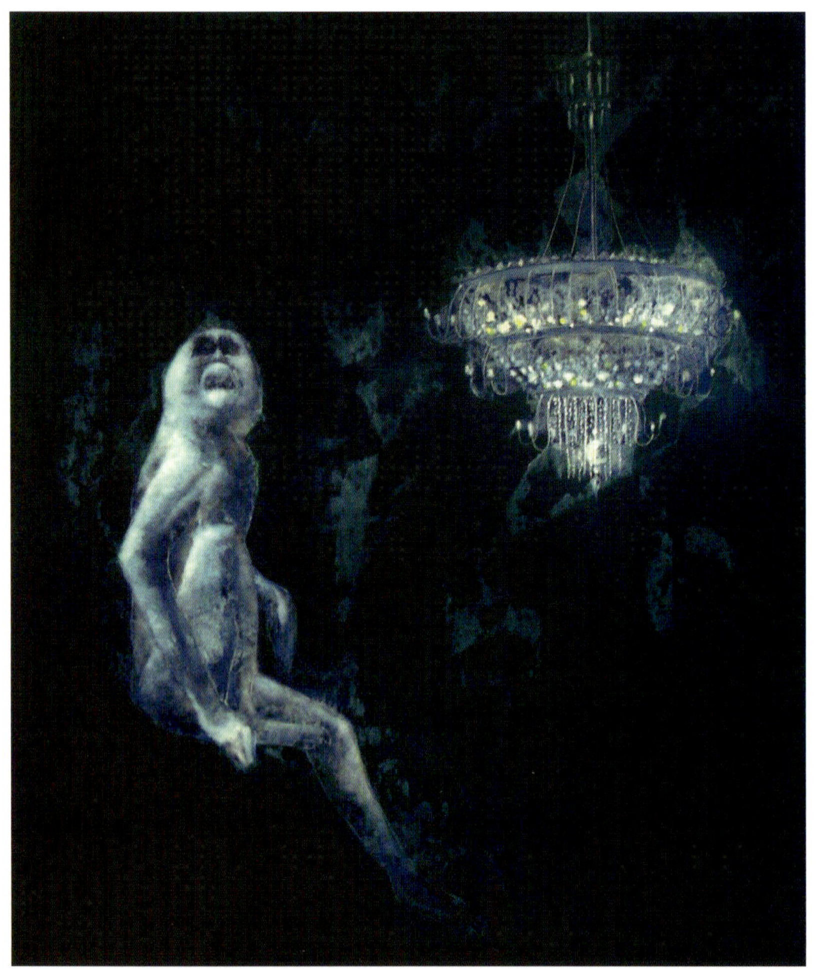

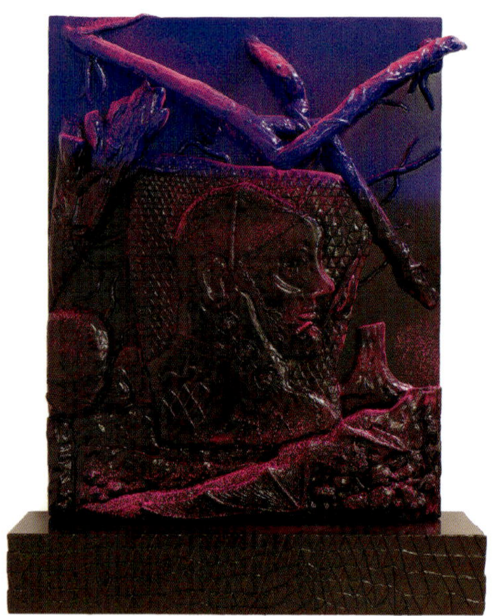

6.26
Mamali Shafahi, *Judgment Night Daddy Kills People*, 2022, installation view at the Parallel Circuits

6.25
Avish Kheberehzadeh, *Untitled*, 2007, a part of the triptych, left panel, 127×101.6 cm, oil on gesso and wood

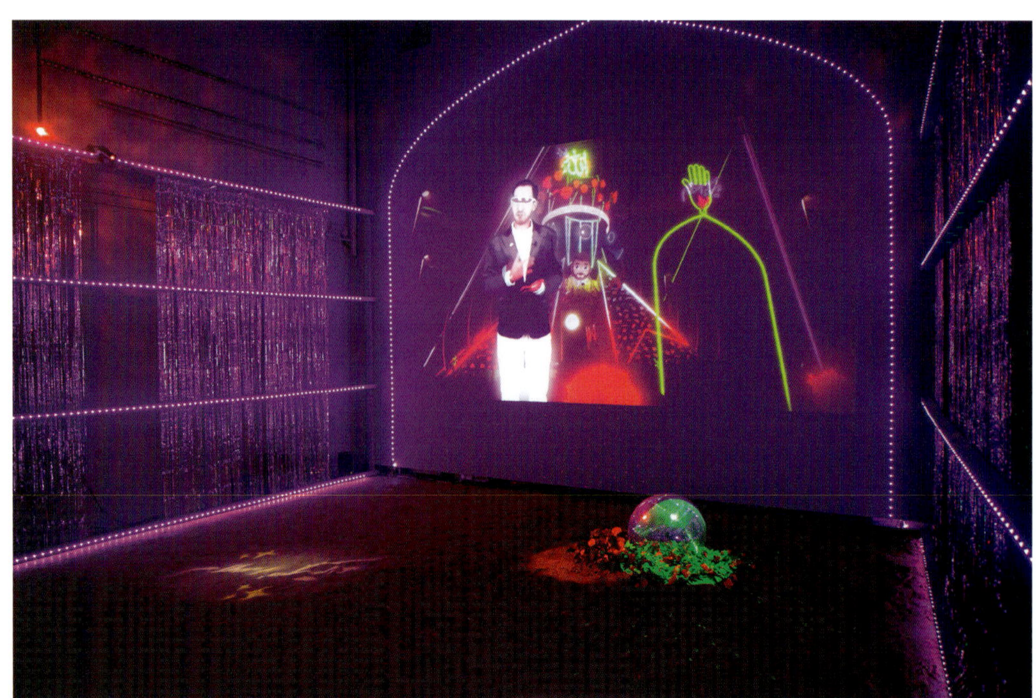

6.27
Bijan Moosavi, *Disco Islam Future Phantasmagoria*, 2022, installation view, Eastside Projects' Second Gallery, Birmingham

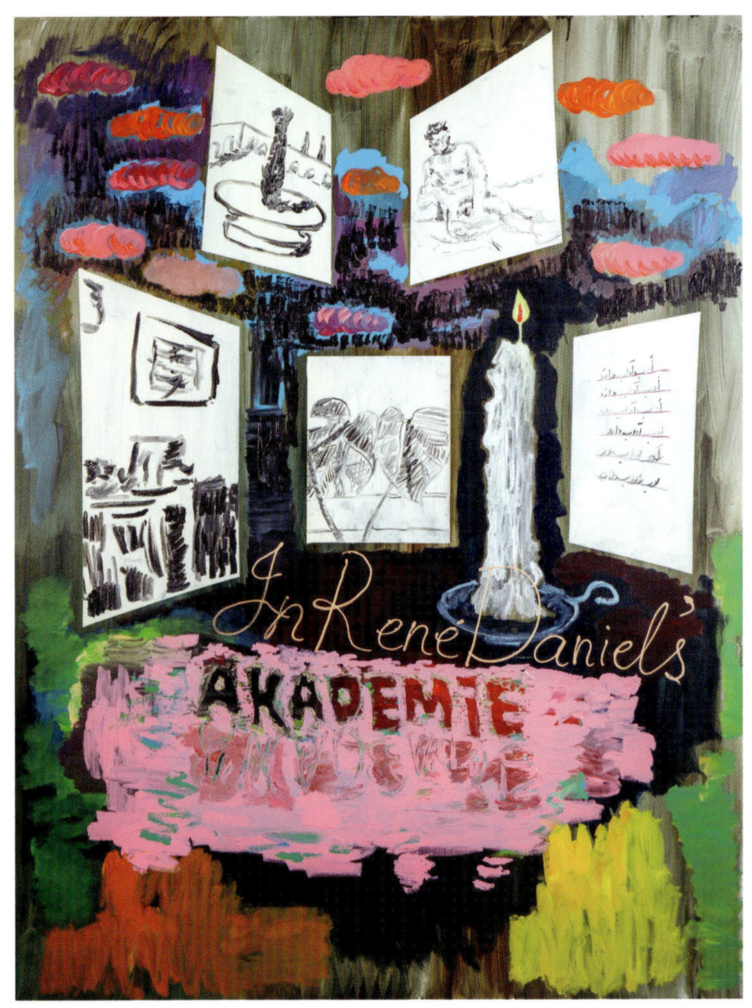

6.28
Sam Samiee, *Al-Hazen A La Daniels
With Reminder on Adab*, 2021,
acrylic on canvas, 200×140 cm

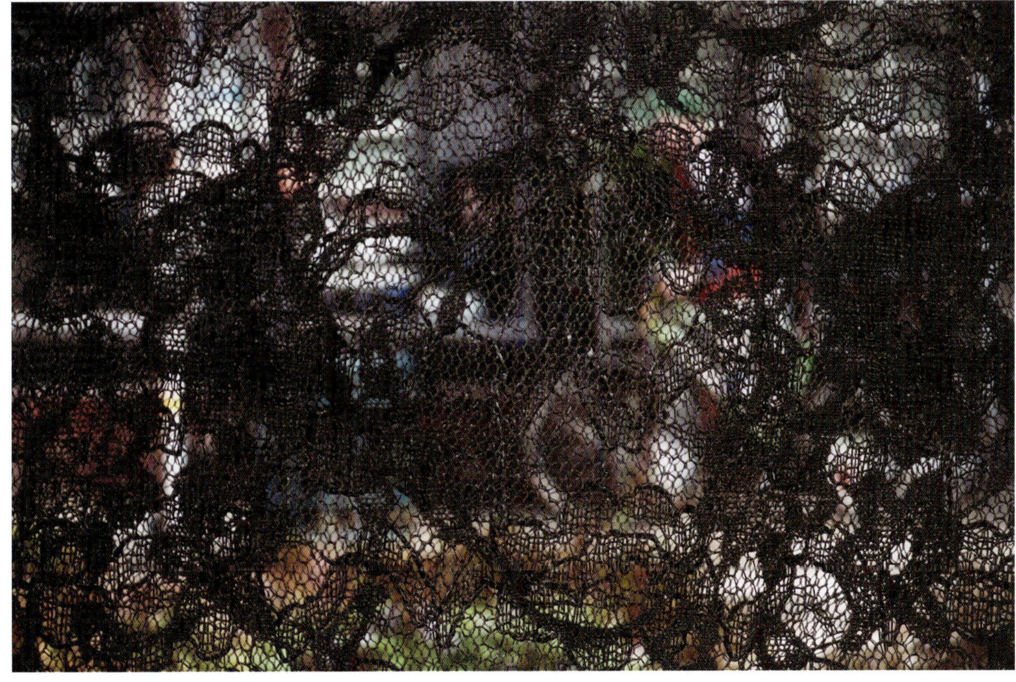

6.29
Ali Ahadi, *Untitled* (*Shit Yes*), 2018,
inkjet print, wooden frame, acrylic,
lace, 46.6×70×5.5 cm

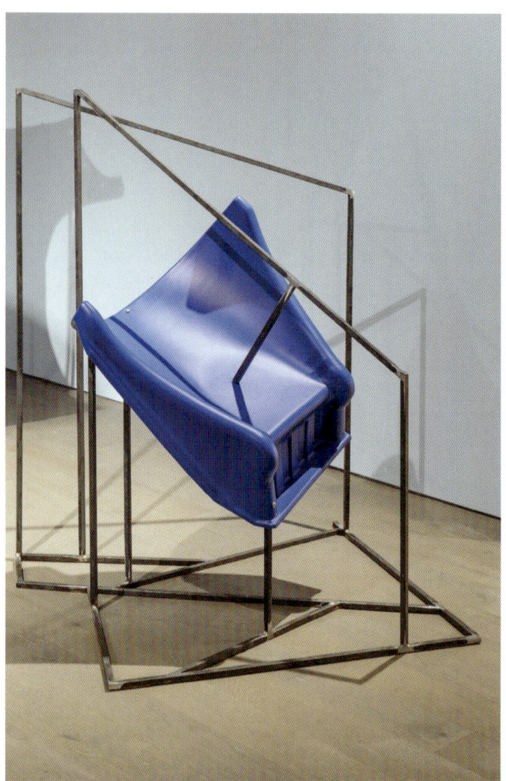

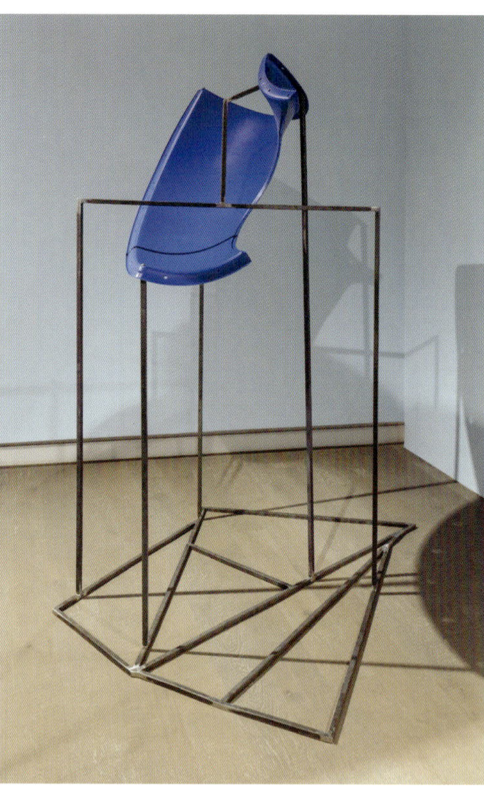

6.30
Ghazaleh Avarzamani, *Strange Temporalities*, 2018, segmented slide on metal armature, sizes vary

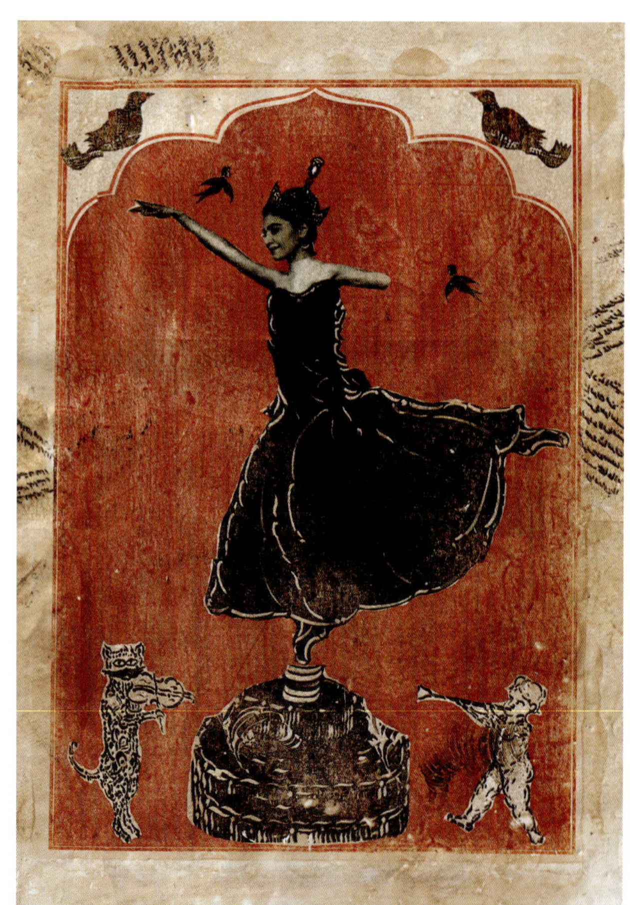

6.31
Mohammad Barrangi, *Dance for Freedom, I saw a girl dancing in Piccadilly Square*, London, 2022, handprint on paper, 49×37 cm

NOTES

1   See Donald Woods Winnicott, *Maturational Processes and the Facilitating Environment: Studies in the Theory of Emotional Development*, London 1965.

2   Stuart Hall, 'Cultural Identity and Diaspora', in Jonathan Rutherford, ed. *Identity: Community, Culture, Difference*, London 1990, p.235.

3   See Helia Darabi, 'Found in Translation: Exile as a Productive Experience in the Work of Iranian Artists', *NuktaArt*, vol. 5, Issue 2, October 2010 http://www.nuktaartmag.com/Nukta/GeneralContent/View/179/Accessed 15.02/2013

4   See Lisa Lowe, "Heterogeneity, Multiplicity: Making Asian-American Differences," *Diaspora*, vol. 1, no. 1, pp.24–44.

5   William Rowe and Vivian Schelling, *Memory and Modernity: Popular Culture in Latin America*, London 1991, p. 231.

6   See Hamid Naficy, *The Making of Exile Cultures: Iranian Television in Los Angeles*, Minneapolis; London 2003; Hamid Naficy, "Phobic Spaces and Liminal Panics: Independent Transnational Film Genre," in Ella Shohat, Robert Stam, ed., *Multiculturalism, Postcoloniality, and Transnational Media*, New Brunswick, N.J., 2003; and Hamid Naficy, *An Accented Cinema: Exilic and Diasporic Filmmaking*, Princeton, Oxford 2001.

7   Hamid Naficy, *The Making of Exile Cultures*, p.8.

8   Ibid, p.223.

9   See Kathleen Stewart, 'Nostalgia – A Polemic', *Cultural Anthropology*, vol. 3, no. 3, August 1988, pp.227, 238.

10 Jean Baudrillard, *Simulations*, Translation into English Paul Foss, Paul Patton, and Philip Beitchman, New York, 1983.

11 Susan Stewart, *On Longing: Narratives of the Miniature, the Gigantic, the Souvenir, the Collection*, Baltimore 1984, p. 145.

12 For further discussion about these works, see Eleanor Heartney, 'Shoja Azari', http://www.artinamericamagazine.com/reviews/shoja-azari/ Accessed 2/06/2013

13 Tabrizian is also a professor of photography at the University of Westminster, London.

14 Anthony Downey, 'Restaging the (Objective) Violence of Images, Reza Aramesh in conversation with Anthony Downey', http://www.ibraaz.org/interviews/5/ Accessed 2/06/2013

15 Ibid.

16 Sasha M. Lee, 'Interview with Babak Golkar', http://babakgolkar.ca/ Accessed 17/01/2013

17 For examination of the concept of liminality in relation to Iranian artists and art, see Peter Cross, 'Inscription and Transcription: Some Notes on the Liminal', *Art Tomorrow*, no. 3, winter 2011, pp.108–113.

Bibliography

Abrahamian, Ervand, *Iran Between Two Revolutions*, Princeton, New Jersey, Princeton University Press, 1982.

Abramovic, Marina and Danto, Arthur C., *Shirin Neshat*, New York, Rizzoli, 2010.

Adamiyyat, Fereydoun, *Andisheh-hay-i Talebuf-i Tabrizi*, Tehran, Intisharat-i Damavand, 1363S/ 1984.

Adhari, M. S. Ali, 'Ali Akbar Khan Naqqash-bashi-Muzayyin al-Dawla', *Payam-i Nuvin* 5, no. 12, 1342S/ 1963–64.

Adle, Shahriar and Zuka, Yahya, 'Notes et Documents sur la phtographie Iranienne et son historire: Les Premiers Daguerreotypistes', *Studia Iranica*, no. 12, 1983, pp. 249-80.

Afsarian, Iman, 'Huviyyat an chizi ast keh beh ijra dar mi-ayad: guft-u-gu ba Mansour Barahimi', *Hirfeh Hunarmand*, no. 5, 1382S/ 2003.

Aghdashloo, Aydin, Mohammad Ehsai's exhibition's catalogue, *Anjoman-i Iran va amrica* (Iran-American Society), Tehran, Isfand 1354S/ Feb-March 1976.

Aydin Aghdashloo, 'Baqi hameh harf ast', *Hunar-i mu'asir*, no. 2, 1372S/ November/ December 1993, pp. 46-48.

Akhavi, Shahrough, *Religion and Politics in Contemporary Iran*, Albany, N.Y., State University of New York Press, 1980.

Al-e Ahmad, Jalal, *Arzishyabi-i shitab-zadeh*, fifth edition, Tehran, n. p., 1999.

——, *Gharb-zadigi*, Tehran, Ravaq 1341S/ 1962

——, Jalal Al-e Ahmad, *Occidentosis: A Plague from the West*, translated into English by R. Campbell, Berkeley, California, Mizan, 1984.

——, 'Tukhm-i seh zardeh-i panjum', in *Adab va hunar-i imruz, kitab-i sivvum*, Tehran, Nashr-i Mitra, 1994, pp. 1377-1386.

Ali, Wijdan, *Modern Islamic Art: Development and Continuity*, Gainesville, University of Florida, 1997.

Ali, Wijdan and Bisharat, E. (eds), *Contemporary Art from the Islamic World*, Amman, London, Scorpion on behalf of Royal Society of Fine Arts, 1989.

Amanat, Abbas, 'Qajar Iran: A Historical Overview', in Layla S. Diba, ed., *Royal Persian Painting: The Qajar Epoch 1785-1825, Two Hundred Years of Painting from the Royal Persian Courts*, New York, I. B. Tauris 1999, pp. 14-29.

Anderson, Benedict, *Imagined Communities: Reflections on the Origin and spread of Nationalism*, London, Verso, 1991.

'An Exposition of Contemporary Iranian Painting' (brochure of Iranian contemporary painting exhibition in Doha, Qatar), 2001.

Anonymous, 'Mohammad Ghaffari hunarmand va naqqash-i buzurg', *Payam-i now*, no. 10, Murdad 1325S/ 1946, p. 82.

——, 'Kamal al-Mulk', *Yaghma*, no. 3, Aban 1329S/ October 1950, p. 339.

——, Introduction to the Second Tehran Biennial (exhibition catalogue), Tehran 1960.

——, Introduction to the Third Tehran Biennial (exhibition catalogue), Tehran 1341S/ 1962.

——, Introduction to the Fourth Tehran Biennial (exhibition catalogue), Tehran 1343S/ 1964.

——, 'Guft-u-gu-i ba naqqashan-i javan', *Sukhan*, no. 11, 12, Murdad & Shahrivar 1343S/ August 1964, pp. 1061-1066.

——, 'Bayaniyeh-i guruh-i naqqashan-i talar-i Qandriz', *Barrasi: mi'mari, naqqashi, mujjasameh-sazi, girafik...*, nos. 6 & 7, 1344S/ 1965.

——, 'Mansour Qandriz murd', *Sukhan*, no. 2, Isfand 1344S/ March 1965, p. 205.

——, 'Az khudiman', *Firdawsi*, no. 574, Isfand 1344S/ March 1965, p. 14.

——, 'Qandriz murd', *Talash*, no. 1, Khurdad 1345S/ June 1966, pp. 75, 76.

——, 'Guft-u-gui ba sh'ir-i naqqash Manuchehr Yektaei', *Talash*, no. 19, Aban-Azaar 1348S/ October-November 1969, pp. 68-73.

——, 'Man hichguneh qiyd va bandi ra baray-i hunarmand nimipaziram', *Firdowsi*, no. 984, Mihr 1349S/ October 1970, pp. 18, 19.

——, Introduction to *Fasli dar hunar; dar bareh-y-i hunar-hay-i tajassumi, hunar-hay-i nimayishi va adabiyyat*, no. 4, summer 1350S/ 1971, no page number.

——, 'Kazemi va giyah va sang', *Talash*, no. 35, Khurdad-Tir 1351S/ June-July 1972, pp. 30-32.

——, 'Kamal al-Mulk sunnat shikan va sunnat guzar', *Hunar va mardum*, no. 150, Farvardin 1354S/ March 1975, pp. 63-67.

——, 'Kamal al-Mulk sunnat shikan va sunnat guzar', *Hunar va mardum*, no. 151, Urdibihisht 1354S/ April 1975, pp. 63-68.

——, 'Kamal al-Mulk sunnat shikan va sunnat guzar', *Hunar va mardum*, no. 152, Khurdad 1354 S/ May 1975, pp. 63-66.

——, 'Kamal al-Mulk sunnat shikan va sunnat guzar', *Hunar va mardum*, no. 155, Shahrivar 1354S/ August 1975, pp. 47-53.

——, 'Pezeshk-Niya naqqash-i zindigi', *Kiyhan*, 2 Azar 2535 = 1355S/ December 1976, p. 9.

——, 'Chahar divari-i [Marco]; guft-u-shinud ba Marcos Grigurian', *Rastakhiz*, 19 Bahman 2535 = 1355S/ January 1977, p. 7.

——, 'Kubism urupai dar iran?' *Rastakhaui* 5 Khurdad 2536 = 1956S/ 1977, p. 7.

——, 'Nihzat-i *Khurus-jangi* va tahavvul-i hunar', *Rastakhiz*, 3 Khurdad 2536 = 1356S/ August 1977, p. 7; & 7 Khurdad 2536 = 1356S/ August 1977, pp. 7, 18.

——, 'Galirihay-i Tehran, *Rastakhiz*', no.825, Bahman 1356S/ January 1978, p. 8.

——, 'Dar muzeh-ha huviyyat-i milli ra justuju kunim', *Javanan-i Rastakhiz*, Farvardın 1357S/ 1978, p. 29.

——, 'Siyri kutah dar nimayishgah-hay-i buzurgdasht-i ayyam-i daheh-i fajr: payam-i vahid-i hunarmandan', *Faslnameh-i hunar*, no. 3, spring & summer 1362S/ 1983, pp. 334-351.

——, 'Guft-u-gu: Gholam Ali Ajalli khattat va naqqash (dunyay-i khuytut, dunyayi 'ajib va hiyrat-angiz)', *Faslnameh-i hunar*, no. 5, winter 1362S/ 1983, spring 1363S/ 1984, pp. 208-223.

——, 'Ustad Ali Mohammad Heydarian: naqqashi fowq-i 'irfan ast', *Kiyhan-i Farhangi*, no. 11, Bahman 1364S/ 1985, pp. 3-10.

——, 'Muzeh-i hunar-hay-i mu'asir dar daheh-i fajr (12-22 Bahman 1365S)', *Hunar-hay-i tajassumi*, no. 14, summer and autumn 1366S/ 1987, pp. 276-281.

——, 'Barr va bahr farakh ast va adami bisyar', *Faslnameh-i hunar*, p. 19, 1369S/ 1990, pp. 5-7.

——, 'Duwumin nimayishgah-i du-salaneh-i naqqashi-i iran', *Mah-nameh-i hunar-hay-i tajassumi*, no. 4, 1372S/ 1993, p. 1.

——, 'Naqqashi dar ruz-hay-i aftabi: pay-i suhbat-i ustad Mahmoud Javadipour beh munasibat-i barguzari-i nimayishgahi az asar-i in hunarmand dar galiri-i kelasik', *Hunar-hay-i tajassumi*, pish-shimareh-i nos. 5 & 6, winter 1993-4, pp. 6-11.

——, 'Harf-hai now baray-i guftan: guft-u-gui samimaneh ba Mehdi Hosseini naqqash va ustad-i danishgah', *Hunar-hay-i tajassumi*, no. 1, spring 1377S/ 1998, pp. 34-41.

——, 'Ba Irani-i durun-gira, ixprisiyunism sazigar ast: guf-u-gu ba hunarmand-i pishkisvat ustad Javad Hamidi', *Hunar-hay-i tajassumi*, no. 52, Tir 1378S/ July 1999, pp. 2-10.

——, 'Parvaneh Etemadi: Representation and Re-creation of Reality', *Tavoos*, no. 1, Tehran, autumn, 1999, pp. 116-119.

——, 'Vurud beh 'arseh-i nuvin: guzarishi az fa'aliyyat-hay-i chand saleh-i akhir-i muzeh-i hunar-hay-i mu'asir', *Hamshahri*, 11 Murdad 1380S/ 2 August 2001.

——, 'Guft-u-gu ba Hamid Severi; agar istifadeh nakunim, "aqab mimanim"', *Hirfeh hunrmand*, no. 2, 1381S/ 2002, pp. 130-133.

Araeen, Rasheed, *The Other Story: Afro-Asian Artists in Postwar Britain,* London, Hayward Gallery, 1989.

Arasteh, R., *Education and Social Awakening in Iran*, Leiden, E. J. Brill, 1962.

Arnheim, R, *Art and Visual Perception: A Psychology of the Creative Eye*, London, Faber, 1967.

Aryanpour, Yahya, *Az saba ta nima*, Tehran, Intisharat-i Amirkabir, 1352S/ 1973.

——, *Az nima ta ruzigar-i ma: tarikh-i adab-i Farsi-i mu'asir*, Tehran, Intisharat-i Zavvar 1374S/ 1995.

Aschenbrenner, E. (ed), *Persian Rugs and Carpets*, Tehran, Farhang-sara (Yasavuli), 1996.

Ashrafi, H., 'Az tarrahi be tarrahi: guzarishi az nimayishgah-i Faramarz Pilaram', *Rastakhiz-i Javanan*, no. 83, Isfand 2535 = 1355S/ 1977, pp. 20-23.

Ashtiani, Esmail, 'Sharh-i hal va tarikh-i hayat-i Kamal al-Mulk', *Hunar va mardum*, no. 7, Ordibehesht 1342 S/ April 1963, pp. 8-19.

Ashuri, Daryoush, *Ma va mudirniyyat*, second edition, Tehran, Mu'assiseh-i farhangi-i sirat, 1377S/ 1998.

Atashi, M., 'Suratgar-i sihr-afarin-i ihsas-ha va andisheh-ha', *hafteh-nameh-i tamasha*, no. 186, 1355, 1975, p. 14.

Avvalin nimdyishgah-i dusdlaneh-i naqqashdn-i iran (First Iranian Painters Biennial) (exhibition catalogue), Tehran, Tehran Museum of Contemporary Art (Department of Biannual), 1370S/ 1991.

Ayatollahi, Habibollah, 'Buhran dar hunar-i imruz-i iran', in *Huvıyyat-i farhangi va hunari: majmu'eh bahs-hay-i kunfirans-i hunar-hay-i tajassumi* (Proceedings of the First Plastic Arts Conference), Tehran 1372S/ 1993, pp. 95-101.

——, 'Naqqashi-khatt hunar-i bi risheh', *Hunar-i mu'asir*, no. 4, Farvardın & Urdibihisht 1373S/ 1994, pp. 12-14.

Badie, Bertrand, *Les deux etats: pouvoir et societe en Occident et en terre d' Islam*, Paris, Fayard, 1986.

Shiva Balaghi, 'Iranian Visual Arts in "The Century of Machinery, Speed and the Atom": Rethinking Modernity', in Shiva Balaghi and Lynn Gumpert (eds), *Picturing Iran: Art, Society and Revolution*, London and New York, I. B. Tauris, 2002.

Banani, A., *The Modernisation of Iran 1921-1941*, Stanford, Stanford U. P., 1961.

Reza Baraheni, 'az aftabi beh aftab-i digar', in *Tarikh-i Muzakkar, Farhang-i hakim va mahkum*, Tehran, Nashr-i Avval, 1363S/ 1984, pp. 177-188.

Barnard, N., *Klim, The Complete Guide: History, Pattern, Technique, Identification,* London, Thames and Hudson, 1993.

Barnlart, R, *Along the Border of Heaven; Sung and Yuan Painting*, New York, Metropolitan Museum of Art, 1983.

Baudrillard, Jean, *Simulations,* translation into English Paul Foss, Paul Patton and Philip Beitchman, New York, Semiotext(e), 1983.

Bayat-Philipp, Mangol, 'Tradition and Change in Iranian Socio-Religious Thought', in Michael E. Bonine and Nikki R. Keddie (eds), *Modern Iran: the Dialectics of Continuity and Change*, New York, State University of New York Press 1981, pp. 37-58.

Bell, Vikki, 'Introduction', in Vikki Bell (ed), *Performativity and Belonging*, London, Sage Publications, 1999.

Bharier, Julian, *Economic Development in Iran 1900-1970*, London, Oxford University Press, 1971.

Bill, James Alban, *The Politics of Iran: Groups, Classes and Modernization*, Columbus, Ohio, Merrill, 1972.

Bonine, M. E. and Keddie, N. et al, *Modern Iran: The Dialectics of Continuity and Change*, eds. M. E. Bonine and N. Keddie, New York, State University of New York Press, 1981.

Boroujerdi, Mehrzad, 'Gharbzadegi: The Dominant Intellectual Discourse of Pre- and Post-Revolutionary Iran', in Smith K. Farsoun and Mehrdad Mashayekhi (eds), *Iran: Political Culture in the Islamic Republic*, London and New York, Routledge, 1992, pp. 30-56.

——, *Iranian Intellectuals and the West: The Tormented Triumph of Nativism*. New York, Syracuse University Press, 1996.

Butler, Judith, *Bodies That Matter: On the Discursive Limits of 'Sex'*, New York, London, Routledge 1993.

Bydler, Charlotte, 'Pax Anglo-Americana: A Plea for a Cosmopolitan History of Contemporary Art', in *Ethnic Marketing* (exhibition catalogue), Tehran, Toseh Publishing, 2006, pp. 26-31.

Cabanne, Pierre, 'Un Lettrisme Sacré', *Combat*, no. 7987, 23 Mars 1970, p. 5.

Campbell, J. R. and A. Rew, *Identity and Affect: Experiences of Identity in a Globalising World,* London and Sterling, VA, Pluto Press, 1999.

Sheila Canby, 'Farangi saz: The Impact of Europe on Safavid Painting', in Jill Tilden (ed), *Silk & Stone: The Art of Asia*, London, Hali Publications Limited 1996, pp. 46-59.

Carey, F., ed., *Collecting the 20th Century*, Frances Carey, London, British Museum Press, 1991.

Carrière, J. C., *La Porte Sous La Fontaine* (The Door Underlying the Fountain) (exhibition catalogue), Paris, August 2001.

Catalogue of the Exhibition, *On the Occasion of Seventh Asian Games Exhibition of: works by Contemporary Iranian Artists, Painting, Sculpture, and Design*, Tehran, Shahrıvar 1353S/ September 1974.

Chalipa, Kazem, 'Now-avari va tanawu'-talabi', *Naqsh* (a special magazine series published on the occasion of each Iranian Painting Biennial, commencing with the second), no. 1, 1372S/ 1993, p.5.

Chelkowski, Peter, 'Narrative Painting and Recitation in Qajar Iran', *Muqarnas*, vol. 6, 1989, pp. 98-111.

Chelkowski, Peter and Dabashi, Hamid, *Staging a Revolution: The Art of Persuasion in the Islamic Republic of Iran*, London, Booth-Clibborn, 2000.

Chelkowski, Peter, 'The Art of Revolution and War: The Role of the Graphic Arts in Iran', in Shiva Balaghi and Lynn Gumpert (eds), *Picturing Iran: Art, Society and Revolution*, London, I. B. Tauris, 2002, pp. 127-142.

Clark, John Anthony, *Modern Asian Art*, North Ryde, NSW, Distributed by Craftsman House in association with G+B Arts International, 1998.

Clark, John, 'Asian Modernism', in Yashodhara Dalmia (ed), *Contemporary Indian Art, Other Realities*, Mumbai, Marg Publications, 2002.

Cottam, R. W., *Nationalism in Iran*, London, University of Pittsburgh Press, 1979.

Cross, Peter, 'Inscription and Transcription: Some Notes on the Liminal', *Art Tomorrow*, no. 3, winter 2011, pp. 108-113.

Curzon, G. N., *Persia and Persian Question*, London, Longmans, Green & Co. 1892.

Daftari, Fereshteh, 'Another Modernism: An Iranian Perspective', in Shiva Balaghi and Lynn Gumpert (eds), *Picturing Iran: Art, Society and Revolution*, London and New York, I. B. Tauris, 2002, pp. 39-87.

Dalvand, Ahmad Reza, 'Junbish-i now-pay-i naqqashi', *Gardun*, spring 1370S/ 1991, pp. 73-77.

——, 'Ba naqqashan va hunarmandan-i mu'asir', *Dunyay-i Sukhan*, no. 1370S/ 1991, pp. 90-91.

Daneshvari, Abbas, 'Parviz Tanavoli of Existential Purity and Sophistication', *Art Tomorrow*, no. 5, summer 2011, pp. 179-183.

Darabi, Helia, 'Found in Translation: Exile as a Productive Experience in the Work of Iranian Artists', *NuktaArt*, vol. 5, Issue 2, October 2010, http://www.nuktaartmag.com/Nukta/GeneralContent/View/179/ Accessed 15/02/2013.

——, 'Mahmoud Bakhshi Makhar', *Art Press*, no. 17, May/June/July 2010, pp. 72-74.

Dehbashi, Ali, *Nameh-hay-i Kamal al-Mulk*, Tehran, Intisharat-i Buzurgmihr, 1987.

Denny, W. B., 'Reflection of Paradise in Islamic Art', in Sheila S. Blair and Jonathan M. Bloom (eds), *Images of Paradise in Islamic Art*, Hanover, Hood Museum of Art, Dartmouth College, 1991, pp. 33-65.

Diba, Kamran, 'Iran', in Wijdan Ali and E. Bisharat (eds), *Contemporary Art from the Islamic World*, Amman, London, Scorpion on behalf of Royal Society of Fine Arts, 1989, pp. 150-156.

Diba, Layla S., 'Tasvir-i qudrat va qudrat-i tasvir', *Iran Nameh*, vol. XVII, no. 3, summer 1999, pp. 423-452.

——, 'Muhammad Ghaffari: The Persian Painter of Modern Life', *Iranian Studies*, vol. 45, no. 5, September 2012, pp. 645-659.

——, 'The Power of Images: Qajar Photography and its Relationship to Iranian Art', in Reza Sheikh and Carmen Pérez González (eds), *History of Photography Journal*, Special Issue 'The First Hundred Years of Iranian Photography', vol. 37, no. 1, winter 2013.

Donzel, E. Van, Lewis, B., and Pellat, Ch. (eds), *The Encyclopaedia of Islam* (New Edition), vol. 4, Leiden, E. J. Brill, 1978.

Dorraj, M., 'Populism and Corporatism in Post-revolutionary Iranian Political Culture', in Smith K. Farsoun and Mehrdad Mashayekhi (eds), *Iran: Political Culture in the Islamic Republic*, London and New York, Routledge, 1992, pp. 214-233.

Ebrahim, M., 'Baztabai az zharfay-i andisheh: nazari bar nukhustin nimayishgah-i du-salaneh-i naqqashan-i iran dar muzeh-i hunar-hay-i mu'asir', *Faslnameh-i hunar*, no. 21, winter 1370S/ 1991, spring 1371S/ 1992, pp. 38-45.

Ehsai, M., 'Mohammad Ehsai; naqqash', *Rastakhiz-i Javanan*, no. 100, Tir 2536 = 1355S/ 1977, pp. 28-30.

Ehyayi, Z., 'Higher Education in Iran', *Kiyhan-i Farhangi*, June-July 1998, no. 143, pp. 50-53.

Ekhtiar, Maryam, 'From Workshop to Bazaar to Academy: Art Training and Production in Qajar', in Layla S. Diba (ed), *Royal Persian Painting: The Qajar Epoch 1785-1825, Two Hundred Years of Painting from the Royal Persian Courts,* New York, I. B. Tauris, 1999, pp. 50-65.

Elgar, F., *L'Enchantement Mystique*, (exhibition catalogue), Galerie C. Renault, 28 September-27 October 1965.

Emami, Karim, '*nimayishgah-i asar-i Qandriz*' (Qandriz's exhibition brochure in the Borghese Gallery), Tehran, 1345S/ 1966.

——, 'Modern Persian Artists', in Ehsan Yarshater and Richard Ettinghausen (eds), *Iran Faces the Seventies*, New York, Praeger Publishers, 1971, pp. 349-364.

——, 'Saqqakhaneh School Revisited', in Saqqakhaneh (exhibition catalogue), Tehran 1356S/ 1977.

——, 'Art in Iran XI Post-Qajar', in Ehsan Yarshater (ed), *Encyclopaedia Iranica*, vol. II, London and New York, Routledge & Kegan Paul, 1987, pp. 640-646.

Epstein, Arnold Leonard, *Ethos and Identity*, London, Transaction Publishers, 1978.

Eriksen, Thomas Hylland, 'The Cultural Context of Ethnic Differences', *Man* 26(1), 1991, pp. 127–144.

——, *Ethnicity and Nationalism*, London, Pluto Press, 1993.

Etemadi, E., 'Owj va nuzul-i naqqashi-i mudirn dar iran', *Hunar-hay-i tajassumi*, summer/ winter 1378S/ 1999, pp. 112-114.

Ettinghausen, Richard, 'An Introduction to Modern Persian Painting', in *Iran Faces the Seventies*, Ehsan Yarshater and Richard Ettinghausen (eds), New York, Praeger Publishers, 1971, pp. 341-348.

Evans, Jessica and Hall, Stuart, *Visual Culture: The Reader*, London, Thousand Oaks, and New Delhi, Sage Publications Ltd, 1999.

Fabian, Johannes, 'The Other Revisited', in Johannes Fabian, *Memory against Culture, Argument and Reminders*, Durham and London, Duke University Press Books, 2007.

Falk, S. J., *Qajar paintings; Persian Oil Paintings of the 18th and 19th Centuries,* London, Sotheby Park-Bark-Bernet Publications Limited, 1972.

Faraj, Maysaloun (ed), *Strokes of the genius: Contemporary Iraqi Art*, London, Saqi Books, 2001.

Faroughi, F., 'Chira kubism dar Iran ba burji az mukhalifat ru-beh-ru shud?' *Rastakhiz*, 3 Diy 2536 = 1356S/ 1977, p. 22.

Farsoun, Samih K. and Mashayekhi, Mehrdad, *Iran: Political Culture in the Islamic Republic*, London and New York, Routledge, 1992.

Ferrier, R.W. et al, *The Arts of Persia*, New Haven & London, Yale University Press, 1989.

First Iranian Painters Biannual: 19 Nov-19 Dec 1991, Tehran, Tehran Museum of Contemporary Art, Niavaran Cultural Centre, Azadi Cultural Centre (exhibition brochure), Tehran 1370S/ 1991

Fischer, M., *Iran: From Religious Dispute to Revolution*, Cambridge, Massachusetts and London, Harvard University Press, 1980.

Fischer, M.J. and Abedi, M., *Debating Muslims: Cultural Dialogues in Postmodernity and Tradition*, Madison: University of Wisconsin Press, 1990.

Fisher, Jean, 'The Syncretic Turn, Cross-cultural Practices in the Age of Multiculturalism', in Zoya Kocur and Simon Leung (eds), *Theory in Contemporary Art since 1985*, Malden (MA), Oxford, Victoria, Blackwell Publishing, 2005, pp. 233–241.

Flood, Finbarr Barry, 'From the Prophet to Postmodernism? New World Orders and the End of Islamic Art', in Elizabeth Mansfield (ed), *Making Art History: A Changing Discipline and its Institutions*, London, Routledge, new edition 2007.

Foroughi, Mohamad Ali, 'Namehi dar bareh-i Kamal al-Mulk', *Iran Nameh*, vol. 17, no. 3, summer 1999, pp. 536-551.

Fortier, Anne-Marie, 'Re-Membering Places and the Performance of Belonging(s)', in Vikki Bell (ed), *Performativity and Belonging*, London, Sage Publications, 1999.

Foster, H., *Recoding: Art, Spectacle, Cultural Politics*, Seattle, WA, Bay Press, 1989.

Foucault, Michel, 'The Subject and Power', in Hubert L. Dreyfus (ed) *Michel Foucault: Beyond Structuralism and Hermeneutics*, Chicago, University of Chicago Press, 1983.

Frascina, Francis and Harris, Jonathan (eds), *Art in Modern Culture: an Anthology of Critical Texts*, London, Phaidon Press Limited, 1999.

Galloway, David, 'The Global Vision of Parviz Tanavoli', *Art Tomorrow*, no. 5, summer 2011, pp. 172-175.

Gheissari, Ali, *Iranian Intellectuals in the Twentieth Century*, Austin USA, University of Texas Press, 1998.

Golshiri, Barbad, *And I Regurgitate And I Gulp It Down* (exhibition catalogue), 2011.

Goudarzi, Mostafa, 'Dar-amadi bar naqqashi-i mu'asir-i iran', *Hunar-hay-i tajassumi*, no. 2, summer 1377S/ 1998, pp. 62-69.

——, 'rah-i chuharum', *Hunar-hay-i tajassumi*, no. 2, summer 1377S/ 1998, pp. 4-14.

——, 'Dar-amadi bar naqqashi-i mu'asir-i iran', *Hunar-ha-yi tajassumi*, no. 2, summer 1377S/ 1998, pp. 62-69.

Goudarzi, Morteza, *Naqqashi-i inqilab, hunar-i muta'ahid-i ijtima'i-i dini- inqilabi*, Tehran, intisharat-i farhangistan-i hunar, 1390S/ 2011.

Goudarzi, Morteza, *Girafik-i inqilab, hunar-i muta'ahid-i ijtima'i-i dini-inqilabi*, Tehran, intisharat-i farhangistan-i hunar, 1390S/ 2011.

Grabar, Oleg, *The Formation of Islamic Art*, New Haven and London, Yale University Press, 1987.

Grigorian, Marcos, Introduction to the First Tehran Biennial catalogue (exhibition catalogue), Tehran, Idareh-i intisharat va ravabit-i 'oumumi-i kull-i hunar-hay-i zibay-i kishvar, 1958.

Gruber, Christiane, 'Media/ting Conflict: Iranian Posters from the Iran-Iraq War (1980-88)', in Jaynie Anderson (ed), *Crossing Cultures: Conflict, Migration, Convergence*, Proceedings of the 32nd Congress of the International Committee of the History of Art, Melbourne 2009, pp. 710-715.

Guerman, M., *Art of the October Revolution*, compiled and introduced by Mikhail Guerman, Leningrad, Aurora Art Publishers, 1986.

Gumpert, Lynn, 'Introduction', in Shiva Balaghi and Lynn Gumpert (eds), *Picturing Iran: Art, Society and Revolution*, London and New York, I. B. Tauris, 2002, pp. 11-16.

Gupta, Suman, *Social Constructionist Identity Politics and Literary Studies*, Basingstoke, New York, Palgrave Macmillan, 2007.

Guzideh'i az asar-i avvalin nimdyishgah-i dusdlaneh-i naqqashan-i iran (Selection of Works of the First Iranian Painter's Biennial), Tehran, Markaz-i hunar-hay-i tajassumi-i vizarat-i farhang va irshad-i islami, 1371S/ 1992.

Hakimi, Michael, unpublished notes, quoted in: Kempkes, Anke, *Black Palms: Signs of the Times in Michael Hakimi's Pictures and Installations*, Ars Viva 04/05 – Zeit, catalogue, Kulturkreis der deutschen Wirtschaft, BDI e.V., 2005.

Hall, Stuart, 'Cultural Identity and Diaspora', in Jonathan Rutherford (ed), *Identity: Community, Culture, Difference*, London, Lawrence & Wishart, 1990, pp. 223–237.

——, 'Introduction', in Stuart Hall and Paul du Gay (eds), *Questions of Cultural Identity*, London, Thousand Oaks, CA, Sage Publications, 1996.

Hanaway, W., 'The Symbolism of Persian Revolutionary Posters', in Barry M. Rosen (ed), *Iran since the Revolution: Internal Dynamics, Regional Conflict, and The Superpowers*, Boulder, Columbia University Press, 1985.

Harrison, Charles, *Art in Theory 1900-1990; An Anthology of Changing Ideas*, Charles Harrison and Paul Wood (eds), Oxford (UK), Cambridge (USA), Basil Blackwell Ltd, 1995.

——, *Conceptual Art and Painting: Further Essays on Art & Language*, Cambridge, MA and London, MIT Press, 2001.

Heartney, E., 'Art & Politics: Modernity and Revolution', in *Art in America*, February 2003, pp. 50-53.

Hill, D., *Islamic Architecture and Its Decoration AD 800-1500*, with an introductory text by Oleg Grabar, London, R. MacLehose and Company Ltd, The University Press Ltd, 1967.

Hobsbawmn, Eric and Ranger, Terence (eds), *The Invention of Tradition*, Cambridge, Cambridge University Press, 1983.

Hooglund, Eric (ed), *Twenty Years of Islamic Revolution: Political and Social Transition in Iran since 1979*, Syracuse, New York, Syracuse University Press, 2002.

Hosseini, Mansoureh, in *Huviyyat-i farhangi va hunari: majmu'eh bahs-hay-i kunfirans-i hunar-hay-i tajassumi* (Proceedings of the First Plastic Arts Conference), Tehran 1372S/ 1993.

Hosseini Rad, Abdolmajid, A., 'Shikl-hay-i hunar-i sunnati va naqqashi-i mu'asir-i iran', *Hunar-hay-i tajassumi*, no. 2, 1377S/ 1998, pp. 136-144.

——, 'Chand kalimeh dar bareh-i naqqashi-i mu'asir-i iran', *Hunar-hay-i tajassumi*, no. 7, winter 1378S/ 2000, pp. 180-191.

——, 'Naqqashi-i now-giray-i Iran dar hich kuja-yi in jahan-i pahnavar na-istada ast,' *Naqsh* (series for the Fifth Painting Biennial), no. 25, 1379/ 2000, p. 8.

——, *Ru'ya-y-i firishtigan: Bayan-i tamsili dar naqqashi i now-gira-y-i iran* (Symbolic Expression in Iranian Modernist Painting) (exhibition catalogue), Tehran 2000.

Hunar-i Iran fara-suy-i marz-ha, Catalogue of Contemporary Iranian Art's Exhibitions outside the Country 1999-2001, Tehran, Tehran Museum of Contemporary Art, 2001.

Hunar-i qudsi majmu'eh sukhanrani-hay-i duvumin kunfirans-i hunar-hay-i tajassumi (Proceedings of the Second Plastic Arts Conference), Tehran 1373S/ 1994.

Hunter, Shireen T., *Iran after Khomeini*, New York, Praeger, 1992.

Huviyyat-i farhangi va hunari: majmu'eh bahs-hay-i kunfirans-i hunar-hay-i tajassumi (Proceedings of the First Plastic Arts Conference), Tehran, anjuman-i hunar-hay-i tajassumi (kumiteh-i intisharat), 1372S/ 1993.

Iran Contemporary Painting; a Selection of the Works: Third Iran Painting Biennial, Tehran, Plastic Arts Society in Cooperation with the Tehran Museum of Contemporary Arts, 1376S/ 1997.

Iranian Contemporary: An Exhibition in Association with the Tehran Museum of Contemporary Art (catalogue of the exhibition of Contemporary Iranian Art at Christie's), 19-23 May 2002.

Issa, Rose (ed), *Iranian Contemporary Art*, London, Booth-Clibborn Editions, 2001.

I'timad al-Saltaneh (Sani' al-Dowleh), M. H. K., *Ruznameh-hay-i Mira'at al-Safar va urduy-i humayun*, Introduction by Iradj Afshar, Abdollah Foradi, Tehran, Intisharat-i Gulshan, 1363S/ 1984.

——, M. H. K., *Matla' al-Shams*, vol. 3, Introduction by Teymour Borhan Limoudehi, Tehran, Intisharat-i farhhang-Sara, 1363S/ 1984-5.

Jadval-i guzarish-i 'amalkard-i nigar-khaneh-hay-i shahr-i tihran dar sal-i 1377, Markaz-i hunar-hay-i tajassumi-i kishvar (report), Tehran, 1998.

Jahanbagloo, Ramin, *Iran va Mudirniteh; Guft–u-guhai ba pazhuhishgaran-i irani va khariji dar zamineh-i ruyarui-i iran ba dastavard-hay-i jahan-i mudirn*, Tehran, Nashr-i Guftar, 1379S/ 2000.

——, 'guf-u-gu ba Ramin Jahanbagloo', *Hirfeh hunrmand,* no. 4, 2002, pp. 129-133.

——, (ed), *Iran Between Tradition and Modernity*, Lanham, MD, Lexington Books, 2004.

Jalali, Reza, 'guft-u-gu ba ductur Namvar Motlagh dabir-i farhangistan-i hunar: tafakkuri khas nisbat beh jahan-i islam', *Sharq Newspaper*, no. 382, 1383S/ 2004, p. 14.

Jamalzadeh, Mohammad Ali, 'Kamal al-Mulk', *Hunar va mardum*, no. 35, Aban 1344 S/ October 1965, pp. 6-19.

Jelloun, T. B., 'Sur un Ciel de Soie', *Le Monde Newspaper*, no. 23-24 Mai, 1976, pp. 23-24.

Jones, Amelia, 'Body', in Robert S. Nelson and Richard Shiff (eds), *Critical Terms for Art History*, Chicago, London, University of Chicago Press, 2003.

Jorjani, R., 'Nimayishgah-i hunar-hay-i zibay-i iran', *Sukhan*, no. 1, Farvardin 1325S/ March 1946, pp. 24-31.

Jowdat, Mohammad Reza and Pakbaz, Ruin, 'Nimayishgah-i Pakbaz va Qandriz', *Kitab-i sal-i talar-i iran*, Tehran, intisharat-i talar-e iran, 1344S/ 1965, pp. 27-34.

Kamshad, H., *Modern Persian Literature*, Cambridge, Cambridge University Press, 1996.

Kamal al-Mulk, Second Edition, Tehran, Visarat-i Irshad-i Islami, Muzeh-i hunar-hay-i mu'asir, 1362S/ 1983.

Karimov, L, *Persian Rugs Motifs for Needlepoint*, New York, Dover, 1975.

Karimzadeh Tabrizi, Mohammad Ali, *Ahval va asar-i naqqashan-i qadim-i iran va barkhi az mashahir-i nigaragari-i hind va 'usmani,* vol. 1, London, Interlink Longaph Ltd, 1985.

Kashani-Sabet, F., *Frontier Fictions: Shaping the Iranian Nation, 1804-1946*, Princeton, NJ, Princeton University Press, c.1999.

Kashefi, Jalaloddin, 'Naqqashi-i mu'asir-i iran (3)', *Faslnameh hunar*, no. 15, 1372S/ 1993, pp. 46-129.

——, 'Anasur-i hamgin dar kalbud-i shikl va rang', *Faslnameh hunar*, no. 15, spring 1367S/ 1998, pp. 46-129.

Katouzian, Homa, *The Political Economy of Modern Iran: Despotism and Pseudo-Modernism 1926-1979*, New York, New York University Press, 1981.

Keddie, Nikki R., *Iran: Religion, Politics and Society*, collected essays, London, Frank Cass and Company Limited, 1980.

——, *Roots of Revolution: An Interpretive History of Modern Iran*, New Haven, London, Yale University Press, 1981.

—— (ed), *Modern Iran: Roots and Results of the Revolution*, New Haven, Yale University Press, 2006.

Keddie, Nikki R., and Hooglund, Eric (eds), *The Iranian Revolution and the Islamic Republic*, New York, Syracuse University Press, 1986.

Keelan, Siumee H., 'Ensuring Visibility: Art, History and Patronage', in Fran Lloyd (ed), *Contemporary Arab Women's Art: Dialogue of the Present*, London, The Women's Art Library, 1999, pp. 51-57.

Kehrer, Michaela, 'How Culture Sells: Examples from National and International Marketing Perspectives', in *Ethnic Marketing* (exhibition catalogue), Tehran, Toseh Publishing, 2006, pp. 18-24.

Keshmirshekan, Hamid, 'Neo-Traditionalism and Modern Iranian Painting: The *Saqqa-khaneh* School in the 1960s', *Iranian Studies*, vol. 38, no. 4, December 2005, pp. 607–630.

——, 'Discourses on Postrevolutionary Iranian Art: Neotraditionalism during the 1990s', *Muqarnas*, vol. 23, 2006, pp. 131–157.

——, 'Contemporary Iranian Art: The Emergence of New Artistic Discourses', *Iranian Studies*, vol. 40, no. 3, 2007, pp. 335-366.

——, 'Saqqa-khana School of Art', *Encyclopaedia Iranica* (London, New York, 2008), http://www.iranicaonline.org/articles/saqqa-kana-ii-school-of-art

——, 'Modern and Contemporary Iranian Art: Developments and Challenges', in Hossein Amirsadeghi (ed), *Different Sames: New Perspectives in Contemporary Iranian Art*, London 2009.

——, 'The Paradigms for Contemporaneity in Iranian Art', *Art Tomorrow*, no. 1, spring 2010, pp. 112-125.

——, 'The New Wave of Iranian Art: Tendencies and Origins', *Art Press* no. 17, May/June/July 2010, pp. 22-35.

——, 'The Question of Identity vis-à-vis Exoticism in Contemporary Iranian Art, *Iranian Studies*, vol. 43, no. 4, September 2010, pp. 489–512.

——, 'Reproducing Modernity: Post-revolutionary Art in Iran since the Late 1990s', in Hamid Keshmirshekan (ed), *Amidst Shadow and Light: Contemporary Iranian Art and Artists*, Hong Kong, Liaoning Creative Press, 2011, pp. 44-65.

——, 'Globalisation and the Question of Identity: Discourses on Contemporary Iranian Art During Past Two Decades', in ibid, pp. 64-81.

—— (ed), *Amidst Shadow and Light: Contemporary Iranian Art and Artist*, Hamid Keshmirshekan, Hong Kong, Liaoning Creative Press, 2011.

——, 'Calligraphic Texts and Varieties in Modern and Contemporary Iranian Art', *Art Tomorrow*, no. 5, summer 2011, pp. 166-182.

——, 'Contemporary or Specific: The Dichotomous Desires in the Art of Early 21st Century Iran', *Middle East Journal of Culture and Communication*, no. 4, 2011, pp. 44-71.

——, 'Seeing Twofold: Locality and Trans-locality in the Art of Contemporary Iran', *Art Tomorrow*, no. 3, winter 2011, pp. 143-148.

——, 'The Concealed Layers of Meaning: Barbad Golshiri's Art', *Art Tomorrow*, no. 5, summer 2011, pp. 92-95.

——, 'Beauty versus Reality: Nosratollah Moslemian's Art in Different Stages', Art Tomorrow, no. 7, winter 2012, pp. 140-146.

——, 'Neo-calligraphism and Its Varieties in Modern and Contemporary Iranian Art', in Venetia Porter and Mariam Rosser-Owen (eds), *Metalwork and Material Culture in the Islamic World: Art, Craft and Text*, London: I. B. Tauris, 2012, pp. 441-460.

——, 'Reclaiming Cultural Space: Artist's Performativity versus State's Expectations in Contemporary Iran', in Staci Gem Scheiwiller (ed), *Performing the Iranian State: Cultural Representations of Identity and Nation*, London, New York, Anthem Press, 2013, pp. 145-155.

Khatami, Seyyed Mohammad, 'Hunar-i risheh-yafteh az adyan', *Faslnameh-i hunar*, no. 3, 1362S/ 1983, pp. 10-17.

Khatibi, Abdelkebir and Sijelmassi, Mohammed (eds), *The Splendour of Islamic Calligraphy*, London, Thames and Hudson, 1996.

Khemir, S., 'Mobile Identity and the Focal Distance of Memory', in Fran Lloyd (ed), *Displacement & Difference: Contemporary Arab Visual Culture in the Diaspora*, London, Easter Art Publishing, 2001, pp. 43-51.

Khoshroo, Abolghasem, 'Sukhanrani-i aghay-i muhandis Abulghasim Khoshroo dar marasim-i iftitahiyyeh-i duwumin kunfirans-i hunarhay-i tajassumi dar muzeh-i Hunar-hay-i Mu'asir', in *Hunar-i qudsi majmu'eh sukhanrani-hay-i duvumin kunfirans-i hunar-hay-i tajassumi* (Proceedings of the Second Conference of Plastic Arts), Tehran 1373S/ 1994, pp. 29-32.

Khosrokhavar, Farhad, 'Postrevolutionary Iran and the New Social Movements', in Eric Hooglund (ed), *Twenty Years of Islamic Revolution: Political and Social Transition in Iran since 1979*, Syracuse, New York, Syracuse University Press 2002, pp. 3-18.

Kuspit, Donald, *The End of Art*, New York, Cambridge University Press, 2004.

Langaroudi, H., 'Naqqashi mikunam ta istighaseh kunam beh dargah-i ui keh taqsim napazir ast; nigahi guzara beh negar-khaneh-hay-i tihran', *Intikhab*, no. 575, Wednesday Farvardin 29 1380S/ March 2001, p. 10.

Lawrence, L. A., 'Letter- Word- Art', *Aramco World*, vol. 48, no.2, March/April 1977, pp. 34, 35.

Lazarian, J, 'Goft-u-gu ba Marcos Grigorian', *Bukhara*, no. 16, Bahman/Isfand 1379S/ Jan/Feb 2000.

Lee, Sasha M., 'Interview with Babak Golkar', http://babakgolkar. ca/ Accessed 17/01/2013

Lefevre, J., *The Persian Carpet, Tiles that Bind: A Social History of the Iranian Carpet,* London, Lefevre & Partners, 1977.

Lenczowski, G., *Iran under the Pahlavis*, Stanford, CA, Hoover Institution Press, 1978.

Le Salon d'Automne de Paris Galeries de Section Iranienne, Nukhustın nimayishgah-i hunari-i biynul-milali-i Tihran: naqqashi, mujassameh-sazi, mi'mari (The First Tehran international art exhibition: Painting, Sculpture and Architecture), beh ihtimam-i anjuman-i milli-i ravabit-i farhangi, 30 Azar-11 Bahman 1353S/ 1974.

Lloyd, Fran (ed), *Contemporary Arab Women's Art: Dialogues of the Present*, London, The Women's Art Library, 1999.

—— (ed), *Displacement & Difference: Contemporary Arab Visual Culture in the Diaspora*, London, Eastern Art Publishing, 2001.

Lowe, Lisa, 'Heterogeneity, Multiplicity: Making Asian-American Differences', *Diaspora*, vol. 1, no. 1, pp 24-44.

Ludwig, H., *Aspects of Oriental Ornamentation and Twentieth Century Art*, in World Culture and Modern Art: the Encounter of 19th and 20th Century European Art and Music with Asia, Africa, Oceania, Afro- and Indo-America, Exhibition on the Occasion of the Games of the XXth Olympiad Munich 1972, Bruckmann Publishers, 1972, pp. 67-77.

Lynton, Norman, *The Story of Modern Art*, Oxford, Phaidon 1980.

Mahboubi Ardakani, Hossein, *Tarikh-i tahavvulat-i danishgah-i tihran va mu'assisat-i ali-i amuzishi-i iran dar 'asr-i khujasteh-i Pahlavi*, Tehran, 1350S/ 1971.

——, *Muqaddamehi dar bab-i ashnayi-i iran ba mazahir-i tamaddun-i gharbi*, Tehran, Daftar-i Mutali'at va Barnameh-rizi-i Farhangi, Vizarat-i Farhang va Hunar, 1976.

——, *Tarikh-i mu'assisat-i tamadduni-i jadid dar iran*, Tehran, Silsileh-i intisharat-i Danishgah-i Tehran, 1975-1989.

Marcus, George, *Writing Culture: The Poetics and Politics of Ethnography,* James Clifford and George E. Marcus (eds), Berkeley, CA, London, University of California Press, 1986.

Marefat, M., 'The Protagonists Who Shaped Modern Tehran', in Chahriar Adle and B. Hourcade (eds), *Téhéran, Capitale bicentenaire*, Paris and Téhéran Institut Français de Recherche en Iran, 1992, pp. 95-125.

Martin, D. C., 'The Choices of Identity', *Social Identities*, vol. 1, no. 1, 1995, pp. 5–20.

Martín Alcoff, Linda and Mohanty, Satya P., 'Introduction', in Linda Martín Alcoff and Satya P. Mohanty, et al (eds), *Identity Politics Reconsidered*, New York, Basingstoke, Palgrave Macmillan, 2006.

Mashayekhi, Mehrdad, 'The Politics of Nationalism and Political Culture', in Smith K. Farsoun and Mehrdad Mashayekhi (eds), *Iran: Political Culture in the Islamic Republic*, London and New York, Routledge 1992, pp. 82-115.

Matin-Asgari, Afshin 'The Intellectual Best-sellers of Post-Revolutionary Iran: On Backwardness, Elite-killing, and Western Rationality', *Iranian Studies*, vol. 37, no. 1, winter 2004, pp. 73-88.

Matsuda, M. K., *The Memory of the Modern*, New York, Oxford University Press, 1996.

Menashri, D., *Education and the Making of Modern Iran*, Ithaca, Cornell University Press, 1992.

Meskoob, Shahrokh, *Iranian Nationality and the Persian Language 900-1900*, translated into English by Michael C. Hillmann, Washington DC, Mage, 1992.

——, 'Dar bareh-i naqqashi-i qajar', *Iran Nameh*, vol. XVII, no. 3, summer 1999, pp. 405-421.

Milani, A., 'Sayyid Fkhroddin Shadman va mas'aleh-i tajaddud', *Iran-shinasi*, no. 2, 1374S/ 1995, pp. 261-79.

Millward, William G., 'Traditional Values and Social Changes in Iran', *Iranian Studies*, vol. 4, no. 1, 1971, pp. 2-11.

Mir Emadi, Manijeh, 'Parviz Tanavoli', *Tavoos*, no. 1, Tehran, autumn 1999, pp. 128-137.

——, 'Jalil Ziapour (1299-1378)', *Tavoos*, no. 2, winter 2000, pp. 118-123.

——, 'Zhazeh Tabatabaei', *Tavoos*, nos. 5 & 6, autumn 2000 & winter 2001, pp. 18-31.

Mirfattah, A, 'Beh Aydin va baray-i nasl-i pishtaz', *Hunar-i Mu'asir*, no. 2, Azar/Dey 1372S/ Nov/Dec 1993, p. 49.

Mirsepassi, Ali, *Intellectual Discourse and the Politics of Modernisation: Negotiating Modernity in Iran*, Cambridge, Cambridge University Press, 2000.

Mitchell, W. J. T., *Picture Theory: Essays on Verbal and Visual Representation*, London, University of Chicago Press, 1994.

Modern, Iranian Art, Basle Switzerland (exhibition catalogue), 16-21 June 1976.

Mohajer, M, 'Na-gufteh-ha', *Hunar-i Mu'asir*, no. 2, Azar/Diy 1372S/ Nov/Dec 1993, p. 39.

——, 'Nimayishgah-hay-i buzurg va biennial-hay-i naqqashi-i tihran', *Hunar-hay-i tajassumi*, no. 1, spring 1377S/ 1998, pp. 42-73.

——, 'Avvalin nimayishgah-i dusalaneh-i naqqashan-i Iran', *Hunar-hay-i tajassumi*, no .2, summer 1377S/ 1998, pp.118-127.

——, 'Duvvumin nimayishgah-i du-salaneh-i naqqashi', *Hunar-hay-i tajassumi*, no. 3, autumn 1377S/ 1998, pp. 109-119.

Mojabi, Javad, 'Zenderoudi's Current Exhibition', *Ittila'at*, no. 15120, October 1976.

——, 'Pilaram naqqashi bi aram ast', *Ittila'at*, no. 152338, Sunday 24th Bahman 2535 = 1355S/ February 1976, p. 17.

——, 'Naqqashani keh dustishan dashteh-am', *Gardun; vizheh nameh-i hunar-i naqqashi*, bahar 1370S/ spring 1991, pp. 78-92.

——, *Pioneers of Contemporary Persian Painting: First Generation*, translated into English by Karim Emami, Tehran, Iranian Art Publishing, 1997.

Momayyez, Morteza, 'Heydarian ustad-i mumtaz-i danishgah-i tihran', *Ayandeh*, no. 16, Murdad 1369S/ 1990, pp. 600-601.

——, 'Tvaqqu' va vaqi'iyyat: guftari dar bareh-i avvalin nimayishgah-i du-salaneh-i naqqashan-i iran', *Kilk*, no. 24, 1370S/ 1991, pp. 146-155.

——, 'Faculty of Fine Arts', in Ehsan Yarshater (ed), *Encyclopaedia Iranica*, vol. X, New York, Bibliotheca Persica Press, 1999, pp. 142-143.

Moradi, A., 'Ayandeh-i naqqashi-i iran rowshan nist: guft-u-gu ba 'Ruin Pakbaz', naqqash, nivisandeh va pazhuhishgar', *Bahar*, 14 May 2000, p. 7.

Moslemian, Nosratollah, 'Chiguneh yik hunarmand mitavanad shuru' beh naqqashi kunad', *Dunyay-i Sukhan*, no. 1370S/ 1991, pp. 91, 92.

——, 'Interview with artists', *Gardun*, nos. 19 & 20, 1994, p. 68.

Motahhari, Morteza, *Khadamat-i mutaqabil-i islam va iran* (The Mutual Services of Islam and Iran), 13th edition, Tehran, Sadra Publishing Co 1366S/ 1987.

Moya, Paula M. L., 'What's Identity Got to Do with It?' in Linda Martín Alcoff et al (eds), *Identity Politics Reconsidered*, New York, Basingstoke, Palgrave Macmillan, 2006.

Mu'ayyir al-Mamalik, Dust 'Ali Khan, *Vaqayi' al-Zaman (khatirat-i shikariyyeh): kitab-i hashtum (qajariyya)*, Tehran, Nashr-i tarikh-i iran, 1363S/ 1984.

——, *Yad-dasht-hayi az zindigani-i khususi-i Nassir al-Din Shah: kitab-i nuhum (qajariyya)*, Tehran, Nashr-i tarikh-i iran, 1363S/ 1984.

——, *Rijal-i 'asr-i nassiri: Kitab-i dahum (qajariyya)*, Theran, Nashr-i tarikh-i iran, 1363S/ 1984.

Muzeh-i hunar-hay-i mu'sair-i tihran harim-i arzish-hay-i paydar (catalogue of the Tehran Museum of Contemporary Arts), Tehran, Muzeh-i hunar-hay-i mu'asir-i tihran ba hamkari-i anjuman-i hunar-hay-i tajassumi, 1373S/ 1994.

Naficy, Hamid, *An Accented Cinema: Exilic and Diasporic Filmmaking*, Princeton, Oxford, Princeton University Press, 2001.

Naficy, Hamid, *The Making of Exile Cultures: Iranian Television in Los Angeles*, Minneapolis, London, University of Minnesota Press, 2003.

Naficy, Hamid, 'Phobic Spaces and Liminal Panics: Independent Transnational Film Genre', in Ella Shohat, Robert Stam (eds), *Multiculturalism, Postcoloniality, and Transnational Media*, New Brunswick, NJ, Rutgers University Press, 2003.

Nigareh: guzidehi az asar-i hunarmandan-i mu'asir, Tehran, Markaz-i hunar-hay-i tajassumi-i vizarat-i irshad-i Islami, Muzeh-i hunar-hay-i mu'asir, 1362S/ 1983.

Najafi, Rasool, 'Education and the Culture of Politics in the Islamic Republic of Iran', in Samih K. Farsoun and Mehrdad Mashayekhi (eds), *Iran: Political Culture in the Islamic Republic*, New York, Routledge, 1992.

Naqqashi-i muc'sir-i iran (Iran Contemporary Painting, catalogue of the Second Iranian Painting Biennial), Tehran, anjuman-i hunarhay-i tajassumi ba hamkari-i markaz-i hunar-hay-i tajassumi, 1373S/ 1994.

Naqsh Newsletters Issues nos. 1, 2, 3 & 4 on the occasion of the Second Iranian Painting Biennial (1993); 3 & 4 on the Third Iranian Painting Biennial (1995); 2, 3, 6, 7 & 8 on the Fourth Iranian Painting Biennial (1997); 2, 3, 4 & 5 on the Fifth Iranian Painting Biennial (2000); and 1 & 2 on The First International Painting Biennial of the Islamic World, Tehran, Museum of Contemporary Arts.

Naraqi, Ehsan, *Ancheh khud dasht,* Tehran, Amir Kabir, 2535 = 1355S/ 1976.

Nasr, Seyyed Hossein, *Art and Spirituality*, New Delhi (Delhi), Gandhi National Centre for Arts, Oxford University Press, 1990.

Navaei, A., 'Mukhtasari az ahval va asar-i Kamal al-Mulk afarinandeh-i ziba'i', *mah-nameh-i Ittila'at*, nos. 4 & 5, Tir and Murdad 1329S/ June and July 1950, p. 9.

Nowshirvani, V. F., 'Economy ix-x under the Islamic Republic', in Ehsan Yarshater (ed), *Encyclopaedia Iranica*, vol. VIII, Costa Mesa, California, Mazda Publishers, 1998, pp. 156-163.

Pahlavan, Cyrus, 'Nigahi beh nimayishgah-hay-i du salaneh-i naqqashi dar iran (1337-1370)', *Iran Nameh*, no. 4, autumn 1371S/ 1992, pp. 635-654.

Pakbaz, Ruin and Jowdat, Mohammad Reza, Fa'aliyyat-i ma keh dar Talar-i Iran shikl migirad, *Kitab-i sal-i Talar-i iran*, Tehran, intisharat-i talar-e iran, 1344S/ 1965, pp. 1-8.

——, 'Nimayishgah-i dasteh jam'i-i naqqashi', *Kitab-i sal-i talar-i iran*, Tehran: intisharat-i talar-e iran, 1344S/ 1965, pp. 9-26.

Pakbaz, Ruin, *Contemporary Iranian Painting and Sculpture*, translated into English by S. Melkonian, Tehran, Vizrat-i Farhang va Hunar (High Council of Culture and Art), 1974.

——, 'Kamal al-Mulk sunnat shikan-i buzurg', *Tamasha*, no. 185, 1355S, 1976, pp. 64, 65.

——, 'Mururi bar naqqashi va piykareh-sazi-i mu'asir-i iran: seh nuqteh-i 'atf dar naqqashi-i mu'asir', *Javanan rastakhiz*, no. 80, 23 Diy 2535 = 1355S/ December 1976, pp. 28-29 & 49.

——, 'Chihreh-i az Qandriz', *Gardun; vizheh nameh-i hunar-i naqqashi*, bahar 1370S/ spring 1991, pp. 50-62.

——, 'Taqabul ba tahajum-i farhangi', *Hunar-i mu'dsir*, no. 3, 1372S/ 1993, pp. 69-72.

——, *Encyclopaedia of Art*, Tehran, Farhang Moaser Publishers, 1378S/ 1999

——, 'Contemporary Art of Iran', *Tavoos*, no. 1, autumn 1999, pp. 168-191.

——, 'Pishgaman-i naqqashi-i mudirn dar Iran', in Ramin Jahanbagloo (ed), *Iran va Mudirniteh; Guft—u-guhai ba pazhuhishgaran-i irani va khariji dar zamineh-i ruyarui-i iran ba dastavard-hay-i jahan-i mudirn*, Tehran, Nashr-i Guftar, 1379S/ 2000, pp. 137-150.

——, 'Mudirnism ya now-avari', *Hunar-hay-i tajassumi*, no. 7, winter 1378S/ 2000, pp. 168-173.

——, *Naqqashi-i iran az dır-baz ta imruz*, Tehran, Nashr-i Naristan, 2000.

——, 'Biographies of Artists', in Rose Issa (ed), *Iranian Contemporary Art,* London, Booth-Clibborn Editions, 2001, pp. 127-137.

——, 'The Originality of Repetition', in Ruin Pakbaz and Yaghoub Emdadian (eds), *Charles Hossein Zenderoudi*, Tehran, Tehran Museum of Contemporary Art, 2001, pp. 28, 29.

Pakbaz, Ruin and Emdadian, Yaghoub (eds), *Beh bagh-i hamsafaran:* (Pioneers of Iranian Modern Painting: Houshang Pezeshknia, Sohrab Sepehri, Hossein Kazemi), Tehran, Nazar Printing & Publishing Cultural & Research Institute, 2001.

—— (eds), *Charles Hossein Zenderoudi*, Tehran, Tehran Museum of Contemporary Art, 2001.

—— (eds), *Pioneers of Iranian Modern Art: Massoud Arabshahi*, Tehran, Tehran Museum of Contemporary Art, 2001.

Palangi, Nasser, 'Memories of Khorramshahr', *Tavoos*, no. 2, winter 2000, pp. 178-185.

Parham, Cyrus (ed), *The Splendour of Iran*, Volume III, Islamic Period, London, Booth-Clibborn Editions, 2001.

Parsa, M., *Social Origins of the Iranian Revolution*, New Brunswick, NJ, Rutgers University Press, 1989.

Pesaran, Hashem, 'Economy ix in the Pahlavi Period' in Ehsan Yarshater (ed), *Encyclopaedia Iranica*, vol. VIII, Costa Mesa, California, 1998, pp. 143-156.

Pilaram, Faramarz, 'Na az har khanandeh taranehi', *Rastakhiz-i Javanan*, no. 100, Tir 2536 = 1356S/ July 1977, pp. 20, 21.

——, 'Interview with Faramarz Pilaram', *Kiyhan*, Thursday 4th Farvardın 2536 = 1356S/ March 1977, p.12.

Porter, Venetia, *Word into Art: Artists of the Modern Middle East,* London, The British Museum Press, 2006.

Qandriz, Mansour, 'Dowreh-i qajar', *Intighad-i Kitab*, no. 8, Isfand 1343S/ March 1965, p. 86.

——, 'Man beh suhulat-i bayan va azadi-i iradeh iman daram', *Firdowsi*, no. 714, 1344S/ 1965, pp. 12, 16.

——, 'mushkil-i hunarmand va mukhatab', *Gardun; vizheh nameh-i hunar-i naqqashi*, bahar 1370S/ spring 1991, pp. 40-43.

Raby, Julian, *Qajar Portraits*, New York, London: I. B. Tauris, 1999.

Rahmati, Hamid, 'Miyan-i du karaneh-i na-piyda...', *Dunyay-i Sukhan*, no. 74, May 1997, pp. 62, 63.

Rahnavard, Zahra, 'Huviyyat-i gumshudeh va dayalug-i jahani', *Hunar-i mu'asir*, no. 3, Bahman & Isfand 1372S/ 1993, pp. 65-66.

Rajabi, Mohammad Ali, 'Huviyyat va haqiqat-i naqqashi-i imruz', *Hunar-i mu'asir*, no. 3, Bahman & Isfand 1372S/ 1994, pp. 66-68.

Ram, Haggai, 'Mythology of Rage: Representations of the Self and the "Other" in Revolutionary Iran', *History and Memory*, vol. 8, no. 1, spring/summer 1996, pp. 67-87.

——, 'Multiple Iconographies: Political Posters in the Iranian Revolution', in Shiva Balaghi and Lynn Gumpert (eds), *Picturing Iran: Art, Society and Revolution*, London and New York, I. B. Tauris 2002, pp. 89-103.

Ramadan, Khaled D., 'Introduction', in Khaled D. Ramadan (ed), *Peripheral Insider: Perspectives on Contemporary Internationalism in Visual Culture*, Copenhagen 2007.

Rastegar, K., 'Naqqashi ya'ni taqlid az zibayi-hay-i tabi at', *Rudaki*, nos. 37 & 38, Aban & Azar 1353S/ October & November 1974, pp. 32, 34.

Razavi, A, 'Jilveh-i hunar-i mu'asir-i iran', *Hunar-i Mu'asir*, no. 2, Azar/Diy 1372S/ November/December 1993, pp. 40-41.

Razi, A., 'Beh yik-sivvum-i qiymat-i hunarmand: yad-dashti bar nimayishgah-i Massoud Arabshahi dar galiri-i Seyhoun', *Hunar-i Mu'asir*, no. 1, Mihr/Aban 1372S/ September/October 1993, pp. 6-7.

Restany, Pere, *The Man of True and Just Measure in Communication* (catalogue of the Exhibition), Paris, August 2001.

Rivière, M., *Interview with Charles Hossein Zenderoudi* (catalogue of the Musée Bernay), 1995, pp. 95-97.

Robinson, B. W., 'Persian Painting Under the Zand and Qajar Dynasties', in *The Cambridge History of Iran,* vol. VII, 'From Nader Shah to the Islamic Republic', Cambridge, Cambridge University Press, 1991, pp. 870-89.

Rochechouart, Julien M. de, 'Quant aux paintures que les Persans produisent eux-mêmes, c'est à faire grincer les dents', in *Souvenir d'un voyage en Perse*, Paris 1867.

Rogoff, Irit, 'The Where of Now', *Art Tomorrow,* no. 3, winter 2011, pp. 152-158.

Rosen, Barry B. M. (ed), *Iran since the Revolution: Internal Dynamics, Regional conflict, and the Superpowers*, Boulder, Columbia University Press, 1985.

Roushangar, Majid (ed), *Contemporary Persian Painting, Oveissi, Nasser*, vol. I, Tehran, Murvarid Publishing House, 1966.

Rowe, William and Schelling, Vivian, *Memory and Modernity: Popular Culture in Latin America*, London, Verso Books, 1991.

Safwat, Nabil F., *The Art of the Pen: Calligraphy of the 14th to 20th centuries;* The Nasser D. Khalili Collection of Islamic Art, Vol. V, Oxford, New York, The Nour Foundation in Association with Azimuth Editions and Oxford University Press, 1996.

Said, Edward, *Orientalism*, New York, Vintage Books, 1978.

——, *Culture and Imperialism*, New York, Knopf, 1993.

Sami Azar, Alireza, 'Buzurgtarın muzeh-i khavar-i miyaneh budjeh nadarad', *Abrar*, no. 27, Tir 1380S/ 18 July 2001.

——, 'An Investigation into Different Series of Works by Aydin Aghdashloo', *Art Tomorrow*, no. 2, summer 2010, pp. 163-167.

Saqafi, Morad, 'Shahr va 'arzeh-i hunar: nigahi beh tajrubeh-i talar-i qandriz', *Guft-u-gu*, no. 4, 1375S/ 1996, pp. 37-53.

Sarkouhi, Faraj, 'Daheh-i shast: Adabiyyat va hunar dar gir va guriz', *Adineh*, no. 75, 1369S/ 1990, pp. 66-71.

——, 'Aya tahavuli dar rah ast?' *Gardun; vizheh nameh-i hunar-i naqqashi*, bahar 1370S/ spring 1991, pp. 73-77.

Sattari, Jalal, *Ramz-andishi va hunar-i qudsi*, Tehran, Nashr-i Markaz, 1367S/ 1998.

——, *Dar bi dowlati-i farhang: Nigahi beh fa'aliyyat-hay-i farhangi va hunari dar baz-pasin sal-hay-i nizam-i pishin*, Tehran, Nashr-i Markaz, 1379S/ 2000.

Scarce, J., 'The Arts of the Eighteenth to Twentieth Centuries', in *The Cambridge History of Iran,* vol. VII, From Nader Shah to the Islamic Republic, Cambridge, Cambridge University Press, 1991, pp. 890-958.

Schimmel, Annemarie, *Calligraphy and Islamic Culture*, London, Tauris, 1990

Sepanloo, Mohammad Ali, *Nivisandigan-i pishrow-i iran az mashrutiyat ta 1350: tarikhcheh-i ruman, qisseh-i kutah, nimayishnameh va naqd-i adabi dar iran-i mu'asir*, Tehran, Intisharat-i Nigah, 1366S/ 1987.

Shabahang, Darab Behnam and Dehbashi, Ali, et al (eds), *Yad-nameh-i Kamal al-Mulk: majmu'eh maqalat az nivisandigan-i mukhtalif*, Tehran, Nashr-i Chakameh, 1366S/ 1987.

Shadman, Seyyed Fakhroddin, 'Taskhir-i tamaddun-i farangi', in *Arayish va pirayish-i zaban*, Tehran, chap-khaneh-i iran, 1326S/ 1947.

Shariati, Ali, *On the Sociology of Islam*, translated to English by Hamid Algar, Berkeley, California, Mizan Press, 1979.

——, *Tshayyu'-i 'alavi va tashayyu'-i safavi, Majmu'eh asar*, no. 9, Tehran, daftar-i gid-avari va sazman-dihi asar-i duktur Ali Shariati, 1360S/ 1981.

——, *Rowshanfikr va mas'aleh-i u dar jsmi'eh, Majmu'eh asar*, no. 20, Tehran, daftar-i gid-avari va sazman-dihi asar-i duktur Ali Shariati, 1361S/ 1982.

——, *Baz-shinasi-i huviyyat-i irani-islami, majmu'eh*, vol.27, Tehran, Elham, 1361S/ 1983, pp. 79-225.

Sharifi, M., 'Nimayishi az tahavvul va tatavvur-i yik shukuh', *Tavoos*, nos. 5 & 6, autumn 2000 & winter 2001, pp. 74-85.

Shayegan, Daryoush, *But-hay-i zihni va khatireh-hay-i azali*, Tehran, Amir Kabir, 2535 = 1355/ 1976.

——, *Asiya dar barabar-i gharb* (Asia Facing the West), Tehran, Amir Kabir, 2536 = 1356S/ 1977.

——, *Cultural Schizophrenia: Islamic Society Confronting the West*, translated from French by John How, London, Saqi Books, 1992.

——, 'At the Cutting Edge of Intersecting Worlds,' in Rose Issa (ed), *Iranian Contemporary Art*, London, Booth-Clibborn Editions 2001, pp. 9-11.

Sheil, Lady, *Glimpses of Life and Manners in Persia*, London, J. Murray, 1856.

Sheykh, Hossein, 'Kamal al-Mulk', *Hunar va mardum*, no. 150, Farvardin 1354S/ March 1975, p. 65.

Shirvanlou, Firouz, Faramarz Pilaram's exhibition's catalogue, at the Saman Gallery, Tehran, October 1977, p. 12.

Shohat, Ella, *Talking Visions: Multicultural Feminism in a Transnational Age*, Cambridge, MA, London, MIT Press, New York, New Museum of Contemporary Art, 1998.

Siavoshi, S., *Liberal Nationalism in Iran*, Boulder, Westview Press, 1990.

Smith, R. M., *Persian Art*, London, Chapman and Hall Ltd, 1876.

Smith, Edward Lucie, 'Contemporary Art in Iran and its Relation to Other Non-European Art', in Hamid Keshmirshekan (ed), *Amidst Shadow and Light: Contemporary Iranian Art and Artists*, Hong Kong, Liaoning Creative Press, 2011, pp. 34–43.

Smith, Terry, 'What is Contemporary Art? Contemporaneity and Art to Come', *Konsthistorisk Tidskrift*, vol. 71, nos. 1 & 2, 2002, pp. 3–15.

——, 'Contemporary Art and Contemporaneity', *Critical Inquiry*, vol. 32, no. 4, summer 2006, pp. 681–707.

Soheyli Khansari, Ahmad, *Kamal-i hunar* (Perfection of Art: Life and Works of Mohammad Ghaffari Kamal-ol-Molk (1847-1940), Tehran: Elmi Publishing Co, Soroush Press, 1989.

Sohofi, Mohammad, 'Introduction to the First Plastic Art Conference of Iran', in *Huviyyat-i farhangi va hunari· majmu'eh bahs-hay-i kunfirans-i hunar-hay-i tajassumi* (Proceedings of the First Plastic Arts Conference), Tehran, anjuman-i hunar-hay-i tajassumi (kumiteh-i intisharat), 1372S/ 1993, p. 5.

Sorush, Abdolkarim, 'Seh farhang', *Ayandeh-i Andısheh*, nos. 3 & 4, 1369S/ 1990, pp. 50-59.

——, *Qabz va bast-i ti'uri-i shari'at*, Tehran: Mu'asseseh-i farhangı-i Sirat, 1370S/ 1991.

Stewart, Kathleen. 'Nostalgia – A Polemic', *Cultural Anthropology*, vol. 3, no. 3, August 1988, pp. 227-241.

Stewart, Susan, *On Longing: Narratives of the Miniature, the Gigantic, the Souvenir, the Collection,* Baltimore, Johns Hopkins University Press, 1984.

Tabrizi, Sadegh, 'Saqqa-khaneh az anja pa girift (interview with Artist)', *Hunar-hay-i tajassumi*, no. 6, 1377S/ 1998.

——, 'Piydayish-i talar-i Iran, tavallud-i maktab-i Saqqa-khaneh' (Proceedings of the Conference on Modern Iranian Art), Tehran, 2005.

Tadjvidi, Akbar, *L'art Moderne En Iran*, Teheran, Ministère Iranien de la Culture et des Arts, 1967.

Tajalli-i ihsas (Manifestation of feeling: a selection of paintings by Iranian female artists), Tehran, Iran Visual Arts Association, 1374S/ 1995.

T'am-i Ru'ya; nigahi beh asar-i panjumin nimayishgah-i du-salaneh-i naqqashi-i mu'asir-i iran (The Fifth Iranian Contemporary Painting Biennial's catalogue), Tehran, Nazar, 1379S/ 2000.

Tanavoli, Parviz, 'Atelier Kaboud', in David Golloway (ed), *Parviz Tanavoli: Sculptor, Writer & Collector*, Tehran, Iran Art Publishing, 2000.

Taylor, J., *From Modernization to Modes of Production: A Critique of the Sociologies of Development and undevelopment*, London, Macmillan, 1979.

The Dream of Angels (catalogue of the exhibition titled 'Symbolic Expression in Iranian Modernist Painting'), Tehran, Nazar Painting & Publishing Cultural Research Institute, 1379S/ 2000.

The First International Contemporary Drawing Exhibition (catalogue of the exhibition held 6 Dec 1999–10 Jan 2000 at the Tehran Museum of Contemporary Arts), 2000.

The Fourth Tehran Biennial catalogue, Tehran, Intisharat-i vizarat-i farhang va hnar, 1343S/ 1964.

The Second Tehran Biennial catalogue, Tehran, Idareh-i ravabit-i biynulmilali va intesharat-i hunar-hay-i zibay-i kishvar, Farvardin, 1339S/ 1960.

The Second Iranian Painting Biennial (exhibition brochure) Tehran, Intisharat-i muzeh-i hunar-hay-i mu'ir-i tihran, 1372S/ 1993.

The Third Tehran Biennial catalogue, Tehran, Intisharat-i hunar-hay-i zibay-i kishvar, 1341S/ 1962.

Thomas, Julian, *Time, Culture and Identity: An Interpretative Archaeology*, London, New York, Routledge, 1996.

Vafa, J., *Liberal Nationalism and Educational Politics in Iran*, Michigan, London, University Microfilms International Ann Arbor, 1977.

Vaziri, Mostafa, *Iran as Imagined Nation: The Construction of National Identity*, New York, Paragon House, 1993.

Vernoit, Stephen, *Occidentalism*: *Islamic Art in the 19th Century: The Nasser D. Khalili Collection of Islamic Art*, vol. 23, New York, Nour Foundation in association with Azimuth Editions and Oxford University, 1997.

Weintraub, Linda, Danto, Arthur, and McEvilley, Thomas (eds), *Art on the Edge and Over Searching for Art's Meaning in Contemporary Society*, New York, Third printing, Art Insight Inc, 1996.

Wertime, John T., *Sumak Bags of Northwest Persia*, Christine Davis (ed), London, L. King in association with Hali Publications, 1998.

Williams, Patrick and Chrisman, Laura, *Colonial Discourse and Post-colonial Theory; A Reader*, Patrick Williams and Laura Chrisman (eds), New York, Columbia University Press 1994, p. 14.

Willson, Peter Lemborn, 'The Saqqakhaneh', in *Saqqakhaneh* (exhibition catalogue), Tehran 1356S/ 1977, pp. 16-22.

Winnicott, Donald Woods, *Maturational Processes and the Facilitating Environment: Studies in the Theory of Emotional Development*, Karnac, London, New York, Hogarth Press Ltd, 1965.

Yarshater, Ehsan, 'Nimayishgah-i biyinal-i naqqashı va piykar-sazi dar kakh-i Abyaaz', *Sukhan*, no. 1, Farvardin 1337S/ March 1958, pp. 82-84.

——, 'Contemporary Persian Painting', in Richard Ettinghausen and Ehsan Yarshater (eds), *Highlights of Persian Art*, New York, Westview Press, 1979, pp. 362-377.

Yarshater, Ehsan, Ettinghausen Richard (eds), *Iran Faces the Seventies*, New York, Praeger Publishers, 1971.

Zabih, S., *Iran since the Revolution*, London, Croom Helm, 1982.

Zehtab, Zahra, 'Guft-u-gu ba pishkisvat-i khushnivısi, ustad Mohammad Ehsai', *Khabar-nameh-i hunar-hay-i tajassumi*, no. 25, Tehran, Isfand 1375S/ March 1996, pp. 1-6.

——, 'Guft-u-gu ba hunarmand-i naqqashi-khatt ustad Nasrollah Afjai', *Khabar-nameh-i hunar-hay-i tajassumi*, no. 26, Tehran, Farvardin 1376S/ March 1997, pp. 1-7.

——, 'Beh dunbal-i dirakht-i kaj va daftarcheh-i naqqashi: guft-u-gu ba ustad-i naqqash-i pishkisvat Mansoureh Hosseini', *Khabar-nameh-i hunar-hay-i tajassumi*, no. 38, Tehran, Urdibihisht 1377S/ April 1998, pp. 1-6.

Zenderoudi, Hossein, '*Mudi Libre*', no. 9401, 9 April 1971, p. 1.

——, 'Musahibeh ba Zenderoudi (Zenderoudi's Interview)', *Tamasha Magazine*, Series 3, no. 146, Diy 1353S/ January 1974, pp. 23-25.

——, *Catalogue of the Musée Bussuel*, Meaux 1988.

Ziapour, Jalil, 'Ba Heydarian yik bar-i digar tabi'at ra shinakhtim', *Ittila'at*, 5 Diy 2536 = 1356S/ 1977, p. 17.

Zoka, Syrous, 'Dar jahan-i danish va hunar', *Sukhan*, no. 1, Urdibihisht 1341S/ April 1962, p. 115-122.

——, 'Dar jahan-i danish va hunar: nimayishgah-hay-i bahar', *Sukhan*, series 14, nos. 8 & 9, April 1964, pp. 843-847.

——, 'Dar jahan-i danish va hunar', *Sukhan*, nos. 8 & 9, Urdıbihesht & Khurdad 1343S/ 1964, pp. 837-847.

Zuka, Yahya, 'Mirza Abu'l Hassan Sani' al-Mulk Ghaffari', *Hunar va mardum*, no. 11, Shahrivar 1342S/ August 1963.

Zolghadr, Tirdad, 'Ethnic Marketing: An Introduction', in *Ethnic Marketing* (exhibition catalogue), Tehran, Toseh Publishing, 2006, pp. 10-15.

Credits

All the photographs were provided either
by the institutions, owners or the artists.

CHAPTER ONE
Museum of Fine Arts, Sa'ad Abad Palace: 1, 9
Malek Museum: 3, 7
Arman Estepanian collection: 4
Golestan Palace: 6, 8, 12
Tehran Museum of Contemporary Art (TMoCA): 10, 19–21, 23, 24
Niavaran Museum: 11
Majlis Museum: 13, 14, 15
Museum of National Arts: 25, 26
Behzad Museum: 27

CHAPTER TWO
TMoCA: 4, 5, 6, 10, 11, 13, 14–17, 22, 27, 28
Iranian Academy of Arts: 8
Massoud Akhavan collection: 7, 23
Tania and Arash Goharbin collection: 18
Ali Mousakhani collection: 20
Kerman Museum: 24
Saeed Kouros collection: 25

CHAPTER THREE
Tanavoli collection: 1, 2, 3, 4, 10, 14
British Museum: 5
Iranian Academy of Arts: 6, 34, 37, 38, 40
Metropolitan Museum: 15
Khalili Collection: 20
TMoCA: 22, 24, 26, 28, 30, 31, 33, 42, 48, 49, 52–55, 57, 62–66,
    74–76, 78–85, 87–94, 96, 98–104, 106, 107, 109–118, 120, 121,
    126–131, 133
Niavaran Museum: 27, 32
Massoud Akhavan collection: 29, 59, 60, 61
Museum of Fine Arts, Sa'ad Abad Palace: 41
Saeed Kouros collection: 46, 47
Amir Hossein Zandi collection: 51
Tania and Arash Goharbin collection: 95
Nader Mobargha collection: 105
Hamidreza Pejman collection: 108
Smithsonian Museum: 125

CHAPTER FOUR
Howzeh-i hunari: 7–12
TMoCA: 13, 15–19, 21–25, 31, 33, 35–39, 43, 47–50, 52
Massoud Akhavan collection: 44
Saeed Kouros collection: 46

CHAPTER FIVE
TMoCA: 4, 7
Massoud Akhavan collection: 29
Hamidreza Pejman collection: 40
Nader Mobargha collection: 41

CHAPTER SIX
Alireza Parsadmehr collection: 13

Index